THE ROUTLEDGE HANDBOOK OF VOLUNTEERING IN EVENTS, SPORT AND TOURISM

This timely handbook examines the most contemporary, controversial, and cutting-edge issues related to the involvement of volunteers in the fields of events, sport, and tourism.

Split into thematic sections, the primary areas covered include key disciplinary approaches to understanding volunteerism, international contexts, managing volunteers, the impacts and legacies of volunteering, and future trends in these sectors including online and digital volunteering. Commonalities and differences of volunteering in these sectors are drawn out throughout the volume. A diverse range of case studies are examined including the 2007 UEFA Under-21 Championship hosted by Poland, the development of the Appalachian National Scenic Trail, the Vancouver, London, and PyeongChang Olympic Games, Belgium's National Day in 2019, the Puffing Billy Railway in Australia, as well as many other examples looking at destination services organizations, museums, grassroots associations, corporate events, community events, and visitor attractions.

Drawing on the academic and practical expertise of over 50 authors from across the globe, the handbook provides an invaluable resource for all those with an interest in volunteering in these sectors, encouraging dialogue across disciplinary boundaries and areas of study in order to advance volunteering research and practice in the fields of events, sport, and tourism.

Kirsten Holmes is a Professor at Curtin University, Australia, and is an international expert in volunteering in events, sport, and tourism contexts. She has written extensively on volunteering within events, tourism, and more generally. Kirsten's research has been funded by the Australian and UK Governments, the Australian Research Council, and the International Olympic Committee. She is currently investigating the event legacies of the Olympic Games 1988–2000 for the International Olympic Committee. She is currently Chair of the Council for Australasian Tourism and Hospitality Education (CAUTHE) and a member of Volunteering Western Australia's research committee. She also has expertise in developing sustainable events and festivals, and is the lead author of the Routledge textbook *Events and Sustainability* (2015).

Leonie Lockstone-Binney is an Associate Professor and Research Director in the Department of Tourism, Sport and Hotel Management at Griffith University, Australia. Leonie's research relates to event and tourism volunteering, having published over 70 peer-reviewed articles and received competitive research funding from the Australian Research Council and the International Olympic Committee. Leonie is Associate Editor of the *Journal of Hospitality and Tourism Management* and has roles on the editorial boards of *Event Management*, the *International Journal of Event and Festival Management*, and *Frontiers in Sports and Active Living*.

Karen A. Smith is Professor of Tourism Management in the Wellington School of Business and Government at Te Herenga Waka – Victoria University of Wellington, New Zealand. Karen's research concerns volunteers and their management in the tourism and events sectors, and more broadly in non-profit organizations and employer-supported volunteering. Karen is a past-Chair of Volunteering New Zealand and was made a Member of the New Zealand Order of Merit for her services to education and volunteering.

Richard Shipway is an Associate Professor in the Department of Sport and Event Management at Bournemouth University, UK. His research interests focus on sport tourism, Olympic studies, the impacts and legacies of international sport events, crisis and disaster management for sport, volunteering at mega sports events, and sport ethnography. His previous work has explored a series of Olympic related research themes ranging from resident perception studies to Olympic tourism. Richard's other research interests are linked to the experiences of endurance athletes, most notably distance runners and cyclists. He is the Regional Editor (Europe) for the *International Journal of Event and Festival Management (IJEFM)* and Reviews and Commentaries Editor for the *Journal of Sport and Tourism*. Since 2010 Richard has served on the Economic and Social Research Council (ESRC)'s high profile Peer Review College, refereeing grant proposals within social sciences.

THE ROUTLEDGE HANDBOOK OF VOLUNTEERING IN EVENTS, SPORT AND TOURISM

Edited by
Kirsten Holmes, Leonie Lockstone-Binney,
Karen A. Smith and Richard Shipway

Routledge
Taylor & Francis Group

LONDON AND NEW YORK

First published 2022
by Routledge
2 Park Square, Milton Park, Abingdon, Oxon OX14 4RN

and by Routledge
605 Third Avenue, New York, NY 10158

Routledge is an imprint of the Taylor & Francis Group, an informa business

British Library Cataloguing-in-Publication Data
A catalogue record for this book is available from the British Library

Library of Congress Cataloging-in-Publication Data
Names: Holmes, Kirsten, editor. | Lockstone-Binney, Leonie, editor. | Smith, Karen A., 1973– editor. | Shipway, Richard, editor.
Title: The Routledge handbook of volunteering in events, sport and tourism / edited by Kirsten Holmes, Leonie Lockstone-Binney, Karen A Smith, and Richard Shipway.
Other titles: Handbook of volunteering in events, sport and tourism
Description: New York: Routledge, 2022. | Includes bibliographical references and index.
Identifiers: LCCN 2021022776 (print) | LCCN 2021022777 (ebook) | ISBN 9780367417093 (Hardback) | ISBN 9781032127248 (Paperback) | ISBN 9780367815875 (eBook)
Subjects: LCSH: Voluntarism.
Classification: LCC HN49.V64 R677 2022 (print) | LCC HN49.V64 (ebook) | DDC 302/.14—dc23
LC record available at https://lccn.loc.gov/2021022776
LC ebook record available at https://lccn.loc.gov/2021022777

ISBN: 9780367417093 (hbk)
ISBN: 9781032127248 (pbk)
ISBN: 9780367815875 (ebk)

DOI: 10.4324/9780367815875

Typeset in Bembo
by codeMantra

CONTENTS

List of figures   ix
List of tables   x
List of contributors   xi

1 Introduction   1
   Kirsten Holmes, Karen A. Smith, Leonie Lockstone-Binney and
   Richard Shipway

PART 1
Disciplinary approaches to volunteering   13

2 Economics and volunteering   15
   Megan Haddock

3 Geography, place and international development volunteering   31
   Amanda Davies

4 How a political ecology lens can help assess and improve
   conservation volunteer tourism   40
   Kerry E. Grimm, Emilie Wiehe and Robyn Bath-Rosenfeld

5 Psychology of volunteering   56
   Darja Kragt

6 Volunteering in international sports events from a public
   administration perspective   68
   Robert Gawłowski and Patrycja Gulak-Lipka

PART 2
Volunteering in tourism and sport 81

7 Destination service volunteering 83
Karen A. Smith, Anna Karin Olsson and Kirsten Holmes

8 Visitor attraction: volunteering in cultural heritage tourism in
Aotearoa New Zealand 96
Jane Legget

9 Herding 6,000 volunteers 112
Robert S. Bristow

10 Deconstructing volunteer tourism 122
Snigdha Kainthola, Pinaz Tiwari and Nimit R. Chowdhary

11 The freefall of volunteer leaders in Australian grassroots associations 133
Christel Lorraine Mex

12 Volunteering in community sports organisations and associations 144
Geoff Nichols

PART 3
Volunteering at events 159

13 Enhancing volunteer skills through mega sport events: evidence from
London 2012 Olympic Games 161
Niki Koutrou

14 London, Vancouver, and PyeongChang Olympics: a comparison of
volunteer motivations 174
Chulhee Kang, Femida Handy and Sang-uk Park

15 Volunteering at community events: from volunteering *for* an event to
volunteering *as* an event 190
Elias Delanoeye, Sam Gorleer and Lesley Hustinx

16 Volunteering and charity fundraising events 202
Tim Brown

17 Helping through sport and events within corporate volunteering:
benefits for volunteers and companies 214
Barbara Józefowicz

18 Volunteering at business events: insights from China   223
    Hongxia Qi

PART 4
Managing volunteers   **235**

19 Designing a volunteer program   237
    Graham Cuskelly and Michelle Hayes

20 Volunteer stewardship management models for volunteer programs   249
    Lucas C.P.M. Meijs

21 Volunteer motivation   258
    Katja Petrovic and Arthur A. Stukas

22 Volunteer recruitment and selection: evidence from the visitor
    attraction sector   271
    Giancarlo Fedeli and Linda Cigurova

23 Exploring retention and rewards in community sport volunteering   286
    Nadina Ayer and John R. Cooper

24 The role of organisational culture in sustaining volunteers in heritage
    attractions: the case of Puffing Billy Railway   298
    Josephine Pryce

PART 5
Impacts and legacies of volunteering   **317**

25 Understanding volunteering impact and legacy, a sustainability
    approach   319
    Andrew Adams and John Deane

26 "It's just a fun day out really": perceptions of volunteering and
    mega–event volunteer legacy   332
    Ellie May

27 Creating a social legacy from event volunteering   346
    Robert Rogerson, Fiona Reid and Rafaelle Nicholson

28 Widening the scope of evaluating volunteer tourism: beyond impact
    measurement   360
    Simone Grabowski-Faulkner, Phoebe Everingham and Tamara Young

PART 6
Critical issues in volunteering 373

29 Ethics of volunteering in tourism: ethics of the heart 375
   Konstantinos Tomazos

30 Diversity and inclusion in sport volunteering 389
   Ryan Storr

31 Intercultural learning or just having fun? What volunteer tourism
   providers can learn from educational volunteering programmes to
   enhance intercultural competencies 400
   Olga Junek and Celine Chang

32 Service learning and volunteering: a case study of service learning in
   Chinese business events volunteering 416
   Guoyang Chen and Hongxia Qi

33 Volunteering and obligation: positive and negative 425
   Robert A. Stebbins

34 Glocal citizenship: lofty ideals in regional space 434
   Faith Ong

PART 7
New directions in volunteering research 445

35 Profiling research on volunteering in events, sport and tourism 447
   Andrzej Lis and Mateusz Tomanek

36 Trends in volunteering 460
   Colin Rochester

37 Informal volunteering 473
   Lili Wang

38 Methods for researching volunteers 485
   Richard Shipway and Leonie Lockstone-Binney

39 The future of volunteering and work 500
   *Tom Baum, Leonie Lockstone-Binney, Karen A. Smith,
   Richard Shipway and Kirsten Holmes*

Index 511

FIGURES

2.1	Forms of work and the 2008 SNA	17
4.1	Interactions and flows in typical Conservation Volunteer Tourism (CVT) projects	42
4.2	Interactions and flows in more equitable Conservation Volunteer Tourism (CVT)	43
7.1	Destination service volunteering settings and roles	90
9.1	The AT logo	115
9.2	Hikers are guided by the rectangular white blaze on trees and stones. Note the work of the volunteer trail maintainer who has cleared downed trees away from the trail path	117
16.1	Typology of charity event volunteering	209
22.1	Volunteer recruiting methods	277
22.2	Volunteer selection methods	279
24.1	The Puffing Billy Railway journey from Belgrave to Gembrook	301
29.1	Proliferation of projects	378
35.1	Productivity in research on volunteering in events, sport and tourism	450
38.1	Volunteering at the Virgin Money London Marathon	491
38.2	Observational guidelines for volunteering	492
38.3	Unstructured interview questions and *aide memoires* for volunteering research	493
38.4	Interview questions and prompts	494
38.5	Volunteering experience, feeling and knowledge questions	495

TABLES

6.1	Different perspectives to volunteering in international sports events	75
8.1	Summary of categories of visitor attractions	96
8.2	Key characteristics of three major cultural heritage attractions managing volunteer programmes in Auckland, New Zealand	100
12.1	Sports club participation and participation in voluntary work that supports sporting activity (people 15 years and over)	147
14.1	Summary of motivations components at Olympic events using SEVMS	177
14.2	Volunteers at Olympic Games	178
14.3	Summary of methods: Vancouver, London, and PyeongChang	179
14.4	Sample characteristics: Vancouver, London, and PyeongChang	180
14.5	Rankings of motivation items: comparisons	181
14.6	Significant differences in means of motivations: Vancouver, London, and PyeongChang	183
14.7	Standardized comparison based on original components of the SEVMS scale	185
15.1	Event volunteer sample characteristics ($n = 252$)	196
15.2	Motivations for participating in the event and importance of specific project features ($n = 252$)	197
20.1	Volunteer Stewardship Framework applied to events, sport, and tourism	250
21.1	Motivations to volunteer identified in the events, sport, and tourism fields	260
22.1	Interview respondents' profile	277
24.1	Dimensions of organisational culture as used in this study	304
24.2	Themes from the analysis of the raw secondary data from 2016 VSS and 2018 Consultancy Document	307
24.3	Strategic Initiatives from 2019 PBR Business Plan, aligned to OC dimensions	311
27.1	Social indicators of events	350
31.1	Characteristics of commercial and non–commercial international volunteering providers	407
34.1	Typology of global citizenship	435
35.1	Most productive contributors to research on volunteering in events, sport, and tourism	452

CONTRIBUTORS

Andrew Adams is a senior academic in the Department of Sport and Event Management at Bournemouth University, UK. His research focuses on critical volunteer management, social justice, human rights and sustainability. Andrew is co-author of the book *Who Owns Sport?*

Nadina Ayer is a Lecturer (Academic) in Sport Management in the Department of Sport and Event Management at Bournemouth University, Poole, UK. Her research interests include online communities, interpersonal and group dynamics, participation and leadership in sport, and marketing and management of sport and outdoor recreation.

Robyn Bath-Rosenfeld has her Master's in Environmental Science and Policy from Northern Arizona University in the United States. She studies citizen science and its role in conservation research in Latin America. She currently lives in Oregon, working as an environmental educator.

Tom Baum is Professor of Tourism Employment in the University of Strathclyde in Scotland. He has researched, consulted and taught in the area of work and employment across more than 45 countries worldwide and has published extensively in the area, including on the role of volunteers in tourism, hospitality and events. Tom holds two doctorates in tourism labour market studies.

Robert S. Bristow is a recreation geographer by training and experience, Rob has taught over 30 years and published over 65 papers in books, journals, government documents and conference proceedings. He also completed a 2,000 mile hike of the Appalachian Trail in 1975. Besides natural resource planning, Rob has an interest in the lighter form of dark tourism called Fright Tourism.

Tim Brown is Programme Leader for Events Management at the University of Chester in the UK. Tim has over 15 years' experience working in the events industry and 11 in higher education. Tim's research is focused on charity fundraising, events management and operations, the economic impact of events and the socio-cultural impacts of events.

Celine Chang is Professor of Human Resources Management at Munich University of Applied Sciences, Department of Tourism in Germany. Her research interests include leadership and talent management in tourism as well as intercultural competence development through educational programmes such as international volunteer services.

Guoyang Chen is a PhD student at Victoria University of Wellington in New Zealand. After completing a Master's degree in Events Management in the UK, he worked as a Volunteer Advisor in Cape Town, SA for two years before his PhD study. His research interests include volunteer tourism, role identity and experiential learning.

Nimit R. Chowdhary is a Professor and Head of the Department of Tourism and Hospitality Management at Jamia Millia Islamia in India. He is an avid researcher and author with nine books and more than 115 papers to his credit. He has more than 25 years of experience of teaching, research, training and consultancy. His interests are in destination management, tourism marketing, entrepreneurship and tour guiding and leadership. He is a recipient of AICTE Career Award for Young Teachers; SIDA Fellowship, Sweden; Guest Scholarship, Sweden; Linnaeus Palme Exchange Programme Grants, Sweden; PIMG Research Excellence Award, Gwalior; Scholars' Grant (EMTM), Erasmus Mundus, Europe, among others. Recently he was chosen for prestigious LEAP programme at Oxford University.

Linda Cigurova is a Research Assistant at the Moffat Centre for Travel and Tourism Business Development, Glasgow Caledonian University, with research experience and applied background in the area of volunteering in tourism in Scotland. She holds a BA in International Business and Tourism Management and is currently undertaking a Masters in Social Research.

John R. Cooper is President of the KW Sports Council and Chairperson of KidSport KW Chapter in Waterloo, Ontario, Canada. He has 40 years of professional and volunteer experience in managing sport. His research interests include women in sport, inclusive sport and community youth sports clubs.

Graham Cuskelly is a Professor Emeritus, Department of Tourism, Sport and Hotel Management at Griffith University in Australia. His research areas of expertise include the management of sport and event volunteers and organizational behaviour, community sport development, sport policy and governance.

Amanda Davies is a lecturer and researcher in human geography, demography and planning at the University of Western Australia. With a disciplinary background in geography, Professor Davies' research focuses on examining population growth, distribution and patterns of demographic change. Her work also focuses on exploring the social, economic and environmental issues related to rural re-population and community development.

John Deane is Assistant Dean Quality Assurance and Enhancement at University of Wales, Trinity St David. His research interests include sport and leisure marketing, volunteer management and operations management of sport events.

Elias Delanoeye is a PhD candidate in the Department of Sociology at Ghent University in Belgium. He researches the role played by organizational mechanisms and features in the production and reproduction of inequality through volunteering in order to develop a demand-side perspective on inequality in the field of volunteering.

Phoebe Everingham is an early career researcher and sessional staff member at the University of Newcastle, Australia. She draws on multi-disciplinary perspectives such as human geography, sociology and anthropology and tourism management studies. Her work centres on intercultural encounters within tourism spaces and the possibilities for emotions and affect to unsettle neocolonial power dynamics.

Giancarlo Fedeli is a Senior Researcher at the Moffat Centre for Travel and Tourism Business Development, Glasgow Caledonian University, Scotland. He obtained his PhD in Marketing and Technology adoption in the Visitor Attraction sector. His research lies in the areas of digital marketing and (dis)information in tourism. He has undertaken over 60 research and consultancy assignments both in the UK and internationally. He is the Principal Investigator for several major EU projects and his research has been published in top-tier journals including *Annals of Tourism Research*.

Robert Gawłowski is a Professor at WSB University in Toruń, Poland. His research has focused on public management, public administration and new trends in public sector. In recent years, he has devoted increasing attention to research of delivering public services.

Sam Gorleer is a PhD candidate in the Department of Sociology at Ghent University, Belgium. His research is situated within the field of Blood Economy and is aimed primarily at developing a comprehensive understanding of the structural determinants of blood donation in Europe.

Simone Grabowski-Faulkner is a Senior Lecturer in Management and International Business at the University of Technology Sydney. She has a PhD and first class Honours degree in Tourism Management and a BA (International Studies). Her research spans volunteerism, sustainability, tourist behaviour, cross-cultural psychology, community, disability and diversity management.

Kerry E. Grimm is an environmental social science research consultant and adjunct faculty at Northern Arizona University in the United States. She studies human dimensions of restoration and conservation, specifically community and private landowner conservation approaches, including conservation volunteer tourism. Much of her research occurs in the Caribbean, Latin America and the Western United States.

Patrycja Gulak-Lipka is Assistant Professor at Nicolaus Copernicus University in Toruń, Poland. Being a former professional athlete, her research is primarily focused on sports management issues. Her recent research relates to sustainability etc. She is currently a part of an international research group devoted to a project related to leadership in cross-cultural contexts.

Megan Haddock in her role at the Johns Hopkins Center for Civil Society Studies worked with the UN to develop international standards for the measurement of volunteering. She is co-author of *Explaining Civil Society Development: A Social Origins Approach* (Johns Hopkins University Press, 2017) and author of several articles on volunteering.

Femida Handy is Professor of Nonprofit Studies at the School of Social Policy and Practice, University of Pennsylvania in the United States, and Director of its PhD program in Social Welfare. She recently completed her six-year term as the Editor-in-chief of the *Nonprofit and Voluntary Sector Quarterly*. Dr Handy's research is collaborative and interdisciplinary. She has widely published on a wide range of topics that focus on the economics of the nonprofit sector, and won multiple awards for her publications. Her recent co-authored work is a book on *Ethics for Social Impact* (2018).

Michelle Hayes is a Research Assistant in the Department of Tourism, Sport and Hotel Management at Griffith University in Australia. Her research areas include sport communication, athletes' use of social media, and sport organizations' management of social media impacts.

Kirsten Holmes is Professor at Curtin University, Australia, and is an international expert in volunteering in events, sport and tourism contexts. She has written extensively on volunteering within events, tourism and the not-for-profit sector more generally. Kirsten's research has been funded by the Australian and UK Governments, the Australian Research Council, and the International Olympic Committee. She is currently investigating the event legacies of the Olympic Games 1988–2000 for the International Olympic Committee. She is currently Chair of the Council for Australasian Tourism and Hospitality Education (CAUTHE) and a member of Volunteering Western Australia's research committee. She also has expertise in developing sustainable events and festivals and is the lead author of the Routledge textbook *Events and Sustainability* (2015).

Lesley Hustinx is an Associate Professor in the Department of Sociology at Ghent University, Belgium. Her primary research fields are social theory, political sociology and the third sector. Her research focuses on the consequences of late-modern social change for citizenship and voluntary solidarity.

Barbara Józefowicz is an Assistant Professor in the Faculty of Economic Sciences and Management at Nicolaus Copernicus University in Toruń, Poland. Her current research interests focus on organizational behaviour, in particular on trust in team management, diversity and inclusion, and corporate volunteering programs.

Olga Junek teaches across the disciplines of tourism, hospitality and events in Australian and German Universities, which has given her a broad perspective on international education. She has collaborative networks within the tourism and events industry and her research interests include international education and students as well as travel behaviour, including voluntourism.

Snigdha Kainthola is a doctoral researcher in the Department of Tourism and Hospitality Management, Jamia Millia Islamia, India. Post her MBA in tourism, she has worked in the tourism sector for two years as a tour leader. Her core areas for research are spiritual tourism, overtourism and management. She has contributed different chapters related to overtourism in different books under well-known publications.

Chulhee Kang is Professor of Philanthropy & Nonprofit Organization Studies at the School of Social Welfare, Yonsei University in South Korea, and former Dean of the School of Social Welfare. He recently served as the President of the Korean Academy and on the editorial board member of *Nonprofit and Voluntary Sector Quarterly*. Dr Kang designed the Community Chest of Korea (the largest public charity organization in Korea), the Honor Society (the largest major donors' circle in Korea), and Giving Korea (a bi-annual national survey on giving and volunteering). Dr Kang's research covers a wide range of topics that include nonprofit organizations, charitable giving and volunteering. His recent book is titled *Understanding Citizens' Altruistic Behaviors in Korea* (2019).

Niki Koutrou is a Senior Lecturer in Sport Management at Bournemouth University, UK. Her research focuses on social legacies, sport policy, and sustainability. Niki is also the Principal Investigator of a project funded by the IOC/Olympic Studies Centre that aims to explore the volunteering legacy of the Athens 2004 Games.

Darja Kragt is a Lecturer in Work Psychology at the University of Western Australia School of Psychological Science. Her research is focused on investigating attraction, retention and leadership among emergency services volunteers. Darja's other research interests include identity processes in leadership development and retirement transitions.

Jane Legget is Associate Director, Cultural Heritage at the New Zealand Tourism Research Institute, Auckland University of Technology. She has worked within the museum and heritage management sectors and in academe in Great Britain and New Zealand. She has enjoyed working alongside volunteers in diverse cultural heritage attractions.

Andrzej Lis is an Assistant Professor at Nicolaus Copernicus University, Poland, the executive editor of the *Journal of Corporate Responsibility and Leadership*, and an author of numerous publications in management studies, with the focus on knowledge management, positive organizational scholarship, corporate social responsibility, public management and logistics, and sport management.

Leonie Lockstone-Binney is an Associate Professor and Research Director for the Department of Tourism, Sport and Hotel Management at Griffith University, Australia. Leonie's research relates to event and tourism volunteering having published over 70 peer-reviewed articles and received competitive research funding from the Australian Research Council and the International Olympic Committee. Leonie is Associate Editor of the *Journal of Hospitality and Tourism Management* and has roles on the editorial boards of *Event Management*, the *International Journal of Event and Festival Management* and *Frontiers in Sports and Active Living*.

Ellie May is a Senior Lecturer in the School of Events, Tourism and Hospitality Management at Leeds Beckett University in the UK. Ellie completed her PhD in 2017 which explored volunteers' experiences at the London 2012 Paralympic Games. Her research interests include volunteering, sport event volunteering, mega events and disability sport.

Lucas C.P.M. Meijs is Professor of Strategic Philanthropy and Volunteering at RSM, Erasmus University, the Netherlands. His research focuses on volunteer management, corporate community involvement and service learning. He has served for six years as the first non-North American editor of *Nonprofit and Voluntary Sector Quarterly*.

Christel Lorraine Mex is an Adjunct Research Associate with Flinders University (Australia) having completed her PhD in 2019. She is currently an elected member with the

City of Norwood Payneham & St Peters, President of Community Alliance SA and a Working Group member for South Australia's Volunteering Strategy.

Geoff Nichols is an Honorary Senior Lecturer in Sport and Leisure Management at the University of Sheffield. Geoff's main research interests are volunteers in sports clubs and events, management of sports clubs run by volunteers and the volunteering legacy of sports events. Since 2009, he has chaired the UK's Sports Volunteering Research Network.

Rafaelle Nicholson is Senior Lecturer in Sport and Sustainability at Bournemouth University. She is the author of *Ladies and Lords: A History of Women's Cricket in Britain* (Peter Lang, 2019). She is also a freelance journalist who writes for ESPNCricinfo, *Wisden* and *The Guardian*, and runs her own women's cricket website, CRICKETher.

Anna Karin Olsson is Assistant Professor in Business Administration at University West, School of Business, Economics and IT, in Sweden. Anna's recent publications cover issues such as volunteers in tourism settings, place innovation, urban regeneration, cultural heritage, stakeholder collaboration, women entrepreneurs and social media.

Faith Ong is a lecturer in the Tourism discipline at The University of Queensland in Australia. Her research interests lie in the role of tourism and events as tools of social change, focusing on inclusivity for marginalized communities in events and tourism. Faith has published in volunteer tourism, sustainability and critical events.

Sang-uk Park is Executive Director of FrameC Research Institute in Seoul, South Korea and Executive Director of the Baehwa Senior Welfare Center in Tae-an, South Korea. He conducted the survey regarding motivations on volunteers for the PyeongChang Olympic and Paralympic Games with the Seoul Volunteer Center. Dr Park has conducted research on a wide range of topics including citizens' volunteering and human service organizations.

Katja Petrovic obtained her PhD in social psychology (examining the relationship of religiosity and volunteerism) at La Trobe University in Australia. Her research interests include religiosity, spirituality and their effect on prosocial and antisocial behaviour.

Josephine Pryce is an Associate Professor at James Cook University in Australia. Her research interest in the 'sustainability of working lives' captures many aspects of 'work', including paid work, voluntary work and the notion of occupation. Her research enables her to learn about people from all walks of life and to contribute to making a difference in the everyday and working lives of people, their well-being, sustained labour markets, workforce trends and 'the future of work'.

Dr Hongxia Qi is an Adjunct Research Fellow at Victoria University of Wellington. Her research interests include event volunteering and MICE, especially in the China context.

Fiona Reid was a Lecturer in Sport and Event Management at Glasgow Caledonian University until 2020. Her research focuses on sport volunteers and voluntary sport clubs. She is now an Independent Researcher and Director of Bayfirth Research.

Colin Rochester has been involved in the practice and study of voluntary action since 1968. His recent books include *Volunteering and Society in the 20th Century* (with Angela Ellis Paine and Steven Howlett, 2010), *Rediscovering Voluntary Action* (2013) and *Handbook on Hybrid Organisations* (edited with David Billis, 2020).

Robert Rogerson is Academic Director of the Institute for Future Cities at the University of Strathclyde, focusing on innovative research into the development of sustainable, liveable cities globally. Having been Legacy Research Coordinator for the 2014 Glasgow Commonwealth Games, he authored the definitive account of the Games – *Glasgow's Commonwealth Games: Behind the Scenes.*

Richard Shipway is an Associate Professor in the Department of Sport and Event Management at Bournemouth University, UK. His research interests focus on sport tourism, Olympic studies, the impacts and legacies of international sport events, crisis and disaster management for sport, volunteering at mega sports events and sport ethnography. His previous work has explored a series of Olympic-related research themes ranging from resident perception studies to Olympic tourism. Richard's other research interests are linked to the experiences of endurance athletes, most notably distance runners and cyclists. He is the Regional Editor (Europe) for *the International Journal of Event and Festival Management (IJEFM)* and Reviews and Commentaries Editor for the *Journal of Sport and Tourism.* Since 2010 Richard has served on the Economic and Social Research Council (ESRC)'s high profile Peer Review College, refereeing grant proposals within social sciences.

Karen A. Smith is Professor of Tourism Management in the Wellington School of Business and Government at Te Herenga Waka – Victoria University of Wellington in New Zealand. Karen's research concerns volunteers and their management in the tourism and events sectors, and more broadly in non-profit organizations and employer-supported volunteering. Karen is a past-Chair of Volunteering New Zealand and was made a Member of the New Zealand Order of Merit for her services to education and volunteering.

Robert A. Stebbins received his PhD in Sociology in 1964 from the University of Minnesota. He has taught at Presbyterian College (1964–1965), Memorial University of Newfoundland (1965–1973), the University of Texas at Arlington (1973–1976) and the University of Calgary (1976–1999). In 2000, he was appointed Professor Emeritus at the University of Calgary. Stebbins served as President of the Social Science Federation of Canada (1991–1992), after having served as President of the Canadian Sociology and Anthropology Association (1988–1989).

Ryan Storr is a Lecturer and Academic Course Advisor in Sport Development at Western Sydney University in Australia. His PhD thesis investigated community sport volunteers and their engagement with diversity work. Dr Storr's current research interests are primarily related to LGBT+ inclusion in sporting contexts.

Arthur A. Stukas, PhD (Minnesota, 1996), is an Associate Professor in the Department of Psychology and Counselling and the Centre for Sport and Social Impact at La Trobe University in Australia. Art's research focuses on volunteerism and community service, social interactions and social relationships, and stigma and prejudice.

Pinaz Tiwari is a research scholar in the Department of Tourism and Hospitality in Jamia Millia Islamia, India. She has worked in the tourism sector for two years after her MBA in tourism. Her interest areas are in tourism marketing, destination management, tourism education and stakeholders' capacity development. She has contributed to different chapters related to overtourism in different books under well-known publications.

Mateusz Tomanek is an Assistant Professor at Nicolaus Copernicus University in Poland, the editor-in-chief of the *Quality in Sport* journal, the chairman of the organizing committee of the International Scientific Conference *Quality in Sport* and author of numerous publications in sport management.

Konstantinos Tomazos is a Senior Lecturer in International Tourism at the University of Strathclyde Business School, UK. His work places emphasis on new trends and niches in tourism and their effect on the tourism industry, local recipients and other stakeholders. He has presented and published on different forms of tourism, and the process that takes new tourism niches from the margins to the mainstream. More specifically, his work focuses on the realm of alternative tourists, volunteer tourists, tourism micro-niches and 'next-gen' travellers.

Lili Wang is Associate Professor in Nonprofit Leadership and Management at the School of Community Resources and Development, Arizona State University in the United States. Her research interests include volunteering and charitable giving, institutional philanthropy and cross-sector collaboration.

Emilie Wiehe is a PhD candidate in Geography at the University of Guelph, Ontario in Canada. Her doctoral research is focused on the political ecology of marine conservation and the blue economy in Mauritius. In addition to her doctoral research, Emilie has conducted research on volunteer tourism on the island.

Tamara Young is an Associate Professor of Tourism in the College of Human and Social Futures, University of Newcastle, Australia. Her interdisciplinary research is situated in critical tourism studies and extends knowledge on the lived experience of travelled and travelling cultures. Tamara's research focuses on both the production and consumption of cultural tourism experiences in Australia and the Asia-Pacific region, with a focus on particular subcultural forms of travel including youth tourism, backpacker tourism, volunteer tourism and Indigenous cultural tourism.

1

INTRODUCTION

Kirsten Holmes, Karen A. Smith, Leonie Lockstone-Binney
and Richard Shipway

Volunteering in events, sports and tourism

Volunteering is an essential component of the events, sports and tourism (EST) sectors. Volunteers underpin a range of core EST services that contribute to the liveability and vibrancy of destinations for visitors and residents alike. From running local sporting clubs, to directing visitors at local information centres, to planning community events and delivering development projects abroad, the multitude of contributions of EST volunteers cannot be ignored.

Volunteering can be defined in many ways – as unpaid work, civil society or serious leisure (Rochester et al., 2010). The dominant understanding of what constitutes volunteering varies across different countries, with the unpaid work perspective taking precedence in Anglo-Saxon countries, while volunteering as civil action is the leading view in Nordic countries. While there is no accepted definition, there is general agreement among researchers that volunteering is a multi-dimensional concept, and the most frequently cited definition comes from Cnaan, Handy and Wadsworth (1996, p. 371). Cnaan et al. present four elements of volunteering, which form the basis of a definition, each dimension presented on a continuum:

- free choice (free will, relatively uncoerced, obligation to volunteer);
- remuneration (none at all, none expected, expenses reimbursed, stipend/low pay);
- structure (formal, informal); and
- intended beneficiaries (benefit/help others, usually strangers; benefit/help friends or relatives; benefit oneself, as well).

These dimensions mean that different forms of volunteering sit on a spectrum ranging from pure to broad. This gives rise to many 'grey' areas where it is not clear whether an activity is understood to be volunteering by the participant or the beneficiaries. Research has shown that some forms of volunteering are perceived by society more widely as more volunteer-like than others (Haski-Leventhal et al., 2018). This perception is based on the cost of volunteering to the participant; the more it costs the participant in terms of time and resources, the more volunteer-like the activity is perceived to be. This means that most of the activities

DOI: 10.4324/9780367815875-1

undertaken by volunteers in the EST sectors in supporting the leisure activities of beneficiaries, could also be classified as a form of leisure for the volunteer and, as such, may be perceived as less serious compared to volunteering efforts that support essential services such as health provision and emergency response.

The contribution of EST volunteers is difficult to quantify. In respect of events, volunteers are involved in a wide range from local community events and festivals to mega-events, the latter being one about which there has been a lot written (Smith et al., 2014). They are also involved in most sports, particularly at grassroots level. Indeed, in some Western Anglo countries, sport volunteering makes up nearly a third of all formal volunteering (ABS, 2019). Volunteering within tourism takes place in two distinct settings: host volunteers and guest volunteers (Holmes et al., 2010). Host volunteers are involved in a range of services for tourists. These include various roles at attractions, meet-and-greet programmes, visitor information centres, tour guiding and emergency services. Guest volunteers are primarily volunteer tourists. Volunteer tourism as a phenomenon was first described in detail by Wearing (2001) and has now developed into a substantial sub-field, as Chapter 35 of this handbook demonstrates. Paradoxically, some volunteers provide visitor services at some distance from their home, combining both host and guest roles. An example would be campground hosts, who operate national park campsites (Weiler & Caldicott, 2020), see Chapter 7.

Research on volunteering in EST has grown substantially in recent years. Some aspects such as mega-event volunteer programmes and volunteer tourism have received substantial attention from researchers, whereas others, including destination service volunteering (Chapter 7), and fundraising and business events (Chapters 16 and 18 respectively), have been largely overlooked. Most research on EST volunteering is also very siloed. Papers on mega-event volunteer programmes are published in events and occasionally tourism journals, sports volunteer researchers publish in sports journals whereas, volunteer tourism studies are published in tourism journals. There are few studies that examine issues across different sectors. Research has predominantly examined formal volunteering in the EST sectors, whereby individuals volunteer through an organisation. In contrast, informal volunteering, where individuals help within their neighbourhood, has received little attention to the point where we know very little about this (see Chapter 37).

In addition, there is a significant gap between the EST body of research on volunteering and more generalist studies from the not-for-profit sector. There is much that EST researchers could learn from these generalist studies, rather than the predisposition to look inwards and describe volunteering only in narrow reference to EST volunteering studies. This predisposition in part explains the ongoing drive to develop specialist EST volunteering instruments (as noted in Chapters 5 and 40), when generalist measures such as the Volunteer Functions Inventory (VFI) (Clary et al., 1998) are widely applicable and reliable, as Chapter 21 demonstrates. It is notable that there is a body of work on volunteer tourism within tourism studies and a separate body of work on international volunteering within the not-for-profit literature. Both approach the phenomena differently, with tourism researchers seeing volunteer tourists as tourists who volunteer, and not-for-profit researchers perceiving them as volunteers who travel internationally. Both approaches also favour different methodologies, with a predominance of qualitative case study work on volunteer tourism and a preference for large-scale macro studies on international volunteering.

This handbook is timely in bringing these various forms of volunteering within EST together. The chapters highlight similarities and differences, which enable a more macro perspective on the challenges facing the future of EST volunteering and volunteer-involving organisations. In addition, we have included chapters from leading researchers working in the generalist not-for-profit space (including Haddock, Chapter 2; Meijs, Chapter 20; Rochester, Chapter 36; Wang, Chapter 37; chapter co-authors Handy and Kang, Chapter 14; Hustinx, Chapter 15; and Stukas, Chapter 21). These chapters draw on the wider body of literature on volunteering and will enable broader cross-fertilisation. If we are to advance our knowledge of EST volunteering – and volunteering more generally – such interdisciplinary perspectives are essential. One challenge that emerges from different forms of EST volunteering is how to leverage short-term and episodic volunteering into both bounce-back and longer-term commitments. This is a challenge for both event legacy planning and volunteer tourism providers. Sharing and comparing experiences and approaches to harnessing recognised volunteer energy for future volunteer assignments would be highly beneficial for the sustainability of both local and international forms of EST volunteering.

Structure of handbook

The handbook is divided into seven parts, which we outline below.

Part 1 – Disciplinary approaches to volunteering

The study of volunteerism is multi-disciplinary, and Part 1 sets the foundation for the handbook by reviewing how different disciplines have examined EST volunteering. The different disciplinary approaches are presented in alphabetical order, beginning with economic approaches. Economists view volunteering as unpaid work and are primarily concerned with measuring volunteering and establishing its value. In Chapter 2, Haddock discusses the challenges involved and merits in arriving at an internationally accepted definition of volunteering work. This definitional clarity allows for volunteering efforts to be measured alongside the range of economic data collected by international statistical bodies, with the potential to bring the economic contributions of volunteers to the fore. Furthering this recognition, Haddock moves on to explore the potential of relating EST volunteering to international standard statistical classifications of occupations, industries, goods and services and sector-relevant satellite accounts. Haddock concludes by discussing various methods for calculating the economic value of volunteering, dedicated studies of which are underutilised in respect of EST volunteering, with Solberg's (2003) valuation of a cohort of major sporting event volunteers being a notable exception.

Drawing on a review of the international development scholarship, in Chapter 3 Davies argues that geography fundamentally affects the nature of volunteering as it promotes mobility of individuals, ideas, knowledge and resources between geographies. Davies argues that the geographic divide often associated with international and other (domestic) forms of volunteering should be avoided to prevent dichotomous framings of volunteer spaces, particularly in respect of international development as being a one-way movement of knowledge, resources, values and practices from the global North to the global South. The dominance of the global North perspective of volunteering in general, and in relation to EST volunteering specifically, is noted elsewhere in this handbook (see, for example, Chapter 39). In Chapter 4, Grimm, Wiehe and Bath-Rosenfeld critique conservation volunteer tourism through the lens of political ecology, proposing that the latter can help to assess the former. They introduce two models which examine power dimensions and contrasting access to opportunities, and highlight that these models can assist researchers and practitioners to examine and identify places of inequity that, if addressed, will help facilitate more ethical conservation volunteer tourism.

Chapter 5 explores the psychology of volunteering, with Kragt examining the application of psychological theories to understand the latent motivations for people becoming and remaining volunteers. In respect of the recruitment phase, Kragt discusses appeals based on the functional approach to volunteering of which the aforementioned VFI is the dominant instrument for assessing the psychological functions volunteers seek to have met through volunteering (Clary et al., 1998). Adaptions of the VFI contextualised to EST volunteering are outlined. Kragt explores, amongst other theories, the importance of the psychological contract for understanding how volunteers' expectations can be fulfilled to ensure their ongoing retention. Finally, psychological understandings of demographic and individual factors affecting volunteering are discussed. Kragt argues this is an important area where the lack of EST specific studies should be addressed to better understand the role of such factors in volunteer recruitment and retention. We acknowledge some confirmatory overlap between Kragt's chapter and Chapter 21 on volunteering motivation by Petrovic and Stukas.

The final disciplinary lens covered in this part is public administration. In Chapter 6, Gawlowski and Gulak-Lipka provide a case study of the dynamics of local public administration working in respect of an international sporting event (the UEFA Under 21 Championship hosted by Poland in 2017). They highlight that two different management paradigms were at play. UEFA, as the international sporting organisation that owned the event, demonstrated top-down New Public Management (NPM) (Nesbit, Christensen & Brudney, 2017), keeping tight control over a number of decisions as to how the local volunteer workforce in the city of Bydgoszcz were recruited and managed. In contrast, the local public administration demonstrated network governance aimed at building cooperation with UEFA and other host city stakeholders. For the local administration, there were perceived benefits in terms of the professionalisation of their volunteer management practice. The impacts of NPM are also discussed in Chapter 39 of the handbook in relation to the future of volunteering and work.

Part 2 – Volunteering in tourism and sport

Parts 2 and 3 bring in the EST context by considering the wide range of organisational types and forms of volunteering in these areas. Part 2 focuses on tourism and sports contexts including host volunteering within destinations and volunteer tourism. Chapter 7 by Smith, Olsson and Holmes begins this part by examining the destination services organisations which promote and facilitate tourism in a destination, and where the volunteers are often the first 'hosts' that tourists meet in the destination. The authors review the relatively small body of research on volunteering in six destination settings: visitor information centres, meet-and-greet programmes, destination tourism associations, destination tour guiding, campground hosting, and emergency and rescue services. Smith et al.'s model of destination service volunteering identifies four roles where volunteers make contributions to destination management and the visitor experience: destination planning, risk management, visitor welcome and orientation, and interpretation, and they highlight that these volunteers are involved in the co-creation of visitor experiences. The chapter concludes with a research agenda for this largely overlooked form of tourism volunteering.

Chapters 8 and 9 are concerned with volunteering in two contrasting types of attractions: museums and protected natural areas. In Chapter 8, Leggat examines the volunteer cohorts associated with three distinct museums located in Auckland, New Zealand. Across these cultural institutions, it is reported that the museums are managing a predominantly older population of volunteers and are facing difficulties in attracting younger people to volunteer at these visitor attractions. Leggat's chapter also suggests that New Zealand's indigenous and diverse multicultural populations are not represented in the composition of the museum volunteers, which are overrepresented by European New Zealanders. Leggat concludes by calling for qualitative research to investigate ways and means of developing more inclusive and representative museum volunteer cohorts. Turning from museums to nature-based attractions, in Chapter 9, Bristow recognises that many protected areas, operated by both public agencies and non-governmental organisations, are increasingly depending on the support of volunteers, with 'Friends of the Park' groups being a common management strategy. Chapter 9 presents a case study of the development of the Appalachian National Scenic Trail, an almost 3,500 km long trail site in the United States. Bristow considers the philosophic roots of the Appalachian Trail and demonstrates how volunteer efforts have been central to the Trail throughout its 100-plus year history; a reliance on volunteers, which continues to this day. The chapter outlines the comprehensive volunteer management structure which exists to support (herd) 6,000 volunteers as they undertake trail and facility maintenance, construction and repair, corridor monitoring, administration and leadership, protection of natural and cultural resources, education, outreach and interpretation.

Chapter 10 on deconstructing volunteer tourism sees Kainthola, Chowdhary and Tiwari critique and debate some of the opportunities for tourists to facilitate constructive change for both local communities and environments. They revisit scholarly understandings of volunteer tourism and tourist motivations, and discuss how an ideology of neo-liberalism has influenced and impacted volunteer tourism. The chapter also discusses the extent to which volunteer tourism promotes a culture whereby rich, white people from developed countries travel to 'help' poor, usually non-white people in developing countries. This is one of a number of chapters that recognises ethical questions related to EST volunteering (see Chapter 29 for an in-depth discussion on the ethics of volunteer tourism, but also, for example, Chapter 7, which focuses on the involvement of volunteers in commercial destination contexts).

In Chapters 11 and 12, Mex and Nichols in turn shift the focus to leisure and sport associations and grassroots organisations. Both chapters provide an overview of the relevant sector before outlining challenges facing volunteers in these organisations, particularly succession planning for committee members. Chapter 11 by Mex highlights the decline of volunteer leaders in Australian grassroots associations and argues that despite the importance of these associations in civil society, membership numbers are declining and fewer members are willing to become leaders. Key issues and messages relating to overcoming 'red tape' and bureaucracy, greater accessibility to volunteering infrastructure and capacity building programmes to enable positive outcomes, and the supportive cultures within grassroots association are discussed. In Chapter 12, Nichols scrutinises sports clubs managed by volunteers, termed as community sports organisations in Europe, Australia and Canada, and community sports associations in the United States of America. The chapter introduces a selection of broader leisure debates relating to measuring volunteering, evaluating the contribution of volunteering to society, the balance between altruism and self-interest in volunteers' motives, and the position of the voluntary sector in the EST sectors, whereby competition for time, enthusiasm and expenditure is intense. In doing so, Nichols' discussion of community sports organisations highlights themes which run through the study of volunteering and other chapters in this handbook.

Part 3 – Volunteering at events

Part 3 turns the attention to the study of event volunteering. This separate part highlights both the dependency of the events sector on volunteers as well as the substantial body of work on event volunteering. The part begins with Chapters 13 and 14, which use the Olympic Games as case studies (also see Chapters 26 and 27 for further mega-sporting events examples), followed by a series of chapters on volunteering at events which have been much-less researched: community events (Chapter 15), charity fundraising events (Chapter 16), corporate volunteering at events (Chapter 17) and business events (Chapter 18).

Using a case study of the London 2012 Olympic Games, Koutrou asked volunteers to retrospectively reflect on their experiences at the Games. Chapter 13 discusses the outcomes of volunteering in relation to skill enhancement and highlights the extent to which mega-sport events are hubs of volunteering activity that allows volunteers to enhance knowledge, skills, networks and career prospects. Koutrou argues that to achieve some of the broader social legacies at mega-sports events, more supportive structures and institutional arrangements are needed by host governments, Local Organising Committees and other stakeholders to ensure that volunteers can be effectively mobilised to support their local communities and other activities beyond the event. In Chapter 14, Kang, Handy and Park bring in the non-Western perspective by comparing cohorts of volunteers at the Vancouver, London and Pyeong Chang Olympic Games. Kang and colleagues note that the literature on Olympic volunteers is predominantly from English-speaking countries, which means that cultural differences in volunteer participation are often overlooked. To address this imbalance, the authors undertook a study of volunteer motivation at the Pyeong Chang Olympic Games in the Republic of Korea, which has a fairly recent history of volunteering. The findings are compared with similar studies from the Vancouver Winter and London Summer Olympic Games. While there were some significant differences between the volunteer cohorts, these could be the result of demographic or geographic factors rather than cultural. The study highlights the challenges of conducting comparative work across different mega-events taking place in diverse cultural, economic, geographic, political and temporal contexts.

Moving away from mega sporting events, Chapter 15 turns our attention to community events and an interesting conceptualisation of these. Delanoye, Gorleer and Hustinx acknowledge the accepted view of event volunteering as *volunteering for an event*, whereby volunteers contribute to the leadership and/or operational success of an event. This view is contrasted with the emergent perspective of events at which people can *volunteer as an event*. Delanoye, Gorleer and Hustinx use the global emergence of National Days of Service (NDS) and a particular case example of the 2019 NDS held in Belgium to illustrate points of difference. At this event, a series of one-day volunteering opportunities were offered in tandem with an existing multi-day festival. People were able to engage in short term volunteer opportunities as part of the event, in addition to celebrating and promoting the act of volunteering. Survey findings suggested that the Belgium NDS event attracted a diverse group of volunteers, including people who had not previously volunteered before. As such, Delanoye, Gorleer and Hustinx suggest that *volunteering as an event* may provide an appealing entry-point for people with limited volunteering experience, in addition to offering an opportunity for more experienced volunteers to celebrate their acts of volunteering. Brown, in Chapter 16, then explores the interaction between volunteering and charity fundraising events. He identifies the critical support role of volunteers within the third sector, the extent that charities are reliant on their support, and how charities can best manage this valuable resource. The chapter discusses trends of volunteering with charities and charity events, the economic significance of charity events, and outlines a proposed typology for understanding charity event volunteering.

In Chapter 17, Józefowicz uses two case studies of corporate volunteering event projects to identify both the individual and organisational benefits of corporate volunteering.

The chapter highlights that volunteering activities can help strengthen positive relationships among employees, enhance their experience of meaningfulness at work, develop employee competencies, improve levels of organisational commitment, whilst also helping to improve the image of socially responsible employers. The part then concludes with Qi's Chapter 18 on volunteering at business events in China. The perspectives within the chapter are important and contribute to the event volunteering literature as it moves the discussion of scholarly attention from volunteering in Western countries, to that of China. Findings are examined from a project on student volunteering at business events and key aspects of the volunteering experiences are discussed. This includes the consideration of a commercialisation trend within volunteering at business events, and consequently blurred boundaries with other activities. The students' event volunteering is organised collectively, and within this Chinese context, monetary rewards for volunteering are common.

Part 4 – Managing volunteers

Volunteers are not paid but still their work needs to be organised (Holmes & Smith, 2009). This ensures that their time is not wasted and that the fundamentals are in place to underpin a satisfactory volunteering experience, whilst adhering to mandatory conditions such as insurance and training. Part 4 provides an overview of the volunteer management process from programme design (Chapters 19 and 20), volunteer motivation (Chapter 21), recruitment and selection (Chapter 22), to organisational culture, retention and reward (Chapters 23 and 24).

Cuskelly and Hayes (Chapter 19) begin this part by outlining the process for designing a successful volunteer programme in the EST sectors. Organisations should begin with a rationale for volunteer involvement, and they highlight that a successful volunteer programme requires leadership and should be integrated into the wider organisation. Following these initial components are developing job descriptions, induction and training materials, assigning suitable roles that meet the needs of volunteers, identifying recruitment and retention strategies, and incorporating evaluation strategies for volunteers and the programme. The chapter considers virtual and episodic volunteering and also stresses the importance of meeting the needs of volunteers and reducing barriers to involvement. Chapter 20 sees Meijs take the volunteer stewardship management model he developed with colleagues (Brudney, Meijs & van Overbeeke, 2019) and applying this to events to argue that not all events should manage volunteers in the same way. The volunteer stewardship framework considers both an organisation's access to volunteer energy and the guidance provided to volunteers. The chapter reviews the four management models as they pertain to events. Whereas mega–events should generally apply a programme management approach, frequently held smaller local events should apply a member management approach. Meijs then considers dual or shared volunteer management models which can support events to develop strategies to engage with new sources of volunteer energy such as corporations, educational institutes, family volunteering and single volunteers.

Volunteering motivations feature in a number of chapters, but are the specific focus of Chapter 21 by Petrovic and Stukas. Stukas, as one of the seminal authors of the VFI (Clary et al., 1998), discusses how the functional approach to understanding volunteering motivations can provide a framework for creating persuasive communications to convince individuals to take up volunteering. Petrovic and Stukas note research support for this contention and go on to suggest that messages that appeal to an individual's primary motivations for volunteering will be more persuasive than those focusing on less salient motives. Through motive fulfilment, the authors also demonstrate the merits of the functional approach linked to volunteer satisfaction and commitment, in support of these positive retention outcomes. The chapter concludes in suggesting that future research may seek to identify additional motivations, beyond the VFI, which are applicable to understanding volunteer recruitment and retention in the under-researched fields of continuous sport volunteering and volunteer tourism.

Fedeli and Cigurova examine evidence of widespread recruitment and selection practices applied in the Scottish visitor attraction sector in Chapter 22. Drawing on a mixed methods study, the authors highlight that the extent of formalised recruitment and selection practices in the sector varied considerably, with unsurprisingly, larger operations adopting more formalised practices. Fedeli and Cigurova noted that the sheer need for volunteers to support smaller visitor attractions, in light of their significant recruitment challenges, does not sit well with the institution of formal practices. The authors go on to make a series of recommendations for the sector including the increased use of social media to support recruitment efforts and the tailoring of recruitment and selection practices and associated documentation to the unique characteristics of individual visitor attractions.

The final two chapters in this part consider aspects of volunteer retention and reward. In Chapter 23, Ayer and Cooper focus on community sport volunteers in Canada. They point out that turnover can be challenging for organisations dependent on the ongoing commitment of volunteers and highlight that the need to find new ways to retain volunteers is imperative to ensure organisational success. Volunteers in their study reported that feeling rewarded and recognised were important, with the role of others, good fit and ability to reach personal goals being the main reasons for continuing volunteering. Ayer and Cooper also explored resignation, including why volunteers cease volunteering, and how resignations can be prevented. Sustaining volunteer involvement is also a central thread of Chapter 24 where Pryce investigates the organisational culture of a heritage attraction involving volunteers. She presents a case study of the Puffing Billy railway in Australia to identify and understand the dimensions of organisational culture that impact volunteers. Themes include planning and leadership, communication, being valued, relationships and work satisfaction, as well as strategic and operational changes in the heritage organisation. The research highlights the organisational values, commitment and challenges in attracting, engaging and maintaining volunteers at heritage attractions, akin to some of the themes to emerge from Chapters 8 and 22.

Part 5 – Impacts and legacies of volunteering

Exploring the unique interactions between the EST sectors, Part 5 scrutinises the diverse impacts and legacies of volunteering. The part commences with Chapter 25 and an overview from Adams and Deane who adopt a sustainability approach to help develop a better understanding of the dual concepts of impact and legacy. They approach this by suggesting that both volunteering impact and legacy are in a state of coopetition concerning aspects of philosophy, outcome and output. Through an examination of individual and community-based sustainability, they proceed to contest that the very soul of volunteering, 'altruism', is perhaps under threat from broader neoliberal forces and processes.

Utilising the perspectives of a mega and large-scale sports event, Chapter 26 by May highlights how the development of a volunteer legacy was an integral part of the strategy for hosting the London 2012 Olympic and Paralympic Games. The chapter also examines how the event was perceived as an opportunity to increase volunteering within the local community. Through a series of in-depth interviews with volunteers, the chapter explores the various conceptualisations of volunteering before and after the event, and how these understandings impacted the volunteers' future engagement in volunteering. In doing so, May demonstrates that understanding conceptualisations of volunteering and the relationship to future intentions has an important role in achieving positive legacy outcomes. Rogerson, Reid and Nicolson (Chapter 27) also critique the volunteering impact and legacies associated with high profile global sports events. Using the case of the 2014 Commonwealth Games held in Glasgow, Scotland, they engage in a broader discussion about how event volunteering can be leveraged to generate wider social legacies. Drawing insights from an event volunteer programme, which sought to enhance social connectedness, the chapter explores how social legacies can be generated and considers the implications for future event volunteer management.

In contrast, and within the context of exploring the immersive experiences associated with volunteer tourism, in the last chapter of this part (Chapter 28), Young, Grabowski-Faulkner and Everingham examine some of the challenges associated with impact measurement and the broader impacts on host communities, destinations and supply chains associated with volunteer tourism. They propose that impact measurements in volunteer tourism are difficult to capture and they suggest that rather than quantifying impacts, volunteer tourism impacts are better evaluated in contexts that account for the emerging possibilities for connecting across cultural differences.

Part 6 – Critical issues in volunteering

A critical lens has rarely been applied to studies of EST volunteering. Primarily, volunteering is seen as a 'good thing', and studies have tended to take a top-down managerial perspective, examining how volunteers can be better managed for the benefit of the organisation. Volunteer tourism has been the exception in this body of research, with concerns around the short-term nature of volunteer assignments particularly in developing countries and the deployment of Western, unskilled volunteers with suggestions of neo-colonialism (Holmes, 2014, also see Chapter 10). Critical studies have started to grow within the event studies literature as well. This part, which identifies critical issues related to EST volunteering, considers ethics (Chapter 29), diversity and inclusion (Chapter 30), intercultural and service learning (Chapters 31 and 32), volunteering and obligation (Chapter 33) and global citizenship (Chapter 34).

Tomazos (Chapter 29) begins by considering the ethical dimensions of EST volunteering. Generally, volunteering is thought to be a 'good thing' but some EST contexts throw up ethical concerns, particularly volunteer tourism (see also Chapter 28). Tomazos provides a strong theoretical framework of what constitutes ethical and moral behaviour, noting the dilemmas facing volunteer tourists as they seek to navigate these challenges. Discussions of diversity and inclusion have largely been absent in the literature on EST volunteering, which makes Chapter 30 an important contribution to this volume. Storr critiques the role of volunteers in relation to diversity work in sport organisations and the policies for diversity and inclusion in the sports sector. Data from two Australian studies are presented to provide an account of the experiences of volunteers from diverse backgrounds. First, the experiences of community sport volunteers involved in specialist cricket teams for athletes with intellectual disabilities are presented; and the second is research with a group of lesbian, gay, bisexual and trans (LGBT+) volunteers who facilitated and coordinated the Australian Football League (AFL) LGBT+ supporter groups. Storr argues that policymakers and sports administrators need to be more proactive in supporting volunteers who are committed to diversity, and also makes recommendations for future research on volunteering within diverse communities.

Chapter 31 by Junek and Chang investigates how rarely studied North-North volunteer tourism programmes facilitate intercultural learning among participants. While intercultural learning is often posited as a benefit of volunteer tourism, there has been little evidence of how this occurs or what volunteer tourism organisations can do to facilitate this form of learning. This chapter examines the work of non-governmental organisations (NGOs) offering international voluntary service programmes for young people and what commercial providers would need to do to emulate the intercultural learning built into the NGOs' programmes. In Chapter 32, Chen and Qi examine how volunteering for university students at business events in China enables mutually beneficial service learning to occur. While volunteering as service learning has received considerable attention in some countries, it has rarely been considered in a Chinese context or within an EST setting. Chen and Qi use the context of Events Management students to uncover the differences between service learning and volunteering, and also identify the different roles of the three stakeholders: students, universities and host organisations. In tandem with Qi's Chapter 18, Chen and Qi's contribution to this volume brings in several new perspectives including the Chinese context and the involvement of volunteers in the commercial EST sector.

Stebbins examines the role of obligation in volunteering in Chapter 33 and contemplates the contrasting positive and negative perceptions of the term within. Following this debate, he gravitates towards the more positive interpretations of 'obligation', given that volunteering is understood as an agreeable responsibility, as part of an event, sport or tourism activity. In doing so, Stebbins also explores the rise of volunteering as leisure, examines the nature of obligation as usually met when volunteering, and concludes by considering the implications of obligatory volunteering in the personal lives of participants. Given Cnaan, Handy and Wadsworth's (1996) definition of volunteering as involving free will, this takes us into broader forms of volunteering. Volunteer-involving organisations do need to impose some level of obligation if their volunteers are to work with defined parameters and provide necessary services such as meeting cruise ship arrivals or delivering a guided tour of botanic gardens. Indeed, we might ask to what extent the volunteers in Chen and Qi's study (Chapter 32) experienced obligation?

Ong's chapter on turning international volunteer tourism into domestic, glocal volunteering concludes this part. Chapter 34 is timely, given the travel restrictions resulting from COVID-19. Ong considers the opportunities for domestic volunteer tourism and how this could create a more ethical and sustainable context for tourists to give back to their communities.

Part 7 – New directions in volunteering research

The final part looks at trends in volunteering and volunteering research, including an overview of EST volunteering research (Chapter 35), trends in volunteering generally (Chapter 36) and specifically regarding informal volunteering (Chapter 37), as well as research methods adopted by EST volunteering researchers (Chapter 38). The book concludes with Chapter 39's forward-focused stance on the future of volunteering, work and the impacts of COVID-19.

Lis and Tomanek begin this part with a bibliometric analysis of the extant research on EST volunteering. The analysis in Chapter 35 reveals three distinct periods to date in the progression of EST volunteering research including a start-up phase (2000–2007), growth phase (2008–2014) and a more recent shakeout or stabilisation phase (2015–2020). This analysis goes on to reveal the most productive (in terms of yearly number of publications and the number of received citations) researchers in the entirety of the EST volunteering field and in the various sub-fields (i.e., sports, events and tourism) and the top contributing countries and institutions. In analysing core studies in the EST field, Lis and Tomanek highlight that their research sample indicates two separate research branches, with the focus on tourism volunteering and volunteering in sport, and few studies straddling both. They go onto to suggest that event volunteering studies make a linking 'bridge' to these two sub-fields.

In Chapter 36 Rochester provides a summary of trends affecting volunteering, drawing on both generic not-for-profit literature as well as specific issues for the EST sectors. A significant challenge for the author is identifying trends during a significant global event – the COVID-19 pandemic – which is impacting on how individuals volunteer and how organisations involve volunteers. Many of the identified trends are long-term changes, which continue to influence the ways in which we volunteer. These include demographic, economic and social trends such as the growth of consumerism and ageing population. These trends have generated new ways in which individuals can volunteer and engage, such as online. The EST sector has both benefited from some trends (such as episodic volunteering underpinning the growth in events) and struggled to adapt to others, like the corresponding decrease in longer-term traditional volunteering, which has underpinned sports clubs and community associations (see Chapters 11 and 12). Chapter 37 sees Wang examine one trend in-depth – informal volunteering, which in terms of numbers far exceeds the contribution of formal volunteering conducted through organisations (ABS, 2019). To date, there has been no consideration in published research of informal volunteering in the EST sectors; however, there is growing interest in this form of helping out from non-profit researchers and governments. Wang provides a thorough grounding in issues related to understanding this phenomenon as well as setting out an agenda for future research on this topic. This is one trend that has been accelerated as a result of COVID-19, with neighbourhood groups sprouting up to respond to the needs of others in their locality.

The research informing this Handbook draws on a range of methodologies, and in Chapter 38 Shipway and Lockstone-Binney review how research on EST volunteering has been conducted to date. In doing so, they note dominant methodological approaches within different EST sectors and provide guidance for researchers on selecting appropriate methods. This chapter will be particularly valuable to those new to researching EST volunteering, including students. The key message emanating from this chapter is that volunteering research, especially in the EST domains, is far richer for the wide variety of views and insights that these variety of methods can generate.

Lastly, in Chapter 39, Baum joins the four editors to consider the future of EST volunteering. The chapter begins by considering how general trends in work and employment impact on volunteering; these include changing population structures, and technological, social and political change. In this context, the conceptualisation of volunteering as unpaid work, and the consequences of this view, are debated. We draw on issues raised in the rest of this volume to identify challenges specific to volunteering in the EST sectors. Finally, these challenges are placed in the context of COVID-19 to consider both threats and opportunities for the future of EST volunteering.

Concluding thoughts

This handbook has been written during the COVID-19 pandemic and we are conscious that the pandemic's appearances in selected chapters are rather fleeting given the scale of its impact on EST volunteering. In some cases, this is a reflection of chapters based on research undertaken pre-pandemic; in others it is a signal that the full impacts are not yet understood. Some planned chapters we had hoped to include could not be completed due to disrupted fieldwork when events were cancelled, volunteer tourism trips postponed and sporting activities severely curtailed.

We acknowledge many of the contributors have been negatively affected by the illness; some have been sick themselves or had loved ones who have been ill. We are grateful for the contributors who were able to work through the challenges of COVID-19 and the additional work and family commitments many were facing due to lockdowns and restrictions, not least the demands of remote learning and teaching. But throughout this we have also seen resilience and hope, not least in the contributions that volunteers are making to their communities; many of these volunteers may have more usually been involved in events, sport and tourism volunteering, but have redirected their efforts to other areas. The re-emergence of travel, sport and events will offer opportunities to re-engage volunteers, who, we believe, will be central to the re-emergence of these sectors. As researchers, we also have an important role to play in advancing knowledge and practice related EST volunteering and its COVID-safe practice.

This handbook is dedicated to our colleagues who have suffered due to the COVID-19 pandemic.

References

Australian Bureau of Statistics. (2019). *General Social Survey*. ABS.

Brudney, J. L., Meijs, L. C., & van Overbeeke, P. S. (2019). More is less? The volunteer stewardship framework and models. *Nonprofit Management and Leadership, 30*(1), 69–87. https://doi.org/10.1002/nml.21358

Clary, E. G., Snyder, M., Ridge, R. D., Copeland, J., Stukas, A. A., Haugen, J., & Miene, P. (1998). Understanding and assessing the motivations of volunteers: A functional approach. *Journal of Personality and Social Psychology, 74*, 1516–1530. https://doi.org/10.1037/0022-3514.74.6.1516

Cnaan, R. A., Handy, F., & Wadsworth, M. (1996). Defining who is a volunteer: Conceptual and empirical considerations. *Nonprofit and Voluntary Sector Quarterly, 25*, 364–383. https://doi.org/10.1177/0899764096253006

Haski-Leventhal, D., Oppenheimer, M., Holmes, K., Lockstone-Binney, L., Alony, I., & Ong, F. (2018). Conceptualisation of volunteering among non-volunteers: Expanding definitions and dimensions using net-cost. *Non-Profit and Voluntary Sector Quarterly, 48*(2), 30S–51S. https://doi.org/10.1177/0899764018768078

Holmes, K. (2014). Voluntourism: International trends. In J. Warburton & M. Oppenheimer (Eds.) *Volunteers and volunteering in Australia* (pp. 117–130). Federation Press.

Holmes, K., & Smith, K. A. (2009). *Managing volunteers in tourism: Attractions, destinations and events.* Butterworth-Heinemann.

Holmes, K., Smith, K., Lockstone-Binney, L., & Baum, T. (2010). Dimensions of tourism volunteering. *Leisure Sciences, 32*(3), 255–269. https://doi.org/10.1080/01490401003712689

Nesbit, R., Christensen, R. K., & Brudney, J. L. (2017). The limits and possibilities of volunteering: A framework for explaining the scope of volunteer involvement in public and nonprofit organizations. *Public Administration Review, 78*(4), 502–513. https://doi.org/10.1111/puar.12894

Rochester, C., Ellis-Paine, A., Howlett S., & Zimmeck M. (2010). *Volunteering in the 21st century.* Palgrave Macmillan.

Smith, K. A., Baum, T., Holmes, K., & Lockstone-Binney, L. (2014). Introduction to event volunteering. In K. A. Smith, L. Lockstone-Binney, K. Holmes, & Baum, T. (Eds.) *Event volunteering: International perspectives on the event volunteering experience* (pp. 1–15). Routledge.

Solberg, H. A. (2003). Major sporting events: Assessing the value of volunteers' work. *Managing Leisure, 8*, 17–27. https://doi.org/10.1080/1360671032000075216

Wearing, S. (2001). *Volunteer tourism: Experiences that make a difference.* CABI Publishing.

Weiler, B., & Caldicott, R. (2020). Unpacking the factors that contribute to successful engagement of stakeholders in volunteer campground host programme. *Tourism Recreation Research, 45*(2), 247–264. https://doi.org/10.1080/02508281.2019.1640445

PART 1

Disciplinary approaches to volunteering

2

ECONOMICS AND VOLUNTEERING

Megan Haddock

Introduction

The giving of time to one's community, to an organisation, or to another person, can be such a natural or necessary part of life that it may seem at odds with attempts by social scientists to define and measure the concept. It can feel cold and clinical when economists fuss about the boundaries of the definition of volunteering and try to pin measurements and economic valuation on its expression. Furthermore, many have worried that applying definitions and economic measures to volunteering will flatten out the rich textures of its manifestations and that local conceptualisations will be lost to flat bar graphs and excel spreadsheets.

And yet, definition and measurement also offer important opportunities to identify where and how volunteering manifests, and how it changes communities and the people who do it. With robust data we might be able to discern why it flourishes or withers and use this information to develop enabling policy environments for volunteering. Documenting the contributions volunteering makes and telling the story of volunteering helps it to be understood. Where it is understood, it can be recognised and supported and its environments can be changed and corrected if needed.

Significant progress has been made in the last ten years to bring our understanding of the scope and scale of volunteering into focus. This chapter will provide an overview of the conceptualisation of volunteering in economic terms, will explain how this concept fits into the international statistical system, and will provide practical guidance for using this system to improve understandings of volunteerism.

Definitions of volunteering

Definitions of volunteering serve different purposes depending on who is using them. The context of this discussion is the set of international standards employed by national governments around the world to benchmark and measure changes in national economic and labour developments over time. The connotations of each word in the definition were carefully considered before they were adopted by the international statistical community, the audience of their intended use. These definitions might inform public policy, legal environments, and

DOI: 10.4324/9780367815875-3

15

organisational management in other contexts, but were not designed for these purposes. Alternative wordings and definitions may be more appropriate in other settings.

No matter the context, defining volunteering turns out to be more difficult than expected. Almost everyone has an idea of what volunteering is – they think they know it when they see it – and yet most people have difficulty defining volunteering without using the term itself. Undertaken in leisure time, it is nevertheless a form of productive activity that produces value to others (Stebbins, 2009). Pursued for no monetary compensation, it produces both tangible and intangible benefits not only for its beneficiaries but also for the volunteers and the organisations that they support when it is carried out in that context (Wilson, 2012). Supposed to be undertaken as a matter of free will, it is often motivated by a sense of personal, cultural, religious, or other obligation. Treated by statistical authorities as a form of unpaid work, it is nevertheless believed to perform important social functions by promoting social integration, civic participation, and sentiments of altruism (Haddock, Sokolowski & Salamon, 2018). Identifying an act as volunteering is somehow a matter of degree along a continuum (Cnaan, Handy & Wadsworth, 1996); the boundaries are indeed "permeable" (Hustinx, Cnaan & Handy, 2010).

Definitions of volunteering and attempts to measure it have been in existence at the national level in a handful of countries for a few decades. However, the definitions employed have varied, making it difficult, if not impossible, to compare the resulting data. What is more, nearly all of these definitions included within their scope only activities carried out through organisations, ignoring what turns out to be the vast majority of volunteer work, which is that carried out directly by individuals for others outside the context of an organisation (United Nations Volunteers, 2018). And even so, data on organisation-based volunteering are not captured in administrative data (as is the case for employment data), leaving us with surveys as the primary mechanism for the collection of this information. Where surveys have been used, national measures have been often very limited in their scope, sometimes measuring only headcounts of volunteers and overlooking the activities volunteers do or how much time they gave to the effort (Salamon, Sokolowski & Haddock, 2011).

The challenge before the international statistical community, therefore, has been to identify a definition that is wide enough to capture the varied range of volunteering activities that exist globally and is yet narrow enough with clear boundaries to give the term meaning. The need for a definition became more apparent when volunteering was mentioned as an optional variable in guidance issued for the economic measurement of the non-profit sector in the system of national accounts (SNA) (United Nations, 2003), as a measure of non-monetary support flowing into these organisations. It became clear that countries choosing to publish these so-called "satellite accounts" of the non-profit sector were omitting the contribution of volunteers not because they did not think it important, but because they had no guidance for how to collect and report on these data.

The internationally accepted economic definition of volunteer work

Major progress was made in 2011 with the publication by the International Labour Organization of a *Manual on the Measurement of Volunteer Work* (ILO, 2011) and subsequent adoption by, with minor modification, the 19th International Conference of Labour Statisticians (ICLS) in 2013, a gathering of the global labour statistical community that meets only

Intended destination of production	for own final use		for use by others					
	Own-use production work		Employment (work for pay or profit)	Unpaid trainee work	Other work activities	Volunteer work		
Forms of work	Of services	Of goods				in market and non-market units	in households producing	
							Goods	Services
Relation to 2008 SNA	*Activities within the SNA production boundary*							
	Activities inside the SNA General production boundary							

Figure 2.1   Forms of work and the 2008 SNA

once every five years to debate and update global labour measurement standards. Closing the loop, the ICLS definition has been fed back into the United Nations (UN) guidance for economic measures of the non-profit sector in the system of national accounts (*United Nations Satellite Account on Nonprofit and Related Institutions and Volunteer Work*) when it was revised in 2018 (United Nations, 2018).

The definition of volunteering adopted in 2013 came in the context of a wider clarification of the definition of work by the global labour statistical community. The *Resolution concerning statistics of work, employment and labour underutilization* (19th ICLS, 2013) defines the statistical concept of work for reference purposes and provides operational concepts, definitions and guidelines for a distinct subset of work activities, referred to as forms of work. In this context, volunteer work was identified as one of the five forms of work, as noted in Figure 2.1.

The full text of the 19th ICLS Resolution's (2013, p. 8) definition of volunteer work is provided below:

37. Persons in volunteer work are defined as all those of working age who, during a short reference period, performed any unpaid, non-compulsory activity to produce goods or provide services for others, where:
    a   "any activity" refers to work for at least one hour;
    b   "unpaid" is interpreted as the absence of remuneration in cash or in kind for work done or hours worked; nevertheless, volunteer workers may receive some small form of support or stipend in cash, when below one third of local market wages (e.g. for out-of-pocket expenses or to cover living expenses incurred for the activity), or in kind (e.g. meals, transportation, symbolic gifts);
    c   "non-compulsory" is interpreted as work carried out without civil, legal or administrative requirement, that are different from the fulfilment of social responsibilities of a communal, cultural or religious nature;
    d   production "for others" refers to work performed:
        i   through, or for organizations comprising market and non-market units (i.e. organization-based volunteering) including through or for self-help, mutual aid or community-based groups of which the volunteer is a member;
        ii   for households other than the household of the volunteer worker or of related family members (i.e. direct volunteering).

38 Excluded from volunteer work:

    a   community service and work by prisoners ordered by a court or similar authority, compulsory military or alternative civilian service;

    b   unpaid work required as part of education or training programmes (i.e. unpaid trainees);

    c   work for others performed during the working time associated with employment, or during paid time off from an employee job granted by the employer.

39 Essential items that should be collected for national accounts and sectoral analyses of volunteer work include the working time associated with each relevant activity cluster, the industry, occupation, and type of economic unit (market units/non-market units/ households).

This definition slightly revised and narrowed the definition of volunteer work provided in the 2011 ILO *Manual on the Measurement of Volunteer Work* by moving the boundary of activity considered to be in-scope to households other than the household of the volunteer worker *or of related family members* (i.e., direct volunteering). The original boundary had been set strictly at the household, i.e., activity conducted for those outside the household, regardless of relationship to the volunteer, was considered in-scope.

A revised ILO Manual definition incorporating the changes in Resolution 1 would thus likely read:

Unpaid non-compulsory work; that is, time individuals give without pay to activities performed either through an organization or directly for others outside their own household or for related family members.

In addition, this definition also makes clear that volunteer work includes that carried out for self-help, mutual aid or community-based groups, which had not been explicitly stated in the 2011 document. And indirectly, the adoption of unpaid trainee work as a form of unpaid work for others further clarifies what is sometimes a confusing boundary for volunteer work.

Five years later, the 20th International Conference of Labour Statisticians adopted a *Resolution concerning statistics on work relationships* (20th ICLS, 2018) that clarified the relationships among the five forms of work identified in Figure 2.1 above, including the two forms of volunteer work:

> Direct volunteers are workers who, on their own account or in partnership with others, and independently of any organization or community group, perform any unpaid, non-compulsory activity to produce goods or provide services for other households. Excluded from this group are workers who produce goods or services for consumption by members of the worker's own household or family.
>
> Organization-based volunteers are workers who perform any unpaid non-compulsory activities to produce goods or provide services for others through or for any type of organization or community group, including market and non-market units. (a) Included in this group are workers who produce goods or provide services for others through or for self-help, mutual aid, or community-based groups. (b) Excluded from this group are: (i) unpaid trainee workers; (ii) workers performing unpaid compulsory activities.
>
> *(20th ICLS, 2018, p. 13)*

The acceptance of volunteering by the 19th ICLS in combination with the recognition of the role of volunteers in achieving the 17 Sustainable Development Goals (SDGs) as part of

Agenda 2030 resolution (UNGA, 2015) has generated a number of new measurement tools by the ILO that support countries interested in measuring volunteering and publications that report on the resulting data. This revised Labour Force Survey (LFS) survey module, LFS integration guide, and model questions for a census and rapid survey platforms are reported on the ILO's dedicated website for volunteer work (https://ilostat.ilo.org/topics/volunteer-work/) (ILO, 2020a, 2020b).

Volunteer work in the international statistical system

The acceptance of an international definition of volunteer work has two major statistical and economic consequences. First, it enables social scientists to produce internationally comparable estimates of its scale and characteristics and to begin to produce analyses of the results to date. Second, acceptance into the international statistical system connects volunteer work to an entire universe of other economic data, making it theoretically possible for data on volunteering to be reported in connection with other data on a host of industries, products, and occupations, including those connected to events, sport, and tourism.

The scale of volunteering globally

As a first step in using the international definition of volunteer work, researchers were able to conservatively estimate the global scale of volunteer work. Based on the latest comparative data, if the time volunteers around the world gave was collectively converted into measures of full-time workers employed in an imaginary country, it would be the fifth largest workforce of any country in the world. This is roughly equivalent in size to the total employment in Indonesia, two-thirds the total employment in the United States and is 50% larger than the total employment in the Russian Federation and Japan (United Nations Volunteers, 2018). Only a third of volunteer work takes place by people who give their time to organisations; as the UNV report shows, approximately 70% of volunteer activity is carried out directly by individuals for friends and neighbours outside the volunteer's family (United Nations Volunteers, 2018).

Put another way, the global volunteer workforce is over half as large as global employment in manufacturing, nearly as large as all employment in construction, and four times larger than the workforce in mining, gas, electricity, and water supply (note that these data do not include China for which employment data are not available) (United Nations Volunteers, 2018). In Organisation for Economic Co-operation and Development (OECD) countries, where agriculture employs far smaller proportions of the workforce, the volunteer workforce stands out even more starkly as engaging 70% of all workers in manufacturing, and more workers than construction, agriculture, and banking and insurance (United Nations Volunteers, 2018).

These global data can be broken down by region, at the national and sub-national level, and disaggregated by demographic characteristics, most notably gender and age where the data are most available and comparable. The story these figures tell becomes more interesting the more we cut and slice the available data. The production of this massive set of globally comparative data in the UNV 2018 report is impressive, and yet they represent only the beginning of what is possible in connecting measures of volunteering to other systems within the global data infrastructure.

Connecting volunteer work to a universe of other data

Underpinning the economic data that we have all come to depend on for basic knowledge about our daily existence in the market, such as rates of employment, gross domestic product, and information about occupations, products, and services in the economy, is a web of connected and interwoven standards and codes nearly universally accepted, though adopted to varying degrees, by nearly every country in the world. Any lack of adoption of the core standards is primarily a matter of national capacity, with a lack of resources for statistical personnel and data collection instruments being the primary barriers. Most countries aspire to their full adoption, and the result is a common statistical language spoken by national accountants and statisticians the world over, in countries large and small, with which they communicate about their economies and labour forces, where the most valued currency is an accurately measured phenomenon.

It is into this environment that the definition of volunteer work (ILO, 2011), and a set of guidelines for its measurement, have been accepted. Thus initiated, the data collected can potentially be connected to a wealth of information collected and classified by the same statistical bodies. This section provides a review of these, with a focus on those most connected to the topic of this Handbook.

Data on occupations – ISCO-08

What kind of work do volunteers do? As noted earlier in the chapter, volunteering is a form of unpaid work. This work can therefore be classified according to the International Standard Classification of Occupations-08 or ISCO-08 (ILO, 2012). Where alternative classification systems are used, they are all aligned with ISCO-08 and can be cross walked to it. Data are first assigned to Major Groups, which are broken out into Sub-major, Minor, and Unit Groups. Appendix II.A (pp. 67–69) of the ILO Manual on the Measurement of Volunteer Work provides a list of disinctive volunteer work activities at the Unit Group level coded to ISCO-08, many of which are especially relevant to the activities associated with sports, events, and tourism, including:

- 2432 Leading of conferences
- 265 Creative and performing artists
- 2652 Perform music, sing, contribute or display work of art at a cultural event
- 2655 Act at a cultural event
- 3332 Event planners, organizers, or managers
- 3422 Coach, referee, judge, or supervise a sports team
- 343 Artistic, cultural and culinary associate professionals
- 3521 Broadcasting and sound and vision recording technicians
- 4419 Provide assistance to other managing or planning an event
- 8322 Driving, providing car, taxi, or van transportation to people or transporting goods
- 9112 Clean up after an event

Many other codes are potentially relevant to the sports, events, and tourism industries and so they are not all replicated here. The point here and for the sections below is that these codes make it possible to sort and organise data on volunteering in a way that enables comparisons of volunteer work.

Data on industries – ISIC-Rev. 4

In which field does the volunteer carry out their work? Like ISCO-08 for the classification of occupations, the International Standard Industrial Classification of All Economic Activities Revision 4 (ISIC Rev. 4) is the highly detailed classification of economic industries (United Nations, 2008). Where alternative classification systems are used, they are all aligned with ISIC Rev. 4 and can be cross walked to it. Data are first assigned to Sections, which are broken out into Divisions, Groups, and Classes. Because ISIC was not designed with the charitable sector in mind, it can be somewhat clunky for those with an interest in third sector organisations and volunteering to manoeuvre. It also lacks sufficient detail in Sections Q (Human Health and Social Work Activities) and R (Arts, Entertainment, and Recreation) and requires coding down to the Group level of detail to allow for meaningful comparison.

For these reasons, the Satellite account on non-profit and related institutions and volunteer work (United Nations, 2018) has published an International Classification of Non-profit and Third Sector Organizations (ICNP/TSO) that reorganises the relevant ISIC Rev. 4 codes and provides additional detail where needed, making the resulting data more accessible for researchers and stakeholders with an interest in the third sector and volunteering. Working under the presumption that the work of most volunteers in sports, events, and tourism would be organised by third sector organisations, a non-exhaustive list of codes is useful for identifying and coding the work of volunteers by industry and is presented in Appendix A.

Data on consumer products: goods and services – CPC Ver. 2.1

What goods and services are produced by volunteer work? The Central Product Classification (CPC) Version 2.1 classifies the goods and services that are the result of production in any economy (United Nations, 2015). This is often closely related to the industry in which the production takes place and the occupation of the worker, but that is not always the case. It is useful in studying transactions in goods and services in detail and can also be used as a basis for developing lists of goods and services for specific purposes, and specifically mentions tourism statistical surveys in this context.

The CPC consists of ten major Sections, which are further subdivided into Divisions, Groups, Classes, and Subclasses. Sections 6–9 are likely to be the most relevant to the connection of volunteer work in the context of events, sports, and tourism. Specific divisions and groups of interest are outlined in Appendix A.

Related satellite accounts

Other industries have recognised the power of leveraging the international statistical system to highlight their specific contribution, including the tourism, sports, and culture sectors. Guidance materials for the development of statistical publications highlighting the contribution of each have been or are currently in development. The contribution of volunteer work to each of these is mentioned briefly but is not fully integrated given the relatively recent arrival of volunteering to the international standards. The stage is set, however, for any country with the data available to connect the dots. A brief review of the available publications is provided below.

Tourism statistics

Because tourism is vital to the economies of so many countries and regions, guidance for the development of a satellite account on tourism within the international statistical system was one of the first to be discussed and is now well advanced in using the data systems described here to highlight the contributions of tourism to national economies. This effort has also benefited from sponsorship by the UN World Tourism Organization (UNWTO), which warehouses and publishes international data on tourism. The adoption of volunteering as a form of work now enables connecting the data on volunteering to that on tourism. For example, Annex 3 of the *International Recommendations for Tourism Statistics 2008* provides a list of tourism characteristic activities (tourism industries) and grouping by main categories according to ISIC Rev. 4 (United Nations, 2010b). Statisticians can now more easily highlight which volunteering matches up with the codes listed there.

The recommendations do briefly recognise the connection between volunteering and tourism already, for example, volunteer work is mentioned as a purpose for trips, although it unhelpfully groups this with travel related to investigative work and migration possibilities; undertaking any other temporary non-remunerated activities not included elsewhere etc. (United Nations, 2010b). To better integrate these data, volunteer work will need to be separately identified as a purpose for a trip, and a possible next step could be harmonising tourism employment survey modules, which were designed to link basic employment data with the closely related *Tourism Satellite Account: Recommended Methodological Framework* 2008 (United Nations, 2010a), and with the information collected by the volunteer work survey modules. Like the satellite account for non-profit and third sector institutions, the tourism satellite account provides a framework for governments seeking to separately present economic data on tourism in their countries that are comparative internationally.

Sports accounts

The European Commission set up a European Union (EU) Working Group on Sport and Economics in 2006 and worked with the Sport Industry Research Centre at Sheffield Hallam University to develop a common European approach for measuring the economic importance of sport and since then a handful of European countries have constructed sports satellite accounts (European Commission, 2018).

Like the tourism data, connecting volunteer work to the employment data in sports could prove to be relatively straightforward and would benefit both fields of interest. As an example, the available data from 2012 indicate that sport is "an employment-intensive economic activity, therefore generating a greater sport share in employment than in GDP" (European Commission, 2018, p. 9). According to the European Commission report, sports-related employment was about 2.72% of total employment while sport-related GDP was about 2.12% of total GDP within the EU. Indeed, half of the employment in the comparative satellite account was connected with "sports education" (European Commission, 2018, Table 4). Given that a large share of sports clubs and sports-education organisations are registered as non-profit organisations that engage significant number of volunteers, one would assume that this understanding of the sports industry being "employment-intensive" would only increase if data on volunteer work were to be included.

For its part, the EU Expert Group on the Economic Dimension of Sport (XG ECO), during the development of the sport satellite account guidance documents, recognised the potential value of measuring volunteer work in the context of sport, and made specific mention of its measurement in recommendations for ongoing efforts to develop sports satellite accounts. They noted,

> accurate data on employment in sport, as well as on the weight of the sports economy in the global GDP and its components are often missing. For this reason, the work in

progress led by Eurostat aiming at developing harmonized indicators on sports volunteering, participation in sport events, sports balance on goods and services is essential.

(European Commission/Sport, 2014, p. 8)

Culture accounts

Like the sports and tourism accounts, efforts are underway to produce guidance on the development of culture satellite accounts. The UNESCO Institute for Statistics (UIS), in collaboration with the UN Statistics Division, is developing international recommendations for compiling culture satellite accounts. Importantly, the proposed global standard is strongly connected to sports and tourism accounts and considers them in relation to the proposed culture satellite account. The challenge will be to present this information in a way that does not double count the results because there is significant overlap. In Austria, for example, data from the initial half of tourism in that country is sport-related (European Commission, 2013).

In 2009, UIS published *The 2009 UNESCO Framework for Cultural Statistics* that offers important insight into what the satellite account will include. This framework recognises the contribution of volunteer work to culture employment and industries though it was published prior to the adoption of the international definition of volunteer work. This publication does offer important guidance for the identification of cultural occupations, which were not developed with volunteering in mind but are nevertheless relevant.

Data uses: calculating the economic value of volunteering

Once the basic data on volunteering have been collected, coded, tallied, and connected to other industries, occupations, and products, it becomes possible to conduct additional calculations of interest, including the rate of volunteering and the economic value of volunteer time.

Volunteer rate

The volunteer rate is an expression of the percentage of the population that engages in volunteer work and is achieved by dividing the number of volunteers by the number of people in the population. Though it seems straightforward, this calculation can become complicated by discussions of exactly who belongs in the population in the denominator. At the country level, this population would typically include all persons over 15 years of age, or the age that might be considered both the legal working age and when minors are able to make uncoerced decisions. Weighting factors for different population sub-groups should also be taken into account when calculating the final rate.

The economic value of volunteering

Economic theory poses the dilemma as to why people volunteer their services for free and to benefit others when rational man is primarily motivated by self-interest (Freeman, 1997; Katz & Rosenberg, 2005; Meier & Stutzer, 2008). The application of a monetary value to the time that people give to organisations and to their neighbours serves two primary purposes. First, for national economic accountants, it contributes to their calculations of the non-market value of goods and services by non-profit and charitable organisations operating in the market. On the books, the number of paid staff does not reflect the true number of workers because it does not account for those not being paid. The output these unpaid workers produce does appear in the market, however, distorting reality in the national accounting system. The second purpose for estimating the economic value of volunteering is for advocacy and recognition purposes. Because conceptualisations vary considerably, putting the efforts of volunteering into monetary terms can serve as a useful mechanism to demonstrate recognition of the contributions of the volunteers themselves, thereby garnering the attention of supporters, stakeholders, policymakers, potential funders and donors, and the broader community.

The replacement cost approach

The replacement cost method is the most commonly used approach for estimating the economic value of volunteer work and is the method recommended by the ILO *Manual on the Measurement of Volunteer Work* (2011). This method asks, "what would it have cost to have paid someone to do this work that has been done without remuneration?" The question is hypothetical and assumes the theoretical funding to pay for the work is available and that individuals would accept the work if paid. The exercise is intended to be intellectual, and not political in nature. The benefit of economic valuations is that they are nearly universally understood among the population and easy to compare to other economic conceptualisations. The downside is that they are limited in scope. It should go without saying that economic valuations do not reflect the full scope of the value of volunteering to people and communities, which includes other rewards and consequences over the short and long term.

The processes used to assign a value to volunteer time range from simple to very complex. The degree of complexity employed depends on three factors: the level of detail available in the data, the resources available to carry out the work, and the interest in the task.

At the organisational level, particularly in smaller organisations, where good records of volunteering hours and activities are kept, it can be somewhat straightforward to provide a rather precise estimation of the value of a volunteer's time. The replacement wages here are calculated by identifying the type of volunteer activity carried out and applying to the number of hours the local going rate for paid work of that kind, and ideally at the same level of skill that it is being provided by the volunteer (Kragt & Holtrop, 2019).

This very specific estimation of the economic value is known as the "specialist" approach (Mook & Quarter, 2003) and is optimal in its level of precision. But this approach is usually only possible at the individual level where people keep track of their work and at the organisational level where good records of the amount and type of volunteer work are kept. Applying the specialist wage becomes more time consuming and challenging the farther one moves out from the individual organisation because it requires a precise level of detail on the number of volunteers and hours worked, and also on the jobs that each volunteer does, the occupational structure of the workforce, and the wages associated with various occupations, which themselves vary by region.

Because of the complexity of applying a precise specialist wage, most efforts to produce an economic value of volunteering generalise the data to some degree. For example, the average wage of workers in a particular field might be used for all volunteers in that same field, instead of the specific wage of an occupation for a specific volunteer activity. Other examples of the "generalist wage" (Mook & Quarter, 2003) include the average wage in the economy as a whole or the average wage in the fields in which volunteers most usually work.

As a sector relevant exemplar of the economic valuation of volunteering, Solberg (2003) highlighted varying valuations of volunteers' time spent working at a major sporting event. The study found that an opportunity cost model, based on volunteers' own reports of the wage they could attract for their diverted time, resulted in a considerably lower valuation of labour contributed in comparison to what it would have cost to pay the volunteer worker market wages. Solberg (2003) suggests that the lower value of the opportunity cost model resulted from the majority of sport event volunteers undertaking the activity during their leisure time rather than using working time to volunteer. This principle is likely to apply to all tourism, sport, and event volunteering, where non-wage active personnel, such as retirees and students, are major contributors (Smith, Lockstone-Binney & Holmes, 2020). This study highlights the variations that can result from using different approaches and cautions those against using the opportunity cost approach in making estimations of the value of volunteering in tourism, sport, and event volunteering.

Discussions of the economic value of volunteering often lose the forest in the discussion of the trees. Unless you are a national accountant or national labour statistician attempting to make very precise estimations for your country, making your best estimation with the resources you have available and keeping the reason that an economic value is being applied to the fore is a good rule of thumb to follow. It is important to try to be as specific as the data allow, but where the data are not available and generalisations must be made, this author recommends erring on the side of a lower estimate in order to avoid accusations of inflating the results erroneously.

Measurement at the organizational level

The inclusion of volunteer work in international statistical systems has significant implications for the collection and reporting of data for national governments, who must consider the cascade of interlocking changes that must be made within the larger system to keep it all in harmony. The impacts of these changes on organisations are likely negligible, however, except for perhaps the policy changes that might result from the increased recognition of volunteering. Nevertheless, the lessons from the international standards can inform and guide organisations in their measurement endeavours.

National level data must rely on household surveys for the collection of information in order to capture both the organisation-based work and the direct volunteer work individuals do on their own. The sheer amount of information makes it a challenge to code and report at any level of detail. Organisations, however, have much more flexibility and access to information than national governments and the ability to gather administrative data about the volunteer work being carried out under their organisational auspices.

Organisations interested in estimating the value of volunteer time should seek to capture the following variables at minimum:

1   The number of people who volunteered (headcount)
2   The number of hours volunteered
3   The types of volunteer work activities (jobs)
4   The field of activity of the work
5   The institutional setting of the work

Additional variables, including the demographics of the volunteers are strongly recommended. Ideally, organisations should establish systems within their administrative structures to capture this information directly in real time so that estimates do not need to be made in retrospect that require individuals to recall what they did and report this information to an interviewer. This is sometimes not possible, and indeed becomes more challenging the larger the organisation, event, or activity becomes.

While daunting, estimating the amount, character, and economic value of volunteering generated by complicated international organisations is possible. Both the International

Red Cross and Red Crescent Societies (IFCRC, 2011) and Rotary International (Salamon, Haddock & Sokolowski, 2019) have carried out major projects to estimate the amount, character, and economic value of the volunteer work of their members and affiliates worldwide. The Rotary example is particularly demonstrative. Here, a survey that utilised the ICLS definition of volunteering was sent via email by Rotary's President to a carefully selected sample of Rotary club leaders in every Rotary region around the world. Club leaders were asked to distribute the surveys, either in electronic or paper form, to all of their club members to mimic the compulsory nature of labour force surveys. The survey asked respondents to recall and report information about each time they volunteered in the previous four weeks. Responses were then tallied, weighted by region, and adjusted to account for potential non-response bias. In the end, Rotary International was able to conservatively estimate that its 1.2 million members give nearly 47 million hours of volunteer effort in a typical year and that the value was conservatively USD $850 million per year.

The Rotary International example offers a more complicated methodology than most organisations will require, but it provides important lessons for organisations that are similar to those utilised by national governments, which are:

1   Make sure that the reasons for the measurement of volunteering is clarified and accepted internally and let this guide the design of the data collection and communication strategy.
2   Utilise existing administrative systems for the collection of data as much as possible.
3   Minimise the number of variables being sought to ensure high quality information.
4   Gather data at a level of detail that will provide sufficiently useful information, but not at such a level that it hampers data collection and analysis.
5   Limit the requirement of individuals to recall and report on their own activities.
6   Use a conservative approach when estimating the economic value.

Conclusion

The development of data on volunteer work has been likened to building a house, where

> the foundation stones of volunteering studies consist of reliable and systematically comparable information on how much volunteering, and of what kind, is taking place. This involves the actual number of people engaged in volunteer activities during a reference period of interest and the amount of time they spend on those activities.
> *(Salamon, Sokolowski & Haddock, 2018, p. 37)*

From there, researchers can

> add the outer shell composed of wall panels, the roof, the doors and the windows. Of these three sections, only the last one is fully visible to most observers, yet without the solid foundation and structure the resulting edifice would be as shaky as a house of cards.
> *(Salamon et al., 2018, p. 37)*

With the adoption of volunteer work into the international statistical infrastructure, the foundation has started to be poured. The next step is in our hands, and that is to leverage the international statistical system to the advantage of volunteer work, including in the fields of events, sports, and tourism. Additionally, there is broad scope to examine the economics of volunteering in these fields, given the dearth of extant studies (Smith et al., 2020).

Appendix A

Relevant ISIC rev. 4 codes for volunteer work in sports, events, and tourism by industry

Section A: culture, communication, and recreation activities

Group A10	Culture and Arts	
Sub-group	A11	Performing and visual arts
	A12	Museums, zoos, parks, historical sites and similar institutions
Group A20	Sports and recreation	
Sub-group	A21	Sports Activities
	A22	Amusement and recreation services

Group A30   Information and communication services

Section E: environmental protection and animal welfare activities

Group E10	National resource management and protection	
Sub-group	E11	Land or water management activities
	E12	Pollution abatement and control activities
	E13	Eco-tourism
	E14	Eco-farming and forestry
	E19	National resource management and protection, n.e.c.,

Group E20   Animal health and welfare activities

Section G: civic, advocacy, political, and international activities

Group   G10   Civic, advocacy and social participation activities

Sub-group	G11	Social advocacy
	G12	Environmental conservation and animal welfare advocacy
	G13	Social clubs and similar member-serving activities
Group G20	Political activities	
Group G30	International activities	

Section L: other activities

Group L30	Accommodation, catering, and food services
Group L40	Trade activities
Group L50	Transportation and storage activities
Group L60	Financial and insurance activities
Group L70	Real estate activities

Relevant CPC version 2.1 classifications for the goods and services produced by volunteer work in the context of events, sports, and tourism

Division 64 Passenger transport services
641 Local transport and sightseeing transportation services of passengers

Division 63 Accommodation, food and beverage services
855 Travel arrangement, tour operator and related services
Group 929 Other education and training services and educational support services
Cultural education services
Sports and recreation education services
Division 93 Human health and social care services
959 Services furnished by other membership organizations
Religious services
Services furnished by political organizations
Services furnished by human rights organizations
Services furnished by environmental advocacy groups
Other special group advocacy services
Other civic betterment and community facility support services
Services provided by youth associations
Grant-giving services
Cultural and recreational associations (other than sports or games)
Other civic and social organizations
Division 96 Recreational, cultural and sporting services
962 Performing arts and other live entertainment event presentation and promotion services
963 Services of performing and other artists
964 Museum and preservation services
965 Sports and recreational sports services
969 Other amusement and recreational services

References

19th International Conference of Labour Statisticians. (2013). *Resolution I: Resolution concerning statistics of work, employment and labour underutilization.* ICLS-Resolution-I-[STATI-131114-1]-En.docx. https://www.ilo.org/wcmsp5/groups/public/—dgreports/—stat/documents/normativeinstrument/wcms_230304.pdf

20th International Conference of Labour Statisticians. (2018). *Resolution I: Resolution concerning statistics on work relationships.* https://www.ilo.org/wcmsp5/groups/public/—dgreports/—stat/documents/meetingdocument/wcms_648693.pdf

Cnaan, R., Handy, F., & Wadsworth, M. (1996). Defining who is a volunteer: Conceptual and empirical considerations. *Nonprofit and Voluntary Sector Quarterly, 25*(3), 364–383. https://doi.org/10.1177/0899764096253006

European Commission Directorate-General for Education, Youth, Sport and Culture. (2013). *Sport satellite accounts. A European project: New results.* https://doi.org/10.2766/47303. https://op.europa.eu/en/publication-detail/-/publication/d44cae16-23bc-4cee-8bc8-f1411c447464

European Commission/Sport. (2014). *Practical guidance on how to encourage transparent and long-term investment in sport, including EU funding, based inter alia on 2012 Recommendations on sustainable financing of sport, including state aid.* EU Expert Group on the Economic Dimension of Sport (XG ECO). https://ec.europa.eu/transparency/regexpert/index.cfm?do=groupDetail.groupDetailDoc&id=27176&no=1

European Commission Directorate-General for Education, Youth, Sport and Culture. (2018). *Study on the economic impact of sport through sport satellite accounts.* https://doi.org/10.2766/156532. https://op.europa.eu/en/publication-detail/-/publication/865ef44c-5ca1-11e8-ab41-01aa75ed71a1/language-en/format-PDF/source-71256399

Freeman, R. B. (1997). Working for nothing: The supply of volunteer labour. *Journal of Labor Economics, 15*(1, pt. 2), 140–166.

Haddock, M. A, Sokolowski, S. W., & Salamon, L. M. (2018). Measuring direct volunteering: Current and future prospects. In *13th International Conference of the International Society for Third*

Sector research working paper. July 2018 https://cdn.ymaws.com/www.istr.org/resource/resmgr/wp18/direct_volunteering_paper_ha.pdf

Hustinx, L., Cnaan, R. A., & Handy, F. (2010). Navigating theories of volunteering: A hybrid map for a complex phenomenon. *Journal for the Theory of Social Behaviour, 40*(4), 410–434. https://doi.org/10.1111/j.1468-5914.2010.00439

International Labour Organization. (2012). *International standard classification of occupations ISCO-08.* Geneva: United Nations.

International Labour Organization. (2011). *Manual on the measurement of volunteer work.* Geneva: United Nations.

International Labour Organization. (2020a). *ILO volunteer work add-on module LFS integration guide (v1) for PAPI and CAPI.* Geneva: United Nations.

International Labour Organization. (2020b). *ILO LFS add-on module on volunteer work (v1) for PAPI and CAPI.* Geneva: United Nations.

International Federation of Red Cross and Red Crescent Societies. (2011). *The value of volunteers: Imagine how many needs would go unanswered without volunteers.* Geneva: Red Cross Red Crescent. https://www.ifrc.org/Global/Publications/volunteers/IFRC-Value%20of%20Volunteers%20Report-EN-LR.pdf

Katz, E., & Rosenberg, J. (2005). An economic interpretation of institutional volunteering. *European Journal of Political Economy, 21*, 429–443. https://doi.org/10.1016/j.ejpoleco.2004.06.004

Kragt, D., & Holtrop, D. (2019). Volunteering research in Australia: A narrative review. *Australian Journal of Psychology, 71*(4), 342–360. https://doi.org/10.1111/ajpy.12251

Meier, S., & Stutzer, A. (2008). Is volunteering rewarding in itself? *Economica, 75*, 39–59.

Mook, L., & Quarter (2003). *How to assign a monetary value to volunteer contributions.* Knowledge Development Centre, Canadian Centre for Philanthropy.

Salamon, L. M., Haddock, M. A, & Sokolowski, S. W. (2019). *The scope and scale of Rotary volunteering.* Baltimore, MD: Johns Hopkins Center for Civil Society Studies. https://my.rotary.org/en/document/scope-and-scale-rotary-international-volunteering-johns-hopkins-report

Salamon, L. M., Sokolowski, S. W., & Haddock, M. A. (2011). Measuring the economic value of volunteer work globally: Concepts, estimates, and a roadmap to the future. *Annals of Public and Cooperative Economics, 82*(3), 217–252. https://doi.org/10.1111/j.1467-8292.2011.00437.x

Salamon, L. M., Sokolowski, S. W., & Haddock, M. A. (2018). *The scope and scale of global volunteering. Current estimates and next steps.* A Background Paper for the 2018 State of The World's Volunteerism Report: The Thread That Binds. United Nations Volunteers.

Solberg, H. A. (2003). Major sporting events: Assessing the value of volunteers' work. *Managing Leisure, 8*, 17–27. https://doi.org/10.1080/1360671032000075216

Smith, K. A., Lockstone-Binney, L., & Holmes, K. (2019). Revisiting and advancing the research agenda for event volunteering. In J. Armbrecht, E. Lundberg & T. G. Andersson (Eds.), *A research agenda for event management* (pp. 126–153). Northampton, MA: Edward Elgar Publishing.

Stebbins, R. A. (2009). Would you volunteer? *Social Science and Public Policy, 46*, 155–159. https://doi.org/10.1007/S12115-008-9186-1

UNESCO Institute for Statistics. (2009). *The 2009 UNESCO framework for cultural statistics.* Montreal: United Nations. http://uis.unesco.org/sites/default/files/documents/unesco-framework-for-cultural-statistics-2009-en_0.pdf

United Nations. (2003). *Handbook on non-profit institutions in the system of national accounts.* New York: United Nations.

United Nations. (2008). *International standard industrial classification of all economic activities, Revision 4.* Department of Economic and Social Affairs Statistics Division Statistical Papers Series M No. 4/Rev.4. New York: United Nations

United Nations. (2010a). *Tourism satellite account: Recommended methodological framework 2008.* Publication ST/ESA/STAT/SER.F/80/Rev.1. New York: United Nations.

United Nations. (2010b). *International recommendations for tourism statistics 2008.* ST/ESA/STAT/SER.M/83/Rev.1. New York: United Nations.

United Nations. (2015). *Central product classification (CPC) version 2.1.* Department of Economic and Social Affairs Statistics Division Statistical Papers Series M No. 77, Ver.2.1. New York: United Nations.

United Nations. (2018). *Satellite account on nonprofit and related institutions and volunteer work.* New York: United Nations.

UNGA [United Nations General Assembly]. (2015). *Transforming our world: The 2030 agenda for sustainable development.* New York: United Nations.

United Nations Volunteers. (2018). *2018 state of the world's volunteerism report: The thread that binds.* Bonn: United Nations Volunteers.

Wilson, J. (2012). Volunteerism research: A review essay. *Nonprofit and Voluntary Sector Quarterly, 41,* 176–212. https://doi.org/10.1177/0899764011434558

3

GEOGRAPHY, PLACE AND INTERNATIONAL DEVELOPMENT VOLUNTEERING

Amanda Davies

Introduction

A review of volunteering through a geographic lens enables us to consider how place can inform the nature of volunteering. It also lets us consider how volunteering can shape the development of places. While the action of volunteering occurs world over, the activities people undertake and the reasons for this do vary between places. At the most basic level, this variability is informed by the characteristics of places, such as population size and formality of settlement, demographics, environmental features and the nature and location of institutional capital. Volunteering can be easier in some places than others, due to the presence (or absence) of Non-Government Organisations (NGOs) and/or volunteering organisations which shape the nature and extent of volunteering. Also shaping variability is the fact that in some places the demand for volunteer provided services and activities is greater than others (Skinner, 2014). Demand is often most acute in places where, for reasons of policy, geographic remoteness, community size and formality, essential and social services are not provided by government or the market.

While the scholarship that purposefully seeks to examine the role of place in shaping volunteering is contextually limited, the rich and diverse examples of volunteering reported across the volunteering literature highlights the role that place plays in shaping the performance of volunteering, and, in turn, the assemblages of place(s). To learn more about the relationship(s) between place and volunteering, this chapter provides an overview of selected scholarship on international development volunteering. It is acknowledged that the scholarship reporting on international development volunteering is extensive, with contributions over at least five decades, from a range of disciplines, drawing on diverse geographical, cultural and political contexts. It is also acknowledged that key themes stemming from and relevant to the scholarship on international development volunteering have been covered in other chapters of this Handbook. However, as argued in this chapter, material reporting on international development volunteering provides particular insight into the role of place in informing volunteering. Across this thematically expansive research are rich case studies that highlight how overlapping geographies including relational remoteness, community size and formality, environmental features as well as social, cultural and political factors necessitate, enable and shape volunteering. As such, this chapter's review of international development

DOI: 10.4324/9780367815875-4

volunteering is structured to focus on illuminating material that is particularly relevant to understanding how place shapes the role and nature of volunteering.

Evolution of international development volunteering

Characterisations of international development volunteering range from being an altruistic activity through to being a purposeful state sponsored, racialised effort to align contested geographies to neoliberal values (St-Amant et al., 2018). As such, the scholarship examining the multiple and contested experiences of international development volunteering provides a useful starting point for considering how geography shapes volunteering. Fundamentally, international development volunteering is a form of volunteering which sees people volunteer to travel to an international destination and participate in developing or delivering infrastructure, services and activities for the purpose of 'developing' places. Much of the literature reporting on international development volunteering centres on North to South volunteering, with Baillie Smith et al. (2018) finding that within this literature, the global North is characterised as a site for sending volunteers, resources and knowledge and the global South as a place needing development, hosting volunteers and receiving knowledge. Therefore, at this broadest definitional level, the geographic construct of the global North and global South informs the positioning of international development volunteering.

Modern forms of international development volunteering have roots in colonialism and missionary activity, with missionary work still forming a significant component of the organised international development volunteering activity today. Non-secular, state sponsored or organised international volunteering emerged in the early 20th century primarily as a response to natural disasters and war recovery (Georgeou, 2012). Lough (2015) highlighted the role that international workcamp movements had in response to World War 1 in stimulating a broader understanding of international voluntary service. These early voluntary service movements established the foundations for modern international development volunteering (Devereux, 2008; Georgeou, 2012). During the 1950s, international volunteering was being articulated as a component of international development aid and relations systems of various governments (Sobocinska, 2017). Devereux (2008, pp. 359–360) summarised international volunteering for development as involving 'humanitarian motivation; reciprocal benefit; living and working under local conditions; long-term commitment; local accountability and North-South partnerships; and linkages to tackle causes rather than symptoms'. Sobocinska (2017) identified that this secular form of international development volunteering involved organising governments selecting particular countries and locations in which to work based on motivations to strengthen transnational diplomacy in particular geographic regions. In effect, early forms of international development volunteering were shaped by the geographic location and trade relationships between countries.

As international development volunteering has expanded, scholars have argued that, in some instances, volunteering has shifted away from reflecting bilateral arrangements between countries to volunteers being a collective – acting within a global civil society (Georgeou, 2012). Building on this broader conceptualisation of international volunteering, others have argued that international development volunteering can support nation building through the extension of international boundaries (Krishna & Khondker, 2004). In reviewing the recent scholarship in international development volunteering, Lough and Tiessen (2018) identified that scholars were continuing to conceptualise volunteering by the two broad historically relevant aims – the volunteer as beneficiary and the community as beneficiary. Sub-typologies of volunteering, dependent on the specific program aims, include, inter alia: volunteering for mutual aid, philanthropic volunteering, civic service, volunteer activism and advocacy, volunteer tourism, cross-cultural volunteering, student volunteering/service-learning and volunteer workcamping (Lough & Tiessen, 2018). Importantly, across the evolving and contested definitions of international development volunteering, the places that are involved in volunteering, both sending and receiving, shape volunteering.

Sites for international development volunteering

International development volunteering is site specific – it does not occur anywhere and everywhere and at all times. The geographic location of volunteering effort is not simply a factor of the geographic location of need. Given that international development volunteering emerged, in a large part, as a state strategy for strengthening international relations and the deployment of aid, the sites where international development volunteering occurs tend to reflect the geo-political networks of various countries (Sobocinska, 2017; Thompson et al., 2020). These relationships have also impacted, overtime, access to communities and on ground networks which are critical for supporting international development volunteering (Devereux, 2008). Research reporting on the functions and legacies of international volunteering development programs highlight how factors such as civil conflict, accessibility, climate, culture, religion and the history and legacy of past NGO and not-for-profit involvement in communities impacts where and how international development volunteers can engage in communities (Sherraden et al., 2008; Thompson et al., 2020).

Present day, while there is variability, most typically sites for international development volunteering are places where NGOs and not-for-profit development and aid agencies, including secular groups, are operating. For NGOs and not-for-profits, their places of operation are determined by a complex of geographic, political and cultural factors that generate site specific need and also impact access. NGOs, not-for-profit and other aid agencies can only operate in locations where their networks provide the foundation for the necessary political and institutional capital for access into the community (Sherraden et al., 2006).

Lough and Tiessen (2018) also highlighted the importance of the difference in program models between different NGOs and not-for-profits. They commended

> in broad terms, some forms of gap year volunteering or "volunteer tourism" by unskilled young people can strengthen cross-cultural communication but are also associated with a variety of poor to negative community-level outcomes including potential harm they may cause by acting on situations they do not fully understand… Likewise, research documents that "professional volunteering" by those who are highly skilled can be effective at building local capacity, producing tangible social capital, filling gaps in services, and forming sustainable development partnerships but may be less successful at developing relationships when performed over a short duration.
>
> *(p. 105)*

Furthermore, their study concluded that programs that specifically recruit different skills to match program aims have greater success and impact. Therefore, attention must be given to understanding the place-based needs of the community as well as the volunteer population.

Relationships between the sending and recipient communities

The framing of international development volunteering as a simple transactional arrangement whereby volunteers from the global North, for altruistic reasons, deliver services to the global South has been extensively critiqued within the academic scholarship. The dichotomous constructions of the volunteer and recipient and the homogenous framing of the global North and South places the power in the relationship with the volunteer from the global North. Challenging narrow dichotomos farmings, research over the last two decades has revealed a diversity of complex ways of being and doing volunteering (Smith et al., 2010; DeVerteuil et al., 2020).

It is now well understood that multiple and overlapping geographies impact where and how NGOs and not-for-profits can engage in international development (Burrai et al., 2014). However, arguably less well understood is how NGOs and not-for-profits extend and re-interpret these geographies and how these geographies, in turn, shape volunteers' actions and relationships between the host community and their home(s). Researchers examining the role of organisations that manage international development volunteering have found that these organisations have a core role in establishing and reproducing, over time and space, a narrative of separation between the volunteer sending and recipient communities, and a narrative of the volunteer as the 'giver' and host community as 'recipient' (Georgeou, 2012; Sullivan, 2017). For example, St-Amant et al. (2018), in reviewing health worker international volunteering, found that in some forms volunteering had been positioned as a commodity with some NGOs considering the volunteer as a client of the volunteering experience. Such critiques challenge the notion of involvement in international development volunteering as an altruistic activity where participants give of their time and skills fundamentally for the benefits of others.

Extending the notion of the volunteer as a client, studies on international development volunteering have revealed how, through volunteering, the volunteer can seek and gain 'benefits' in terms of personal growth, adventure and status. For example, a review by Tiessen and Heron (2012) of Canadian youth who had been involved in international development volunteering found that the primary focus of the youth in reflecting on their own experience of volunteering was on personal growth. The participants viewed this as the most significant positive impact from their volunteering, more so than an impact on the community in which they volunteered. The potential to gain career advancement from participation was found to be a significant motivator for some for involvement in international volunteering (Tyler et al., 2018). Jones (2010), in highlighting the positioning of involvement in international development volunteering as beneficial to the volunteer, noted the extent of program evaluation instruments focused on the transferrable skills participants could gain through involvement in programs. Extending this, Smith et al. (2012) found that a deterrent to participation in international development volunteering was a lack of recognition of the skills gained through volunteering participation.

With some organised international volunteering experiences linked to university entry or progression, the reason why individuals become involved in volunteering is shaped by their own position in their home society and access to resourcing. Indeed, in considering healthcare professionals, access to the opportunity to participate in international volunteering – which was promoted as a mechanism for skill development – was found to be restricted to those individuals who were able to afford the costs of participation (Tyler et al., 2018). McBride and Lough (2010) found that for the US population who had reported participation in international development volunteering in the 2005 Current Population Survey, there was an overrepresentation of young, white, highly educated people without children in the home, participating and an overrepresentation of men participating in general. Driving this demographic imbalance were a complex combination of underlying socio-economic factors that were further complicated by the variety of different types of international development volunteering possible –from short to long term and from highly skilled work to that requiring more generalised skills. Sorting through the driving factors of demographic imbalance, McBride and Lough (2010) suggested that, in part, the demographic overrepresentation of young, white, educated people could result from volunteering organisations selecting volunteers with particular skills that were in short supply in the host location (McBride & Lough, 2010).

Critical reflections on the characterisation of place

In critically reviewing the characterisation of the relationship between volunteers and volunteer organisations with recipient communities, researchers have further expanded knowledge about relational understandings of place. In examining both the performance of international development volunteering and the positioning of such activities within marketing materials by international volunteering development agencies, scholars have critically positioned international volunteering as a modern extension of colonialism, a form of racialised development (Calkin, 2014; Simpson, 2004; Sullivan, 2017). Giving rise to such characterisations is an underlying tendency in volunteering programs to position recipient communities as 'underdeveloped' – needing development – with the resourcing, knowledge and skills for this development required to come from a more developed nation (Calkin, 2014). Of this dichotomous construction of global spaces, Sobocinska (2017, p. 50) wrote,

> Development Volunteering was an expression of modernization theory's reconceptualization of 'backwardness' as a state of mind, which could be shifted through the presence and influence of a 'developed' person. The cultural chauvinism underpinning this notion, which located Western society as the ideal towards which all nations and people should progress, was mostly unspoken but always present in situations where young and mostly inexperienced volunteers were placed in positions of power and authority. Many receiving nations were conscious of this undertone: strong anti-Peace Corps movements in Nigeria and Indonesia, as well as regular critiques of VGS [Volunteer Graduate Scheme] and VSO [Voluntary Service Overseas] in other nations, reveal that many people regarded Development Volunteering as a form of neo-colonialism.

International development volunteering is informed by neoliberal ideologies (Baillie Smith & Laurie, 2011). As noted above, 'opportunities' are marketed to potential volunteers as an opportunity to expand their experiences and develop soft skills that might make them more employable or more likely to gain access to a desired education provider (Smith et al., 2010). Vrasti and Montsion (2014, p. 336) argued of international volunteering that

> rather than treat it as a spontaneous act of virtue, we insist that volunteerism is a carefully designed technology of government the purpose of which is to align individual conduct with neoliberal capital's double injunction of market rationality and social responsibility.

However, Griffiths (2016) cautioned against characterisations of the volunteer as passive subjects of capitalism, arguing the limitations of affording volunteers only limited subjectivity.

While noting the neoliberal framing of international development volunteering, Griffiths (2016, p. 175) makes the concise point 'volunteers, before all else, volunteer'.

International volunteer tourism and place

Providing useful insight into the complex geography of international development volunteering, and how this is shaped by place, is the literature that examines international volunteering tourism. This body of work challenges the dichotomy between the volunteer's home and destination. While volunteer tourism is covered elsewhere in this Handbook, it is important to highlight that this body of work has revealed that through tourist encounters with places, individuals can gain familiarity with place and understandings of the roles for international volunteers (Holmes et al., 2010). Qi (2020) found that different cultural contexts, which are manifested in place, impact how individuals conceptualise volunteering and engage in volunteering tourism. Keese (2011), in examining volunteer tourism, concluded that the geographic features of destinations informed an individual's decision to participate in international development volunteering and where to participate.

Holmes et al. (2010, p. 267), in reviewing tourism volunteering argued that 'given the nature of current and projected demographic and social change within many developed economies, forms of volunteering are likely to gain pace as key elements within the social support and leisure fabric of countries'. They proposed that volunteer tourists would play an increasingly important role in providing volunteer services. The spatial distributions of this international volunteer effort would, therefore, be informed by and inform the spatial distribution of tourism. The link between place and volunteering has been further explored in work examining ecotourism. Across this extensive literature the relationship between the physical and cultural characteristics of the destination and the volunteers' willingness to participate are made clear. Galley and Clifton (2004), for example, examined research ecotourism in Southeast Sulawesi. In reviewing the demographic characteristics and motivations of those who sought to volunteer to participate in ecotourism related research they identified participants had similar characteristics to those participating more broadly in international volunteering. Participants tended to be young and previously well-travelled and educated (Galley & Clifton, 2004). For ecotourist volunteers, the physical characteristics of the destination were of fundamental importance in their decision to volunteer.

The dimensions and impacts of international volunteering for events and sports has also been well documented in the academic literature and is reported on throughout this Handbook. While it is not within the scope of this chapter to review this literature, it can be noted that through such forms of international volunteering, individuals can develop their awareness of places and cultures. For example, research by Qi et al. (2018) found that those with greater awareness and understanding of cultural differences were the most satisfied with their international volunteering experience. Of particular relevance to this chapter was the finding that volunteers' cross cultural skills were based on each individual's own knowledge and attitude to different cultures – often informed by prior interaction or visitation to different places (Qi et al., 2018). Smith et al. (2014) in reviewing the long term benefits for international sport volunteers found that volunteers' desire to travel to the destination and engage in an immersive cultural experience was the primary motivator for international volunteering. They also noted that those that volunteered for a longer duration were the most satisfied with their experiences and longer-term benefits. Another dimension explored in the literature that examines event and sport volunteering, is the impact of sports and events on the places in which events are held. Again, while a review of this literature is not within the scope of this chapter, and is more thoroughly addressed elsewhere in this Handbook, at this juncture it is useful to highlight that research has revealed how volunteers at events, particularly mega events, can disrupt the functions, culture and physical characteristics of places – with positive and negative outcomes (Benson & Wise, 2017).

Conclusion

This chapter examined the research reporting on international development volunteering to highlight the critical role of place in shaping the performance of volunteering. While it was not the intent of this paper to fully account for the contested positionings of international development volunteering, or indeed resolve these, it is noteworthy that across these contested conceptualisations there is an understanding that international development volunteering involves the transition of values and practices between geographies (Laurie & Smith, 2018). Indeed, Mangold's (2012) exploration of young German participants in a year-long volunteer program found that over the duration of the program the volunteers and members of the local community engaged in a complex series of ongoing social and cultural exchanges where geographies became intertwined. Importantly, the geographies that shape volunteering are informed by variability in the spatial and temporal characteristics between places. On this matter, Laurie and Baillie Smith (2018) found, when examining five different projects over a six year timeframe, it was the existing geographies of volunteering and development that fostered a geographical fixity in volunteering.

To fully understand the role of place in shaping volunteering or indeed the nature and impacts of international development volunteering, it is critical to avoid dichotomous understandings of place. There is a need to challenge the geographical imaginary that often frames volunteering – particularly international development as being a one way movement of knowledge and resources from the global North to the global South. The relational turn in human geography provides a useful theoretical lens to support moving away from dichotomous framings of volunteering, volunteers and volunteer spaces to re-entangle the geographic, political, cultural, historical, economic and humanistic relationships between and across places (DeVerteuil et al., 2020).

Geographic imaginations inform how volunteering activities are conducted and who is involved. However, irrespective of the factors underpinning involvement in international development volunteering, this activity promotes mobility of individuals, ideas, knowledge and resources between geographies. This, in turn, shapes the relationship between places and the longer-term outcomes for the different places involved. To further extend knowledge about international development volunteering, and the relationship between place and volunteering, Griffiths (2016) proposed that constructing understandings of volunteering through the performance of volunteering would facilitate richer and ultimately more useful insights. Such an approach would enable the 'hosts' to be actively written into accounts of volunteering and the temporal and unbounded spaces that inform the voluntary actions of individuals in place to be revealed.

References

Baillie Smith, M., & Laurie, N. (2011). International volunteering and development: Global citizenship and neoliberal professionalisation today. *Transactions of the Institute of British Geographers, 36*(4), 545–559.

Baillie Smith M., Laurie N., & Griffiths M. (2018). South–South volunteering and development. *Geographical Journal, 184*(2), 158–168. https://doi.10.1111/geoj.12243

Benson, A. M., & Wise, N. (Eds.) (2017). *International Sports Volunteering*. London: Routledge.

Burrai, E., Font, X., & Cochrane, J. (2014). Destination stakeholders' perceptions of volunteer tourism: An equity theory approach. *International Journal of Tourism Research*, *17*(5), 451–459. https://doi:10.1002/jtr.2012

Calkin, S. (2014). Mind the 'gap year: A critical discourse analysis of volunteer tourism promotional material. *Global Discourse*, *4*(1), 30–43. https://doi:10.1080/2326995.2013.855008

Devereux, P. (2008). International volunteering for development and sustainability: outdated paternalism or a radical response to globalisation? *Development in Practice*, *18*(3), 357–370. https://doi.org/10.1080/09614520802030409

DeVerteuil, G., Power, A., & Trudeau, D. (2020). The relational geographies of the voluntary sector: Disentangling the ballast of strangers. *Progress in Human Geography*, *44*(5), 919–937. https://doi:10.1177/0309132519869461

Galley, G., & Clifton, J. (2004). The motivational and demographic characteristics of research ecotourists: Operation Wallacea volunteers in Southeast Sulawesi, Indonesia. *Journal of Ecotourism*, *3*(1), 69–82. https://doi.org/10.1080/14724040408668150

Georgeou, N. (2012). *Neoliberalism, Development and Aid Volunteering*. Abingdon: Routledge.

Griffiths, M. (2016). An opinion piece. A response to the special issue on volunteer tourism: The performative absence of volunteers. *Journal of Sustainable Tourism*, *24*(2), 169–176. https://doi.10.1080/09669582.2015.1071382

Holmes, K., Smith, K. A., Lockstone-Binney, L., & Baum, T. (2010). Developing the dimensions of tourism volunteering. *Leisure Sciences*, *32*(3), 255–269. https://doi.org/10.1080/01490401003712689

Jones, E. (2010). 'Don't worry about the worries': Transforming lives through international volunteering. In E. Jones (Ed.) *Internationalisation and the student voice: Higher education perspectives* (pp. 83–97). Abingdon: Routledge.

Keese, J. (2011). The geography of volunteer tourism: Place matters. *Tourism Geographies: An International Journal of Tourism Space, Place and Environment*, *13*, 257–279. https://doi.org/10.1080/14616688.2011.567293

Krishna, K. C., & Khondker, H. H. (2004). National-building through international volunteerism: A case study of Singapore. *The International Journal of Sociology and Social Policy*, *24*(1–2), 21–55. https://doi:10.1108/01443330410790957

Laurie, N., & Baillie Smith, M. (2018). Unsettling geographies of volunteering and development. *Transactions of the Institute of British Geographers*, *43*(1), 95–109. https://doi.org/10.1111/tran.12205

Lough, B. J. (2015). *The evolution of international volunteering*. United National Volunteering Program. https://core.ac.uk/download/pdf/233233153.pdf

Lough, B. J., & Tiessen, R. (2018). How do international volunteering characteristics influence outcomes? Perspectives from partners organisations. *Voluntas*, *29*, 104–118. https://doi.org/10.1007/s11266-017-9902-9

Mangold, K. (2012). 'Struggling to do the right thing': Challenges during international volunteering. *Third World Quarterly*, *33*(8), 1493–1509. https://doi.org/10.1080/01436597.2012.698137

McBride, A. M., & Lough, B. J. (2010). Access to international volunteering. *Nonprofit Management and Leadership*, *21*(2), 195–208. https://doi.org/10.1002/nml.20020

Qi, H. (2020). Conceptualising volunteering in tourism in China. *Tourism Management Perspectives*, *33*, https://doi.org/10.1016/j.tmp.2019.100618

Qi, H., Smith, K. A., & Yeoman, I. (2018). Cross-cultural event volunteering: Challenge and intelligence. *Tourism Management*, *69*, 596–604. https://doi.org/10.1016/j.tourman.2018.03.019

Tiessen, R., & Heron, B. (2012). Volunteering in the developing world: The perceived impacts of Canadian youth. *Development in Practice*, *22*(1), 44–56. https://doi.org/10.1080/09614524.2012.630982

Tyler, N., Chatwin, J., Byrne, G., Hart, J., & Bryn-Davis, L. (2018). The benefits of international volunteering in a low-resource setting: Development of a core outcome set. *Human Resources for Health*, *16*, 69. https://doi.org/10.1186/s12960-018-0333-5

Sherraden, M. S., Lough, B., & McBride, A. M. (2008). Effects of international volunteering and service: Individual and institutional predictors. *Voluntas: International Journal of Voluntary and Nonprofit Organizations*, *19*, 395–421. https://10.1007/s11266-008-9072

Sherraden, M. S., Stringham, J., Sow, S. C., & McBride, A. M. (2006). The forms and structure of international voluntary service. *Voluntas: International Journal of Voluntary and Nonprofit Organizations*, *17*, 156–173. https://doi.org/10.1007/s11266-006-9011-7

Simpson, K. (2004). 'Doing development': The gap year, volunteer-tourists and the popular practice of development. *Journal of International Development*, *16*(5), 681–692. https://doi:10.1002/jid.1120

Skinner, M. W. (2014). Ageing, place and voluntarism: Towards a geographical perspective on third sector organisations and volunteers in ageing communities. *Voluntary Sector Review, 5*(2), 161–179. https://doi.org/10.1332/204080514X14020630062723

Smith, C., Pettigrew, L. M., Seo, H.-N., & Dorward, J. (2012). Combining general practice with international work: Online survey of experiences of UK GPs. *JRSM Short Reports, 3*(7), 1–8. https://doi.org/10.1258/shorts.2012.012054

Smith, F. M., Timbrell, H., Woolvin, M., Muirhead, S., & Fyfe, N. (2010). Enlivened geographies of volunteering: Situated, embodied and emotional practices of voluntary action. *Scottish Geographical Journal, 126*(4), 258–274. https://doi:10.1080/14702541.2010.549342

Smith, N. L., Cohen, A., & Pickett, A. C. (2014). Exploring the motivations and outcomes of long-term international sport-for-development volunteering for American Millennials. *Journal of Sport & Tourism, 19*(3–4), 299–316. https://doi.org/10.1080/14775085.2016.1143865

Sobocinska, A. (2017). How to win friends and influence nations: The international history of development volunteering. *Journal of Global History, 12,* 49–73. https://doi:10.1017/S1740022816000334

St-Amant, O., Ward-Griffin, C., Berman, H., & Vainio-Mattila, A. (2018). Client or volunteer? Understanding neoliberalism and neo-colonialism within international volunteer health work. *Global Qualitative Nursing Research, 5,* 1–16. https://doi/pdf/10.1177/2333393618792956

Sullivan, N. (2017). International clinical volunteering in Tanzania: A postcolonial analysis of a global health business. *An International Journal for Research, Policy and Practice, 13*(3), 310–324. https://doi.org/10.1080/17441692.2017.1346695

Thompson, S., Sparrow, K., Hall, J., & Chevis, N. (2020). Volunteering for development: What does best practice look like. *Development in Practice, 30*(7), 972–978. https://doi.org/10.1080/09614524.2020.1787351

Vrasti, W., & Montsion, J. M. (2014). No good deed goes unrewarded: The values/virtues of transnational volunteerism in neoliberal capital. *Global Society, 28*(3), 336–355, https://doi.org/10.1080/13600826.2014.900738

4

HOW A POLITICAL ECOLOGY LENS CAN HELP ASSESS AND IMPROVE CONSERVATION VOLUNTEER TOURISM

Kerry E. Grimm, Emilie Wiehe and Robyn Bath-Rosenfeld

Introduction

In recent years, given the need for labour and lack of funding, many conservation and scientific research projects have turned to travelling volunteers to help them accomplish goals and generate revenue (Brightsmith, Stronza & Holle, 2008; Gray, Campbell & Meeker, 2016; Liu & Leung 2019). Conservation volunteer tourism (CVT) can be considered an extreme form of ecotourism because unlike traditional ecotourists, conservation volunteer tourists not only want to see and monetarily support nature but also work on projects to save the environment, improve sustainability, and possibly assist local communities (Cousins, Evans & Sadler, 2009b; Gray & Campbell, 2007; Grimm, 2013). Volunteers most often select projects that involve charismatic fauna (e.g. sea turtles), exciting destinations (e.g. Costa Rica), or iconic ecosystems (e.g. rainforest) (Cousins, Evans & Sadler, 2009a; Ellis, 2003; Lorimer, 2010). Usually, CVT sending organisations are in the Global North, and the direction of volunteers illustrates a one-way flow from the Global North to the Global South (Lorimer, 2009). Therefore, CVT projects can involve multiple actors (e.g. international volunteer tourists, community members, CVT organisations), some of whom may be in close human-environment contexts for extended periods of time.

With the growth of CVT, research on the subject has also increased. It is not the intention of this chapter to detail all CVT research, but we briefly highlight major topics researchers have examined (for a review, see Wearing & McGehee, 2013; Wearing, Young & Everingham, 2017). These include volunteer motivations (Campbell & Smith, 2005; Grimm & Needham, 2012b) and values (Campbell & Smith, 2006), as well as positive and negative impacts that volunteers have on projects (Brondo, 2015; Foster-Smith & Evans, 2003; Guttentag, 2009; Wearing, 2001). Researchers also have examined various aspects of CVT promotional material, such as its role in recruitment, influence on volunteers, and discourse (Cousins et al., 2009a; Grimm & Needham, 2012a). Other work has examined CVT as citizen science (Brightsmith et al., 2008; Gray et al., 2017; Roques, Jacobson & McCleery, 2018). Although not specific to CVT, an increasing amount of research has examined volunteer tourism through the lens of neoliberal development and governmentality (Smith, 2014; Vrasti & Montsion, 2014), geographies of care and compassion, and the politics of affect (Brondo, 2019; Griffiths, 2015; Mostafanezhad, 2013b). Another strand has explored whether or not volunteer tourism and CVT foster

DOI: 10.4324/9780367815875-5

cross-cultural understanding (Dillette, Douglas, Martin & O'Neill, 2017; Kirillova, Lehto & Cai, 2015; Liu & Leung, 2019; Raymond & Hall, 2008) and promote global citizenship (Butcher & Smith, 2015; Lorimer, 2010; Lyons, Hanley, Wearing & Neil, 2012). Despite the wealth of research on CVT, the majority of researchers have collected data from volunteers and organisations, with relatively few studies examining CVT from the local perspective (Brondo, 2015; Lupoli & Morse, 2015). However, some have extended their work to community members or local project staff to better understand their impressions of benefits and disadvantages of CVT (Gray & Campbell, 2007; Gray et al., 2017; Grimm, 2013; Lupoli & Morse, 2015; Mostafanezhad, 2015; Ravensbergen, 2016).

In response to Benson and Wearing's (2011) claim that tools are needed to evaluate sociocultural impacts in assessing outcomes of volunteer tourism projects, Grimm (2013) proposed that "one possible tool could be a political ecology framework, which has been applied to numerous studies examining conservation projects, and more recently ecotourism" (p. 265). McGehee (2014) also noted that political ecology (PE) could be an area for further study. Although, not referring to PE specifically, Henry and Mostafanezhad (2019) stated that a multi-scalar perspective of volunteer tourism would allow research to not only focus on one node of contact, such as the onsite-encounter, but also the local, regional, national, and global context in which volunteer tourism exists. However, despite extensive use of PE to analyse ecotourism (Belsky, 1999; Campbell, Gray & Meletis, 2007; Fletcher, 2019) and the fact that many CVT researchers have explored topics of interest to PE, few explicitly use a PE lens. Those who have, examined discourse, neoliberal conservation, goal prioritisation, spread of Western knowledge and ideals, and the depoliticisation of what is a highly politicised environment (Brondo, 2015, 2019; Gray et al., 2016; Grimm, 2013; Mostafanezhad, 2015; Vrasti, 2013). However, just like CVT research has not engaged much with PE, Brondo (2019) explained that few political ecologists have turned to CVT, despite the growing importance of volunteer tourists in conservation efforts and CVT's potential impacts on local people.

Building on work that has addressed these recognised gaps in CVT and PE research, our chapter demonstrates how PE can help assess CVT projects. Throughout the chapter, we refer to a model that illustrates how key PE concepts predominantly function in many CVT projects (Figure 4.1) described in the literature. We use this model to illuminate power and inequities in access between CVT actors. A second model demonstrates how a more sustainable, equitable, and socially-just CVT could function if these factors were addressed, and throughout the text, we use examples of CVT projects to illustrate ways some of these weaknesses have been addressed (Figure 4.2). These models do not capture every actor or interaction in CVT, nor every PE component, but they provide a starting point for applying PE to assess CVT.

Political ecology

PE is a wide and varied field that broadly combines ecological concerns and political economy to examine how power circulates discursively and materially across scales to impact resource access and environmental change (Neumann, 2015; Robbins, 2012; Svarstad, Benjaminsen & Overå, 2018). Researchers have applied PE to critically examine conservation and environmental concerns, most often in the Global South and increasingly in the Global North (Watts, 2015). Central to PE are interactions and power dimensions between actors, including state or national institutions/actors, local communities, NGOs, and households (Neumann, 2015; Robbins, 2012; Svarstad et al., 2018). PE recognises that certain

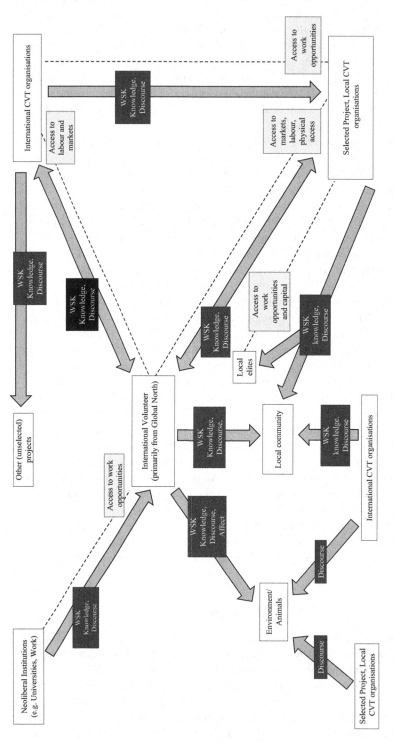

Figure 4.1 Interactions and flows in typical Conservation Volunteer Tourism (CVT) projects

Actors directly or indirectly involved with CVT (white boxes), selected PE components (black boxes), and types of access opportunities (grey boxes). Arrows indicate dominant flow of power across scales and between actors specific to PE components on the arrow; bidirectional arrows indicate a more even flow of power between actors. Dashed lines indicate relationships between actors in terms of access; actors benefiting from the access opportunity has the grey box next to their name. International CVT organisations and Selected projects/Local CVT organisations appear in two boxes each for model clarity. WSK indicates western scientific knowledge, and international CVT organisations refers to both for-profit sending organisations and international organisations directly involved in CVT.

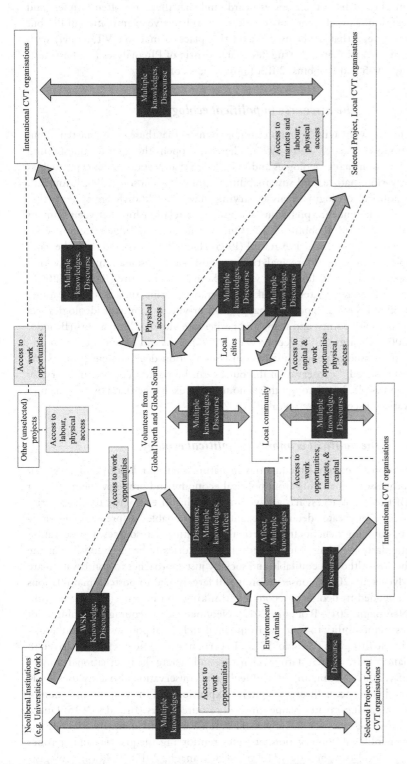

Figure 4.2 Interactions and flows in more equitable Conservation Volunteer Tourism (CVT)

Actors involved directly or indirectly with CVT (white boxes), select PE components (black boxes), and types of access opportunities (grey boxes). Arrows indicate the dominant flow of power across scales and between actors specific to those PE components on the arrow; bidirectional arrows indicate a more even flow of power between actors. Dashed lines indicate relationship between actors in terms of access. Actors benefitting from access in the relationship has the box with access type next to them. International CVT organisations and Selected projects and Local CVT organisations appear in two boxes each for model clarity; international CVT organisations refers to both for-profit sending organisations and international organisations directly involved in CVT; "Multiple knowledges" includes western scientific knowledge (WSK), traditional and local ecological knowledges, and cultural knowledge; and volunteers include those from the Global North and South.

groups of people might not have their voices heard, and that there are often winners and losers in any intervention. This chapter is by no means an exhaustive examination of PE, but rather provides key concepts that can be used as a starting place to analyse CVT, namely with a focus on the discursive and material struggles characteristic of PE analyses (see Perreault, Bridge & McCarthy, 2015 and Robbins, 2012, for overviews of PE).

The discourse in political ecology

Discursive PE, which draws heavily from Foucault, recognises that there is not one truth, but rather a plurality of views (Peet & Watts, 1996). Thereby, it opens the door for questioning globally disseminated, dominant ideologies and knowledge that pertain to concepts such as community, conservation, nature, and sustainability (Agrawal & Gibson, 1999; Campbell, 2002). Discursive political ecologists analyse varying views and knowledge systems that actors hold, and how different interpretations can influence relationships between humans and with nature (Bryant, 1998; Robbins, 2012). One dominant knowledge system is western scientific knowledge (WSK), which Agrawal (1995) claimed is "divorced from the daily livelihoods of people and aims at a more analytical and abstract representation of the world" (p. 15). WSK has often led to a dichotomous view of humans and nature (Robbins, 2012). In addition, discursive PE interrogates how taken-for-granted terms, such as 'conservation', and neoliberal discourses, such as 'poor-but-happy', can privilege dominant ideologies and WSK but neglect other viewpoints, and shape and perpetuate views of local actors (Brondo, 2015; Campbell, 2002; Grimm, 2013; Peet & Watts, 1996). This can have material ramifications for relationships among people involved in conservation development projects. As Mostafanezhad (2015) stated, "conservation discourses can be contest[ed] within everyday interactions between people. It is through these moments of exchange that power dynamics mediating conservation discourses are revealed" (p. 241).

The political economy in political ecology

PE also draws attention to material inequalities in nature-society relations and equity in decision-making processes. Emanating from political economy and property theory, Ribot and Peluso's (2003) theory of access has allowed many political ecologists to characterise unequal resource access in greater detail and examine what enables or prevents individuals and groups from enjoying benefits from particular activities or resources. Conservation interventions, particularly area-based approaches, have historically been established at the cost of local livelihoods. Although equitable and socially just approaches to conservation are possible (Zafra-Calvo et al., 2017), conservation is still largely tied to postcolonial relations and is currently embedded in neoliberal economic thinking and policies (e.g. ecotourism, protected areas) (Neumann, 2015; Robbins, 2012). Neoliberalism encourages devolution of the state and can restrict its ability to fund environmental and social policies that would support conservation in the first place (Brondo, 2015). In turn, non-state actors may be driven to intervene, gain financially from their status as charities, and dictate the international conservation agenda (Duffy, 2002; Neumann, 2015). Neoliberal conservation also aptly uses WSK to protect species and ecosystems through capitalist expansion and the commodification of nature while often imparting greater blame on local resource users (Brondo, 2015; Duffy, 2002; Fairhead, Leach & Scoones, 2012; Gray et al., 2016). Varied and unequal social impacts have resulted from neoliberal conservation, at times reinforcing inequalities and at times providing benefits to local communities (Holmes & Cavanagh, 2016). Political ecologists have also highlighted problems that can be encountered with community participation if it is donor-driven and tokenistic or risks reinforcing existing inequalities (Mowforth & Munt, 2016; West, 2006).

Discursive tensions in CVT

CVT discourse

Applying PE to CVT, we first examine the global movement and multiple scales of discourse and knowledge, focusing on how they function off-site and on-site in much of the researched CVT (refer to Figure 4.1). We should note that in this chapter, because of similarities of how they function in CVT, international CVT organisations refers to both international organisations directly involved in CVT and for-profit volunteer tourism sending organisations, of which CVT might only be a part of their project offerings. To locate a place, project, and even CVT organisation, most volunteers use the internet; therefore, keyword optimisation is necessary for project success (Cousins et al., 2009a; Grimm & Needham, 2012a). While useful for locating projects, inherent problems exist with this method. Volunteers tend to trust professional, organised, and well-designed websites (Grimm & Needham, 2012a). Smaller, local projects might find difficulty in recruiting volunteers if they do not have capacity for website design and connections to trusted international CVT organisations that assist with advertisement and recruitment (Grimm & Needham, 2012a). Certain types of projects might be prioritised over others that are scientifically valid, and perhaps even more important for conservation, but do not include elements like charismatic megafauna, contact with animals, or exciting destinations (Cousins et al., 2009a; Lorimer, 2010). Program descriptions and mission statements may be loaded with global discourses of biodiversity conservation and sustainable development, using scientific jargon to sound legitimate, while also employing buzzwords, such as "conservation in the cloud forest" or "sea turtles and surf in Costa Rica" (Cousins et al., 2009a; Grimm & Needham, 2012a; Lorimer, 2010). In addition, destination priority is given to countries that are safer and enjoy certain levels of development (Lorimer 2009; Steele & Scherrer, 2018). Given competing interests, projects may have to balance representation of their conservation objectives and destination characteristics, often prioritising elements that will attract volunteers (Grimm & Needham, 2012a). Final selection by volunteers demonstrates the power they have in perpetuating which projects continue to gain support and grow, as their payment helps fund both the project and future volunteer recruitment (Grimm & Needham, 2012a).

International CVT organisations and local projects are also in a place of power to create or perpetuate discourse about the environment, local actors, and volunteers. Images in promotional material might not accurately represent marginalised people (Simpson, 2004) or capture the full complexities of environmental issues, such as national politics or local context. Mostafanezhad (2015) described a CVT project where the founder acknowledged the brochures advertised projects that sought to enhance environmental awareness for local people, but his agenda did not always align with environmental concerns of the local community, again demonstrating how certain goals can be prioritised. Discourse can also present volunteers from Global North countries as difference-makers (Lorimer, 2010), useful and needed (Simpson, 2004), or more extreme, as saviours, in turn perpetuating the othering of those in the Global South. These moral economies set up a dichotomy where the volunteer is a 'giver' who compassionately provides aid to the 'receiver' (Mostafanezhad, 2013b). Although, much work on the helping discourse is not specific to CVT research

(Mostafanezhad, 2013a; Simpson, 2004; Vrasti, 2013), since CVT projects may involve interactions with local actors and aim to help them take better care of their environment, the helping discourse applies. In addition, Lorimer (2010) explained discourse around the 'global citizen' demonstrates power because although it purports that people can go anywhere to make a difference, middle-upper class individuals from the Global North tend to be the ones who access these opportunities due to aspects such as money and visas (Gray et al., 2017; Lyons et al., 2012).

In some cases, global discourse may lead to negative expectations or experiences of local residents, places, or the project. Images of wild landscapes without people may generate volunteer disappointment because they do not match the reality of far-flung places, such as the Arctic or African savannah (Cousins et al., 2009b; Saville, 2019); tourists can also perpetuate the eco-imaginary by adding to these representations on social media (Saville, 2019). Key concepts, such as conservation, may also be subject to differing interpretations and can lead to dissatisfaction with, and judgement of, the project and staff (Cousins et al., 2009a; Grimm, 2013). Discursive myths of poverty (Vrasti, 2013) can generate volunteer expectations of local residents, such as beliefs that local people are less knowledgeable and care less about the environment because their poverty does not allow them to focus on such concerns (Grimm, 2013). In addition, CVT volunteers may have limited interaction with local actors if their project location is removed from the actual community (e.g. forested preserve), and therefore representations are not challenged. Even when there is interaction, it might be superficial, in turn further reaffirming expectations of the other and not allowing a more critical exploration of why things might be as they are (Simpson, 2004). For example, volunteer expectations of how individuals should interact with the environment and animals can lead to judgement of actions such as hunting and fishing (Guttentag, 2009).

Knowledge

PE also allows exploration of how knowledge functions in CVT. To create long-term funding for research projects, many scientists use CVT to fund and provide personnel for data collection and conservation tasks for longer-term projects (Brightsmith et al., 2008; Cousins, 2007; Gray & Campbell, 2007). The dominance of the Global North's scientific discourse can push out local or traditional ecological knowledge, insinuating that local knowledge is inferior to WSK (Mostafanezhad, 2015). By supporting CVT over local labour and stewardship, WSK can devalue the local knowledge of the communities intertwined with protected areas and endangered species (Brondo, 2015). PE also can illuminate problems with access to knowledge, as providing data and publications to the communities involved in CVT has been limited (Chapman et al., 2015). In this respect, CVT has often been blamed for carrying out 'parachute science', where the research is extractive and little is done to build capacity at a local level (Hart, Leather & Sharma, 2020).

Volunteers may also see themselves as the saviours of animals, and thus carry a presumption that they know more about these species and their protection than local stewards (Brondo 2015; Hart et al., 2020). Gray et al. (2017) found that many volunteers described themselves as "knowledge generators and providers, and local residents as recipients of this knowledge" (p. 207). Local governments or projects may also perceive that volunteers are more capable at collecting scientific data over local community members (Gray et al., 2017). However, volunteers do not need to be experts, or even have any conservation experience, to invest in the CVT experience (Guttentag, 2009; Raymond & Hall, 2008). CVT participants are often there to gain knowledge and experience for their resume, but due to the privileging of WSK, they can take on the role of experts over local actors even when they hold incorrect knowledge (Brondo, 2015; Gray et al., 2017; Grimm, 2013).

This is not to say that CVT volunteers cannot change their views. Crall et al. (2012) contended that volunteers engaged in citizen science may leave with heightened scientific literacy in a specific project and an increased desire to participate in environmental actions. In addition, there is evidence of research outputs with involvement of local scientists, providing important information to guide local conservation science (Bath-Rosenfeld, 2019; Roques et al., 2018) (Figure 4.2). These studies illustrate the promise for the positive impact CVT can have in project locations, as well as for returning volunteers, and their potential impact on their communities.

Political economic considerations in CVT

Local involvement and resident perceptions

PE can also illuminate existing and future paths towards an ethical approach to tourism by allowing us to examine interactions between and among actors at the project and in the surrounding community (refer to Figure 4.1). Benefits to the host community are presented as one of the crucial elements of volunteer tourism ventures, and ensuring local involvement has been a recurring focus in the literature (Wearing & McGehee, 2013). While desirable from an ethical standpoint, local involvement must also be critically assessed in light of different power relations between actors and whether the CVT intervention is always a win-win scenario. Despite this need, studies on the role and integration of host communities in CVT specifically remain few and far between (Guttentag, 2009; Wearing & McGehee, 2013). Authors attribute this dearth of information to the difficulty in establishing what 'community' is, who constitutes the host in various CVT locations, and what is the full range of stakeholders (Wearing & McGehee, 2013; Zahra & McGehee, 2013). The degree of involvement of local actors and the benefits derived from such involvement may significantly vary from one location to the next and can be affected by the particular historical, social, and economic contexts surrounding CVT establishment. These contexts, in turn, affect power relations between different local and international actors and help determine access of local residents to the benefits provided by CVT. Types of access include but are not limited to access to capital, markets, labour, and work opportunities (Ribot & Peluso, 2003).

As mentioned above, although several researchers have indicated a need for greater attention to resident perceptions, only some studies provide a glimpse of CVT's challenges and benefits to resident communities. For many existing programs, the economic incentive is often the dominant benefit (Gray & Campbell, 2007; Gray et al., 2017; Vrasti, 2013), and in other projects, benefits derived from intercultural exchange or expectation thereof take priority (Dillette et al., 2017; Senko et al., 2011). One way that residents are able to derive an economic benefit comes from hosting volunteers (Gray et al., 2016; Vrasti, 2013), hosting a research project (Brightsmith et al., 2008), or even developing and implementing a project (Grimm, 2013). In contrast to other types of volunteer tourism, CVT does not necessitate volunteer and resident interactions, so families hosting volunteers may be the most extensive aspects of their local involvement (Kirillova et al., 2015). Economic benefits may also come from logistics and infrastructure, such as providing boat rides for research (Senko et al., 2011).

Yet, even in contexts where these types of benefits are possible or where communities are supportive of CVT development, authors acknowledge its limits. For example, Senko et al. (2011) pointed out that direct economic benefits and cash transfers were likely to be minimal. Part of this is attributed to the distance of volunteer activities from villages. In Baja California Sur, Mexico, due to this distance, most residents interviewed were not even aware of the existence of a CVT venture led by Earthwatch for a decade (Senko et al., 2011). Further, in the development of CVT, benefits tend to be unevenly distributed (Ravensbergen, 2016), often favouring those who already have certain facilities such as boats or property (Grimm, 2013; Senko et al., 2011). This is consistent with similar critiques of conservation and ecotourism development, which argue that they are most likely to benefit local elites. It also illustrates the role physical access and access to capital play in mediating how and whether local residents derive material benefits from CVT (Belsky, 1999; Mowforth & Munt, 2016; Ribot & Peluso, 2003).

Neoliberalism and access to benefits derived from CVT

Also similar to ecotourism, CVT has been critiqued as aiding in the neoliberalisation of conservation (Brondo, 2015; Gray et al., 2016). Debate has been ongoing on whether CVT provides a commodified or decommodified experience (Benson & Wearing, 2011; Gray et al., 2016). While there are longstanding major actors that act as international CVT sending organisations and providers on the ground, many CVT activities function with smaller local organisations (Cousins et al., 2009a; Lorimer, 2010), and the sector has been found to be increasingly commercialised (Coghlan & Noakes, 2012). This leads to different bargaining powers between international CVT organisations and their local counterparts. In South Africa, Cousins et al. (2009b) revealed these power dynamics, with international CVT organisations often determining the terms of the activity and the fee. In doing so, they retain access to markets, that is fee-paying volunteers, and labour, preventing local counterparts from benefiting equitably (Brondo, 2015; Cousins et al., 2009a; Grimm & Needham, 2012a; Lorimer, 2009).

Neoliberal processes also help dictate the terms of access to work opportunities. Indeed, neoliberal logic is partly what encourages young professionals, as mentioned above, to seek to gain skills and experience in the form of volunteerism to build their resumes (Gray et al., 2017). By doing so, CVT not only recreates neo-colonial relations but also replaces paid, skilled jobs by volunteers who are not always properly trained (Brondo, 2015; Gray et al., 2017; Hart et al., 2020). Authors have also found that local recruitment in managerial and scientific staff was limited (Gray et al., 2017). Therefore, access to work opportunities is limited by the types of social relations existing in many CVT ventures.

Beyond neoliberalism, recent scholarship has encouraged PE to consider how emotions and affect mediate resource access and conflict (Sultana, 2015). Several CVT scholars have examined how affect mediates the relationship between volunteers and the more-than-human environment in which they immerse themselves (Brondo, 2019; Conran, 2011; Griffiths, 2015; Lorimer, 2010). These affective encounters are presented as either transcending power dynamics or augmenting social and economic inequalities. Authors tie CVT to the commodification of experiences of nature (Brondo, 2019; Cousins et al., 2009b), where affective encounters and caring for species determine much of the volunteers' experience (Brondo, 2019). Affect is seen here to create value by drawing in volunteers who seek thrill and care in their experiences (Brondo, 2019; Cousins et al., 2009b) and to displace existing more-than-human relationships mediated by local ecological knowledge and culture (Brondo, 2019). However, as discussed below, affective encounters can lead also to more equitable and just CVT when the transformative learning potential of CVT is fully explored (Coghlan & Weiler, 2018; Henry, 2019).

Towards a more sustainable, equitable, and just CVT

One of the goals of CVT is to offer a type of tourism that provides benefits for local communities and the environment, as well as for the volunteer. Existing research and the PE framework have illuminated that this is not always the case. By examining the PE model of most CVT (Figure 4.1) and CVT research that has discussed examples of more socially conscious CVT, we see areas that can be strengthened or changed to lead to more sustainable, equitable, and just CVT. This is illustrated in the revised model (refer to Figure 4.2). Specifically, if CVT wants to achieve these goals, it should look to places where power, discourse, knowledge, and people can move in multiple directions, as well as increasing access to opportunities. In this section, we present some suggestions for CVT that strives towards an ideal form of tourism. However, we encourage other researchers and CVT organisations and projects to use our model to generate additional suggestions, especially place and context specific approaches. We do not suggest that PE can or will rectify all problems associated with CVT.

Volunteers

One of the first ways to potentially address the dominance of volunteers from the Global North participating in CVT is to support the bidirectional movement of volunteers, thereby offering similar opportunities and benefits to those not from the Global North. Some research has begun to examine volunteers from non-Western countries (Lo & Lee, 2011; Pan, 2017). CVT projects and organisations can assist with some of these challenges on a national and international scale. For example, the reserve in Ecuador that Grimm researched offered a lower price to nationals who wanted to volunteer. Alternatively, some volunteer payment can be set aside to provide scholarships to support volunteers from the Global South to volunteer internationally or locally, or receive project-related professional development and trainings (Gray et al., 2017), depending on cultural preferences. For example, the reserve owner told Grimm that in Ecuador many people prefer paid work to volunteering. Partnering with local schools might increase the chance of opportunities being shared more equitably among those in a community. In addition, CVT organisations could facilitate the acquisition of visas and passports, as many work abroad programs do for recent students (e.g. CIEE, BUNAC).

As noted above, even though volunteers might come with expectations that they hold more knowledge about the site, there is evidence that they learn from their experience (Crall et al., 2012). To further increase the bidirectionality of knowledge, projects and organisations can provide training or mini-lectures, including those given by local experts. Grimm (2013) described how the reserve owner provided volunteers with local and national context in weekly talks where topics included Ecuadorian politics, environmental laws, and waste infrastructure; some volunteers referred to this information in their interviews when detailing challenges the region faced. Also, many projects already include training about tasks, but they can ensure the rationale of the CVT project is clearly explained and linked to the environmental goals of the project, thereby increasing volunteer conservation knowledge. Although this can be tiring for projects with high volunteer turnover, technology allows for interactive training videos that volunteers could watch ahead of time; they could then ask project staff any remaining questions.

In addition, even though volunteer tourism is driven by neoliberalism and post-Fordist consumer tastes, affective encounters may offer possibilities to transcend and momentarily flatten out relations (Griffiths, 2015). Such a perspective takes into account the lived experience and transformative potential of CVT for volunteers (Coghlan & Weiler, 2018), host communities, and the non-human world, and acknowledges that not all experiences and encounters can be qualified as a commodified tourism experience. Encouraging reflection about the affective aspects of the CVT experience in training can further support volunteers in thinking critically about their position during and after their trip (Henry, 2019).

Community

Community needs and opportunities should be considered more in CVT. This would include providing greater access to work opportunities and the selling of goods to volunteers and projects, as well as including their social and environmental needs in project goals. Several authors have proposed the need for monitoring and evaluation frameworks, which assess the degree of local involvement and benefit to local communities (Gilfillan, 2015; Lupoli & Morse, 2015; Steele & Scherrer, 2018). Through a participatory approach with sending organisations and host communities, Lupoli and Morse (2015) developed separate sets of sociocultural, economic, and environmental indicators, and contrasted which indicators were prioritised for each group. Their findings showed that expectations of community involvement were actually lower among the host community, who instead prioritised biodiversity-related indicators. Steele and Scherrer (2018) encouraged volunteer organisations to enable host communities to prioritise needs and determine what is ethical in their locality. These could include greater work opportunities, but projects and organisations should make sure they are not just selecting certain community members who have more connections (i.e., they should aim to the spread the wealth). For example, the scientist running an Earthwatch project in the Canadian Rockies (Eisenberg et al., 2019) hired field technicians from the Fort Belknap Indian Community, providing them with opportunities to add fieldwork to their resumes and access work opportunities in a community with one of the highest poverty rates in Canada. Going a step further, local NGOs or projects can empower themselves and identify ways to access volunteers as labour to meet their own goals, perhaps focusing on more transient volunteers like backpackers (Frilund, 2018). They could also liaise directly with universities and conservation organisations for long-term research goals in equal partnerships recognising multiple knowledges.

CVT organisations and projects

In addition, projects and CVT organisations can help dismantle some of the discourses that perpetuate inequities and/or lead to problems at sites. Some might argue that by not ascribing to, and repeating, these dominant discourses, projects and organisations might not attract as many volunteers. However, research shows that false expectations created by promotional material can lead to volunteer dissatisfaction on-site (Grimm & Needham, 2012b; Smith & Font, 2014). Projects may struggle if international CVT organisations set them up for failure since they often have little control of the discourse shared in promotional material (Grimm & Needham, 2012a). A more equitable CVT would allow projects to have a role in crafting their promotional material and providing pre-trip information (McGehee, 2014) to reduce on-the-ground conflict. Information can still advertise attractive qualities of the location and project, but also provide greater ecological information and avoid misrepresentations of the place, project, and local people. CVT organisations can also explore ways to support other projects, including projects that might not initially garner volunteer attention but provide ecological benefits for the area.

Projects and organisations can also allow for greater inclusion of community feedback on representations. This becomes even more important if the project is run by non-local actors. Collaborations with community members might allow for a shift from the helper discourse to more of a partnership discourse, which might in turn alter volunteer expectations and views before arriving on-site. Gray et al., (2017) proposed that local residents and volunteers learn alongside each other, changing discourse from local residents as project recipients to project participants.

Countering dominant knowledge systems, both who does science and what knowledge systems exist to address environmental issues, can also be addressed by CVT organisations and projects. Although global biodiversity discourse might be difficult to challenge because it attracts volunteers, once on-site, projects can expose volunteers to multiple knowledge systems. There are varying levels of how this can be accomplished, including collaboratively working alongside local residents and integrating traditional or local ecological knowledge to demonstrate how different knowledges complement each other in addressing ecological issues. The aforementioned Earthwatch project in the Canadian Rockies incorporated traditional ecological knowledge throughout the project to examine the roles of indigenous burning and bison, a culturally sacred animal, in native prairie restoration, (Eisenberg et al., 2019). After research is completed, findings should be openly available to the community to help them in work they might want to conduct and to give back to those who assisted in their project. Recent manuscripts have set new guidelines for researchers to share their findings to improve conservation endeavours in their research areas (Chapman et al., 2015; Durant et al., 2019).

Conclusion

All tourism is not without its challenges, but CVT purports to strive towards a more ethical method of travelling. In many ways it does, but as researchers have illustrated, weaknesses still exist that need to be addressed. PE has long been an effective lens to uncover inequity in access and power; therefore, it can be useful in identifying areas where CVT needs to improve and opens the door for approaches to rectify these problems. The models illustrated in this chapter provide a starting place for researchers, and even practitioners, to examine CVT and identify places of inequity that should be addressed in order to work toward more ethical CVT.

References

Agrawal, A. (1995). Indigenous and scientific knowledge: Some critical comments. *Indigenous Knowledge and Development Monitor, 3*, 3–5.

Agrawal, A., & Gibson, C. C. (1999). Enchantment and disenchantment: The role of community in natural resource conservation. *World Development, 27*(4), 629–649. https://doi.org/10.1016/S0305-750X(98)00161-2

Bath-Rosenfeld, R. J. (2019). *Engaging Citizen Scientists to Determine the Importance of Non-Agricultural Fruiting Trees for Seed-Dispersing Frugivores on Working Landscapes in Southern Costa Rica.* Dissertation. Northern Arizona University.

Belsky, J. M. (1999). Misrepresenting communities: The politics of community-based rural ecotourism in Gales Point Manatee, Belize. *Rural Sociology, 64*(4), 641–666. https://doi.org/10.1111/j.1549-0831.1999.tb00382.x

Benson, A. M., & Wearing, S. (2011). Volunteer tourism: Commodified trend or new phenomenon? In O. Moufakkir & P. M. Burns (Eds.), *Controversies in Tourism* (pp. 242–252). CABI. https://doi.org/10.1079/9781845938130.0000

Brightsmith, D. J., Stronza, A., & Holle, K. (2008). Ecotourism, conservation biology, and volunteer tourism: A mutually beneficial triumvirate. *Biological Conservation, 141*, 2832–2842. https://doi.org/10.1016/j.biocon.2008.08.020

Brondo, K. V. (2015). The spectacle of saving: conservation voluntourism and the new neoliberal economy on Utila, Honduras. *Journal of Sustainable Tourism, 23*(10), 1405–1425. https://doi.org/10.1080/09669582.2015.1047377

Brondo, K. V. (2019). Entanglements in multispecies voluntourism: Conservation and Utila's affect economy. *Journal of Sustainable Tourism, 27*(4), 590–607. https://doi.org/10.1080/09669582.2018.1477784

Bryant, R. L. (1998). Power, knowledge and political ecology in the third world: A review. *Progress in Physical Geography, 22*(1), 79–94. https://doi.org/10.1191/030913398674890974

Butcher, J., & Smith, P. (2015). *Volunteer Tourism.* Routledge.

Campbell, L. M. (2002). Science and sustainable use: Views of marine turtle conservation experts. *Ecological App, 12*(4), 1229–1246. https://doi.org.10.2307/3061048

Campbell, L. M., Gray, N. J., & Meletis, Z. A. (2007). Political ecology perspectives on ecotourism to parks and protected areas. In K. S. Hanna, D. A. Clark, & S. Slocombe (Eds.), *Transforming Parks and Protected Areas: Policy and Governance in a Changing World* (pp. 200–221). Routledge. https://doi.org/10.4324/9780203961902

Campbell, L. M., & Smith, C. (2005). Volunteering for sea turtles? Characteristics and motives of volunteers working with the Caribbean Conservation Corporation in Tortuguero, Costa Rica. *Mast, 3*(2), 169–193. http://www.seaturtle.org/PDF/CampbellLM_2005_MAST.pdf

Campbell, L. M., & Smith, C. (2006). What makes them pay? Values of volunteer tourists working for sea turtle conservation. *Environmental Management, 38*(1), 84–98. https://doi.org/10.1007/s00267-005-0188-0

Chapman, J. M., Algera, D., Dick, M., Hawkins, E. E., Lawrence, M. J., Lennox, R. J., Rous, A., Souliere, C. M., Stemberger, H. L. J., Struthers, D. P., Vu, M., Ward, T., Zolderdo, A., & Cooke, S. J. (2015). Being relevant: Practical guidance for early career researchers interested in solving conservation problems. *Global Ecology and Conservation, 4*, 334–348. https://doi.org/10.1016/j.gecco.2015.07.013

Coghlan, A., & Noakes, S. (2012). Towards an understanding of the drivers of commercialization in the volunteer tourism sector. *Tourism Recreation Research, 37*(2), 123–131. https://doi.org/10.1080/02508281.2012.11081697

Coghlan, A., & Weiler, B. (2018). Examining transformative processes in volunteer tourism. *Current Issues in Tourism, 21*(5), 567–582. https://doi.org/10.1080/13683500.2015.1102209

Conran, M. (2011). They really love me!: Intimacy in volunteer tourism. *Annals of Tourism Research, 38*(4), 1454–1473. https://doi.org/10.1016/j.annals.2011.03.014

Cousins, J.A. (2007). The role of UK-based conservation tourism operators. *Tourism Management, 28*(4), 1020–1030. https://doi.org/10.1016/j.tourman.2006.08.011

Cousins, J. A., Evans, J., & Sadler, J. (2009a). Selling conservation? Scientific legitimacy and the commodification of conservation tourism. *Ecology and Society, 14*(1). https://doi.org/10.5751/ES-02804-140132

Cousins, J. A., Evans, J., & Sadler, J. P. (2009b). "I've paid to observe lions, not map roads!" - An emotional journey with conservation volunteers in South Africa. *Geoforum, 40*(6), 1069–1080. https://doi.org/10.1016/j.geoforum.2009.09.001

Crall, A. W., Jordan, R., Holfelder, K., Newman, G. J., Graham, J., & Waller, D. M. (2012). The impacts of an invasive species citizen science training program on participant attitudes, behavior, and science literacy. *Public Understanding of Science, 22*(6), 745–764. https://doi.org/10.1177/0963662511434894

Dillette, A. K., Douglas, A. C., Martin, D. S., & O'Neill, M. (2017). Resident perceptions on cross-cultural understanding as an outcome of volunteer tourism programs: The Bahamian Family Island perspective. *Journal of Sustainable Tourism, 25*(9), 1222–1239. https://doi.org/10.1080/09669582.2016.1257631

Duffy, R. (2002). *A Trip Too Far Ecotourism, Politics and Exploitation.* Earthscan.

Durant, S. M., Groom, R., Kuloba, B., Samna, A., Muzuma, U., Gadimang, P., Mandisodza-Chikerema, R., Ipavec, A., Mitchell, N., Ikanda, D., & Msuha, M. (2019). Bridging the divide between scientists and decision-makers: How behavioural ecologists can increase the conservation impact of their research? *Philosophical Transactions of the Royal Society B: Biological Sciences, 374*(1781). https://doi.org/10.1098/rstb.2019.0011

Eisenberg, C., Anderson, C. L., Collingwood, A., Sissons, R., Dunn, C. J., Meigs, G. W., Hibbs, D. E., Murphy, S., Dakin Kuiper, S., SpearChief-Morris, J., Little Bear, L., Johnston, B., &Edson, C. B. (2019). Out of the ashes: Ecological resilience to extreme wildfire, prescribed burns, and indigenous burning in ecosystems. *Frontiers in Ecology and Evolution*, 7(November), 1–12. https://doi.org/10.3389/fevo.2019.00436

Ellis, C. (2003). When volunteers pay to take a trip with scientists—Participatory environmental research tourism (PERT). *Human Dimensions of Wildlife*, 8(1), 75–80. https://doi.org/10.1080/10871200390180172

Fairhead, J., Leach, M., & Scoones, I. (2012). Green Grabbing: A new appropriation of nature? *Journal of Peasant Studies*, 39(2), 237–261. https://doi.org/10.1080/03066150.2012.671770

Fletcher, R. (2019). Ecotourism after nature: Anthropocene tourism as a new capitalist "fix." *Journal of Sustainable Tourism*, 27(4), 522–535. https://doi.org/10.1080/09669582.2018.1471084

Foster-Smith, J., & Evans, S. M. (2003). The value of marine ecological data collected by volunteers. *Biological Conservation*, 113(2), 199–213. https://doi.org/10.1016/S0006-3207(02)00373-7

Frilund, R. (2018). Teasing the boundaries of 'volunteer tourism': Local NGOs looking for global workforce. *Current Issues in Tourism*, 21(4), 355–368. https://doi.org/10.1080/13683500.2015.1080668

Gilfillan, D. (2015). Short-term volunteering and international development: An evaluation framework for volunteer tourism. *Tourism Analysis*, 20(6), 607–618. https://doi.org/10.3727/108354215x14464845877878

Gray, N. J., & Campbell, L. M. (2007). A decommodified experience? Exploring aesthetic, economic and ethical values for volunteer ecotourism in Costa Rica. *Journal of Sustainable Tourism*, 15(5), 463–482. https://doi.org/10.2167/jost725.0

Gray, N. J., Campbell, L. M., & Meeker, A. (2016). Decommodifying neoliberal conservation: A political ecology of volunteer tourism. In S. Nepal & J. Saarinen (Eds.), *Political Ecology and Tourism* (pp. 55–67). Routledge.

Gray, N. J., Meeker, A., Ravensbergen, S., Kipp, A., & Faulkner, J. (2017). Producing science and global citizenship? Volunteer tourism and conservation in Belize. *Tourism Recreation Research*, 42(2), 199–211. https://doi.org/10.1080/02508281.2017.1300398

Griffiths, M. (2015). I've got goose bumps just talking about it!: Affective life on neoliberalized volunteering programmes. *Tourist Studies*, 15(2), 205–221. https://doi.org/10.1177/1468797614563437

Grimm, K. E. (2013). Doing "conservation": Effects of different interpretations at an ecuadorian volunteer tourism project. *Conservation and Society*, 11(3), 264–276. https://doi.org/10.4103/0972-4923.121029

Grimm, K. E., & Needham, M. D. (2012a). Internet promotional material and conservation volunteer tourist motivations: A case study of selecting organisations and projects. *Tourism Management Perspectives*, 1(1), 17–27. https://doi.org/10.1016/j.tmp.2011.12.007

Grimm, K. E., & Needham, M. D. (2012b). Moving beyond the "I" in motivation: Attributes and perceptions of conservation volunteer tourists. *Journal of Travel Research*, 51(4), 488–501. https://doi.org/10.1177/0047287511418367

Guttentag, D. (2009). The possible negative impacts of volunteer tourism. *International Journal of Tourism Research*, 11, 537–551. https://doi.org/10.1002/jtr.727

Hart, A. G., Leather, S. R., & Sharma, M. V. (2020). Overseas conservation education and research: The new colonialism? *Journal of Biological Education*, 1–6. https://doi.org/10.1080/00219266.2020.1739117

Henry, J. (2019). Pedagogy, possibility, and pipe dreams: Opportunities and challenges for radicalizing international volunteering. *Journal of Tourism and Cultural Change*, 17(6), 663–675. https://doi.org/10.1080/14766825.2018.1515215

Henry, J., & Mostafanezhad, M. (2019). The geopolitics of volunteer tourism. In D. T. Timothy (Ed.), *Handbook of Globalisation and Tourism* (pp. 295–304). Edward Elgar Publishing Limited. https://doi.org/10.4337/9781786431295.00037

Holmes, G., & Cavanagh, C. J. (2016). A review of the social impacts of neoliberal conservation: Formations, inequalities, contestations. *Geoforum*, 75, 199–209. https://doi.org/10.1016/j.geoforum.2016.07.014

Kirillova, K., Lehto, X., & Cai, L. (2015). Volunteer tourism and intercultural sensitivity: The role of interaction with host communities. *Journal of Travel and Tourism Marketing*, 32(4), 382–400. https://doi.org/10.1080/10548408.2014.897300

Liu, T. M., & Leung, K. K. (2019). Volunteer tourism, endangered species conservation, and aboriginal culture shock. *Biodiversity and Conservation*, *28*(1), 115–129. https://doi.org/10.1007/s10531-018-1639-2

Lo, A. S., & Lee, C. Y. S. (2011). Motivations and perceived value of volunteer tourists from Hong Kong. *Tourism Management*, *32*(2), 326–334. https://doi.org/10.1016/j.tourman.2010.03.002

Lorimer, J. (2009). International conservation volunteering from the UK: What does it contribute? *Oryx*, *43*(3), 352–360. https://doi.org/10.1017/S0030605309990512

Lorimer, J. (2010). International conservation "volunteering" and the geographies of global environmental citizenship. *Political Geography*, *29*(6), 311–322. https://doi.org/10.1016/j.polgeo.2010.06.004

Lupoli, C. A., & Morse, W. C. (2015). Assessing the local impacts of volunteer tourism: Comparing two unique approaches to indicator development. *Social Indicators Research*, *120*(2), 577–600. https://doi.org/10.1007/s11205-014-0606-x

Lyons, K., Hanley, J., Wearing, S., & Neil, J. (2012). Gap year volunteer tourism. Myths of Global Citizenship? *Annals of Tourism Research*, *39*(1), 361–378. https://doi.org/10.1016/j.annals.2011.04.016

McGehee, N. G. (2014). Volunteer tourism: Evolution, issues and futures. *Journal of Sustainable Tourism*, *22*(6), 847–854. https://doi.org/10.1080/09669582.2014.907299

Mostafanezhad, M. (2013a). The geography of compassion in volunteer tourism. *Tourism Geographies*, *15*(2), 318–337. https://doi.org/10.1080/14616688.2012.675579

Mostafanezhad, M. (2013b). The politics of aesthetics in volunteer tourism. *Annals of Tourism Research*, *43*, 150–169. https://doi.org/10.1016/j.annals.2013.05.002

Mostafanezhad, M. (2015). "They came for nature": A political ecology of volunteer tourism development in Northern Thailand. In S. S. Finney, M. Mostafanezhad, G. C. Pigliasco, & F. W. Young (Eds.), *At home and in the field: Ethnographic encounters in Asia and the Pacific Islands* (pp. 209–215). University of Hawai'i Press. https://doi.org/10.21313/hawaii/9780824847593.003.0035

Mowforth, M., & Munt, I. (2016). *Tourism and Sustainability: Development, Globalisation and New Tourism in the Third World* (4th ed.). https://doi.org/10.4324/9781315795348

Neumann, R. P. (2015). Nature conservation. In T. Perreault, G. Bridge, & J. McCarthy (Eds.), *The Routledge Handbook of Political Eeology* (pp. 391–405). Routledge. https://doi.org/10.4324/9781315759289

Pan, T. J. (2017). Personal transformation through volunteer tourism: The evidence of Asian students. *Journal of Hospitality and Tourism Research*, *41*(5), 609–634. https://doi.org/10.1177/1096348014538048

Peet, R., & Watts, M. (1996). Liberation ecology: Development, sustainability, and environment in an age of market triumphalism. In R. Peet & M. Watts (Eds.), *Liberation Ecologies: Environment, Development, and Social Movements* (pp. 1–45). Routledge.

Perreault, T., Bridge, G., & McCarthy, J. (2015). *The Routledge Handbook of Political Ecology*. Routledge. https://doi.org/10.4324/9781315759289

Ravensbergen, S. (2016). *Marine Conservation and Volunteer Tourism: Examining Community Perceptions in Sarteneja, Belize*, Master's thesis, University of Guelph. http://atrium.lib.uoguelph.ca/xmlui/handle/10214/9858

Raymond, E. M., & Hall, C. M. (2008). The development of cross-cultural (mis)understanding through volunteer tourism. *Journal of Sustainable Tourism*, *16*(5), 530–543. https://doi.org/10.2167/jost796.0

Ribot, J. C., & Peluso, N. L. (2003). A theory of access. *Rural Sociology*, *68*(2), 153–181. https://doi.org/10.1111/j.1549-0831.2003.tb00133.x

Robbins, P. (2012). *Political Ecology: A Critical Introduction*. John Wiley & Sons Ltd.

Roques, K. G., Jacobson, S. K., & McCleery, R. A. (2018). Assessing contributions of volunteer tourism to ecosystem research and conservation in southern Africa. *Ecosystem Services*, *30*, 382–390. https://doi.org/10.1016/j.ecoser.2017.12.014

Saville, S. M. (2019). Tourists and researcher identities: Critical considerations of collisions, collaborations and confluences in Svalbard. *Journal of Sustainable Tourism*, *27*(4), 573–589. https://doi.org/10.1080/09669582.2018.1435670

Senko, J., Schneller, A. J., Solis, J., Ollervides, F., & Nichols, W. J. (2011). People helping turtles, turtles helping people: Understanding resident attitudes towards sea turtle conservation and opportunities for enhanced community participation in Bahia Magdalena, Mexico. *Ocean and Coastal Management*, *54*(2), 148–157. https://doi.org/10.1016/j.ocecoaman.2010.10.030

Simpson, K. (2004). "Doing development": The gap year, volunteer-tourists and a popular practice of development. *Journal of International Development*, *16*(5), 681–692. https://doi.org/10.1002/jid.1120

Smith, P. (2014). International volunteer tourism as (de) commodified moral consumption. In M. Mostafanezhad & K. Hannam (Eds.), *Moral Encounters in Tourism* (pp. 11–45). Ashgate Publishing Limited.

Smith, V. L., & Font, X. (2014). Volunteer tourism, greenwashing and understanding responsible marketing using market signalling theory. *Journal of Sustainable Tourism, 22*(6), 942–963. https://doi.org/10.1080/09669582.2013.871021

Steele, J., & Scherrer, P. (2018). Flipping the principal-agent model to foster host community participation in monitoring and evaluation of volunteer tourism programmes. *Tourism Recreation Research, 43*(3), 321–334. https://doi.org/10.1080/02508281.2018.1457251

Sultana, F. (2015). Emotional political ecology. In R. L. Bryant (Ed.), *The International Handbook of Political Ecology* (pp. 633–645). Edward Elgar Publishing Limited. https://doi.org/10.4337/9780857936172

Svarstad, H., Benjaminsen, T. A., & Overå, R. (2018). Power theories in political ecology. *Journal of Political Ecology, 25*, 350–425. https://doi.org/10.2458/v25i1.23044

Vrasti, W. (2013). *Volunteer Tourism in the Global South - Giving Back in Neoliberal Times*. Routledge. https://doi.org/10.1080/14766825.2014.969960

Vrasti, W., & Montsion, J. M. (2014). No good deed goes unrewarded: The values/virtues of transnational volunteerism in neoliberal capital. *Global Society, 28*(3), 336–355.

Watts, M. J. (2015). Now and then: the origins of political ecology and the rebirth of adaptation as a form of thought. In T. Perreault, G. Bridge, & James McCarthy (Eds.), *The Routledge Handbook of Political Ecology* (pp. 19–50). Routledge.

Wearing, S. (2001). *Volunteer Tourism: Experiences That Make a Difference*. CABI Publishing.

Wearing, S., & McGehee, N. G. (2013). Volunteer tourism: A review. *Tourism Management, 38*, 120–130. https://doi.org/10.1016/j.tourman.2013.03.002

Wearing, S., Young, T., & Everingham, P. (2017). Evaluating volunteer tourism: Has it made a difference? *Tourism Recreation Research, 42*(4), 512–521. https://doi.org/10.1080/02508281.2017.1345470

West, P. (2006). *Conservation Is Our Government Now: The Politics of Ecology in Papua New Guinea*. Duke University Press. https://doi.org/10.1215/9780822388067

Zafra-Calvo, N., Pascual, U., Brockington, D., Coolsaet, B., Cortes-Vazquez, J. A., Gross-Camp, N., Palomo, I., & Burgess, N. D. (2017). Towards an indicator system to assess equitable management in protected areas. *Biological Conservation, 211*(A), 134–141. https://doi.org/10.1016/j.biocon.2017.05.014

Zahra, A., & McGehee, N. G. (2013). Volunteer tourism: A host community capital perspective. *Annals of Tourism Research, 42*(2006), 22–45. https://doi.org/10.1016/j.annals.2013.01.008

5

PSYCHOLOGY OF VOLUNTEERING

Darja Kragt

Introduction

The literature on volunteering is extensive and spans a variety of topics and disciplines, including sociology, management, psychology, and political science. The different disciplines aid in bettering our understanding of the diverse and differentiated process of volunteering. Yet, as concluded by previous reviews, the diversity of perspectives is confusing and leads to a lack of sufficient theoretical rigour (Kragt & Holtrop, 2019). This chapter presents the psychological perspective on volunteering. Whereas sociologists are concerned with group processes, and management scholars are focused on organising and administration, psychologists try to understand the individual volunteering experiences and behaviour by asking: what motivates people to volunteer? What benefits do individuals obtain from engaging in volunteering? What factors influence whether they stay with their volunteering organisation, seek a better volunteering experience elsewhere, or withdraw from volunteering altogether? And finally, how do individuals differ in their experiences of volunteering? A variety of psychological theories help to answer these and other questions about people who volunteer and those who do not. This chapter offers a brief overview of the most noteworthy conceptual propositions and empirical findings in this domain. Keeping with the theme of the Handbook, illustrative empirical studies have been sought from research on events, sports, and tourism volunteering, where available.

The chapter is particularly centred on the experiences of the individual volunteer. Benefits and the value of volunteering are often discussed from a societal and organisational point of view, that is, highlighting the important contributions that volunteers make to their communities. However, research has recognised that volunteers derive great benefits from the activity, in the form of psychological, social and human capital. In fact, Holmes (2009) compared volunteering benefits derived by organisations, recipients, and volunteers and found that volunteers were the primary beneficiaries of volunteering activities. Research has convincingly demonstrated that all volunteers report higher levels of personal well-being (i.e., happiness and life satisfaction) and social well-being (i.e., participation and reciprocity; Mellor et al., 2009). More specifically, volunteering behaviour was positively related to well-being among mega-event volunteers (Wu & Li, 2019). Better well-being outcomes among volunteers are said to occur because volunteering is a form of active social engagement. Volunteering also

DOI: 10.4324/9780367815875-6

contributes to the development of human and social capital, particularly by increasing individual's social connectedness. For example, sports volunteering has been found to foster human capital and encourage practical and intellectual connectedness amongst young people (Kay & Bradbury, 2009). Social connectedness, in turn, promotes greater social solidarity and social cohesion, which then also leads to better well-being.

Thus, studying volunteering from an individual-based perspective remains an important and worthy challenge for researchers. It is hoped that this chapter will inform the reader about well-established psychological theories that could be applied to explain different volunteering phenomena, and thus help in guiding researchers to design and conduct rigorous and impactful studies. This chapter is organised in three sections: motivation to become a volunteer; challenges of volunteer retention; and individual differences in volunteering.

Becoming a volunteer

Increasingly, volunteering organisations compete to attract and recruit volunteers. Unsurprisingly, a large portion of the research literature on volunteering is concerned with understanding why individuals become volunteers. There are several theoretical approaches in the volunteering literature that try to explain volunteer motivation, but the most dominant is the functional approach.

Functional approach

The functional approach to volunteer motivation suggests that individuals have different reasons to engage in the same volunteer activity. The Volunteer Functions Inventory or VFI (Clary et al., 1998) is the most commonly used tool and it measures six broad categories of motivation or psychological functions met through volunteering. These functions are: values (i.e., volunteering to express pro-social values), understanding (i.e., volunteering to learn), enhancement (i.e., volunteering for personal growth), career (i.e., volunteering for career-relevant experience), social (i.e., volunteering to strengthen social relationships), and protective (i.e., volunteering to alleviate personal problems).

Although the VFI promises to deliver a unified approach to studying volunteer motivation, many researchers, particularly in the sporting, leisure, and tourism domains have attempted to modify the inventory, arguing that these volunteering groups have unique motivations. For example, Kim, Zhang, and Connaughton (2010b) argued that youth sports organisations are unique in that most volunteers are parents, while volunteering requires specialised knowledge and skills. Accordingly, the authors conducted two studies to modify the VFI for application in these organisations. The results confirmed the original factor structure of the VFI, but 12 items were deleted from the original scale due to low relevance to the youth sport setting. This resulted in a new Modified Volunteer Functions Inventory for Sports (MVFIS) scale. Furthermore, Kim, Zhang, and Connaughton (2010a) showed that MVFIS scores also significantly differed between volunteers at different youth sports organisations and events (e.g. international, national, local, and special-needs). Specifically, volunteers working at the international and special-needs sport events displayed higher motivations in all six factor areas than those volunteering for the national and local organisations.

Similarly, other research suggests that event volunteers have distinct reasons for volunteering, such as the need to associate with and support an event (Treuren, 2009). Monga (2006) investigated volunteer motivation in a sample of South Australian event volunteers and found the main reason for volunteering to be an affective relation or affiliation with the key features of the event. The second main reason was that volunteering felt gratifying, followed by altruism towards the community, personal development, and solidarity with traditions or close others. In an attempt to resolve some of the confusion in the use of different inventories to assess volunteer motivation, Kim, Fredline, and Cuskelly (2018) neatly compared the content of the VFI to four event volunteer specific inventories and confirmed that all these inventories overlapped to a degree. However, the event volunteer specific inventories also included aspects unique to event volunteering. Overall, these findings support the need for a more nuanced understanding of volunteer motivation in different contexts. Yet researchers should be cautious in developing more fine-grained inventories and measurement tools, as this presents a significant challenge for generalisability.

Interestingly, it appears that managers have a differing perception of volunteer motivations. Kay and colleagues (2017) surveyed managers of non-profit leisure events about volunteer motivations and derived a much broader typology of 14 motivations. Considering the managerial perspective is important, because ultimately they play a key role in volunteer attraction, but also in ensuring that volunteer expectations are satisfied, so that the initial level of motivation is maintained. Future research could attempt to compare volunteer reported motivations to the perceptions of their managers to identify any potential gaps and misalignments. Additional details on the VFI are contained in Chapter 22 of this Handbook.

Other approaches to volunteer motivation

Whereas the VFI aims to identify different motivations volunteers have, the motivational profiling approach extends this work to identify distinct profiles of volunteers, based on the configuration of their motivations. For example, Dolnicar and Randle (2007) analysed Australian census data that contained the 12 main reasons why people volunteer. They found that the reasons for volunteering clustered into six distinct profiles. 'Classic volunteers' want to do something useful, help others, and gain personal satisfaction. 'Dedicated volunteers' are motivated by a wide and less focused range of reasons. 'Personally involved volunteers' volunteer because they know someone in the organisation, such as their child. 'Volunteers for personal satisfaction' and 'altruists' mainly want to help the community, and 'niche volunteers' have a few specific and less common motivators, such as gaining work experience.

Similarly, Kim et al. (2018) investigated how reasons for volunteering cluster together, using survey data from Queensland sporting event volunteers. As a theoretical framework they used the incentives approach, which distinguishes three broad underlying volunteer motives: normative incentives (comparable to the VFI 'values' motive) describing a genuine concern for others and a desire to help; affective incentives (comparable to the VFI 'social' motive) describing social benefits; and utilitarian incentives (somewhat comparable to VFI 'understanding' and 'career' motives) describing tangible benefits, such as work experience and skills (Knoke & Prensky, 1984). Additionally, Kim et al. (2018) measured some reasons that are specific to sports volunteers, such as the love for sports. They found that the volunteering motives formed four distinct clusters: (1) material benefit seekers, (2) sports and community enthusiasts, (3) altruists, and (4) career and social relationship seekers. This study also uncovered some sociodemographic differences between the profiles, for example, career and social relationship seekers were younger and mostly unemployed or employed in a part-time job. Material benefit seekers and career and social relationship seekers were also more likely to be first-time volunteers. Similarly, another study found three key motivational profiles among event volunteers: instrumentalists, who volunteer for material benefits; conscripts, who volunteer with some reluctance; and enthusiasts, who enjoy the volunteering experience (Treuren, 2014).

Finally, continuity theory is a novel perspective on volunteer motivation and is particularly relevant to sports and event volunteering. Continuity theory suggests that individuals maintain well-being by maintaining established patterns of behaviour during status transitions and throughout life in order to preserve role stability (Atchley, 1989). Cuskelly and O'Brien (2013) applied continuity theory to study players transitioning from playing roles into non-playing volunteering roles, such as administration and coaching. They found that former players were motivated to continue their involvement in and connection to sport, and to preserve their sense of identity and existing relationships.

Studying volunteer motivation is important to improve attraction and recruitment outcomes. However, volunteer motivation to join an organisation will also affect volunteers' subsequent experiences. For example, motivation was found to positively relate to volunteer experiences and satisfaction among volunteers at a mega-sporting event (Giannoulakis, Wang & Felver, 2015). Hence, understanding what functions individuals seek to satisfy by becoming a volunteer is important to improving subsequent volunteer retention, which is discussed in the next section of this chapter.

Remaining a volunteer

Volunteer retention is a major topic of interest among both practitioners and academics. Turnover rates among volunteers are particularly high in the first year after joining (Kragt & Holtrop, 2019), which brings about personal, financial, and psychological costs. Volunteer retention is a massive challenge in event volunteering, since engagement occurs at distinct points of time, rather than continuously. There are several psychological theories, which offer insights into the processes and mechanisms of volunteer retention.

Psychological contract

The notion of psychological contract (PC) is grounded in social exchange theory, and is described as a subjective cognitive state that refers to the development and maintenance of the relationship between the individual and the organisation (Taylor, Darcy, Hoye & Cuskelly, 2006). In a volunteering context, PC encompasses volunteer's expectations about the volunteering role and experience (Rousseau, 1995). In contrast to the traditional employment contract, PC is implicit, shaped by the volunteer experience, and can be unique for every volunteer (Stirling, Kilpatrick & Orpin, 2011). PC is critical to volunteer retention, because its *fulfilment* or *breach* will affect volunteers' willingness to remain in the role. A study of World Expo event volunteers found that PC fulfilment was positively related to volunteer satisfaction, which in turn predicted future intention to volunteer (Wang & Yu, 2015).

There are two main types of psychological contracts: transactional (i.e., monetary exchange) and relational (i.e., social exchange). Although relational contract appears more relevant to volunteering, research has found support for both forms. For example, Harman and Doherty's (2014) study of volunteer youth sport coaches found that they expected the club to provide fundamental resources and administration (transactional) and coach support (relational).

Remarkably, volunteer expectations may significantly differ from an administrator's expectations. Taylor et al. (2006) found that rugby club volunteers focused on the relational contract expectations, such as rewards, sufficient power and responsibility, training and development, and pleasant social environment. On the other hand, volunteer administrators were overly focused on transactional aspects, such as adherence to professional, legal, and regulatory standards. Paradoxically, volunteer administrators were also club volunteers.

The PC perspective is particularly useful in studying volunteering, because it investigates the fulfilment of initial expectations, thus connecting volunteer recruitment experiences to retention outcomes. However, research so far has failed to investigate PC as a dynamic construct that changes over time. For example, volunteers might update their expectations after initial experiences with the organisation, and this might impact upon PC fulfilment.

Self-determination theory

Self-determination theory (SDT; Deci & Ryan, 1985) proposes a continuum of motivations that underlie human behaviour. Intrinsic motivation refers to freely engaging in an activity, because it is inherently interesting or enjoyable. Extrinsic motivation refers to doing something for instrumental reasons, such as acquiring a reward (Millette & Gagné, 2008). SDT also suggests that extrinsic motivation varies in the extent to which it is self-determined and distinguishes four types: external and interjected regulation; identified and integrated regulation (Deci & Ryan, 1985). The former two are completely and somewhat externally controlled, respectively, hence are referred to as 'controlled motivation'. The latter two reflect motivation that is somewhat and completely self-determined, respectively, hence are called 'autonomous motivation'.

Finally, SDT also identified three basic psychological needs: autonomy, relatedness, and competence (Deci & Ryan, 2000). The need for autonomy refers to an individual's desire to have the freedom to carry out an activity in their chosen way; the need for belongingness refers to an individual's need to relate and connect with people around them; and the need for competence refers to the extent to which an individual feels capable of performing effectively in their role. Previous research has shown that when volunteers experience high levels of autonomy and competence, they are less likely to consider leaving the organisation (Haivas, Hofmans & Pepermans, 2013).

Although SDT is a motivational theory, it has been primarily applied to study *existing* volunteers and how the features of the volunteering experience impact on volunteer outcomes, rather than studying *potential* volunteers and what attracts them to volunteering in the first place. An early qualitative study of SDT among volunteers at a large sporting event found that participants reported intrinsic motivation towards volunteering, but also extrinsic motivation towards some volunteering tasks (Allen & Shaw, 2009). Participants also perceived satisfaction of their psychological needs through volunteering. In another study, autonomous motivation was positively related to work effort among volunteers (Bidee et al., 2013).

Other research has established that autonomous motivation mediates the relationship between needs satisfaction and volunteer outcomes. For example, autonomy and competence needs are related to autonomous motivation, which in turn predicts work engagement among volunteers (Haivas et al., 2013). Interestingly, autonomy and competence needs were directly (rather than indirectly related) and negatively related to intention to quit. Another study of volunteers at the Special Olympics tested a process model, whereby competence was related to intrinsic motivation, in turn related to satisfaction, and in turn related to intention to continue volunteering (Wu, Li & Khoo, 2016).

SDT has also been studied in the context of volunteer leadership. Autonomy-supportive leadership involves behaviours that aim to address volunteers' psychological needs, for example, encouraging personal initiative, offering opportunities for choice, taking others' perspective into account, providing optional challenges, supporting people's competences, and facilitating social interactions (Gagné, 2003). Unsurprisingly, autonomy-supportive leadership was positively related to autonomous motivation and negatively related to controlled motivation among sport event volunteers (Wu & Li, 2019). Furthermore, autonomous motivation was negatively related to emotional exhaustion and positively related to life satisfaction, whereas the impacts of controlled motivation were opposite. In another study, need satisfaction and autonomous motivation serially mediated the link between autonomy-supportive leadership and volunteer satisfaction (Oostlander, Güntert & Wehner, 2014).

Overall, SDT is one of the most researched and established motivational theories in volunteering literature. However, studies frequently report inconsistent and conflicting findings. It would be worthwhile to pursue research that integrates SDT with other established theories, in order to investigate volunteer experiences more comprehensively. For example, Güntert, Strubel, Kals, and Wehner (2016) combined the functional approach to volunteer motivation and SDT; and found that whereas some motives (i.e., values, understanding) are positively related to self-determined motivation, others (i.e., career) are negatively related. Furthermore, self-determined motivation mediated the relationship between motives and satisfaction.

Commitment and identification

Organisational commitment and organisational identification are both broadly defined as the extent to which individuals see themselves as members of a particular organisation, identify with organisational goals and wish to remain an organisational member (Kreiner & Ashforth, 2004). Commitment and identification are conceptually distinct, yet both are underpinned by social identity theory (Tajfel & Turner, 1979), which argues that individuals think of themselves as psychologically linked to the groups and organisations to which they belong. For example, pride and respect in organisations were positively related to organisational identification and commitment among volunteers (Boezeman & Ellemers, 2007).

Cuskelly and colleagues have conducted many studies to investigate commitment among sport and event volunteers. Overall, they found that organisational commitment was a strong predictor of volunteer turnover (Cuskelly & Boag, 2001), however, its level among volunteers was found to decline over time (Cuskelly, Harrington & Stebbins, 2002). Researchers have also identified various antecedents of volunteer commitment. For example, a study of a sporting event in Norway found that organisational commitment was predicted by older age, satisfaction with contribution and recognition, and personal connection to the sport (Mykletun & Himanen, 2016). In turn, commitment predicted intention to volunteer at future events, along with higher levels of education and a personal connection to sport. Ringuet-Riot, Cuskelly, Auld, and Zakus (2014) distinguished between core and peripheral volunteers in sporting organisations. Core volunteers held a formal office and were found to be more committed, as opposed to peripheral volunteers, who only provided an occasional contribution.

Importantly, the organisation is not the only foci of commitment in the volunteering context. Other foci can include the cause, the community supporting the cause, the volunteer role, or the work team (Engelberg, Zakus, Skinner & Campbell, 2012). Furthermore, foci of commitment differently predict aspects of volunteer performance. For example, organisational commitment predicted involvement, whereas role commitment predicted knowledge among youth sport volunteers (Engelberg, Skinner & Zakus, 2011). Other research found that commitment among event volunteers was related to the particular event and the specific sport (i.e., golf) (MacLean & Hamm, 2007). Other research suggests that volunteer identification with an event is primarily achieved through communication with patrons and also with other staff members and artefacts (i.e., clothing) (Tornes & Kramer, 2015).

Theory of planned behaviour

The Theory of Planned Behaviour (TPB) proposes that human behaviour, such as volunteering, follows from behavioural intentions (Ajzen, 1991). In turn, intentions are formed by three considerations: attitudes, subjective norms, and perceived behavioural control. *Attitudes* reflect if an individual thinks executing the intended behaviour will have positive or negative consequences. *Subjective norms* reflect if an individual thinks he/she is expected to perform the behaviour. *Perceived behavioural control* (PBC) reflects the individual's perception of the difficulty of the intended behaviour, which is often equated to a person's self-efficacy.

Research on sports, event, and tourism volunteers has generally applied the TPB theory to study their intention to volunteer again (rather than investigating why they joined in the first place). The results are somewhat mixed. One study of sporting event volunteers found that attitudes, subjective norms, and PBC were related to the intention to return to volunteer, with PBC being the strongest predictor (Lee, Won & Bang, 2014). Another study of mega-event volunteers found that PBC positively influenced both volunteering intention and behaviour, but attitude and subjective norms did not influence intention (Wu & Li, 2019).

Most recently, the TPB has been examined in relation to tourism volunteering. A study of participants in a non-profit global volunteer tourism program found that attitudes, subjective norms, and PBC were positively related to re-participation intention (Meng, Chua, Ryu & Han, 2020). Furthermore, the study also included the norm activation model and personal values approach. The norm activation model proposes that personal norms influence pro-social behaviour (Schwartz, 1977). Study results suggested that TPB variables mediated the relationship between values, norms, and intention to re-participate. In a follow-up meta-analysis, Manosuthi, Lee, and Han (2020) found that supplementing the TPB with the norm activation model only marginally increased the predictive power.

Another interesting example of theoretical integration is a study by Li and Wu (2019), who combined the TBP and SDT. They found that autonomous motivation positively predicted attitudes and PBC, but controlled motivation was negatively related to both. Attitudes and PBC were then positively related to intention.

Demographic and individual differences in volunteering

A chapter on the psychological perspective on volunteering would be incomplete without a section on individual differences. Although the primary impetus in volunteering research has been to understand antecedents and outcomes of volunteering at the group level, some researchers have considered demographic and individual differences.

Demographic differences

Volunteers represent a distinct population group in that they typically have higher income, higher education, and more social resources (Kragt & Holtrop, 2019; Wilson, 2000). This is consistent with socio-structural resources theory, which argues that individuals have different levels of access to opportunities and resources, and thus undertake different roles in society (Warburton & Stirling, 2007). Thus, the extra resources available to those of higher socioeconomic status facilitate volunteering.

Within the volunteering population, some demographic differences have been observed as well. For example, men are more likely to volunteer in sports/hobby organisations, whereas women are more likely to volunteer for welfare, community, and health organisations (Gray, Khoo & Reimondos, 2012). Some researchers have argued that men and women volunteer at sporting events for different reasons, i.e., women volunteer to improve their social capital and to become involved in useful networks, whereas men are more driven by intrinsic interest in the sports as such (Skirstad & Hanstad, 2013). Another study suggested that observed gender differences in motivation and commitment to sport event volunteering might be due to gender roles and their attribution to volunteering context, which is consistent with social role theory (Hallmann, Zehrer, Fairley & Rossi, 2020).

Furthermore, there are significant age-related differences in volunteering both in terms of types of volunteering activity and outcomes. For example, mid-age adults are more likely to volunteer in sports/hobby and educational organisations, because they have children participating in these organisations (Gray et al., 2012). Volunteering also results in different outcomes, for example, it can be especially beneficial for well-being in older adults. This is consistent with socioemotional selectivity theory, which proposes that individuals place a greater importance on emotionally meaningful activities as they age (Carstensen, 2006). In seeking to satisfy their emotional goals, older adults turn to volunteering, because it contributes to the needs and welfare of others. Consistent with this, hours spent volunteering have been positively related to psychological well-being and life satisfaction in older adults (Windsor, Anstey & Rodgers, 2008). On the other hand, younger adults volunteer primarily to satisfy their career and learning goals.

Individual differences

Personality traits are stable individual characteristics, and despite the popularity of research on personality, it has been rarely studied in relation to sports, event, or tourism volunteering. However, findings from the more general volunteering context shed some light on how personality traits shape volunteering behaviour. For example, extraversion was found as a positive predictor of any volunteering activity, whereas agreeableness only predicted informal volunteering, while openness to experience – only online volunteering (Ackermann, 2019). Furthermore, agreeableness and extraversion were found to relate to volunteering through pro-social value motivation, suggesting there is a benefit in studying personality and motivation together (Carlo, Okun, Knight & de Guzman, 2005).

Researchers have also investigated how personality types (i.e., configurations of personality traits) are associated with volunteering. For example, an over-controlled personality type is characterised by high levels of generally negative affect and by social withdrawal, whereas under-controlled personality types are described as unsympathetic, aggressive, lacking in emotional control, and are low in conscientiousness. Unsurprisingly, Matsuba, Hart, and Atkins (2007) found that both over-controlled and under-controlled personality types were associated with less volunteering.

Extending SDT findings in the volunteering context, Oostlander et al. (2014) studied the impact of individual difference in *locus of causality*. Locus of causality is defined as a stable and trait-like tendency to generally experience social contexts as autonomy-supportive (termed as autonomy orientation) or controlling (termed as control orientation; Deci & Ryan, 1985). The results revealed that the relationship between autonomy-supportive leadership and volunteer motivation was moderated by the strength of autonomy and control orientation. Specifically, volunteers with a strong autonomy orientation showed higher autonomous motivation under less conditions compared to volunteers with a weak autonomy orientation.

In line with identity theory, role identity is a self-definition derived from the social or structural role that an individual occupies (Stryker & Burke, 2000). Because individuals vary in the extent to which they internalise a social role as self-identifying, role identity can be sought of as an individual difference. Social psychologists have investigated volunteer identity as an additional factor that helps to explain volunteering outcomes, particularly retention. An early study established that volunteer role identity was positively related to volunteer performance (i.e., hours worked) and intent to remain (Grube & Piliavin, 2000).

Furthermore, a study of Italian volunteers found that role identity fully mediated the relationship between attitudes and norms and behavioural intentions to volunteer (i.e., TPB factors), which in turn predicted actual volunteering behaviour after three years (Marta, Manzi, Pozzi & Vignoles, 2014). A study among 2000 Sydney Olympic Games volunteers found that they continued to identify with their role 12 years after the event, and the identity was grounded in the experiences of friendship and teamwork, knowledge and learning, a sense of connection, and ownership over the event (Fairley, Green, O'Brien & Chalip, 2014).

Overall, demographic and individual differences appear to be an important area of research in volunteering. Particularly, the noted lack of such studies in the events, sports, and tourism volunteering contexts should be addressed in order to more fully understand the role of such differences in volunteer attraction and retention.

Conclusion

The aim of this chapter was to provide a brief overview of psychological perspectives on volunteering. Several noteworthy psychological theories have been reviewed and illustrative empirical findings have been provided. While some of these theories have been studied quite extensively (i.e., Self-determination Theory, Functional Approach to motivation), others have received little attention. There appear to be several fruitful research directions for more comprehensive understandings of volunteering. First, as suggested, integration of different psychological theories allows for generation of new insights into volunteers' motivation and outcomes. Furthermore, as noted by previous commentators, a major drawback of the current literature on volunteering is that it frequently is solely focused on one stage with little regard to how experiences at one stage influence and/or are influenced by experiences at other stages (Kragt & Holtrop, 2019). Thus, theoretical integration that also considers how the volunteering experience unfolds over time should be considered by researchers.

Second, one of the major concerns identified is a lack of methodological rigour in studying motivation among events, sport, and tourism volunteers. For example, instead of using a single, empirically validated measurement instrument, such as VFI, researchers are prone to developing (but often not validating) their own instruments. Instead, different types of volunteers should be studied through the lens of individual differences, which is currently under-explored in events, sport, and tourism volunteering research. Overall, it is hoped that the present chapter has offered some suggestions and directions for new and exciting research on volunteering in these contexts.

References

Ackermann, K. (2019). Predisposed to volunteer? Personality traits and different forms of volunteering. *Nonprofit and Voluntary Sector Quarterly, 48*(6), 1119–1142. https://doi.org/10.1177/0899764019848484

Ajzen, I. (1991). The theory of planned behavior. *Organizational Behavior and Human Decision Processes, 50*(2), 179–211.

Allen, J. B., & Shaw, S. (2009). "Everyone rolls up their sleeves and mucks in": Exploring volunteers' motivation and experiences of the motivational climate of a sporting event. *Sport Management Review, 12*(2), 79–90. https://doi.org/10.1016/j.smr.2008.12.002

Atchley, R. C. (1989). A continuity theory of normal aging. *The Gerontologist, 29*(2), 183–190.

Bidee, J., Vantilborgh, T., Pepermans, R., Huybrechts, G., Willems, J., Jegers, M., & Hofmans, J. (2013). Autonomous motivation stimulates volunteers' work effort: A self-determination theory approach to volunteerism. *Voluntas, 24*(1), 32–47. https://doi.org/10.1007/s11266-012-9269-x

Boezeman, E. J., & Ellemers, N. (2007). Volunteering for charity: Pride, respect, and the commitment of volunteers. *Journal of Applied Psychology, 92*(3), 771–785. https://doi.org/10.1037/0021-9010.92.3.771

Carlo, G., Okun, M. A., Knight, G. P., & de Guzman, M. R. T. (2005). The interplay of traits and motives on volunteering: Agreeableness, extraversion and prosocial value motivation. *Personality and Individual Differences, 38*(6), 1293–1305. https://doi.org/10.1016/j.paid.2004.08.012

Carstensen, L. L. (2006). The influence of a sense of time on human development. *Science, 312*(5782), 1913–1915. https://doi.org/10.1126/science.1127488

Clary, E. G., Snyder, M., Ridge, R. D., Copeland, J., Stukas, A. A., Haugen, J., & Miene, P. (1998). Understanding and assessing the motivations of volunteers: A functional approach. *Journal of Personality and Social Psychology, 74*(6), 1516–1530. https://doi.org/10.1037//0022-3514.74.6.1516

Cuskelly, G., & Boag, A. (2001). Organisational commitment as a predictor of committee member turnover among volunteer sport administrators: Results of a time-lagged study. *Sport Management Review, 4*(1), 65–86. https://doi.org/10.1016/S1441-3523(01)70070-8

Cuskelly, G., Harrington, M., & Stebbins, R. A. (2002). Changing levels of organizational commitment amongst sport volunteers: A serious leisure approach. *Leisure, 27*(3–4), 191–212. https://doi.org/10.1080/14927713.2002.9651303

Cuskelly, G., & O'Brien, W. (2013). Changing roles: Applying continuity theory to understanding the transition from playing to volunteering in community sport. *European Sport Management Quarterly, 13*(1), 54–75. https://doi.org/10.1080/16184742.2012.744767

Deci, E. L., & Ryan, E. M. (1985). *Intrinsic motivation and self-determination in human behavior.* New York: Plenum Press.

Deci, E. L., & Ryan, R. M. (2000). The "what" and "why" of goal pursuits: Human needs and the self-determination of behavior. *Psychological Inquiry, 11*(4), 227–268. https://doi.org/10.1207/S15327965PLI1104_01

Dolnicar, S., & Randle, M. (2007). What motivates which volunteers? Psychographic heterogeneity among volunteers in Australia. *Voluntas, 18*(2), 135–155. https://doi.org/10.1007/s11266-007-9037-5

Engelberg, T., Skinner, J., & Zakus, D. H. (2011). Exploring the relationship between commitment, experience, and self-assessed performance in youth sport organizations. *Sport Management Review, 14*(2), 117–125. https://doi.org/10.1016/j.smr.2010.05.003

Engelberg, T., Zakus, D. H., Skinner, J. L., & Campbell, A. (2012). Defining and measuring dimensionality and targets of the commitment of sport volunteers. *Journal of Sport Management, 26*(2), 192–205. https://doi.org/10.1123/jsm.26.2.192

Fairley, S., Green, B. C., O'Brien, D., & Chalip, L. (2014). Pioneer volunteers: The role identity of continuous volunteers at sport events. *Journal of Sport & Tourism, 19*(3–4), 233–255. https://doi.org/10.1080/14775085.2015.1111774

Gagné, M. (2003). The role of autonomy support and autonomy orientation in prosocial behavior engagement. *Motivation and Emotion, 27*(3), 199–223. https://doi.org/10.1023/A:1025007614869

Giannoulakis, C., Wang, C.-H., & Felver, N. (2015). A modeling approach to sport volunteer satisfaction. *International Journal of Event and Festival Management, 6*(3), 182–199. https://doi.org/10.1108/IJEFM-04-2014-0010

Gray, E., Khoo, S.-E., & Reimondos, A. (2012). Participation in different types of volunteering at young, middle and older adulthood. *Journal of Population Research, 29*(4), 373–398. https://doi.org/10.1007/s12546-012-9092-7

Grube, J. A., & Piliavin, J. A. (2000). Role identity, organizational experiences, and volunteer performance. *Personality and Social Psychology Bulletin, 26*(9), 1108–1119. https://doi.org/10.1177/01461672002611007

Güntert, S. T., Strubel, I. T., Kals, E., & Wehner, T. (2016). The quality of volunteers' motives: Integrating the functional approach and self-determination theory. *The Journal of Social Psychology, 156*(3), 310–327. https://doi.org/10.1080/00224545.2015.1135864.

Haivas, S., Hofmans, J., & Pepermans, R. (2013). Volunteer engagement and intention to quit from a self-determination theory perspective. *Journal of Applied Social Psychology, 43*(9), 1869–1880. https://doi.org/10.1111/jasp.12149

Hallmann, K., Zehrer, A., Fairley, S., & Rossi, L. (2020). Gender and volunteering at the Special Olympics: Interrelationships among motivations, commitment, and social capital. *Journal of Sport Management, 34*(1), 77–90. https://doi.org/10.1123/jsm.2019-0034

Harman, A., & Doherty, A. (2014). The psychological contract of volunteer youth sport coaches. *Journal of Sport Management, 28*(6), 687–699. https://doi.org/10.1123/JSM.2013-0146

Holmes, K. (2009). The value of volunteering: The volunteer's story. *Australian Journal on Volunteering, 14,* 50–58.

Kay, P., Polonsky, M. J., & Inglis, J. (2017). Understanding managerial perspectives of volunteering at nonprofit leisure events: A comparison of typologies within open gardens Australia. *Journal of Nonprofit & Public Sector Marketing, 29*(1), 64–97. https://doi.org/10.1080/10495142.2017.1293586

Kay, T., & Bradbury, S. (2009). Youth sport volunteering: Developing social capital? *Sport, Education and Society, 14*(1), 121–140. https://doi.org/10.1080/13573320802615288

Kim, E., Fredline, L., & Cuskelly, G. (2018). Heterogeneity of sport event volunteer motivations: A segmentation approach. *Tourism Management, 68,* 375–386. https://doi.org/10.1016/j.tourman.2018.04.004

Kim, M., Zhang, J. J., & Connaughton, D. P. (2010a). Comparison of volunteer motivations in different youth sport organizations. *European Sport Management Quarterly, 10*(3), 343–365. https://doi.org/10.1080/16184741003770198

Kim, M., Zhang, J. J., & Connaughton, D. P. (2010b). Modification of the volunteer functions inventory for application in youth sports. *Sport Management Review, 13*(1), 25–38. https://doi.org/10.1016/j.smr.2009.04.005

Knoke, D., & Prensky, D. (1984). What relevance do organization theories have for voluntary associations? *Social Science Quarterly, 65*(1), 3–20.

Kragt, D., & Holtrop, D. (2019). Volunteering research in Australia: A narrative review. *Australian Journal of Psychology, 71*(4), 342–360. https://doi.org/10.1111/ajpy.12251

Kreiner, G. E., & Ashforth, B. E. (2004). Evidence toward an expanded model of organizational identification. *Journal of Organizational Behavior, 25*(1), 1–27. https://doi.org/10.1002/job.234

Lee, Y.-j., Won, D., & Bang, H. (2014). Why do event volunteers return? Theory of planned behavior. *International Review on Public and Nonprofit Marketing, 11*(3), 229–241. https://doi.org/10.1007/s12208-014-0117-0

Li, C., & Wu, Y. (2019). Understanding voluntary intentions within the theories of self-determination and planned behavior. *Journal of Nonprofit & Public Sector Marketing, 31*(4), 378–389. https://doi.org/10.1080/10495142.2018.1526745

MacLean, J., & Hamm, S. (2007). Motivation, commitment, and intentions of volunteers at a large Canadian sporting event. *Leisure/Loisir, 31*(2), 523–556. https://doi.org/10.1080/14927713.2007.9651394

Manosuthi, N., Lee, J.-S., & Han, H. (2020). Predicting the revisit intention of volunteer tourists using the merged model between the theory of planned behavior and norm activation model. *Journal of Travel & Tourism Marketing, 37*(4), 510–532. https://doi.org/10.1080/10548408.2020.1784364

Marta, E., Manzi, C., Pozzi, M., & Vignoles, V. L. (2014). Identity and the theory of planned behavior: Predicting maintenance of volunteering after three years. *The Journal of Social Psychology, 154*(3), 198–207. https://doi.org/10.1080/00224545.2014.881769

Matsuba, M. K., Hart, D., & Atkins, R. (2007). Psychological and social-structural influences on commitment to volunteering. *Journal of Research in Personality, 41*(4), 889–907. https://doi.org/10.1016/j.jrp.2006.11.001

Mellor, D., Hayashi, Y., Stokes, M., Firth, L., Lake, L., Staples, M., . . . Cummins, R. (2009). Volunteering and its relationship with personal and neighborhood well-being. *Nonprofit and Voluntary Sector Quarterly, 38*(1), 144–159. https://doi.org/10.1177/0899764008317971

Meng, B., Chua, B.-L., Ryu, H. B., & Han, H. (2020). Volunteer tourism (VT) traveler behavior: Merging norm activation model and theory of planned behavior. *Journal of Sustainable Tourism, 28*(12), 1947–1969. https://doi.org/10.1080/09669582.2020.1778010

Millette, V., & Gagné, M. (2008). Designing volunteers' tasks to maximize motivation, satisfaction and performance: The impact of job characteristics on volunteer engagement. *Motivation and Emotion, 32*(1), 11–22. https://doi.org/10.1007/s11031-007-9079-4

Monga, M. (2006). Measuring motivation to volunteer for special events. *Event Management, 10*(1), 47–61. https://doi.org/10.3727/152599506779364633

Mykletun, R. J., & Himanen, K. (2016). Volunteers at biking race events. *Sport, Business and Management: An International Journal, 6*(3), 246–273. https://doi.org/10.1108/SBM-12-2014-0051

Oostlander, J., Güntert, S. T., & Wehner, T. (2014). Linking autonomy-supportive leadership to volunteer satisfaction: A self-determination theory perspective. *Voluntas, 25*(6), 1368–1387. https://doi.org/10.1007/s11266-013-9395-0

Ringuet-Riot, C., Cuskelly, G., Auld, C., & Zakus, D. H. (2014). Volunteer roles, involvement and commitment in voluntary sport organizations: Evidence of core and peripheral volunteers. *Sport in Society, 17*(1), 116–133. https://doi.org/10.1080/17430437.2013.828902

Rousseau, D. M. (1995). *Psychological contracts in organizations: Understanding written and unwritten agreements.* Thousand Oaks: SAGE.

Schwartz, S. H. (1977). Normative influences on altruism. *Advances in Experimental Social Psychology, 10*(1), 221–279.

Skirstad, B., & Hanstad, D. V. (2013). Gender matters in sport event volunteering. *Managing Leisure, 18*(4), 316–330. https://doi.org/10.1080/13606719.2013.809188

Stirling, C., Kilpatrick, S., & Orpin, P. (2011). A psychological contract perspective to the link between non-profit organizations' management practices and volunteer sustainability. *Human Resource Development International, 14*(3), 321–336. https://doi.org/10.1080/13678868.2011.585066

Stryker, S., & Burke, P. J. (2000). The past, present, and future of an identity theory. *Social Psychology Quarterly, 63*(4), 284–297. https://doi.org/10.2307/2695840

Tajfel, H., & Turner, J. C. (1979). An integrative theory of intergroup conflict. In W. G. Austin & S. Worchel (Eds.), *The social psychology of intergroup relations* (pp. 33–47). Monterey, CA: Brooks/Cole.

Taylor, T., Darcy, S., Hoye, R., & Cuskelly, G. (2006). Using psychological contract theory to explore issues in effective volunteer management. *European Sport Management Quarterly, 6*(2), 123–147. https://doi.org/10.1080/16184740600954122

Tornes, M., & Kramer, M. W. (2015). The volunteer experience in temporary organizations: Volunteer role negotiation and identification in a pop-culture convention. *Communication Studies, 66*(5), 590–606. https://doi.org/10.1080/10510974.2015.1073165

Treuren, G. (2009). The associative-supportive motivation as a factor in the decision to event volunteer. *Leisure, 33*(2), 687–711. https://doi.org/10.1080/14927713.2009.9651458

Treuren, G. J. M. (2014). Enthusiasts, conscripts or instrumentalists? The motivational profiles of event volunteers. *Managing Leisure, 19*(1), 51–70. https://doi.org/10.1080/13606719.2013.849506

Wang, C., & Yu, L. (2015). Managing student volunteers for mega events: Motivation and psychological contract as predictors of sustained volunteerism. *Asia Pacific Journal of Tourism Research, 20*(3), 338–357. https://doi.org/10.1080/10941665.2014.889027

Warburton, J., & Stirling, C. (2007). Factors affecting volunteering among older rural and city dwelling adults in Australia. *Educational Gerontology, 33*(1), 23–43. https://doi.org/10.1080/03601270600846824

Wilson, J. (2000). Volunteering. *Annual Review of Sociology, 26*(1), 215–240. https://doi.org/10.1146/annurev.soc.26.1.215

Windsor, T. D., Anstey, K. J., & Rodgers, B. (2008). Volunteering and psychological well-being among young-old adults: How much is too much? *The Gerontologist, 48*(1), 59–70. https://doi.org/10.1093/geront/48.1.59

Wu, Y., & Li, C. (2019). Helping others helps? A Self-Determination Theory approach on work climate and wellbeing among volunteers. *Applied Research in Quality of Life, 14*, 1099–1111. https://doi.org/10.1007/s11482-018-9642-z

Wu, Y., Li, C., & Khoo, S. (2016). Predicting future volunteering intentions through a self-determination theory perspective. *Voluntas, 27*(3), 1266–1279. https://doi.org/10.1007/s11266-015-9570-6

6

VOLUNTEERING IN INTERNATIONAL SPORTS EVENTS FROM A PUBLIC ADMINISTRATION PERSPECTIVE

Robert Gawłowski and Patrycja Gulak-Lipka

Introduction

Volunteering is a multifaceted phenomenon at a global scale. It is commonly recognised as giving time and energy to third parties, which can bring benefits not only for volunteers, but also organisations, communities, clubs, and society at large. However, the crucial thing is that this kind of behaviour is driven by the free will of participants and a lack of monetary benefits. Public sector volunteering is defined as a voluntary activity that is sponsored and organised by a government agency (Musick & Wilson, 2008). It takes place in a formal setting where volunteers are involved in ongoing responsibilities for service delivery or organisational maintenance for the benefit of agency clients and are unpaid for their time and work, which is not mandated or coerced (Brudney, 1999).

In recent years, public administration has experienced many challenges in terms of changing social circumstances, IT advances, public participation and/or financial constraints. During this time, volunteering has become increasingly important in terms of both public service delivery and public administration. In the first instance, a distinct kind of volunteering can be found in such areas as: parental involvement in schools (Limerick & Burgess-Limerick, 1992), auxiliaries in public hospitals (Jones, 2004; Neuberger, 2008), community policing (Karlovic & Sucic, 2017; Terpstra, 2008; van Eijk, Steen & Verschuere, 2017) and social services (Brudney & Meijs, 2014; Son & Wilson, 2012). In the second instance, volunteering has received increasing recognition by public agencies, which have implemented strategic policies in order to attract more and more volunteers (Blackmore, 2005; Brudney, 1999; Gazley & Brudney, 2005). The challenge, however, is how best to integrate volunteers into existing arrangements as the relationship between volunteers and public agencies may not always be an easy one (Dover, 2010).

This article explores the process of cooperation between international sports organisations and public administrations in order to identify and explain how public administrations can and should involve themselves in international sporting events.

DOI: 10.4324/9780367815875-7

This chapter is organised as follows. Section 'Methodology' discusses the methodological assumptions that were taken into account during the research process. Section 'Volunteering in public administration and sport' explores different faces of volunteering in both sport and public administration in order to discern the expectations underpinning this phenomenon. The penultimate section presents different approaches that are being used in terms of volunteering management. Last but not least, the final section presents a case study by which the authors identify and explain how public administration can and should be involved in international sporting events. The chapter ends with some concluding remarks.

Methodology

Volunteering in sport is a long-standing research perspective. Topics covered include sport volunteering as a means of creating, developing and maintaining social capital (Nicholson & Hoye, 2008), measurement of volunteer motivations relating to sports events (Giannoulakis, Wang & Gray, 2007), investigation of volunteering legacies (Doherty, 2010), gender matters in sport event volunteering (Skirstad & Hanstad, 2013) and volunteer management (Wicker, 2017), among many others. The role of the public sector in sport event volunteering has been rarely taken into consideration (Krajňáková et al., 2018). Hoye and others analyse how government policy and legislation impacts on the ways in which volunteer activities are undertaken in sport (Hoye et al., 2019). The limited research on this topic is quite surprising taking into consideration the fact that the cooperation of both public and private organisations is crucial in the planning and delivery of international sporting events.

Due to the lack of analysis about volunteering in international sporting events from a public administration perspective, the authors adopted a case study method. As Yin notes "the more that your question seeks to explain some contemporary circumstances (e.g., how or why), the more that case study research will be relevant" (2018, p. 14). This is an appropriate tool to explore this specific kind of cooperation and moreover to stay sensitive to the context, detail and complexity of this phenomenon. We used a combination of techniques within the overall case study approach, which are considered common to qualitative research (Hoeber & Shaw, 2017). First, a semi-structured interview was conducted with the person responsible for managing volunteers during the analysed UEFA U-21 event and many others hosted by the City of Bydgoszcz, Poland. The aim of this interview was to identify public sector actor justification and motivations to engage in volunteering during the sporting event alongside the tangible impacts that the public administration was hoping to achieve. The interviewed person was the leader responsible for the volunteering process from the preparation part of the event, a few months before the official opening, until the close of the event. The interview lasted two hours and was conducted on 29 July 2020. Second, the authors analysed a collection of documentary evidence from the Centre of Volunteerism in Bydgoszcz (voluntary unit set up by the City of Bydgoszcz), as well as some toolkits prepared by UEFA, which allowed us to identify room for cooperation between the public administration and the international sport organisation, UEFA. The data was analysed using a qualitative approach, which has been identified as a method that can give new insight into topics related to volunteerism (e.g. see Byers, 2013). The next step of the research was to compare the public sector perspective on volunteering with the private organisation perspective. This cross-checking approach aimed to better understand different perspectives of volunteering, which is very useful in terms of foreseeable cooperation between both parties.

Volunteering in public administration and sport

Sport is an industry where volunteering is very common at many different levels. There are a variety of opportunities to volunteer and serve locally including coaching and supporting kids or amateur clubs through initiatives that give the possibility to engage and build strong social networks. As a result, in different communities, volunteering plays a big role in building social capital (Cuskelly, 2008). This means that volunteering not only relies on helping others, but it also supports the volunteer to learn new knowledge and skills. There are many great opportunities to volunteer, especially during large-scale sporting events. The majority of research on sport volunteering focuses on volunteerism and volunteer management in the context of sport organisations and sport events (Wicker, 2017). In more depth, such research can reflect several different perspectives: the individual volunteer perspective, the institutional perspective of entities involved, as well as from a multi-level and policy perspective (Wicker & Hallmann, 2013; Wilson, 2012).

Nowadays, no mega sport event can be run without the support of volunteers (Baum & Lockstone-Binney, 2007). They are a very important component of sport ventures and support the work of employed, paid staff. Their engagement in the successful delivery of an event is not cost free, but the benefits of volunteer service significantly exceed expenditures, consistently providing a return to the organisation (Segal & Weisbrod, 2002; Whitley, Everhart & Wright, 2006). As major events tend to be very complex, with many areas to cover, organisers seek to engage voluntary staff to help. For example, reports from a mega-event such as the 2012 London Olympic Games showed that over 70,000 volunteers were involved along with 130,000 paid staff to make this event happen (Thareja & Campbell, 2015). This can be compared with the total number of tickets sold, i.e., 8,800,000 and the number of athletes competing during the 2012 Games, almost 7,500 (Thomas Insights, 2019) to whom volunteer assistance was offered. Their appearance and work are noticeable in venues alongside athletes and referees, on the side of the audience assisting spectators and making their experience enjoyable (Ringuet, 2012). As Ringuet lists, there is a wide variety of volunteer responsibilities which range from media roles and statistics support, security, venue branding, ticketing, registration, social and children's activities, as well as a variety of tasks related to event operations and event risk management. This implies that in practice, volunteers are engaging with spectators, athletes, staff and contractors, thus the final outcome of a mega sport event is vastly dependent on the quality of their service (Green & Chalip, 2004).

The large range of duties available for volunteers, number of ventures and people to coordinate, all entail effective teamwork among the individuals and organisations involved in the realisation of mega sport events. As Roche (2000) states, mega-events are best described as large-scale cultural events, both commercial and sport endeavours, which are characterised by their international significance, mass popularity, recognition and dramatic character that evokes the emotions of participants. Behind every sport mega-event stand large international organisations like FIFA, UEFA, FIBA and the International Olympic Committee. Their regulations and requirements mandate how the event is carried out and their representatives are the direct link between the organisation and the host city.

The place and importance of volunteerism in public management has changed during recent decades as public administration paradigms have also done so (Jo, 2020; Parris & Peachey, 2012; Til, 2009). In traditional, bureaucratic-oriented public administration, the main focus was on legal regulations and the most common features of public administration were: anonymity, neutrality, seniority and last but not least, legality (Weber, 1957). In this respect, voluntary engagement was seen more like an additional and unimportant support of public administration rather than an important asset bringing better quality public services. This bureaucratic-legalistic model is meant to be strictly top-down, where frontline employees implement messages from above (Hughes, 1994). This way of thinking about public administration was too narrow to give room for public administration improvement. As a result, in many Anglo-Saxon countries, public administration experienced the New Public Management (NPM) revolution (Lapuente & van de Walle, 2020). The main concept of this new paradigm was based on a new set of rules taken from private sector management. Privatisation of public services, quality management in public services, strategic planning and evaluation of public policy were fertile ground for incremental changes introduced since the very late 1980s. The pace and scale of public administration reform differ across different geographies. However, there is no doubt that the main point of public administration research has moved from legal regulation to final products measured by quality of public services and/or cost-benefit analyses (Politt, Thiel & Homburg, 2007). Taking this into consideration, volunteerism has been viewed as part of the solution to improve the quality of public service delivery (Gawlowski, 2018). Citizens, as well as non-governmental organisations (NGOs), have the potential to exert positive influence on public management. Devoting their free time, spending private financial resources, presenting their knowledge and ideas for improvement is only a part of this story. Public administration cannot be simply equal to private management due to the fact that these two sectors operate according to different rules (Mazur, 2018). Although there are critics of the new public management, the aspects that have gained traction include management flexibility and the evaluation of received outcomes.

The limits of NPM have pushed many scholars and practitioners towards new ways of public management (Bovaird & Loeffler, 2016; Meijer, 2016; Osborne, Radnor & Strokosch, 2016; Sześciło, 2015; Thomas, 2012; Voorberg, 2017). It is described as collaborative management or public governance and in principle is based on strong and meaningful cooperation with third parties such as: NGOs, private companies, voluntary groups and/or citizens. As Bingham suggested "collaboration suggests a closer relationship, it suggests that participants 'colabour', it entails a new structure, shared resources, defined relationships, and communication. Collaboration also involves creating, enhancing, and building on social and organizational capital in pursuit of shared purposes" (2009, p. 279). Researchers focusing on collaboration highlight such elements as: (1) process (Lawrance & Phillips, 2002); (2) structure (Mandell & Steelman, 2003; Sowa, 2008); (3) participants (Ansell & Gash, 2007; Mullin & Daley, 2009) and last but not least (4) the outcome process (Agranoff & McGuire 2003; O'Leary, Gerrard & Bingham, 2006).

Bearing this in mind, the importance of volunteering in public administration is constantly growing and is a fruitful inspiration for new public management tools. Therefore, it appears important to recognise such research perspectives as public service motivation (Parrado et al., 2013), through which the coproduction of public services helps to engage citizens directly in public service delivery (Alford & Head, 2017; Bovaird, 2007; Gawlowski, 2018); innovation in public administration and last but not least, participation in public administration. In all of these examples, volunteering appears to offer formal and informal implications for public service delivery. In each situation, there are at least a handful of tools that allow public administrators to manage the process of volunteering.

Involving volunteers in public administration

Involving volunteers into public administration can be justified in different ways. First and foremost is the consideration of the financial constraints and growing societal expectations in terms of public service quality. Given the limited means to deliver public services, public administrators are seeking new and innovative ways to do more for less or at least properly prioritise goals that need to be meet (Nesbit, Christensen & Brudney, 2017). Second, based on ideological grounds, volunteers enhance the responsiveness of government and also reduce the role of government (Sundeen, 1990). In this respect, civil engagement in public service delivery is a means to build more transparent and trusted relations between public administration and citizens. As Taylor (2002) pointed out, civil engagement in community life offers resources, social glue and is seen as an essential part of society. The most prominent justification of volunteerism was made by Robert Putnam in his famous work concerning social capital in which he strongly highlights the importance of networks, trust and civil engagement. According to his research, there was no doubt that efficient and high performing public services were possible only in the context of bridging social capital in local and/ or regional communities (Putnam, 2000). It is worth mentioning that in contradiction to this kind of social capital is bonding social capital, which is best exemplified by sporting fans clubs (Morgan, 2013; Tacon, 2014). The peril of this kind of social capital is the fact that the social glue mentioned earlier is based on the social exclusion of other members. As a result, this kind of social community can engender conflicts, fear and even social disorder, which stands in contradiction with bridging social capital (Adams, 2011). Last, but not least, the reason why it is worth engaging volunteers to the public administration is expected improvements in the quality of services. There is no doubt that a public service is a specific kind of relation between provider and recipient. Given that, it is not only public administrations that are responsible for creating public value. An important role is also played on the side of citizens. According to this, there is no good teacher without a dedicated student nor is there is no safe neighbourhood without mutual cooperation between police and citizens (Sorensen & Torfing, 2018; Strokosch & Osborne, 2020). In this respect, the role of volunteers is an additional asset that might leverage public services on the next level for both benefits. The way to do this is through a mutual learning process that helps civil servants to better understand citizens' expectations and moreover allows citizens to learn how the public service is run (Dover, 2010). In this respect, volunteering in public administration is under intense scrutiny from very different approaches, such as: knowledge sharing (Chen & Hsieh, 2015) and public service motivation (Leisink, Knies & van Loon, 2018).

According to empirical research, we can highlight that public service provides quite a unique motivation to engage volunteers in this environment. Working for the public good, organising support for vulnerable people or entertainment for local communities prompts people to spend their free time more easily rather than in the private sector (Hardyman, Kitchener & Daunt, 2019). Therefore, public service motivation is associated with more time spent volunteering, increased frequency and higher levels of volunteering intensity (Eriksson & Nordgren, 2018). However, most variance is explained by volunteering intensity. Costello et al. suggest that how the individual perceives they exert volunteering intensity in terms of hours volunteered may be useful among public service motivated volunteers (Costello, Homberg & Secchi, 2020).

Case study

In order to answer the research questions, the authors analysed a case study of an international sporting event that was hosted by the City of Bydgoszcz, Poland. The city of 350,000 inhabitants is located in the central part of Poland. For many Poles, Bydgoszcz is a city associated with sport where many national and international sporting events are organised.

It is partly a result of good sporting infrastructure maintained by the local government as well as long-lasting experience in hosting these kinds of events. Bydgoszcz has hosted the 2019 European Athletics Championships, the 2009 Basketball European Championships, the 2009 European Universities Rowing Championships and many more, which means that the public administration appears to be experienced in organising such international events. This is also in part a result of meeting the standards of the International Association of Athletics Federation as well as UEFA and FIFA. The case described below aims to present where there is room for cooperation between public administration and sports organisations in terms of volunteering.

The event taken into consideration was the Under-21 UEFA Championship or UEFA U-21 hosted by Poland between 15–30 June 2017. Bydgoszcz was one of the major destinations where matches of Group B took place. From the local administration perspective, preparations started at the end of 2016. This is when the Mayor of Bydgoszcz appointed the special organisation team responsible for coordination and organisation of UEFA Euro U-21 matches. The Local Organising Committee (LOC) for the event was set up based on an internal by-law document dated 9 December 2016 (Mayor Order nr 597). Members nominated to the LOC came from different local council departments as well as external institutions responsible for local security, police, crises management, public transport and the sport venue Zawisza, where all events took place. The main tasks of the LOC were: cooperation and coordination work among different institutions such as the Polish Football Association and UEFA, preparing additional events for tourist and football fans, promotion of the city of Bydgoszcz and, last but not least, arranging safety requirements during the whole event. Most importantly, a special coordinator was appointed in terms of volunteering in order to promote cooperation with NGOs.

This internal by-law document decreed on 9 December 2016 can be analysed from two dimensions. First, it shows a number of issues taken into consideration during the event, which may be indicative of those pertinent to other international sports events. Such tasks as: local security, marketing and promotion, public transport, crisis management and volunteering were city responsibilities to be delivered. For these reasons, the local government administration considered the international sports event to be a multi-phased project, which needed a much more helicopter view than the other events it hosted. Second, there is no doubt that the aim to set up such a unit as the LOC was about mitigating the silo-effects of public administration.

Managing volunteering during UEFA Euro U-21 was one of those tasks that were divided between two entities – local government and UEFA. According to the semi-structured interview with the coordinator responsible for volunteering, there were two important goals from the city council perspective. The first was to learn how to manage volunteers during international events to benefit other planned events over the long run. As the volunteer coordinator said:

> Before UEFA EURO21 volunteering was managed from one project to the next one. Therefore, there was a lack of general approach that allow us to think about volunteering more strategically. We were aware of the fact that there is a room to improve it, however, knowledge how to deal with it was very appreciated.

The second one was to promote the City Centre for Volunteering among the local community. From this respect, the first goal could be met by cooperation with UEFA due to the fact that the organisation provided fixed manual instructions based on past events. Therefore,

UEFA took a mentoring position, which meant leading and coordinating volunteering management step by step. It would be fair to say that planning, execution and evaluation activities were entirely supervised by UEFA, however, local government played an important role in terms of delivering each task. UEFA, as the international sport organisation, left little room for bottom-up initiatives from the local government. Each aspect of volunteering management followed UEFA's pre-determined volunteer management plan. It was more like top-down management process. The way the volunteers were trained, dressed and communicated to was decided by UEFA. Each day was precisely planned and evaluated in order to minimise any risk of mistakes.

It would not be an exaggeration to say that the coordinator working for the local administration on a daily basis was de facto delegated to by the international organisation. The main reason for choosing this way of working was the fact that U-21 Championships took place in several cities simultaneously. Therefore, having the same way of planning and executing volunteering vastly simplified the whole process. In order to pursue the given strategy, the LOC and especially the local coordinator of volunteers, were responsible to prepare daily reports which were sent to the national coordinator of volunteering based in the Polish Association of Football. The only thing that was managed by the local government was the process of recruiting and communicating with the local community. Pursuing communication with local schools, NGOs and different kinds of communities remained an additional value for the public administration and enabled civil servants to maintain cooperation after the event. Bearing this in mind, local government provided an intensive communication campaign in order to build a long list of volunteers, which was successful. Learning know-how of volunteering management, promotion of the City Centre of Volunteering (a unit of the public administration) among the local community and finally building the first group of devoted volunteers enabled the local administration to improve the quality of volunteering management. The proof of that was the fact they continued to utilise the City Centre of Volunteering during the subsequent events mentioned above. As the volunteer manager said:

> UEFA Euro U-21 gave us all we need to set up new organisation responsible for volunteering. After this event we have knowledge, manuals and first success. Continuity of this type of work seemed to be a natural step and no one had doubt that it is a useful tool in public management.

A great deal of responsibility of the local volunteering coordinator was also related to the training and preparation of recruited volunteers. Each host city, with its own volunteering coordinator, required approximately 115 volunteers to be recruited for a variety of tasks. The entire event, which took place in six different cities, attracted a total of 1,818 volunteer applications and in Bydgoszcz, 233. What could be seen as a challenge to the local volunteering coordinator and leaders was the fact that among the applicants, only 37% were inhabitants of the host cities and surrounding regions, and 63% came from different regions (data provided by the interviewed volunteer manager). Interestingly, 1% of applicants came from a different country, among which we can list Brazil, Ecuador, Indonesia and Zimbabwe.

According to the event volunteer manual, the volunteer training process involved several stages. The first stage was directed to all volunteer coordinators and leaders representing all U-21 host cities, which was aimed at developing crucial soft skills needed for effective teamwork, task delegation and general communication. The next stage involved introducing the entire group of recruited volunteers to the specific aspects of the tournament, as well as first aid training. The last stage of the training was supposed to familiarise volunteers with the topography of the city and event venues in order to assist athletes and visitors. This last stage was particularly the responsibility of the local authorities and the local volunteer coordinator in Bydgoszcz.

Discussion and conclusions

Given the presented case study, it is plain that managing volunteering by international sport organisations and local public administrations is based on different perspectives. Preparation, execution and evaluation of the sporting event by the international organisation was seen as a highly sophisticated and professional project, which was precisely described in manuals, calendars and strategies. This set of toolkits was tailormade for each partner in terms of their responsibilities. However, there was quite a different attitude from the public administration perspective. First, it was much more complicated in terms of the number of public providers that needed to be involved in the project (e.g. police, fire brigade, crisis management, PR, promotion). Second, it was not only a time-limited project, but also part of a broader strategy being pursued in order to develop social capital and civil engagement. As a result, two different public management paradigms were experienced as detailed in Table 6.1. The international sporting organisation could be described as taking a New Public Management position (Nesbit et al., 2017). However, the public administration was more interested in network governance and a more horizontal approach. Therefore, typical tools that were implemented by the public administration were concentrated on building cooperation and coordination.

There was a window of opportunity for cooperation between the international sport organisation and the public administration possible. In this respect, the public administration was more open to implement the measures proposed or even sometimes, the strong advice from UEFA, by seeing in this guided strategy some advantages in learning new tools of management. The case study presents the volunteer management insights of the UEFA Euro U–21 in Bydgoszcz and the authors believe it clearly reflects two perspectives: the sport and public administration perspectives of organising such events. Such events, played on a

Table 6.1 Different perspectives to volunteering in international sports events

	Public administration	*International sports organisation*
Objectives	Engage local community with the event and build social capital; Coproduction of public service; Transfer of knowledge about volunteering management; Promotion of the city	Promotion Public trust
Partners for cooperation	Local governments departments; Other public institutions (Police, Transport Companies, Fire Brigade); NGOs	National sport organisation Central/Local government
Management tools	Legal instruments; Inter–organisation cooperation; Outsourcing	Toolkits Evidence/report based decisions One tool fits all
Management paradigm	Bureaucracy; Network governance	New public governance

Source: Own study.

regular basis, bring together large-scale international organisations on one side and public administrations of the host city on the other side, thus being representative of varying and sometimes conflicting management paradigms.

Disclosure statement and funding

No potential conflict of interest was reported by the authors. This work was not supported by any external source. The authors take all responsibility for the preparation and conduct of research.

References

Adams, A. (2011). Between modernization and mutual aid: The changing perceptions of voluntary sports clubs in England. *International Journal of Sport Policy and Politics, 3*(1), 23–43. https://doi.org/10.1080/19406940.2010.544663

Agranoff, R., & McGuire, M. (2003). *Collaborative public management.* Washington, DC: Georgetown University Press.

Alford, J., & Head, B. (2017). Wicked and less wicked problems: A typology and a contingency framework. *Policy and Society, 36*(3), 397–413. https://doi.org/10.1080/14494035.2017.1361634

Ansell, C., & Gash, A. (2007). Collaborative governance in theory and practice. *Journal of Public Administration Research and Theory, 18*(4), 543–571. https://doi.org/10.1093/jopart/mum032

Baum, T., & Lockstone-Binney, L. (2007). Volunteers and mega sporting events developing a research framework. *International Journal of Event Management Research, 3*(1), 29–41.

Blackmore, A. (2005). *The reform of public services: The role of the voluntary sector.* London: NCVO.

Blomgren Bingham, L. (2009). Collaborative governance: Emerging practices and the incomplete legal framework for public and stakeholder voice. *Journal of Dispute Resolution, 2009*(2), 1–58. https://scholarship.law.missouri.edu/jdr/vol2009/iss2/2.

Bovaird, T. (2007). Beyond engagement and participation: User and community co-production of public services. *Public Administration Review, 67*(5), 846–860. https://doi.org/10.1111/j.1540-6210.2007.00773.x

Bovaird, T., & Loeffler, E. (Eds.). (2016). *Public management and governance.* New York: Routledge.

Brudney, J.L. (1999). The effective use of volunteers: Best practices for the public sector. *Law and Contemporary Problems, 62*(4), 219–255.

Brudney, J. L., & Meijs L. (2014). Models of volunteer management: Professional volunteer program management in social work. *Human Service Organizations: Management, Leadership & Governance, 38,* 297–309. https://doi.org/10.1080/23303131.2014.899281

Byers, T. (2013). Using critical realism: A new perspective on control of volunteers in sport clubs. *European Sport Management Quarterly, 13*(1), 5–31. https://doi.org/10.1080/16184742.2012.744765

Chen, C.-A., & Hsieh, C.-W. (2015). Knowledge sharing motivation in the public sector: The role of public service motivation. *International Review of Public Administration, 81*(4), 812–832. https://doi.org/10.1177/0020852314558032

Costello, J., Homberg, F., & Secchi, D. (2020). The public service motivated volunteer: Devoting time or effort? *Nonprofit and Voluntary Sector Quarterly, 49*(5), 1–26. https://doi.org/10.1177/0899764020911200

Cuskelly, G. (2008). Volunteering in community sport organizations: Implications for social capital. In M. Nicholson & R. Hoye (Eds.), *Sport and social capital* (pp. 187–206). London: Routledge.

Doherty, A. (2010). The volunteer legacy of a major sport event. *Journal of Policy Research in Tourism, Leisure and Events, 1*(3), 185–207. https://doi.org/10.1080/19407960903204356

Dover, G. J. (2010). Public sector volunteering: Committed staff, multiple logics, and contradictory strategies. *Review of Public Personnel Administration, 30*(2), 235–256. https://doi.org/10.1177/0734371X09360180

Eriksson, E. M., & Nordgren, L. (2018). From one-sized to over-individualized? Service logic's value creation. *Journal of Health Organization and Management, 32*(4), 572–586. https://doi.org/10.1108/JHOM-02-2018-0059

Gawlowski, R. (2018). Co-production as a tool for realization public services. *Public Governance, 44*(2), 71–81. https://doi.org/10.15678/ZP.2018.44.2.05

Gazley, B., & Brudney, J. L. (2005). Volunteer involvement in local government after September 11: The continuing question of capacity. *Public Administration Review, 65*, 131–142. https://www.jstor. org/stable/3542548

Giannoulakis, C., Wang, C.-H., & Gray, D. (2007). Measuring volunteer motivation in mega-sporting events. *Event Management, 4*(11), 191–200. https://doi.org/10.3727/152599508785899884

Green, B. C., & Chalip, L. (2004). Paths to volunteer commitment: Lessons from the Sydney Olympic Games. In R. Stebbins & M. Graham (Eds.), *Volunteering as leisure/leisure as volunteering: An international assessment* (pp. 49–67). Oxfordshire: CABI Publishing.

Hardyman, W., Kitchener, M., & Daunt, K. L. (2019). What matters for me! User conceptions of value in specialist cancer care. *Public Management Review, 21*(11), 1687–1706. https://doi.org/10.1080/14 719037.2019.1619808

Hoeber, L., & Shaw, S. (2017). Contemporary qualitative research methods in sport management. *Sport Management Review, 20*, 4–7. https://doi.org/10.1016/j.smr.2016.11.005

Hoye, R., Cuskelly, G., Auld C., Kappelides, P., & Misener, K. (2019). *Sport volunteering*. London: Routledge.

Hughes, O. E. (1994). *Public management and administration*. New York: Palgrave Macmillan.

Jo, S. (2020). Schools for democracy? The relationship between nonprofit volunteering and direct public participation. *International Public Management Journal, 24*, 67–85. https://doi.org/10.1080/10 967494.2020.1839610

Jones, H. (2004). *Volunteering for health: A research report produced for the Welsh Assembly Government*. Wales Council for Voluntary Action.

Karlovic, R., & Sucic, I. (2017). Security as the basis behind community policing: Croatia's community policing approach. In P. S. Bayerl, R. Karlovic, B. Akhgar & G. Markarian (Eds.), *Community policing: A European perspective. Strategies, best practices and guidelines* (pp. 125–138). Switzerland: Springer.

Krajňáková, E., Šimkus, A., Pilinkiene, V., & Grabowska, M. (2018). Analysis of barriers in sports volunteering. *Journal of International Studies, 11*(4), 254–269. https://doi.org/10.14254/ 2071-8330.2018/11-4/18

Lapuente, V., & van de Welle, S. (2020). The effects of new public management on the quality of public services. *Governance. An International Journal of Policy, Administration, and Institutions, 33*(3), 461–475. https://doi.org/10.1111/gove.12502

Lawrance, T., & Phillips, N. (2002). Understanding cultural industries. *Journal of Management Inquiry, 11*(4), 430–441. https://doi.org/10.1177/1056492602238852

Leisink, P. L. M., Knies, E., & van Loon, N. (2018). Does public service motivation matter? A study of participation in various volunteering domains. *International Public Management Journal*. https://doi. org/10.1080/10967494.2018.1428254

Limerick, B., & Burgess-Limerick, T., (1992). Volunteering and empowerment in secondary schools. *Nonprofit and Voluntary Quarterly, 21*(1), 19–37. https://doi.org/10.1177/089976409202100103

Mandell. M., & Steelman, T. (2003). Understanding what can be accomplished through interorganizational innovations: The importance of typologies, context and management. *Public Management Review, 5*(2), 197–224. https://doi.org/10.1080/1461667032000066417

Mayor Order - Zarządzenie nr 597/ 2016 Prezydenta Miasta Bydgoszczy z dnia 9 grudnia 2016 roku w sprawie powołania Lokalnego Komitetu Organizacyjnego ds. Koordynacji działań związanych z przygotowaniem i przeprowadzeniem na terenie Bydgoszczy meczów Mistrzostw Europa EUFA EURO U21 Polska 2017.

Mazur, S. (Ed.). (2018). *Public policy and the neo-Weberian state*. New York: Routledge.

Meijer, A. (2016). Co-production as a structural transformation of the public sector. *International Journal of Public Sector Management, 29*(6), 596–611. https://doi.org/10.1108/IJPSM-01-2016-0001

Morgan, H. (2013). Sport volunteering, active citizenship and social capital enhancement: What role in the "Big society"? *International Journal of Sport Policy and Politics, 5*(3), 381–395. https://doi.org/1 0.1080/19406940.2013.764542

Mullin, M., & Daley, D. (2009). Working with the State: Exploring interagency collaboration within a federalist system. *Journal of Public Administration Research and Theory, 19*(4), 757–778. https://doi. org/10.1093/jopart/mup029

Musick, M. A., & Wilson, J. (2008). *Volunteers. A social profile*. Bloomington: Indiana University Press.

Nesbit, R., Christensen, R. K., & Brudney, J. L. (2017). The limits and possibilities of volunteering: A framework for explaining the scope of volunteer involvement in public and nonprofit organizations. *Public Administration Review, 78*(4), 502–513. https://doi.org/10.1111/puar.12894

Neuberger, J. (2008). Volunteering in the public services: Health and social care. *Baroness Neuberger's review as the government's volunteering champion.* London: Cabinet Office, Office of the Third Sector.

Nicholson, M., & Hoye, R. (2008). Sport and social capital: An introduction. In M. Nicholson & R. Hoye (Eds.), *Sport and social capital* (pp. 1–18). London: Routledge.

O'Leary, R., Gerrard C., & Bingham L. B. (Eds.) (2006). Symposium on collaborative public management. *Public Administration Review, 66*(S1), 6–9. https://www.jstor.org/stable/4096565

Osborne, S., Radnor, Z., & Strokosch, K. (2016). Co-production and the co-creation of value in public services. *Public Management Review, 18*(5), 639–653. https://doi.org/10.1080/14719037.2015.1111927

Parrado, S., van Ryzin, G., Bovaird, T., & Loffler, E. (2013). Correlates of co-production: Evidence from a five-nation survey of citizens. *International Public Management Journal, 16*(1), 85–112. https://doi.org/10.1080/10967494.2013.796260

Parris, D. L., & Peachey, J. W. (2012). Building a legacy of volunteers through servant leadership: A cause-related sporting event. *Nonprofit Management & Leadership, 23*(2), 259–276. https://doi.org/10.1002/nml.21047

Politt, C., Thiel, S., & Homburg, V. (2007). *New public management in Europe. Adaptation and alternatives.* New York: Palgrave Macmillan.

Putnam, R. (2000). *Bowling alone: The collapse and revival of American community.* New York: Simon and Schuster.

Ringuet, C. (2012). Volunteers in sport: Motivations and commitment to volunteer roles. *Aspetar Sports Medicine Journal, 1*(2), 154–161.

Roche, M. (2000). *Mega-events and modernity: Olympics and expos in the growth of global culture.* London: Routledge.

Segal, L. M., Weisbrod, B. A. (2002). Volunteer labor sorting across industries. *Journal of Policy Analysis and Management, 21*(30), 427–447. https://doi.org/10.1002/pam.10053

Skirstad, B., & Hanstad, D. V. (2013). Gender matters in sport event volunteering. *Managing Leisure, 18*(4), 316–330. https://doi.org/10.1080/13606719.2013.809188

Son, J., & Wilson, J. (2012). Volunteer work and hedonic, eudemonic, and social well-being. *Sociological Forum, 27*(3), 658–681. https://www.jstor.org/stable/23262183

Sorensen, E., & Torfing, J. (2018). The democratizing impact of governance networks: From pluralisation, via democratic anchorage, to interactive political leadership. *Public Administration, 96*(2), 1–16. https://doi.org/10.1111/padm.12398

Sowa, J. E. (2008). The collaboration decision in nonprofit organizations: Views from the frontline. *Nonprofit and Voluntary Sector Quarterly, 38*(6), 1003–1025. https://doi.org/10.1177/0899764008325247

Strokosch, K., & Osborne, S. P. (2020). Co-experience, co-production and co-governance: An ecosystem approach to the analysis of value creation. *Policy & Politics, 48*(3), 425–442. https://doi.org/10.1332/030557320X15857337955214

Sundeen, R. A. (1990). Citizens serving government: The extent and distinctiveness of volunteer participation in local public agencies. *Nonprofit Voluntary Sector Quarterly, 19*(4), 329–344. https://doi.org/10.1177/089976409001900404

Sześciło, D. (2015). Governance in public services. In S. Mazur (Ed.), *Public governance* (pp. 286–301). Warsaw: Scholar Publishing House.

Tacon, R. (2014). Social capital and sports clubs. In A. Christoforou & J. B. Davis (Eds.), *Social capital and economics: Social values, power, and social identity* (pp. 236–261). London: Routledge.

Taylor, M. (2002). *Public policy in the community.* Basingstoke: Palgrave.

Terpstra, J. (2008). Police, local government, and citizens as participants in local security networks. *Police Practice and Research, 9*(3), 213–225. https://doi.org/10.1080/15614260701797520

Thareja M., Campbell S. (2015). *Volunteer programme best practices – London Olympics,* www.metavalue.co.uk/wp-content/uploads/2015/07/Volunteer-programme-best-practice-London-Olympics.pdf [accessed: 21.08.2020].

Thomas, J. (2012). *Citizen, customer, partner: Engaging the public in public management.* New York: M.E. Sharp Inc.

Thomas Insights (2019). *2012 London Olympics by the numbers,* https://www.thomasnet.com/insights/2012-london-olympics-by-the-numbers/ [accessed: 30.06.2020].

Til, J. V. (2009). A paradigm shift in third sector theory and practice: Refreshing the well-springs of democratic capacity. *American Behavioral Scientist, 52*(7), 1069–1081. https://doi.org/10.1177/0002764208327675

Yin, R. K. (2018). *Case study research and applications: Designs and methods.* Los Angeles: SAGE Publications.

Weber, M. (1957). *Essays in sociology.* London: Routledge.

Whitley, E. M., Everhart, R. M., Wright, R. A. (2006). Measuring return on investment of outreach by community health workers. *Journal of Health Care Poor Underserved. 17*(1 Suppl), 6–15. https://doi.org/10.1353/hpu.2006.0015

Wicker, P. (2017). Volunteerism and volunteer management in sport. *Sport Management Review, 20*(4), 325–337. https://doi.org/10.1016/j.smr.2017.01.001

Wicker, P., & Hallmann, K. (2013). A multi-level framework for investigating the engagement of sport volunteers. *European Sport Management Quarterly, 13*, 110–139. https://doi.org/10.1080/16184742.2012.744768

Wilson, J. (2012). Volunteerism research: A review essay. *Nonprofit and Voluntary Sector Quarterly, 41*(2), 176–212. https://doi.org/10.1177/0899764011434558

van Eijk, C., Steen, T., & Verschuere, B. (2017). Co-producing safety in the local community: A Q-methodology study on the incentives of Belgian and Dutch members of neighbourhood watch schemes. *Local Government Studies, 43*(nr 3), 323–343. https://doi.org/10.1080/03003930.2017.1281803

Voorberg, W. (2017). *Co-creation and co-production as a strategy for public service innovation: A study to their appropriateness in a public sector context.* Rotterdam: Erasmus University.

PART 2

Volunteering in tourism and sport

7

DESTINATION SERVICE VOLUNTEERING

Karen A. Smith, Anna Karin Olsson and Kirsten Holmes

Introduction

Volunteering is a global phenomenon of importance to tourism settings. Volunteers are often viewed as a 'hidden workforce' (Kemp, 2002) who take on a range of roles, frontline and behind-the-scenes, and are hence involved in various interactions with visitors and other stakeholders at destinations, attractions and events (Olsson, 2012; Olsson, Therkelsen & Mossberg, 2016). Tourism volunteering is defined here as volunteering where individuals are working or making efforts for free, carried out within a tourism setting (Olsson et al., 2016; Smith & Holmes, 2012). Many destinations are dependent on volunteers as an unpaid workforce, and as financial and social resources (Bussell & Forbes, 2002; Jago & Deery, 2002). While there is a growing body of research on volunteering in tourism, this has been dominated by research on volunteer tourists, those travelling to a destination to volunteer. In Holmes and Smith's model of tourism volunteer engagements (Holmes & Smith, 2009) we refer to this as 'guest' volunteering. Conversely, 'host' volunteering is that which is typically undertaken by those living at the destination. Research has focused on host volunteering at events and attractions, both natural (e.g. conservation volunteers in national parks) and cultural (e.g. volunteers in art galleries and museums). Less attention has been paid to those volunteering in destination service organisations, which we define as "organisations promoting and facilitating tourism in a destination" (Smith & Holmes, 2012, p. 563).

The concept of a tourism destination is wide and may refer to places that are visited by tourists hence embracing smaller or larger geographical units such as a city, a region, an island or a country (Cho, 2000). Destinations are based on complex networks of stakeholders who come together to offer holistic visitor experiences (Fyall & Garrod, 2019; Olsson, 2016; Olsson, Bernhard & Friedrichs, 2018). Destination stakeholders can thus be viewed as actors within an integrated system (Olsson, 2016), who may participate in collaborative decision-making and the sharing of responsibility and benefits (Li & Hunter, 2015). Stakeholders may be categorised into sectors such as public, private and volunteer (Yang, 2014); here we focus on volunteers as stakeholders, and specifically those involved in volunteering which promotes and facilitates tourism in a destination.

DOI: 10.4324/9780367815875-9

The chapter critiques the extant literature on destination service volunteering by first establishing the importance of this form of volunteering. Second, we review the limited studies on volunteering in destination service settings, namely visitor information centres, meet-and-greet programmes, destination tourism associations, destination tour guiding, campground hosting, and emergency and rescue services. Where appropriate, parallels are drawn with other forms of tourism volunteering. A model of destination service volunteering settings and roles is presented, and a research agenda for destination service volunteering is proposed.

Destination service volunteering

Focusing on organisations that operate to promote and facilitate tourism experiences, destination service volunteers may therefore be found at various locations within a destination. This includes arrival points and transport hubs (e.g. airports, ports and train stations), visitor information centres (also known as convention and visitor bureau) and some accommodation facilities (e.g. campground hosts). They may also work across the destination, such as in tour guiding roles, part of emergency response teams (e.g. coastguards or mountain rescue), or in tourism associations. Many tourism volunteers perform operative roles 'on-stage'; others are active in strategic and leadership roles as board members or are involved in roles behind-the-scenes (Holmes & Edwards, 2008; Olsson, 2012; Smith & Holmes, 2009). While many VOLUNTEERS offer their time and skills on an ongoing basis all year round, DESTINATION SERVICE volunteers may instead be involved on a seasonal basis to correspond with the destination's visitor fluctuations (Smith & Holmes, 2009, 2012). While some volunteering may be episodic, for example when search-and-rescue volunteers are called out to an incident, these highly skilled volunteers are likely to have an ongoing commitment to training and other professional development.

It is well-established that staff have an impact on visitor experience (see, for example, Schliephack, Moyle & Weiler, 2013). Thus, earlier research shows that host volunteers, i.e., local residents engaging in their home community, often have a direct impact on visitors' experiences by transmitting their enthusiasm, passion and interest (Holmes & Smith, 2009; Jago & Deery, 2002). Host volunteers may lack professional tourism training, yet they contribute as vital social resources of their community and are often motivated by place attachment, pride and emotional ties (Bernhard, Olsson & Lundh Snis, 2020; Olsson et al., 2016; Smith & Holmes, 2012; Snis, Olsson & Bernhard, 2021). Volunteer roles are often multiple and overlapping within networks of stakeholders (Getz, Andersson & Larson, 2006), including volunteers acting as co-creators of visitor experiences (Olsson, 2016). Volunteers may then act as co-creators at the destination when taking part in service encounters, undertake destination marketing as supporters or advocates, take leadership roles as members of boards or committees and make suggestions for improvements (Olsson & Gellerstedt, 2014; Olsson et al., 2016).

Destination service volunteers hence have a critical role at destinations in significantly affecting the visitor experience. On one hand their roles include welcoming visitors when they arrive at the destination and promoting destination activities, while on the other hand they are integral in destination safety and emergency rescues in order to save visitors' lives. The distinctions between volunteers and paid staff, residents and visitors are often not clear-cut (Garrod et al., 2012) and they all operate within a destination experience-scape with physical, social and sensory settings, focusing on the individual visitor experience of the destination's offerings (Olsson, 2016).

Destination volunteering settings

Volunteers are involved in various settings within destinations, each linked to different roles such as visitor welcome and orientation, destination planning and management, the interpretation and co-creation of a destination experience, and risk management and safety of the destination. Six settings will be discussed in turn, before presenting a model of destination service volunteering.

Visitor information centres

Visitor information centres have multiple functions; as well as acting as information hubs promoting the destination and providing information to facilitate visitors' experiences, they also have a social and community role (Fallon & Kriwoken, 2003; Pearce, 2004). Visitor centres can be staffed by paid employees and/or volunteers and may be run by the public sector, a private or commercial business, a destination marketing organisation, or jointly run by several organisations (Smith & Holmes, 2012). Knowledgeable and friendly staff are of key importance to users of visitor information centre services, but in Draper (2018) they were an area where convention and visitor bureaux underperformed. With many visitor information services heavily dependent on volunteer labour (Smith & Holmes, 2012), understanding the role and performance of volunteers is important.

Research on volunteering at visitor centres has largely taken a supply-side or management perspective. This includes a number of Australian studies, which evaluate volunteer centre staffing models. Smith and Holmes (2012) found four main reasons for visitor centre management to involve volunteers: need (related to a public-sector funding model); community involvement, ownership and support for the information centre as part of the destination and tourism more generally; positive impacts of volunteers on the visitor experience; and the personal qualities and motivations of volunteers. The local labour market, and the availability (or not) of paid staff can also influence staffing decisions. In rationalising the involvement of volunteers, visitor centre managers in Smith and Holmes' research commonly made comparisons between paid staff and volunteers and this also featured in other studies. Deery et al. (2007) highlighted the advantages and limitations of volunteer staff: their local knowledge and availability enable a visitor centre to offer a personal service, but this has to be balanced with volunteers' work patterns (often irregular or infrequent shifts), their resistance to change and the need for ongoing training and clear communication processes. Jago and Deery (2002) more directly compared the costs and management of paid staff and volunteers in two visitor centres. Their study shows that collaboration and teamwork between paid staff and volunteers are vital and that deployment of appropriate volunteers may provide means of cost containment while maintaining quality of service.

Smith and Holmes (2012) argue that volunteers can act as a bridge between the destination's tourism sector and the local community, reflecting Pearce's (2004) idea of visitor centres having an important community integration function. Alonso and Liu (2013) also present volunteering at visitor centres as an example of community and civic involvement. In their case study of four visitor centres in the Blackwood River Valley, an emerging tourism destination in rural Western Australia, they argue that volunteering leads to benefits for strengthening both bonding and collaboration among members of the community. This can impact on community initiatives, including tourism development and promotion, and also on building the social fabric of the community, including civic pride, local identity and relationships corresponding to destinations studies in Norway and Sweden (Snis et al., 2021).

Despite motivation being a dominant feature of research on volunteer tourism and events (Wearing & McGehee, 2013; Smith, Lockstone-Binney & Holmes, 2019), there is surprisingly little research on the reasons why destination service volunteers are involved. In a visitor information centre context, again in Australia, Anderson and Cairncross (2005) found that motivations relating to learning, experiences and using skills and knowledge were important for volunteers. Interestingly, the visitor centre manager in that study also identified a strong social motivation for the volunteering, although volunteers rated this as less important. Smith and Holmes (2012) also sought a managerial perspective on motivations by considering what makes visitor centre volunteering attractive. Important aspects included that the volunteering is enjoyable, in part due to interacting with visitors who are themselves enjoying a holiday or leisure trip. They also identified a strong social aspect and that this volunteering appeals to local residents who want to showcase their hometown or region.

Destination associations

In contrast to the growing body of research on visitor information centre volunteering, our second destination services setting – destination associations – is currently represented by a single study by Paraskevaidis and Andriotis (2017). They studied two voluntary tourism associations in Northern Greece where the associations were involved in tourism development and planning initiatives, both on their own (e.g. reviving and hosting local events) and jointly with local authorities. Association membership was drawn from the local community and members were motivated to volunteer to achieve both collective benefits for the community and individual self-interest. While community benefits appeared more important than tourism benefits specifically, these volunteers did expect "a desirable indirect reciprocal exchange" (p.35) including economic, social and environmental rejuvenation of their area, and thus tourism is a means to achieve this. Place attachment was a reason for volunteering for the tourism association members. Though this was also evident in the visitor centre context, however, we draw a distinction between the destination planning role of the former and the destination orientation and interpretation roles of the latter.

Meet-and-greet programmes

Destination service volunteers are also present at meet-and-great programmes based at transport hubs including airports, train stations and ports, particularly meeting cruise ships, however, this role has received very little attention from researchers (Holmes & Smith, 2009). Yet, the importance of these volunteers as the first members of the host community whom tourists meet and who welcome tourists into the destination, deserves consideration (Nichols, Ralston & Holmes, 2017). As with visitor information centres, there are different models of operation of meet-and-greet programmes, and volunteering schemes may involve not-for-profit, public and private sector stakeholders. For example, a commercial transport hub such as an airport may run its own volunteer programme, or work with an independent voluntary organisation, or a local council body, potentially involving the destination marketing organisation or local information bureau. Smith and Holmes (2010) found that meet-and-greet volunteers at key transport hubs in Perth, Western Australia were attracted to these volunteering opportunities because of the interactions with tourists and the appeal of working at an international airport or port.

The visitor welcome and orientation role fulfilled by meet-and-greet volunteers means there is some overlap with those in destination guiding roles. For example, Qian and Yarnal's study (2010) on students volunteering as tour guides at a university campus in the United States has a strong meet-and-greet element. Student guides were introducing potential applicants and their families to the university as an organisation but also to the campus as a destination. These volunteers had dynamic motivations that changed between starting and continuing as a tour guide: initial motivations were typically altruistic, related to supporting the university and potential applicants, but having fun, making friends and personal satisfaction were more important as time progressed.

Destination tour guides

In contrast with the some of the other destination settings discussed in this chapter, there is a strong body of tourism research on tour guiding, both paid and unpaid guides (Weiler & Black, 2015). However, much of the work on volunteer guides is on tour guiding in attractions, either nature-based settings such as national parks (e.g. Evans, Carter Ching & Ballard, 2012) or cultural sites including art galleries, museums and historic sites where volunteer guides may be called docents (e.g. Hanley, Baker, & Pavlidis, 2018; Modlin, Alderman & Gentry, 2011; Potter, 2016; Stamer, Lerdall & Guo, 2008). There is much less consideration of volunteer guides involved at the destination level, for example across a city, although there are some studies on destination tour guides who are paid (e.g. Seyitoğlu, 2020).

Bryon (2012) proposed a taxonomy of tour guide organisations based on research in Flanders. Each type of guiding organisation operating in the destination had different target groups for their tours and used different interpretation and storytelling techniques. Volunteers were present in the typology as 'alternative guiding'. These alternative guiding associations were generally not-for-profit organisations with volunteer guides who were deeply engaged with their community. Love of their city was a strong motivation, but Bryon also identified that "they want to emancipate tourists, affect changes in tourists' personal lives and teach them to look beyond the alleged 'traditional tourist story'" (p. 35). Here Bryon, and his research participants, draw a distinction between paid 'official guides' and volunteers. These alterative guides do not necessarily align with the official destination narratives and, indeed, may deliberately present a story that is at odds with the destination's official marketing narrative. By integrating personal stories and their experience of their community, these volunteer guides are, Bryon argues, adding complexity and layers to the interpretation of the destination. This aligns with Olsson et al.'s (2016) Nordic study on volunteers and storytelling where tour guides may apply storytelling to enhance the visitor experience (Olsson et al., 2016). Weiler and Black (2015) also point to the changing demands and expectations of tourists and that guides need to "become more highly skilled experience-brokers, including embracing technology to choreograph memorable experiences" (p. 364). Fukuyasu et al.'s study (2020) of Japanese sightseeing volunteer guide organisations suggests this can be challenging when community-based volunteers are ageing and need specific support to engage in social media and technology.

Richardson's (2015) research on walking tour guides in New York offers another perspective on the destination volunteering experience. These volunteer tour guides had all been directly affected by the September 11 terrorist attacks, as survivors, family members of victims, rescue workers or local residents. The guides identified four benefits from volunteering. Much like the visitor centre volunteers discussed earlier, they valued the opportunities to meet tourists from around the world and share personal stories, however here they were sharing their experiences of the September 11 attacks rather than making recommendations of local attractions and activities. The other benefits were ability to educate, telling their stories in a way that helped them and others make sense of the events and draw positives from the experience, and a healing and therapeutic aspect as they shared their own story and engaged with the experiences of the other volunteers and visitors.

Lamont, Kennelly and Weiler (2018) present a different aspect to volunteer tour guiding, that of an eight-day packaged tour run by a commercial tour operator. In their study, the volunteer nature of the tour guiding is contentious, not least because the volunteer status of the guides was not immediately disclosed to the tour participants. Various service delivery issues are identified by the customers. These include disorganisation and poor communication, dissatisfaction with guides' knowledge and skills, and unsatisfactory dispute resolution. Lamont et al. (2018) postulate on the extent to which the volunteer-status of the guides contributed to the perceptions of service delivery and customer satisfaction, but also note that the absence of financial rewards means tour managers may not have the same management tools available to both control and support the volunteer staff compared to if they had been paid.

Campground hosts

Accommodation settings can also be a location for volunteer efforts, although, again, there is little research available. An exception is Weiler and Caldicott's study (2020) of campground hosts in a national park in the Australian Northern Territories. They took a stakeholder engagement approach to analysing the establishment of a volunteer campground host programme, drawing on participant observation and the perceptions of three stakeholder groups: national park employees, volunteer camp hosts and park visitors. The programme was positively evaluated, with camp hosts both maintaining the campgrounds and providing information to visitors. The volunteers were considered to improve both the visitor experience and the workload of rangers. While the interpretation role overlaps with the other destination settings discussed here, these camp host volunteers differed as rather than being drawn from the local community, they were themselves travellers (although they were reluctant to identify as 'tourists'). Many were older 'Grey Nomad' travellers (see Leonard & Onyx, 2009) and volunteering for a short period (such as a few weeks) rather than a full season or on an ongoing basis.

Emergency and rescue settings

The final destination service setting example is emergency rescue services volunteers, who are a key part of the emergency response to accidents and natural disasters including "fire, rescue, medical care and relief" (McLennan & Birch, 2005, p. 101). While emergency services are not designed specifically for tourists, their existence makes the destination a safer place to visit. Moreover, tourists may be unaware of local dangers such as coastal rip currents and can end up disproportionately receiving these services (De Nardi & Wilks, 2007). There is some research on volunteers in emergency rescue services, which typically frames these as emergency volunteers rather than relating them to tourism destination management (Fahey, Walker & Lennox, 2003; Fahey, Walker & Sleigh, 2002, Fallon & Rice 2015; Hall & Innes, 2008; O'Connell, 2006; Rice & Fallon, 2011).

Surf lifesaving patrols at popular beaches are perhaps the emergency and rescue volunteers most visible to tourists. To take the example of one Australian state, over 34,000 volunteers were members of Surf Life Saving Queensland (SLSQ) in 2019/20, donating 333,918 hours to patrol the state's extensive coastline. These volunteers undertook 2,555 rescues and performed over 660,000 preventative actions (SLSQ, 2020). International tourists are an 'at risk' group in relation to drowning and De Nardi and Wilks (2007) detail a range of safety initiatives undertaken by SLSQ on the Gold Coast and targeted at Japanese tourists. Although volunteers are not specifically mentioned, this programme will have been largely delivered by SLSQ volunteers. In addition to extended patrols, the programme included destination-based activities such as a beach walk to orientate and educate Japanese (and other) visitors. In addition, the *Staying Alive surf safety campaign* is based at the Gold Coast's main international airport to meet-and-greet visitors with information about both the destination and beach safety messages.

Emergency volunteers are typically highly trained while simultaneously being unpaid amateurs (Yarnal & Dowler, 2002). The need for emergency response volunteers can be particularly acute in rural areas, which are often also nature-based tourism destinations, but also where studies have found that recruiting and retaining volunteers in these locations is challenging (see, for example, Haug & Gaskins, 2012; McLennan & Birch, 2005). The Israeli desert is an example of a remote area, which is popular with tourists for outdoor pursuits such as hiking. Uriely et al. (2002) studied members of the Fast Israeli Rescue and Search Team (FIRST) and found that volunteers were motivated by being able to assist tourists hiking in these destinations. At the same time, volunteers were themselves hikers and the opportunity to be involved in challenging physical situations also motivated their participation. Hall and Innes' (2008) study of Australian surf lifesavers' motivations also found volunteers were primarily motivated by intrinsic motivation and rewards, namely participation in the structured training programme provided by surf lifesaving and volunteers' awareness of the contribution that surf lifesavers make to community safety. Despite these interviewees being based at Queensland beaches, that latter motivation was focused on serving their community and, unlike the FIRST volunteers in Uriely et al.'s (2002) research, tourists were not specifically identified in Hall and Innes' study (2008).

A model of destination service volunteering

In this chapter we have identified six destination settings where these volunteers can engage; comparing across these settings we identify four roles where volunteers are making contributions to a destination's management and the visitor experience. First, volunteers can be involved in destination planning, illustrated by the members of local tourism associations. Second, emergency and rescue service volunteers are key elements of a destination's risk management, both preventing situations that put tourists at risk (e.g. beach patrols by surf life savers) and emergency responses when tourists are in danger (e.g. search-and-rescue services). Third and fourth are contributions to the visitor experience at the destination; this can be divided into welcome and orientation activities to aid visitors on arrival and in the navigation of the destination, and interpretation roles. While meet-and-greet volunteers focus on the former, other roles can include both orientation and interpretation elements; this applies to volunteers in visitor centres, destination tour guides and campground hosts. In such roles, we argue that volunteers actively co-create the visitor experience with the tourists. Most obviously, this is through interactions with visitors at the destination, for example, the welcome and interpretation roles, but also through destination planning and interactions that influence visitors' risk-taking behaviours.

Figure 7.1 illustrates these destination management aspects and also incorporates the host–guest volunteering distinction in our earlier model of tourism volunteer engagements (Holmes & Smith, 2009). The new model highlights that most destination service settings can be classified as host volunteering, with local residents engaging in their home community.

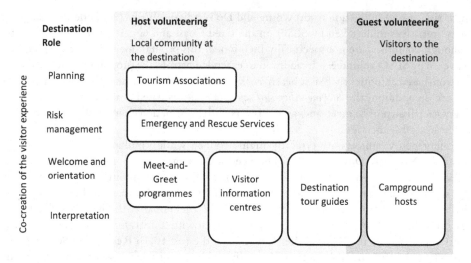

Figure 7.1 Destination service volunteering settings and roles

These organisations mainly recruit from their local community (Smith & Holmes, 2012). Indeed, place is very important to these volunteers. Many are motivated to volunteer through their relationship to a place, their love for the place and their desire to share and showcase this to visitors. This is evident in the studies of visitor information centres (Alonso & Liu, 2013; Smith & Holmes, 2012), voluntary tourism associations (Paraskevaidis & Andriotis, 2017) and alternative tour guiding (Bryon, 2012). This has also been a feature in other host volunteering settings, for example, tourist attractions and events (Olsson, 2012; Olsson et al., 2016); heritage attractions (Bernhard et al., 2020; Smith, 2003; Snis et al., 2021) and trail guides in nature reserves (Evans et al., 2012). Long-term residents such as host volunteers typically bring a wealth of local and sometimes expert knowledge about the destination, and this contributes to the visitor experience through their interpretation and orientation roles. In Holmes and Smith (2009), we also argue that host volunteering can be attractive to new migrants to a place as a way of integrating into their new community.

Figure 7.1 also acknowledges that, in some cases, destination service volunteers can themselves be tourists and therefore be classified as guest volunteering. This was evident in Weiler and Caldicott's work on campground hosts where these were travellers who volunteered, and in Lamont et al.'s (2018) study of volunteer tour guides on an extended trip, these volunteers were themselves travelling as part of their role.

Conclusion and research agenda

This chapter concludes with a research agenda for destination service volunteering. This chapter has already highlighted that there has been more research on guiding and visitor information centres compared to settings such as meet-and-greet programmes, accommodation hosting and tourism associations. In addition, extant research on emergency and rescue service volunteering rarely explicitly considers the tourism setting. However, while there is certainly merit in further research in all these settings, as well as comparing across destination settings and between these volunteers and other tourism volunteering, in this conclusion we take a different approach. The research agenda draws on the framework used by Wicker (2017) in her review of sport volunteerism and volunteer management by considering different perspectives on destination service volunteering: individual, institutional, multi-level and policy perspectives.

First, the individual perspective focuses on volunteerism as individual behaviour (Wicker, 2017). In research on sport, events and tourism volunteering more generally (see, for example, Holmes & Smith, 2009; Smith et al, 2019; Wicker, 2017), individuals have been a focus of volunteering research, particularly the motivations to volunteer. The destination volunteering studies cited here show this is also the case, with reasons for volunteering (or benefits of volunteering in Richardson, 2015) dominating (cf. Anderson & Cairncross, 2005; Hall & Innes, 2008; Qian & Yarnal, 2010; Uriely et al., 2002). Other aspects of the individual perspective are largely missing, for example, understanding volunteer commitment and intentions, satisfaction and experiences, and wellbeing. Developing our understanding of these volunteers' sense of place and social connections could further leverage destination services' community and social roles (Pearce, 2004). Who volunteers, and who we study, is also important. Within sport, Wicker (2017) found that research focused on volunteers in 'leading positions' had dominated, but within destination services, attention has been on those in service delivery roles (e.g. guides), whereas governance roles, including board members, have been largely overlooked.

The second perspective is organisational and includes studies understanding the structure and operations of destination service organisations (for example, Bryon, 2012; De Nardi & Wilks, 2007; Deery et al., 2007; Jago & Deery, 2002). While some of these studies have included comparison of more than one organisation, they are limited to one aspect of the destination context (e.g. guiding associations in Bryon, 2012) and research considering destination services more collectively could reveal further commonalities and differences regarding this form of volunteering and its organisation. Few of the extant studies specifically study the volunteer management aspects of these organisations (unlike sports studies where this was more dominant, Wicker, 2017) and there is scope to further investigate how volunteers are recruited, trained and rewarded. Destination services can also involve the public and private sector, in addition to non-profit or voluntary sector organisations; as demonstrated in the visitor information and meet-and-greet sections above, these sectors may be working together within the destination context. Lamont et al.'s study (2018) of a commercial tour operator using volunteer guides and Smith and Holmes (2012) identifying the 'need' rationale for local councils to staff visitor centres with volunteers both raise questions about the ethics of such an arrangement. Destinations provide other situations where the costs and benefits of an organisation involving volunteers could have a strong ethical consideration. This could include the perspectives of the volunteers themselves, as well as service users (i.e., visitors and tourists) and community members, and suggests an approach related to Wicker's third perspective: multi-layered.

Both Lamont et al. (2018) and Weiler and Caldicott (2020) adopted a multi-layered perspective, drawing on different sources within their studies. Lamont et al.'s (2018) study included interviews with the tourists who were clients of the volunteer tour guides and the visitor perspective is an area ripe for further study within other destination settings. This could include how volunteers' impact the visitor experience, including how to create the environment at the destination in which consumers can have experiences (Mossberg, 2007) and how volunteers are co-creators of these experiences (Olsson, 2016).

Weiler and Caldicott (2020) also demonstrate the value of multiple stakeholder perspectives (including, in their study, park visitors, staff and volunteers), and we support their call for future research to include the voice of the host community, including indigenous peoples. While many destination service volunteers are drawn from the local community (see Figure 7.1), the views of the wider host community are important for understanding the service provided by volunteers and attitudes towards tourism in the community more generally (see Alonso & Nyanjom, 2016, for an example of a wider community perspective on volunteering). Weiler and Caldicott (2020) also included some analysis of programme materials in their study (e.g. volunteer recruitment, orientation and training materials, and programme evaluations) and make brief mention of the destination's management plan, however, Wicker's fourth perspective – policy – has largely been overlooked in relation to volunteering in destination services. This is perhaps surprising given the strong body of work on destination policy and planning, and the recognition of including the diversity of destination stakeholder groups (Fyall & Garrod, 2019; Olsson, 2016). Analysing how, if at all, volunteering is framed within destination policymaking therefore warrants attention, including volunteering in relation to other destination stakeholders, and destination resilience, competitiveness and sustainability (see Bernhard et al., 2020; Fyall & Garrod, 2019; Snis et al., 2021). This could also include exploration of smart destinations (Jovicic, 2019; Snis et al., 2021), the role of destination services and within this, volunteers, particularly as technology may be challenging for some volunteers (Fukuyasu et al., 2020).

To conclude, this chapter has argued that volunteers engaging in destination service settings have been overlooked compared to those in other tourism contexts. This is despite the role they can play in destination planning, risk management, visitor welcome and orientation, and destination interpretation. While we have argued that some destination service volunteers are themselves tourists, most are drawn from the destination's local community and are a key stakeholder. Their role as a bridge between the tourism sector and residents (Smith & Holmes, 2012), and potential ambassadors for tourism within a community is particularly vital as destinations start to rebuild tourism after the impacts of the COVID-19 pandemic. The need for a welcoming presence at transport hubs and within the destination is, more than ever, an opportunity for volunteers to be part of creating meaningful and memorable visitor experiences.

References

Alonso, A. D., & Liu, Y. (2013). Local community, volunteering and tourism development: the case of the Blackwood River Valley, Western Australia. *Current Issues in Tourism, 16*(1), 47–62. https://doi.org/10.1080/13683500.2011.644770

Alonso, A. D., & Nyanjom, J. (2016). Volunteering, paying it forward, and rural community: A study of Bridgetown, Western Australia. *Community Development, 47*(4), 481–495. https://doi.org/10.1080/15575330.2016.1185449

Anderson, E., & Cairncross, G. (2005). Understanding and managing volunteer motivation: Two regional tourism cases. *Australian Journal on Volunteering, 10*(2), 7–17.

Bernhard, I., Olsson A K., & Lundh Snis, U. (2020). Inclusive place innovation as a means for local community regeneration, In I. Bernhard, U. Gråsjö & C. Karlsson (Eds.), *Diversity, Innovation and Clusters: Spatial Perspectives* (pp. 57–80). Edward Elgar Publishing.

Bryon, J. (2012). Tour guides as storytellers – from selling to sharing. *Scandinavian Journal of Hospitality and Tourism, 12*(1), 27–43. https://doi.org/10.1080/15022250.2012.656922

Bussell, H., & Forbes, D. (2002). Understanding the volunteer market: The what, where, who and why of volunteering. *International Journal of Nonprofit and Voluntary Sector Marketing, 7*(3), 244–257. https://doi.org/10.1002/nvsm.183

Cho, B. H. (2000) Destination, In J. Jafari (Ed.), *Encyclopaedia of Tourism* (pp.144–145) Routledge.

De Nardi, M. & Wilks, J. (2007). Tourist water safety: surflife-saving initiatives for the Japanese inbound market. *Journal of Vacation Marketing, 31*(3), 275–283. http://doi.org/10.1177/1356766707077700

Deery, M., Jago, L., Mistilis, N., D'Ambra, J., Richards, F., & Carson, D. (2007). *Visitor information centers: Best practice in information dissemination.* CRC for Sustainable Tourism.

Draper, J. (2018). Applying importance-performance analysis to services of a visitor information center. *Tourism and Hospitality Research, 18*(1), 84–95. https://doi.org/10.1177/1467358415627300

Evans, E., Carter Ching, C., & Ballard, H. L. (2012). Volunteer guides in nature reserves: Exploring environmental educators' perceptions of teaching, learning, place and self. *Environmental Education Research, 18*(3), 391–402. https://doi.org/10.1080/13504622.2011.624585

Fahey, C., Walker, J., & Lennox, G. (2003). Flexible, focused training: Keeps volunteer ambulance officers. *Australasian Journal of Paramedicine, 1*(1). https://ajp.paramedics.org/index.php/ajp/article/view/74

Fahey, C., Walker, J., & Sleigh, A. (2002). Training can be a recruitment and retention tool for emergency service volunteers. *Australian Journal of Emergency Management, 17*(3), 3–7.

Fallon, B. J., & Rice, S. M. (2015). Investment in staff development within an emergency services organisation: Comparing future intention of volunteers and paid employees. *The International Journal of Human Resource Management, 26*(4), 485–500. https://doi.org/10.1080/09585192.2011.561222

Fallon, L. D., & Kriwoken, L. K. (2003). Community involvement in tourism infrastructure - The case of the Strahan Visitor Centre, Tasmania. *Tourism Management, 24*(3), 289–308. https://doi.org/10.1016/S0261-5177(02)00072-9

Fukuyasu, M., Hasegawa, Y., Urata, M., Endo, M., & Yasuda, T. (2020). Supporting the social media transmission via social media of local sightseeing volunteer guides. *Journal of Global Tourism Research, 5*(2), 149–154. https://doi.org/10.37020/jgtr.5.2_149

Fyall, A., & Garrod, B. (2019). Destination management: A perspective article. *Tourism Review, 75*(1), 165–169. https://doi.org/10.1108/TR-07-2019-0311

Garrod, B., Fyall, A., Leask, A., & Reid, E. (2012). Engaging residents as stakeholders of the visitor attraction. *Tourism Management, 33*(5), 1159–1173. https://doi.org/10.1016/j.tourman.2011.11.014

Getz, D., Andersson, T., & Larson, M. (2006). Festival stakeholder roles: Concepts and case studies. *Event Management, 10*(2–3), 103–122. https://doi.org/10.3727/152599507780676689

Hall, J., & Innes, P. (2008). The motivation of volunteers: Australian surf lifesavers. *Australian Journal on Volunteering, 13*(1), 17–28.

Hanley, J., Baker, S., & Pavlidis, A. (2018). Applying the value-creation framework to a community museum volunteer project: Implementing a digital storytelling programme at the Mudgeeraba Light Horse Museum. *Annals of Leisure Research, 21*(1), 74–94. https://doi.org/10.1080/11745398.2016.1265459

Haug, J. C., & Gaskins, J. N. (2012). Recruiting and retaining volunteer EMTs: From motivation to practical solutions. *International Journal of Sociology and Social Policy, 32*(3/4), 197–213. https://doi.org/10.1108/01443331211214767

Holmes, K., & Edwards, D. (2008). Volunteers as hosts and guests in museums. In K. D. Lyons & S. Wearing (Eds.), *Journeys of Discovery in Volunteer Tourism: International Case Study Perspectives* (pp. 155–165). CABI Publishing.

Holmes, K., & Smith, K. A. (2009). *Managing Volunteers in Tourism: Attractions, Destinations and Events.* Butterworth-Heinemann.

Jago, L., & Deery, M. (2002). The role of human resource practices in achieving quality enhancement and cost reduction: An investigation of volunteer use in tourism organisations. *International Journal of Contemporary Hospitality Management, 14*(5), 229–236. https://doi.org/10.1108/09596110210433754

Jovicic, D. Z. (2019). From the traditional understanding of tourism destination to the smart tourism destination. *Current Issues in Tourism, 22*(3), 276–282. https://doi.org/10.1080/13683500.2017.1313203

Kemp, S. (2002). The hidden workforce: Volunteers' learning in the Olympics. *Journal of European Industrial Training, 26*(2/3/4), 109–116. https://doi.org/10.1108/03090590210421987

Lamont, M., Kennelly, M., & Weiler, B. (2018). Volunteers as tour guides: A stakeholder–agency theory case study. *Current Issues in Tourism, 21*(1), 58–77. https://doi.org/10.1080/13683500.2015.1055715

Leonard, R., & Onyx, J. (2009). Volunteer tourism: The interests and motivations of grey nomads, *Annals of Leisure Research, 12*(3–4), 315–332. https://doi.org/10.1080/11745398.2009.9686827

Li, Y., & Hunter, C. (2015). Community involvement for sustainable heritage tourism: A conceptual model. *Journal of Cultural Heritage Management and Sustainable Development. 5*(3), 248–262. https://doi.org/10.1108/JCHMSD-08-2014-0027

McLennan, J., & Birch, A. (2005). A potential crisis in wildfire emergency response capability? Australia's volunteer firefighters. *Global Environmental Change Part B: Environmental Hazards, 6*(2), 101–107. https://doi.org/10.1016/j.hazards.2005.10.003

Mossberg, L. (2007). A marketing approach to the tourist experience. *Scandinavian Journal of Hospitality and Tourism, 7*(1), 59–74. https://doi.org/10.1080/15022250701231915

Nichols, G., Ralston, R., & Holmes, K. (2017). The 2012 Olympic Ambassadors and sustainable tourism legacy. *Journal of Sustainable Tourism, 25*(11), 1513–1528. https://doi.org/10.1080/096695 82.2017.1291648

O'Connell, S. (2006). How to value an Australian icon: The economic and social value of surf lifesaving in Australia. *Australian Journal on Volunteering, 11*(1), 76–79.

Olsson, A. K. (2012). Spatial aspects of member retention, participation and co-creation in tourism settings. *International Journal of Nonprofit and Voluntary Sector Marketing, 17*(3), 231–247. https://doi.org/10.1002/nvsm.1426

Olsson, A. K. (2016). Canals, rivers and lakes as experiencescapes: Destination development based on strategic use of inland water. *International Journal of Entrepreneurship and Small Business, 29*(2), 217–243. https://doi.org/10.1504/IJESB.2016.078696

Olsson, A. K., Bernhard, I., & Friedrichs, Y. V. (2018). Approaches to inclusive networking in place development-an illustration from six smaller Scandinavian cities. *International Journal of Innovation and Regional Development, 8*(3), 259–280. https://doi.org/10.1504/IJIRD.2018.097213

Olsson, A. K., & Gellerstedt, M. (2014). Doing good at a nonprofit tourist attraction. *International Journal of Culture, Tourism and Hospitality Research, 8*(1), 74–91. https://doi.org/10.1108/IJCTHR-07-2012-0051

Olsson, A. K., Therkelsen, A., & Mossberg, L. (2016). Making an effort for free–volunteers' roles in destination-based storytelling. *Current Issues in Tourism, 19*(7), 659–679. https://doi.org/10.1080/1 3683500.2013.784242

Paraskevaidis, P., & Andriotis, K. (2017). Altruism in tourism: Social exchange theory vs altruistic surplus phenomenon in host volunteering. *Annals of Tourism Research, 62*, 26–37. https://doi.org/10.1016/j.annals.2016.11.002

Pearce, P. L. (2004). The functions and planning of visitor centres in regional tourism. *Journal of Tourism Studies, 15*(1), 8–17.

Potter, A. E. (2016). "She goes into character as the lady of the house": Tour guides, performance, and the Southern plantation. *Journal of Heritage Tourism, 11*(3), 250–261. https://doi.org/10.1080/17438 73X.2015.1100626

Qian, X. L., & Yarnal, C. (2010). The dynamics of motivations to volunteer as campus tour guides. *Annals of Leisure Research, 13*(1–2), 298–319. https://doi.org/10.1080/11745398.2010.9686849

Rice, S., & Fallon, B. (2011). Retention of volunteers in the emergency services: Exploring interpersonal and group cohesion factors. *The Australian Journal of Emergency Management, 26*(1), 18–23.

Richardson, K. M. (2015). Sharing stories of the 9/11 experience: An exploratory study of the Tribute Walking Tour Program. *Journal of Loss and Trauma, 20*(1), 22–33. https://doi.org/10.1080/153250 24.2013.819276

Schliephack, J., Moyle, B., & Weiler, B. (2013). Visitor expectations of contact with staff at a protected site. *Annals of Leisure Research, 16*(2), 160–174. https://doi.org/10.1080/11745398.2013.796908

Seyitoğlu, F. (2020). Tourists' perceptions of the tour guides: The case of gastronomic tours in Istanbul. *Anatolia, 31*(3), 393–405. https://doi.org/10.1080/13032917.2020.1735462

Smith, K. A. (2003). Literary enthusiasts as visitors and volunteers. *International Journal of Tourism Research, 5*(2), 83–95. https://doi.org/10.1002/jtr.419

Smith, K. A., & Holmes, K. (2009). Researching volunteers in tourism: Going beyond. *Annals of Leisure Research, 12*(3–4), 403–420. https://doi.org/10.1080/11745398.2009.9686831

Smith, K. A., & Holmes, K. (2010). Volunteers and tourism destination services: Challenging the limits of tourism volunteering research. In S. Crispin et al. (Eds.), *Proceedings of the 20th Annual Conference Council for Australian University Tourism and Hospitality Education (CAUTHE)* (17 pp.) University of Tasmania.

Smith, K. A., & Holmes, K. (2012). Visitor centre staffing: Involving volunteers. *Tourism Management, 33*(3), 562–568. https://doi.org/10.1016/j.tourman.2011.06.010

Smith, K. A., Lockstone-Binney, L., & Holmes, K. (2019). Revisiting and advancing the research agenda for event volunteering. In J. Armbrecht, E. Lundberg & T. G. Andersson (Eds.), *A Research Agenda for Event Management* (pp. 126–153). Edward Elgar Publishing.

Snis, U. L., Olsson, A. K., & Bernhard, I., (2021). Becoming a smart old town–How to manage stake-holder collaboration and cultural heritage. *Journal of Cultural Heritage Management and Sustainable Development*. https://doi-org.ezproxy.server.hv.se/10.1108/JCHMSD-10-2020-0148

Stamer, D., Lerdall, K., & Guo, C. (2008). Managing heritage volunteers: An exploratory study of volunteer programmes in art museums worldwide. *Journal of Heritage Tourism*, *3*(3), 203–214. https://doi.org/10.1080/17438730802138949

Surf Life Saving Queensland (SLSQ) (2020). *Annual Report 2019/20*. SLSQ.

Uriely, N., Schwartz, Z., Cohen, E., & Reichel, A. (2002). Rescuing hikers in Israel's deserts: Community altruism or an extension of adventure tourism? *Journal of Leisure Research*, *34*(1), 25–36. https://doi.org/10.1080/00222216.2002.11949958

Wearing, S., & McGehee, N. G. (2013). Volunteer tourism: A review. *Tourism Management*, *38*, 120–130. https://doi.org/10.1016/j.tourman.2013.03.002

Weiler, B., & Black, R. (2015). The changing face of the tour guide: One-way communicator to choreographer to co-creator of the tourist experience. *Tourism Recreation Research*, *40*(3), 364–378. https://doi.org/10.1080/02508281.2015.1083742

Weiler B., & Caldicott, R. (2020). Unpacking the factors that contribute to successful engagement of stakeholders in a volunteer camphost programme. *Tourism Recreation Research*, *45*(2), 247–264. https://doi.org/10.1080/02508281.2019.1640445

Wicker, P. (2017). Volunteerism and volunteer management in sport. *Sport Management Review*, *20*(4), 325–337. https://doi.org/10.1016/j.smr.2017.01.001

Yang, R. J. (2014). An investigation of stakeholder analysis in urban development projects: Empirical or rationalistic perspectives. *International Journal of Project Management*, *32*(5), 838–849. https://doi.org/10.1016/j.ijproman.2013.10.011

Yarnal, C. M., & Dowler, L. (2002). Who is answering the call? Volunteer firefighting as serious leisure. *Leisure/Loisir*, *27*(3–4), 161–189. https://doi.org/10.1080/14927713.2002.9651302

8

VISITOR ATTRACTIONS

Volunteering in cultural heritage tourism in Aotearoa New Zealand

Jane Legget

Introduction

Visitor attractions are a complex mainstay of the tourism sector and, for many, volunteers are a key operational asset. Attractions come in many forms and cover an almost limitless range of themes, mostly, but by no means always, related to their location and its natural and cultural history. Such is their diversity that Leask (2008, 2010, 2016) has noted the challenges of finding an internationally recognised definition. Her summary of visitor attraction categories (Leask, 2010; see Table 8.1 below) remains a useful representation. For the purposes of this chapter, Hu and Wall's (2005, p. 619) definition of a visitor attraction will serve: "a permanent resource, either natural or human-made, which is developed for the primary purpose of attracting visitors", while noting that sometimes other community functions may also be served by the same organisation. Weaver and Lawton (2010) cite other features for consideration including: ownership, orientation, scarcity, markets, authenticity, carrying capacity and status. In the context of heritage, tangible and intangible, movable and immovable are also pertinent aspects, as is locality.

Table 8.1 Summary of categories of visitor attractions

Visitor attraction categories	Include but are not limited to:
Theme parks/amusement parks	Water parks, amusements, themes
Museums and galleries (Cultural heritage)	Art, cultural, historical, collections-based museums, virtual museums, open-air museums
Natural heritage	Gardens, national parks, forests
Animals	Safari, farms, zoos, aquariums
Visitor centres	Cultural, industrial and transport centres
Religious sites	Chapels, cathedrals, churches, temples, sacred sites
Heritage	Castles, forts, historic houses, heritage visitor centres, monuments, industrial suites, dark heritage sites, archaeological sites, military sites and music centres

Source: Adapted from Leask (2010, p. 157).

DOI: 10.4324/9780367815875-10

Attractions can vary in scale of operation and in type of legal entity. These affect *how* volunteers contribute. Attractions may be wholly man-made and run as commercial businesses or remote unstaffed natural or cultural heritage sites of outstanding beauty and/or historical significance cared for on a voluntary basis by passionate residents and/or indigenous traditional guardians or both. The largest enterprises include Disneyland's internationally distributed theme-parks, where thematic content transcends their location. In contrast, an early missionary's cottage on New Zealand's Chatham Islands can attract a mere handful of adventurous visitors for whom the 1870 homestead's appeal is partly its isolated setting in a dramatic landscape (Jenkins, 2017). Cultural attractions may be the major pull factor for tourists to leave home (primary attractors), or they can be serendipitous discoveries with their own special charm encountered at, or en route to, a holiday destination (secondary attractors). Sometimes it is the volunteers themselves who become the attraction, especially if they are known to be welcoming local knowledge holders with great stories to tell (Kelly, Savage, Landman & Tonkin, 2002; Wallace, 2006).

Cultural heritage (however defined) makes many contributions to the tourism sector as visitor attractions, often conferring an image and identity on a place, with an emphasis on 'authenticity' and atmosphere, often carefully constructed (Bonn, Joseph-Mathews, Dai, Hayes & Cave, 2007; Dekel & Vinitzky-Seroussi, 2017). 'Heritage' can be just one aspect of a tourism or hospitality business, often as the selling point – for example, a hotel or restaurant housed in a castle, a historic homestead, a restored church or other historic building preserved and adapted for a new use but retaining characteristic features to enhance the experience of traditional accommodation or regional cuisine. Mainstream 'heritage attractions' often take pride of place in their communities, confirming their distinctive identity, and transforming the host destination through economic and social benefits. A well-managed visitor attraction needs a 'social licence' from the host community to operate successfully (Edwards & Trafford, 2016), balancing the requirements for a sustainable enterprise and community support, particularly in New Zealand where responsive relationships with the indigenous Maori are increasingly recognised as important (McCarthy, 2011). Local volunteers can play a pivotal role in achieving this equilibrium.

Depending on the nature and population of the host community, the volunteers' level of involvement in a heritage visitor attraction will vary according to the origin and organisation of the operation. Volunteers may have total responsibility for the attraction, or they may support staff in a professionally managed enterprise. While the roles of customer service, bookings, visitor management, cash handling and general administration are common to many tourism operations and may be undertaken by volunteers, many heritage attractions, such as museums and nature-based attractions, also fulfil additional specialist functions, such as conservation, that require academic knowledge, technical and research skills.

The focus of this chapter is museums which are public non-profit operations, deeply rooted in their place, and frequently having other purposes (Kotler & Kotler, 2000) beyond providing satisfying experiences for international and domestic tourists, although importantly these latter contribute operating income. It is visitors who consume the 'heritage experiences' but it is frequently volunteers who assist in creating and delivering these.

Firstly, the New Zealand museum scene is briefly introduced, differentiating rural and small town contexts from the urban centres. Next, findings from a survey of volunteers at three metropolitan museums are outlined. These are then discussed in the context of the policy imperatives for inclusion of diverse communities, particularly how volunteers' characteristics and involvement/motivations are likely to relate to the concept of cultural capital. The chapter identifies how this may contribute to understanding the lack of social and ethnic diversity in the dominant volunteer cohort.

Museums as cultural heritage visitor attractions in Aotearoa New Zealand

New Zealand is said to have one of the highest densities of museums and art galleries per head of population (McCarthy, 2014), and these form the bulk of the cultural tourism attractions regularly open to tourists. Today, there are thought to be over 500 museums, galleries and heritage sites open to the public. The proportions remain at c. 60% small operations wholly run by volunteers, while another 30% have 1–5 paid staff (McCarthy, 2014). The remaining 10% still vary greatly in staff numbers but are professional institutions, almost all receiving public funding and supported by volunteers in some aspects of their work. In 2014, 83% of museums benefitted from volunteers, collectively contributing 143,445 hours (Museums Aotearoa, 2015).

Little and local

New Zealand's museums rely heavily on volunteers – in roles ranging from ownership (often through incorporated historical societies or independent charitable trusts), governance and management to day-to-day operations (e.g., see Smith, 2019). In smaller communities and suburbs, volunteer-run museums are often seasonal, have limited opening hours, and may be housed in repurposed heritage buildings, which limit the scope of activities and facilities for both visitors and hosts. Their volunteers' attachment to place and history is both their strength and their weakness when serving tourists. Their deep local knowledge is a major asset: the volunteers make the human connections for visitors between local landmarks, buildings, monuments and stories. Sometimes, though, a well-meaning enthusiast narrowly focused on certain topics fails to address visitors' needs and interests, leading to a less than positive tourism experience. These local history museums may be thought of as accidental tourist attractions which are still evolving.

While the smaller museums serve important social purposes for local people in uncovering and sharing their community's history (see e.g. Auckland Council, 2020), their volunteer team may lack a full understanding of tourists' expectations. In country towns, heritage volunteers have few, if any, training opportunities. Online training may not be practicable if the broadband service is poor and if older volunteers (usually the majority) have limited information technology skills. If a volunteer's primary affiliation is with museums and local history, then they would look for practical training and support through the New Zealand History Federation (2021) or public libraries or resources from the museum agency, National Services Te Paerangi (see e.g. NSTP, 2006). Yet it is the tourist visitors who contribute to their meagre resources with admission fees, donations and occasional purchases of books or family history research services. These modest ventures welcome tourists, orient them to the area and provide visitor information in a friendly informal style, which compensates for a lack of tourism industry sophistication.

Metropolitan museums

In New Zealand's largest cities, the cultural heritage institutions take seriously their position in the tourism scene. Each is professionally run and sustainably financed with well-developed volunteer programmes enabling them to deliver high quality visitor experiences, along with other services for city residents and businesses. Tourism is New Zealand's largest industry. National museums, art galleries and cultural attractions face strong competition from New Zealand's landscape and outdoor adventures, which are the main drawcards for many international tourists (Stats NZ, 2021). The Museum of New Zealand Te Papa Tongarewa (Te Papa) opened as the new national museum in Wellington in 1998 and has since made a positive impact on the capital's tourism profile (Carey, Davidson & Sahli, 2013). Other museums have subsequently benefitted from actively engaging with the tourism market. Auckland's museums are increasingly popular with visitors as they provide useful introductions to the nation's history, art and nature, especially Maori culture. An increase in the ethnic diversity of visitors to Te Papa has also been a notable feature of the museum's audience (Davidson & Sibley, 2011). Has this shift been echoed in the volunteer cohorts of metropolitan museums?

Research approach

Given the contributions of volunteers to museums that market themselves to tourist audiences in New Zealand, little attention has been paid to volunteers' characteristics and motivations since Wilson (1999). The findings outlined in this chapter are from a study undertaken in 2014 to gain insights into volunteers' characteristics and motivations at three museums (Chen, 2014), subsequently discussed by Chen, Liu and Legget (2019). Volunteers were surveyed to gather descriptive data on their demographics and roles. To elicit information about their motivations a tailored version of Clary, Snyder, Ridge, Copeland, Stukas, Haugen and Miene's (1998) Volunteer Functions Inventory (VFI) was included. On a five-point Likert scale, informants indicated their level of agreement with 30 randomised statements relating to possible motivational factors that led them to volunteer (Chen, 2014, pp. 92–93; Chen et al., 2019, p. 139). The statements were analysed according to Clary et al.'s (1998) six motivational factors: Values, Understanding, Protective, Enhancement, Career and Social Functions. Each function had five associated statements, and mean levels of agreements for each function are reported.

To investigate the reliability of these findings, Cronbach's Alpha values were calculated, indicating strong internal consistency. The reliability coefficient across the 30 motivational statements was 0.928, and those across the six functions ranged from 0.700 to 0.935 (Chen, 2014, pp. 52–53; Chen et al, 2019, pp. 133–134), thus achieving the generally acceptable level of 0.7 (Helms, Henze, Sass & Mifsud, 2006). The response rate of 39% (p. 177) from a census of the three museums' volunteer populations (Chen, 2014, p. 68; Chen et al., 2019, p. 131) exceeded the 30% deemed acceptable for self-complete questionnaires (Dillman, 1978). Volunteers could choose either paper or online versions of the survey.

Three Auckland museums: volunteering in bicultural operations in a multicultural context

Auckland was the gateway destination for 2,741,398 international visitors in 2018–2019 (Auckland Tourism, Events and Economic Development, 2019), representing 70.1% of the country's international tourists. The city also catered for 5,385,333 domestic visitors in 2018–2019 (ATEED, 2019), enticed by the cosmopolitan attractions – lively café culture, shopping, restaurants, festivals, concerts, sporting events, exhibitions and maritime activities. Museums are increasingly promoted as visitor attractions, alongside the city's culturally diverse attractions.

The three museums surveyed were established Auckland institutions offering different heritage experiences and collections: Auckland War Memorial Museum, Auckland Art Gallery and the New Zealand Maritime Museum. They have increasingly engaged with the tourism sector since 2000 (Auckland Museum appointed its first dedicated tourism manager in 2005). They highlight New Zealand's history and culture and that of the neighbouring Pacific Islands (see Table 8.2). Each museum receives its core revenue from the local authority, Auckland Council, throughlocal residential and business taxes. These annual contributions do not cover all costs; therefore, each generates further income from a variety of activities, including (but not limited to) gift shops, merchandising, cafés, venue hire, lectures, performances, special paid-for events, research services and guided tours. Each charges admission for out-of-town visitors, with a regime of concessions for Aucklanders. Auckland Council regards these museums as core elements of its tourism portfolio appealing to different visitor audiences but recognises that they are also public services for residents and researchers. Each museum manages a team of volunteers to undertake a variety of roles and tasks contributing directly or indirectly to the visitors' experiences.

The annual visitor numbers indicate the scale of these attractions. In 2017–2018, all three museums were operating at full capacity. Auckland Museum hosted 931,487 visitors (Auckland Museum, 2018); Auckland Art Gallery 545,782 (Regional Facilities Auckland, 2018); and the Maritime Museum 160,000 (Regional Facilities Auckland, 2018). Auckland Museum has since closed its galleries for extensive renovations and each site had to reduce services during the Covid-19 pandemic in 2020.

In 2017, Auckland was home to 1.65 million people, of whom 40% were born outside New Zealand (Auckland Tourism, Events and Economic Development, 2017). With 220 different ethnicities represented, its population is described as 'superdiverse' or 'polydiverse' (Cameron & Poot, 2019). In 2019, 77% of museum visitors nationally were European New

Table 8.2 Key characteristics of three major cultural heritage attractions managing volunteer programmes in Auckland, New Zealand

Museum (year founded) and website	Building & location	Collections & themes	Staffing
Auckland War Memorial Museum Tamaki Paenga Hira (1852), commonly referred to as Auckland Museum. https://www.auckland museum.com/	Neoclassical heritage building, on hilltop in central public park.	Maori culture, NZ social history, Pacific cultures, Natural history, Military history.	275 volunteers supporting full-time staff and part-time/casual staff.
Auckland Art Gallery Toi o Tamaki (1888). https://www.aucklandart gallery.com/	Victorian French-style building with award-winning extension (2011) in city centre.	NZ, Pacific and international art: old masters and contemporary works.	50 volunteers supporting full-time staff and part-time/casual staff.
New Zealand Maritime Museum Hui te Ananui o Tangaroa (1993). https://www.maritimemuseum.co.nz/	Purpose-built industrial-look structure on wharf, downtown waterfront.	NZ maritime history, migration, fishing, Pacific watercraft, heritage boats, including operating vessels.	166 volunteers supporting full-time staff and part-time/casual staff.

Zealanders and 11% were Maori (Museums Aotearoa 2019). Consequently, many residents will not identify strongly, if at all, with the city's heritage. This means that New Zealanders with deeper roots, including the indigenous Maori and European New Zealanders, have more direct links to and interests in New Zealand's cultural history, and are more likely to engage with its museums.

Maori culture and Maori collections have particular appeal for international visitors, but Maori, including those living overseas and returning to connect with family, now feature more frequently among museum visitors, as Maori revitalise their culture. Museums in New Zealand have pioneered bicultural ways of working, in response to the national imperative to honour the 1840 Treaty of Waitangi – *Te Tiriti o Waitangi* (McCarthy, 2011). The Treaty between the Crown (Government) and Maori chiefs is regarded as a nation-founding document, but it was rarely honoured (Orange, 2015). Instead, Maori were disempowered and deprived of natural and cultural resources, traditional rights to land and cultural practices. Since the 1980s, past wrongs have been formally acknowledged by the Government, leading to negotiations for redress through settlements with individual *iwi* (tribes). Museums that hold many important *taonga tukuiho* (ancestral treasures) have established partnerships with local *iwi*. They have co-developed bicultural museum practices to manage *taonga* Maori in culturally appropriate ways, and have established Maori in governance, management and operational roles, as well as expert advisors (see, for example, Cotton & Merito, 2017; McCarthy, 2011). Maori have also built many successful tourism ventures and have influenced national and local tourism policy.

Museums have adopted the Maori concepts of *manaakitanga* (hosting visitors with warmth, generosity and concern for well-being) and *kaitiakitanga* (stewardship of cultural and natural resources). Also central tenets of New Zealand's tourism policy (Ministry of Business, Innovation and Employment & Department of Conservation, 2019), these translate readily to the museum context as guiding principles. Museums' public-facing roles care for the visitors, while back-of-house roles take care of the heritage collections and add value through research and respectful display, handling and storage. Volunteers at the three Auckland museums work mainly in front-of-house roles, looking after visitors, but others contribute behind the scenes to the development of the products for tourist consumption and specialist operational roles. The museums have devised training and management approaches to work with the range of individuals volunteering in this sector of cultural tourism (see, e.g. NSTP, 2006) and each places a strong emphasis on recognition and respect for Maori values.

Who volunteers in Auckland's tourist-oriented museums?

In Aotearoa New Zealand, volunteers are the lifeblood of most cultural heritage attractions but to realise fully the value that they contribute it is important to understand who they are and what motivates them. The findings from Chen (2014), also discussed by Chen et al. (2019), are reported briefly here to build the profile of these museum volunteers, starting with the demographic data: age, employment status, gender, ethnicity, educational attainment and income.

Considering age first, as anticipated by other studies including Kelly et al. (2002) and Deery, Jago and Mair (2011), the majority (71.6%) of volunteers were people over 60 years old (Chen, 2014, pp. 38, 86; Chen et al., 2019, p. 132). When including 51–60 year-olds, older volunteers represented 75% of the sample population. The low response in the 18–20 age group (2 = 1.1%) likely reflects the increased costs of tertiary study and students' need for part-time paid employment. All three museums employ young people as casual staff, mainly in front-of-house and event support roles. Chen (2014), while participating as a graduate student, worked as a casual visitor host at the Maritime Museum, developing skills and knowledge related to their future career direction.

Regarding employment status, only 19 (10.7%) respondents had full-time work, with 28 (15.8%) working part-time, factors which can constrain opportunities to volunteer (Chen, 2014, pp. 40, 89; Chen et al., 2019, p. 132). Over half the respondents (57.1%) were fully retired with more time to follow their own interests.

Data on gender was also sought. Responding volunteers were predominantly female (67%) (Chen, 2014, pp. 38, 86; Chen et al., 2019). When analysed by museum, findings showed that the two older museums had attracted more women (Chen, 2014, p. 55; Chen et al., 2019, p. 134). At Auckland Museum, 79% were women, while Auckland Art Gallery's cohort comprised 94% women (Chen et al., 2019, p. 134), echoing findings by Stamer, Lerdal and Guo (2008). At the Maritime Museum, only established in 1993, male volunteers comprised 85% of its volunteer team, reflecting the strong participation by men in Auckland's sailing culture and their associated skills for maintaining and sailing heritage vessels (Chen, 2014, p. 65; Chen et al., 2019, p. 134).

While Auckland's population is superdiverse, the dominant culture was over-represented in the response on ethnicity. Over 90% self-identified as European New Zealanders (Chen, 2014, pp. 38, 43, 87; Chen et al., 2019, p. 132). Again, this might be expected, given that museums are institutions from a Western tradition. Stamer et al. (2008) noted a similar lack of diversity at the National Museum of Singapore, where 79% of volunteers were expatriates and likely more familiar with museums, with only 21% of volunteers Singaporeans. In Auckland, the volunteers included just two Maori (1.2%), three Pacific Islanders (1.7%) and eight self-identifying as Asians (4.7%), far below their proportions in the city's population (Chen, 2014, p. 87; Chen et al., 2019, p. 132). Auckland Museum now actively recruits Mandarin-speaking volunteers to train as tour guides to serve Chinese visitors, both residents and international tourists (Auckland Museum, 2020).

As informal learning environments, museums provide for both educational and leisure experiences. The Auckland museums attracted well-educated volunteers. Over half of the respondents (54.8%) had Bachelor's degrees or higher qualifications (Master's degrees 15.4% and doctorates 2.3%) (Chen, 2014, pp. 38–39, 87; Chen et al., 2019, p. 132). A further 25.7% had attained tertiary diplomas or certificates, while 13 volunteers were current students. Volunteering in these settings offered opportunities for further learning, including both subject knowledge and new skills. As cultural tourism venues with an educational role, museums are a natural choice for visitors pursuing 'serious leisure' (Stebbins, 1996). Given Smith's (2003) observation in literary heritage sites that volunteers are also audiences for heritage attractions and that museums visitors are generally better educated, it follows that volunteering at museums appeals to those with tertiary qualifications and that they engage intellectually with the subject matter in their museums.

When asked about income, over a quarter (26.4%) 'preferred not say' (Chen, 2014, pp. 40–41). Two-thirds (67%) of those responding reported their income as over NZ$ 65,000 (Chen, 2014, pp. 40, 90; Chen et al., 2019, p. 135). When those with incomes of NZ $50,000 or more were included, the figure was 79%, indicating the predominance of higher income levels. The median income in Auckland in 2013 was NZ $29,600. Only 10% reported incomes less than NZ $20,000 (Chen, 2014, p. 40).

Employment status and age influence the levels of contribution and commitment that volunteers can make. These museums had some longstanding volunteers: 27 (15.5%) respondents had volunteered at their museum for over ten years (including three with over 20 years' service); 36 (20.7%) served 6–10 years; while nearly half (86) had volunteered 1–5 years (Chen, 2014, pp. 41–42, 88; Chen et al., 2019, p. 134). These years of volunteering indicate strong engagement with the museums, their purposes, themes and functions. Furthermore, 38.6% of respondents were members of the museums' Friends organisations (Chen, 2014, pp. 43, 91).

Income and educational attainment levels suggest that the majority of the volunteers accumulated significant resources of cultural capital, which likely contributed to their choice of volunteering activity (Harflett, 2015). Not possessing such resources may be a barrier to a more diverse volunteer cohort at these museums.

What are the volunteers' roles and functions?

The tasks offered at the museums appeal to volunteers' varied interests, skills and personalities as well as their availability. Volunteers at the Art Gallery are generally art lovers engaged in 'serious leisure' (Yang, 2015), while the Maritime Museum attracts both the hobby sailor and those qualified in marine trades and professions. For front of house roles, fluency in English is expected while knowledge of other languages is welcomed, especially at Auckland Museum which hosts the most international visitors among the three sites.

Half of the respondents (85 = 51%) interacted directly with visitors, either leading tours of the galleries or as hosts welcoming them, staffing the entrance desk, providing information and directing visitors around the museum buildings (Chen, 2014, pp. 43, 90; Chen et al., 2019, p. 132). A further 5%, mostly women, undertook administrative functions which might involve telephone contact, but generally covered clerical work, updating membership lists, filing and sorting papers (Chen, 2014, p. 44; Chen et al., 2019, p. 132). At Auckland Art Gallery, the sole task of the overwhelmingly female (94%) volunteer team was to deliver gallery tours (Chen, 2014, p. 44; Chen et al., 2019, p. 132). These included scheduled daily public tours of the long-term exhibitions, pre-booked group tours and themed tours of special exhibitions. These volunteers were already interested in art but received full training about the artworks on display. They were keen to assist the gallery by sharing their love and knowledge of the arts and to support their community.

The 11% of volunteers undertaking operational tasks, of whom 95% were men, have still some engagement with tourists (Chen, 2014, p. 45; Chen et al., 2019, p. 132). Male volunteers predominated at the Maritime Museum (85%), many with relevant sailing and boat building experience. They carried out on-going maintenance on heritage vessels and crewed the boats (Chen, 2014, pp. 44–45; Chen et al., 2019, p. 132). They took visitors out into the Waitemata Harbour for a sail on a regular schedule. In addition to boat handling skills, they needed to be familiar with maritime rules, safety and the history of the vessels and life on the harbour. They needed communication skills not only for narrating local stories to visitors of many nationalities, but also for imparting safety information and for working effectively with fellow crew members.

Those involved with collections and exhibitions (16%) worked mainly behind the scenes (Chen, 2014, p. 44; Chen et al., 2019, p. 132). Of these, 72% were women and 28% men. Their tasks varied from academic research on collections, preparing objects for storage or exhibitions, to data entry for collection records or contributing to exhibition installations. A further 20% reported engaging in other duties (Chen, 2014, p. 44; Chen et al., 2019, p. 132). Task areas included library work (the three museums have substantial specialist libraries), supporting educational programmes for school groups, assisting military history researchers or undertaking scientific work with natural history curators.

In exchange for training its volunteers, the museums expect a minimum period of commitment, which may vary for each role. The minimum at the Maritime Museum is three months, while two years is required for tour guides at Auckland Museum. Each museum rosters their volunteers to meet its visitation patterns and needs. For instance, during the 2018–2019 cruise season, Auckland received 238,975 passengers (Stats NZ, 2019). Auckland Museum serves the cruise companies' onshore excursion programmes. When cruise ships are in port, the museum provides multiple concurrent guided tours (for which they charge fees), starting as early as 8.00 a.m., thanks to the flexibility and willingness of its volunteer guides. Another example of responsiveness is the museum's Flying Squad which helps through 'episodic volunteering' (Holmes & Smith, 2009) on an 'as needed' basis with time-critical jobs three to four times per year. Examples include photocopying, filing, preparing resource packs, "stuffing envelopes or even skewering marshmallows" (Auckland Museum, 2020).

Why do they volunteer?

Museum volunteers generally have a keen interest in one or more of the topics displayed at their museum and value their museum as a community institution that they want to support. There are many reasons for contributing their time and energy. The 177 informants indicated their level of agreement with the 30 randomised motivational factor statements, tailored from Clary et al.'s Volunteer Functions Inventory (1998). Fourteen statements were re-worded to reflect the New Zealand museum context for the research (Chen, 2014, pp. 92–93; Chen et al., 2019, p. 139). The volunteers' self-reported motivations were analysed according to the six tailored VFI functions. They are presented briefly here in descending order of levels of agreement: Values, Understanding, Protective, Enhancement, Career and Social Functions.

The Values function rated highest with a mean of 3.29 (SD = 0.550) (Chen, 2014, p. 52; Chen et al., 2019, p. 133). These Auckland volunteers were principally driven by altruism, wanting to help others. They worked to assist their museum to deliver good experiences for visitors but also to achieve its larger goal of protecting and sharing the heritage collections and knowledge. Since they themselves enjoyed the museums, they wanted visitors to benefit as they had.

The Understanding function produced a mean agreement level of 3.25 (SD = 0.587) (Chen, 2014, p. 52; Chen et al., 2019, p. 133). This showed that, as mostly well-educated people, the volunteers were still interested in learning – whether it was more about how their museum works, gaining new perspectives, hands on experience or exploring their own strengths. Exposure to the wide range of visitors requires learning how to deal with a variety of people, something which may be especially important to an older cohort of volunteers.

Agreement on the Protective function was almost as strong: 3.22 (SD = 0.604) (Chen, 2014, p. 52; Chen et al., 2019, p. 133). Protective factors supported these volunteers' well-being. Museums do offer an escape from normal life, affording opportunities to connect socially with new people – whether visitors, the museum's staff or fellow volunteers. All of these, together with exhibitions and collection topics, add interest to volunteers' lives and can make people feel better about themselves.

The Enhancement function achieved a slightly lower agreement level: 3.09 (SD = 0.793) (Chen, 2014, p. 52; Chen et al., 2019, p. 133). The museum volunteers reported positively that they benefitted from feeling valued and needed by the museums, where they felt better about themselves. Additionally, they made new friends and their volunteering helped to increase their self-esteem.

The Career and Social functions were less important motivators for the respondents volunteering at these three museums: respectively 2.41 (SD = 1.112) and 2.25 (0.914) (Chen, 2014, p. 52; Chen et al., 2019, p. 133). Given the predominance of older people, many retired, gaining experience to augment a curriculum vitae or get a 'foot in the door' at a potential workplace had little resonance. They were mostly beyond thinking about new career options or making contacts to foster their progress in their chosen field of employment. Volunteering used to be the standard entry point to a career in museums, as the present author can attest, and still is the case in some countries (e.g., see Pacesila, 2020). The changing structure of funding for tertiary study means younger people face strong competition for the rare internship opportunities – paid or otherwise – and so now seek paid employment, even on casual contracts, in preference to unpaid ones in New Zealand's cultural heritage attractions. Internships, which take various forms, are managed separately at these museums (Remer, 2005).

The more positive levels of agreement with the Values, Understanding, Protective and Enhancement functions indicated this mostly well-educated group were less concerned about pressures from their social groups to volunteer. They had made their decisions to volunteer based on their own willingness to serve the community, their individual interests and other benefits, rather than being influenced by family and friends. It also suggests that these factors might augment their stocks of cultural capital to act and support their well-being through intellectual engagement and social connection.

Discussion

The characteristics, roles and motivations outlined here for these urban museum volunteers have implications for the ways the museums recruit, train, retain and operate with their volunteers. The mode of volunteering fits well within Stebbins' (1996) dimensions of 'serious leisure' as 'formal' and 'non-occupational', and each museum has developed its own training and management practices to sustain an engaged cohort.

Most volunteers have established interests in the museums' themes, most are well-educated, older and possibly long socialised towards museum visiting, although this was not investigated. Most have made independent decisions to offer their services to the museums.

These museums have themselves made determined efforts to diversify their audiences, but the volunteer programmes had not yet attracted members of Auckland's different cultural groups. Engaging with cultural diversity in public sector institutions is an increasingly important aspect of public policy in New Zealand and in seeking grants from funding bodies. Therefore, developing a multicultural volunteer cohort has both strategic and social imperatives.

Differing levels of cultural capital, in the Bourdieusian sense, could be part of the explanation for limited success to date (Harflett, 2015). Bourdieu's concept of cultural capital is relevant to museum volunteers, having been developed through his study of art gallery visitors (Bourdieu, 1984). Harflett (2015) emphasises the cultural tastes, preferences and practices (including cultural participation) that individuals accumulate over time, which comprise Bourdieu's cultural capital and develop further in museum visiting, also apply in volunteering at heritage attractions. This type of cultural capital is more likely to be possessed by white, middle-class people, acquired through their experiences of leisure (Harflett, 2015). Possession of cultural capital appears to be a relevant resource for the museum volunteer.

Policy imperatives

National and local government policy development increasingly addresses concepts of cultural well-being and cultural identity. The New Zealand Government's Living Standards Framework for assessing policy implementation progress now includes 'cultural identity' as a key domain to be monitored: "As a bicultural country, with obligations under Te Tiriti o Waitangi, and as a multicultural country with an immigrant background, the Treasury believes that it is important to recognise that culture matters to our well-being" (The Treasury, 2019b, p. 3). 'Social connection' is another monitored domain where volunteering is relevant. The Living Standards Framework recognises the value of natural, human, social and financial/physical capital. The Treasury and Ministry of Cultural Heritage have discussed a potential fifth stock: 'cultural capital' (The Treasury, 2019a), which recognises both visiting and volunteering in museums as cultural production and engagement of value for public investment in 'cultural well-being'.

Local governments in New Zealand have been required to report annually on their contributions to social, economic, environmental and cultural well-being in their communities since the Local Government Act 2002. Their museums and galleries are frequently cited as contributing to local government well-being outcomes, through their visitor numbers and diversity, educational programmes, creative opportunities, Maori cultural engagement, place-making and identity-building and community pride. Involvement of volunteers and participation in tourism are also reported respectively as social and economic well-being outcomes.

Museums strategically align their public accountability reporting with public policy thinking, even when it is not yet Government policy. For example, Auckland Museum's active response to Auckland's diverse populations include *He Korahi Maori: Strategic Pathways* (Auckland Museum, 2016a) and *Teu Le Vaa: the Pacific Dimension at Auckland Museum* (Auckland Museum, 2016b), which guide museum policy and practice and were co-developed with Maori and Pacific community leaders. The three Auckland museums report on volunteer hours contributed annually, as well as figures around visitor participation, and are active in attracting diverse audiences, as well as successfully recruiting for staff and governance, representative of Auckland's multicultural communities.

Social inclusion has long been a goal of museums (e.g., see Sandell, 1998). In relation to museums, the 'bridging' dimensions of social capital conceived by Putnam (2000) are regarded as a positive benefit of museum visiting; paradoxically, the 'bonding' dimension created through community formation among the volunteers may deter members of cultural minorities (Murzyn-Kupisz & Dzialek, 2013). The findings from Chen's 2014 research suggest that resources of cultural capital held by current volunteers may play a role in limiting the potential diversity of volunteers, since minority communities' stocks of 'capital' manifest differently.

Cultural and social capital resources possessed by volunteers

Harflett (2015) has identified cultural capital as a key resource for volunteers in England's National Trust, which manages a large portfolio of cultural and natural heritage places open to the public including historic houses and protected areas of landscape and coast. Her research shows that possession of social, economic and cultural capital are important characteristics of the Trust's volunteers. While her research was undertaken in rural settings, her findings resonate with the findings from Chen's (2014) research. Volunteering in the heritage sector, including museums, is 'serious leisure' (Stebbins, 1996) and it attracts people well-endowed with 'cultural capital' (Harflett, 2015). The Values, Understanding, Protective and Enhancement functions which more strongly motivated the Auckland volunteers can also boost cultural capital and contribute to social well-being.

The majority of these urban museums' volunteers had high levels of educational attainment and income (Chen, 2014, pp. 56–57; Chen et al., 2019), thus social and economic resources to devote to their museum duties, travel into town, park cars (if relevant), social ease with their fellow volunteers and active interest in their museums' subject matter. The fact that the majority were retired or semi-retired (Chen, 2014, p. 56) also means that they have the time and are freer from other social or cultural obligations. They also made their decisions to volunteer independently: the statement attracting least agreement overall (only 21.8% positive agreement) was: *People I'm close to want me to volunteer* (Chen, 2014, pp. 50–51; Chen et al., 2019, p. 136).

As Harflett notes (2015), Bourdieu's notion of cultural capital builds on social origins and 'takes time to accumulate'. These volunteers may have grown up visiting museums, especially if they were residents locally for many years, given the longevity of Auckland Museum founded in 1852 and Auckland Art Gallery founded in 1888. Auckland Museum, for example, also serves as the regional war memorial, honouring the fallen from the two World Wars. It was built by public subscription in 1929, when almost every family contributed financially and had relations memorialised there. It remains the site for annual commemorations on ANZAC Day (Australian and New Zealand Army Corps). Many New Zealanders are emotionally invested in the museum over two or more generations, but it does not hold the same significance for newer migrants.

Harflett (2015) emphasises that volunteers 'bring their personal interests with them', and this is a factor which the museums would consider in their recruitment and allocation of duties.

The highest rated statement (97.2% positive agreement) of the VFI in the 2014 study was: *Volunteering adds interest to my life* (Chen, 2014, p. 62; Chen et al., 2019, p. 136), which, while not specifying where the interest lies, may suggest intellectual and social engagement and the drive for this kind of cultural participation. Holmes (2003) and Stebbins (1995) also recognise pre-existing interests as drivers for volunteering. Stebbins (1996) highlighted volunteering as a dimension of 'serious leisure' applicable to museum volunteering. This combines both leisure interests and altruism also common in New Zealand's well-established sports volunteering. For migrant groups, support through their churches and temples, takes priority for volunteering for many cultural minorities. Auckland's heritage institutions cannot compete, despite holding collections from many cultures. Museums can satisfy the altruistic motivation of volunteering without carrying the burden of social expectation prevalent in some communities.

The museums have standing as 'nonprofit heritage brands' (Curran, Taheri, Macintosh & O'Gorman, 2016), partly derived from their respect in the community and long-held affection of those who grew up with them: not only heritage institutions, but non-commercial institutions with their own heritage. While Curran et al. (2016) studied the Scouts organisation, their findings resonate strongly, especially since the museum volunteers committed themselves for several years of service. Retention ranged from less than 1 year to more than 20 years, with almost half volunteering from 1 to 5 years (Chen, 2014, pp. 41–42, 87; Chen et al., 2019, p. 135). The sense that museums endure through generations may also appeal to their older volunteer cohort (Chen, 2014, pp. 38, 86; Chen et al., 2019, p. 132). In terms of cultural capital, the volunteers could be regarded as building an inter-generational legacy, benefitting their descendants, among others.

The second most highly rated statement was: *Doing volunteer work makes me feel I am contributing to the community* (93.81% positive agreement) (Chen, 2014, p. 50; Chen et al., 2019, p. 133). Equally, older volunteers may be averse to change, and perceive museums as changing only gradually and are therefore stable places to work. Museums may be places where their stock of cultural capital therefore has continuing personal validity, contributing to their longer service.

Conclusions

The phenomenon of the visitor attraction is extraordinarily varied, and it follows that an attraction's needs for volunteers and the recruits available will be equally wide-ranging. Urban museums and art galleries in tourism destinations compete with other cultural attractions for both visitors and volunteers. Auckland Museum, Auckland Art Gallery and the New Zealand Maritime Museum have succeeded in building loyal and socially cohesive teams. The volunteers are initially drawn by personal motivations such as interest or experience in a subject covered in the museum's collections or service to the community. They stay because of the well-managed volunteer programmes and the sense of belonging to a worthwhile endeavour. Whether their participation is regular, occasional or episodic, they are altruistically motivated to contribute, they benefit personally from the social connectedness and the inherent interest of their duties and they enhance their pre-existing stock of cultural capital.

The volunteers are successfully managed at each attraction, as their long service attests. They have many learning opportunities and feel part of a community (Stamer et al., 2008). They undertake satisfying tasks and feel valued. Harflett's (2015) observation that the cultural capital that each volunteer brings is more likely to be possessed by white, middle-class people, accumulated over time through their experiences of leisure rings true for these three museums.

This means that the current volunteer cohorts are not representative of Auckland's superdiverse population. Generally, these volunteers are older, well-educated and retired or semi-retired. More women undertook hosting, guiding visitors around exhibition galleries, and administration roles, while more men worked as operational volunteers, particularly at the less traditional Maritime Museum, which attracted volunteers with practical sailing experience. Most volunteers belonged to the majority culture, but this may change, in response to the multicultural makeup of the museum staff, museums' increasing engagement with ethnic communities in co-curating exhibitions and events and public policy imperatives. Online collections, new types of volunteers with information technology skills (e.g., see Beel et al., 2017; Claisse, Ciolfi & Petrelli, 2017; Coleman & Nankervis, 2015), visitors with new research interests and a new history curriculum to be introduced in 2022 may hold promise for building a new kind of volunteer force. This may apply to both the well-established institutions featured in this chapter and smaller rural heritage museums. Until then, recruitment strategies are likely to draw from the same pool of people possessing a solid stock of cultural capital and their volunteer profile is unlikely to change.

Qualitative research akin to Harflett's (2015) but conducted in urban heritage attractions would offer valuable insights for developing more inclusive and representative volunteer cohorts. Similarly, investigating whether and how current volunteers acknowledge museums' gradual shift into the tourism industry as cultural attractions might also offer understandings for recruiting people more interested in supporting the tourism focus rather than engaging predominantly with the heritage dimension.

Acknowledgements

I wish to thank Xiaohua (Rico) Chen for granting me the opportunity to revisit his master's thesis findings (Chen, 2014) and my colleague Dr Claire Liu with whom I had the pleasure of co-supervising Chen's research and co-authoring Chen et al. (2019).

References

Auckland Council. (2020). *Auckland heritage counts 2020 annual summary*. https://www.knowledgeauckland.org.nz/media/1924/aucklands-heritage-counts-2020.pdf

Auckland Museum. (2016a). *He Korahi Maori: Strategic pathways*. Retrieved from: https://www.aucklandmuseum.com/your-museum/about/he-korahi-maori-a-maori-dimension-auckland-museum

Auckland Museum. (2016b). *Teu Le Vaa: The Pacific dimension at Auckland War Memorial Museum*. Retrieved from: https://www.aucklandmuseum.com/your-museum/about/teu-la-va-the-pacific-dimension-at-auckland-museum

Auckland Museum. (2018). *Annual report 2017–2018 Tāmaki Paenga Hira Auckland War Memorial Museum*. Retrieved from: http://www.aucklandmuseum.com/getmedia/6ea91f22-24b5-4074-b61a-01ff18818270/Auckland-Museum-Annual-Report-2017-2018.pdf

Auckland Museum. (2020). *Become a volunteer guide*. Retrieved from: https://www.aucklandmuseum.com/your-museum/get-involved/volunteer/volunteer-guides

Auckland Tourism, Events and Economic Development (2017). *Auckland growth monitor*. Retrieved from: Auckland Growth Monitor (aucklandnz.com)

Auckland Tourism, Events and Economic Development. (2019). *Auckland destination overview March 2019*. Retrieved from: https://www.aucklandnz.com/sites/build_auckland/files/media-library/documents/Auckland-Destination-Overview-March-2019.pdf

Beel, D. E., Wallace, C. D., Webster, G., Nguyen, H., Tait, E., Macleod, M., & Mellish, C. 2017). Cultural resilience: The production of rural community heritage, digital archives and the role of volunteers. *Journal of Rural Studies, 54*, 459–468. https://doi.org/10.1016/j.jrurstud.2015.05.002

Bonn, M. A., Joseph-Mathews, S. A., Dai, M., Hayes, S., & Cave, J. (2007). Cultural attraction atmospherics: creating the right environment for the heritage/cultural visitor. *Journal of Travel Research, 45*(3), 345–354. https://doi.org/10.1177/0047287506295947

Bourdieu, P. (1984). *Distinction: A social critique of the judgement of taste*. Routledge.

Cameron, M. P., & Poot, J. (2019). Towards superdiverse Aotearoa: Dimensions of past and future ethnic diversity in New Zealand and its regions. *New Zealand Population Review, 45*, 18–45. https://population.org.nz/app/uploads/2019/12/NZPR-45_whole-doc-final.pdf

Carey, S., Davidson, L., & Sahli, M. (2013). Capital city museums and tourism flows: An empirical study of the Museum of New Zealand Te Papa Tongarewa. *International Journal of Tourism Research, 15* (6), 554–569. https://doi.org/10.1002/jtr.1874

Chen, X. (2014). *Understanding volunteers in cultural tourism organizations in New Zealand: Exploring demographics and motivational factors* (A dissertation submitted to Auckland University of Technology in partial fulfilment of the requirements for the degree of Master of Hospitality Management). Auckland University of Technology, Auckland, New Zealand. http://hdl.handle.net/10292/7948

Chen, X., Liu C., & Legget, J. (2019). Motivations of museum volunteers in New Zealand's cultural tourism industry. *Anatolia, 30*(1), 127–139. https://doi.org/10.1080/13032917.2018.1542521

Claisse, C., Ciolfi, L., & Petrelli D. (2017). Containers of stories: Using co-design and digital augmentation to empower the museum community and create novel experiences of heritage at a house museum. *The Design Journal, 20*(sup1), S2906–S2918, https://doi.org/10.1080/14606925.2017.1352801

Clary, E. G., Snyder, M., Ridge, R. D., Copeland, J., Stukas, A. A., Haugen, J., & Miene, P. (1998). Understanding and assessing the motivations of volunteers: A functional approach. *Journal of Personality and Social Psychology, 74*(6), 1516–1530. https://doi.org/10.1037/0022-3514.74.6.1516

Coleman, J., & Nankervis, A. (2015). The missing link: Volunteers, museums and researchers in the digital age. *The Journal of the Inclusive Museum, 8* (1), 11–23. https://eds.a.ebscohost.com/eds/pdfviewer/pdfviewer?vid=1&sid=358669a8-924b-476a-b1a1-6617d74739c6%40sdc-v-sessmgr02

Cotton, E., & Merito, E. (2017). The Treaty of Waitangi and Tamaki Paenga Hira Auckland war memorial museum. In R. Bell, M. Kawharu, K. Taylor, M. Belgrave, & P. Meihana (Eds.), *The treaty on the ground: Where are we headed and why it matters* (pp. 233–253). Massey University Press.

Curran, R., Taheri, B., MacIntosh, R., &. O'Gorman, K. (2016). Nonprofit brand heritage: Its ability to influence retention, engagement and satisfaction. *Nonprofit and Voluntary Sector Quarterly, 45*(6), 1234–1257. https://doi.org/10.1177%2F0899764016633532

Davidson, L., & Sibley, P. (2011) Audiences at the "new" museum: Visitor commitment, diversity and leisure at the museum of New Zealand Te Papa Tongarewa, *Visitor Studies, 14*(2), 176–194, https://doi.org/10.1080/10645578.2011.608009

Deery, M., Jago, L., & Mair, J. (2011). Volunteering for museums: The variation in motives across volunteer age groups. *Curator: The Museum Journal, 54*(3), 313–325. https://doi.org/10.1111/j.2151-6952.2011.00094.x

Dekel, I., & Vinitzky-Seroussi, V. (2017). A living place: On the sociology of atmosphere in home museum. *European Journal of Cultural and Political Sociology, 4*(3), 336–362 https://doi.org/10.1080/23254823.2017.1332486

Dillman, D. A. (1978). *Mail and telephone surveys (Vol. 3).* John Wiley.

Edwards, P., & Trafford, S. (2016). Social licence in New Zealand—what is it? *Journal of the Royal Society of New Zealand, 46* (3–4), 165–180. https://doi.org/10.1080/03036758.2016.1186702

Harflett, N. (2015). "Bringing them with personal interests": The role of cultural capital in explaining volunteers. *Voluntary Sector Review, 6*(1), 3–9. https://dx.doi.org/10.1332/2040805 15X14241616081344

Helms, J. E., Henze, K. T., Sass, T. L., & Mifsud, V. A. (2006). Treating Cronbach's Alpha reliability coefficients as data in counseling research. *The Counseling Psychologist, 34*(5), 630–660. https://doi.org/10.1177/0011000006288308

Holmes, K. (2003). Volunteers in the heritage sector: A neglected audience? *International Journal of Heritage Studies, 9*(4), 341–355. https://doi.org/10.1080/1352725022000155072

Holmes, K., & Smith, K. (2009). *Managing volunteers in tourism: Attractions, events and destinations.* Elsevier.

Hu, W., & Wall, G. (2005). Environmental management, environmental image and the competitive tourism attraction. *Journal of Sustainable Tourism, 13*(6), 617–635. https://doi.org/10.1080/09669 580508668584

Jenkins, M. (2017). *Chatham Islands economic profile – final report.* Chatham Islands Council. Retrieved from: Chatham-Islands-Economic-Profile-Report-2017.pdf (cic.govt.nz).

Kelly, L., Savage, G., Landman, P., & Tonkin, S. (2002). *Energised, engaged, everywhere: older Australians and Museums - a report for the Australian Museum, Sydney, and the National Museum of Australia.* Retrieved from: https://media.australian.museum/media/dd/Uploads/Documents/2591/fullreport.baa24bf.pdf

Kotler, N., & Kotler, P. (2000). Can museums be all things to all people? Missions, goals, and marketing's role, *Museum Management and Curatorship, 18*(3), 271–287. https://doi.org/10.1080/09647770000301803

Leask, A. (2008). The nature and role of visitor attractions. In A. Fyall, B. Garrod, A. Leask, & S. Wanhill (Eds.) *Managing visitor attractions* (2nd ed., pp. 3–15). Butterworth-Heinemann.

Leask, A. (2010). Progress in visitor attraction research: Towards more effective management. *Tourism Management, 31* (2), 155–166. https://doi.org/10.1016/j.tourman.2009.09.004

Leask, A. (2016). Visitor attraction management: A critical review of research 2009–2014. *Tourism Management, 57*, 334–361. https://doi.org/10.1016/j.tourman.2016.06.015

McCarthy, C. (2011). *Museums and Maori: Heritage professionals, Indigenous collections, current practice.* Te Papa Press.

McCarthy, C. (2014). Museums - Museums in New Zealand culture. Retrieved January 17, 2021 from *Te Ara - the Encyclopaedia of New Zealand.* Retrieved from: http://www.TeAra.govt.nz/en/museums/page-1

Ministry of Business, Innovation and Employment & Department of Conservation. (2019). *New Zealand-Aotearoa government tourism strategy.* Retrieved December 20, 2020 from https://www.mbie.govt.nz/dmsdocument/5482-2019-new-zealand-aotearoa-government-tourism-strategy-pdf

Murzyn-Kupisz, M., & Dzialek, J. (2013). Cultural heritage in building and enhancing social capital. *Journal of Cultural Heritage and Sustainable Development, 3*(1), 35–54. https://doi.org/10.1108/20441261311317392

Museums Aotearoa (2015). *2014 Sector Survey.* Retrieved from: https://www.museumsaotearoa.org.nz/sites/default/files/2020-06/Museums%20Aotearoa%20Sector%20Survey%20report%202014.pdf

Museums Aotearoa (2019). *2019 National Visitor Survey*. Retrieved from: https://www.museumsaotearoa.org.nz/sites/default/files/2020-07/2019NVS.PNG

National Services Te Paerangi (2006). *He Rauemi Resource Guides: Working with volunteers*. Museum of New Zealand Te Papa Tongarewa. Retrieved from: https://www.tepapa.govt.nz/sites/default/files/29-managing-volunteers.pdf

New Zealand History Federation (2021). Retrieved from: https://www.nzhistoricalsocieties.org.nz.

Orange, C. (2015). *The Treaty of Waitangi*. Bridget Williams Books.

Pacesila, M. (2020). Volunteering in the heritage sector: Opportunities and trends. *Management and Economics Review, 5*(1), 91–107. http://mer.ase.ro/files/2020-1/5-8.pdf

Putnam, R. (2000). *Bowling alone: the collapse and revival of American community*. Simon & Schuster.

Regional Facilities Auckland. (2018). *Regional Facilities Auckland Annual Report for the year ended 30 June 2018*. Retrieved December 20, 2020 from https://drive.google.com/file/d/1HLyw0UeYId x2oo2SPcHe7_PFkB3vk48t/view

Remer, A. (2005) What is (not) an internship? *Te Ara: Journal of Museums Aotearoa, 32*(2), 32–34.

Sandell, R. (1998). Museums as agents of social inclusion. *Museum Management and Curatorship, 17*(4), 401–418. https://doi.org/10.1080/09647779800401704

Smith, K. A. (2003). Literary enthusiasts as visitors and volunteers. *International Journal of Tourism Research, 5*(2), 83–95. https://doi.org/10.1002/jtr.419

Smith, P. (2019). *The contributions and motivations of Auckland volunteer heritage organisations. A report submitted in partial fulfilment of the requirements for the degree of Master of Urban Planning (Professional) and Heritage Conservation*. Unpublished Masters Thesis: The University of Auckland.

Stamer, D., Lerdal, K., & Guo, C. (2008). Managing heritage volunteers: An exploratory study of volunteer programmes in art museums. *Journal of Heritage Tourism, 3*(3), 203–214. https://doi.org/10.1080/17438730802138949

Stats NZ (2019). *Cruise ship traveller and expenditure statistics: Year ended June 2019*. Retrieved January 23, 2021. https://www.stats.govt.nz/information-releases/cruise-ship-traveller-and-expenditure-statistics-year-ended-june-2019

Stats NZ (2021). *International visitor survey – Activities*. Retrieved January 20, 2021 from http://nzdotstat.stats.govt.nz/wbos/Index.aspx?DataSetCode=TABLECODE7576

Stebbins, R. A. (1995). Cultural tourism as serious leisure. *Annals of Tourism Research, 23*(4) 948–950. https://doi.org/10.1016/0160-7383(96)00028-X

Stebbins, R. A. (1996). Volunteering: A 'serious leisure' perspective. *Nonprofit and Voluntary Sector Quarterly, 25*, 211–224. https://doi.org/10.1177/0899764096252005

The Treasury (2019a). *Culture, well-being and the Living Standards Framework: A perspective*. Retrieved March 21, 2021 from https://treasury.govt.nz/publications/dp/dp-19-02

The Treasury (2019b). *Our country, our future, our people. The Living Standards Framework: Dashboard update*. Retrieved from: Living Standards Framework: Dashboard Update -12 December 2019 (treasury.govt.nz)

Wallace, M. A. (2006). *Museum branding*. Altamira Press.

Weaver, D., & Lawton, L. (2010). *Tourism management* (4th ed.). John Wiley.

Wilson, L. M. (1999). *For love, not money: Volunteers in New Zealand museums: A thesis submitted in partial fulfillment of the requirements for the degree of Master of Arts in Museum Studies at Massey University*. http://hdl.handle.net/10179/6612

Yang, J. (2015). The art and culture companions: Art museum volunteering as serious leisure in Finland. *International Journal of the Inclusive Museum, 7*(3/4), 9–20. https://doi.org/10.18848/1835-2014/CGP/v07i3-4/58337

9

HERDING 6,000 VOLUNTEERS

Robert S. Bristow

Introduction

Every winter in January, a group of some 100 volunteers gather in a local school's cafeteria in Massachusetts on a weekend. They are brought together by a team of a dozen leaders, also volunteers, to hear about the previous years' accomplishments and plans for the upcoming season. For this group, in 2019, nearly 10,000 hours of volunteer service were recorded (Massachusetts AT Committee, 2020).

Who are these dedicated volunteers? These are the Appalachian Trail volunteers and they are joined by thousands of other volunteers to plan, manage and otherwise take care of the Appalachian Trail (AT) in the eastern part of the United States. Every year some 6,000 volunteers do trail maintenance, natural and cultural resource monitoring, oversee campsites and 260 lean-tos that offer overnight accommodations for thousands of hikers. Overall, it is estimated that 240,000 hours of volunteer efforts contribute to the health of the AT every year (Bowman, 2021). They are the eyes and ears of the AT and are responsible for protecting this valuable and historic resource. Like any Friends group, they also do fundraising, public relations work and other efforts more associated with most non-profit groups (Baker et al., 2010; McArdle, 2020). Yet this dedicated group of volunteers is spread apart by over 3,500 km (nearly 2,200 miles) in 14 states. Some of the volunteers are neighbours of the trail while others may need to travel hours to get to the footpath they help watch over.

The AT is an extremely popular hiking trail that is within a day's drive for about one half of the United States' population. Thousands of hikers visit the park for an afternoon walk, a weekend backpack, while others start a journey to become one of the honoured 2,000 milers by putting one foot in front of the other some 5 million times. Over 20,000 hikers from around the world can make that claim and about half of those were in the last decade, encouraged by many things including the best-selling novel and movie *A Walk in the Woods* by Bill Bryson and *Wild* based on the memoir by Cheryl Strayed with a movie starring Reese Witherspoon.

So how do 6,000 volunteers take care of 3,500 km of trail? The rest of this chapter follows this path. First we trace its 100 year history, from the humble proposal in regional planning to today as a premier volunteer managed foot trail. Volunteers have been an essential element throughout this history. A foundation of natural resource planning and management in our

DOI: 10.4324/9780367815875-11

parks and protected areas is introduced in the next section of this chapter. Trail related strategies are found next by discussing a more sustainable approach to protect those resources. Then recognising the lack of funding in many of our parks and protected areas, the essential role of volunteers is highlighted. Examples of the type of volunteer efforts will be discussed and we will conclude with strategies for volunteer groups that may not have 6,000 members.

Parks and protected area planning and management

A preponderance of trail related research has been based on parks and protected areas (Godtman Kling et al., 2017). Within this umbrella, two main themes are found. First, we have visitor impact studies that affect the user experience and the natural environment (Anderson et al., 1998; Cole et al., 1987; Eagles & McCool, 2002; Hammitt et al., 2015). Next, there are management concerns directed toward resource protection such as soil, habitats, invasive species, encroachments and pollution (Benninger-Truax et al., 1992; Collinge, 1996; Manning, 1979). To address these broad reaching influences, a more holistic management approach to resource changes in parks and protected areas is found in research by Cole (1989), and later in Hammitt et al. (2015), where the impacts are not just confined to the specific resource impacts, i.e., trails, campsites, so popular with hikers, but a more ecological approach that includes the entirety of the cultural and natural resources throughout the park. Despite this grand goal, trails must receive attention due to their concentrated use (Manning, 1979).

Beginning earnestly in the 1970s and coincidentally tied to the tremendous interest in hiking spurred by the writings of Collin Fletcher and Edward Abbey, and a global awareness following the first Earth Day, we begin to note more research specifically on trails. Early writings in recreation geographies, not tourism geographies, marked the initial entry in resource protection of the footpaths weaving through the countryside, thus permitting hikers to enjoy a more rural experience (Coppock & Duffield, 1975; Cosgrove & Jackson, 1972; Lavery, 1974). Yet, these studies were concerned about the explosive use in recreation and concentrated research efforts in the understanding of demand (Lavery, 1975), and less on the need for sustainable management for these trail resources.

The development of trail guidelines for design, construction and maintenance appeared when Birchard and Proudman (1981) prepared one of the earliest set of instructions. Additional research by Cole et al. (1987) provided yet another comprehensive guide to identify, document and mitigate trail impacts in backcountry areas.

Moving forward, much of the research into trail management continues to investigate the human impacts and strategies for alleviation. For example, Marion and Leung (2004) emphasised the need for professional trail planning and management. Strategies exemplified in the early work of Birchard and Proudman (1981) had been field tested and became accepted methods by many trail maintaining organisations.

For parks and protected areas, since many trails extend well beyond the heavily used 'front country', park managers have begun to use the efforts of volunteers for monitoring changes (Timothy & Boyd, 2015). The initial application of volunteer trail management may have focused on litter or brush removal; tasks that did not require great attention by the managers. Nevertheless, this effort identified an approach to meet the needs of trail work, when declining budgets directed managers to concentrate time and money to the highest used areas in parks and protected areas.

Today literature continues to exalt the economic, societal and environmental benefits of trails (Ward-Perkins et al., 2019; World Tourism Organization, 2019). Recognising the task of planning and managing trail resources, both of these references recommend the building of partnerships to encourage the engagement and support of the local stakeholders, a theme that this chapter will build on in the next section.

Historical background

In 1916, the National Park Service (NPS) was established in the United States. This federal agency set the stage for the planning and management of many of the nation's natural and cultural landmarks for the future. Shortly after the formation of the NPS, Benton MacKaye, a regional planner wrote "The Appalachian Trail: A Project in Regional Planning" for the *Journal of the American Institute of Architects* (MacKaye, 1921). His proposal suggested a land management strategy for the eastern mountain range of North America and was based on four ideas.

First, there was the trail. Utilising the many existing trails found in the Appalachian Mountains, it was simply the matter of linking these footpaths into the one AT. Recognising that 2,000 miles is extremely long, MacKaye suggested that the trail length be organised into shorter segments to aid in the local volunteer management of the trail resource.

Second, MacKaye proposed the construction of shelter camps on the trail, each about a day's walk between them. Volunteers would be responsible for the construction and maintenance of these structures often called lean-tos.

Third, MacKaye (1921, p. 328) envisioned the establishment of community groups along the route whose role would be providing a place for the urban dwellers to escape the cities for "for recreation, for recuperation and for study". This idea was uniquely driven to encourage regional planning, yet still would be supported by the volunteering nature of the participants.

Lastly would be the establishment of food and farm camps giving citizens another way to give "back to the land" (MacKaye, 1921, p. 328). The temporary visitors would need food to eat and wood to construct the communities found in the rural mountains in order to be sustainable.

Shortly after this proposal, in 1925 the Appalachian Trail Conference (ATC) was founded by MacKaye and other like-minded outdoor enthusiasts (Anderson, 2002; King, 2000). Thus a regional not-for-profit organisation was established that linked volunteers from local communities in order to plan and manage the AT (Appalachian Trail Conservancy, 1981).

Construction of the trail was started during the 1920s by the weekend volunteers who left the city to work and play following the philosophical theme of MacKaye. The time to build the 2,000 mile trail was delayed by many things. For example, two competing volunteer groups in Massachusetts independently built two parallel trails in that state, and needlessly delayed the final route (Waterman & Waterman, 2019). The Berkshire Hills Conference attempted the first statewide trail route in Massachusetts from 1928 to 1931. In 1931, the Appalachian Mountain Club built a trail route to the east, duplicating much of the earlier work. To address this, Myron Avery, then ATC Chair, coerced the Massachusetts' volunteers and finally oversaw trail construction from 1932 to 1935. From this example, it became clear that local management of the trail, as envisioned by MacKaye, would still need guidance and direction from the national volunteer leadership. To finish the task, one central vision was needed to bond the local volunteers and the final section of trail was blazed on 14 August 1937 in central Maine.

Since the 1930s, the trail route had frequently changed due to the urban sprawl and competing land use demands (Fisher & Durrance, 1972; Foster, 1987). By the 1960s frequent

Figure 9.1 The AT logo
Source: Author.

relocations and land owner disputes riddled the route of the trail. The historic 'handshake' agreements between the trail volunteers and land owners meant the future of the trail was threatened (Bureau of Outdoor Recreation, 1966). During this period the popularity of the AT drew 1 million visitors in 1966.

Recognising this threat, in 1968 the National Trails System Act (NTSA Public Law 90-543) and an amendment of the Act in 1978 secured the necessary funds to secure a permanent route for the trail that would preserve the character of the AT corridor. The Act also acknowledged the importance of "volunteer citizen involvement in the planning, development, maintenance, and management" of the nation's trails (Cerveny et al., 2020, p. 18). To prepare for these efforts, the law established the formal working relationship between the Appalachian Trail Conference (now Conservancy) and the National Park Service and other federal land management agencies. The Appalachian Trail shifted from being an informally managed trail park to being part of the National Park System offering federal protection and funding (Mittlefehldt, 2010, 2013). Unique in federal land use planning, the management of the trail system began to be a true partnership between the federal, state and local agencies whose land the trail passed and the local citizen-volunteer trail-maintaining groups. This formalised a long term relationship that has made the AT one of the premier hiking experiences available to the public and a model for other long distance trails around the world (Burch, 1979; Bristow, 1998, 2004).

Fueled by the NTSA, the National Park Service began acquiring lands on both sides of the trail to secure a permanent and protected route. Exterior corridor boundary surveys were conducted between 1979 and 2005 as part of the NPS land protection program. The acquired corridor was essential to protect not only the trail but the surrounding natural and cultural landscapes (Leonard, 1979; Yahner et al., 1995). Today the trail is fully protected and the iconic AT symbol (Figure 9.1) is found at nearly every road crossing, representing the route of the Appalachian Trail through the mountains.

AT volunteer management

True to the philosophy of MacKaye, local volunteer management continues today, guided by formal agreements between the public land agencies whose land the trail traverses and those volunteers engaged in the daily management of the trail. The informal, but guiding *Foundation Document: Appalachian National Scenic Trail* confirms the importance of the volunteer acknowledging that the AT was "(c)onceived, designed, and constructed by volunteers..." and that "(v)olunteers are the soul of the Trail..." (NPS, 2015, p. 5). The foundation document reinforces the importance of volunteers to the AT, from MacKaye's origin to present day needs.

The AT organisational plan is the important document that guides volunteer management. For the AT, the overriding document is the *Appalachian Trail Comprehensive Plan* (ATC, 1981). This document identified the resource to be protected and management philosophy, including the cooperative arrangements with the list of government and volunteer partners.

Once the federal guidelines are established and the underlying foundation is understood, specific guidelines for volunteers can be prepared. Guiding the volunteers is the *Appalachian Trail Conservancy Volunteer Leadership Handbook* (ATC, 2016). The handbook provides a historical view of the volunteer trail management and lists all the federal regulations that support the cooperative arrangement.

From these AT guidelines, the local management plan addresses the specific issues facing the trail in that geographical area. It identifies the chief public and private partners who cooperatively work to protect and manage the AT. This is important since often local park managers will have a detailed understanding of the local social and natural environments. These officials are versed in the laws and regulations needed to protect the trail. This guidance is important to the volunteer. The partnership goes both ways between the local park ranger and the trail volunteer. For example, it is interesting to note one misunderstanding between land managers and the volunteers. Brian (1982), reported that park rangers were not expecting the volunteer efforts for the AT and that the trail clearing of branches and paint blazing were thought to be acts of vandalism having failed to recognise the volunteer efforts of trail clearing and blazing. Today, management policies will direct the volunteer to specific procedures and the appropriate tools to complete the task to eliminate any misunderstanding of the volunteer role.

For example, in 2019, the Berkshire Chapter of the Appalachian Mountain Club has updated their comprehensive management plan for the trail in Massachusetts (Massachusetts AT Committee, DCR & ATC, 2019). This cooperative agreement between the maintaining trail club and the federal government has the stated purpose, among others, to guarantee the role of the trail volunteer in the management process.

This is a large task supported by the team of volunteers described in the introduction. On average, every year some 10,000 volunteer hours are recorded for Massachusetts where there are 4,661 hectares of land protecting the corridor of the trail. About half of the corridor is NPS lands while the other half are state lands found in State Parks and State Forests. Other parcels include conservation easements, or town properties. The time and effort of these volunteer efforts is important evidence and expected to be reported as part of the volunteer's responsibility in the shared partnership with the federal government. Records are collected each fiscal year, ending 30 September (ATC, 2016).

It should be emphasised that the role of volunteers is clearly identified in all layers of documentation, from the federal government down to the local trail club. This is an incredibly important bond, recognising the role and necessity of the volunteer and the Appalachian Trail. Further, volunteers are supported and granted significant roles in protecting the national scenic trail. The NPS expects the local volunteer to adhere to the policies needed to protect the AT, and in turn, the volunteer is supported by the NPS for training, supplies and even money to support the purchase of materials related to the maintenance of the trail.

One unique and interesting element of the agreement between the federal government and the volunteer is how environmental impacts are addressed on the trail. Most projects on public lands are subject to laws and regulations pertaining to the environment, and these factors are directed by the National Environmental Policy Act, NEPA (1970) in the US. The agreement between the federal government and the volunteers, as briefly described above, provide for a categorical exclusion for NEPA regulations for routine trail maintenance, provided these actions follow procedures and those of the local management plan. Again this is a tremendous responsibility for the trail volunteer, instilled by decades of cooperation between the federal government and the volunteer. Larger projects may have an impact on the natural environment and therefore will need to go through a review process before the volunteers can proceed.

Volunteer descriptions

Most trail groups' efforts tend to focus on the volunteer doing trail maintenance. While this is extremely important it is not the only task. The ATC and NPS have formalised five volunteer tasks for the Appalachian Trail. Each is described by identifying duties and responsibilities, training and resources needed and physical demands and working conditions.

First is trail work that requires not only training in the tools of the trade, but also knowledge of prescribed trail design. There are many guides for trail building and maintenance, and interested readers are directed to *Trail design, construction, and maintenance* (Birchard & Proudman, 1981). But issues about first aid, health in the woods (e.g. Lyme disease caused by ticks, poisonous plants), the physical ability to hike several miles and carrying the equipment for the task are essential too. Evidence of this work is illustrated in Figure 9.2.

The second task for volunteers is corridor monitoring (ATC, 2011). Since the land acquisition program of the 1980s and 1990s, much of the protected lands are under federal ownership. For the national park lands, the corridor monitoring program finds the volunteer bushwhacking through the woods on the alert for encroachments. Since this work is

Figure 9.2 Hikers are guided by the rectangular white blaze on trees and stones. Note the work of the volunteer trail maintainer who has cleared downed trees away from the trail path
Source: Author

away from the trail, damage to the corridor is frequently averted by the careful eyes of the volunteer. Bristow (2019) describes this volunteer effort encouraging adventure tourists to follow suit.

Acknowledging the task of 'herding' volunteers as noted in the title of this chapter, there is a role of volunteer administration and leadership. Not all volunteer work is found on the Trail. Record keeping, coordination of multiple projects, partnering with government, NGOs and local citizens require an attention to detail, and this is necessary to be successful. Office work includes GIS and GPS spatial mapping of resources, fundraising and other tasks prescribed by the *Appalachian Trail Conservancy Volunteer Leadership Handbook* (ATC, 2016).

Money is always a concern and the AT, like most parks and protected areas could always use some more. One important opportunity for trail funding is the ability to use matching 'labour' costs to leverage financial support from organisations that embrace trail related recreation and conservation. AT volunteers can calculate the 'volunteer' wages using the Independent Sector website (https://independentsector.org/). Nationwide, this is currently $27.20 US an hour, but some AT states are higher. While some of this volunteer effort may be inside, outside trail work frequently contributes significantly to match funds.

It is clear that the trail is much more than a footpath. The natural and cultural resources found in the corridor and adjacent lands also contribute to the experience. Natural resource volunteers track environmental trends of wildlife habitats, rare and non-native species, water quality and other natural systems. For cultural resources the task is relatively new as there is a trail wide interest in protecting the AT under federal guidelines called the National Register of Historic Places (https://www.nps.gov/subjects/nationalregister/index.htm) due to the unique cultural history of the landscape. This will ensure that both the natural environment (through NEPA) and cultural resources will be protected.

Education, outreach and interpretation volunteers link the trail with the citizenry. For example, Leave No Trace (http://LNT.org) is a message of sustainability in these educational moments. If volunteers can expand visitor knowledge of hiking it will support the importance of the natural greenway envisioned by MacKaye. This message is important to sustain the health of the trail.

In sum, the responsibilities are broad enough to cater to the wide interests of the volunteers. For those seeking physical labour, trail work will meet those demands. Those confined to the inside can support the trail through administration, fundraising or coordination of the many projects undertaken throughout the year. There are enough tasks for the 6,000 volunteers found along a 3,500 km trail.

Conclusion

It may seem that the formality of the NPS and ATC relationship is strict; yet given the massive responsibility of thousands of trail volunteers who contribute to the well-being of the trail as well as the reciprocal support from the federal government, it is in the best interest for the trail. There are several issues that any Friends group may still find important.

Volunteer recruitment is vital. Historically, most recent retirees and baby boomers may volunteer their efforts (Bruyere & Rappe, 2007; Musick & Wilson, 2007; Okun & Schultz, 2003). While the percentage of elderly volunteers may be lower than other age cohorts, the total number of hours by volunteers continues to grow (Corporation for National and Community Service, 2006). Yet despite these numbers, three concerns need our attention. First, the volunteers are ageing (Bruyere & Rappe, 2007). The demographics of this team of AT volunteers tend to be older. With age, we find that the physical labour needed to do difficult trail work is challenging (Trauntvein, 2011), let alone any other physical activities (Willems & Dury, 2017). Financial issues are also a concern for retirees since their income may decrease (Musick & Wilson, 2007). For the trail volunteers to be sustainable, new younger stewards need to become engaged on the AT.

Younger individuals will join the efforts often through their membership in church or outdoor organisations. Frequently, we find urban youth oriented groups organised to provide valuable labour needed on the trail.

New initiatives are preparing the next generation of trail stewards. The Appalachian Trail Conservancy has established a Next Generation Advisory Council, made up of 14 to 16 young, diverse leaders between the ages of 18 and 30 who serve two-year terms. These young women and men are selected to address the reality that America's growing, diverse population is underrepresented in many conservation organisations (Taylor et al., 2019). To encourage additional youth support, the ATC has a pro-rated dues structure based on age as well.

A second issue is more positive. AT communities are new in the volunteer efforts for the AT. Designation as an 'AT Community' serves to enhance local economic development, engage the citizens as trail stewards, assist in conservation planning and promote the AT as a resource and asset. For too long, the trail may have been viewed as a collecting point for backpackers. The 'AT Community' program promotes a close neighbourly connection with the trail similar to MacKaye's food and wood camps since they support the local economy. Currently, over 40 towns are found along the 3,500 km route. A similar idea could be found for any park, where a local town joins forces with park management to work cooperatively to protect the park they share.

MacKaye's original dream has been realised. Volunteers built the trail and still manage it today. Lean-tos and other lodging opportunities are found along the entire route. Community camps are now found in the many trail towns along the way offering local support and provisions for the hikers. The spirit of the Trail, born out of the volunteer efforts of the 1920s has grown to become an experience and something beyond a simple hiking trail. Perhaps nowhere else in the world have volunteers contributed to a monumental dream that has become the AT.

Finally, there is the Trail Magic, the unique volunteer efforts of neighbors of the AT (Bratton, 2012). Here we find individuals offering hikers rides into town to pick up supplies, leaving water at unreliable springs and otherwise helping to continue the spirit of Mackay's utopian world that we call the AT.

It is now the time that all users of natural resources take a role of protecting these special places. Voluntourism is fine away from home, but we need to think global, and volunteer local. National parks around the world provide the strongest protection of our natural treasures (Wright, 1996). What remains is the protection that volunteers can supply. The rewards of volunteering are enormous (Martinez & McMullin, 2004) and management should do what it can to facilitate volunteers in the task to care for our parks and protected areas.

References

Anderson, D. H., Lime, D. W., & Wang, T. L. (1998). *Maintaining the quality of park resources and visitor experiences. A handbook for managers.* University of Minnesota.

Anderson, L. (2002). *Benton MacKaye: Conservationist, planner, and creator of the Appalachian Trail.* Johns Hopkins University Press.

Appalachian Trail Conservancy (ATC). (1981). *Comprehensive plan for the protection, management, development and use of the Appalachian National Scenic Trail.* Appalachian Trail Conservancy.

Appalachian Trail Conservancy. (2011). *A.T. corridor stewardship field: A guide to corridor monitoring and boundary maintenance for volunteers.* Appalachian Trail Conservancy.

Appalachian Trail Conservancy. (2016). *Appalachian trail conservancy volunteer leadership handbook.* Appalachian Trail Conservancy.

Baker, M. L., Dhungel, S., Davenport, M. E., Leahy, J. E., & Bridges, C. A. (2010). An exploratory investigation of the roles friends groups play in national park management. *Journal of Outdoor Recreation, Education, and Leadership, 2*(3), 285–300.

Benninger-Truax, M., Vankat, J. L., & Schaefer, R. L. (1992). Trail corridors as habitat and conduits for movement of plant species in Rocky Mountain National Park, Colorado, USA. *Landscape Ecology, 6*(4), 269–278. https://doi.org/10.1007/BF00129705

Birchard, W., & Proudman, R. D. (1981). *Trail design, construction, and maintenance.* Appalachian Trail Conservancy.

Bowman, J. (2021, January 5). *Media room.* Appalachian Trail Conservancy. Retrieved January 5, 2021 from https://appalachiantrail.org/our-work/about-us/media-room/

Bratton, S. P. (2012). *The spirit of the Appalachian trail: Community, environment, and belief.* University of Tennessee Press.

Brian, C. (1982). New Handshake: Management Partnerships along the Appalachian Trail. *Parks and Recreation. 17*(6), 62, 36–42.

Bristow, R. S. (1998). Volunteer-based recreation land management. *Parks and Recreation. 33*(8), 70–77.

Bristow, R. S. (2004). Volunteer-based recreation land management: The eyes and ears for the Appalachian Trail. In I. Camarda (Ed.), *Global challenges of parks and protected area management* (pp. 71–78). Carlo Delfino.

Bristow, R. S. (2019). Altruistic adventure voluntourism: Help manage the park you visit. In I. Jenkins (Ed.), *Adventure Tourism* (pp. 145–154). CABI.

Bruyere, B., & Rappe, S. (2007). Identifying the motivations of environmental volunteers. *Journal of Environmental Planning and Management, 50*(4), 503–516. https://doi.org/10.1080/09640560701402034

Burch Jr, W. R. (1979). Long distance trails. The Appalachian trail as a guide to future research and management needs. *Long distance trails. Symposium on the Appalachian Trail,* 11–13 October, 1977. Yale University.

Bureau of Outdoor Recreation. (1966). *Trails for America: Report on the nationwide trails study.* United States Department of Interior, Bureau of Outdoor Recreation.

Cerveny, L., Derrien, M., & Miller, A. B. (2020). Shared stewardship and national scenic trails: Building on a legacy of partnerships. *International Journal of Wilderness, 26*(2), 18–33.

Cole, D. N. (1989). Recreation ecology: What we know, what geographers can contribute. *The Professional Geographer, 41*(2), 143–148. https://doi.org/10.1111/j.0033-0124.1989.00143.x

Cole, D. N., Petersen, M., & Lucas, R. C. (1987). *Managing wilderness recreation use: Common problems and potential solutions.* US Department of Agriculture, Forest Service, Intermountain Research Station.

Collinge, S. K. (1996). Ecological consequences of habitat fragmentation: Implications for landscape architecture and planning. *Landscape and Urban Planning, 36*(1), 59–77. https://doi.org/10.1016/S0169-2046(96)00341-6

Coppock, J., & Duffield, B. (1975). *Recreation in the countryside: A spatial analysis.* St. Martin's Press.

Corporation for National and Community Service. (2006). *Volunteer growth in America: A review of trends since 1974.* Retrieved from https://www.nationalservice.gov/pdf/06_1203_volunteer_growth.pdf

Cosgrove, I., & Jackson, R. (1972). *The geography of recreation and leisure.* Hutchinson.

Eagles, P. F., & McCool, S. F. (2002). *Tourism in national parks and protected areas: Planning and management.* CABI.

Fisher, R. M., & Durrance, D. (1972). *The Appalachian Trail.* National Geographic Society.

Foster, C. H. (1987). *The Appalachian National Scenic Trail: A time to be bold.* Appalachian Trail Conservancy.

Godtman Kling, K., Fredman, P., & Wall-Reinius, S. (2017). Trails for tourism and outdoor recreation: A systematic literature review. *Turizam: međunarodni znanstveno-stručni časopis, 65*(4), 488–508.

Hammitt, W. E., Cole, D. N., & Monz, C. A. (2015). *Wildland recreation: Ecology and management.* John Wiley & Sons.

King, B. (2000). Trail years. In R. Rubin (Ed.). *Special 75th Anniversary Issue, July 2000 – Appalachian Trailway News* (pp. 2–16, 52–63). Appalachian Trail Conservancy.

Lavery, P. (1974). *Recreational geography.* David and Charles.

Lavery, P. (1975). The demand for recreation: A review of studies. *The Town Planning Review, 46*(2), 185–200. https://www.jstor.org/stable/40103100

Leonard, R. (1979). Protecting the long trail resource: A problem analysis. In W. R. Burch Jr, (Ed.), *Long distance trails. The Appalachian trail as a guide to future research and management needs. Long distance trails. Symposium on the Appalachian Trail*, 11–13 October, 1977 (pp. 84–102). Yale University.

MacKaye, B. (1921). An Appalachian trail: A project in regional planning. *American Institute of Architects, 9*(October), 325–330.

Manning, R. E. (1979). Impacts of recreation on riparian soils and vegetation. *Journal of the American Water Resources Association, 15*, 30–43. https://doi.org/10.1111/j.1752-1688.1979.tb00287.x

Marion, J. L., & Leung, Y. F. (2004). Environmentally sustainable trail management. In R. Buckley (Ed.), *Environmental impacts of tourism* (pp. 229–244). CABI.

Martinez, T. A., & McMullin, S. L. (2004). Factors affecting decisions to volunteer in nongovernmental organizations. *Environment and Behavior, 36*(1), 112–126. https://doi.org/10.1177/0013916503256642

Massachusetts AT Committee, Massachusetts Department of Conservation and Recreation, and the Appalachian Trail Conservancy. (2019). *Local management plan for the Appalachian trail in Massachusetts*. Berkshire Chapter, Appalachian Mountain Club, AT Committee. On file.

Massachusetts AT Committee. (2020). *Report at the 2019 Mass AT volunteer gathering*. Massachusetts AT Committee.

McArdle, K. (2020). Multiple case study of nonprofit partnerships in North Carolina's coastal state parks. *Coastal Management, 48*(1), 38–56. https://doi.org/10.1080/08920753.2020.1694474

Mittlefehldt, S. (2010). The people's path: Conflict and cooperation in the acquisition of the Appalachian Trail. *Environmental History, 15*(4), 643–669. https://www.jstor.org/stable/25764487

Mittlefehldt, S. (2013). *Tangled roots: The Appalachian Trail and American environmental politics*. University of Washington Press.

Musick, M. A., & Wilson, J. (2007). *Volunteers: A social profile*. Indiana University Press.

National Park Service. (2015). *Foundation document*, USDI, NPS. Retrieved from https://www.nps.gov/appa/getinvolved/upload/APPA-Foundation-Document-2015.pdf

Okun, M. A., & Schultz, A. (2003). Age and motives for volunteering: Testing hypotheses derived from socioemotional selectivity theory. *Psychology and Aging, 18*(2), 231. https://doi.org/10.1037/0882-7974.18.2.231

Taylor, D. E., Paul, S., & McCoy, E. (2019). Diversity, equity, and inclusion and the salience of publicly disclosing demographic data in American environmental nonprofits. *Sustainability, 11*(19), 5491. https://doi.org/10.3390/su11195491

Timothy, D. J., & Boyd, S. W. (2015). *Tourism and trails: Cultural, ecological and management issues* (Vol. 64). Channel View Publications.

Trauntvein, N. (2011). *Volunteerism at urban park and recreation agencies: Examining the role of volunteers' socio-demographic characteristics, motivations, organizational identity, and satisfaction on volunteer participation outcomes*. [Unpublished doctoral dissertation], University of Pennsylvania.

Ward-Perkins, D., Beckmann, C., & Ellis, J. (2019). *Tourism routes and trails: Theory and practice*. CABI.

Waterman, L., & Waterman, G. (2019). *Forest and crag: A history of hiking, trail blazing, and adventure in the Northeast Mountains*. SUNY Press.

Willems, J., & Dury, S. (2017). Reasons for not volunteering: Overcoming boundaries to attract volunteers. *The Service Industries Journal, 37*(11–12), 726–745. https://doi.org/10.1080/02642069.2017.1318381

World Tourism Organization. (2019). *Walking tourism – Promoting regional development*, UNWTO, Madrid. https://doi.org/10.18111/9789284420346.1

Wright, R. G. (1996). *National parks and protected areas: Their role in environmental protection*. Blackwell Science Ltd.

Yahner, T. G., Korostoff, N., Johnson, T. P., Battaglia, A. M., & Jones, D. R. (1995). Cultural landscapes and landscape ecology in contemporary greenway planning, design and management: A case study. *Landscape and Urban Planning, 33*(1–3), 295–316. https://doi.org/10.1016/0169-2046(94)02024-A

10

DECONSTRUCTING VOLUNTEER TOURISM

Snigdha Kainthola,
Pinaz Tiwari and Nimit R. Chowdhary

Introduction

Volunteering has long been an integral element of society. With the onset of globalization, its powerful presence is evident in the tourism industry. The increasing popularity of volunteer tourism (VT), volunteerism or voluntourism is evident in academic literature, press, and global trends (Eckardt, Font & Kimbu, 2019; Sin, 2009; Wearing & McGehee, 2013). It is based on the idea that tourists engage in pleasurable vacations while contributing constructively to the destination and the welfare of locals (Everingham, 2015). As with other forms of tourism, volunteer tourists are driven by several objectives. The primary motive identified by academic studies is altruism, which has proved to be paramount in volunteer tourism (Brown, 2005; Pompurová et al., 2020; Unger, 1991). Hence it is also referred to as altruistic tourism (Weaver, 2015). Besides, the objectives of volunteer tourists are also influenced by egoistic and individualistic principles (Benson & Seibert, 2009). Volunteers are further motivated by the desire for personal growth, transformation, curriculum vitae or CV-building, and the pursuit of tourism (Crossley, 2019; Magrizos, Kostopoulos & Powers, 2021).

Voluntourism has a strong influence on macro-cultural trends, such as increasing awareness towards the sustainability of the environment and the growing sentiment towards the welfare of others (Uriely, Reichel & Ron, 2003). Volunteer tourists have a wide range of activities that they can indulge in during their trip such as teaching, volunteering in an event, and preserving the environment. Volunteers opt for activities compatible with their skill sets, availability of time, and their objectives. Voluntourism can be a trip designed solely for volunteering, or volunteer activities can be a part of the vacation. Undoubtedly, there is a strong influence in developing this sector by initiatives of firmly established organizations, both non-profit and profit-making agencies. The role of organizations leading projects is fundamental for successful execution (Coghlan, 2008). The heterogeneity of volunteer tourists results in multiple motivations of tourists implying that organizations have to consider the aims and needs of tourists and cater to them efficiently, whilst also considering the local population.

Volunteer tourism embraces an array of varied experiences that attracts tourists from all age groups and different backgrounds (Coghlan, 2006). Traditionally deemed under niche tourism, voluntourism is increasingly considered as an alternative (Mcintosh & Zahra, 2007), or mass niche tourism (Thompson & Taheri, 2020). Several authors postulate volunteer

DOI: 10.4324/9780367815875-12

tourism to be closer to sustainable and responsible tourism where tourists willingly participate in supporting the local community as a part of their travel (Meng et al., 2020b). However, these claims are difficult to corroborate with tangible, concrete facts, and research is still in its infancy. Also, although volunteer tourists possess compassionate motives for volunteering in the third world or developing countries, the idea of them being the 'giver' or 'helping', serves to reproduce neo-colonial binaries (Simpson, 2004). Such a belief downgrades local cultures and people and puts the volunteers at a podium where development is synonymous with their culture (Simpson, 2004). Increasingly volunteer tourism has received denunciation from media and scholarly literature for fostering neoliberal ideas that ignore issues of structural inequality and social justice (Godfrey et al., 2019).

Various authors have proposed several definitions to explore the concept of VT. This chapter deconstructs the concept of volunteer tourism and expounds on its various dimensions via a review of the literature and highlights the diverse reasons for tourists to indulge in volunteer activities during their leisure time. The chapter further elucidates on several contemporary debates on the pros and cons of voluntourism while exploring its several contemporary aspects.

Defining volunteer tourism

Traditionally considered a niche sector, volunteer tourism has outgrown its cocoon (Butcher, 2011; Stainton, 2016). Thompson and Taheri (2020) categorize it under a 'mass niche'. As research on volunteer tourism continues to expand, it becomes even more challenging to define the concept. Since previous scholars have not been successful in advancing an unanimously accepted definition, the advocation of new definition continues to emerge in scholarly literature (Taplin, Dredge & Scherrer, 2014). One of the first attempts to define volunteer tourists is evident in the research by Wearing (Hustinx et al., 2016). Wearing (2001, p. 1) defined volunteer tourists as people who "volunteer in an organised way to undertake holidays that might involve aiding or alleviating the material poverty of some groups in society, the restoration of certain environments or research into aspects of society or environment". However, authors, including Bussell and Forbes (2002) advocate that it is difficult to define a volunteer due to no conventional norms in volunteering. Uriely et al. (2003) believe that as much as the definition proposed by Wearing stands true, it only focuses on 'micro-social' influences of volunteer tourism. It misses out on the 'macro-cultural trends', such as the rising sensitivity towards sustainability and the desire to help others. Also, Wearing does not take cognizance of the locals engaged in volunteer activities, which are essential in enabling volunteer tourism.

Most researchers advocate the property of exchange involved in volunteer tourism, where tourists respond to the costs and benefits (Unger, 1991). Such a perception of a volunteer elucidates that the definition is shaped by the relative cost incurred and the benefits achieved during the process by the volunteer. The definitions based on the element of interchange believe that volunteers weigh the returns that they receive from volunteering work in comparison to the resources they invest in the process. The higher the cost borne during volunteering, the efficiency of the volunteer is believed to be more considerable, and intentions are judged to be real (Cnaan, Handy & Wadsworth, 1996). Although the doctrine around volunteering is that it involves contributions from the participants without coercion, such a simplistic definition negates the possibilities of other scenarios of obligation. Cnaan et al. (1996) demonstrate that volunteering can be both, out of sheer 'free will' or through obligation. The 'involuntary volunteering' includes mandatory service imposed by the government or employer-directed volunteer work (Bailey & Russell, 2012). As opposed to government-mandated volunteering, employer-led volunteering is paid for by the office. It caters to the long-term goal of an organization. Volunteer work also ranges from receiving no remuneration to acquiring a small stipend for their services.

Eddins and Cottrell (2013) consider volunteer tourists as the unacknowledged heroes of progress. Accordingly, volunteer tourism is perceived in a two-dimensional manner. At the centre of this definition is the fact that 'holidaymakers' volunteer their time to work on projects that are established to enhance the environment of an area or local community. The second dimension focuses on the development of the participant through the intrinsic rewards of contributing to such projects (Callanan & Thomas, 2005). McGehee and Santos (2005, p. 1) define volunteer tourism as "utilizing discretionary time and income" to help others while travelling. However, volunteering is not necessarily conducted in leisure time as opposed to the fundamental characteristic of tourism. For example, a natural crisis or a catastrophe necessitates the involvement of volunteers in periods other than their 'discretionary' time (Wearing, Beirman & Grabowski, 2020). Brown (2005) uses a different lens to understand volunteer tourists. He emphasized the role of tour operators in promoting volunteering. Travellers consider their own volition and time while volunteering through activities that suit them the best (Crossley, 2019), guided by their social and cultural backgrounds.

Elements of volunteer tourism

The exponential rise in the 'guilt-conscious' individuals can be attributed to tourists who are more sensitive towards the environment (Callanan & Thomas, 2005). Many began to steer away from the much-criticized mass tourism and in the process propagated new forms of tourism which are more responsible and sustainable. Volunteer tourism fits in such a paradigm that facilitates a form of travel that is more considerate of the local community and benign for the environment. The sector is strongly dependent on the support of tourists aiming to contribute positively to society. Central to volunteer tourism is the belief that travel can positively contribute to destinations and work towards improving the lives of local communities (Sin, 2009).

Increasingly, Volunteer tourism projects are abundantly available globally, which are organized by different types of 'sending organisations' (Raymond & Hall, 2008). These include private agencies, non-governmental organizations, conservation agencies, universities and colleges, and government (Broad, 2003; Ellis, 2003). The non-profit organizations and other agencies providing volunteer projects to tourists have a decisive role in shaping and developing the sector since they have a decisive role in marketing, managing, and administering volunteer activities in the destinations (Steele, Dredge & Scherrer, 2017). Administrators of volunteer projects must be aware of the heterogeneity of their participants, along with the need of the local community to successfully execute the project (Han, Lee, Meng, Chua, & Ryu, 2020). The consideration of motivations of participants, their skill sets, and the cultural and social background of the destination is an essential prerequisite for organizations to deliver successful, meaningful results (Coghlan, 2006).

The section below deconstructs the motivations for volunteer tourism and highlights the advantages and disadvantages of this complex sector.

Motivations of the volunteers

Volunteer tourism is a multi-dimensional concept full of contradictions (McGehee, 2012). Although initial research on VT involves considerable work on the motivations of volunteer tourists (e.g., see Benson & Seibert, 2009; Brown, 2005; Unger, 1991), research is still nascent (Hustinx, 2001). While the altruistic motivations of the volunteers are acknowledged by a majority of researchers (Han, Lee, Meng, Chua, & Ryu, 2020; Han, Lee & Hyun, 2020; Mustonen, 2006; Rehberg, 2005), it is not void of several other self-centred objectives of tourists. McGehee and Santos (2005) highlight that altruism must be the central motive of tourists to be considered volunteers, along with the pursuit of tourism. Bussell and Forbes (2002) advocates that selfless motives drive participants. However, several studies demonstrate that there are overlapping objectives of tourists, which are subject to change with time (Magrizos et al., 2021). Wearing (2001) classified the motivations of volunteer tourists in seven categories, while the predecessors like Andereck et al. (2012), Benson and Seibert (2009) accepted and further added to Wearing's list. The lists of motivations largely include the dominant emotion of altruism, desire to travel and seek adventure, development on personal and professional aspects, building up networks with other volunteers and locals, and to experience cultural immersion.

Brown (2005) indicated the strong motivation for personal enrichment, identity formation, and a way of expressing self. Also, the work highlighted the desire of participants to promote peace and witness local culture. The wish of seeking camaraderie, thrill, and novelty were recognized as distinct motivations specific to volunteer tourism. Not central to the altruistic motives, these motivations are directed towards the development of self. Another strong motivator is the zeal for experiential knowledge and to satisfy curiosity (Andereck et al., 2012; Polus & Bidder, 2016). The host community is considered anchor points for knowledge and new experiences, and volunteers believe these encounters can trigger personal growth and meaning-making projects (Kontogeorgopoulos, 2017; Shalbafian & Zarandian, 2019; Zahra, 2006). A large number of scholars advocate that the endeavours of tourists are legitimate only when the positive result is visible for locals and the destination (Beirman et al., 2018; Crossley, 2019; Mostafanezhad, 2013).

Since volunteers are self-driven, they freely opt to indulge in volunteer tourism with altruistic or egoistic reasons, or maybe both (Bailey & Russell, 2010). Volunteer tourism provides a variety of benefits to participants, primarily based on the activities they choose. Often volunteers embark on trips for CV-building and to enlarge career opportunities (McGloin & Georgeou, 2015). Volunteer tourists can be classified under 'experiential' or 'experimental' tourist (Cohen, 1979), who are in pursuit of much broader encounters than recreation in their trip. Volunteers consciously engage in experiences that allow them substantial interaction with locals. Participants are further driven by spiritual motivations (Shalbafian & Zarandian, 2019; Zahra, 2006). The work of Vada et al. (2020) demonstrates that the communion formed due to contact with natural and social environments influences the well-being of tourists. Irrespective of the motivations of tourists, volunteer tourism aims to improve the economic, environmental, and social conditions of the destination.

Advantages

The soul of volunteer tourism lies in the intention of the tourists. The resolve to contribute towards the welfare of the society by employing sustainable environmentally friendly approaches form a strong basis for volunteer tourism (Shalbafian & Zarandian, 2019). Volunteer tourism embraces a bilateral experience for tourists (Wearing, 2001), where the benefit is available for locals as well as for the contributors (Polus & Bidder, 2016). The stronger motivation of bringing a positive change in society by tourists encourages them to engage in activities outside of their comfort zone. The innate characteristic of altruism of volunteer tourism provides meaningful impacts for all stakeholders and the environment, listed below.

Tourist oriented

The significant impact of volunteering on tourists is personal. The interactions with locals and other volunteers open the doors to new experiences, which can lead to an accumulation of wisdom, and provide opportunities to explore the self. The challenges, chance of introspection, networking, and novel experiences develop greater awareness of self and transformation (Magrizos et al., 2021). Also, volunteers feel more confident and empowered on return from volunteering, knowing that they can make a difference in the world with their efforts. The endeavour further equips volunteers to deal with challenges efficiently (Brown, 2005). Wearing (2001) highlights volunteer tourism as a leverage to promote self-development. The process may further help in enlarging the self-image of the person, and to use the volunteer experience for self-presentation.

Volunteer tourism also brings like-minded people with common goals together (Comerford & Fambrough, 2002). It provides them with a platform for networking. Henderson and Presley (2003) advocate that volunteering is closely linked to the formation of social networks, which encourages the generation of social support for an individual and at times provides them with the validation they might have been seeking for years. Also, volunteer tourism experiences have the power to influence the perception of the participant towards society and encourage awareness of global issues (Bailey & Russell, 2012). This awareness brings a long-lasting impact and domino effect in the public as participants can become propagators of responsible behaviour (Magrizos et al., 2021).

A significant change is also conspicuous in the behaviour and belief system of volunteers, prominent being a higher level of tolerance and self-efficacy (McGehee & Santos, 2005). Further, leisure volunteering allows the voice of participants to be heard. The innate quality of volunteer tourism is that it provides a platform for discovering balance and self in life through experiences, which are not always freely available. It can lead to skill development and CV enhancement (Arai & Pedlar, 1997).

Local community oriented

With the involvement of volunteer tourists, the host community can experience a rise in pro-social values, increased consciousness, and a heightened rate of activism (Bailey & Russell, 2012). They find support and an outlet to voice their opinion. Lee (2020, p. 10) revealed that locals experience positive emotions such as "happiness, content, optimism" due to intermingling with participants. The experience provided enjoyment and a break from monotonous routines. The efforts of volunteers in teaching and educating locals to endorse their development allow new and enhanced skill sets that they can utilise to procure a livelihood. Also, in several cases, the local people are provided with monetary benefits to provide them with sudden relief (Galley & Clifton, 2004).

The tasks of volunteers uplift the spirits of the local community and evoke hope for a better future. The host community receives recognition, and interaction with other people which infuses them with confidence (Lee, 2020). Further, the locals are motivated with the altruistic values of the volunteers, encouraging them to adopt positive principles from tourists. The engagement in volunteer activities makes them aware of their potential and helps them in finding meaning and happiness in life. Involvement in volunteer work also provides the courage to fight for themselves and others in their society.

Destination oriented

Volunteer tourism works parallel with the ideology of sustainability, and hence helps in preserving the environment (Han, Lee, Meng, Chua, & Ryu,2020). Further, it also propagates awareness towards nature and its resources, encouraging responsible behaviour by society (Steele et al., 2017). The activities of volunteer tourists help in restoring the natural state of the destination. During a catastrophe, volunteers help not just people, but also assist with rebuilding the destination (Wearing et al., 2020). Several economic, social, and environmental benefits of volunteer tourism are visible in the destination (Han, Lee, Meng, Chua, & Ryu,2020; Lee, 2020; Steele et al., 2017; Wearing et al., 2020). Volunteer tourism further helps bring attention to objects of historical importance, rendering significant cultural value to them (Pompurová et al., 2020). Given that many volunteer tourism destinations are relatively deprived, one stated benefit of volunteer tourism is that it directs tourism money to destinations that would not typically profit from tourism (Galley & Clifton, 2004). As such, volunteer monetary provision also provides for future projects of the destination (Bargeman, Richards & Govers, 2016), allowing lasting community goals to be achieved (Prince & Ioannides, 2017).

Disadvantages

Volunteer tourists seek authentic trip experiences (Kontogeorgopoulos, 2017) and inadvertently at times participate in the commodification of tourism (Wearing, 2001), cultivating cultural materialism of host communities (Thompson & Taheri, 2020). Also, volunteer tourists often possess utopian and unrealistic desires (Smith & Font, 2014), which makes it difficult for them to have a fulfilling experience. The scope of gaining experience and rendering a constructive impact on destinations sometimes gets limited since volunteer tourists are mostly time-bound. They often get frustrated with the inability of generating significant change on destinations in the restricted time frame available to them (Pompurová et al., 2020).

However, closely linked to altruism, travellers do have self-centred desires which at times adversely impact the efficiency of their volunteer work. Guttentag (2009) criticizes volunteerism for limited involvement of locals, unskilled workforce promoting inefficient work, and for disturbing the economy of host destinations. Since organizations aim to increase profits, they acquire more money from the volunteers and pass little benefits on to the community. Organizations allot work without much consideration of the participant's skill sets resulting in reckless damage. Unskilled participants have the potential to obstruct the successful implementation of projects.

Though interaction amongst volunteers and locals can reproduce meaningful encounters, the negative repercussions are also visibly present. Contact with volunteer tourists has a profound impact on local communities who are more vulnerable to adverse changes. There is a constant fear of the 'demonstration effect' that implies that the host culture is impacted by the culture and wealth of tourists (Guttentag, 2011). Locals may respond to the arrival of tourists by imitating their lifestyles, such as their behaviour, body language, and consumption patterns. This imitation often culminates into discontent due to the disparity in the wealth of the host community and volunteers. Though projecting a large number of positive manifestations in the destination, volunteer tourism needs to be managed and organised, considering these negative impacts. There is a fear of volunteerism turning into a

'Trojan Horse', where the adverse outcomes of the sectors are overlooked, and communities acknowledge only its virtuous side (Butler, 1990).

Further, volunteer tourism is believed to encourage a colonial way of western domination where people from developed countries consider themselves superior to others, and act as givers (Devereux, 2008; Godfrey et al., 2019). Viewing volunteer tourism largely under a sustainable paradigm possessing mostly developmental characteristics is worrisome, especially when the participants are mostly young, untrained, inexperienced, and volunteering for a limited period (Atkins, 2011; Mostafanezhad, 2014; Simpson, 2004). The objective of 'making a difference' may also lead to false hopes in volunteers as it can be challenging to achieve in a small trip (Everingham, 2015), leading to disheartenment and discouragement in future endeavours.

Contemporary viewpoint

The traditional view of volunteer tourism focuses more on the positive impact of the sector (Guttentag, 2009). Thus, the scholarly literature bespeaks of the benefits of volunteer tourism in abundance. The new viewpoint is much more diverse and critical. The current discourse is concerned with the role of volunteer tourism organizations (Eckardt et al., 2019; Steele et al., 2017) and the effect of the sector on locals (Everingham, 2015; Proyrungroj, 2017). The rising popularity of volunteer tourism, increasing competition in the sector, and aggressive marketing by organizations has brought a fear of commercialization of the entire VT sector, which has brought these agencies organizing volunteer tours under the radar. Organizations, at the expense of locals, attempt to fulfil the expectations of their customers (Smith & Font, 2014). Though the benefits rendered from the sector cannot be undermined, volunteer tourism is heavily criticized for fostering a neo-colonialist ideology (Guttentag, 2011; Mostafanezhad, 2014). The backlash emanates from the advocates that believe volunteerism is based on the supposition that people from developed countries automatically have something to offer those in the developing world (Mostafanezhad, 2014).

The development of the sector is dependent on creating stronger bonds between volunteer tourists and host communities, where the voices of both parties are heard. Researchers further elucidate that the host community does not view participants as tourists but as volunteers. Therefore, optimistic intentions from both sides can foster mutual benefits (Everingham, 2015; Griffiths, 2018). Ideally, approaches in projects must be bottom-up (Wearing et al., 2020), helping the underprivileged first. Fortunately, the adverse outcomes of volunteer tourism are avoidable, and with thoughtful planning and management, adversities can be mitigated (Wearing et al., 2020; Wearing & McGehee, 2013). For instance, substantial reckless damage can be avoided with a considerate allotment of tasks to volunteers with the right skill sets, or by training volunteers briefly beforehand. Raymond and Hall (2008) suggest the development of programmes which are more sensitive and benign for local communities. The approach of projects must be more focused towards learning rather than restricted to mere experiences. The contemporary research further emphasises the importance of cultural immersion during volunteer tours.

The critical aspect of volunteer tourism is the confrontation with the issues of a different country which may not immediately be a pleasant experience. However, the bigger picture involves rewarding experiences for volunteer tourists through their engagement of resources for the upliftment of a society (Bailey & Russell, 2010).

Conclusion

The volunteering of tourists in local communities as a part of their travel (Sin, 2009), renders multiple benefits for all stakeholders involved. Volunteer tourism is situated in a paradigm that is opposed to regular mass tourism and closer to sustainable, alternative, and niche tourism. It provides travel options that are more benign to the local community and advantageous for the whole of the destination (Han, Lee, Meng, Chua, & Ryu,2020). Volunteer tourism is increasingly being considered as responsible and contributing pro-social behaviour in developing countries (Meng et al., 2020a). The expanding popularity of this form of tourism is being met by a proliferation of organizations from the private, public, and non-profit sectors offering a range of projects that can be pursued worldwide. Often volunteers pay a hefty amount for the privilege of volunteering. Even with a constant fear of contributing more to the organizing agencies of volunteer tours, the primary motivation of altruism amongst the volunteers can bring positive change in the destination. Despite heavy criticism for the neo-liberal discourse by the media, the sector continues to grow extensively.

Volunteer tourists primarily hail from developed, affluent countries and travel to the developing or under-developed countries, which inherently fuels the power dynamics between the local communities and volunteer tourists (Eddins & Cottrell, 2013). However, this generalization is too simplistic. Uriely et al. (2003) propose that volunteer tourism must incorporate the local community which can volunteer in the tourism sector along with tourists. A multifaceted partnership is essential to be forged between the host community, volunteer tourists, public sector, and volunteer tourism organizations, to develop a successful and sustainable volunteer tourism industry. Fostering intercultural exchange under the framework of mutuality is vital in diminishing the neo-colonial binaries.

References

Andereck, K., McGehee, N.G., Lee, S., & Clemmons, D. (2012). Experience expectations of prospective volunteer tourists. *Journal of Travel Research, 51*(2), 130–141. https://doi.org/10.1177/0047287511400610

Arai, S.M., & Pedlar, A.M. (1997). Building communities through leisure: Citizen participation in a healthy communities initiative. *Journal of Leisure Research, 29*(2), 167–182. https://doi.org/10.1080/00222216.1997.11949792

Atkins, S.G. (2011). Smartening-up voluntourism: SmartAid's expansion of the personality-focused performance requirements form (PPRF). *International Journal of Tourism Research, 14*(4), 369–390. https://doi.org/10.1002/jtr

Bailey, A.W., & Russell, K.C. (2010). Predictors of interpersonal growth in volunteer tourism: A latent curve approach. *Leisure Sciences: An Interdisciplinary Journal, 32*(4), 352–368. https://doi.org/10.1080/01490400.2010.488598

Bailey, A.W., & Russell, K.C. (2012). Volunteer tourism: Powerful programs or predisposed participants? *Journal of Hospitality and Tourism Management, 19*(1), 123–132. https://doi.org/10.1017/jht.2012.14

Bargeman, B., Richards, G., & Govers, E. (2016). Volunteer tourism impacts in Ghana: A practice approach. *Current Issues in Tourism, 21*(13), 1486–1501. https://doi.org/10.1080/13683500.2015.1137277

Beirman, D., Upadhayaya, P.K., Pradhananga, P., & Darcy, S. (2018). Nepal tourism in the aftermath of the April/May 2015 earthquake and aftershocks: Repercussions, recovery and the rise of new tourism sectors. *Tourism Recreation Research, 43*(4), 544–554. https://doi.org/10.1080/02508281.2018.1501534

Benson, A., & Seibert, N. (2009). Volunteer tourism: Motivations of German participants in South Africa. *Annals of Leisure Research, 12*(3–4), 295–314. https://doi.org/10.1080/11745398.2009.9686826

Broad, S. (2003). Living the Thai life - A case study of volunteer tourism at the Gibbon Rehabilitation Project, Thailand. *Tourism Recreation Research, 28*(3), 63–72. https://doi.org/10.1080/02508281.2003.11081418

Brown, S. (2005). Travelling with a purpose: Understanding the motives and benefits of volunteer vacationers. *Current Issues in Tourism, 8*(6), 479–496. https://doi.org/10.1080/13683500508668232

Bussell, H., & Forbes, D. (2002). Understanding the volunteer market: The what, where, who and why of volunteering. *International Journal of Nonprofit and Voluntary Sector Marketing, 7*(3), 244–257. https://doi.org/10.1002/nvsm.183

Butcher, J. (2011). Volunteer tourism may not be as good as it seems. *Tourism Recreation Research, 36*(1), 75–76. https://doi.org/10.1080/02508281.2011.11081662

Butler, R.W. (1990). Alternative tourism: Pious hope or Trojan Horse? *Journal of Travel Research, 3*, 40–45. https://doi.org/10.1177/004728759002800310

Callanan, M., & Thomas, S. (2005). Volunteer tourism - Deconstructing volunteer activities within a dynamic environment. In M. Novelli (Ed.), *Niche Tourism - Contemporary issues, trends and cases* (pp. 183–200). Routledge. https://doi.org/10.1016/b978-0-7506-6133-1.50025-1

Cnaan, R.A., Handy, F., & Wadsworth, M. (1996). Defining who is a volunteer: Conceptual and empirical considerations. *Nonprofit and Voluntary Sector Quarterly, 25*(3), 364–383. https://doi.org/10.1177/0899764096253006

Coghlan, A. (2006). Volunteer tourism as an emerging trend or an expansion of ecotourism? A look at potential clients' perceptions of volunteer tourism organisations. *International Journal of Nonprofit and Voluntary Sector Marketing, 11*, 225–237. https://doi.org/10.1002/nvsm.35

Coghlan, A. (2008). Exploring the role of expedition staff in volunteer. *International Journal of Tourism Research, 10*, 183–191. https://doi.org/10.1002/jtr.650

Cohen, E. (1979). A phenomenology of tourist experiences. *Sociology, 13*(2), 179–201. https://doi.org/10.1177/003803857901300203

Comerford, S.A., & Fambrough, M.J. (2002). Constructing learning sites for solidarity and social action: Gender autobiography for consciousness raising. *Affilia, 17*, 411–428. https://doi.org/10.1177/088610902237359

Crossley, É. (2019). Volunteer tourism: Subjectivity and transformation. *Critical Tourism Studies Proceedings*, Vol. 2019.

Devereux, P. (2008). International volunteering for development and sustainability: Outdated paternalism or a radical response to globalisation? *Development in Practice, 18*(3), 357–370. https://doi.org/10.1080/09614520802030409

Eckardt, C., Font, X., & Kimbu, A. (2019). Realistic evaluation as a volunteer tourism supply chain methodology. *Journal of Sustainable Tourism, 28*(2), 647–662. https://doi.org/10.1080/09669582.2019.1696350

Eddins, E., & Cottrell, S. (2013). Sustainable development and sustainable livelihoods frameworks: Theory and practice in volunteer tourism. *The International Journal of Sustainability Policy and Practice, 9*, 47–60. https://doi.org/10.18848/2325-1166/CGP/v08i01/55360

Ellis, C. (2003). When volunteers pay to take a trip with scientists-participatory environmental research tourism (PERT). *Human Dimensions of Wildlife, 8*, 75–80. https://doi.org/https://doi.org/10.1080/10871200390180172

Everingham, P. (2015). Intercultural exchange and mutuality in volunteer tourism: The Case of Intercambio in Ecuador. *Tourist Studies, 15*(2), 175–190. https://doi.org/10.1177/1468797614563435

Galley, G., & Clifton, J. (2004). The motivational and demographic characteristics of research ecotourists: Operation Wallacea volunteers in Southeast Sulawesi, Indonesia. *Journal of Ecotourism, 3*(1), 69–82. https://doi.org/10.1080/14724040408668150

Godfrey, J., Wearing, S.L., Schulenkorf, N., & Grabowski, S. (2019). The 'volunteer tourist gaze': Commercial volunteer tourists' interactions with, and perceptions of, the host community in Cusco, Peru. *Current Issues in Tourism, 23*(20), 2555–2571. https://doi.org/10.1080/13683500.2019.1657811

Griffiths, M. (2018). Writing the body, writing others: A story of transcendence and potential in volunteering for development. *The Geographical Journal, 184*(2), 115–124. https://doi.org/10.1111/geoj.12200

Guttentag, D. (2009). The possible negative impacts of volunteer tourism. *International Journal of Tourism Research, 11*(6), 537–551. https://doi.org/10.1002/jtr.727

Guttentag, D. (2011). Volunteer tourism: As good as it seems? *Tourism Recreation Research, 36*(1), 69–74. https://doi.org/10.1080/02508281.2011.11081661

Han, H., Ariza-Montes, A., Tirado-Valencia, P., & Lee, S. (2020). Volunteering attitude, mental well-being, and loyalty for the non-profit religious organization of volunteer tourism. *Sustainability, 12*(11), 1–16. https://doi.org/10.3390/su12114618

Han, H., Lee, S., & Hyun, S.S. (2020). Tourism and altruistic intention: Volunteer tourism development and self-interested value. *Sustainability, 12*(5), 1–14. https://doi.org/10.3390/su12052152

Han, H., Lee, S., Meng, B., Chua, B.L., & Ryu, H.B. (2020). The relative importance of volunteer tourism (sustainable/pro-social form of tourism) motivation factors for young tourists: A descriptive analysis by continents, gender, and frequency. *Sustainability, 12*(10), 1–21. https://doi.org/10.3390/SU12104002

Henderson, K.A., & Presley, J. (2003). Globalization and the values of volunteering as leisure. *World Leisure Journal, 45*(2), 33–37. https://doi.org/10.1080/04419057.2003.9674314

Hustinx, L. (2001). Individualisation and new styles of youth volunteering: An empirical exploration. *Voluntary Action, 3*(2), 57–76.

Hustinx, L., Shachar, I.Y., Handy, F., & Smith, D.H. (2016). Changing nature of formal service program volunteering. In D.H. Smith, R.A. Stebbins, & J. Grotz (Eds.), *The Palgrave handbook of volunteering, civic participation, and nonprofit associations* (1st ed., pp. 349–365). Palgrave.

Kontogeorgopoulos, N. (2017). Finding oneself while discovering others: An existential perspective on volunteer tourism in Thailand. *Annals of Tourism Research, 65*, 1–12. https://doi.org/10.1016/j.annals.2017.04.006

Lee, H.Y. (2020). Do the locals really feel good? Understanding wellbeing in volunteer tourism from the perspectives of host communities in Mongolia. *Journal of Tourism and Cultural Change*. https://doi.org/10.1080/14766825.2020.1800022

Magrizos, S., Kostopoulos, I., & Powers, L. (2021). Volunteer tourism as a transformative experience: A mixed methods empirical study. *Journal of Travel Research, 60*(4), 878–895. https://doi.org/10.1177/0047287520913630

McGehee, N.G. (2012). Oppression, emancipation, and volunteer tourism: Research propositions. *Annals of Tourism Research, 39*(1), 84–107. https://doi.org/10.1016/j.annals.2011.05.001

McGehee, N.G., & Santos, C.A. (2005). Social change, discourse and volunteer tourism. *Annals of Tourism Research, 32*(3), 760–779. https://doi.org/10.1016/j.annals.2004.12.002

McGloin, C., & Georgeou, N. (2015). 'Looks good on your CV': The sociology of voluntourism recruitment in higher education. *Journal of Sociology, 52*, 1–15. https://doi.org/10.1177/1440783314562416

Mcintosh, A.J., & Zahra, A. (2007). A cultural encounter through volunteer tourism: Towards the ideals of sustainable tourism? *Journal of Sustainable Tourism, 15*(5), 541–556. https://doi.org/10.2167/jost701.0

Meng, B., Chua, B.L., Ryu, H.B., & Han, H. (2020a). Volunteer tourism (VT) traveler behavior: Merging norm activation model and theory of planned behavior. *Journal of Sustainable Tourism, 28*(12), 1947–1969. https://doi.org/10.1080/09669582.2020.1778010

Meng, B., Ryu, H.B., Chua, B.L., & Han, H. (2020b). Predictors of intention for continuing volunteer tourism activities among young tourists. *Asia Pacific Journal of Tourism Research, 25*(3), 261–273. https://doi.org/10.1080/10941665.2019.1692046

Mostafanezhad, M. (2013). The geography of compassion in volunteer tourism. *Tourism Geographies: An International Journal of Tourism Space, Place and Environment, 15*(2), 318–337. https://doi.org/10.1080/14616688.2012.675579

Mostafanezhad, M. (2014). Volunteer tourism and the popular humanitarian gaze. *Geoforum, 54*, 111–118. https://doi.org/10.1016/j.geoforum.2014.04.004

Mustonen, P. (2006). Volunteer tourism: Postmodern pilgrimage? *Journal of Tourism and Cultural Change, 3*(3), 160–177. https://doi.org/10.1080/14766820608668493

Polus, R.C., & Bidder, C. (2016). Volunteer tourists' motivation and satisfaction: A case of Batu Puteh Village Kinabatangan Borneo. *Procedia - Social and Behavioral Sciences, 224*, 308–316. https://doi.org/10.1016/j.sbspro.2016.05.490

Pompurová, K., Sokolová, J., Cole, D., Marčeková, R., & Kožiak, R. (2020). Are visitors interested in volunteer tourism? Evidence from Slovakia. *Entrepreneurship and Sustainability Issues, 7*(4), 3339–3353. https://doi.org/http://jssidoi.org/jesi/

Prince, S., & Ioannides, D. (2017). Contextualizing the complexities of managing alternative tourism at the community-level: A case study of a Nordic Eco-village. *Tourism Management, 60*, 348–356. https://doi.org/10.1016/j.tourman.2016.12.015

Proyrungroj, R. (2017). Host-guest relationship in the context of volunteer tourism. *European Journal of Tourism Research, 16*, 177–200.

Raymond, E.M., & Hall, C.M. (2008). The development of cross-cultural (mis)understanding through volunteer tourism. *Journal of Sustainable Tourism, 16*(5), 530–543. https://doi.org/10.1080/09669580802159610

Rehberg, W. (2005). Altruistic individualists: Motivations for international volunteering among young adults in Switzerland. *Voluntas: International Journal of Voluntary and Nonprofit Organizations, 16*(2), 109–122. https://doi.org/10.1007/s11266-005-5693-5

Shalbafian, A.A., & Zarandian, N. (2019). Volunteer tourism: An approach to realize spirituality (a new look of Iranian pro-poor tourism). *International Journal of Tourism and Spirituality, 4*(1), 9–32. https://doi.org/10.22133/IJTS.2019.95828

Simpson, K. (2004). "Doing development": The gap year, volunteer-tourists and a popular practice of development. *Journal of International Development, 16*, 681–692. https://doi.org/10.1002/jid.1120

Sin, H.L. (2009). Volunteer Tourism – "Involve me and I will learn"? *Annals of Tourism Research, 36*(3), 480–501. https://doi.org/10.1016/j.annals.2009.03.001

Smith, V.L., & Font, X. (2014). Volunteer tourism, greenwashing and understanding responsible marketing using market signalling theory. *Journal of Sustainable Tourism, 22*(6), 942–963. https://doi.org/10.1080/09669582.2013.871021

Stainton, H. (2016). A segmented volunteer tourism industry. *Annals of Tourism Research, 61*, 256–258. https://doi.org/10.1016/j.annals.2016.09.011

Steele, J., Dredge, D., & Scherrer, P. (2017). Monitoring and evaluation practices of volunteer tourism organisations. *Journal of Sustainable Tourism, 25*(11), 1674–1690. https://doi.org/10.1080/09669582.2017.1306067

Taplin, J., Dredge, D., & Scherrer, P. (2014). Monitoring and evaluating volunteer tourism: A review and analytical framework. *Journal of Sustainable Tourism, 22*(6), 874–897. https://doi.org/10.1080/09669582.2013.871022

Thompson, J., & Taheri, B. (2020). Capital deployment and exchange in volunteer tourism. *Annals of Tourism Research, 81*. https://doi.org/10.1016/j.annals.2019.102848

Unger, L.S. (1991). Altruism as a motivation to volunteer. *Journal of Economic Psychology, 12*(1), 71–100. https://doi.org/10.1016/0167-4870(91)90044-T

Uriely, N., Reichel, A., & Ron, A. (2003). Volunteering in tourism: Additional thinking. *Tourism Recreation Research, 28*(3), 57–62. https://doi.org/10.1080/02508281.2003.11081417

Vada, S., Prentice, C., Scott, N., & Hsiao, A. (2020). Positive psychology and tourist well-being: A systematic literature review. *Tourism Management Perspectives, 33*, 100631. https://doi.org/10.1016/j.tmp.2019.100631

Wearing, S. (2001). *Volunteer Tourism: Experiences that make a difference*. CABI Publishing.

Wearing, S., Beirman, D., & Grabowski, S. (2020). Engaging volunteer tourism in post-disaster recovery in Nepal. *Annals of Tourism Research, 80*, 102802. https://doi.org/10.1016/j.annals.2019.102802

Wearing, S., & McGehee, N.G. (2013). Volunteer tourism: A review. *Tourism Management, 38*, 120–130. https://doi.org/10.1016/j.tourman.2013.03.002

Weaver, D. (2015). Volunteer tourism and beyond: Motivations and barriers to participation in protected area enhancement. *Journal of Sustainable Tourism, 23*(5), 683–705. https://doi.org/10.1080/09669582.2014.992901

Zahra, A. (2006). The unexpected road to spirituality via volunteer tourism. *Tourism, 54*(2), 173–185.

11

THE FREEFALL OF VOLUNTEER LEADERS IN AUSTRALIAN GRASSROOTS ASSOCIATIONS

Christel Lorraine Mex

Introduction

I love the club I belong to, and volunteering has given me so many great opportunities that I would never have dreamt of. However, if you don't have a good spine (committee), none of this can happen!!

(survey respondent)

The genesis of this research began with anecdotal observations during my role as the first General Manager of the Office for Volunteers in South Australia (2001–2004), then as Executive Officer of the State's *Volunteering Strategy* (2013–2015), and currently as an elected official for my local council. Through this real-life experience, I witnessed numerous annual general meetings of community groups where few members volunteered to join the committee. To find answers to these problems, I completed a PhD as part of an Australian Research Council funded project entitled *Creating and Sustaining a Strong Future for Volunteering in Australia* (LP140100528).

Most Australians are involved in or touched by a grassroots association (Mex, 2019). Whether to enjoy a hobby, sport or generally serve the community, these undertakings cannot occur without volunteer leaders who coordinate activities and lead others. This chapter specifically examines the volunteer leaders of grassroots associations (GAs) and, by extension, regular members, to determine why leadership nominations are declining. It also identifies motivations and barriers to leadership, and what interventions can assist GAs in becoming more sustainable into the future.

In their qualitative study of volunteer groups in Australia, Leonard and Onyx (2003, p. 195) found community organisations were a "valuable source of both strong and loose ties" and provided members with opportunities to expand their networks. A leading scholar of GAs, David Horton Smith (2000, p. 7) defines them as:

...locally based, significantly autonomous, volunteer-run, formal nonprofit (i.e., voluntary) groups that manifest substantial voluntary altruism as groups and use the associational form of organization and, thus, have official memberships of volunteers who perform most, and often all, of the work/activity done in and by these nonprofits.

DOI: 10.4324/9780367815875-13

A volunteer leader is defined as any member of a committee or board of a GA who does not earn a salary or receive remuneration. Nesbit et al. (2017b, pp. 915–916) described leaders of associations as "providing shared vision, direction and strategy; focus on motivating and developing people without the use of formal reward" and "may include board members and chairs, elected volunteer officers, committee chairs [and] informal leaders".

Regular members of GAs, by contrast, are defined as individuals who join an association to participate in the activities of the association but do not partake in any leadership responsibilities. Van Puyvelde et al. (2017) found some associations were 'commoditizing membership' by selling benefits such as access to facilities, training, or social programs. Others have penned numerous terms to describe these 'chequebook' members of associations, such as 'free-riders', 'slacktivists' and 'pay 'n' players' (Holmes & Slater, 2012; Howard & Gilbert, 2008; Kristofferson, White & Peloza, 2014).

In South Australia, GAs have been experiencing a long-term decline of members since 1985 (Mex, 2019) and the participation rate of people who serve on committees has fallen from 17% in 2006 to 14% in 2016 (Harrison Research, 2016a). Many grassroots organisations are struggling, especially with replenishing their management committees. According to the *General Social Survey* published by the Australian Bureau of Statistics (2019), volunteering rates have declined from 36.2% in 2010 to 28.8% in 2019. In addition, the survey also found involvement in social groups had fallen significantly in the same period, from 62.5% to 50.0%. The decline of volunteering in Australia has been an ongoing trend, with participation dropping during periods of economic downturn, particularly in the 1990s, with service clubs, sport and social clubs, and youth organisations such as Scouts and Guides, being significantly affected (Lyons, 2001). As the retiring president of the now-closed South Australian Association of School Parent Clubs, Jenice Zerna explained to a local newspaper, she "and other long-serving committee members were simply worn out", with "most people saying we don't have the time to go to meetings and things like that" (Williams, 2016).

The evidence from both the literature and data uncovered in this study suggests that fewer people are nominating to join volunteer committees in Australia. This reflects similar patterns elsewhere (Nesbit et al., 2017b; Posner, 2015). If the leadership ranks of Australia's grassroots organisations are in freefall, can these organisations survive? Was Putnam (2000) right to imply this type of volunteering will die out with the 'long civic generation', as will those who Goss (1999, p. 379) described as the "civic torchbearers" for civil society? Or as others believe, it could be merely a case of the natural 'wax and wane' of group evolution (Fischer, 2005; Wuthnow, 1998), with people volunteering in different ways and other group settings (Rotolo & Wilson, 2004).

Review of the literature

There is little academic research on GAs, and even less on their leaders (Schneider & George, 2011; Soteri-Proctor et al., 2017). Most of the studies are written from the perspective of nonprofit associations that employ staff and engage volunteers through formal volunteer programs (Kunreuther & Edwards, 2011; Ockenden & Hutin, 2008; Oppenheimer & Warburton, 2014; Posner, 2015). Brudney and Meijs (2009) maintained that poor volunteering experiences could damage the reputation of volunteer-involving associations across communities and reduce the pool of people willing to volunteer. As Posner (2015) observed in his study of sporting associations in the USA, volunteer leaders' poor behaviour is a significant problem due to the vast numbers of volunteers who are influenced by these leaders. GAs are becoming increasingly important worldwide, and there is a considerable lack of research on the characteristics and criteria for selecting their leaders (Nesbit et al., 2017b). This, in turn, makes it more challenging for them to recruit leaders and build internal positive relationships within their associations (Hoye, 2006).

Leaders of GAs create organisations or take up leadership roles out of a sense of community need and personal passion. Many do not understand the extent of accountability and governance required upon incorporation. As Rochester (1999, p. 18) pointed out, "management concepts such as control and supervision are alien to these kinds of organizations, which operate on the basis of teamwork and personal leadership". In her in-depth case study of a Canadian softball league, Sharpe (2003) concluded that professionalism was a significant factor in the decline of its membership. Volunteer leaders, who lead other association members, operate with restricted authority, especially since they are not paid employees and do not function under a command and control system (Bowers, 2012). Hemming (2011, p.104) observed that many GAs do not bother with official rules or formalities in their early years, and "[y]ou don't find many clubs or societies with positions such as 'meeting organiser', 'head person' or 'she who invites speakers'".

While governance obligations and regulations may appear to be necessary and protect individuals, it introduces red tape for leaders and committee members of small associations (Hutchison & Ockenden, 2008; King, 2017; Oppenheimer, 2001; Pearce, 1993). This has been cited why some people leave volunteering and leadership positions (Brueckner, Holmes & Pick, 2017; Hedley, 1995; Kreutzer & Jager, 2011). In their report on the impact of public policy on volunteering, Hutchison and Ockenden (2008, p. 7) found the formalisation of management structures in small associations "may also threaten the inclusiveness of volunteering and sideline volunteers from decision-making processes".

Despite the challenges, some GA leaders stay in leadership roles to keep their associations going. In the sport volunteer sector, Nichols (2005) called these leaders 'stalwarts', with their main motivations being a combination of altruism, recreation and self-development, while detecting their numbers declined due to over-work. Cnaan (1991) found most leaders of small associations are uncontested at elections due to the lack of rewards of such positions, and it was similarly difficult to find members to volunteer and serve on management committees. More recently, Nesbit et al. (2017b) concurred, committee or board members are often recruited through personal social networks with selection criteria which is "often ambiguous and quite open-ended, usually favouring individuals who are seemingly competent, willing to serve, and have time for the position" (p. 919). These dynamics can lead to oligarchical tendencies, with committee members facing little change year after year and associations being driven by a small elite (Paull & Redmond, 2011; Perkins & Poole, 1996). In some cases, committee members of grassroots associations gradually become entrenched and develop into what Huxley (1962, p. 152) dubbed "village Napoleons", managing their organisations in an undemocratic and dictatorial fashion. With the same people putting their hand up to lead year after year, often because nobody else does, members can become complacent and defer to the experience and passion of existing (and in many cases) founding leaders. It can lead to apathy and passivity amongst members (Knoke & Wood, 1981).

Given the extra demands and time commitments placed on volunteer committee members of GAs, it is often difficult to recruit leaders and replenish retiring committee members. This may be because these roles are more demanding than task-based or episodic volunteering with little extra reward (Bowlby & Lloyd Evans, 2011; Wanwimolruk, 2014). Due to high-level skills in communication, organisation and networking, volunteer leaders tend to do much more work compared to other volunteers and tend to experience burnout, particularly when they do not receive adequate recognition or achieve their goals for the association

(Baggetta, Han & Andrews, 2013; Nesbit et al., 2017a; Ockenden & Hutin, 2008; Pearce, 1993; Rochester, 1999).

In his survey of over 8,000 sport volunteers in the UK, Nichols (2005) found the sector was over-dependent on a small number of volunteers who contributed most of the work. The most demanding roles involved leadership and coordination. Holmes et al. (2015) proposed organisations are better placed to convert people to volunteering when they recognise the barriers to volunteering and identify interventions that could help potential volunteers become more willing, capable and available to volunteer. It can be surmised from the literature that recent complexities of committee work have flow-on consequences to the quality of leadership in GAs. Poor leadership has a negative effect on regular members' attitude, their commitment and the recruitment and retention of future leaders.

Methods

This study aimed to identify motivations and barriers to volunteer leadership in grassroots associations and explore potential recruitment strategies. A mixed-methods research approach was implemented with 12 focus groups and a survey of association members in South Australia. The focus groups were held in 2016 in three demographically diverse local government areas and were held with volunteer leaders and regular members of GAs. Participants were from diverse interest areas including sport, arts, civic associations, recreation clubs, health services, emergency services and environmental groups. The survey was conducted in 2017–2018 with questions informed by the focus group findings, through an email invitation to a list of 5,000 associations in South Australia. A little over 1,500 people responded to the survey, with 75% of the respondents from grassroots associations. There was a great diversity of sectors included, with sport, the arts, community development and recreation all well represented.

Demographically, most of the respondents were from older age segments of the population which mirrored the profile of volunteers in South Australia, where the largest age group of volunteers ranges from 65 to 74 (Harrison Research, 2016a). Just over half of the respondents were female (55%), which is also a similar ratio to all of South Australian volunteers (Harrison Research, 2016b). Most respondents were frequent volunteers, serving or participating in their association at least once a week. Most respondents volunteered with groups that were quite small, with 65% having less than 100 members. There were over 5,000 written comments within the survey which added rich qualitative data. This engagement with the questions demonstrated a solid interest in the survey's subject matter by the respondents.

Results

The main themes emerging from the data included motivations for joining committees, barriers keeping potential leaders from serving and leadership behaviours. These themes will now be addressed in more detail.

Regarding the motivations for joining committees, the focus group participants agreed the most significant reason was to have fun and meet new people. One committee member said, "we have a really good group of people who I've met through doing this ... and I get a buzz out of it". Enjoyment was followed closely by self-satisfaction as a significant benefit of committee membership, strongly aligned to secondary motivations of a sense of responsibility to the association and wanting to see it succeed. "You're helping other people who need help and I think that's most important", said one committee member. Several of the participants mentioned they could influence outcomes for the association by being on the committee and make things happen. As a young committee member said, "I was frustrated with the governance and the structure in place, and rather than complaining about it ... I got involved". Helping to build their career was mentioned by a few participants, and comments were similar to those about building skills. A regular member said if she joined a committee it would, "help me find a job".

The survey respondents had similar views, but 90% reported pursuing their interests and using their skills were the top reasons they joined committees, closely followed by being a crucial part of their social life and learning new things. Many also reported being on a committee gave them a sense of identity and helped them feel needed. This concurs with Chetkovich and Kunreuther's (2006) findings of those who felt strongly about an issue, or express themselves in meaningful ways, often volunteered to lead associations.

In both the focus group and survey, regular members of associations were asked why they do not join committees, and committee members were questioned why they believed members did not participate. Focus group participants from both cohorts reported the primary barrier to joining committees was the misuse of power and internal politics, followed by lack of time, red tape and a lack of self-confidence. Research in Australia identified workplace bullying as an issue for volunteers and paid employees (Paull & Omari, 2015), and negative volunteer experiences are a barrier to future volunteering (Brudney & Meijs, 2013; Warburton & Paynter, 2006). The mental anguish participants experienced through committee work was quite disturbing, as a regular member from a focus group reported:

> ... the politics can be so draining and I'm just shying away from it now. I want to be able to sleep at night without worry, worry, worry', and 'people who lie and backstab, they are poisonous on committees – and they tend to gravitate towards positions they see as powerful too.

The survey data revealed the current availability of volunteer leaders for GAs is quite disturbing. Sixty-seven percent of respondents reported their associations were experiencing difficulty recruiting leaders, compared to 49% from associations with paid staff. Also, 78% of respondents from GAs reported minimal turnover in leadership, compared to 66% from larger nonprofit organisations. When asked what the main barriers were for people joining committees, the fear of responsibility was reported as a leading factor, followed closely by the lack of time, perceived lack of skills, disliking committee politics and personality conflicts.

Another significant barrier to joining committees was the phenomenon of 'red tape'. Red tape has also been well documented in the literature as a major barrier to volunteering in general (Haski-Leventhal, Meijs & Hustinx, 2009; Obar, Zube & Lampe, 2012; Sharpe, 2003; Warburton & McDonald, 2009). The evidence of red tape raised in the focus groups ranged from macro-level regulations of state and local governments to self-imposed antiquated committee procedures embedded in constitutions. Survey participants elaborated on red tape over 200 times in open-ended comments, reporting that it made their work too complicated, took too much time and was a significant impediment. Both focus group participants and survey respondents gave many examples of rules described as red tape, imposed by government authorities. Examples include a focus group participant who said, "by the time you've done the health hazards, the food handling, risk assessments, you're snowed under with the red tape", and another survey responded complained "people are fed-up with the red tape that has been foisted on volunteers".

Due to historical reasons and a reluctance to change, some committees bring unnecessary bureaucracy and red tape upon themselves. The increasing complexity of leading GAs, brought on by increased awareness of risk management and legal issues, requires a continuous updating of skills. Perhaps without these skills, leaders of GAs become too rule-bound and fall back on command and control methods they experienced as employees. Focus group participants confirmed that the culture of committees could be too formal. As two regular members said, "You can't just slip in a random comment about something, you have to always put it on the agenda beforehand" and, "it was all so officious and rule-bound". Whether these rules and regulations come from an external government authority or are imposed by the committee themselves, they need to be recognised as a significant barrier to committee work. The barrier of red tape has frequently been cited in the literature as a reason why people leave volunteering and leadership positions (Brueckner et al., 2017; Kreutzer & Jager, 2011).

Another barrier reported, especially by regular members, was a lack of self-confidence to nominate for committees which stemmed from a sense of alienation and "not feeling good enough". One hundred sixty-seven survey respondents provided comments regarding the issue, with one committee member commenting "[some people] feel they are inadequate to the task", and, "a lack of confidence and self-belief is a significant factor". Nine focus group participants were 45 years of age or under. While often mentioning this feeling of alienation, they were also exasperated by what was perceived as old-fashioned and boring meeting procedures. Two under-35 year old regular members from focus groups said, attending meetings, "it's a little bit daunting", and "it's a bit of a spectacle…ridged, alienating and separatist". The presence of over-formality in meeting procedures seemed to increase the young regular members' feelings that they did not have the skills to be leaders.

Focus group participants cited good leadership as the most essential success factor for retaining committee members. They mentioned several attributes of good leaders, including conflict resolution skills, seeing the big picture and not getting bogged in minutiae and practical chairing skills. Other characteristics included the ability to delegate and motivate others, set direction, organise tasks and create a good culture by "selling the vision… to be part of something". Some young committee members across the focus groups concurred and saw good leadership as being flexible and enabling. They cited examples of where they introduced changes such as specific working groups, breaking down roles, dealing with strong personalities and "leading from behind". This concurs with Boehm and Staples (2005) qualitative study, which found that successful leaders of GAs were visionary, had good relationships with followers and emphasised collaboration.

Similarly, survey respondents rated good leadership highly with over 80% rating positive attitude, mutual respect and good communication as attributes of successful committees. There were many comments in the survey relating to behaviours, with many complaining about personal experiences with poor leadership. For example, committee members saying, "committees need people without personal agendas", "looking at the big picture and what's best for all". There were quite a few comments in the survey, especially by regular members, suggesting that flexibility was an essential attribute for committees, such as having "imagination, open-mindedness", "willingness to change", "inclusiveness" and "[being] open to recruiting new members with different skills and characteristics". A significant challenge for GAs that have a concentration of power with the same people serving a committee year after year, includes the 'burn-out' of existing committee members leading to inflexibility, which is a barrier to prospective committee members (Baggetta et al., 2013). As two focus group participants said, "It really got driven on the back of a couple of individuals who just worked tirelessly", and, "the same person has been in the chair for 25 years, and there is nothing in the constitution to make him resign, and it's pretty frustrating for people if they feel like they have something to offer".

Other reasons given for committee difficulties were a general declining of association membership and an ageing membership. These two are related as many participants observed young people are not joining associations, which gradually reduces the total number of association memberships, making the general pool of willing committee members much smaller. This pattern supports Putnam's (2000) argument about the decline of the 'long civic generation'. One committee member in a focus group said, "Our club was a very big club back 32 years ago, it's now down to about 45 members". Other committee members had the same concerns stating, "Committees haven't got new blood, younger blood, coming through", and, "I think that what exercises all of our minds in every group I've been involved in, is how to get younger people involved and I don't know what the answer is". The survey showed similar results, with 78% of GA respondents agreeing that their associations have mostly the same individuals serve on their committees year after year. There were several comments made by survey respondents regarding oligarchic behaviours, such as "it's hard to change a culture when the same people have done things the same way for years". Many of the above reasons for committee difficulties are interrelated and can lead to barriers to committee participation. It poses the question, if improved governance and leadership could address these barriers, can more regular members be recruited to be leaders of GAs?

Discussion

Volunteer committees in GAs are groups of people, sometimes strangers, coming together to advance a common cause. Nesbit et al. (2017b, pp. 915–916) acknowledged the importance of these volunteer leaders as they "provided shared vision, direction and strategy ... without the use of formal reward and punishment systems". Leaders of GAs need to demonstrate a variety of useful leadership practices to attract and retain people to their committees (Kouzes & Posner, 2003), but they have the added challenge of having to do this without offering a salary (Wilson, 1973 cited in Andrews et al., 2010). Unlike larger non-governmental organisations (NGOs), these GAs do not have the support of human resource managers and access to training opportunities to build the capacity of volunteer leaders. Associations with paid staff often provide training in leadership practices to develop the capacity of leaders. The findings from this study indicated GAs would benefit from this training. However, leaders of these organisations are operating on their own without support in an increasingly volatile and changing environment.

The data identified many incidences of the misuse of power in committees including personality clashes, bullying behaviours, internal politics and governance malpractice. This outranked 'lack-of-time' as the largest barrier to joining committees, especially by regular members. This finding is related to the primary motivations for people joining committees in the first place. Individuals agreed to take up committee positions for personal satisfaction, enjoyment and making new friends. Suppose major barriers are not addressed, such as misuse of power and poor governance. In that case, it is logical to expect people will not join committees experiencing these problems as they are seeking a positive experience from their volunteering. Most GAs operate at a local level, and it does not take long for word-of-mouth to publicise committee problems across a community. It can be assumed that many committees are unaware of their reputations due to the 'group think' that comes with oligarchic behaviours. Hence the significant barrier of misuse of power could go unnoticed in grassroots committees. As Posner (2015) found in his study of sporting clubs, the attitude of regular members of associations was heavily impacted by their leaders' behaviour.

The data reveals a set of cause and effect relationships concerning the issues facing GAs today. When discussing barriers to join committees and committee difficulties, participants and respondents often talked as though they were one and the same. This was the case regarding 'red-tape', which is both a barrier and a difficulty and can be imposed from outside or created by outdated internal governance procedures. Conversely, the reasons why people served on committees were often factors for success, such as enjoyment and a sense of satisfaction which help give organisations a good reputation and high membership levels.

Learnings from the data and literature indicate improving committee culture and policies should remove some of the barriers to serving on volunteer committees. GAs facing difficulties could consider improving their leadership practices, which may also increase membership numbers. This, in turn, would increase the recruitment pool for new committee members. For this to happen, more support needs to be available for volunteer leaders to improve their leadership practices so they can prepare for inevitable changes that are impacting GAs. As Baggetta et al. (2013) observed, more investment is needed in training leaders to improve committees' collective skills.

Conclusion

There are many online resources, workshops and support programs on offer for the non-profit sector. Still, the focus group and survey data showed little evidence GAs were aware of these services. These services include training offered by the volunteering infrastructure which includes the Volunteering Australia network, Our Community, Connecting Up, Pro-Bono Australia and State Government programs such as StarClub in South Australia. Despite their shared constituency, it appears these service providers may be working in isolation. If all training providers were to work together in an integrated approach with increased government support, there would be cascading benefits for GAs. All levels of Government, by funding the volunteering infrastructure and aligning existing services, could support a new capacity building program across Australia. This could be delivered in partnership with local councils, regional development boards, business enterprise centres and the volunteer infrastructure.

However, for this to be successful GAs themselves need the motivation to participate in the program. This means the leaders of GAs must recognise the need for further education to adapt to a changing world. The biggest challenge for GAs facing a decline of members and leader nominations is to recognise there is a problem and that the root of the problem might be poor organisational culture and negative behaviours. Trzcinski and Sobeck (2012) found associations who were willing to change and listen to their members were more likely to succeed and even grow. As Barnes and Nelson (2014, p. 15) remind us, "by looking ahead and breaking with tradition when necessary, associations can cultivate membership growth and engagement".

The importance of GAs should be more acknowledged by all levels of government and the volunteering infrastructure. Without the thousands of small sporting clubs, craft groups, resident groups, men's sheds, service clubs, advocacy and self-help groups, many Australians would be living in isolation, with consequences for mental and physical health. Our democracy would also be weakened as fewer people are engaged in civic society. The leaders of GAs, who are vital to civil society, need capacity building and access to support. This assistance, in the form of education, training and policy improvements, will help their organisations become more sustainable for the long-term benefit of Australian society.

References

Australian Bureau of Statistics (2019). *General social survey summary results.* Australian Bureau of Statistics.

Andrews, K.T., Ganz, M., Baggetta, M., Han, H., & Lim, C. (2010). Leadership, membership, and voice: Civic associations that work. *American Journal of Sociology, 115*(4), 1191–1242. https://doi.org/0002-9602/2010/11504-0006$10.00

Baggetta, M., Han, H., & Andrews, K.T. (2013). Leading associations: How individual characteristics and team dynamics generate committed leaders. *American Sociological Review, 78*(4), 544–573. https://doi.org/10.1177/0003122413489877

Barnes, J., & Nelson, J. (2014). *Exploring the future of membership.* ASAE Foundation.

Boehm, A., & Staples, L. (2005). Grassroots leadership in task-oriented groups: Learning from successful leaders. *Social Work with Groups, 28*(2), 77–96, https://doi.org/10.1300/J009v28n02_06

Bowers, K.M. (2012). *An Exploration of the Leadership Behavior of Volunteer Leaders.* PhD Thesis, Indiana Wesleyan University.

Bowlby, S., & Lloyd Evans, S. (2011). Between state and market: The non-profit workforce in a changing local environment. *Social Policy and Society, 10*(3), 417–427. https://doi.org/10.1017/S1474746411000133

Brudney, J.L., & Meijs, L. (2009). It ain't natural: Toward a new (natural) resource conceptualization for volunteer management. *Nonprofit and Voluntary Sector Quarterly, 38*(4), 564–581. https://doi.org/10.1177/0899764009333828

Brudney, J.L., & Meijs, L. (2013). Our common commons: Policies for sustaining volunteer energy. *Nonprofit Policy Forum, 4*(1), 29–45. https://doi.org/10.1515/npf-2012-0004

Brueckner, M., Holmes, K., & Pick, D. (2017). Out of sight: Volunteering in remote locations in Western Australia in the shadow of managerialism. *Third Sector Review, 23*(1), pp. 29–49. https://search.informit.org/doi/10.3316/informit.812787283013878

Chetkovich, C.A., & Kunreuther, F. (2006). *From the ground up: Grassroots organizations making social change.* Cornell University Press.

Cnaan, R.A. (1991). Neighborhood-representing organizations: How democratic are they? *The Social Service Review, 65*(4), 614–634. https://www.jstor.org/stable/30012431

Fischer, C.S. (2005). Bowling alone: What's the score? *Social Networks, 27*(2), 155–167. https://doi.org/10.1016/j.socnet.2005.01.009

Goss, K.A. (1999). Volunteering and the long civic generation. *Nonprofit and Voluntary Sector Quarterly, 28*(4), 378–415. https://doi.org/10.1177/0899764099284002

Harrison Research (2016a). *Volunteering in South Australia, unpublished data.* Office for Volunteers.

Harrison Research (2016b). *Volunteering in South Australia.* Office for Volunteers.

Haski-Leventhal, D., Meijs, L., & Hustinx, L. (2009). The third party model: Enhancing volunteering through governments, corporations and educational institutes. *The Journal of Social Policy, 39*(1), 139–158. https://doi.org/10.1017/S0047279409990377

Hedley, R. (1995). Inside the voluntary sector. In J.D. Smith, C. Rochester & R. Hedley (Eds.), *An introduction to the voluntary sector* (pp. 97–111). Routledge.

Hemming, H. (2011). *Together: How small groups achieve big things.* Hachette.

Holmes, K., Haski-Leventhal, D., Lockstone-Binney, L., Meijs, L., & Oppenheimer, M. (2015). *Identifying potential volunteers: Introducing the convertibles.* Paper presented to ARNOVA, Chicago.

Holmes, K., & Slater, A. (2012). Patterns of voluntary participation in membership associations: A study of UK heritage supporter groups. *Nonprofit and Voluntary Sector Quarterly, 41*(5), 850–869. https://doi.org/10.1177/0899764011420881

Howard, M.M., & Gilbert, L. (2008). A cross-national comparison of the internal effects of participation in voluntary organizations. *Political Studies, 56*(1), 12–32. https://doi.org/10.1111/j.1467-9248.2007.00715.x

Hoye, R. (2006). Leadership within Australian voluntary sport organization boards. *Nonprofit Management and Leadership, 16*(3), 297–313. https://doi.org/10.1002/nml.108

Hutchison, R., & Ockenden, N. (2008). *The impact of public policy on volunteering in community-based organizations.* Institute for Volunteering Research.

Huxley, A. (1962). *Island: A novel.* Chatto & Windus.

King, D. (2017). Becoming business-like: Governing the nonprofit professional. *Nonprofit and Voluntary Sector Quarterly, 46*(2), 241–260. https://doi.org/10.1177/0899764016663321

Knoke, D., & Wood, J.R. (1981). *Organized for action: Commitment in voluntary associations.* Rutgers University Press.

Kouzes, J.M., & Posner, B.Z. (2003). *The Leadership Practices Inventory (LPI).* John Wiley & Sons.

Kreutzer, K., & Jager, U. (2011). Volunteering versus managerialism: Conflict over organizational identity in voluntary associations. *Nonprofit and Voluntary Sector Quarterly, 40*(4), 634–661. https://doi.org/10.1177/0899764010369386

Kristofferson, K., White, K., & Peloza, J. (2014). The nature of slacktivism: How the social observability of an initial act of token support affects subsequent prosocial action. *The Journal of Consumer Research, 40*(6), 1149–1166. https://www.jstor.org/stable/10.1086/674137

Kunreuther, F., & Edwards, M. (2011). Grassroots associations. In M. Edwards (Ed.), *The Oxford handbook of civic society* (pp.55–67). Oxford University Press.

Leonard, R., & Onyx, J. (2003). Networking through loose and strong ties: An Australian qualitative study. *Voluntas, 14*(2), 189–203. https://doi.org/10.1023/A:1023900111271

Lyons, M. (2001). *Third sector: The contribution of nonprofit and co-operative enterprises in Australia.* Allen & Unwin.

Mex, C. (2019.) *Stepping up or stepping out? Volunteer leaders in Australian grassroots associations.* PhD Thesis, Flinders University, South Australia.

Nesbit, R., Moldavanova, A., Cavalcante, C.E., Jochum, V., & Lin, N. (2017a). Conducive meso-and micro-contexts influencing volunteering. In D.H. Smith, R.A. Stebbins & J. Grotz (Eds.), *The Palgrave Handbook of volunteering, civic participation and nonprofit associations* (pp. 607–631). Palgrave Macmillan.

Nesbit, R., Rimes, H., Smith, D.H., Akhter, S., Akingbola, K., Domaradzka-Widla, A., Kristmundsson, O.K., Malunga, C., & Sasson, U. (2017b). Leadership and management of associations', In D.H. Smith, R.A. Stebbins & J. Grotz (Eds.), *The Palgrave Handbook of volunteering, civic participation and nonprofit associations* (pp. 915–949), Palgrave Macmillan.

Nichols, G. (2005). Stalwarts in sport. *World Leisure Journal, 47*(2), 31–37. https://doi.org/10.1080/04419057.2005.9674393

Obar, J.A., Zube, P., & Lampe, C. (2012). Advocacy 2.0: An analysis of how advocacy groups in the United States perceive and use social media as tools for facilitating civic engagement and collective action. *Journal of Information Policy, 2,* 1–25. https://doi.org/10.5325/jinfopoli.2.2012.0001

Ockenden, N. & Hutin, M. (2008). *Volunteering to Lead: A study of leadership in small, volunteer-led groups.* Institute for Volunteering Research.

Oppenheimer, M. (2001). 'We all did voluntary work of some kind': Voluntary work and labour history. *Labour History,* (81), 1–11. https://www-jstor-org.helicon.vuw.ac.nz/stable/pdf/27516800.pdf?refreqid=excelsior%3Aa0be87a3bb78f5e8f3b9eb91bf253144

Oppenheimer, M., & Warburton, J. (2014). *Volunteering in Australia.* The Federation Press.

Paull, M., & Omari, M. (2015). Dignity and respect: Important in volunteer settings too! *Equality, Diversity and Inclusion: An International Journal, 34*(3), 244–255. https://doi.org/10.1108/EDI-05-2014-0033

Paull, M., & Redmond, J. (2011). Succession in community organisations: Newcomers and the 'purple circle'. *Third Sector Review, 17*(2), 1–14. https://search.informit.org/doi/10.3316/informit.824274991288342

Pearce, J.L. (1993). *Volunteers: The organizational behavior of unpaid workers.* Routledge.

Perkins, K.B., & Poole, D.G. (1996). Oligarchy and adaptation to mass society in an all-volunteer organization: Implications for understanding leadership, participation, and change. *Nonprofit and Voluntary Sector Quarterly, 25*(1), 73–88. https://doi.org/10.1177/0899764096251006

Posner, B.Z. (2015). An investigation into the leadership practices of volunteer leaders. *Leadership & Organization Development Journal, 36*(7), 885–898. https://doi.org/10.1108/LODJ-03-2014-0061

Putnam, R.D. (2000). *Bowling alone: The collapse and revival of American community.* Simon & Schuster.

Rochester, C. (1999). One size does not fit all: Four models of involving volunteers in small voluntary organisations. *Voluntary Action, 1,* 8–20.

Rotolo, T., & Wilson, J. (2004). What happened to the 'long civic generation'? Explaining cohort differences in volunteerism. *Social Forces, 82*(3) 1091–1121. https://www.jstor.org/stable/3598367

Schneider, S.K., & George, W.M. (2011). Servant leadership versus transformational leadership in voluntary service organizations. *Leadership & Organization Development Journal, 32*(1), 60–77. https://doi.org/10.1108/01437731111099283

Sharpe, E.K. (2003). It's not fun any more: A case study of organizing a contemporary grassroots recreation association. *Society and Leisure, 26*(2), 431–452. https://doi.org/10.1080/07053436.2003.10707630

Smith, D.H. (2000). *Grassroots Associations*. SAGE Publications.

Soteri-Proctor, A., Smith, D.H., Pospíšilová, T., Roka, K., & Yu, P. (2017). Local or grassroots associations: Micro-associations. In D.H. Smith, R.A. Stebbins & J. Grotz (Eds.), *The Palgrave Handbook of volunteering, civic participation and nonprofit associations* (pp. 807–835). Palgrave Macmillan.

Trzcinski, E., & Sobeck, J.L. (2012). Predictors of growth in small and mid-sized nonprofit organizations. *Administration in Social Work, 36*(5), 499–519. https://doi.org/10.1080/03643107.2011.627492

van Puyvelde, S., Cornforth, C., Dansac, C., Guo, C., & Smith, D.H. (2017). Governance, boards, and internal structures of associations. In D.H. Smith, R.A. Stebbins & J. Grotz (Eds.), *The Palgrave Handbook of volunteering, civic participation and nonprofit associations* (pp. 894–914), Palgrave Macmillan.

Wanwimolruk, M. (2014). *Volunteerism: Alive and well or dying quietly?* Royal New Zealand Plunket Society.

Warburton, J., & McDonald, C. (2009). The challenges of the new institutional environment: An Australian case study of older volunteers in the contemporary non-profit sector. *Ageing and Society, 29*(5), 823–840. https://doi.org/10.1017/S0144686X09008484

Warburton, J., & Paynter, J. (2006). *Barriers and benefits of volunteering for seniors*. National Seniors Productive Ageing Centre, Brisbane, Queensland.

Williams, T. (2016). Parent group has been a class act but bell is tolling. *The Advertiser*, 25 October 2016.

Wuthnow, R. (1998). *Loose Connections: Joining together in America's fragmented communities*. Harvard University Press.

12

VOLUNTEERING IN COMMUNITY SPORTS ORGANISATIONS AND ASSOCIATIONS

Geoff Nichols

Defining community sport organisations and volunteering

In common with volunteer led organisations, it is difficult to define community sport organisations (CSOs) and therefore difficult to measure them. There is not a clear distinction between a CSO and an informal group who play sport together. For example, at what point does a group of people who meet weekly to go running constitute a CSO? This presents a difficulty in deciding the degree of formality required for an organisation to qualify as a CSO. One defining characteristic is affiliation to a national governing body (NGB) of sport but an early survey of sports clubs in Scotland (Allison, 2001) noted that a football club may, or may not, be affiliated. If it is not affiliated, this limits the use of NGB records to quantify clubs or use as a sampling frame in surveys. Further, a CSO may be a group of friends who compete in a five-a-side league in a sports centre; or it may just be a group who meet weekly to play football. In either case, there will not be a record of these informal associations. In CSOs the distinction between formal and informal is not distinct, but is a matter of degree. Even the CSOs who are affiliated to NGBs vary in the degree of formality, as measured by the adoption of a range of formally defined processes (Nichols, 2015).

The difficulty in defining a CSO reflects a general difficulty of defining volunteering as formal or informal and of measuring informal volunteering. In their review of six UK surveys between 1982 and 2012, Lindsey et al. (2018) note the inconsistency of distinguishing between 'formal volunteering', defined as taking place in an organisation, and 'informal volunteering', defined as out of an organisation, for example, supporting a relative. This inconsistency makes it difficult to compare results across surveys. This has become more important in measuring CSOs and their role in contributing to sports participation because in England there has been a trend away from participation in clubs and towards informal participation, out of the club structure (Harris, Nichols & Taylor, 2017).

Alternative approaches to conceptualising CSOs

The theoretical conceptualisation of CSOs has implications for the research questions asked and the policy implications derived from these. Specifically, analysis starting from economic theory and theory applied to for-profit organisations can be contrasted with analysis starting

DOI: 10.4324/9780367815875-14

from sociological or political theory. An economic approach to CSOs, and any volunteer led organisation, has defined them in a residual sense, as meeting needs that have not been met by the public and commercial sectors. For example, Weisbrod (1978) analysed the voluntary sector as meeting the demand for goods where there is insufficient consensus on their value to justify public provision or to make such provision effectively. A particular justification for this in leisure has been that the extremely varied leisure preferences of individuals can be best met by small groups acting collectively (Gratton & Taylor, 1991). Within this economic framework, non-profit organisations are defined as ones which do not distribute their surplus resources to those in control of the organisation (Steinberg, 2006). The dominance of this perspective in the USA is reflected in the titles of American textbooks, such as Powell and Steinberg's (2006) *The Non-profit Sector* and in journal titles such as *Non-profit and Voluntary Sector Quarterly.*

The starting point of this approach leads to theory used in the analysis of paid work and for-profit organisations being applied to the non-profit sector. One implication is that volunteering and its contribution to society can be attributed a monetary value and this may be used to advocate its importance in policy. A study in England (Taylor et al., 2003) estimated the value of the time contributed by formal and informal sports volunteers together at over £14 billion in 2002. In that study, CSOs accounted for the large majority, 83% of the hours and value contributed to formal volunteering in sport, although the study was careful to note that this did not imply the sports volunteers could be replaced by paid workers. Representing the well-being benefits of volunteering experienced by the volunteers themselves in monetary terms can also be used to try and promote volunteering, by making potential volunteers aware of these benefits (Sport England, 2016, discussed below). A further implication of starting analysis from theory applied to paid work is that advice on managing volunteers tends to adapt human resource management practices from the for-profit sector (for example, McCurley, Lynch & Jackson, 2012).

In contrast, a sociological or political approach to CSOs conceptualises them as an association of individuals grouped together to attain some purpose or govern some activity defined by them as important to their interests. Politically, advocates of associational democracy claim that the active involvement of volunteers can empower them and the communities they are providing services for, and devolving the provision of public services to voluntary self-governing associations maximises human liberty (Nichols, Forbes, et al., 2015). Thus, the type of association represented by a CSO has been seen as a characteristic of associational democracy (Hirst, 1994) and facilitated by a pluralist society. This is illustrated by the seminal study of the voluntary sector in leisure by 'Hoggett and Bishop' (1985) in which they described volunteer led organisations as "organising around enthusiasms". The driving force of the organisation is the enthusiasms of the members, which are expressed collectively. Thus, in CSOs the collective enthusiasm is for some form of sport, for example, a love of cricket or football. While an economic approach distinguishes between for profit and not-for-profit organisations by how surplus resources are distributed (to those in control of the organisation or to the members of the organisation), a sociological approach distinguishes the private, public, and voluntary sectors of provision by their driving forces. Billis (2010) defined these respectively as: generating profit, achieving social objectives, and the values and enthusiasms of the members. This distinction is particularly useful in understanding organisations, such as CSOs, in which volunteers take roles of governance and delivery, and in which they determine the strategic aims of the organisation. This contrasts with organisations in which governance is by paid managers and volunteers only take roles of delivery, although these may also be defined as non-profit from an economic perspective.

The sociological perspective applies concepts such as social capital and social inclusion to understand CSO membership and its benefits (for example, Nichols, Tacon & Muir, 2013; Ibsen, Nichols & Elmose-Østerlund, 2016). This perspective is critical of rational systems approaches applied to management of CSOs in which volunteers are regarded as resources to be managed, rather than as the driving force of the enthusiasms which gives the organisation its purpose (Rochester, 2013; Schulz, Nichols & Auld, 2011). The contention of this section is that an economic approach has dominated studies of the voluntary sector as a provider of society's needs. However, alternative sociological or political perspectives offer useful insights. While there is only scope to contrast the implications of the two approaches briefly, this is especially relevant to understanding CSOs.

The numbers of CSOs and their importance as a context for volunteering

The numbers of CSOs

Difficulties in defining a CSO make it harder to estimate how many CSOs there are, and their importance as a context for volunteering. In England, estimates have been made through surveying national governing bodies of sport (NGBs). In most countries the NGBs are representative bodies of the relevant clubs and provide a structure for competition, and an administrative structure at national, regional, and county levels. This is common across Europe (Ibsen et al., 2016). Using NGB records, the most recent estimate in 2017 (Shibli & Barrett, 2017) concluded there were 74,233 CSOs in England. Association Football accounted for 30% of these, and ten sports accounted for 76% of all CSOs. A comparison with the previous English survey in 2015, using the same 60 NGBs in each year, suggested an increase of 3% of CSOs over these two years. However, this change is unreliable because of changes in the way individual NGBs record the number of affiliated clubs. Comparisons of estimates of the number of CSOs in England, which again used telephone interviews with NGBs in 2002 and 2009 (Taylor et al., 2003; Taylor, Barrett & Nichols, 2009), show a decline in the number of clubs by 15%. This is consistent with the trends away from club participation noted above (Harris et al., 2017).

The role of CSOs in sports participation and volunteering

Estimates of the importance of CSOs for sports participation and volunteering can be made from national surveys, or from surveys of CSOs. In the first case, the surveys are rarely conducted with the purpose of examining the role of CSOs, so the results do not give this detail. For example, using European-wide surveys, Table 12.1 shows the percentage of the population in different countries who take part in sports in a club and who participate in voluntary work that supports sport.

The variations between countries, in levels of sports participation in clubs and in sports related volunteering, will reflect different levels of overall sports participation and the importance of the CSO structure. However, the survey asking about volunteering did not specify the context, so we cannot tell from this the proportion of sports related volunteering which takes place in CSOs. This is illustrated by Norway, which exhibits low sport participation in clubs, but high sports volunteering. This is because participation may take place out of clubs, for example skiing events (a popular sport in Norway) and in schools. These other

Table 12.1 Sports club participation and participation in voluntary work that supports sporting activity (people 15 years and over)

	Sports club participation (%)	Participation in voluntary work that supports sport (%)
Netherlands	27	18
Switzerland	25	22
Denmark	25	18
Germany	24	10
Belgium	16	9
France	16	7
Austria	13	12
EU (average)	12	7
United Kingdom	11	10
Spain	7	4
Italy	7	3
Norway	7	25
Hungary	7	6
Greece	5	3
Poland	3	3

Adapted from: Breuer, C., Hoekman, R., Nagel, S., & van der Werff, H. (Eds.) (2015). *Sports clubs in Europe: A cross-national comparative perspective* (p. 423). Springer. (nineteen countries are included in the source).

contexts for sports participation are supported by volunteers. Neither does the table show the proportion of sports participation that takes place in CSOs.

Although national surveys may not give details of volunteering in CSOs, they generally show that sport related volunteering is important. For example, the Eurobarometer *75.2 Voluntary Work* survey (European Parliament, 2011) shows that of those who 'have a voluntary activity on a regular or occasional basis', the most common of 15 categories of activity is 'sports club or club for outdoor pursuits' (24%). Similarly, the most recent survey of volunteering in the UK (McGarvey et al., 2019) found that sport/exercise, was the fourth most significant area of volunteering, taken part in by 15% of volunteers. Even the latest survey of sports participation and volunteering in England, *Active Lives* (Sport England, 2020) asks about six volunteer roles, but not where they take place. Thus, it is not possible to quantify the amount of volunteering in a sports club.

The most precise results on volunteering in CSOs from national surveys are from one conducted in England in 2002 (Taylor et al., 2003), specifically to research sport volunteering. It found that 14.8% of adults in England volunteered for sport. Volunteering in CSOs accounted for 75% of all formal sport-related volunteering, so was by far the most important context. Although there has been a decline in the number of CSOs since, it is still likely that they are the most significant context for sport volunteering.

Alternative estimates of sports participation and volunteering have been made from surveys of CSOs. These have to be qualified by how representative the samples are of CSOs: it is probable that the larger and more formally organised CSOs will be more likely to respond to surveys, thus inflating the results. Nevertheless, in 2015, it was possible to use the same questionnaire in surveys of CSOs across ten European countries as part of a study of social inclusion and volunteering in sport clubs in Europe (Breuer et al., 2017). From this study the median number of adult members in a CSO varied between 45 in Spain to 270 in the Netherlands. This survey categorised volunteers as 'in fixed positions' or 'not in fixed positions', and estimated volunteers as a proportion of members in each of the ten countries. The volunteers in fixed positions as a proportion of members varied from 13% in Germany to 23% in Spain. The variation may reflect different structures of CSOs, or interpretations of the question. The same survey estimated the proportion of paid staff to members, which varied between 1% and 5%. This confirms that CSOs are heavily reliant on volunteers for their management and delivery.

Surveys of CSOs in England in 2009, 2011, 2013, and 2017 gave similar results for the number of volunteers, adult members, and junior members per club, thus giving a broadly consistent picture, despite the different samples. Estimates of the number of volunteers were 21, 20, 24, and 37 volunteers respectively. The same surveys showed ranges of between 104 and 120 adult members, and 83 and 107 junior members per club. Rather than suggesting trends, the different survey results probably illustrate that none of the samples accurately represented CSOs and that each relied on one respondent in a CSO having accurate information. They may also illustrate differences in the prompts used. This is always a difficulty researching volunteering as a prompt for volunteering in general will elicit a different response to prompts for a set of defined roles. Thus, an apparent increase in the number of volunteers between 2013 and 2017 is likely to illustrate differences in the survey methods. The same English surveys have distinguished between adult members who play and those who do not. This is useful in showing the CSO members who are just volunteers supporting the participation of others, or who are just members for the social benefits. For example, the 2013 survey found that only 68 of the 114 adult members played sport. Despite minor differences in the survey results, there is a consistent picture of clubs being important for adult and junior participation.

The broader contribution of CSOs to society

Thus, a clear contribution of CSOs is the opportunity for people to participate in sport, with its associated benefits for physical and mental health. The 2017 survey of English clubs (Sport and Recreation Alliance, 2017) found the annual membership fees to be £108 for adults participating in sport, and £68 for juniors. There may be additional match fees, however these figures were compared to average membership of a health and fitness gym, which was £579. Thus, volunteers are providing opportunities for participation at a much cheaper rate than the commercial sector of leisure. Enabling young people to develop sporting skills, confidence, commitment, and sporting capital will encourage participation in later life (Rowe, 2015). One would expect these benefits to be especially important for those for whom cost is the greatest barrier. Thus, one might expect CSOs to play a role in government policies to promote health (Sport England, 2016).

As the large proportion of non-playing adult members suggests, CSOs provide a reward of conviviality for members in common with many organisations led by volunteers. A recent survey of club members across Europe found this reward was more important than sporting success (Elmose-Østerlund et al., 2017). A CSO can be a source of social capital, "a set of relationships and shared values created and used by multiple individuals to solve collective problems in the present and future" (Ostrom, 2009, p. 22). A decline in the numbers of CSOs might reflect a decline in collective social capital, as Putnam put it (2000), more 'bowling alone'. In contrast to the claims that CSO participation may contribute to social capital, commentators have noted that volunteering and membership of CSOs may have a limited impact as members are not representative of society in terms of gender, age, ethnicity, and social class (Doherty & Misener, 2008; Vermeulen & Verweel, 2009). So there is no automatic process by which clubs contribute to bridging social capital, that is links between different groups, although they contribute to bonding between people with similar enthusiasms (Nichols, Tacon & Muir, 2013).

It has been argued that by facilitating volunteering, CSOs can contribute to rewards of life satisfaction and health, both for the volunteers themselves, and through the further sports participation it facilitates (Fujiwara, Kudrna & Dolan, 2014). As noted above, the contribution of volunteering can be attributed a monetary value and this can be used to advocate for political support. For example, in England an estimate of the contribution of volunteers in CSOs to society was made by the 'Join In' report (2014) which estimated a contribution of £53bn per year. This was achieved by adding up the economic value of the time given by the volunteers, the value of the personal well-being, mental and physical benefits to the volunteers themselves, and the participation capacity and benefits that every volunteer enabled through providing opportunities for others to take part in sport. Of course, adding up these three components produced the maximum possible estimate of the contribution which was considerably greater than the 2002 estimate of £14bn (Taylor et al., 2003). As an example of associational democracy it has been argued that CSOs can generate a spillover effect from participation in the club, to participation in the democratic process of broader society. These arguments are rehearsed in Ibsen et al. (2019) but without demonstrating evidence of the effect, it would be very hard to substantiate.

The relation of CSOs to government policy

Overall, government support for CSOs can be made for all the reasons discussed above, but there are considerable methodological difficulties in showing a causal relationship between policy interventions and outcomes. For example, how exactly would a subsidy of CSO use of public facilities contribute to health promotion or an increase in general well-being? Consequently, policy is influenced by the, mainly positive, value judgements which have promoted sport in general since the 19th century (Coalter, 2007). A further difficulty is in incorporating volunteer led organisations into policy initiatives. For example, a survey of English CSOs in 2009 found very few had any idea of what government policy for sport was (Harris, Mori & Collins, 2009), so if they had contributed to these policy aims it was as an incidental by-product of their activity. On the other hand, case studies of English clubs have showed how they have used government grants for initiatives such as promoting sports participation for women and young people (see, example, Nichols & James, 2017).

Across Europe, CSOs are integrated into government policy by varying degrees. For example, in Denmark, CSOs are much more reliant on direct and indirect public support. They receive free use of local government sports facilities and are reimbursed for two thirds of the cost of using private facilities for members below the age of 25. Local government also provides a fee to CSOs for each member aged 25 and under. Possibly the greater independence of CSOs from government in England is a consequence of their historical development in which they have always been autonomous from the state (Ibsen et al., 2016).

Motivations and barriers to volunteering in CSOs

Examining the motivations of volunteers in CSOs illustrates the difficulties of researching volunteer motivations in general and the balance between altruism and self-interest.

A review of motivations of volunteers in sport (Nichols, 2017) aggregated the results of 12 surveys, although limitations were that they used different prompts and questions, different samples, and were conducted between 1997 and 2014. As in all research into volunteers' motives, responses reflect social desirability. In summary, the motivations were:

> being a parent of a child participating in a sports club and wanting to help friends and family; social benefits such as conviviality; giving something back to the community; wanting to remain involved with the sport after retiring from playing; enthusiasm, or passion, for a sport; attachment to a club and a desire to see it do well; using existing skills and learning new ones; satisfaction with achievements as a volunteer; pride in helping a club do well; and to enhance one's own employability.
>
> *(Nichols et al., 2019, p. 6)*

An important aspect of volunteering in CSOs is the overlap between sports participation and volunteering. Although the surveys were not all about volunteers in CSOs, five of these ten motives specifically link sports volunteering with sports participation, of the volunteer or their children, or with affiliation to the sports club.

Developing volunteering – a balance of altruism and self-interest?

The motivations above include a combination of self-interest and altruism, although as in all volunteer research one has to be wary of socially acceptable responses to questionnaire prompts. Cnaan, Handy and Wadsworth's (1996) influential research into the meaning of volunteering concluded that the key defining characteristic was for it to be at the altruistic end of this dimension. The link between sports participation and volunteering in CSOs means that CSOs may offer the context in which the habit of volunteering can be developed in young people. Values and identities developed at this age will remain fairly constant, while individuals' circumstances and opportunities change. This draws on insights from research which showed how volunteering changed over people's lives (Brodie et al., 2011) but was directed by fairly constant values as they reacted to different circumstances and opportunities.

Sport may offer parallel pathways through participation and volunteering. For example, a young person may be introduced to sport at school or in a club. They may be socialised into an expectation of volunteering to support the organisation in which participation takes place and carry this over to university. While they are aware sports volunteering can be a marketable experience the other rewards may then influence the decision to volunteer later in life when they have a young family. Volunteering in a CSO will provide other rewards. Identification with a club grows as people continue to volunteer as a member of the club committee after their children have stopped participating in the club and left home, providing a sense of purpose and social rewards in retirement. Thus, motivations to volunteer change in response to circumstances and experience, but depend on an understanding of the value of volunteering established at an early age (Nichols et al., 2019).

However, volunteering, including in CSOs, can be promoted by government as 'selling' volunteering by treating individuals as motivated by self-interest and extrinsic rewards (Sport England, 2016). This is consistent with the hegemonic conception of volunteering and individuals within economic theory as pursuing competitive self-interest (see Weisbrod, 1978). In contrast, research has identified a range of values present in individuals across all societies. These include having concern for the welfare of all (Rowarth, 2017). In general, a contrast between economists and sociologists is that the former believe preferences are private and constant while the latter believe values can be internalised through socialisation. If values can be socialised, the dominant conception of the individual as a consumer (Shrubsole, 2012) is self-fulfilling. In practice, policy to promote volunteering will use a balance between self-interest and altruism, reflecting the position of different people on Cnaan et al.'s spectrum (1996), with the proviso that promoting volunteering through self-interest could inculcate those values.

The position of CSOs in the leisure market

We can think of the leisure market as the private, public, and voluntary sectors of provision (Roberts, 2016). These sectors of provision are competing for time, enthusiasm, and spending power. In the voluntary sector the act of volunteering to create leisure opportunities for others, for example, managing a sports club, is at the same time a leisure experience for the volunteer (Nichols, Holmes & Baum, 2013). Thus, the competition for time applies both to the producer of leisure, the volunteer, and the consumer, the CSO member.

This competition has intensified. When surveys ask why people do not volunteer in sport, or in anything else, the most common responses are they do not have enough time, which is often qualified by the socially acceptable responses of the competing time at paid work or with the family. Time diary studies support this for some people. In the UK they show "the substantial increases in overall workloads over the last 50 years have been in the main a feature affecting those who are more highly educated, in higher status jobs and in dual-career households with small children" (Gershuny & Sullivan, 2019, p. 300). The household time budget has been strained by the substantial increase in the proportion of women in the workforce since the 1970s such that couples who might have worked roughly a combined total of five or six days a week in the 1950s now work seven or eight days. At the same time "parents are dedicating substantially more time to their children" (Bregman, 2017, p. 136). So, for these people, the constraint of available time on volunteering is real. However, for the population as a whole, time diaries in the UK show a very small increase in leisure time between 1961 and 2015. Thus, the perceived lack of time to volunteer needs another explanation.

In the 1990s Robinson and Godbey (1997), again basing their analysis of time use on diary studies, attributed a perceived lack of time to an inescapable bombardment of new opportunities to use it. This forced individuals to make ever more choices with their leisure time. Since then, these 'opportunities' have grown exponentially. A handful of technology companies such as Facebook, Twitter, Snapchat, YouTube, and Instagram have built highly addictive functions into their technology which has become continually accessible on mobile phones. It is estimated that "people touch, swipe or tap their phone 2,617 times a day" (Lewis, 2017, p. 26). As Rosenstein, the inventor of Facebook's 'like' button noted, "Everyone is distracted...all of the time" (Lewis, 2017, p. 27). A consequence is that a handful of tech companies control the attention of billions of people (Harris, 2017). The competition for attention is accentuated as these companies compete with each other for advertising revenue. The implications on leisure are enormous and under-researched. For example, the cohort of young people who were adolescents at the same time as mobile devices for accessing the internet became commonly used display a rise in mental health problems, an increased concern with personal safety, an unwillingness to engage with conflicting ideas, and a decline in civic involvement (Twenge, 2017). The implications for how we think, what we think, and the political process, are huge (Lewis, 2017).

Thus a barrier to sports volunteering and sports participation is available time, and that time has been successfully competed for by the private sector. It is interesting to relate this insight to changes in sports participation. In England, a decline in traditional team sports has been balanced by an increase in sports participation as an individual or a small group, such as running, cycling, and keep fit activities (Harris et al., 2017). Contributory factors include: a fragmentation of leisure time across the population, a trend towards individualism in a post-modern society, and a decline in civic engagement. However, it is the traditional team sports, such as cricket and association football, which take most time, and require two full teams and officials to commit to that shared time. There has been a considerable increase in private gym membership, which can cater for the fragmented availability of time. The overall conclusion is that the private sector is winning the competition for time, expenditure, and enthusiasm.

Why are there not CSOs in the USA in comparison to Europe?

A different competitive balance between the private, public, and voluntary sectors may also account for the complete lack of CSOs for adults in the USA. A review in 2007 commented that, "there is not a sports club tradition in the United States that is comparable to the kind found elsewhere in the world" (Sparvero, Chalip & Green, 2007, p. 248). Another review concluded that:

> sport in North America (including Canada to a lesser degree) is characterized by [...] commercialization, professionalization and media involvement. [...] Much sport in North America is driven by a concern with developing a commercially viable, elite focused and professionally oriented entertainment spectacle" [with] "little emphasis on sport for all.
>
> *(Slack & Parent, 2006, p. 486)*

Many communities have sports leagues for baseball and American football, which are for children. The two most prominent are Little League for baseball and softball, and Pop Warner Leagues for American football, which are franchise organisations, unlike NGBs in Europe or Australia. As in Europe, sports opportunities are also offered by national youth organisations, supported by volunteers, but these are not for adults. The main aim of these organisations is the development of young people through sport. Volunteers support these organisations, but there is little information available. Similarly, in Canada, the major community sport of hockey is focused on developing young people through hockey, supported by adult volunteers, rather than adult clubs which have junior sections, which is the more common situation in Europe.

Differences in CSOs between countries in Europe, the role of volunteers, and their relation to government, can be understood through their different historical development and more lately, their position on a welfare state typology, which is reflected in the level of social inequality (Ibsen et al., 2016). Historical influences are illustrated in England. Briefly, codified sport in its modern form was developed as a consequence of rules being agreed between groups of public (fee-paying, private) schools to permit competition. These were enshrined in the national governing bodies of sport, such as the Football Association (FA), which were founded towards the end of the 19th century (Nichols & Taylor, 2015). The philanthropic tradition was one of the roots of voluntary action (Rochester, 2013) within the changing "total social organisation of labour" (Taylor, 2005). An ethos of volunteer led organisations was enshrined in the word 'amateur' in many of the newly founded NGBs. Other European countries had their own traditional sports but the clubs structure and codified sports in England had a major influence. While traditional national sports (such as gymnastics in Germany, and shooting and skiing in Norway) had also been organised in club structures, to these were added sports codified in England, especially association football (Ibsen et al., 2016). Most clubs were formed for adult participants, and then extended to offer junior sections. Clubs developed independently of the state and from the commercial sector in leisure.

A second explanation of differences is provided by an adaption of Esping-Andersen's (1990) welfare state typology in which states can be distinguished by the extent of redistribution of wealth and the level of universality of solidarity. Esping-Andersen (1990, pp. 21–22) distinguished between three main types of welfare state:

- The Liberal (Anglophone) welfare state (USA as the most typical – a low level of redistribution and welfare rights).
- The Conservative/Corporatist welfare state (Germany as the most typical).
- The Universalist welfare state (Sweden as the most typical – a high level of redistribution and welfare rights).

Of course, this is a more recent influence than the historical factors. We have already noted how CSOs in Denmark are strongly linked to government polices to promote sports participation, through their high levels of direct and indirect subsidies. The welfare state typology is related to the level of income inequality, and universalist welfare states have lower levels of inequality. Across Europe higher inequality is associated with lower levels of sports participation, leisure time, volunteering, and generalised trust (Veal, 2016; Veal & Nichols, 2017).

Extending these insights to the USA, in an "historical overview of philanthropy, voluntary associations and non-profits organisations in the United States", Hall (2006) highlights the instability of society in the USA at the time corresponding to before, and during, the development of CSOs and NGBs in Europe, and coinciding with industrialisation. Individual states enacted their own legislations to govern associations and federalism would have made the establishment of national level organisations more difficult. The development of national level organisations was also limited by the size of the country, the Civil War (1861–1865), and a disrupted society, which continued to be divided sharply by race. Large numbers of immigrants between the 1830s and 1890s brought their own different cultures. Society was divided by religion and national identity, and parts of the country were colonised at a different pace, resulting in considerable differences between the slave states in the South, the North Eastern seaboard, and the more recently colonised Mid-West. In contrast, modern sport in European countries could develop from more homogeneous cultural traditions and in relatively more stable circumstances.

Hall also notes that in the decades leading up to the civil war there was a "penetration of market values into every aspect of American life" (2006, p. 41). De Tocqueville foresaw the emergence of an "aristocracy of manufactures whose members would take on the power of administrators of a vast empire" (de Tocqueville, 1988, p. 187). These are key points because while the voluntary sector in Europe flourished as people had more free time and money, at the same time, there was a low level of public provision and the private sector was not so well developed. Thus, the voluntary sector could expand into this space. In contrast, between 1870 and 1930, the USA was experiencing a rapid expansion in professional sports franchises (Burden & Church, 2012) and the commercial sector gained dominance. An explanation for this domination of market values and the commercial sector in general is the more rapid pace of industrialisation, the consolidated power of capitalist interests, and the fragmented cultural base of the new society. A general explanation is that a hegemonic view of leisure as consumption prevailed over one of leisure as experience generated from one's own resources (Clarke & Critcher, 1985). Further, in comparison to the other factors influencing the more recent development of CSOs in Europe, the USA has a very low level of state intervention in the market, and is one of the most unequal countries in the world. This corresponds to low levels of sports participation, leisure time, and volunteering (Veal, 2016; Veal & Nichols, 2017).

Thus in the USA, the development of CSOs was restricted by the ideological dominance of the free market and the ability of the private sector to expand rapidly into a leisure market for time and resources, which had not previously been colonised by the voluntary sector. At the same time, the role of the state reflects a view that the private sector should be favoured, which extends to state support for commercial sport. For example, corporate sponsorship of stadiums is categorised as philanthropy rather than advertising so it is exempt from taxation, college athletics departments may have taxpayer-subsidised loans to pay for stadium construction, and college sports are also exempt from business income tax on their commercial activities. In the competitive US leisure market for time, money, and enthusiasm, the private sector is more dominant than in other countries.

Conclusion

CSOs are important as they provide opportunities to play sport for adults and juniors, with its associated benefits. In Europe they are a major context for sports volunteering. The limited scope of this chapter has developed discussions which relate to volunteering in general. CSOs illustrate the difficulties of defining a volunteer led organisation and volunteering, and thus difficulties of measurement. The one example of a national survey dedicated to sports volunteering was able to identify the numbers of volunteers in CSOs. In other surveys it has been necessary to extrapolate from general surveys of volunteering, or surveys of CSOs themselves. Surveys of CSOs are limited by the need to use NGB records as sampling frames, the willingness of CSOs to respond, the consistency of the way questions are asked, and are reliant on one respondent in a CSO having the information required.

These difficulties of measurement compound the difficulties of evaluating the contribution to society. Depending on the assumptions built into aggregations of volunteering, sports participation, and its broadest social benefits, these can be made to produce very big claims for the benefits of CSOs and volunteers. However, these never consider potential negative impacts of sports volunteering which might include the strain on individual volunteers and the 'opportunity cost' of using that time somewhere else. Contrasting economic and sociological conceptualisations of volunteering draws attention to the implications of these for the way CSOs are understood and for policy. There are many studies of the motivations of volunteers in CSOs but these illustrate the difficulties of trying to aggregate surveys with different questions. They do illustrate the particular relationship between sports participation and sports volunteering and the debate between altruism and self-interest, and raise considerations of how best to promote volunteering.

The overall picture of organisations competing in a market for time, spending, and enthusiasm suggests the private sector is gaining dominance. In particular, understandings of the power and influence of social media over the last ten years are a critical research question. The implications for volunteering and leisure are very significant. Lastly, comparing the USA with Europe showed how the lack of CSOs in the USA can be attributed to historical factors, especially at the time the voluntary sector was developing in Europe.

Different levels of state intervention in the market, and more recently, of inequality, also play a part. While brief mention has been made of CSOs in Australia and their limited existence in Canada, the discussion has been limited to roughly a seventh of the world's population in high-income countries (Rosling, Rosling & Rönnlund, 2018). The way leisure is thought of in developed countries is as a product of disposable income, time, and technology. This underpinned the emergence of CSOs in Europe at the end of the 19th century. The potential in countries coming up to this level of development will depend on the balance between the three sectors of leisure provision. This historical perspective suggests that in the countries where it exists, the network of CSOs is a valuable cultural resource, which appears to be stable, but may be more fragile than we think. It is difficult to see how this network of organisations could be established in present day society, given the pressures on volunteering and the changed leisure market. It is the legacy of particular historical circumstances.

References

Allison, M. (2001). *Sport clubs in Scotland: Research Report 75.* Sport Scotland.

Billis, D. (Ed.) (2010). *Hybrid organizations and the third sector: Challenges for practice, theory and policy.* Macmillan International Higher Education.

Bregman R. (2017). *Utopia for realists: How we can build the ideal world.* Hachette.

Breuer, C., Feiler, S., Llopis-Goig, R., Elmose-Østerlund, K., Bürgi, R., Claes, E., Gebert, E., Gocłowska, S., Ibsen, B., Lamprecht, M., Nagel, S., Nichols, G., Perényi, S., Piątkowska, M., Scheerder, J., Seippel, Ø., Stamm, H., Steinbach, D., van der Roest, J.-W., ... van der Werff, H. (2017). *Characteristics of European sports clubs. A comparison of the structure, management, voluntary work and social integration among sports clubs across ten European countries.* Department of Sports Science and Clinical Biomechanics, University of Southern Denmark.

Brodie, E., Hughes, T., Jochum, V., Miller, S., Ockenden, N., & Warburton, D. (2011), *Pathways through participation: What creates and sustains active citizenship?* National Council for Voluntary Organisations.

Burden, W., & Church, A.G. (2012). Sport in North America. In M. Li, E. Macintosh, & G.A. Bravo (Eds.), *International sport management.* Human Kinetics.

Clarke, J., & Critcher, C. (1985). *The devil makes work.* MacMillan.

Cnaan, R., Handy, F., Wadsworth, M. (1996). Defining who is a volunteer: Conceptual and empirical considerations. *Nonprofit and Voluntary Sector Quarterly, 25*(3), 364–383. https://doi.org/10.1177/0899764096253006

Coalter, F. (2007). *A wider social role for sport: Who's keeping the score?* Routledge.

Doherty, A., & Misener, K. (2008). Community sport networks. In M. Nicholson & M.R. Hoye (Eds.), *Sport and social capital* (pp. 114–141). Butterworth-Heinemann.

Elmose-Østerlund, K., Ibsen, B., Nagel, S., Scheerder, J., Breuer, C., Claes, E., Feiler, S., James, M., Llopis-Goig, R., Nichols, G., Perenyi, S., Piątkowska, M., Seippel, Ø., Steinbach, D., van der Roest, J.-W., & van der Werff, H. (2017). *Explaining similarities and differences between European sporTs Clubs: An overview of the main similarities and differences between sports clubs in ten European countries and the potential explanations.* Centre for Sports, Health and Civil Society, Department of Sports Science and Clinical Biomechanics, University of Southern Denmark.

Esping-Andersen, G. (1990). *The three worlds of welfare capitalism.* Polity Press.

European Parliament, Directorate-General for Communication, Directorate for relations with citizens (2011). *European Parliament Special Eurobarometer 75.2, Voluntary work.* https://www.europarl.europa.eu/pdf/eurobarometre/2011/juillet/04_07/SA_en.pdf

Fujiwara, D., Kudrna, L., & Dolan, P. (2014). *Quantifying and valuing the wellbeing impacts of culture and sport.* Department for Culture, Media and Sport. https://www.gov.uk/government/uploads/system/uploads/attachment_data/file/304899/Quantifying_and_valuing_the_wellbeing_impacts_of_sport_and_culture.pdf

Gershuny, J., & Sullivan, O. (2019). *What we really do all day: Insights from the centre for time use research.* Pelican.

Gratton, C., & Taylor, P. (1991). *Government and the economics of sport.* Longman.

Hall, P.D. (2006). A historical overview of philanthropy, voluntary associations and non-profit organisations in the United Sates, 1600–2000. In W. Powell & R. Steinberg (Eds.), *The non-profit Sector: A research handbook* (pp.32–65). Yale University Press.

Harris, S., Nichols, G., & Taylor, M. (2017). Bowling even more alone: Trends towards individual participation in sport. *European Sport Management Quarterly, 17*(3), 290–311. https://doi.org/10.108 0/16184742.2017.1282971

Harris, S., Mori, K., & Collins, M. (2009). Great expectations: Voluntary sports clubs and their role in delivering national policy for English sport. *VOLUNTAS: International Journal of Voluntary and Nonprofit Organizations, 20*(4), 405–423. https://doi.org/10.1007/s11266-009-9095-y

Harris, T. (2017). How a handful of tech companies control billions of minds every day. https://www.ted.com/ talks/tristan_harris_how_a_handful_of_tech_companies_control_billions_of_minds_every_day

Hirst, P. (1994). A*ssociative democracy.* Polity Press.

Hoggett, P., & Bishop, J. (1985). *The social organisation of leisure.* Sports Council.

Ibsen, B., Elmose-Østerlund, K., Feiler, S., Breuer, C., Seippel, Ø., van der Roest, J.-W., & Scheerder, J. (2019). Democratic participation in voluntary associations: A multilevel analysis of sports clubs in Europe. *VOLUNTAS: International Journal of Voluntary and Nonprofit Organizations, 30*(5), 1148–1163. https://doi.org/10.1007/s11266-018-00088-y

Ibsen, B., Nichols, G., & Elmose-Østerlund, K. (2016). *Sports club policies in Europe. A comparison of the public policy context and historical origins of sports clubs across ten European countries.* University of Southern Denmark. http://www.sdu.dk/en/om_sdu/institutter_centre/c_isc/forskningsprojekter/sivsce/ sivsce_publications

Join In (2014). *Hidden diamonds: Uncovering the true value of sport volunteers.* Join In.

Lewis, P. (2017, October 17). Everyone is distracted all of the time. *The Guardian Weekly.* https://www. pressreader.com/uk/the-guardian-weekly/20171027/281505046465121

Lindsey, R., Mohan, J., Bulloch, S., & Metcalfe, E. (2018). *Continuity and change in voluntary action: Patterns, trends and understandings.* Policy Press.

McCurley, S. Lynch, R. and Jackson, R. (2012). *The complete volunteer management handbook.* Directory of Social Change.

McGarvey, A., Jochum, V., Davies, J., Dobbs, J., & Horning, L. (2019). *Time well spent.* NCVO. https://www.ncvo.org.uk/policy-and-research/volunteering-policy/research/time-well-spent

Nichols, G. (2017). *Volunteering in community sports associations: A literature review.* Brill. https://doi. org/10.1163/24054933-12340015

Nichols, G., Forbes, D., Findlay-King, L., & MacFadyen, G. (2015). Is the asset transfer of public leisure facilities in England an example of associative democracy? *Administrative Sciences, 5*(2), 71–87. https://doi.org/10.3390/admsci5020071

Nichols, G., Hogg, E., Knight, C., & Storr, R. (2019). Selling volunteering or developing volunteers. *Voluntary Sector Review, 10*(1), 3–18. https://10.1332/204080519X15478200125132

Nichols, G., Holmes K., with Baum, T. (2013a). Volunteering as leisure; leisure as volunteering. In T. Blackshaw (Ed.), *The Routledge International handbook of leisure studies* (pp. 456–467). Routledge.

Nichols, G., & James, M. (2017). *Social inclusion and volunteering in sports clubs in Europe: Findings for policy makers and practitioners in England and Wales.* University of Sheffield. https://www.sheffield.ac.uik/ management/staff/nichols/index

Nichols, G., Tacon, R., & Muir, A. (2013). Sports clubs' volunteers: Bonding in or bridging out? *Sociology, 47*, 350–367. https://doi.org/10.1177/0038038512441278

Nichols, G., & Taylor, P. (2015). Sport clubs in England. In C. Breuer, R. Hoekman, S. Nagel, & H. van der Werff (Eds.), *Sport clubs in Europe: A cross-national comparative perspective.* (pp. 141–167). Mulier Institute.

Ostrom, E. (2009). What is social capital? In V.O. Bartkus & J.H. Davis (Eds.), *Social capital: Reaching out, reaching in* (pp. 17–38). Edward Elgar.

Putnam R. (2000). *Bowling alone: The collapse and revival of American community.* Simon & Schuster.

Powell, W., & Steinberg, R. (2006). Introduction. In W. Powell & R. Steinberg (Eds.), *The non-profit sector: A research handbook* (pp. 1–12). Yale University Press.

Roberts, K. (2016). *The business of leisure.* Palgrave.

Robinson, J., & Godbey, G. (1997). *Time for life: The surprising ways Americans use their time.* Pennsylvania State University Press.

Rochester, C. (2013). *Rediscovering voluntary action.* Palgrave.

Rosling, H., Rosling, O., & Rönnlund, A.R. (2018). *Factfulness: Ten reasons we're wrong about the world– And why things are better than you think.* Sceptre.

Rowarth, K. (2017). *Doughnut economics: Seven ways to think like a 21st century economist,* Random House.

Rowe, N. (2015). Sporting capital: A theoretical and empirical analysis of sport participation determinants and its application to sports development policy and practice. *International Journal of Sport Policy and Politics*, 7(1), 43–61. https://doi.org/10.1080/19406940.2014.915228

Schulz, J., Nichols, G., & Auld, C. (2011). Issues in the management of voluntary sports organisations and volunteers. In B. Houlihan & M. Green (Eds.), *Handbook of sports development* (pp.432–445) Routledge.

Shibli, S., & Barrett, D. (2017). *Measuring the affiliated sport club market.* Unpublished report for Sport England.

Shrubsole, G. (2012). *Consumers outstrip citizens in the British media.* Open Democracy.

Slack, T., & Parent, M.M. (2006). *Understanding sport organizations: The application of organization theory.* Human Kinetics.

Sparvero, E., Chalip, L., & Green, B.C. (2007). United States. In: B. Houlihan & M. Green (Eds.), *Comparative elite sport development: Systems, structures and public policy* (pp. 242–272). Butterworth-Heinemann.

Sport and Recreation Alliance (2017). *Sports Club Survey Report, 2017.* Sports and Recreation Alliance.

Sport England. (2016). *Volunteering in an active nation.* Sport England.

Sport England. (2020). *Research, volunteering research.* Active Lives Adult Survey. Workforce. https://www.sportengland.org/know-your-audience/demographic-knowledge/workforce#research

Steinberg, R. (2006). Economic theories of non-profit organisations. In W.W. Powell & R. Steinberg (Eds.), *The non-profit sector: A research handbook* (pp. 117–139). Yale University Press.

Taylor, P., Barrett, D., & Nichols, G. (2009). *CCPR Survey of Sports Clubs 2009.* Project Report, Central Council of Physical Recreation, Sheffield Hallam University http://shura.shu.ac.uk/5090/

Taylor, P., Nichols, G., Holmes, K., James, M., Gratton, C., Garrett, R., Kokolakakis, T., Mulder, C., & King, L. (2003). *Sports volunteering in England 2002.* Sport England. https://www.sportengland.org/media/40043/valuing-volunteering-in-sport-in-england-final-report.pdf

Taylor, R. (2005). Rethinking voluntary work. In L. Pettinger, J. Parry, R.Taylor, & M. Glucksmann (Eds.), *A new sociology of work?* (Sociological review monographs) (pp. 119–135). Blackwell.

Tocqueville, A. de. (1988). The ancien regime. Dent. In P.D. Hall (2006). *A historical overview of philanthropy, voluntary associations and non-profit organisations in the United States, 1600–2000.* In W. Powell & R. Steinberg (2006) *The non-profit sector: A research handbook* (pp. 32–65). Yale University Press.

Twenge, J. (2017). *iGen: why today's super-connected kids are growing up less rebellious, more tolerant, less happy - and completely unprepared for adulthood - and what that means for the rest of us.* Simon & Schuster.

Veal, A.J. (2016). Leisure, income inequality and the Veblen effect: Cross-national analysis of leisure time and sport and cultural activity. *Leisure Studies*, 35(2), 215–240. https://doi.org/10.1080/0261 4367.2015.1036104

Veal, A.J., & Nichols, G. (2017). Volunteering and income inequality: Cross-national relationships. *VOLUNTAS: International Journal of Voluntary and Nonprofit Organizations*, 28, 379–399. https://doi.org/10.1007/s11266-016-9818-9

Vermeulen, J., & Verweel, P. (2009). Participation in sport: Bonding and bridging as identity work. *Sport in Society*, 12(9), 1206–1219. https://doi.org/10.1080/17430430903137886

Weisbrod, B.A. (1978). The voluntary non-profit sector. Lexington Books. In C. Gratton & P. Taylor (1991). *Government and the economics of sport.* Longman.

PART 3

Volunteering at events

13

ENHANCING VOLUNTEER SKILLS THROUGH MEGA SPORT EVENTS

Evidence from London 2012 Olympic Games

Niki Koutrou

Introduction

Mega sport events (MSEs), like the Olympic Games present an organisational and financial challenge for their hosts. Volunteers typically comprise the largest pool of personnel at MSEs, and their work in core service delivery is integral to the event's success and feasibility (Hoye et al., 2020). As such, they undertake a variety of duties, which are deemed crucial to support the event's operations, and their skills and knowledge complement those of the existing paid employees of the event (Allen & Shaw, 2009). London hosted the Games in 2012 and utilised 70,000 volunteers or Games Makers (GM) for a plethora of operational roles including hospitality, event, medical and athletes' services, transportation, and accreditation (Dickson & Benson, 2013). It was reported that out of these 70,000 volunteers, 40% were volunteering for the first time (Dickson & Benson, 2013). MSEs of this calibre attract individuals for different reasons compared to regular, long-term volunteers in sport clubs or other regional or national voluntary organisations. For example, a study by Koutrou and Pappous (2016) showed five main drivers for volunteering motivation in the context of the London 2012 Games: patriotism and community values, career orientation (gaining skills and developing networks), love of sport and the Olympic Games (desire to be part of a once-in-a-lifetime opportunity), interpersonal contacts (desire to build social networks and to make friendships) and personal growth (increase volunteer self-esteem and self-development). This study also offered insights to policymakers as to how a volunteering legacy of an MSE and its social benefits could have been leveraged and maximised, while transferring volunteer efforts across activities beyond the Games.

Research has shown that volunteering and other informal and extracurricular activities contribute to an individual's learning process, or personal and professional integration through tasks that are active, enjoyable, relevant, desirable and transferable to potential working situations (Handy et al., 2010). Non-formal learning, in particular, aims to train "active citizens" and "to create and use knowledge effectively and intelligently, on a continually changing basis" in knowledge societies (European Commission, 2000, p. 7). This type of learning often occurs unintentionally, and neither does it take place in organised settings nor is it systematised (Khasanzyanova, 2017).

DOI: 10.4324/9780367815875-16

Volunteering in sport, among other outcomes, enables participants to invest in their human capital, develop social capital, enhance or grow their social networks and integrate into their local communities (Kay & Bradbury, 2009; Welty Peachey et al., 2013). Further, career orientation, skill development and enhancing employment prospects features as one of the most prominent and consistent reasons to volunteer at an MSE enabling individuals to forge links with potential employers and capitalise on the social and professional networks these may bring (Koutrou & Pappous, 2016).

Despite the potential of MSE volunteering to foster the development of skills, knowledge and networks, this issue has not yet been adequately examined by researchers (Schugurensky, 2013). Little is known as to how this is being achieved in the context of MSEs and the various cultural contexts in which they operate, what particular skills volunteers develop as part of their engagement with the MSE, and how they perceive this new acquired knowledge and skills to be of benefit for their future personal and professional development as well as social capital acquisition (Bruening et al., 2015).

This chapter aims to enhance our understanding of the types of educational, skill-based, personal and professional benefits MSE volunteers accrue. In so doing, a case study of a group of London 2012 Games Makers is discussed. The findings are part of a study involving an open-ended online survey with 77 Games Makers that took place in April 2016, four years after the London 2012 Games. Participants were asked to reflect retrospectively on the skills and the benefits that were developed as part of their experience at the Games. To that end, the following question was answered: what types of learning and skills are acquired by individuals through MSE volunteering? Examining social perceptions on the knowledge and skills developed through volunteering is important, as this can affect individuals' decision to volunteer and commit to voluntary action in the future; thus, potentially create a volunteer legacy (Friedland & Morimoto, 2005). Moreover, a better understanding of volunteer perceptions in relation to skill development and employability could help to direct future policy decisions with regard to the social and human capital value that MSEs bring for host communities (Snyder & Omoto, 2008).

Background: the contribution of volunteering at MSEs in skills-enhancement

Distinguishing skills

Skills are distinguished between hard and soft. In an ever-changing and demanding job market, employers focus on skill-based approaches to learning, by expecting graduates and job seekers to have developed a skillset that is readily transferrable to the workplace (Grugulis, 2007).

Soft skills

Soft skills represent the ways someone goes about carrying out their duties, and how the results of their work are produced and communicated (Grugulis, 2007). Soft skills are not occupation-specific, rather, they are deemed more generic and applicable to various situations. As such, they are deemed transversal and foster interactions with others. Soft skills could be acquired and developed throughout an individual's lifespan by engaging in both academic and associative activities, for example, volunteering, education, sport, jobs, hobbies and interests. There is lack of consensus among researchers as to the typology of soft skills. Crosbie (2005) identified eight types of soft skills: cooperation/teamwork skills;

communication skills; initiative; leadership ability; planning and organising skills; personal mastery; coaching; and presentation skills. Jain (2009), on the other hand, identified seven types of soft skills: (1) communicative skills; (2) thinking skills and problem-solving skills; (3) team work force; (4) lifelong learning and information management; (5) entrepreneur skills; (6) ethics, moral and professionalism; and (7) leadership skills. Khasanzyanova (2017) discussed four categories of skills: Personal (efficiency, reliability, identification with the company); Communicational (ability to initiate a discussion, to build a social network); Interpersonal (sense of responsibility, team spirit, awareness of the hierarchy); and those that relate to expressing values (solidarity, resourcefulness, passion, understanding).

Another sub-category of soft skills includes personal attributes that describe all these character traits that, if developed, could prepare individuals for any type of career and workplace issues. Personal attributes include handling stress, commitment, adaptability, trustworthiness and integrity. Research suggests that individuals who engage in extra-curricular work or associative activities alongside their studies are more likely to have developed most of the skills needed to be successful in the workplace such as organisational citizenship, leadership ability, productivity, communication, interpersonal and teamworking skills (Handy et al., 2010). In particular, volunteering can serve as a means for individuals to demonstrate the acquisition of such desirable and transferable attributes to employers, which are likely to be unobservable in standalone job applications (Handy et al., 2010; Katz & Rosenberg, 2005).

Hard skills

Hard skills are considered more tangible compared to soft skills and refer to skills and knowledge that are job-specific, represent technical know-how and are required for a set career route (Grugulis, 2007). Hard skills are normally developed and acquired through engagement in formal education or training as well as in subject-specific work environments. For example, for those who aspire to a career in event management, hard skills could be acquired through involvement in the planning, logistics, catering, hospitality, venue health and safety areas of an event for employees or volunteers to upkeep with the latest industry trends.

Skills development beyond formal education has increasingly been the focus of national and European policy makers (Souto-Otero & Shields, 2016). Involvement in volunteering is thought to bring about skill development benefits and is one of the key motivations to engage in voluntary work (Paine et al., 2013). Engagement in voluntary work is perceived by volunteers as leading to positive skills outcomes and enhancing both 'hard' and 'soft' skills (Hirst, 2001; Nichols & Ralston, 2011b; Souto-Otero & Shields, 2016). Hard skills developed by volunteering are more industry-specific (Hirst, 2001), and since they are often associated with the acquisition of formal qualifications, are more easily observable than soft skills. These types of skills for volunteers may include competences in customer services, foreign languages, information technology, and data processing and analysis among others (Jastrzab et al., 2004; Rochester et al., 2009).

Soft skills developed through volunteering are generally considered more important, and include time management, leadership development, communication, teamwork and motivation (Jastrzab et al., 2004; Rochester et al., 2009). However, the skill outcomes of volunteering, in particular those that relate to soft skills development are harder to measure (Gornostaeva & McGurk, 2013), and do not necessarily provide volunteers with a relevant skillset that employers seek (Souto-Otero & Shields, 2016). These issues have largely been left unexplored by past research.

In addition, the evidence that volunteering or other associative experiences lead to subsequent paid employment or even securing job interviews is slight (Hirst, 2001; Khasanzyanova, 2017). It is also argued that individual characteristics (age, gender, motivations to volunteer) and circumstances (volunteer role, frequency and quality of volunteering, employment history) may account for any employment effects of volunteering (Hirst, 2001; Paine et al., 2013).

Nonetheless, studies highlight positive perceptions on the contribution of voluntary work in accruing job-related benefits for individuals. Hirst (2001) identified that 88% of unemployed respondents remained positive that their volunteering experience would lead them in finding employment and lead to career progression. Similarly, Hill (2009) highlighted that almost 90% of employers believed volunteering as important for the career progression of their existing employees, while 81% of them viewed prospective applicants with volunteering experience more favourably in their hiring decisions.

Studies on the potential benefits of voluntary work for the unemployed concluded that participants accrued skill development in general employability areas such as self-presentation, maintaining positive attitude, good time-keeping, motivation and confidence to engage in job search activities as well as other psychological benefits such as an increased self-esteem and sense of purpose (Gay, 1998; Hirst, 2001; Rochester et al., 2009).

While the employability skills developed by volunteering may seem more specific, research suggests that volunteering leads to social capital development through enabling volunteers to form and broaden their social networks and relationships (Catts, 2005). Through voluntary work, individuals develop networks with others, develop a sense of belonging to social groups, and in the process, improve their sense of self-worth, purpose and confidence (Nichols & Ralston, 2011a). Nichols and Ralston (2011a) also argue that volunteering promotes social inclusion of the economically disadvantaged through establishing social contacts that could lead to career and networking benefits that might compensate for the lack of material resources. Moreover, Glyptis (1989) suggested that volunteering helps individuals become more resourceful through an increased "capacity to use their own and social resources to develop interests and pursue activities which yield personal and social satisfactions" (p. 161).

Volunteering at MSEs

An interplay between altruistic, individualistic and social factors explains motivations to volunteer in sport or regular volunteer settings (Haski-Leventhal et al., 2010; Koutrou & Downward, 2016). However, MSE volunteering attracts individuals who are not necessarily affiliated to a particular sport. They particularly desire to experience a unique event 'behind the scenes', contribute to helping the event's success and show pride in their country and host community or meet people, make friends and networks that may bring about excitement or opportunities for career development and improving one's curriculum vitae (Dickson & Benson, 2013; Koutrou & Pappous, 2016).

Volunteering at the Olympic Games and other MSEs has grown in significance in recent years with a large number of people being interested to provide their support as volunteers. Indeed, such undertakings have grown in size and complexity and present a major challenge for organisers and the host community. As such, volunteers with their time, efforts and expertise provide an integral and cost-efficient resource to stage them (Hoye et al., 2020). Hosting the Olympic Games in particular requires substantial financial resources and diverting public funds to support the staging of the MSE is common practice among host governments (Minnaert, 2014). This essentially leads to public scrutiny, and many host communities justify this expenditure along the lines of employment and skill development opportunities that the event may bring for the local population, particularly for the socially or economically disadvantaged (Minnaert, 2014). Kemp (2002) notes that the Sydney 2000 Games provided volunteers with the opportunity to form a social community with people from different backgrounds in a "unique social context for cooperation and learning" (p. 111), which enabled them to develop feelings of "being needed" and "being socially recognised". Kemp (2002) also emphasised the benefits Olympic volunteering may bring in leading younger individuals into wider social participation, in instilling confidence for females who prioritised family over their career, to enhance their employability and social skills and in enabling the retired and older individuals to develop a sense of purpose through making use of their extensive skillset and experience. As Smith (2008) emphasises, MSE volunteering can widen participation in community life and enhance prospects for unengaged individuals to access the labour market as long as their skills and expectations are appropriately matched to the available volunteer roles and activities. Moreover, Smith (2008) concluded that generally Olympic volunteers consider the sense of being part of a wider community, even for a short period of time, as the most important outcome of their experience.

However, with regard to volunteering and the opportunities it leads to for employability after the Games, research suggests that individuals with a stronger social or financial stability are more likely to volunteer (Dickson & Benson, 2013; Koutrou & Pappous, 2016; Minnaert, 2014). Despite this evidence, recent MSEs-hosting national and local governments adopted 'active labour market' policies (ALMP) that viewed the role of event volunteering as more instrumental in tackling unemployment and social exclusion in areas that were socially and economically deprived (Hill, 2009; Lee, 2010; Nichols & Ralston, 2011a; Smith, 2008). This was the case for the Sydney and London Games, as well as the 2002 Manchester Commonwealth Games, where arrangements were made between public and private institutions to support volunteer recruitment and training and to pursue ALMP goals, particularly among the socially disadvantaged. For the 2002 Manchester Commonwealth Games, a pre-volunteer program was established to encourage the socially excluded to volunteer for the event, and obtain post-games employment. Following the games, a post-event volunteer project was funded to continue the success of the pre-volunteer program, the Manchester Events Volunteers (MEV), which acted as a broker matching volunteers with available opportunities. The MEV programme successfully enhanced individuals' confidence, skills and employability and facilitated participants' transition into paid employment or harnessed their desire to continue volunteering in the community (Nichols & Ralston, 2011b).

London 2012, in particular, prioritised sustainability, accessibility and inclusion as its key objectives and aimed to diversify the potential employability and training benefits of the event to equally reach a wider spectrum of the population (Minnaert, 2014). Although there was commitment among key London 2012 stakeholder groups to emphasise equity, diversity and inclusivity in the recruitment of the Games workforce, in reality, consensus was not achieved on the specifics of this process (Minnaert, 2014). Further, the evidence suggests the London Olympic Games Organising Committee (LOCOG) limited engagement with the local volunteer sector and other outreach activities, with the exception of 'Personal Best', an independent programme that was publicly funded. This was a pre-volunteering training programme targeting unemployed or low-skilled individuals in order to gain a qualification and a guaranteed volunteer position in the Paralympics (Minnaert, 2014). However, the success of such partnerships in reaching the intended beneficiaries and meeting their aims is often difficult to measure (Smith, 2008). Thus, an opportunity may have been missed to effectively integrate the planning, delivery and legacy phases of the event and thus garner the benefits of MSE volunteer work in the long-run, by making it more inclusive (Nichols & Ralston, 2011a).

Considering the above, it is also worth noting that research on London 2012 Games Makers noted a general discontent with the limited use of their skills, the lack of challenge and low levels of knowledge presented in their roles (Koutrou et al., 2016; Wilks, 2016). It is argued that satisfaction with the roles performed at MSEs, can influence interest in and intention to repeat volunteering in the future, or transfer volunteer efforts across activities (Doherty, 2009; Koutrou, 2018). Thus, to leverage any legacy effects beyond the MSE presupposes that event organisers match volunteer skills, abilities and motivations to the roles available, and offer clear guidance and support to undertake these effectively (Smith, 2008). However, there is still lack of research that examines the skills outcomes of Olympic volunteering. To address this limited line of inquiry, a case study of a pool of volunteers in the context of London 2012 Olympic Games was examined by accounting for volunteer perceptions post-event. The section below discusses the Fleet Transport functional area of the London 2012 Olympics where the volunteer sample of this case study was drawn from.

London 2012 transport volunteering context

LOCOG was a private company responsible for preparing and staging the London 2012 Games. Among the key functional areas in an Olympic Games or MSE context is transport. For London 2012, this functional area was responsible for planning, delivering and funding secure transport services from competition and non-competition venues and Last Mile (spectator routes between transport and venue operations) for its client groups. These included Games Family, athletes, technical officials, Team Officials, Media and Games related workforce. The transport workforce for LOCOG was one of the largest across the entire Games-time operation with approximately 17,000 people. These included 300 LOCOG employees, and the rest were either transport contractor staff or a large number of London 2012 Games Makers. LOCOG Transport was further sub-divided into seven working areas. These included Bus Services, Venue Transport, Fleet Services, Client Services, Workforce, Business and Programme Management, Traffic Management and Parking. Fleet services comprised four, 112 BMW vehicles, as the main London 2012 automotive sponsor, and they aimed to provide a safe, timely, efficient and environmentally sustainable car-based service to Games family members. The author was employed by LOCOG for six months as Fleet Scheduler and Volunteer Coordinator.

This commentary will focus upon Games Makers who assisted with Fleet Services Operations and worked closely with the author during London 2012. These volunteers acted as Fleet Drivers and Olympic Games Family Assistants who were assigned to support specific National Olympic Committees (NOCs), dignitaries and personnel, athletes and the International Olympic Committee (IOC) or its Client Groups during Games times. This is deemed one of the most challenging, highly demanding but yet rewarding volunteer positions in an Olympic Games (Ziemba, 2018).

The volunteers were based at the Park Lane Fleet Depot, which was close to the hotels and other non-competition venues where members of the Games Family resided. The Games-time Fleet Depot volunteer personnel comprised 200 Games Makers. The author contacted them four years after the Games, in 2016, to invite them to take part in an open-ended, web-based survey. The survey among other themes, focused on eliciting the retrospective accounts of the respondents on what they felt they gained from their participation as Games Makers in London, their perceptions about the skills and knowledge they acquired, and how they could use or had used this experience in other spheres of life. The rationale for conducting the study during this time frame was in order to assess the event's impacts ex-post, to consider their long-term value (Minnaert, 2014). The survey was completed by 77 individuals. This comprised 28 females and 49 males. With regard to age at the time of the survey, 40 of the volunteers were 61 years or older, followed by 11 between 51 and 60 years of age, 11 volunteers in the 41–50 age bracket, ten between 18 to 30 years of age and finally five individuals in the 31–40 age category. The section below presents the findings related to volunteer perceptions on the impact of the London Olympics on their skill enhancement.

Skills development through volunteering at London 2012 fleet transport

As mentioned earlier, hard skills include those that present an individual with some functionality and occupational significance. In that respect, evidence from the current sample suggests limited development of hard skills, which mainly focused around areas of familiarity with the vehicles navigation system, driving in around London and other event-related venues and some job-related qualifications including training with the interviewing process for future employment. Below are some representative statements from the participants that reflect this:

> Gaining a qualification in hospitality. The experience of interviews and training has helped in future job interview situations.
>
> *(female GM)*

> I am now Head of Enrichment, a new post created at my school. I co-ordinate activities including volunteering opportunities for pupils and staff, so the experience in London helped with this.
>
> *(female GM)*

Other respondents commented:

> I learned enhanced driving skills, learned to navigate my way around London streets and enjoyed the feeling of pride that came with the success of the 2012 Games.
>
> *(male GM)*

> The prime skills that I developed was being able to negotiate driving around a busy city, use a 'sat nav' and a greater understanding of the geography of London and route knowledge.
>
> *(male GM)*

This familiarity with operational procedures, systems and driving in a big city enhanced participants' confidence in their own abilities to transfer such learning to other situations since it took them 'out of their comfort zone' and could perhaps be seen as a legacy for future volunteering in other similar events or in the community.

Soft skills, on the other hand, are those that are transferable and contribute to the adaptability of individuals to various situations and make up personal and life skills. The experience from the London Games provided individuals with a variety of soft skills and abilities that were or could be further transferred to future employment, volunteering or personal pursuits. The skills that were mentioned by this London 2012 Games Makers sample could be summarised under four broader types in line with the typology proposed by Khasanzyanova (2017). These are personal, communication, interpersonal and those skills that express individual's values. With regard to personal skills, many volunteers claimed to have improved adaptability by "stepping outside their normal roles" and "not being frightened to go up and talk to people".

Another volunteer puts it this way:

> Working to tight timeframes under pressure, getting on with strangers and building a rapport very quickly! Being thrown into unpredictable situations and just getting on with things.
>
> *(female GM)*

Another one noted:

> Following skills, organisation and admin, the ability to get along with all sorts of people, decision making, conflict management and handling pressure, were all enhanced.
>
> *(male GM)*

In addition, several volunteers noted that the experience enabled them to adjust to their circumstances, engender confidence in one's one ability and a sense of self-worth. The statements below illustrate this in detail:

> Personally, volunteering at 2012 was a great help for me adjusting to retirement from a career in public for over 30 years. And I did not go straight to doing nothing.
>
> *(male GM)*

> Met a hugely varied group of volunteers. With training and the subsequent Paralympic Games, I had six months of activity, which helped with the transition to retirement.
>
> *(male GM)*

> Felt part of something big, it was something to look forward to after graduating from university and not being able to get a job, felt pride when everyone banged on about how brilliant the Games Makers were.
>
> *(female GM)*

Other volunteers noted how they effectively carried over the skills and learning they acquired in London 2012 to other future volunteering pursuits. As observed by one respondent,

> Great experience. I now run my school's enrichment programme, which includes all pupils doing something 'for others'.
>
> *(female GM)*

Other participants commented:

> The experience encouraged me to apply to MOLA as a volunteer.
>
> *(male GM)*

> I re-joined Girlguiding and am now a Brownie Leader of a unit in East London.
>
> *(female GM)*

The above quotes illustrate how self-confidence, adaptability, working under pressure and other skills acquired through Games volunteering is an unplanned lasting legacy of volunteering since volunteers were able to use the same in other volunteering or job-related situations following the Games.

The respondents were also able to report that the experience enabled them to develop communication skills through "meeting people from different cultures" and "the ability to deal with everyone on a personal basis". Given the size and appeal of the Games, it is not surprising that volunteers had the opportunity to engage and be exposed to a diverse pool of people and cited this as a skill outcome of their experience. In addition to communication skills, respondents cited development of interpersonal skills such as "being able to socialise and approach people easily" as well as an enhanced sense of responsibility and teamwork. For example, some of the participants noted:

> Confidence of working with people, teamwork, respecting the value of others.
>
> *(male GM)*

> Meeting some amazing people including fellow drivers who have become lifetime friends through shared experience. Loving London and all it stands for. Seeing it at its best.
>
> *(female GM)*

> Helping make the games the best ever, showing off the UK and London as the best country and city in the world. Being part of a successful team.
>
> *(male GM)*

> A sense of pride at having contributed towards such an important event. The ability to share my experiences with both Games Makers and people who were not directly involved.
>
> *(female GM)*

Finally, a number of volunteers reported the experience enabled them to acquire skills that expressed values including solidarity, understanding, rigour and warmth. The participants claimed they had an increased understanding of the issues other people face and they reported an increase in sensitivity, tolerance and awareness of each other's differences in culture, faith, language and disability. The quotes below best illustrate this:

> Mainly it made me more aware of approaching people from all over the world. Everyone was different, but we all had the same purpose of being there as part of a 'Once in a Lifetime' event.
>
> *(male GM)*

> Working with people with disability and gaining an insight into the world seen through their achievements.
>
> *(male GM)*

> Confidence, compassion, care, an enhanced understanding of community, an enhanced love of disability sport. A realisation that I wanted to travel, write and consult as a disability advocate in order to change perceptions.
>
> *(female GM)*

I was based at Gravesend Rugby Club. It was to be used as a base for campers and car-avanners. I thought 'oh no!' stuck here, but it turned out to be one of the best bases for meeting people. People were coming up to me and asking what to do and where to go. 'Come in and have a cup of tea, or a cold beer' was the greeting that I was getting and then I couldn't tell them enough about what was to see and do around this part of the country.

(male GM)

There were instances, however, where some individuals believed that their former experience, skills and training were not acknowledged or appreciated to an appropriate degree by the event organisers. For example, one participant stated:

My skills were not properly utilised. Volunteering at the Games was very inspiring but the actual action fell short of my expectations.

(male GM)

Another participant echoes this view by stating,

I spent a long time waiting round to do nothing. I already had the skills, just not used by London 2012.

(male GM)

This hints that a potential dissatisfaction was present in some of the volunteers who felt that LOCOG did not offer them appropriate opportunities to use their existing skillset and make a difference. It also echoes past research supporting the lack of challenge, and low levels of knowledge in Games volunteering were reported by some London 2012 volunteers (Koutrou et al., 2016; Wilks, 2016).

Discussion and conclusion

The chapter provides insights on the unplanned legacies and outcomes of London 2012 volunteering in relation to skill development and other social benefits. The volunteering impacts that were identified are enduring even four years after the Games. Soft skills were more relevant for this group of volunteers, particularly related to personal, communicational, interpersonal and values-oriented aspects. Some volunteers were also able to make good use of their hard skill development, in particular those that are more active in the labour market and could see a benefit in future employment or job-interview situations.

With regards to soft skills, volunteer post-event evaluations about their personal takeaways from their volunteer journey at London 2012 are compelling. For instance, several volunteers noted an increased appreciation and understanding of each other's differences, respecting the value of others and the opportunity to work with a diverse team. They also recognised the importance of this experience in enabling them to develop an increased sense of purpose. In particular, for older volunteers the experience was integral in helping them transition into retirement by putting their existing skillset into good use. The evidence also suggests that some individuals effectively carried over the acquired skills in other job or volunteering situations within their local communities.

However, as with past research, it seems that individual demographics and circumstances play a role in reaping any employment effects (Hirst, 2001; Paine et al., 2013). For example, the volunteers in this study were primarily of an older age. Thus, this skill development could only be relevant on a personal level enabling them to remain 'active citizens' and develop 'feelings of being needed and socially recognised'. It also seems that the current sample comprised individuals with already strong social ties and financial stability. This puts into question the impact and reach of ALM policies in the context of the London 2012 Games.

Echoing past research, a more coordinated approach between LOCOG, the local volunteer sector, the government and other stakeholders could have enabled hard to reach groups to benefit from the Games by developing human and social capital (Nichols & Ralston, 2015). Moreover, as evident in the volunteer responses and echoing past research, to a certain degree the needs of LOCOG were prioritised over the needs of the volunteers hinting on the limited consideration given in matching the existing volunteer skillset, interests and expectations to the available roles in London 2012 (Koutrou et al., 2016; Nichols & Ralston, 2015). This, however, hinders repeat volunteering as the volunteer role and the contribution made is an important determinant of satisfaction and commitment to volunteering (Koutrou, 2018). Since a considerable number of individuals were volunteering in London for the first time (Dickson & Benson, 2013), it could be argued that the lack of challenge, and the low levels of knowledge presented in some of the volunteer roles was a negative impact for a volunteer legacy in the community out of London 2012 (Wilks, 2016).

The above discussion suggests that while MSE volunteering seems to lead to human and social capital benefits, these are often unplanned and take place without appropriate consideration to what this could mean for individuals and host communities (Koutrou et al., 2016; Nichols & Ralston, 2015). It is also too simplistic to say whether volunteers are aware of these skills and how they could transfer them to other future personal, professional or volunteering situations to benefit themselves and others. A greater consideration of the skills outcomes of volunteering should be given, while more structured and coordinated approaches to achieve these outcomes widely should be given by event organisers, host governments and other stakeholders. In that respect, future Games' organisers could leverage any legacy effects in relation to human and social capital, skill development and employability.

References

Allen, J., & Shaw, S. (2009). Everyone rolls up their sleeves and mucks in: Exploring volunteers' motivation and experiences of the motivational climate of a sporting event. *Sport Management Review*, *12*, 79–90. https://doi.org/10.1016/j.smr.2008.12.002

Bruening, J. E., Peachey, J. W., Evanovich, J. M., Fuller, R. D., Murty, C. J. C., Percy, V. E., Silverstein, L. A., & Chung, M. (2015). Managing sport for social change: The effects of intentional design and structure in a sport-based service-learning initiative. *Sport Management Review*, *18*(1), 69–85. https://doi.org/10.1016/j.smr.2014.07.002

Catts, R. (2005). *Social capital and employability*. University of Sterling, Sterling.

Crosbie, R. (2005). Learning the soft skills of leadership. *Industrial and Commercial Training*, *37*(1), 45–51. https://doi.org/10.1108/00197850510576484

Dickson, T. J., & Benson, A. M. (2013). London 2012 games makers: Towards redefining legacy. *Policy: Creating a lasting legacy from the 2012 Olympic and Paralympic Games*. Retrieved January 20, 2021, from https: //www.gov.uk/government/publications/london-2012-games-maker-survey

Doherty, A. (2009). The volunteer legacy of a major sport event. *Journal of Policy Research in Tourism, Leisure and Events*, *1*(3), 185–207. https://doi.org/10.1080/19407960903204356

European Commission. (2000). *A memorandum on lifelong learning*. Commission staff working paper. SEC(2000) 1832. Brussels: Commission of the European Communities. Retrieved January 26, 2021, from http://pjpeu.coe.int/documents/1017981/1668227/COM_Sec_2000_1832.pdf/ f79d0e69-b8d3-48a7-9d16-1a065bfe48e5

Friedland, L. A., & Morimoto, S. (2005). The changing lifeworld of young people: Risk, resume-padding, and civic engagement. Circle working paper 40. *Centre for Information and Research on Civic Learning and Engagement (CIRCLE), University of Maryland.*

Gay, P. (1998). Getting into work: Volunteering for employability. *Voluntary Action, 1*(1), 55–67.

Glyptis, S. (1989). *Leisure and Unemployment.* Open University Press, Milton Keynes.

Gornostaeva, G., & McGurk, P. (2013). Olympic volunteering for the unemployed: Who benefits and how?. *International Journal of Employment Studies, 21*(1), 5–30.

Grugulis, I. (2007). *Skills, Training and Human Resource Development.* Palgrave Macmillan, Basingstoke.

Handy, F., Cnaan, R. A., Hustinx, L., Kang, C., Brudney, J. L., Haski-Leventhal, D., … & Zrinscak, S. (2010). A cross-cultural examination of student volunteering: Is it all about résumé building?. *Non-profit and Voluntary Sector Quarterly, 39*(3), 498–523. https://doi.org/10.1177/0899764009344353.

Haski-Leventhal, D., Meijs, L., & Hustinx, L. (2010). The third-party model: Enhancing volunteering through governments, corporations and educational institutes. *Journal of Social Policy, 39*(1), 139–158. https://doi.org/10.1017/S0047279409990377.

Hill, M. (2009). *Volunteering and employment: What is the link for unemployed volunteers.* Research Bulletin, Institute for Volunteering Research, London.

Hirst, A. (2001). *Links between volunteering and employability.* Cambridge Policy Consultants, Cambridge.

Hoye, R., Cuskelly, G., Auld, C., Kappelides, P., & Misener, K. (2020). *Sport volunteering.* Routledge.

Jain, P. (2009). Knowledge management for 21st century information professionals. *Journal of Knowledge Management Practice, 10*(2), 1–12.

Jastrzab, J., Giordono, L., Chase, A., Valente, J., Hazlett, A., & LaRock, R. (2004). *Serving country and community: A longitudinal study of service in AmeriCorps.* Abt Associates Inc, Cambridge, MA.

Katz, E., & Rosenberg, J. (2005). An economic interpretation of institutional volunteering. *European Journal of Political Economy, 21*(2), 429–443. https://doi.org/10.1016/j.ejpoleco.2004.06.004.

Kay, T., & Bradbury, S. (2009). Youth sport volunteering: developing social capital? *Sport, Education and Society, 14*(1), 121–140. https://doi.org/10.1080/13573320802615288.

Kemp, S. (2002). The hidden workforce: Volunteers' learning in the Olympics. *Journal of European Industrial Training, 26*(2), 109–116. https://doi.org/10.1108/03090590210421987

Khasanzyanova, A. (2017). How volunteering helps students to develop soft skills. *International Review of Education, 63*(3), 363–379. https://doi.org/10.1007/s11159-017-9645-2

Koutrou, N. (2018). The impact of the 2010 Women's Rugby World Cup on sustained volunteering in the rugby community. *Sustainability, 10*(4), 1030. https://doi.org/10.3390/su10041030

Koutrou, N., & Downward, P. (2016). Event and club volunteer potential: The case of women's rugby in England. *International Journal of Sport Policy and Politics, 8*(2), 207–230. https://doi.org/10.1080/19406940.2015.1102756

Koutrou, N., & Pappous, A. S. (2016). Towards an Olympic volunteering legacy: Motivating volunteers to serve and remain–a case study of London 2012 Olympic Games volunteers. *Voluntary Sector Review, 7*(3), 269–291. https://doi.org/10.1332/096278916X14767760874050

Koutrou, N., Pappous, A. S., & Johnson, A. (2016). Post-event volunteering legacy: Did the London 2012 Games induce a sustainable volunteer engagement?. *Sustainability, 8*(12), 1221. https://doi.org/10.3390/su8121221

Lee, J. (2010). *Labour markets: Volunteering and employability* (Doctoral dissertation, University of the West of Scotland).

Minnaert, M. (2014). Making the Olympics work: Interpreting diversity and inclusivity in employment and skills development pre-London 2012. *Contemporary Social Science, 9*(2), 196–209. https://doi.org/10.1080/21582041.2013.838290

Nichols, G., & Ralston, R. (2015). The legacy costs of delivering the 2012 Olympic and Paralympic Games through regulatory capitalism. *Leisure Studies, 34*(4), 389–404. https://doi.org/10.1080/02614367.2014.923495

Nichols, G., & Ralston, R. (2011a). Lessons from the volunteering legacy of the 2002 Commonwealth Games. *Urban Studies, 49*(1), 169–184. https://doi.org/10.1177/0042098010397400.

Nichols, G., & Ralston, R. (2011b). Social inclusion through volunteering: The legacy potential of the 2012 Olympic Games. *Sociology, 45*(5), 900–914. https://doi.org/10.1177/0038038511413413

Paine, A. E., McKay, S., & Moro, D. (2013). Does volunteering improve employability? Insights from the British Household Panel Survey and beyond. *Voluntary Sector Review, 4*(3), 355–376. https://doi.org/10.1332/204080513X13807974909244

Rochester, C., Donahue, K., Grotz, J., Hill, M., Ockenden, N., & Unell, J. (2009). *A gateway to work. The role of volunteer centres in supporting the link between volunteering and employability.* Institute for Volunteering Research: London.

Schugurensky, D. (2013). Volunteers for democracy. In Duguid, F., Mündel, K., & Schugurensky, D. (eds)., *Volunteer work, informal learning and social action* (pp. 159–176). SensePublishers, Rotterdam.

Snyder, M., & Omoto, A. M. (2008). Volunteerism: Social issues perspectives and social policy implications. *Social Issues and Policy Review, 2*(1), 1–36. https://doi.org/10.1111/j.1751-2409.2008.00009.x

Smith, M. (2008), 'When the games come to town: Host cities and the local impacts of the Olympics', London East Research Institute Working Papers, University of East London, London.

Souto-Otero, M., & Shields, R. (2016). The investment model of volunteering in the EU-27 countries: Volunteering, skills development and employability. A multi-level analysis. *European Societies, 18*(5), 487–513. https://doi.org/ 10.1080/14616696.2016.1228991.

Welty Peachey, J., Cohen, A., Borland, J., & Lyras, A. (2013). Building social capital: Examining the impact of Street Soccer USA on its volunteers. *International Review for the Sociology of Sport, 48*(1), 20–37. https://doi.org/10.1177/1012690211432068.

Wilks, L. (2016). The lived experience of London 2012 Olympic and Paralympic Games volunteers: A serious leisure perspective. *Leisure Studies, 35*(5), 652–667. https://doi.org/10.1080/02614367.2014.993334

Ziemba, T. (2018). Personal growth through volunteering at an international sporting-event-reflections on participation in the PyeongChang winter games. 大分工業高等専門学校紀, *55*, 11–15.

14

LONDON, VANCOUVER, AND PYEONGCHANG OLYMPICS

A comparison of volunteer motivations

Chulhee Kang, Femida Handy and Sang-uk Park

Introduction

The Olympic Games are considered one of the most prestigious mega-sporting events and their existence is widely accepted as the pinnacle in sporting competitions (Gold & Gold, 2011). There exists fierce competition among countries wishing to host both the Summer and Winter Olympics as it brings great prestige to the city winning the bid to host the event, as well as tourists. South Korea won the bid to host the winter Olympics in PyeongChang in 2018 and this was significant as it was the first Asian city in the last two decades to host the games, and only the second Asian country to host a Winter Olympics event.

The capital and labor investments required in putting on the games in the winning cities is significant and often put host cities at financial risk, with major costs overruns that burden tax payers (Andreff, 2012; Flyvbjerg & Stewart, 2012). Not surprisingly many labor inputs have shifted to unpaid labor, i.e., volunteers, in an attempt to both to reduce the costs and engage the local public. The 'Olympic volunteer' was officially defined in 1992, although volunteers first appeared at the Lake Placid Winter Games in 1980, involving some 6,000 volunteers (Moreno, Moragas & Paniagua, 1999). Subsequent host communities formed special committees to organize volunteer efforts in order to help facilitate the games. Indeed, with the ever-growing magnitude of the event, both in size and scope, has increased the demand for volunteers. Furthermore, their roles have expanded from competition assistance, accompanying delegations and individuals, to include public relations, accreditation services, technology and telecommunications, transport, access control, catering, finances, administration etc. including assistance with the many cultural programs and other parallel events held alongside by the hosting cities (Moreno et al., 1999).

Even though volunteers' assignments are not equally glamorous or afford volunteers the opportunity to watch the athletes or participate at the venues where the games take place, many individuals are drawn to volunteering at the Olympics. They are attracted by the allure of the global reputation and the unique opportunities afforded by the Olympics. This may explain some of the reasons why the supply of volunteers far exceeds the demand, as not all those who apply to volunteer are accepted.

So, what motivates volunteers to sign up for the Olympic games? To involve volunteers cost-effectively, it is reasonable to understand why individuals choose to volunteer.

DOI: 10.4324/9780367815875-17

Managing volunteers is critical for the success of the games, hence understanding their motivations enables managers to keep volunteers satisfied and productive (Park & Olson, 2020). While there is a large body of literature investigating volunteer motivations, many have treated the volunteers as a homogenous group regardless of the type of volunteer work undertaken or where it takes place. Thus the findings of this literature may not generalize easily to the Olympic volunteer and provide assistance to volunteer managers.

The extant research on Olympic volunteers is largely limited to the English speaking or western countries where there is a tradition of volunteering. There is a lack of information on Olympic volunteers in other parts of the world. This research examines motivations of South Korean volunteers at the PyeongChang Winter Olympics and fills the gap in this literature and compares the findings to those Olympic volunteers in London and Vancouver.

The data collected in this research used the Special Events Volunteer Motivation Scale (SEVMS), which is the same as that used for the Olympic Games in London 2012 and Vancouver 2010 (Dickson et al., 2014). By using the same instrument for the 2018 PyeongChang Games, we avoid instrument bias when comparing findings related to Olympic volunteers in PyeongChang with those in London and Vancouver. Our findings may enable help host communities in future Olympic sites to recruit and provide satisfactory and personalized volunteer experiences during the games, noting that volunteers in different venues may not respond for similar reasons.

Literature review

Volunteering at the Olympic games for most volunteers is generally subsumed under episodic volunteering, which is defined as a one-off and short-term event volunteering. Macduff, Netting, and O'Connor (2009) suggest that much of the observed volunteering has been trending towards this phenomenon due to changes in the social and economic conditions which have seen a larger influx of individuals willing to make only short-term commitments as volunteers. Hustinx and her colleagues (2010) argued that volunteers who engage in episodic volunteering differ from those who practice the more traditional forms of volunteering, both in demographics and motivations. Cnaan and Handy (2005) center their discussion of episodic volunteering around the idea that volunteer opportunities are now more often designed to accommodate individuals making one-off commitments thereby attracting a more diverse network of people.

Episodic volunteering is prevalent in many large-scale mega-events which are normally reliant on flexible, short-term, and one-off volunteering (Holmes & Smith, 2009). Mega-events, however, also differ significantly in their mission and appeal; and those attracted to volunteer at the Boston Marathon will be motivated for different reasons than those volunteering at the Pope's visit to Philadelphia (Cnaan et al., 2017). The Olympic Games is undeniably the prime mega-sporting event globally, and has over the years engaged hundreds and thousands of volunteers, ranging from 28,000 volunteers in the 1984 Los Angeles Games to nearly 100,000 at the Beijing Games in 2008 (Yan & Chen, 2008).

As with all other types of mega-events, volunteers have a large impact on reducing the price and overhead costs of hosting such an event (Ahn, 2018) but the volunteer programs are not without significant costs of recruitment, screening, training, supervision, evaluation, logistics etc. (Pestereva, 2015). In addition, volunteers often receive gifts, free uniforms, free meals, and transportation with occasional free tickets. Overall, as volunteers are not paid for their labor it does reduce labor costs; additionally, volunteers help to bring communal support and excitement by promoting the event within the community. Creating a cohesive community of volunteers, who often act as ambassadors for the host city, does create a platform for publicity of the host city that serves to increases its global status and attraction as a tourist destination long after the Games (Gursoy & Kendall, 2006). This is why hosting the Olympics has become a competitive process as developing countries are coming to the forefront to try and show-off their political prowess and their economic capabilities (Grix & Lee, 2013). Thus it is critical why volunteers, who are often on the frontline and interact with visitors, continue to remain important agents of the Games' success (Kemp, 2002).

Motives of Olympic volunteers

Volunteers are the face of the Olympic Games and often set the tone for how visitors experience the Games and the venue. Hence it is critical to ensure that volunteers provide a positive experience to visitors. To do so it is not only important to provide them training but understand what motivates them to join, because by doing so managers and planners can enhance the experiences for volunteers, who in turn will provide positive experiences for the visitors to the Olympics.

Although with growth and complexity of the Games there is an increasing demand for volunteers, it is easily satisfied. Indeed the Olympics are able to attract a far larger number of volunteers than they can use. For example, the Winter Olympics in PyeongChang, South Korea had over 90,000 of applicants to volunteer for 22,400 positions (The PyeongChang 2018 Passion Crew, 2018). While the upcoming Chinese Winter Olympics in 2022 expect to use only 40,000 volunteers, it had registered over 600,000 applications by November 2020 for the volunteer positions (China Daily, 2020).

This begs the question, why this attraction? What motivates volunteers to be involved in mega- events, and in particular the Olympic Games?

Motives of those who volunteer in the mega-event context have been researched by scholars and converge principally to include prestige (Coyne & Coyne), the significance of being part of the mega-event, and being involved in the action (Farrell, Johnston, & Twynam, 1998), the socializing aspect with other volunteers who share a common interest (Williams et al., 1995), meeting and learning about other people (Elstad, 1996), giving back to the community (Khoo & Engelhorn, 2011), and pride in country where the mega-event takes place (Kemp, 2002). These motives are varied and depend on the context and nature of the mega-event.

Several studies of Olympic volunteers have also been conducted. One report on Olympic volunteers summed up the motivations as the spirit of solidarity and peace enshrined in the Olympic philosophy, commitment as citizens or members of an association, individual challenge, belonging to and identification with a group, and various individual benefits (Moreno et al, 1999). Dickson, Benson, and Terwiel (2014) found that volunteers for the 2012 London Olympics and the 2010 Vancouver Games were largely motivated due to the focus on the uniqueness of the event, the desire to make the event a success, and to give back to their community. The volunteers at the London 2012 Olympic Games were also motivated by the pride of their city and their ability to help advance their community and gain recognition on the world stage. They also acknowledged the personal benefits such as the social connections and the different opportunities and experiences they gained (Nichols, Ralston, & Holmes, 2017).

To investigate motivations of volunteers at mega-events, researchers have relied on the SEVMS. This scale, first developed by Cnaan and Goldberg-Glen (1991) for human service organization volunteers, was adapted and changed to acknowledge the nature of mega-events and episodic volunteers by Farrell et al. (1998) who proposed SEVMS, as a 28-item

Table 14.1 Summary of motivations components at Olympic events using SEVMS

Authors	Olympic Games	Responses	Number of components and labels (variance)
Giannoulakis et al. (2007)	2004 Summer Athens, Greece	146	3 (46% of variance) Factors: Olympic Related (26%); Egoistic (12%); Purposive (8%)
Khoo and Engelhorn (2011)	2006 Special Olympics, Iowa, USA	289	5 (57.4% of variance) Factors: Purposive (17.1%); Solidarity (14.0%); Commitments (11.0%); External Traditions (8.6%); Family Traditions (6.7%)
Dickson et al. (2013)	Vancouver 2010 Winter & Paralympic Games	2,066	8 (58.3% of variance) Factors: All About the Games (26.03%); Transactional (12.99%); Variety (6.31%); Application (5.01%); Availability (4.33%); Altruistic (3.61%)
Alexander et al. (2015)	London 2012 Summer Games	11,521	7 (66.64% of variance) Factors: Career (13.21%); Value (10.9%) Olympics (10.84%); Enhancement (9.27%); Understanding (8.56%); Social (7.01%); Protective (6.85%)

scale in their study of volunteers at the Canadian Women's Curling Championships in 1996. It has been used by a number of scholars studying large scale sporting events such as the World Junior Curling Tournaments in 1998 (Twynam, Farrell & Johnston, 2002) and the Nordic World Ski Championships in 2010 (Wollebæk, Skirstad & Hanstad, 2014). Table 14.1 provides a brief summary of the findings, and in particular we note the components in the SEVMS identified at previous Olympics events. We use for comparison the two most recently reported uses of the SEVMS, by Dickson et al. (2013) and Alexander, Kim, and Kim (2015) done for the Vancouver and London Olympics, respectively, that use similar survey items in the SEVMS as we do for this study, with minor modifications to accommodate the local language and context.

Theoretical framework

An important discussion on what motivates Olympic Games volunteers is understanding who should be classified as a volunteer according to the Net-Cost Approach. The Net-Cost Approach, according to Handy et al. (2000), suggests that the higher the perceived cost of volunteering is to the individual and the lower the perceived personal benefit, the more they are considered a volunteer. Free will and the acting benefiting others also provide an important basis for what constitutes the perceived definition of a volunteer.

With respect to episodic volunteering for the Olympic Games, due to the related global prestige it provides a unique outlet for the motives of volunteers. Volunteering at the Olympics, we argue, provides many instrumental and personal benefits, such as using this experience on your resume, the social and professional connections made, and the recognition of your peers (Handy et al., 2010). Given that the Olympic Games are such a significant and unique event with competitors arriving from across the globe, volunteering at the Games is likely to produce a halo effect for the volunteers; due to a prestige factor of being associated with the games. Volunteers may then be perceived as special and with a cosmopolitan flair. This halo effect may bring volunteers unique professional and social benefits among their peers and employers. From the data on the supply of individuals who register to be

Table 14.2 Volunteers at Olympic Games

Year S/W	Summer Games	# volunteers Selected/Applications	Winter Games	# volunteers Selected/Applications
2004/2002	Athens, Greece	45,000/160,000	Salt Lake City, USA	22,000/70,000
2008/2006	Beijing, China	100,000/1,000,000	Turin, Italy	18,000/20,000
2012/2010	London, UK	70,000/200,000	Vancouver, Canada	18,500/ 60,000
2016/2014	Rio de Janeiro, Brazil	50,000/240,000	Sochi, Russia	25,000/200,00
2021/2018	Tokyo, Japan	80,000/204,680	PyeongChang, South Korea	22,400/92,656
2024/2022	Paris		Beijing, China	27,000*/870,000

volunteers, as compared to the utilization numbers shows that the supply far exceeds the demand, and this suggests these benefits are not trivial and likely recognized by individuals who wish to volunteer. (see Table 14.2).

Volunteering may thus translate into different benefits for different individuals, and these may vary according to the demographics of the volunteer, i.e., by gender, age, and employment status. For example, we would expect volunteers to be motivated by such instrumental benefits, notwithstanding that these benefits would be at the expense of their time and efforts. We would find such benefits, especially if the benefits are largely instrumental, to attract those individuals most likely to value the benefits. For example, if the volunteers were young they would be more likely to report career oriented benefits that older volunteers who may be more likely to volunteer for other motives.

Olympic Games draw thousands of potential volunteers, and how they are recruited and who is selected to volunteer will vary by each host city, reflecting its culture of volunteering and its population. Thus we expect that volunteers will differ in what motivates them. For example, in the early Olympic Games, volunteer recruitment was done among the Boy Scouts and Army, which produced a very different cadre of volunteers than today. Today volunteers are recruited from all walks in life, and sometimes even come from different countries to volunteer at the Olympics (Moreno et al., 1999). Nevertheless, given the uniqueness of the Games and the numbers of volunteers that participate, it is reasonable to conclude that in most cases the benefits of volunteering for the individual must far exceed the costs. To defray costs to the volunteers, accommodation is sometimes provided, as was the case for student volunteers at the 2014 Sochi Winter Olympics (Vetitnev, Kruglova & Bobina, 2015).

As Table 14.2 shows, Olympic committees do not face a dearth of volunteers. Individuals may be attracted for a variety of reasons, and volunteer managers must be able to discern why they apply and how best to engage the 'right' volunteers. To this end, managers must fathom what motivates applicants and if and how these motivations differ not only across volunteer demographics but also across venues. For example, is a 21 year-old South Korean student applying to volunteer at PyeongChang motivated for similar reasons as a 40 year-old teacher in London, or a 65 year-old retired bank manager in Vancouver?

The focus of our paper, thus, is on the comparison of the motivations across volunteers at the Olympic Games in PyeongChang, London, and Vancouver. We use these three particular venues as the volunteers at each of the Games were given a similar instrument (SEVMS) to measure their motivations as we describe below.

We ask the questions across the three venues: who is likely to volunteer? And what motivates them to volunteer? To compare motivations across venues it is useful to do so with volunteers who have been asked the same questions using the same instruments, as we know otherwise the responses are not easily comparable (Allison et al., 2002; Hall, 2001). Although we do not have individual level data for the other two venues, we compare the demographics at the aggregate level, as well as the ratings on the motivation items in the SEVMS.

Methods

Data and Measurement: To examine for similarities and differences in motivations of Olympic volunteers in different venues (London, Vancouver, and PyeongChang), we used the validated SEVMS based on a standardization into the five-point scale. At all three venues the same instrument was used, thus comparison takes place without the additional bias of differences in questions being asked (Allison et al., 2002). The data for the Vancouver and London Games comes from published literature by Dickson et al. (2013) and Alexander et al. (2015), respectively. For the 2018 PyeongChang Olympic Games, we use the data from responses to the SEVMS fielded at the pre-education session held in Seoul for the 1,000 volunteers with 903 responses received. Tables provides details across the three venues; we present at each of the venues, the methods used (Table 14.3) and sample characteristics (Table 14.4).

Demographics

Comparing demographics of Korean volunteers at PyeongChang (2018) with those in Vancouver (2010) and London (2012), we note that more respondents were females (76.6%), and between 18 and 24 years (70.8%), and 90.1% were students.[1] This is a stark comparison with volunteers surveyed in the Vancouver and London Olympic Games (Table 14.4). This may well be how Olympic committees in each city recruited and selected volunteers as well as self-selection among the population. Due to the differences in the volunteer population, the

Table 14.3 Summary of methods: Vancouver, London, and PyeongChang

	Vancouver 2010	London 2012	PyeongChang (2018)
Approved by	IPC	IPC	POCOG
In-country support	VANOC	LOCOG	POCOG
Ethics approval	University of Canberra	University of Canberra	Seoul Volunteer Center
Instrument	Adaptation of the SEVMS	SEVMS – Vancouver	SEVMS – Vancouver
Item scale	Seven-point Likert	Five-point Likert	Five-point Likert
Survey instrument distribution	Link to a survey emailed to volunteers.	Emailed survey direct to volunteers	Self-administered questionnaires
Survey timing	One month prior	Two days post	Eight months prior
Volunteers surveyed	Olympic and Paralympic	Olympic and Paralympic	Olympic and Paralympic
Volunteer population	19,104	70,000	23,000
Sample /response rate	2,066 (10.8%)	11,451 (16.4%)	902 (3.8%)
References	Dickson et al. (2013)	Alexander et al. (2015)	Current study

Table 14.4 Sample characteristics: Vancouver, London, and PyeongChang

	Vancouver 2010, n = 2,066, %	London 2012, n = 11,451, %	PyeongChang 2018, n = 903, %
Gender			
Female	59.6	59.1	76.4
Male	40.4	40.9	23.6
Age			
16–18 years	N/A	1.0	19.6
18–24 years	4.9	9.8	71.1
25–34 years	10.4	12.5	5.4
35–44 years	13.7	14.5	0.6
45–54 years	26.8	24.1	1.6
55–64 years	31.3	27.4	1.4
> 64 years	12.9	10.6	0.3
Employment status			
Employed full time	55.3	49.5	4.6
Employed part time	11.2	15.4	1.4
Employed casually	2.1	1.6	1.1
Retired	24.6	19.6	0.9
Full time student	3.5	7.6	90.2
Full time career or parent	1.4	1.1	0.3
Unemployed &/or looking for work	2.0	3.0	1.2
Other	N/A	2.2	0.3
Previously volunteered	93.6	80.4	91.0

differences in motivations will not come as a surprise. However, the one thing in common for all three populations is that nearly nine out of ten of the Olympic volunteers had previously volunteered.

Motivations: rankings

We first provide the list of motivations and their aggregate value on the Likert Scale as identified by respondents at each of the venues in Table 14.5, which orders them by rank (Vancouver) and notes their associated ranks at the other venues. The motivations among volunteers for the PyeongChang Olympics, at first glance, appear markedly different when compared to those in London and Vancouver, where there are greater similarities.

However, there are certain similarities worth noting: among the top ten motivations, volunteers in in all three venues chose that "It was the chance of a lifetime" suggesting that they all recognized the draw of the Games and its historic relevance. Other items shared among volunteers are: "wanting to do something worthwhile", and "wanting to help make the Games a success". We also note that the lowest ranked two items are also shared by the volunteers: "didn't have anything else to do with my time" and "being asked by a friend or family member who was going to participate in volunteering work for the Games".

Volunteers at PyeongChang ranked "broadening my horizons" and "gaining knowledge of different languages and cultures". Also, they ranked "I wanted to make new friends"

Table 14.5 Rankings of motivation items: comparisons

Variable labels as per questionnaire	Vancouver		London		PyeongChang	
	Mean	*Rank*	*Mean*	*Rank*	*Mean*	*Rank*
5. It was the chance of a lifetime	4.65	1	4.86	1	4.59	2
30. I wanted to help make the Games a success	4.37	2	4.75	2	4.22	5
20. I was interested in the Games	4.34	3	4.57	3	4.20	6
4. I wanted to do something worthwhile	4.27	4	4.47	5	4.61	1
3. Proud of XX Olympic and the Korea	4.25	5	4.44	6	3.89	11
18. I wanted to be associated with the Games	4.18	6	4.54	4	4.44	3
1. I believed in the principles and values of the Olympic Games	4.18	7	4.44	7	3.72	17
25. I had an interest in sports	4.12	8	4.22	9	3.83	14
11. I wanted to interact with others	3.98	9	4.05	11	4.07	8
15. I wanted to use my skills	3.94	10	4.10	10	3.61	18
24. I wanted give something back to the community	3.91	11	4.02	13	3.80	15
2. I wanted to make a contribution to Olympic and Country	3.89	12	4.04	12	4.28	4
28. I had a passion for the Games	3.71	13	4.25	8	3.94	10
10. I wanted to feel part of the community	3.69	14	3.87	15	3.25	21
13. The Games needed lots of volunteers	3.62	15	4.01	14	3.11	27
23. I wanted to broaden my horizons	3.54	16	3.79	16	4.13	7
17. The Games needed my skills	3.45	17	3.46	19	3.10	28
14. I have past experience providing similar services	3.44	18	3.00	24	2.74	31
8. Volunteering at the Games would make me feel better about myself	3.38	19	3.50	18	3.79	16
26. I wanted to make new friends	3.32	20	3.42	20	3.85	13
6. Volunteering is common in my family	3.31	21	2.73	28	3.12	26
19. Volunteering at the Games is prestigious	3.29	22	3.52	17	3.38	20
36. I wanted to gain skills that I can use in future volunteering situations	3.29	23	3.26	22	3.23	22
31. I wanted to gain knowledge of different languages and cultures	3.12	24	3.11	23	4.01	9

(Continued)

Table 14.5 (Continued)

Variable labels as per questionnaire	Vancouver		London		PyeongChang	
	Mean	*Rank*	*Mean*	*Rank*	*Mean*	*Rank*
27. It was an opportunity to meet elite athletes	2.79	26	2.75	27	3.50	19
7. Most people in my community volunteered	2.79	27	2.22	32	2.23	35
16. I wanted to gain skills that I can use in future employment	2.79	28	2.78	26	2.98	29
9. I have more free time than I used to have	2.74	29	2.68	29	2.28	34
22. I wanted to vary my regular activities	2.73	30	3.41	21	3.87	12
35. I wanted to gain official Games rewards	2.24	31	2.11	33	2.71	32
34. I wanted to establish contacts with experts from the same field	2.06	32	2.44	30	3.22	23
33. I wanted to gain experience which might lead to employment	1.95	33	2.32	31	3.17	25
32. I wanted to make job contacts (networks)	1.91	34	2.08	34	2.90	30
12. I was asked by a friend or family member who was going to volunteer for the Games	1.61	35	1.57	36	2.54	33
21. I did not have anything else to do with my time	1.48	36	1.63	35	1.99	36
Mean of all variables	3.31		3.42		3.49	

higher than their counterparts in Vancouver and London. They were more likely to be inexperienced as they ranked "The Games needed my skills", "I wanted to vary my regular activities", and "I have past experience providing similar services" much lower than volunteers at the other two venues. The PyeongChang volunteers also ranked these items lower than other volunteers – "I believed in the principles and values of the Olympic Games" and "I had an interest in sports", suggesting their motivations were less driven by the nature of the event, but by its stature and uniqueness.

Next, we analyzed using the ANOVA test (F-test) and post-hoc test on volunteers' motivation items to identify statistical differences in the means of items among three groups as we report in Table 14.6. Most items were significantly different across all three groups. We note that certain motivations are more likely to be ascribed to volunteers at the PyeongChang Games who tended to be younger than at the other two Games. For example motivations such as "gaining skills for a future employment", "making job contacts", "establishing contacts with experts in the field", and "gaining knowledge of different languages and cultures" were important to PyeongChang volunteers than London and Vancouver. On the other hand, altruistic motives had significantly lower means for the PyeongChang volunteers than the others, for example, motives such as "I wanted to make a contribution to PyeongChang

Table 14.6 Significant differences in means of motivations: Vancouver, London, and PyeongChang

Question	Vancouver 2010, n = 2,066 Mean (SD)	London 2012, n = 11,451 Mean (SD)	PyeongChang 2018, n = 903 Mean (SD)	ANOVA F-test (welch)	Post-hoc[a] (Games-Howell) difference between groups
Transactional					
33. I wanted to gain experience leading to employment	1.95(1.23)	2.32(1.21)	3.17 (1.12)	349.694***	abc
16. I wanted to gain skills for future employment	2.79(1.43)	2.78(1.26)	2.98 (1.13)	13.443***	aab
32. I wanted to make job contacts (networks)	1.91(1.16)	2.08(1.04)	2.90 (1.09)	273.411***	abc
36. I wanted to gain skills for future volunteering	3.29(1.29)	3.26(1.17)	3.23 (1.03)	0.845	–
34. I wanted to establish contacts with experts	2.06(1.24)	2.44(1.08)	3.22 (1.07)	339.515***	abc
31. I wanted to gain knowledge of different languages and cultures	3.12(1.24)	3.11(1.09)	4.01 (0.92)	395.304***	aab
Altruistic					
2. I wanted to make a contribution to Olympic games and country (UK, CA, KO)	3.89(1.17)	4.04(0.99)	4.28 (0.74)	63.361***	abc
3. I was proud of Olympic games and (UK. CA, KO)	4.25(1.02)	4.44(0.77)	3.89 (0.86)	193.192***	abc
24. I wanted to give back to the community	3.91(1.08)	4.02(0.89)	3.80 (0.91)	31.627***	abc
30. I wanted to help make the Games a success	4.37(0.88)	4.75(0.50)	4.22 (0.72)	393.155***	abc
It's all about the Games!					
25. I had an interest in sports	4.12 (1.06)	4.22(0.94)	3.83 (1.00)	68.444***	abc
20. I was interested in the Games	4.34(0.89)	4.57(0.65)	4.20 (0.79)	147.352***	abc
28. I had a passion for the Games	3.71(1.19)	4.25(0.88)	3.94 (0.85)	234.826***	abc
1. I believe in the principles and values of the Olympic	4.18(0.95)	4.44(0.72)	3.72 (0.82)	380.184***	abc
Tradition					
5. Volunteering is common in my family	3.31(1.28)	2.73(1.22)	3.12 (0.96)	223.150***	abc
7. Most people in my community volunteered	2.79(1.01)	2.22(0.89)	2.23 (0.89)	290.297***	abb
12. I was asked by a friend or family member who was going volunteer for the Games	1.61(1.13)	1.57(0.88)	2.54 (1.22)	273.330***	aab

(Continued)

Question	Vancouver 2010, n = 2,066 Mean (SD)	London 2012, n = 11,451 Mean (SD)	PyeongChang 2018, n = 903 Mean (SD)	ANOVA F-test (welch)	Post-hoc (Games-Howell) difference between groups
Availability					
9. I have more free time than I used to	2.74(1.48)	2.68(1.42)	2.28 (1.01)	65.663***	aab
21. I did not have anything else to do with my time	1.48(0.95)	1.63(0.91)	1.99 (0.98)	86.943***	abc
Application					
17. The Games needed my skills	3.45(1.22)	3.46(0.97)	3.10 (1.00)	56.411***	aab
15. I wanted to use my skills	3.94(1.11)	4.1(0.86)	3.61 (0.98)	117.073***	abc
14. I have past experience providing similar services	3.44(1.37)	3.0(1.28)	2.74 (1.13)	124.629***	abc
13. The Games needed lots of volunteers	3.62(1.26)	4.01(0.93)	3.11 (1.01)	402.872***	abc
Rewards					
29. I would be able to attend an event	2.83(1.32)	2.87(1.22)	3.17 (1.08)	33.407***	aab
35. I wanted to gain official Games rewards (e.g. volunteer uniforms)	2.24(1.24)	2.11(1.06)	2.71 (1.08)	134.755***	abc
27. It was an opportunity to meet elite athletes	2.79(1.27)	2.75(1.16)	3.50 (1.02)	221.318***	aab
19. Being a volunteer at the Games is prestigious	3.29(1.27)	3.52(1.05)	3.38 (1.15)	34.224***	aba
18. I wanted to be associated with the Games	4.18(1.01)	4.54(0.68)	4.44 (0.67)	126.026***	abc
Variety					
11. I wanted to interact with others	3.98(1.00)	4.05(0.87)	4.07 (0.81)	4.921***	abb
22. I wanted to vary my regular activities	2.73(1.31)	3.41(1.11)	3.87 (0.95)	379.51**	abc
23. I wanted to broaden my horizons	3.54(1.24)	3.79(1.00)	4.13 (0.83)	114.347***	abc
8. Volunteering at the Games would make me feel better about myself	3.38(1.18)	3.5(1.07)	3.79 (0.85)	62.700***	abc
26. I wanted to make new friends	3.32(1.17)	3.42(1.05)	3.85 (0.92)	105.284***	abc
10. I wanted to feel part of the community	3.69(1.11)	3.87(0.99)	3.25 (0.98)	181.779***	abc
4. I wanted to do something worthwhile	4.27(0.92)	4.47(0.71)	4.61 (0.58)	75.990***	abc
5. It was the chance of a lifetime	4.65(0.82)	4.86(0.43)	4.59 (0.67)	129.690***	aba

***p < .001 level of significance
a abc Vancouver, London and PyeongChang are all significantly different from each other.
aab Vancouver, London are similar, but PyeongChang is different from them both.
abb London and PyeongChang are similar, but Vancouver is different from them both.
aba Vancouver and PyeongChang are similar, but London is different from them both.

Olympics", "I was proud of PyeongChang Olympic and the Korea", "I wanted to put something back into the community", and "I wanted to help make the Games a success".

In summary, items not related to self-serving motivations but focused on community had much higher means in Vancouver and London than they did for PyeongChang. This may be a reflection of the volunteer population for PyeongChang which was significantly younger than that in London and Vancouver and were mostly students. To younger volunteers who were mostly students, motivational items that were 'transactional,' 'reward', and 'variety' based were more highly valued than by the volunteers in Vancouver and London who tended to be older. PyeongChang volunteers were also more inexperienced as seen in their rankings of their own skills and experiences. On the other hand, they were more interested in learning and making new friends, all rather age-appropriate responses of young student volunteers, hungry for new experiences, and very aware of the prestige of the Games and the instrumental benefits of volunteering to their future professional lives.

SEVMS scale: standardized comparison on original components

Following these findings that several items were differently valued by volunteers at the three Games, we investigate whether these differences are reflected when we standardized our comparison by using the underlying component structure of the SEVMS. By comparing the means of the original components with the means of items in Vancouver and London, we are able to do a standardized comparison and identify the differences in components of volunteers' motivations for PyeongChang, Vancouver, and London volunteers. This allows us to compare the results across the three venues.

For the comparative analyses we conducted an ANOVA and post-hoc tests using the original component structure of the motivation SEVM scale. The eight components identified by researchers are reported in column 1 of Table 14.7. Of these eight components, only the 'availability' component shows no statistical difference among three venues, suggesting that availability of time is an equally valued resource across the board, albeit with a relatively low

Table 14.7 Standardized comparison based on original components of the SEVMS scale

Question	Vancouver 2010, n = 2,066, Mean (SD)	London 2012, n = 11,451, Mean (SD)	PyeongChang 2018, n = 903, Mean (SD)	F-test (Welch)	Post Hoc (Games Howell)
1. Transactional	2.52(1.27)	2.67(1.14)	3.25(1.06)	149.178***	abc
2. Altruistic	4.11(1.04)	4.31(0.79)	4.05(0.81)	75.641***	aba
3. It's all about the Games!	4.09(1.02)	4.37(0.80)	3.92(0.86)	171.981***	abc
4. Tradition	2.57(1.14)	2.17(1.00)	2.63(1.03)	176.846***	aba
5. Availability	2.11(1.22)	2.16(1.17)	2.14(1.00)	1.267	–
6. Application	3.61(1.24)	3.64(1.01)	3.14(1.03)	99.694***	aab
7. Rewards	3.07(1.22)	3.16(1.03)	3.44(1.00)	41.210***	abc
8. Variety	3.70(1.09)	3.92(0.90)	4.02(0.82)	48.876***	abc

***p < .001 level of significance
a abc Vancouver, London and PyeongChang are all significantly different from each other.
  aab Vancouver, London are similar, but PyeongChang is different from them both.
  abb London and PyeongChang are similar, but Vancouver is different from them both.
  aba Vancouver and PyeongChang are similar, but London is different from them both.

mean score. The remaining seven components showed statistical differences across the three venues.

The four components: 'it is all about the Games', 'transactional', 'reward', and 'variety' showed differences among three venues, with the latter three scoring greater importance in PyeongChang, confirming a similar finding form the item rankings. With regard to the 'altruistic' component, volunteers at the London Games reported greater altruistic motivations than the volunteers at the other two venues.

We find that for 'tradition', volunteers in London were significantly less likely to be being motivated by the items related to tradition. In the component related to 'application', PyeongChang volunteers significantly differ from the volunteers in Vancouver and London. Generally, as seen in the analyses of the motivation items, self-serving motivation components had the highest means in PyeongChang, compared to those of Vancouver and London. The 'Altruistic', 'it's all about the Games!', and 'application' components had the lowest means in PyeongChang, compared to those of Vancouver and London. These results indicate that there are certainly different motivations driving Olympic volunteers for the different Olympic Games.

Implications and conclusion

There is a significant gap in the literature that examines volunteer motivations in Olympic Games across different venues. While the Olympics is the same event, each host city and the volunteers they recruit experience the games differently. The purpose of this study was to compare the motivations of the volunteers using the SEVMS, an instrument used in the study of volunteer motivations in the 2010 Vancouver Olympic and Paralympic Winter Games. This research compares the motivations of volunteers at three Olympic or Paralympic Games, with the inclusion of a non-English speaking non-European country, South Korea. Although, the comparison included Winter and Summer Olympic volunteers, and were piloted at different times with respect to the Games, they display many of the similar motivations in London and Vancouver, but many are distinctly different in PyeongChang.

These differences have been attributed to the differences in the demographic characteristics of the volunteers themselves, but may also be attributed to the fact that London (UK) and Vancouver (Canada) are cities in countries that have a longer tradition of volunteering than PyeongChang, which is located in a rural area of Korea. Indeed, where volunteering is more of a tradition, it is natural to find that volunteers are less likely to motivated by instrumental and self-serving motives as in the case of UK and Canada. Whereas in Korea, where volunteering does not have a long historical tradition, volunteers were more likely to be motivated by the factors: 'transactional', 'rewards', and 'variety'. This does not suggest that Koreans are not guided by other reasons such as altruistic motives. Indeed we note that Koreans are more likely to also rate their altruistic motives fairly high (not significantly different from their counterparts in Vancouver). It is the nature of younger volunteers who are largely students to be seeking opportunities for learning and boosting their opportunities in the labor market which is highly competitive in Korea and has unusually high unemployment rates among youth, many of whom are college educated (Sohni, 2019).

Future research will need to investigate whether the differences we have encountered may be explained by the differences in the manner in which volunteers are recruited and selected. In most cases the number of individuals who wished to volunteer far exceeded those selected to volunteer. If the criteria for such selection differ, then it may not come as a surprise that the motivations driving the volunteers also differ. Furthermore, different venues, i.e., large urban cities like London and Vancouver may attract different types of volunteers when compared to PyeongChang which is not located near any large city and thus cannot rely on local volunteers. There is little to do in PyeongChang as compared to London and Vancouver, and so the benefits of volunteering in PyeongChang are attractive to younger volunteers, who are willing to travel and have fewer opportunities for paid employment, and may also be seeking opportunities for volunteering that would enhance their resumes and career opportunities. Thus, for them it is likely that the benefits far exceeded the costs, and were therefore more likely to apply and be selected as volunteers. This may explain the variation in the demographics of volunteers in the three cities.

On the other hand, certain similarities also existed, for example, volunteers in all three cities reported having previous volunteering experiences, which may also be explained as 'previous volunteer experience' being a criterion for selection in all three cities. The standardized comparison indicated that one component was similar across the three venues: 'availability'. While the two items in this factor: "I have more free time than I used to have" and "I did not have anything else to do with my time" showed different intensities across the three cities, their combined score on the scale was not significantly different at the three venues, suggesting that time as a resource was not a constraint for the volunteers.

We do note that previous research has identified several questions for further research and one of them was: examine volunteer motivations for the Olympics which are different in countries where volunteering is less traditional, such as South Korea (Dickson et al., 2013, p. 90). This research begins to provide an initial step towards that understanding as South Korea is a country where volunteering is not a tradition and where the population is non-English speaking. We note that the demographics in each of the venues were different, with the most significant difference in South Korea. It seems that it was mostly young students who were willing to go to a small village, PyeongChang, that had few other attractions. We also noted that the demographic differences may also be a result of recruitment and selection processes – but given our data, we can only speculate – and a result of motivations to volunteer. Demographic differences thus make it hard to explain the variance in motivating factors in this research, except in very general terms, as we cannot tell for sure whether it is a result of the selection process or not. We also cannot be certain if these demographic differences are driven by where the Games are located, cultural differences, or just the fact that younger volunteers apply in greater numbers as they find greater benefits, thereby reducing their net-costs.

Future research will need to understand these processes of recruitment and selection better, as clearly the number who apply to volunteer far exceed those that end up volunteering. It now is not a question of 'who volunteers?' rather 'who is chosen to volunteer?' which may provide a better insight into individuals' motives to volunteer.

We also need further research on the volunteers in non-English speaking countries where volunteering is not a tradition and not as ubiquitous as in the western world. With more data from varied Olympic sites, including their recruiting and selection processes, conclusions can be drawn as to the differences and similarities of volunteer motives which may further allow us to draw valuable generalizations that would be helpful to Olympic volunteer managers.

Acknowledgements

We gratefully acknowledge the efforts of our research assistants: Chang-hoon Pyun from Yonsei University, and Stefanie Ruiz Garret and Julia Greitzer from the University of Pennsylvania.

Note

1 It is similar to Sochi (2014) and Beijing (2008), where most of the volunteers were students.

References

Ahn, Y. J. (2018). Recruitment of volunteers connected with sports mega-events: A case study of the PyeongChang 2018 Olympic and Paralympic Winter Games. *Journal of Destination Marketing & Management, 8*, 194–203. http://doi.org/10.1016/j.jdmm.2017.04.002

Alexander, A., Kim, S. B., & Kim, D. Y. (2015). Segmenting volunteers by motivation in the 2012 London Olympic Games. *Tourism Management, 47*, 1–10. http://doi.org/10.1332/0962789 16X14767760874050

Allison, L. D., Okun, M. A., & Dutridge, K. S. (2002). Assessing volunteer motives: A comparison of an open-ended probe and Likert rating scales. *Journal of Community & Applied Social Psychology, 12*(4), 243–255. https://doi.org/10.1002/casp.677

Andreff, W. (2012). The winner's curse: Why is the cost of mega sporting events so often underestimated? In *International handbook on the economics of mega sporting events.* Eds. Wolfgang Maennig and Andrew Zimbalist (Northampton: Edward Elgar, pp. 37–69).

China Daily (2020). *Over 610,000 apply for 2022 Olympics' volunteer program.* https://www.chinadaily.com.cn/a/202001/02/WS5e0d5e8ba310cf3e355820fa.html

Cnaan, R. A., Daniel Heist, H., & Storti, M. H. (2017). Episodic volunteering at a religious megaevent: Pope Francis's visit to Philadelphia. *Nonprofit Management and Leadership, 28*(1), 85–104. https://doi.org/10.1002/nml.21268

Cnaan, R. A., & Goldberg-Glen, R. (1991) Measuring motivation to volunteer in human services. *The Journal of Applied Behavioral Science, 27*(3), 269–284. http://doi.org/10.1177/0021886391273003

Cnaan, R. A., & Handy, F. (2005). Towards understanding episodic volunteering. *Vrijwillige Inzet Onderzocht, 2*(1), 29–35Dickson, T. J., Benson, A. M., Blackman, D. A., & Terwiel, A. F. (2013). It's all about the games! 2010 Vancouver Olympic and Paralympic winter games volunteers. *Event Management, 17*(1), 77–92.

Dickson, T. J., Benson, A. M., & Terwiel, F. A. (2014). Mega-event volunteers, similar or different? Vancouver 2010 vs. London 2012. *International Journal of Event and Festival Management, 5*(2), 164–179. https://doi.org/10.1108/IJEFM-07-2013-0019

Elstad, B. (1996). Volunteer perception of learning and satisfaction in a mega-event: the casde of the XVII Olympic Winter Games in Lillehammer. *Festival Management and Event Tourism, 4*(3-4), 75-83. https://doi.org/10.3727/106527096792195290

Farrell, J. M., Johnston, M. E., & Twynam, G. D. (1998). Volunteer motivation, satisfaction, and management at an elite sporting competition. *Journal of Sport Management, 12*(4), 288–300. https://doi.org/10.1123/jsm.12.4.288

Flyvbjerg, B., & Stewart, A. (2012). *Olympic proportions: Cost and cost overrun at the Olympics 1960–2012 (June 1).* Saïd Business School Working Papers, Oxford: University of Oxford, 23 pp., http://dx.doi.org/10.2139/ssrn.2238053

Giannoulakis, C., Wang, C-H., & Gray, D. (2007). Measuring volunteer motivation in mega-sporting events. *Event Management, 11*(4), 191–200. https://doi.org/10.3727/152599508785899884.

Gold, J., & Gold, M. (2011). *Olympic cities: City agendas, planning, and the world' games, 1896-2016.* London: Routledge.

Grix, J., & Lee, D. (2013). Soft power, sports mega-events and emerging states: The lure of the politics of attraction. *Global Society, 27*(4), 521–536. https://doi.org/10.1080/13600826.2013.827632

Gursoy, D., & Kendall, K. W. (2006). Hosting mega events: Modeling locals' support. *Annals of Tourism Research, 33*(3), 603–623. https://doi.org/10.1016/j.annals.2006.01.005

Hall, M. H. (2001). Measurement issues in surveys of giving and volunteering and strategies applied in the design of Canada's National Survey of Giving, Volunteering and Participating. *Nonprofit and Voluntary Sector Quarterly, 30*(3), 515–526. http://doi.org/10.1177/0899764001303009

Handy, F., Cnaan, R. A., Brudney, J. L., Ascoli, U., Meijs, L. C., & Ranade, S. (2000). Public perception of "who is a volunteer": An examination of the net-cost approach from a cross-cultural perspective. *Voluntas: International Journal of Voluntary and Nonprofit Organizations, 11*(1), 45–65. https://doi.org/10.1023/A:1008903032393

Handy, F., Cnaan, R. A., Hustinx, L., Kang, C., Brudney, J. L., Haski-Leventhal, D., … & Zrin-scak, S. (2010). A cross-cultural examination of student volunteering: Is it all about résumé build-ing? *Nonprofit and Voluntary Sector Quarterly, 39*(3), 498–523.

Holmes, K., & Smith, K. A. (2009). *Managing volunteers in tourism: Attractions, destinations and events.* Butterworth-Heinemann.

Hustinx, L., Cnaan, R. A., & Handy, F. (2010). Navigating theories of volunteering: A hybrid map for a complex phenomenon. *Journal for the Theory of Social Behaviour, 40*(4), 410–434. https://doi.org/10.1111/j.1468-5914.2010.00439.x

Kemp, S. (2002). The hidden workforce: Volunteers' learning in the Olympics. *Journal of European Industrial Training, 26*(2/3/4), 109–116. http://doi.org/10.1108/03090590210421987

Khoo, S., & Engelhorn, R. (2011). Volunteer motivations at a national Special Olympics event. *Adapted Physical Activity Quarterly, 28*(1), 27–39. http://doi.org/10.1123/apaq.28.1.27

Macduff, N., Netting, F. E., & O'Connor, M. K. (2009). Multiple ways of coordinating volun-teers with differing styles of service. *Journal of Community Practice, 17*(4), 400–423. https://doi.org/10.1080/10705420903300488

Moreno, A. B., Moragas, M., & Paniagua, R. (1999). The evolution of volunteers at the Olympic Games. *Proceedings of the Volunteers*, Global Society and the Olympic Movement, Lausanne, Switzerland, 24–26. https://www.researchgate.net/publication/285663835_The_evolution_of_volunteers_at_the_Olympic_Games

Nichols, G., Ralston, R., & Holmes, K. (2017). The 2012 Olympic Ambassadors and sustainable tourism legacy. *Journal of Sustainable Tourism, 25*(11), 1513–1528. https://doi.org/10.1080/09669582.2017.1291648

Park, H., & Olson, E. (2020). *Volunteer management: The case of Tokyo 2020 Olympic Games.* Open Course Materials. 7. https://lib.dr.iastate.edu/materials/7

Pestereva, N. (2015). University network of volunteer training centers as a social project of the So-chi-2014 Olympic winter games heritage. *Procedia-Social and Behavioral Sciences, 214*, 279–284. http://doi.org.10.1016/j.sbspro.2015.11.646

Sohni, I. (2019). The contentious politics of youth unemployment: Comparing Korea and Taiwan. *The Korean Journal of International Studies, 17*(1), 55–77. http://dx.doi.org/10.14731/kjis.2019.4.17.1.55

The PyeongChang 2018 Passion Crew – Continuing a legacy of Games volunteering. (2018, February 14). Retrieved from https://www.olympic.org/news/the-pyeongchang-2018-passion-crew-continuing-a-legacy-of-games-volunteering

Twynam, G. D., Farrell, J. M., & Johnston, M. E. (2002). Leisure and volunteer motivation at a special sporting event. *Leisure/Loisir, 27*(3–4), 363–377. https://doi.org/10.1080/14927713.2002.9651310

Vetitnev, A., Kruglova, M., & Bobina, N. (2015). The economic dimension of volunteerism as a trend of university research. *Procedia-Social and Behavioral Sciences, 214*, 748–757. http://doi.org/10.1016/j.sbspro.2015.11.710

Williams, P. W., Dossa, K. B., & Tompkins, L. (1995). Volunteerism and special event management: A case study of Whistler's Men's World Cup of Skiing. *Festival Management and Event Tourism, 3*(2), 83–95.

Wollebæk, D., Skirstad, B., & Hanstad, D. V. (2014). Between two volunteer cultures: Social com-position and motivation among volunteers at the 2010 test event for the FIS Nordic World Ski Championships. *International Review for the Sociology of Sport, 49*(1), 22–41. http://doi.org/10.1177/1012690212453355

15

VOLUNTEERING AT COMMUNITY EVENTS

From volunteering *for* an event to volunteering *as* an event

Elias Delanoeye, Sam Gorleer and Lesley Hustinx

Introduction

As the event industry has been expanding throughout the world, community events have grown in both popularity and volume, developing into a notable field of research and aspect of social life in general (Page & Connell, 2012). Events have been described as "…temporary experience[s] based on a unique combination of timing, location, theme, design and ambience created and complemented by participants, spectators and organizers" (Page & Connell, 2012, pp. 11–12). Compared to everyday leisure and tourism activities, events have distinct qualities that arouse special interest and motivation to participate. These qualities endow events with considerable symbolic power, which result in social and economic benefits for the communities and locations in which they take place (Page & Connell, 2012).

Scholars of event studies have noted that events are becoming increasingly institutionalised, evolving from organic, informal, and bottom-up initiatives based on community needs, into more strategically planned events aimed at meeting specific public policy or corporate objectives which are supported by powerful stakeholders (Getz, 2011). Community events can thus take many forms and occur at multiple scales. Moreover, large, one-off events often comprise a constellation of forms and goals, pursued by networks of actors (Getz, 2011; Robertson & Wardrop, 2012). Getz (2011, p. 27), therefore, proposes defining events based on their purpose or function rather than their form. In such a definition, community events are those that strive to engender *communitas*, a feeling of community and cohesion, by celebrating shared values and identities (Getz, 2011; Jepson & Clarke, 2014). As noted by Chalip (2006), by combining celebration and sociability, the sharing of time, space, and activity, many different event activities are able to engender a sense of community among their participants. In this regard, Getz (2011) notes that, because community events have no single 'formalistic' attribute, a single event can potentially combine multiple, converging goals (e.g. personal enjoyment, economic benefits, social interaction, and/or ritual celebration).

The complexity of goals in community events is reflected by the multiplicity of stakeholders that they bring together. Traditionally, such events are often associated with a bottom-up organisation, where the community itself and/or local authorities are the main organisers (Brewster et al., 2009; Eckstein, 2001; O'Sullivan & Jackson, 2002). Given this convergence

DOI: 10.4324/9780367815875-18

of goals, actors from many different fields are becoming increasingly interconnected through their involvement with community events. Increasingly, the public sector has come to play a central role in the coordination of community events, seeking to realise a variety of policy goals by building 'third way' partnerships between civic, public, and market actors, while adopting a partnership approach to enacting social, economic, and spatial policy (Maas, 2020; Robertson & Wardrop, 2012). In this approach, a single event might serve to celebrate place identity, grow social capital, stimulate the local economy (e.g. through tourism, fairs), and the expansion of local infrastructure.

Instrumental or celebratory? Volunteering for an event or as an event

Given their role in celebrating shared identity and social cohesion, small community events have traditionally relied on the communities in which they are held for organisation and volunteering has often been the main driving force (Brewster et al., 2009; Eckstein, 2001; Kristiansen et al., 2015). In recent years, large-scale events have become increasingly reliant on volunteers to complement or even constitute their entire workforce (Monga, 2006). In addition to the operational roles that volunteers often fill at large events, some also offer volunteer opportunities to engage in planning and organisation (Doherty, 2009; Schlenker et al., 2012). In some cases, volunteers serve as event ambassadors (Güntert et al., 2015; Monga, 2006). One strand of the event studies literature approaches event volunteers through the lens of an instrumental model (Getz, 2011), based on traditional volunteer management practices (Brudney et al., 2019). This approach presumes access to a group of volunteers willing to put their skills to use in order to achieve the goals of an organisation and its or-ganisers. It thus presupposes a coincidence of organisational goals and individual volunteer antecedents to explain why volunteers are willing to commit skills and effort to fulfil pre-determined tasks that the organisation needs to accomplish. Although this perspective does address the need to provide volunteers with positive experiences to engender commitment, these pursuits are often framed in terms of their benefits to event organisers by building a pool of people who are willing to *volunteer for an event*.

Within the field of research on volunteering, scholars have become increasingly interested in the phenomenon of as *volunteering as an event*. This type of event volunteering resembles its instrumental counterpart in that it is grounded in a wider trend toward more episodic forms of volunteering, as opposed to more traditional, longer-term forms of volunteering (Hustinx & Lammertyn, 2003). Another characteristic that they share is the increasing in-volvement of third parties (e.g. governments, businesses, and schools) in the creation and organisation of volunteer opportunities (Haski-Leventhal et al., 2010). The most prominent distinguishing feature of *volunteering as an event*, however, is its aim to promote volunteering as an activity, focusing on the engagement of volunteers for the sake of creating meaningful experiences and sustainable community engagement.

One very popular form of third-party volunteering events is the National Days of Service (NDS) that have been implemented by national governments across the globe, for example, Netherlands, United Kingdom, United States, and South Africa (Maas, 2020). Such events are created for the purpose of celebrating volunteering and encouraging as many citizens as possible to volunteer. One important goal of these events is to enlarge the pool of volunteers by enabling short-term, first-hand experiences with volunteering and volunteer organisa-tions as well as positive, one-off experiences that create energy to continue volunteering. To enact these goals, NDS are often organised by central 'home organisations,' which recruit event volunteers and function as gateways to 'host organisations' that offer volunteering activities that are generally concrete, approachable, and focused on interacting with beneficiaries (Christensen et al., 2005; Maas, 2020). The goal here is not necessarily to further the (sometimes mundane, pragmatic) goals of the organisation, but to engage in a hands-on way with its mission and vision.

One main purpose of these events is to offer accessible, meaningful volunteering experiences embedded within a broader celebration of volunteering. As such, NDS can be distinguished from other 'one-off' events (e.g. sporting events; cf. Doherty, 2009; Monga, 2006) according to the principal grounds on which they approach the act of volunteering. The main focus of NDS events is not on achieving pre-specified goals (which would require instrumental management) but on carrying out activities that are expected to cultivate fulfilment and engagement based on attachment to the broader mission of the organisation and, of particular importance to the nature of NDS, the broader community (whether real or imagined) that it celebrates (Rehnborg, 2009). In effect, volunteering is celebrated for the meaning that it creates as a pro-social, community-oriented act, rather than for the effect that it has as a form of accessible labour. When embedded in this way, volunteering appears consistent with the *communitas* that is central to shared meaning-making in community events. Volunteering obviously serves an instrumental role in that volunteers perform services for host organisations who regard such events as tools for recruiting volunteers. Nevertheless, organisations approach NDS volunteers as guests who should have a good time, rather than as interim labourers who are there to do a job.

The design and management of volunteering at community events

The management of volunteers as part of the workforce is a key challenge for event organisers, as many events are heavily dependent on volunteers to work alongside a paid workforce (van der Wagen, 2007). Representing a highly flexible and economically efficient part of the workforce, the significance of a well-managed pool of volunteers has been demonstrated in both the planning and execution of successful events (Schlenker et al., 2012). Knowledge concerning the management of instrumental *volunteers for events* is drawn from the generic literature on volunteering and sporting events (Schlenker et al., 2012). In this type of volunteer engagement, the volunteer management process revolves around the principal elements of human resource management (HRM), focusing largely on planning, recruitment, performance assurance, retention, and separation (Studer & von Schnurbein, 2013). Differences in motivation, interests, and competencies are likely to require the application of different HRM strategies for paid and volunteer staff (Parent, 2008). Despite a general recognition that volunteers and paid staff should be managed in different ways (Hanlon & Jago, 2012), the underlying management practices remain dominated by traditional HRM principles.

In the managerialist approach to event volunteering, the first phase of the management process usually involves recruiting a sufficiently large and competent volunteer workforce. This task is likely to be daunting, given the sometimes 'pulsating' nature of events (Hanlon & Jago, 2012). If performed incorrectly, it could become a significant source of dissatisfaction among volunteers (Ralston et al., 2004). Recruitment strategies depend largely on the size of the event and can include practices ranging from engaging volunteer resource centres to adopting more local methods of recruitment (Schlenker et al., 2012).

The second phase of the management process is best described by Studer and von Schnurbein's (2013) notion of performance assurance within the volunteer workforce. This phase entails the orientation or induction, training, monitoring, and evaluation of volunteers. A detailed overview of each of these steps would exceed the scope of this chapter, as would a summary of the alternative ways in which these steps have been conceptualised in the event literature. We therefore summarise this phase as preparing volunteers so that they can fulfil their tasks successfully and in compliance with the values of the organisation. The final phase is completely devoted to retaining the volunteer workforce by rewarding volunteers and motivating them to return. Both of the latter phases emphasise the need to provide a satisfying volunteer experience, thereby ensuring the success of the event by having satisfied volunteers who perform their tasks accordingly and generating what Bryen and Madden (2006) refer to as 'bounce-back' (i.e., the future re-engagement of episodic volunteers).

While the principles of HRM are strongly grounded in event management literature on the recruitment and retention of volunteers as part of the workforce, researchers have recently highlighted the need to re-negotiate volunteer management strategies based on an alternative and, arguably, more up-to-date view of the volunteer management task (Brudney et al., 2019). This is especially, although not exclusively relevant to recent trends of community-based event volunteering as an essentially non-instrumental type of *volunteering as an event*. This trend is best exemplified by the increasing prevalence of NDS events across the globe. The increasing third-party involvement in this type of community event implies the necessity of additional management tasks that go beyond the general principles of HRM and that arise from a shared responsibility for managing volunteers (Brudney et al., 2019). These current trends in volunteering, including event volunteering, also highlight an alternative emphasis on the generation of positive volunteer experiences as the primary goal in and of itself. While in the case of *volunteering for an event*, volunteer satisfaction can also be considered a reward on its own (Monga, 2006), here in the case of *volunteering as an event*, generating satisfaction takes the primary position in the hierarchy of goals to be achieved.

Despite their differing angles, the creation of satisfying volunteer engagements plays a central role in both types of event volunteering, whether primarily as a means to an end (in the case of *volunteering for an event*) or as the primary goal (in the case of *volunteering as an event*). We therefore focus more specifically on typical design elements of event volunteering that generate positive experiences. Due to its strong resemblance to our own case study, we deliberately focus on elements that could potentially generate satisfaction during one-day temporary episodic volunteering events, as identified in a recent study by Maas (2020) on NDS volunteering.

As the first author to propose the term 'episodic volunteers', Macduff (1990, 2004) argued that episodic volunteers should be given tasks with a short-term orientation, and that they could benefit from having work partners. The importance of social support has also been mentioned within the context of successful one-day engagements (Maas, 2020). Receiving social support has been identified as a driver of many different aspects of the volunteering task that generate satisfying experiences (e.g. enabling meaningful contact with beneficiaries of the services provided by the host organisation). In contrast, a lack of social support might result in feelings of anxiety or uncertainty for one-day volunteers. Similarly, volunteers attach importance to the possibility of receiving feedback and gaining recognition for their work (Maas, 2020). Clear, job-based feedback is also a key element of volunteer satisfaction.

Volunteers also benefit from seeing tangible results of their engagement and experiencing a sense of completion with the tasks that they have performed.

For short-term engagements, volunteers appreciate being told what to do (Maas, 2020). In terms of management, this implies ensuring that the tasks are straightforward and delineated, while also being sufficiently varied in nature to avoid inducing boredom. Having some tasks that demand physical effort could also be beneficial, as it allows volunteers literally to 'feel' that their efforts have contributed to the cause. Such tasks also require sufficient planning and preparation (e.g. estimating the number of volunteers required for specific tasks). Ensuring that everything is well prepared once the volunteers enter the organisation is very important, as a lack of preparation on the part of the host organisation is likely to have a direct negative impact on the experience of one-day volunteers (Maas, 2020).

Case study

This study aims to contribute to the scant literature on volunteering for NDS, a prime example of the phenomenon of *volunteering as an event*. We explore the following research questions:

1   To which volunteer profile does the National Day of Service (NDS) appeal? Does it succeed in attracting new volunteers, or is participation largely limited to volunteers with prior experience in volunteering? What motivates people to participate in NDS events?
2   Which particular design elements of NDS events appeal to volunteers?
3   How do participants rate the personal outcomes of their volunteer experiences? For this research question, we focus on satisfaction with the experience itself, as well as on the intention to volunteer again and/or participate again in similar events.

To answer these questions, we studied the NDS in Flanders. The NDS is a recent addition to a heavily mediatised solidarity festival in Flanders (the Dutch-speaking region of Belgium) known as 'Music for Life', which is held in the week leading up to Christmas Day, 25 December. The event is organised by Flemish Radio and Television (the state-owned regional broadcasting agency) and presented by its subsidiary, Studio Brussels, a popular radio broadcasting organisation. The event takes the form of a festival, combining live music with continuous radio broadcasting and other entertainment. Previous events have focused primarily on fundraising, both through local, grass-roots initiatives and through the donation of proceeds from live music shows at the festival location. Fundraisers are invited to present their campaigns and donations during the event, thus offering a spotlight for promoting their causes and explaining their efforts to the radio audience.

In 2019, a series of one-day volunteering opportunities was offered alongside the fundraising projects for the first time. This made the event (or at least that component of it) an NDS. To streamline the organisation and matching of volunteers and volunteer opportunities, the event organisers partnered with a regional volunteer support organisation (VSO), which acted as an intermediary and was charged with registering, supporting, and connecting volunteers to non-profit organisations (NPOs). Most of these host organisations were situated in the healthcare, welfare, or social sectors. They could register with the VSO and post their volunteering projects on the event site, detailing features including their organisational identity and mission, the tasks that volunteers would be doing, and the beneficiaries for whom they would be working. Volunteers could subsequently apply online for their desired volunteering opportunities, after which the NPO would select the required number of volunteers from the applicant pool.

Volunteering opportunities were scheduled according to the needs and availability of the NPOs and each took the form of one-day volunteering in the weeks surrounding the solidarity festival (5–24 December). Depending on the host organisation, these activities ranged in duration from three hours to an entire day, and they were carried out within the organisation or its immediate surroundings (e.g. local fairs). Each host organisation was required to assign a buddy to each event volunteer. In many cases, this task was performed by regular volunteers of the organisation. Some opportunities were limited to one volunteer, while others could accommodate multiple volunteers. For these opportunities, potential volunteers could apply as groups. Finally, to attract participants, the broadcaster marketed the volunteering opportunities on radio and social media, using both popular websites and sub-pages of the event website.

In an effort to explore this type of event volunteering, we cooperated with the VSO and developed a survey for the participants of the volunteering event. In doing so, we hoped to shed light on the impact of the strong brand of Music for Life on event volunteering, the experiences of these volunteers, and the value of this temporary form of volunteering in creating more durable engagements between volunteers and organisations.

Sample

Data were gathered through a self-administered online questionnaire, co-created with the major partners in the volunteering project (the national broadcaster and the VSO). All volunteers participating in an opportunity through the portal received an email thanking them for their efforts and inviting them to participate in the survey. A follow-up email was sent two weeks later in an effort to increase the response. The content of the questionnaire was intended to combine scientifically valid measures with practical information relevant to the partners in an instrument that could be administered in ten minutes in order to limit the burden on participants. We settled on the following measures: characteristics of the volunteers participating in the event, their prior experiences, why and how they had chosen to volunteer (in general, as well as for specific projects), and how they had experienced their participation. Motivations were measured along a five-point Likert scale based on items derived from the previous research, adapted from the functional perspective to the context of event volunteering (Güntert et al., 2015). Other measures were constructed specially for this study, taking into account issues of scientific validity and practical relevance.

The sampling approach ultimately yielded 252 valid cases (see Table 15.1), which were retained for further analysis, for a final response rate of 27.8% (see Table 15.1). The sample was predominantly female (79% women and 18% men) and older, with a mean age of 45 years (SD = 14.69). The age distribution was somewhat unbalanced with half of the respondents aged between 45 and 64 years. The majority of respondents were either married (45%) or cohabiting (16%). An additional 27% indicated they were single, with 8% divorced, and 3% widowed. A large proportion of the sample had children, either living at home (42%) or living away from home (21%).

The socio-economic status of the sample was typically characterised by a high level of education, with 69% having completed tertiary and 29% having completed secondary education.

Table 15.1 Event volunteer sample characteristics (*n* = 252)

Variables	%	n
Gender		
Female	79.0	199
Male	18.3	46
X	1.6	4
Prefer not to answer	1.2	3
Age (mean = 45, SD = 14.7)		
15–24	13.9	35
25–34	10.3	26
35–44	20.2	51
45–54	23.0	58
55–64	26.6	67
65+	6.0	15
Marital status		
Married	45.2	114
Cohabiting, but not married	15.9	40
Single	27.4	69
Divorced or separated	7.9	20
Widowed	3.2	8
Other	0.4	1
Family situation		
No children	36.5	92
Children living at home	42.1	106
Children who have left home	21.4	54
Occupational status		
Full-time job	38.9	98
Part-time job	18.3	46
Inactive	12.3	31
Retired	15.9	40
Student	11.1	28
Other	3.6	9
Highest education		
Higher education	69.4	175
Secondary education	29.0	73
Primary education	1.6	4

The majority were either employed (39% full-time and 18% part-time) or retired (16%). Of the remaining respondents, 11% were still in school, and 12% were inactive (i.e., of working age but not currently employed or studying). The final 4% of the respondents indicated their working situation as 'other', consisting largely of people who were either receiving replacement incomes or who derived at least part of their income from self-employment.

Findings

Many respondents had prior experience as volunteers, with 32% having volunteered within the one-year reference period (December 2018–December 2019), with a median frequency of 18 times a year. An additional 32% had volunteered but not in the previous year. The remaining 36% had never volunteered. When asked what had motivated them to participate in a volunteering project, the most common responses were a desire to help other people, a desire to contribute and the good feeling provided by volunteering (Table 15.2). These results suggest that respondents in the sample volunteered primarily for altruistic reasons, to participate in the event and because of the expected warm glow of volunteering. Items reflecting ego-protective and career-enhancement motives (Clary et al., 1998) were the least commonly indicated motivations.

The questionnaire also asked respondents to identify specific features of the project that had attracted them by rating various aspects of the activity along a five-point Likert scale. The identity of the organisations played a key role in attracting respondents to apply for specific projects, as indicated by the importance that they assigned to values of the organisation, the specific task package, and the target group of the organisation (Table 15.2). Practical considerations such as the duration, accessibility, and timing of the activity were also identified as important. The respondents attached relatively less importance to the amount of autonomy that they had received during the activity, as indicated by responses to the specific item 'The extent to which I could shape the project myself'. This finding corresponds to those of Maas (2020), who reports that one-day volunteers prefer delineated activities, during which

Table 15.2 Motivations for participating in the event and importance of specific project features (*n* = 252)

Motivations for participating in the event (in order of agreement)	% (Completely) disagree	% Neither disagree nor agree	% (Totally) agree
I want to help other people	0.4	2.8	96.8
I want to contribute to the project	1.6	10.7	87.7
Volunteering makes me feel good/better	2.0	14.3	83.7
I want to try new things in order to develop myself further	6.7	14.7	78.6
I can do hands-on work without further obligations	8.7	13.5	77.8
The Warmest Week allows me to be part of a larger whole	10.3	22.2	67.5
I can meet new people	11.1	22.6	66.3
I think that personal commitment makes more sense than simply giving money for a good cause	6.0	31.7	62.3
Out of curiosity, because I want to have a taste of volunteering	23.4	19.4	57.1
Volunteering is greatly appreciated by the people around me	12.7	39.3	48.0
So that I could think about something else, to escape from my daily struggles	46.8	15.9	37.3
The voluntary work fits in well with my studies or professional interests and skills	40.9	22.2	36.9

(Continued)

Table 15.2 (Continued)

Importance of specific project features* (in order of importance)	% (Very) unimportant	% Neither unimportant nor important	% (Very) important
Values of the organisation	1.6	7.5	90.9
Accessibility of the activity	6.3	16.3	77.4
Task package	5.6	17.9	76.6
Target group of the organisation	9.9	20.2	69.8
Moment (e.g. day, time) when the activity takes place	9.5	22.6	67.9
The opportunity to work with new people	13.9	29.8	56.3
Duration of the activity	15.1	29.0	56.0
Guidance by the organisation	23.8	42.1	34.1
The extent to which I could shape the project myself	34.5	42.1	23.4
The opportunity to work with friends or acquaintances	57.1	29.4	13.5

* Results are based on the responses for the first project selected by the respondent. Because respondents could participate in multiple projects, they could also indicate the relative importance of the following elements for each project. Nevertheless, only a small proportion of our sample had participated in multiple projects. In addition, we found high correlations (average of 0.612) between the importance scores for the various projects when comparing the first two projects, thus indicating that the importance of particular project characteristics was not dependent on the specific nature of the project.

they are told what to do. Relatively less importance was also attached to guidance by the organisation (e.g. being assigned a buddy), despite its frequent mention as a best practice in the literature on episodic volunteering.

In general, respondents assigned overwhelmingly positive ratings to their experiences with the event, with 60% rating their experiences as very positive and 35% rating them as positive. Only 2% rated their experiences negatively. These positive experiences were also apparently widespread, as no significant differences were identified in a series of one-way ANOVAs testing for differences in satisfaction based on gender, age, and prior volunteer experience. These results might thus indicate that the NDS formula offers satisfying volunteer engagements to people without volunteering experience, as well as to those currently or formerly engaged in volunteering. The majority of the respondents were also very likely to recommend the event to friends (as measured on a scale from 1 to 10) with 93% assigning scores higher than 6. This also appeared to be a universal experience, as no significant differences were observed based on gender, age, or experience with volunteering.

The respondents were also eager to participate in upcoming iterations of the same event, as indicated by a mean score of 8.82 (SD = 1.34) on a ten-point scale measuring the intention to volunteer again in the aforementioned context. They were slightly less enthusiastic when asked the same question with regard to their intention to volunteer again outside the context of the event, with a reported mean score of 8.36 and a slightly higher standard deviation (SD = 1.70). This pattern continued when the respondents were asked how likely they were to return to the host organisations as volunteers, with the mean score decreasing to 7.82, with a further increase in the standard deviation (SD = 2.09). Such results might reflect the importance of the 'exceptional' nature of the event, the effects of strong mediatisation and the creation of a narrative of altruism and solidarity on eliciting related behaviours. Given the limitations of our sample and the scope of our study, however, we are unable to provide a more detailed analysis.

Conclusion

This chapter elaborates on the connection between volunteers and community events by providing a limited overview of the literature on events, volunteer management literature, and presenting a case study. Proceeding from Getz's (2011) typology of event purposes, community events have been described as events aimed at celebrating shared values and identities, thereby inducing *communitas*, with reference to feelings of belonging and sharing (Turner, 1974). Given the wide variety of goals and stakeholders associated with such events, however, we assume that the celebration of a shared identity is but one (albeit important) of a potential range of goals. The local community thus serves as the focal point through and for which the event is organised. As a result, volunteers are often the driving force of such community-based events, whether as the actual workforce in the organisation of the events or as the target audience through which the community is celebrated. This distinction led us to distinguish two different types of connections between volunteers and community events. We identify the phenomenon in which the pool of volunteers functions mainly as an alternative, non-paid workforce in the organisation of an event as *volunteering for an event*. In contrast, the phenomenon in which volunteer engagements as such are celebrated as reflecting a shared identity can be identified in terms of *volunteering as an event*, in which the volunteers themselves constitute the target audience of the event.

The case study presented in this chapter clearly reflects the notion of *volunteering as an event*. The one-day volunteering opportunities organised within the context of a heavily mediatised solidarity event, Music for Life, in Flanders shares many similarities with the NDS that have been emerging throughout the world. Prior to 2019, Music for Life had focused primarily on fundraising through local initiatives and the donation of proceeds from live concerts at a different festival location each year. With the addition of a series of one-day volunteering opportunities in 2019, the event aimed to encourage as many citizens as possible to volunteer during short engagements. The event that had previously been known largely for the impressive amounts of money raised now extended its celebration of solidarity to include the numerous hours volunteered by Flemish citizens (Saerens, 2019).

Based on the results of a questionnaire distributed to participants in the volunteering program, the event achieved its primary goal of creating satisfying experiences. The results also indicate that the program attracted a diverse group of volunteers in terms of previous volunteer experience. Both former volunteers and people with no prior volunteering experience participated in the program. These findings suggest that the one-day volunteer opportunities provided an attractive entry-point for people who are inexperienced with volunteering, in addition to offering an opportunity for more experienced volunteers to celebrate the act of volunteering. Based on our findings, we conclude that the construction of a well-suited volunteering narrative, with a clear target group and organisational identity, is a key factor in satisfying volunteers, regardless of prior volunteering experience. This narrative can be further enhanced by linking it to a broader event identity constructed by the organiser of the NDS (in our case, the broadcaster). Our results also demonstrate that the program generated opportunities for longer-term volunteer retention. While this instrumental role was less fundamental in defining the success of the event, it might nonetheless be important in convincing organisations to host volunteers during these kinds of events.

Additional research will be required in order to examine the role of home organisations in similar community events. In our case study, the recruiting organisation presumably played a vital role in attracting volunteers, due to its overall popularity and the high level of media attention devoted to the event. Many respondents explicitly highlighted their motivation to support the broader event, which is very well-known in Flanders, as an important reason for participation. The results of the survey further indicated that the volunteers were less enthusiastic about the prospect of volunteering again outside the context of this well-known event. One important question that remains concerns the impact of the particular qualities of this event compared to the potential of other NDS events. Moreover, a thorough examination of the relationship between the intention to volunteer and actual volunteering behaviour in the future will require a more appropriate research design, based on developments over time. Neither our sample nor our survey design allow any clear conclusions in this regard.

References

Brewster, M., Connell, J., & Page, S. J. (2009). The Scottish highland games: Evolution, development and role as a community event. *Current Issues in Tourism, 12*(3), 271–293. https://doi.org/10.1080/13683500802389730

Brudney, J., Meijs, L., & van Overbeeke, P. (2019). More is less? The volunteer stewardship framework and models. *Nonprofit Management and Leadership, 30*(1), 69–87. https://doi.org/10.1002/nml.21358

Bryen, L., & Madden, K. (2006). *Bounce-back of episodic volunteers: What makes episodic volunteers return?* (Working Paper No. CPNS 32). Centre of Philanthropy and Nonprofit Studies, Queensland University of Technology.

Chalip, L. (2006). Towards social leverage of sport events. *Journal of Sport and Tourism, 11*(2), 109–127. https://doi.org/10.1080/14775080601155126

Christensen, R. K., Perry, J. L., & Littlepage, L. (2005). Making a difference day: An assessment. *The International Journal of Volunteer Administration, 23*(4), 23–30. https://www.ijova.org/docs/ChristensenPerryLittlepage.pdf

Clary, E. G., Snyder, M., Ridge, R. D., Copeland, J., Stukas, A. A., Haugen, J., & Miene, P. (1998). Understanding and assessing the motivations of volunteers: A functional approach. *Journal of Personality and Social Psychology, 74*(6), 1516–1530. https://doi.org/10.1037/0022-3514.74.6.1516

Doherty, A. (2009). The volunteer legacy of a major sport event. *Journal of Policy Research in Tourism, Leisure and Events, 1*(3), 185–207. https://doi.org/10.1080/19407960903204356

Eckstein, S. (2001). Community as gift-giving : Collectivistic roots of volunteerism. *American Sociological Review, 66*(6), 829–851. https://doi.org/10.2307/3088875

Getz, D. (2011). Event studies. In S. J. Page & J. Connell (Eds.), *The Routledge handbook of events* (pp. 27–46). Routledge.

Güntert, S. T., Neufeind, M., & Wehner, T. (2015). Motives for event volunteering: Extending the functional approach. *Nonprofit and Voluntary Sector Quarterly, 44*(4), 686–707. https://doi.org/10.1177/0899764014527797

Hanlon, C., & Jago, L. (2012). Staffing for successful events: Having the right skills in the right place at the right time. In S. J. Page & J. Connell (Eds.), *The Routledge handbook of events* (pp. 304–315). London: Routledge.

Haski-Leventhal, D., Meijs, L., & Hustinx, L. (2010). The third-party model: Enhancing volunteering through governments, corporations and educational institutes. *Journal of Social Policy, 39*(1), 139–158. https://doi.org/10.1017/S0047279409990377

Hustinx, L., & Lammertyn, F. (2003). Collective and reflexive styles of volunteering: A sociological modernization perspective. *Voluntas: International Journal of Voluntary and Nonprofit Organizations, 14*(2), 167–187. https://doi.org/10.1023/A:1023948027200

Jepson, A., & Clarke, A. (2014). Defining and exploring community festivals and events. In A. Jepson & V. A. Wright-St Clair (Eds.), *Exploring community festivals and events* (pp. 1–14). Routledge.

Kristiansen, E., Skirstad, B., Parent, M. M., & Waddington, I. (2015). "We can do it": Community, resistance, social solidarity, and long-term volunteering at a sport event. *Sport Management Review, 18*(2), 256–267. https://doi.org/10.1016/j.smr.2014.06.002

Maas, S. A. (2020). *In the moment of giving: Essays on contemporary forms of private and corporate philantropy* [Doctoral dissertation, Erasmus University]. RSM Dissertations in Management. https://repub. eur.nl/pub/124976/

Macduff, N. (1990). Episodic volunteers: Reality for the future. *Voluntary Action Leadership*, Spring, 15–17.

Macduff, N. (2004). *Episodic volunteering: Organizing and managing the short-term volunteer program.* MBA Publishing.

Monga, M. (2006). Measuring motivation to volunteer for special events. *Event Management, 10*, 47–61. https://doi.org/10.3727/152599506779364633

O'Sullivan, D., & Jackson, M. J. (2002). Festival tourism: A contributor to sustainable local economic development? *Journal of Sustainable Tourism, 10*(4), 325–342. https://doi.org/10.1080/09669 580208667171

Page, S., & Connell, J. (Eds.) (2012). *The Routledge handbook of events.* Routledge.

Parent, M. (2008). Evolution and issue patterns for major-sport-event organizing committees and their stakeholders. *Journal of Sport Management, 22*, 135–164. https://doi.org/10.1123/jsm.22.2.135

Ralston, R., Downward, P., & Lumsdon, L. (2004). The expectations of volunteers prior to the XVII Commonwealth Games, 2002: A qualitative study. *Event Management, 9*(1–2), 13–26. https://doi. org/10.3727/1525995042781084

Rehnborg, S. J. (2009). *Strategic volunteer engagement: A guide for nonprofit and public sector leaders.* The University of Texas. https://www.volunteeralive.org/docs/Strategic Volunteer Engagement.pdf

Robertson, M., & Wardrop, K. (2012). Festivals and events, government and spatial governance. In S. J. Page & J. Connell (Eds.), *The Routledge handbook of events* (pp. 489–506). Routledge.

Saerens, Z. (2019, December 24). *17,5 miljoen euro en 11.000 uur vrijwilligerswerk: De Warmste Week breekt opnieuw records.* VRT NWS. https://www.vrt.be/vrtnws/nl/2019/12/24/de-warmste-week/

Schlenker, K., Edwards, D., & Wearing, S. (2012). Volunteering and events. In S. J. Page & J. Connell (Eds.), *The Routledge handbook of events* (pp. 316–325). Routledge.

Studer, S., & von Schnurbein, G. (2013). Organizational factors affecting volunteers: A literature review on volunteer coordination. *VOLUNTAS: International Journal of Voluntary and Nonprofit Organizations, 24*(2), 403–440. https://doi.org/10.1007/s11266-012-9268-y

Turner, V. (1974). Liminal to liminoid, in play, flow, and ritual: An essay in comparative symbology. *Rice Institute Pamphlet-Rice University Studies, 60*(3). https://hdl.handle.net/1911/63159.

van der Wagen, L. (2007). *Human resource management for events: Managing the event workforce.* Butterworth-Heinemann.

16

VOLUNTEERING AND CHARITY FUNDRAISING EVENTS

Tim Brown

Introduction

The concept of charity, giving and volunteering is not a modern phenomenon, but has been an aspect of society for centuries (Anheier, 2014; Levitt, 2012; Sargeant & Shang, 2017). Charities are evident in ancient cultures, such as Egyptian, Greek and Roman society, through to the development of the first official charities in Europe during the Middle Ages, and to their growth globally in the 19th and 20th centuries (Hanvey & Philpot, 1996; Malik, 2008; Mullin, 1995). Many of the earliest texts, such as the Old Testament and Qur'ān, outline requirements of charitable giving, including financial contributions and volunteering in order to aid others, and are intrinsically linked to religion and socio-cultural values (Bremner, 1996; Sargeant & Jay, 2014). There are also numerous examples of sophisticated coordination and governance of charitable giving in antiquity and the Middle Ages, such as donations, legacies, fundraising, volunteering and events, demonstrating the importance of giving and appropriate management of these funds (Levitt, 2012; Mullin, 1995).

During the last 70 years, there has been a significant growth globally in the number and variety of charities, and the importance of volunteers supporting these causes (Worth, 2016). This exponential growth was due to increasing public needs emerging that were not supported by governments (Levitt, 2012). Charities, therefore, are now bridging the service gaps that are not financed by the public purse, which cover a diverse array of 'purposes' such as medical treatment, medical research, education, sports, support services and even the provision of food (Sargeant & Jay, 2014). In order to deliver services to their beneficiaries, charities have become increasingly reliant on volunteers to support their activities, with tens of millions of volunteers supporting charities across the world (Anheier, 2014; Govekar & Govekar, 2008; Hanvey & Philpot, 1996).

This chapter will examine the importance and reliance on volunteers in relation to charities, the role of volunteers in the context of charity events, motivations for giving, volunteering and supporting charities, and outline a new typology for charity event volunteering.

Recent development of charities

The charity sector, often referred to as the Third Sector (Courtney, 2013), has undergone significant changes in the past 30 years, as charities have become more professionalised

DOI: 10.4324/9780367815875-19

(Anheier, 2014; Sargeant & Jay, 2014; Worth, 2016). This transformation was due to several factors. First, charities recognised a need for change and for improving practices and processes (Driscoll, 2017; Fries, 2017). Second, the public perception and trust in charities has continued to decline due to high-profile scandals, mismanagement and poor practice (Etherington, 2017; Hind, 2017). Third, evolving governance requirements and legislation implemented by successive governments have led to tighter regulation and scrutiny of charities (Driscoll, 2017; Fries, 2017; Philips & Smith, 2011). Finally, charity fundraising strategies have become highly sophisticated and diverse in order to enhance the reputation of charities, increase support for their causes, raise income and deliver services to beneficiaries (Courtney, 2013; Hyde, Dunn, Wust, Bax & Chambers, 2016). The charity sector depends on the goodwill of its staff, volunteers, stakeholders and supporters to ensure that each charity is able to succeed on its mission and purpose and remain economically sustainable, whilst adhering to complex governance and legislation (Etherington, 2017; Levitt, 2012; Sargeant & Shang, 2017).

Like conventional businesses, charities need to raise income to meet organisational costs and provide for stakeholders and beneficiaries (Courtney, 2013). It is estimated that over 85% of charity income comes via fundraising, which includes through donations (regular and ad hoc), sales via charity shops, legacy donations, adverts and marketing campaigns, commercial and corporate partnership activity, and fundraising events (Anheier, 2014; Bremner, 1996; Webber, 2006; Weinstein & Barden, 2017). Of the various fundraising strategies, events have seen a significant growth in the last 20 years (Sargeant & Shang, 2017). In an increasingly competitive market place, charities have to work harder than ever to ensure their cause and brand are recognised and supported, and events are now presenting a new opportunity to reach stakeholders and supporters via events (Cox, 2017; Pitts, 1997; Webber, 2006). From a charity perspective, an *event* is a public facing, profile raising, brand awareness and financially rewarding activity, that for many charities can be critical in their ability to be both successful and sustainable (Bladen, Kennell, Abson & Wilde, 2018; Cox, 2017; Clarke & Norton, 1997; Webber, 2006). Like other event sectors, charities need to work with a wide range of stakeholders, supporters and especially volunteers to guarantee the successful delivery of these fundraising events (Cox, 2017; Sargeant & Jay, 2014).

Volunteers are an integral characteristic of the Third Sector, and charities in particular have become dependent on their volunteer workforce to enable them to deliver on operational activities as well as aid in wider strategic objectives (Courtney, 2013; Hanvey & Philpot, 1996). Volunteers undertake numerous roles, such as being a trustee, assisting in administrative duties, volunteering in retail outlets, supporting marketing initiatives, mentoring or caring for others and aiding fundraising campaigns, including events (Bussell & Forbes, 2002; Pynes, 2004; Worth, 2016). There are numerous motivations aligned to volunteering, and these can be linked to the broader concepts of why people *give* to charity.

Motivations for giving to charity

The concept of *giving* to others is not new and has been a key aspect of human society for millennia (Bremner, 1996; Malik, 2008; Mullin, 1995). The three giving attributes of *philanthropy, charity* and *altruism* are the foundation stones of modern charity (Worth, 2016). According to Sargeant and Jay (2004, p. 2), the term philanthropy originates from the Greek and means 'love of mankind' and they define it as "voluntary giving, voluntary service and voluntary association, primarily for the benefit of others". Anheier (2014, p. 8) outlines that philanthropy is the "voluntary dedication of personal wealth and skills for the benefit of specific causes" and these causes are usually linked to the individuals' personal interests or connections. Charity is defined as focusing on the "relief of the poor, helping the sick, disabled and elderly, supporting education, religion, and cultural heritage" (Anheier 2014, p. 8) among other purposes that benefit the community. The reason people give is due to their altruistic tendencies, whereby they give for the sake of giving, with no desire for reward or recognition (Bremner, 1996). In context to this, giving is therefore the motivation to provide financial or personal assistance (such as volunteering or personal expertise) for the benefit of the charity and its stakeholders, and the notion of voluntary support is central to this (Govekar & Govekar, 2008).

Sargeant and Jay (2014) outline that there are seven aspects of self-interest that are linked to the motivations to giving, and these can be readily aligned to the motivations for volunteering which are intrinsic to the notion of giving (Worth, 2016). The seven aspects of self-interest for giving (including volunteering) are:

1   *Self-esteem*: the motivation to give/volunteer is linked to enhanced emotional impact.
2   *Atonement for sins*: individuals are motivated to give/volunteer by a need to atone for past sins.
3   *Recognition*: individuals are motivated to give/volunteer by the potential of recognition from family, society, media and the organisation being supported.
4   *Access to services*: the motivation to give/volunteer is linked to the potential of benefitting from accessing services in the future. For example, giving to cancer charities.
5   *Reciprocation*: the motivation to give/volunteer is linked to a sense of obligation to organisations that have aided individuals in the past. For example, giving to a hospice for nursing assistance provided to a family member.
6   *In Memoriam*: giving via donations or through volunteering in memory of someone close to the donor, or as a legacy donation.
7   *Tax*: giving/volunteering can be tax deductible.

There is a potential eighth aspect of self-interest that could be added to this list, which is *tangible benefits*. The growth of charity fundraising events is resulting in perceived and material tangible benefits that are received in exchange for the money or support (such as volunteering) that they provide (Clarke & Norton, 1997; Sargeant & Shang, 2017; Weinstein & Barden, 2017). As Anheier (2014, p. 233) outlines, a charity supporter would "derive more tangible benefits by being granted access to exclusive sport or cultural events". Sargeant and Jay (2014, p. 235) support this view and comment that a charity fundraising event

> involves strong elements of exchange, where the donor derives a benefit for the giving…. events provide opportunities for socialising, entertainment, competition, recognition and networking, while raffles, auctions and sales provide opportunities to win prizes or to buy and sell goods.

Therefore, the eighth aspect of self-interest can be defined as:

8   *Tangible benefits:* the motivation to give/volunteer is directly linked to the material benefits that are gained in exchange for the support (financial or volunteering).

From a cynical perspective, this means that donors, supporters and volunteers are not necessarily attracted to the charity due to its brand, mission or values, but due to the benefits that can be attained through their support.

Volunteering for charity

It is well documented that the event industry relies heavily on volunteers to aid in event delivery, as these volunteers offer a flexible, skilled and cost-effective workforce at point of delivery (Goldblatt & Matheson, 2009; Schlenker, Edwards & Wearing, 2015; Van der Wagen & White, 2015). Goldblatt (2011, p. 141) posits that "volunteers are the lifeblood of many events. Without volunteers, these events would cease to exist. In fact, the vast majority of events are entirely volunteer driven", and this is particularly relevant for charities. Within the charity sector it is a fundamental imperative for charities to recruit and utilise volunteers across a range of roles, which include events, without whose support these activities and events would certainly cease to exist (Bladen et al., 2018; Clarke & Norton, 1997; Govekar & Govekar, 2008). It is essential, therefore, for charities to identify volunteering needs in the initial planning stages of their event, and recruit volunteers early to ensure the events are viable and able to be safely delivered, whilst also ensuring that the volunteers are valued and their skills appropriately used (Bowdin, Allen, O'Toole, Harris & McDonnell, 2011; Heitmann & Roberts, 2010; Pynes, 2004). As Bladen et al. (2018, p. 38) highlight, charity events "rely on a steady stream of willing volunteers to maintain effective delivery levels, but failure to attract a suitable profile of volunteer can have a serious impact on the success of event projects".

According to the National Council for Voluntary Organisations (NVCO, 2020), over 11.9 million people in the UK were estimated to have volunteered formally at least once a month in 2018–2019 and over 19.4 million people at least once during the year (NVCO, 2020). The types of volunteering activities were varied and included administrative duties, providing advice or counselling, campaigning for charities, providing transport services, mentoring others and visiting those in need (NVCO, 2020). The NVCO (2020) also outlined that three of the top five most popular volunteering activities were organising events (39%), raising money or taking part in sponsored events (27%), and representing their group, club or organisation at an event (25%). Whilst the NVCO (2020) data represents a wide array of volunteering activities, it assists in highlighting that volunteering is an important socio-cultural activity that aids the community and UK economy as a result (Wakelin, 2013). The data also demonstrates the growing importance of charity events and the support and reliance on volunteers. From a global perspective, the role and importance of volunteers is also evident (Govekar & Govekar, 2008). For example, in the US, it is estimated that approximately 35% of adults volunteer for charity, which equates to over 75 million people (CAF, 2019a). Similarly, in Australia, it is also reported that approximately 35% of adults (6.5 million people) volunteer with a charity (CAF, 2019b), and in Canada 30% of adults (9 million people) have volunteered (CAF, 2019c). Across these global contexts, volunteering to assist in the operational activities of charities is one of the core endeavours undertaken by volunteers, but one of the key initiatives that draw volunteers to support charities is to volunteer for charity events (Hyde et al., 2016; Webber, 2006).

Recruiting the right volunteers is therefore extremely important to the charity and particularly for charity fundraising events. Lockstone-Binney, Holmes, Smith, Baum and Storer (2015, p. 461) comment that "volunteers are integral to the operation and success of many events" and ensuring the appropriate calibre of volunteer is recruited is critical. Anheier (2014) highlights that when recruiting charity volunteers, it is important to consider and treat them differently, as their incentives and motivations for working with the charity are different from paid staff. A critical requirement is in "matching volunteer interests and talents to organisational needs" (Anheier, 2014, p. 402), and similarly to the needs of the charity fundraising event. Charities need to ensure there is a clear structure and process in place for recruiting and training volunteers, aligning skills to the event (or task), appreciating demographic challenges of age and gender, volunteer availability, providing clear communication, and developing recognition and retention strategies (Goldblatt & Matheson, 2009; Lockstone & Smith, 2009; Van der Wagen & White, 2015; Wakelin, 2013). Charities also need to be conscious of motivational factors when recruiting volunteers (Govekar & Govekar, 2008).

It is essential for a charity to provide its volunteers with a clear outline of roles and responsibilities as determined by the event, as this provides clear guidance, ensures the interests and skills of volunteers have been factored in, and thereby aids volunteer empowerment and motivation (Lockstone-Binney et al., 2015; Van der Wagen & White, 2015; Wakelin, 2013). Managing and supervising volunteers is also critical as this can have an effect, both positive and negative, on the service quality and event experience (Getz & Page, 2020). A lack of management and coordination will result in disengaged volunteers, who may feel isolated and lack confidence in their roles, which, in turn, will affect the effectiveness of their contribution to the event, and the quality of the consumer experience if it is a customer-facing role (Van der Wagen & White, 2015). Similarly, micro-managing volunteers will lead to frustration and a lack of trust, which will also result in disengagement and poor performance, as well as increasing dropout rates (Smith & Lockstone, 2009). Overall, there should be a balance between engaging volunteers in roles that match their abilities and interests, positive and proactive management and motivation, and strong communication, which, in turn, can increase retention of volunteers and profitability for the event and charity (Goldblatt & Matheson, 2009; Lockstone & Smith, 2009).

Charity volunteers are often personally and emotionally connected to the charity, which links to aspects of the motivating factors for why volunteers will support one charity over another (Heitmann & Roberts, 2010; Lockstone & Smith, 2009; Webber, 2006). Many charities are also developing strategies to attract younger volunteers to aid the long term sustainability of their volunteer cohort (Sargeant & Shang, 2017). NVCO (2020) highlighted that volunteering is still predominantly undertaken by those aged over 65, with younger people (18 to 24 years) less likely to volunteer, although in Australia and Canada the reverse is true (CAF, 2019a, 2019c). There is also a growing trend of increasing numbers of volunteers assisting in one off events, rather than long term or regular volunteering. This links to episodic volunteering and is an issue that charities need to consider in how they recruit and use their volunteers (Goldblatt & Matheson, 2009; Hyde et al., 2016; Schlenker et al., 2015; Smith & Lockstone, 2009).

Motivation and trends in charity volunteering

There is a significant body of literature that examines the motivational factors behind volunteering for events. Anheier (2014), Bladen et al. (2018), Bowdin et al., (2011), Downward, Lumsden and Ralston (2005), Getz and Page (2020), Heitmann and Roberts (2010), Lockstone and Smith (2009), and Van der Wagen and White (2015), among others, outline a range of reasons as to why people volunteer for events specifically, and these motivational factors can be readily applied to the charity events context.

Anheier (2014) outlines three core motivational factors that influence volunteers to engage with charities. First, is an *Altruistic* motivation, where there is a link to the values and beneficiaries of the charity; second, there are *Instrumental* motives, which are concerned with developing skills, networking and utilising spare time; and third, *Obligation* motives, which are influenced by moral and religious values, or a desire to contribute to the local community (Anheier, 2014; Bussell & Forbes, 2002). Govekar and Govekar (2008) examine five underlying motivational factors that can be attributed to charity volunteers based on the volunteering motivational literature. These include: self-esteem factors; moral and civic duty; religious beliefs and values; facilitation (where volunteers are influenced by peers and causes to volunteer); and social benefits (which is also linked to social capital). These motivational reasons are similar to a number of the charitable self-interest motivational factors as previously outlined by Sargeant and Jay (2014). One key defining characteristic of the charity volunteer, however, is the personal connection with the charity, where the volunteer has either been assisted directly or indirectly by the charity they are supporting (Bladen et al., 2018; Webber, 2006).

An underlying characteristic within charitable volunteering in the UK is the predominance of female volunteers compared to males (Bussell & Forbes, 2002; Dale, 2017; Merrylees, 2018). Historically, it has been noted that women are more likely to volunteer than men, although this trend is changing with the gap closing over the last ten years (NFP Synergy, 2016; NVCO, 2020). In terms of regular volunteering (at least once a month), NVCO (2020) noted there was only a marginal difference with 22% of females volunteering at least once a month, compared to 21% of males. In Australia, a similar pattern emerges with more women volunteering compared to men (AIHW, 2019). In contrast to this, in the US, it is noted that men are more likely to volunteer compared to women (CAF, 2019a).

One significant consideration in terms of gender and volunteering depends upon the type of event and charity (Downward et al., 2005; NVCO, 2020). NFP Synergy (2016, p. 3) outlined key

> differences in the kind of volunteering men and women tend to undertake or the organisations they are likely to volunteer for...... with men more likely to do voluntary work related to sports, rather than areas like health, education, and social services which more women were involved in.

Therefore, an underlying trend in charity event volunteering is that the gender of the volunteer attracted will predominantly depend upon the event context (Dale, 2017; Downward et al., 2005). For example, sporting and physical events are more likely to attract male volunteers, and community oriented events are more likely to attract female volunteers (Downward et al., 2005). The organisational context can also play a part in the gender composition of volunteers, with military and family oriented charities having an even balance of male and female volunteers (Bussell & Forbes, 2002).

Whilst there is a move towards a volunteering equilibrium in terms of gender, it is worth noting the significant gender imbalance within the charity sector workforce (Merrylees, 2018). Like the events industry, the charity sector continues to be predominantly female oriented (Bussell & Forbes, 2002; Merrylees, 2018; Thomas, 2016; Walters, 2017). Of particular concern is that despite this female dominated industry, there is still a gender imbalance that persists at the higher levels of management, which is currently disproportionately male dominated (Dale, 2017; Merrylees, 2018; Thomas, 2016; Walters, 2017).

A final trend affecting both the charity sector and event industry is the decreasing time factors that enable people to volunteer more regularly, resulting in volunteers being far more selective and ad hoc in relation to the events they commit to (Getz & Page, 2020; Goldblatt & Matheson, 2009; Lockstone & Smith, 2009). The rise of episodic volunteering has resulted in a shift, from the more regular and reliable volunteering workforce, to volunteers that are more selective of the events they work on, due to time constraints and volunteer interests (Hyde et al., 2016; Lockstone-Binney et al., 2015; Smith & Lockstone, 2009). This is also reflected in the decline of volunteering and selective volunteering reported by NVCO (2020), as well as the significant difference in volunteering rates depending on age. This is resulting in charities needing to align volunteers to events that meet both the organisational and event needs *as well as* the interests and skills of the volunteer (Sargeant & Shang, 2017; Smith & Lockstone, 2009). This leads to greater empowerment, interest, motivation and engagement by the volunteers, leading to improved event experiences and quality (Bussell & Forbes, 2002; Downward et al., 2005). This means that charities must consider carefully how, why and when they engage with their volunteers, especially given the increase in episodic volunteering (Lockstone & Smith, 2009), and that managing volunteers for charity events has become far more strategic than previously considered (Getz & Page, 2020; Goldblatt & Matheson, 2009; Lockstone & Smith, 2009).

Typology of charity event volunteering

Events have become an integral aspect of the fundraising strategy for many charities, and there is a significant reliance on volunteers for their delivery (Cox, 2017; Hyde et al., 2016). In the last 20 years the volume and diversity of these fundraising events has increased exponentially year on year as they can provide excellent returns on investment (Sargeant & Jay, 2014). According to the Business Visits and Events Partnership (BVEP, 2020), charity fundraising events in the UK are estimated to be worth £7 billion annually, which equates to approximately 10% of all income raised. In contrast to this, it is estimated that in the US, there are more than 1 million charities with an annual cumulative income of over $1.73 trillion dollars (Hyde et al., 2016; Sargeant & Shang, 2017), of which 9% is attributed to income from events (CAF, 2019a), or approximately $155 billion dollars. According to Hyde et al. (2016), similar trends are also evident in Australia and Canada, and it is estimated in Canada that 10% (or $1 billon CAD) is raised from events (CAF, 2019c), and in Australia 15% (or $23 billon AUD) of income is via charitable fundraising events (CAF, 2019b). Fundraising events have therefore become a key marketing and fundraising tool for charities, which build brand awareness, generate income and develop long term supporter journeys (Anheier, 2014; Cox, 2017; Sargeant & Jay, 2014). However, the financial data fails to accurately capture the nuanced categories of fundraising events that charities use, all of which rely on volunteers for their success.

From the charity and events literature there is evidence of a robust and varied array of event activity that charities employ as part of their fundraising strategy, and the role volunteers play in their delivery. A 'typology of charity event volunteering' has been developed (Figure 16.1), which reflects the four distinct types of charity fundraising events that are used by charities and the role of volunteers within these. The typology of event volunteering activities is categorised into four specific domains. These include *Volunteer Events* (Mirehie, Buning & Gibson, 2017; Passingham, 1995; Shaw, 1996); *Organisational Events* (Cox, 2017; Lyes, Palakshappa & Bulmer, 2016; Webber, 2006); *Third Party Events* (Goodwin, Snelgrove, Wood & Taks, 2017; Hendriks & Peelen, 2012; Higgins & Lauzon, 2002; Hyde et al., 2016); and *Collaborative Events* (Sargeant & Shang, 2017; Weinstein & Barden, 2017; Wendroff, 1999; Worth, 2016).

'Volunteer events' are solely developed and delivered by volunteers or supporters of the charity (Passingham, 1995). These events are generally small in scale, local to the volunteer

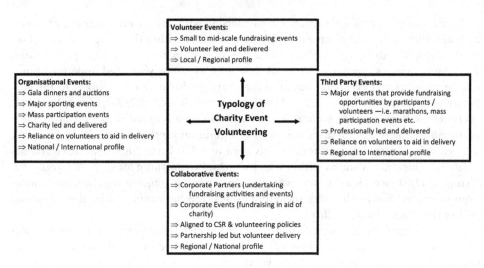

Figure 16.1 Typology of charity event volunteering

organisers and potential audience, and raise modest but not insignificant funds (Sargeant & Shang, 2017). Events include activities such as coffee mornings, fashion shows and wine tastings. The event may or may not have the support of the charity as it is dependent upon how these volunteers interact with the chosen charity (Sargeant & Jay, 2014). Whilst the income from an individual volunteer event will appear modest in isolation, the collective impact of all these events can be significant for the charity. For example, in the UK, the Macmillan's Coffee Morning is a collection of thousands of small coffee events, that raised over £27 million in 2019 alone, and £275 million since 1990 (Macmillan, 2021). From a charity perspective, these events require little direct support, thereby reducing the management burden, whilst maximising the social and economic benefits. From a volunteering perspective, these events provide an opportunity to provide meaningful support for a charity that volunteers are passionate about within their own skill set and time constraints (Courtney, 2013; Webber, 2006).

'Third Party' events are not necessarily designed as fundraising events but provide participants with the opportunity to fundraise (Goodwin et al., 2017; Mirehie et al., 2017). These events are usually designed as mass participation events, and examples include marathons, triathlons, cycling etapes and high endurance events. The London Marathon is considered the largest fundraising event in the world and has raised over £1 billion since its inception in 1981 (Virgin Money London Marathon, 2019). These events enable volunteers to participate on behalf of a charity, raising funds and awareness, whilst engaging in a physical activity (Hendriks & Peelen, 2012; Hyde et al., 2016; Mirehie et al., 2017). The reason behind the growing use of third party events is often that it is cheaper to buy places at the event rather than for a charity to coordinate the event themselves due to the cost, time and expertise required (Goodwin et al., 2017). Charities are increasing the amount of third party events they are purchasing places at, as this is a cost-effective way of maximising a return on investment, increasing brand awareness and reducing internal event workloads (Cox, 2017; Hendriks & Peelen, 2012; Hyde et al., 2016; Mirehie et al., 2017). From an event management perspective, there is a significant reliance on a volunteer workforce to support this type of event, without which these mass participation events would not be possible (Goldblatt, 2011; Van Der Wagen & White, 2015).

'Collaborative events' are managed in partnership with charity and a corporate partner, although they are delivered operationally by volunteers within these organisations (Lyes et al., 2016; Worth, 2016). Collaborative events rely on these corporate partnerships, whereby corporates appoint a charity as their 'charity of the year', and undertake fundraising activities and events on behalf of the charity, which are often linked to the corporate social responsibility policies of the organisation (Cox, 2017; Sargeant & Jay, 2014; Weinstein & Barden, 2017; Wendroff, 1999). Whilst time is invested in cultivating these partnerships, the return on investment can be significant for the charity (Webber, 2006). The growth in corporate partnerships has been noted as being highly lucrative and has created a competitive context within which charities are pitching for support (Sargeant & Shang, 2017). Once secured, however, these partnerships require regular communications to ensure that fundraising, including events, can be maximised by the volunteers within the charity (Worth, 2016).

Finally, 'organisational events' are developed and managed by the charity. These types of events include charity gala dinners, commemorative events, family activities, major sporting events and telethons. These events entail the charity planning, managing and delivering all stages of the event, with the primary aim of raising both funds and their profile (Cox, 2017; Goodwin et al., 2017; Lyes et al., 2016; Passingham, 1995; Weinstein & Barden, 2017; Wendroff, 1999). The charity will aim to underwrite the costs of the event through sponsorship in the first instance to avoid putting organisational funds at risk (Bladen et al., 2018; Bowdin et al., 2011). The charity will also engage with stakeholders to ensure that there is enough support in the wider community for the event to be successfully delivered (Courtney, 2013). Most critically, the charity will actively identify and work with their volunteer bank to ensure there is sufficient human resource support for the event, as without volunteers the event would not be feasible (Bladen et al., 2018).

As the typology indicates, volunteers are integral to the event activities being undertaken, both directly and indirectly by charities. Irrespective of the event type, size or approach being taken, the reliance on volunteers is substantial, and with the growth of events as a critical fundraising strategy, this is placing additional pressure on charities to effectively recruit and manage their volunteers, without whom the events would not happen.

Conclusion

This chapter has highlighted the importance of volunteers in supporting charities and charity events, and that volunteers have become the lifeblood of the sector (Bladen et al., 2018; Goldblatt, 2011; Govekar & Govekar, 2008). Charities must align the right volunteer to the event at an early period in the event process, which considers the event context, gender dynamics, and the volunteer's skills and interests in order to enable a motivated volunteer and successful event outcome (Anheier, 2014; Sargeant & Jay, 2014; Van der Wagen & White, 2015). Charities face numerous challenges, such as regulatory burdens and perceptions of trust (Etherington, 2017; Hind, 2017), and the long term sustainability of charity events may be uncertain due to the decline in volunteers across the sector, the rise in episodic volunteering and the changing demographics of volunteers (Heitmann & Roberts, 2010; Lockstone & Smith, 2009; NVCO, 2020). However, for now, events offer a rich opportunity to raise awareness and income for charities and provide meaningful opportunities for volunteers to support charitable causes (Hyde et al., 2016).

References

AIHW. (2019). *Volunteers*. Australian Institute of Health and Welfare. Retrieved from: https://www.aihw.gov.au/reports/australias-welfare/volunteers

Anheier, H. (2014). *Nonprofit organizations: Theory, management, policy*. London: Routledge.

Bladen, C., Kennell, J., Abson, E., & Wilde, N. (2018). *Events management an introduction* (2nd ed.). London: Routledge.

Bowdin, G., Allen, J., O'Toole, W., Harris, R., & McDonnell, I. (2011). *Events management* (3rd ed.). London: Routledge.

Bremner, R. (1996). *Giving: Charity and philanthropy in history*. London: Transaction Publishers.

Business Visits and Events Partnership (BVEP). (2020). *The UK events industry*. Retrieved from: https://www.businessvisitsandeventspartnership.com/news/bvep-press-releases/801-bvep-launches-report-focused-on-70bn-events-industry

Bussell, H., & Forbes, D. (2002). Understanding the volunteer market: The what, where, who and why of volunteering. *International Journal of Non-profit and Voluntary Sector Marketing, 7*(3), 244–257. https://doi.org/10.1002/nvsm.183

CAF. (2019a). *Charitable giving in the USA 2019: An overview of individual giving in the USA*. Charity Aids Foundation. Retrieved from: https://www.cafonline.org/docs/default-source/about-us-publications/caf-usa-giving-report-2019.pdf

CAF. (2019b). *Australia giving 2019: An overview of charitable giving in Australia*. Charity Aids Foundation. Retrieved from: https://www.cafonline.org/docs/default-source/about-us-publications/caf-australia-giving-report-2019-16master.pdf?sfvrsn=65e49940_2

CAF. (2019c). *Canada giving 2019*. Charity Aids Foundation. Retrieved from: https://www.cafonline.org/docs/default-source/about-us-publications/caf-canada-giving-report-2019.pdf?sfvrsn=c77d9940_4

Clarke, S., & Norton, M. (1997). *The complete fundraising handbook* (3rd ed.). London: Directory of Social Change.

Courtney, R. (2013). *Strategic management in the third sector*. Basingstoke: Palgrave Macmillan.

Cox, K. (2017). Fundraising events. In A. Sargeant & J. Shang (Eds.). *Fundraising principles and practice* (2nd ed., pp. 589–611). Hoboken, NJ: John Wiley & Sons, Inc.

Dale, E. (2017). Fundraising as women work? Examining the profession with a gender lens. *International Journal of Nonprofit and Voluntary Sector Marketing, 22*(2), 1–10. https://doi.org/10.1002/nvsm.1605

Downward, P., Lumsden, L., & Ralston, R. (2005). Gender differences in sports event volunteering: Insights from Crew 2002 at the XVII Commonwealth Games. *Managing Leisure, 10*, 219–236. https://doi.org/10.1080/13606710500348086

Driscoll, L. (2017). The reforming regulator. In M. McGregor-Lowndes & B. Wyatt (Eds.). *Regulating charities: The inside story* (pp. 37–58). Abingdon, Oxon: Routledge.

Etherington, S. (2017). Reflections on modernizing and reforming regulation. In M. McGregor-Lowndes & B. Wyatt (Eds.). *Regulating charities: The inside story* (pp. 59–77). Abingdon, Oxon: Routledge.

Fries, R. (2017). Towards regulation: Modernizing the original charity commission. In M. McGregor-Lowndes & B. Wyatt (Eds.). *Regulating charities: The inside story* (pp. 17–36). Abingdon, Oxon: Routledge.

Getz, D., & Page, S. (2020). *Event studies: Theory research and policy for planned events* (5th ed.). Oxford: Routledge.

Goldblatt, J. (2011). *Special events*. London: Wiley.

Goldblatt, J., & Matheson, C. (2009). Volunteer recruitment and retention: An Australian–USA comparison. In T. Baum, M. Deery, C. Hanlon, L. Lockstone & K. Smith. *People & work in events and conventions: A research perspective* (pp. 138–153). Oxfordshire: CABI.

Goodwin, A., Snelgrove, R., Wood, L., & Taks, M. (2017). Leveraging charity sport events to develop a connection to a cause. *Event Management, 21*(2), 175–184. https://doi.org/10.1080/14775085.20 10.533918

Govekar, P., & Govekar, M. (2008). Volunteer recruitment, retention, development. In A. Sargeant & W. Wymer (Eds.). *The Routledge companion to non-profit marketing* (pp. 361–372). London: Routledge.

Hanvey, C., & Philpot, T. (1996). *Sweet charity: The role and workings of voluntary organisations*. London: Routledge.

Heitmann, S., & Roberts, C. (2010). Successful staffing of events. In P. Robinson, D. Wale & G. Dickinson (Eds.). *Events management* (pp. 113–136). Oxfordshire: Cabi.

Hendriks, M., & Peelen, E. (2012). Personas in action: Linking event participation motivation to charitable giving and sports. *International Journal of Non-profit and Voluntary Sector Marketing, 18*, 60–72. https://doi.org/10.1002/nvsm.1458

Higgins, J., & Lauzon, L. (2002). Finding the funds in fun runs: Exploring physical activity events as fundraising tools in non-profit sector. *International Journal of non-profit and Voluntary Sector Marketing, 8*(4), 363–377. https://doi.org/10.1002/nvsm.226

Hind, A. (2017). New development: Fundraising in UK charities: Stepping back from the abyss. *Public Money & Management Journal, 37*(3), 205–210. https://doi.org/10.1080/09540962.2017.1282238

Hyde, M., Dunn, J., Wust, N., Bax, C., & Chambers, S. (2016). Satisfaction, organisational commitment and future action in charity sport event volunteers. *International Journal of non-profit and Voluntary Sector Marketing, 21*, 148–167. https://doi.org/10.1002/nvsm.1552

Levitt, T. (2012). *Partners for good: Business, government and the third sector.* Abingdon, Oxon: Routledge.

Lockstone, L., & Smith, K. (2009). Episodic experiences: Volunteering flexibility in the events sector. In T. Baum, M. Deery, C. Hanlon, L. Lockstone & K. Smith. *People & work in events and conventions: A research perspective* (pp. 108–126). Oxfordshire: CABI.

Lockstone-Binney, L., Holmes, K., Smith, K., Baum, T., & Storer, C. (2015). Are all my volunteers here to help out? Clustering event volunteers by their motivations. *Event Management, 19*, 461–477. https://doi.org/10.3727/152599515X14465748512605

Lyes, A., Palakshappa, N., & Bulmer, S. (2016). Cause-related events: Fulfilling the objectives of social partnerships. *International Journal of Non-profit and Voluntary Sector Marketing, 21*(4), 286–301. https://doi.org/10.1002/nvsm.1561

Macmillan. (2021). *The world's biggest coffee morning is Macmillan's biggest fundraising event.* Retrieved from: https://coffee.macmillan.org.uk/about/what/

Malik, N. (2008). Defining "charity" and "charitable purposes" in the United Kingdom. *International Journal for Not-for-Profit Law, 11*(1), 36–50.

Merrylees, J. (2018). *Gender equality in the charity sector. Is there strength in numbers?* Retrieved from: https://www.charityjob.co.uk/careeradvice/gender-equality-in-the-charity-sector-is-there-strength-in-numbers/

Mirehie, M., Buning, R., & Gibson, H. (2017). Participation versus nonparticipation in a charity running event. *Event Management, 21*(6), 639–652. https://doi.org/10.3727/152599517X15073047237188

Mullin, R. (1995). *Foundations for fund-raising.* Hemel Hempstead: ICSA Publishing Ltd.

NFP Synergy. (2016). *Volunteering – facts and figures.* Retrieved from: https://nfpsynergy.net/free-report/facts-and-figures-volunteering

NVCO. (2020). *UK civil society almanac 2020: Volunteering overview.* Retrieved from: https://data.ncvo.org.uk/

Passingham, S. (1995). *Organising local events* (2nd ed.). London: The Directory of Social Change.

Philips, S., & Smith, S. (2011). Between governance and regulation: Evolving government third sector relationships. In S. Philips & S. Smith (2011). *Governance and regulation in the third sector: An international perspective* (pp. 1–36). London: Routledge.

Pitts, R. (1997). Regional fundraising events. *Journal of Non-profit and Voluntary Sector Marketing, 3*(1), 28–37. https://doi.org/10.1002/nvsm.6090030104

Pynes, J. (2004). *Human resources management for public and non-profit organisations* (2nd ed.). San Francisco: John Wiley and Sons.

Sargeant, A., & Jay, E. (2014). *Fundraising management: Analysis, planning and practice* (3rd ed.). London: Routledge.

Sargeant, A., & Shang, J. (2017). *Fundraising principles and practice* (2nd ed.). Hoboken, NJ: John Wiley & Sons, Inc.

Schlenker, K., Edwards, D., & Wearing, S. (2015). Volunteering and events. In S. Page & J. Connell (Eds.). *The Routledge handbook of events* (pp. 316–325). London: Routledge.

Shaw, M. (1996). Whatever happened to the pub crawl? A change in attitude to charitable fundraising. *Journal of Non-profit and Voluntary Sector Marketing, 1*(4), 315–321. https://doi.org/10.1002/nvsm.6090010404

Smith, K., & Lockstone, L. (2009). Involving and keeping event volunteers: Management insights from cultural festivals. In T. Baum, M. Deery, C. Hanlon, L. Lockstone & K. Smith (Eds.). *People & work in events and conventions: A research perspective* (pp. 154–170). Oxfordshire: CABI.

Thomas, R. (2016). A remarkable absence of women: A comment on the formation of the new events industry board. *Journal of Policy Research in Tourism, Leisure and Events, 9*(2), 201–204. https://doi.or g/10.1080/19407963.2016.1208189

Van der Wagen, L., & White, L. (2015). *Human resource management for the events industry* (2nd ed.). London: Routledge.

Virgin Money London Marathon. (2019). *First world record for 2020 Virgin Money London Marathon.* Retrieved from: https://www.virginmoneylondonmarathon.com/news-media/latest-news/item/first-world-record-for-2020-virgin-money-london-marathon/index.html

Wakelin, D. (2013). What motivates students to volunteer on events? *Event Management, 17*(1), 63–75. https://doi.org/10.3727/152599513X13623342048185

Walters, T. (2017). Gender equality in academic tourism, hospitality, leisure and events conferences. *Journal of Policy Research in Tourism, Leisure and Events, 10*(1), 17–32. https://doi.org/10.1080/19407 963.2018.1403165

Webber, D. (2006). Understanding charity fundraising events. *International Journal of Non-profit and Voluntary Sector Marketing, 9*(2), 122–134. https://doi.org/10.1002/nvsm.239

Weinstein, S., & Barden, P. (2017). *The complete guide to fundraising management* (4th ed.). Hoboken, NJ: John Wiley & Sons, Inc.

Wendroff, A. (1999). *Special events: Proven strategies for non-profit fundraising.* New York: John Wiley & Sons, Inc.

Worth, M. (2016). *Fundraising principles and practice.* London: Sage Publications Ltd.

17

HELPING THROUGH SPORT AND EVENTS WITHIN CORPORATE VOLUNTEERING

Benefits for volunteers and companies

Barbara Józefowicz

Introduction

Volunteering has many faces. One of these is helping specific beneficiaries, such as other individuals, groups and communities, to solve their problems (Rodell, 2013). Volunteering, especially in its corporate form, has become a popular channel for showing care for social and environmental issues and expressing social responsibility of business (Glavas & Kelly, 2014; Haski-Leventhal, Kach & Pournader, 2019; Mirvis, 2012; Paço & Nave, 2013). Within a growing body of research on corporate volunteering, scholars point out the various benefits to the individual volunteer, the organisation employing a volunteer and the society (e.g., Haski-Leventhal et al., 2018; Wilson, 2000). Through corporate volunteering programmes companies can express their social and environmental responsibility; improve companies' external relations (Booth, Park & Glomb, 2009; Escher & Brzustewicz, 2020; Glińska-Neweś & Górka, 2020; Greening & Turban, 2000; Mirvis, 2012), their employees' organisational commitment (Bartel, 2001; Grant, Dutton & Rosso, 2008; Haski-Leventhal et al., 2019) as well as work-related competencies (Bellé, 2013; Booth et al., 2009; Devereux, 2008; Haski-Leventhal et al., 2019). There is a growing number of companies implementing corporate volunteering as a central component of their strategy (Bussell & Forbes, 2008; Grant, 2012; Shachar et al., 2018). A large increase in corporate volunteering programmes has also been observed in Poland (Responsible Business Forum, 2019). It is estimated that the percentage of the largest companies that have an employee volunteering programme is approximately 16%. Whilst among the medium-sized companies this percentage is around 2%, the same figure as found in large companies ten years ago.

Within volunteering programmes, employees take part in socially and/or environmentally beneficial activities that are encouraged and supported by their employers (Glińska-Neweś et al., 2020; Gratton & Ghoshal, 2003; Muthuri, Matten & Moon, 2009; Paço et al., 2013). Among a large variety of voluntary activities undertaken within corporate volunteering, there are projects related to sport and events. However, the field of corporate volunteering has yet to be empirically examined to a significant extent. Hence, the aim of this chapter is to present specific corporate volunteering projects conducted in the domains of sport and events, and to exemplify the benefits that companies can gain from such initiatives. Such

DOI: 10.4324/9780367815875-20

examples build a better business case for corporate volunteering, and delivering rationales for business engagement in socially responsible initiatives (Carroll & Shabana, 2010).

The chapter begins with a presentation of the theoretical background of corporate volunteering, followed by an overview of the proposed research method and results of the empirical study. Two cases of corporate volunteering projects are presented in more detail, notably, the organisation of a running event, The HeatHouse Run, and corporate volunteers helping at The Enchanted Song Festival for talented disabled people. Based on individual semi-structured interviews with volunteers and coordinators of volunteering programmes in companies, it was found that volunteering activities strengthen positive relationships among employees and their experience of meaningfulness at work, developing employees' competencies, their organisational commitment and the employer's brand image.

Corporate volunteering and its effects – theoretical background

According to Wild (1993), a corporate volunteer programme means any organised company support for employees and their families who wish to volunteer their time and skills in service to the community. Such programmes can be more or less formalised, to a different extent related to the company's strategy, organised individually or collectively and sometimes conducted in cooperation with other organisations (most often with non-governmental organisations, NGOs). The essence of corporate volunteering is that organisations encourage employees to use their time and competencies for actions taken outside the organisation, which are beneficial for the society and environment (Gratton & Ghoshal, 2003; Muthuri et al., 2009; Paço et al., 2013). At the same time, the variety of volunteering projects is significant and limited only by employees' creativity.

Encouraging employees' active involvement in volunteering projects is beneficial for the company for several reasons. Most of all, contemporary stakeholders, such as customers, shareholders, employees and local community require business organisations to demonstrate their corporate social responsibility (Booth et al., 2009; Greening & Turban, 2000; Mirvis, 2012). Showing the company's care for social and environmental problems contributes to building a brand image of socially engaged business, including strengthening the employer's brand which attracts the best candidates to work. Thus, corporate volunteering helps companies gain competitive advantage in the market (e.g., Basil et al., 2009; Plewa et al., 2015).

The results of Deloitte's *2017 Volunteerism Survey* indicate that creating a culture of volunteerism in the workplace may also boost morale, workplace atmosphere and brand perception (Deloitte, 2017). Also, previous research has demonstrated the link between corporate volunteering and positive workplace outcomes (de Gilder, Schuyt & Breedijk, 2005; Peterson, 2004; Plewa et al., 2015). Existing literature in the field provides evidence that employee participation in corporate volunteering is positively and significantly related to their affective commitment in the organisation and job satisfaction (Haski-Leventhal et al., 2019). Corporate volunteering also brings enhancement of employees' sense of work meaningfulness, through providing them an opportunity for networking and relatedness (Gratton & Ghoshal, 2003; Haski-Leventhal et al., 2019) and the opportunity for perceiving their organisations as good corporate citizens (Chaudhary & Akhouri, 2019; Grant & Berry, 2011).

As suggested by various scholars (see Bellé, 2013; Booth et al., 2009; Devereux, 2008; Haski-Leventhal et al., 2019; Wild, 1993) volunteer programmes are also capable of providing employees with the opportunity to enhance job-related skills and improve work attitudes. Findings from Deloitte's *2016 Impact Survey* indicate that volunteering experience may play a significant role in building leadership skills considered to be 'must haves' for successful leaders (Deloitte, 2016, p. 2). Within corporate volunteering, employees can do something different from their daily duties, and hence learn and practice new skills (Haski-Leventhal et al., 2019; Mirvis, 2012; Sundeen & Raskoff, 1994). According to the Responsible Business Forum report (2019), employees who have become involved in volunteer programmes improve their competencies in the areas that employers care most about, that is, cooperation, communication, decision-making and project management. Moreover, due to the very essence of volunteering, employees develop their emotional competencies and awareness of corporate social responsibility (Bartsch, 2012).

Research method

In order to explore the nature and effects of corporate volunteering projects realised in contemporary companies, in May and June 2018 an empirical study was conducted among 18 companies operating in Poland. The research project was funded by the National Science Centre, Poland (DEC-2017/25/B/HS4/01113). The companies were selected from a ranking published by the Responsible Business Forum (Forum Odpowiedzialnego Biznesu, 2017). Out of 62 firms listed in the 2017 rankings, 18 were implementing corporate volunteering programmes. The primary data was collected by semi-structured in-depth individual interviews. In the first step of the study, interviews with the coordinators of volunteer programmes were conducted. The second step was to interview employee-volunteers in five organisations that gave their consent. In two companies, I identified volunteering projects related to sport and events. To ensure anonymity, the names of the companies have been changed and they are referred to as HeatHouse and GlobeBank.

The interview scenario included respondents' perceptions of the company involvement in sustainable development goals, reasons for participating in corporate volunteering, types and goals of projects conducted by employees, and outcomes of the projects. The interviews were audio recorded and transcribed, then independently coded by three researchers. Deductive and inductive coding techniques were employed (Miles, Huberman & Saldana, 2014). Deductive coding was based on researcher-generated codes reflecting issues included in the interview scenario. Inductive in vivo coding was performed based on new codes derived from interviewees' words. After coding, data was classified into categories reflecting specific problems. In this chapter, the nature and results of two volunteering projects related to sport and events were analysed and presented below.

Corporate volunteering in the HeatHouse Run

The HeatHouse is one of the world's leading suppliers of innovative and energy-efficient solutions in the cooling, heating and automotive sector. The HeatHouse Run is a charity running event, which has been organised annually for the past ten years. It is among the key initiatives expressing the company's philanthropy strategy, which prioritises helping children from local communities, specifically in regard to their health, education and sport. The project contributes to several strategic goals of the company, including helping those in need, promoting a healthy and active lifestyle through sport, as well as internal integration and integration with the local community. The run takes place in two locations associated with company units in Poland. The event is held under the patronage of the local government.

HeatHouse employees and their families take part in the event. For each kilometre run by the participant, the company donates a certain amount of money to a charity foundation.

The total sum of money is then spent on charities chosen by the foundation. Sometimes, HeatHouse employees choose the purpose of the donation. Usually, they focus on helping children in need; for example, money can be donated to support the sick children of employees.

The company encourages employees to participate in the project by promoting the Heat-House Run throughout the year. To ensure that this event remains in the employee memory during the year, the company uses various channels of communication, including posters, news on the intranet, articles in a company newspaper and various printouts on information boards. There are also special meetings organised in order to inform employees about the event, before and after the run. A special team composed of representatives of employees supervises the improvement of the project, and all feedback is sent to them.

What sets HeatHouse apart in its charitable activities is that each employee has a direct influence and is able to contribute to the amount and purpose of the donation made after the run. Making such decisions increases employee commitment and their sense of responsibility towards beneficiaries. As part of volunteering work, employees are also involved in the organisation of the run, i.e., they conduct specific tasks related to the course of the run.

Asked about benefits for the company derived from the HeatHouse Run, the coordinator of the project first mentioned the improvement of internal and external relationships. Sample quotes regarding the integration among all company members are:

> We all run together. Starting from the CEO, through office workers to production workers, their families and children, so it is also such a nice form of integration and the fact that no barriers are created. (...) there is also a nice atmosphere at this event, because we are all together, we wear the same outfits and we run together. We are all equally involved. There are no divisions here.
>
> *(Project Coordinator, 25 May 2018)*

> Building of a sense of belonging to the company and the fact that these barriers between managers and workers simply cease to exist during such meetings, and this has such an integrative form.
>
> *(HeatHouse Employee, 11 June 2018)*

Besides increasing the sense of unity and solidarity within the company, there are also benefits concerning external relationships, as indicated by one of the interviewees:

> I think it is also a great benefit for us from these projects, that as a company we have an influence on certain changes that are taking place in our society. And certainly, this cooperation with the local community, because this run seems to bring us closer to this local community, because we get to know the problems and needs of people who live in our area and we try to help them.
>
> *(Project Coordinator, 25 May 2018)*

Among the positive effects of involvement in the HeatHouse Run, the development of volunteers' competencies was also noticed:

> Participation in the run certainly triggered empathy in the employees, (...) - emotional intelligence gains weight here.
>
> *(Project Coordinator, 25 May 2018)*

A person who has worked in a production position so far has not managed any team, during this event he has the opportunity to develop leadership skills.

(HeatHouse Employee, 11 June 2018)

Interestingly, in this case, competency development is associated also with the increasing organisational commitment of employees. As an employee representative mentioned:

It also gives us the opportunity to develop, along with our passions, it gives opportunities for development, not necessarily strictly professional, but to do something that gives us fun, allow us to fulfil our passion, so it certainly strengthens the commitment to the company.

(HeatHouse Employee, 11 June 2018)

In summary, the sport event conducted by HeatHouse within their corporate volunteering programme was evaluated as very successful. It has been organised for many years and every year, attracts employees willing to take part in it and help others through sport activities. The project's success is measured by the number of children who received support and the amount of money raised. It is also measured by the company's good relationship with the local community as well as the local authorities of cities where the company branches are located. The project's significant contribution is perhaps best summarised in the coordinator's words: "I can see only positives here. The fact that employees integrate, get involved and do something good together" (Project Coordinator, 25 May 2018). Although not specified by the interviewees, and perhaps too obvious, there is also an improvement of employee physical condition through participation in sport activities.

The Enchanted Song Festival for talented disabled people as the corporate volunteering project of GlobeBank

GlobeBank is one of the largest and most innovative financial institutions in Poland. It offers complex financial services, supported by modern banking technology. The company is a part of GlobeBank Group with a meaningful presence in ten core markets in Europe and the Americas and is one of the largest banks in the world by market capitalisation. Its purpose is to help people and businesses prosper in a simple, personal and fair way. The GlobeBank mission of building a more responsible bank has been operationalised in a number of commitments supporting this objective. It aims to raise over €120 billion in green financing between 2019 and 2025, as well as financially empowering more than 10 million people over the same period.

GlobeBank has a well-established Employee Volunteering Policy. The policy defines the areas of voluntary activities, describes the procedures and presents indicators related to volunteering. From 2019, all employees of GlobeBank have eight hours a year at their disposal that they can spend on volunteering in three areas resulting from the Employee Volunteering Policy: supporting education and science development, activities for equalising opportunities and building a civil society.

Among many different volunteering activities proposed for the employees, one is participation in the Enchanted Song Festival. It is a popular vocal competition for gifted people with disabilities, organised since 2005 by a charitable foundation led by a well-known Polish actress. The unique idea of this festival is to promote the extraordinary singing talents of people suffering from illness and disability, without indulgence, and providing them with fair competition. In 15 years, over 4,000 applications were submitted to participate in this nationwide vocal competition. Eighty laureates received statuettes and awards totalling over a million Polish zlotys. Seventy-five of the biggest stars of Polish song sang with the finalists. The candidates were assessed by 126 jurors. About 42 million people watched the festival on television.

GlobeBank has been involved in this event for three years. The employee-volunteers are responsible for looking after the participants of the final concert. Moreover, they organise and coordinate events and activities accompanying the Festival, such as sport competitions. Thus, the event represents a combination of both culture and sport. The cooperation between GlobeBank and the foundation organising the Enchanted Song Festival began with the bottom-up initiative of an individual bank employee who had worked before as a volunteer for the foundation. The employee wanted the company he worked for to join this event and to provide financial assistance. Due to his efforts, GlobeBank participates in sharing the costs of organising vocal workshops for participants qualified for the final concert and also sponsors scholarships for the winners of the competition. The cooperation of GlobeBank with the foundation goes beyond the organisation of the festival. An added benefit is that GlobeBank receives substantive support from the foundation in creating other volunteering opportunities for employees and sharing experiences with foundation members.

There are various effects of GlobeBank's involvement in the Enchanted Song Festival; however, strengthening the public image of the company seems to be the most significant. This is how the project coordinator explained it:

> Of course, this is an advantage for us from a marketing point of view. Our logo can be found on advertising materials, on TV etc. But it also gives us the opportunity to show the bank in such a warm light of social activities. Because not everyone knows that we are also very involved. It is certainly a good promotion for us.
>
> *(Project Coordinator, 18 May 2018)*

Among other effects of corporate volunteering perceived from the manager's perspective, there were similar benefits to those noticed at the HeatHouse Run. Relational benefits include both internal and external relationships' improvement, which has been expressed in these words:

> In addition to establishing friendly relations with beneficiaries, employees get to know each other from a different, non-professional side.
>
> *(Project Coordinator, 18 May, 2018)*

Volunteers noted that participation in this project allowed them to get out of the routine of everyday activities at work, especially working in a group:

> Always a suit, desk, client at work. So, there is no time to talk about what we like, about our passions; therefore this is an extra thing I appreciate. I like working in larger group.
>
> *(GlobeBank Employee, 28 May 2018)*

It is worth emphasising the emergence of strong emotional relationships between volunteers and beneficiaries, which result in greater empathy and sensitivity to problems that were not known or noticed before. Moreover, some non-job-related skills of volunteers were revealed: "(…) some of us draw beautifully, others are able to knit something with these children, or make cut-outs" (GlobeBank Employee, 28 May 2018).

In summary, GlobeBank's involvement in the Festival, taking the form of corporate volunteering, has become an opportunity to strengthen positive relationships at work and develop the external relations of the company. It may be argued that due to the nationwide impact of the Festival, the bank's involvement primarily brought benefits for enhancing the image of the company. Nevertheless, the volunteering work of employees also had a significant impact on their relations and competency development.

Conclusion

The cases presented in this chapter demonstrate how employee engagement as corporate volunteers in sports and events can be beneficial for all parties. The results of this qualitative study indicate that participation in volunteering programmes can lead to higher levels of relatedness, both internal and external, image benefits and employees' organisational commitment. The study supports arguments of other researchers that employees prefer to work for companies that are not only focused on their financial results but are also actively involved in their community (Booth et al., 2009; Greening & Turban, 2000; Mirvis, 2012). The findings also align with results of the study conducted by the Responsible Business Forum (2019) indicating that 96% of decision-makers in companies implementing corporate volunteering believe that employees improve their competencies through volunteering work.

The analysis in this chapter sheds light on the corporate form of volunteering in sports and events. Based on the two cases presented, it is argued that together with growing interest in this form of performing social responsibility, the business, sport and event industries can benefit from company engagement in corporate volunteering programmes. Companies encouraging employees to participate in such programmes create a powerful new prospect for volunteering in general.

References

Bartel, C. A. (2001). Social comparisons in boundary-spanning work: Effects of community outreach on members' organizational identity and identification. *Administrative Science Quarterly, 46*(3), 379–413. https://doi.org/10.2307/3094869

Bartsch, G. (2012). Emotional learning: managerial development by corporate volunteering. *Journal of Management Development, 31*(3), 253–262. https://doi.org/10.1108/02621711211208880

Basil, D. Z., Runte, M. S., Easwaramoorthy, M., & Barr, C. (2009). Company support for employee volunteering: A national survey of companies in Canada. *Journal of Business Ethics, 85*(supp. 2), 387–398. http://dx.doi.org/10.1007/s10551-008-9741-0

Bellé, N. (2013). Leading to make a difference: A field experiment on the performance effects of transformational leadership, perceived social impact, and public service motivation. *Journal of Public Administration Research and Theory, 24*(1), 109–136. https://doi.org/10.1093/jopart/mut033

Booth, J. E., Park, K. W., & Glomb, T. M. (2009). Employer-supported volunteering benefits: Gift exchange among employers, employees, and volunteer organizations. *Human Resource Management, 48*(2), 227–249. https://doi.org/10.1002/hrm.20277

Bussell, H., & Forbes, D. (2008). How U.K. universities engage with their local communities: A study of employer supported volunteering. *International Journal of Nonprofit and Voluntary Sector Marketing, 13*, 363–378. https://doi.org/10.1002/nvsm.331

Carroll, A. B., & Shabana, K. M. (2010). The business case for corporate social responsibility: A review of concepts, research and practice. *International Journal of Management Reviews, 12*(1), 85–105. https://doi.org/10.1111/j.1468-2370.2009.00275.x

Chaudhary, R., & Akhouri, A. (2019). CSR perceptions and employee creativity: Examining serial mediation effects of meaningfulness and work engagement. *Social Responsibility Journal, 15*(1), 61–74. https://doi.org/10.1108/SRJ-01-2018-0018

Deloitte. (2016). *2016 Impact Survey: Building leadership skills through volunteerism.* https://www2.deloitte.com/content/dam/Deloitte/us/Documents/us-deloitte-impact-survey.pdf

Deloitte. (2017). *2017 Volunteerism survey: Impacts that matters.* https://www2.deloitte.com/us/en/pages/about-deloitte/articles/citizenship-deloitte-volunteer-impact-research.html

de Gilder, D., Schuyt, T. M., & Breedijk, M. (2005). Effects of an employee volunteering program on the work force: The ABN-AMRO case. *Journal of Business Ethics, 61,* 143–152. https://doi.org/10.1007/s10551-005-7101-x

Devereux, P. (2008). International volunteering for development and sustainability: Outdated paternalism or a radical response to globalisation? *Development in Practice, 18*(3), 357–370. https://doi.org/10.1080/09614520802030409

Escher, I., & Brzustewicz, P. (2020). Inter-organizational collaboration on projects supporting sustainable development goals: The company perspective. *Sustainability, 12*(12), 4969. https://doi.org/10.3390/su12124969

Forum Odpowiedzialnego Biznesu (2017). *Znamy Ranking Odpowiedzialnych Firm 2017- Forum Odpowiedzialnego Biznesu.* http://odpowiedzialnybiznes.pl/aktualno%C5%9Bci/znamy-ranking-odpowiedzialnych-firm-2017/

Glavas, A., & Kelly, K. (2014). The effects of perceived corporate social responsibility on employee attitudes. *Business Ethics Quarterly, 24*(2), 165–202. https://doi.org/10.5840/beq20143206

Glińska-Neweś, A., Brzustewicz, P., Escher, I., Fomina, Y., Józefowicz, B., Katunina, I., Petrykowska, J., & Szostek D. (2020). Company involvement in sustainable development: Proposition of a theoretical framework. In A. Zakrzewska-Bielawska & I. Staniec (Eds.), *Contemporary Challenges in Cooperation and Coopetition in the Age of Industry 4.0.* (pp. 439–451). Springer Proceedings in Business and Economics. https://doi.org/10.1007/978-3-030-30549-9_24

Glińska-Neweś, A., & Górka, J. (2020). Capabilities of corporate volunteering in strengthening social capital. *Sustainability, 12*(18), 7482. https://doi.org/10.3390/su12187482

Grant, A. (2012). Giving time, time after time: Work design and sustained employee participation in corporate volunteering. *Academy of Management Review, 37*(4), 589–615. http://dx.doi.org/10.5465/amr.2010.0280

Grant, A. M., & Berry, J. W. (2011). The necessity of others is the mother of invention: Intrinsic and prosocial motivations, perspective taking, and creativity. *Academy of Management Journal, 54*(1), 73–96. https://doi.org/10.5465/amj.2011.59215085

Grant, A. M., Dutton, J. E., & Rosso, B. (2008). Giving commitment: Employee support programs and the prosocial sensemaking process. *Academy of Management Journal, 51,* 898–918. https://doi.org/10.5465/amj.2008.34789652

Gratton, L., & Ghoshal, S. (2003). Managing personal human capital: New ethos for the 'volunteer' employee. *European Management Journal, 21*(1), 1–10. https://doi.org/10.1016/S0263-2373(02)00149-4

Greening, D. W., & Turban, D. B. (2000). Corporate social performance as a competitive advantage in attracting a quality workforce. *Business and Society, 39,* 254–280; https://doi.org/10.1177/000765030003900302

Haski-Leventhal, D., Kach, A., & Pournader, M. (2019). Employee need satisfaction and positive workplace outcomes: The role of corporate volunteering. *Nonprofit and Voluntary Sector Quarterly, 48*(3), 593–615. https://doi.org/10.1177/0899764019829829

Haski-Leventhal, D., Meijs L. C. P. M., Lockstone-Binney, L., Holmes, K., & Oppenheimer, M. (2018). Measuring volunteerability and the capacity to volunteer among non-volunteers: Implications for social policy. *Social Policy & Administration, 52*(3), 1139–1167. https://doi.org/10.1111/spol.12342

Miles, M. B., Huberman, A. M., & Saldana, J. (2014). *Qualitative Data Analysis: A Methods Sourcebook.* London: Sage.

Mirvis, P. (2012). Employee engagement and CSR: Transactional, relational, developmental approaches. *California Management Review, 54,* 93–117. https://doi.org/10.1525/cmr.2012.54.4.93

Muthuri, J. N., Matten, D., & Moon, J. (2009). Employee volunteering and social capital: Contributions to corporate social responsibility. *British Journal of Management, 20*(1), 75–89. https://doi.org/10.1111/j.1467-8551.2007.00551.x

Paço, D. A., Agostinho, D., & Nave, A. C. (2013). Corporate versus non-profit volunteering—do the volunteers' motivations significantly differ? *International Review on Public and Nonprofit Marketing, 10*(3), 221–233. https://doi.org/10.1007/s12208-013-0101-0

Paço, D. A., & Nave, C. A. (2013). Corporate volunteering A case study centred on the motivations, satisfaction and happiness of company employees. *Employee Relations: An International Journal, 35*(5), 547–559. https://doi.org/10.1108/ER-12-2012-0089

Peterson, D. K. (2004). Benefits of participation in corporate volunteer programs: Employees' perceptions. *Personnel Review, 33*(6), 615–627. https://doi.org/10.1108/00483480410561510

Plewa, C., Conduit, J., Quester, P., & Johnson, C. (2015). The impact of corporate volunteering on CSR image: A consumer perspective. *Journal of Business Ethics, 127*, 643–659. https://doi.org/10.1007/s10551-014-2066-2.

Responsible Business Forum (2019). *III Polish National Research of Corporate Volunteering.* http://odpowiedzialnybiznes.pl/wp-content/uploads/2019/12/raport_III_Og%C3%B3lnopolskie_Badanie_Wolontariatu_Pracowniczego.pdf

Rodell, J. B. (2013). Finding meaning through volunteering: Why do employees volunteer and what does it mean for their jobs? *Academy of Management Journal, 56*(5), 1274–1294. https://doi.org/10.5465/amj.2012.0611

Shachar, I. Y., Hustinx, L., Roza, L., & Meijs L. C. P. M. (2018) A new spirit across sectors: Constructing a common justification for corporate volunteering. *European Journal of Cultural and Political Sociology, 5*(1–2), 90–115. https://doi.org/10.1080/23254823.2018.1435293

Sundeen, R. A., & Raskoff, S. A. (1994). Volunteering among teenagers in the United States. *Nonprofit and Voluntary Sector Quarterly, 23*, 383–403. https://doi.org/10.1177/089976409502400406

Wild, C. (1993), *Corporate Volunteer Programs: Benefits to Business,* Report No. 1029, The Conference Board, New York, NY.

Wilson, J., (2000), Volunteering, *Annual Review of Sociology, 26*, 215–240, https://doi.org/10.1146/annurev.soc.26.1.215

18
VOLUNTEERING AT BUSINESS EVENTS
Insights from China

Hongxia Qi

Introduction

Business events, which refer to meetings, conventions, and exhibitions (including trade and consumer shows), have been called the fastest growing segments of the global tourism industry (Getz, 2008). They are often referred to as the MICE (Meetings, Incentives, Conventions, and Exhibitions) industry. Business events are important catalysts for contemporary society, bringing great economic value as well as cultural prosperity and diversity to the host destinations. According to UFI (2019), in 2018 approximately 32,000 exhibitions were held across over 180 countries, and directly involved 303 million visitors and nearly 5 million exhibitors. These exhibitions supported 1.3 million direct jobs and generated €68.7 billion of direct GDP. These numbers provide a glimpse into the booming business events industry. It has become a global trend that local governments, not only in the US and Europe, but also in Asian regions such as China, are able to promote their area as an international destination for business events (Nwobodo, Ngui & Voon, 2019). Rapid development and global attention on business events have created an increased workforce demand, including volunteers within this field.

This chapter focuses on the volunteering experiences at business events, using data from a larger project on the phenomenon of business events volunteering in China. The chapter first examines the relevant literature on event volunteering and volunteering in the Chinese context. It then continues with a discussion of the experiences of volunteering at business events, by highlighting youths/students as being the main force of volunteering, considers volunteer motivations, and the key features of volunteering at business events in China.

Literature review

Volunteering at business events

Volunteers are an integral part of the workforce at events, and they are increasingly heralded as a key factor underpinning event success (Smith, Wolf & Lockstone-Binney, 2014) and business events are no exception. At business events, there are many roles for volunteers, and they represent the event organiser providing service for attendees and visitors. For example,

DOI: 10.4324/9780367815875-21

this might include volunteers in customer service roles at the registration desk, protocol and language volunteers, and providing operational support for attendees. The large number of volunteers involved in various business events is a valuable workforce. With the continuous growth of the global events industry, the importance of event volunteering has been widely acknowledged. Although studies have investigated sports events and festival volunteerism extensively (e.g., Shipway, Lockstone–Binney, Holmes & Smith, 2019; Smith, Lockstone-Binney, Holmes & Baum, 2014), there have been limited studies exploring volunteering at business events, and with only a few exceptions (e.g., Qi, Smith, & Yeoman, 2018, 2019), the understanding of volunteering at business events is overlooked.

As most business events are reoccurring periodic events, one of the main challenges for organisers is to develop appropriate strategies to recruit, manage, and retain volunteers. Due to the booming of the global business event industry, the models and strategies for recruiting and managing volunteers at business events merit further investigation.

Volunteer motivation at events is one area in which an ample body of research evidence exists. This body of literature demonstrates that event volunteers' motivations are diverse, among which being part of the event, personal development, networking, career orientation, and social motives are the common motives (e.g., Cain, Orlowski & Kitterlin-Lynch, 2021; Dickson, Darcy & Benson, 2017). There is considerable research suggesting that volunteer motivations are associated with the type of event; for example, love of sport has been identified as a widely mentioned motive at sports events (e.g., Hallmann & Harms, 2012). However, understanding on what business events bring to volunteer motivations is still in its infancy. 'Volunteering' is a terminology originating from Western countries and the existing research on volunteering is mainly conducted based on Western/Euro-centric ideologies. Relatively little effort has been devoted to exploring how volunteering manifests similarly or differently in other cultural contexts, leaving a crucial knowledge gap (Hustinx, Cnaan & Handy, 2010). There are different opinions on the conceptualisation of volunteering, depending on various factors such as culture, participants and activity. Taking the issue of payment as an example, although it is widely believed that no financial payment is one characteristic of volunteering, some scholars (e.g., Stunkel & Grady, 2011) have noticed that payment can be a motivation for volunteers in some situations. Whether and how the business event contexts impact the rewards of volunteering remains unexplored. The investigation on this issue will contribute new empirical evidence and insights around the conceptualisation of the phenomenon.

Volunteering in China

The concept of volunteer arrived in China in the early stage of reform and opening up (Cai, 2010). Volunteering in China has only experienced a few decades' developments and most of the ideas of volunteering are transferred from Western countries. The concept of volunteering has become more widely accepted in China since the 2000s especially after the 2008 Beijing Olympic Games. The Olympic Games greatly promoted the development of volunteering and accelerated the pace of legislation of volunteer activities in China (Tang, 2007). However, the voluntary spirit such as *ren ai* (the love thought), *ci shan* (charity), and *xing shan ji de* (one good turn deserves another) has over 2,000 years' history in traditional Chinese culture. The government, through top-down initiatives, is now the main impetus for volunteerism in contemporary China (Xu, 2017). Volunteering is encouraged as a tool to label participants as socially responsible individuals with a superior type of morality and respectable social behaviour (Xu & Ngai, 2011). Volunteer service is promoted as a means of self-development through a discourse that blends concepts of cultural competence and self-realisation with a concern for the common good (Fleischer, 2011). In China, youths, particularly university students, are the main forces of volunteers, especially at national and international events. Taking the 2008 Beijing Olympic and Paralympics Games as an example, the number of applicants from Beijing was 256,000, of which 181,500 (71%) were university students (Zhang, 2008).

Method

The data for this chapter were collected as part of a project on *Student Volunteering at Business Events in China*. This incorporated studying individuals' motivations for being a volunteer at business events, and the conceptualisation of the phenomenon. This qualitative study started with auto-ethnography, followed by in-depth interviews with data triangulation from three groups: student volunteers, business event organisers, and administrators in tertiary educational institutions. In the first stage of auto-ethnography, the researcher herself volunteered and became an 'insider' at two business events in China (the 2016 Shandong Province Entrepreneurship Programs Exhibition and the 25th Qingdao International Fabric and Accessories Procurement Fair) and used the personal experiences to gain a fuller understanding of volunteering in the business events context. Auto-ethnographic data were collected in the form of reflective daily journals during the researcher's volunteer activities at the two business events. Auto-ethnography allowed the researcher to use an individual's personal experience to gain a fuller and balanced understanding of a particular phenomenon from the 'insider' perspective (Ellis & Bochner, 2000). It puts the researcher back into the study, rather than keeping them quietly on the side-lines (Parry & Johnson, 2007). In the second stage of the study, semi-structured interviews captured the perspectives of 20 volunteers, ten business event organisers, and nine education institution administrators. To protect participants' privacy and identities, the names of interviewees were replaced by codes (e.g. V# for volunteers, O# for business event organisers, and A# for administrators). A purposive sampling method was used to approach participants. All interviews were conducted in Mandarin and digitally recorded with the permission of participants. The interviews were linked to auto-ethnography data during the analysis.

A constructivist grounded theory approach guided the analysis process. Initial coding was conducted as the first stage of data analysis with a large number of initial codes. After that, focused coding produced several categories. This process was repeated several times with the deepening of constant comparison. NVivo offered an efficient means to manage and organise the data to support a rigorous data analysis process and was adopted to facilitate the coding process. The findings presented in this chapter reflected the key findings of the project.

Experiences of volunteering at business events in China

Youths/students are the main force of volunteers

This project identified that almost all the on-site volunteers at business events in China were students or recent graduates. As the researcher reflected in her research journal after the 2016 Shandong Province Entrepreneurship Programs Exhibition:

> Having provided volunteer service at so many business events such as Auto Show, Furniture Fair, and Consumer Goods Fair, I notice that most volunteers are students, especially the university students studying event and MICE.
>
> *(Research journal, 19 March 2016)*

This is consistent with the wider volunteer field in China, where young people are the main participants and youth volunteering is encouraged by the government through large, politicised, and collective campaigns as a "technology of power" (Fleischer, 2011; Xu, 2017). Volunteering is one of the most important forms of social practice activities, which is designed to encourage students to connect with the local community, to enhance learning through practice, and to improve their comprehensive ability; it is also one of the most popular ways of public participation in building a harmonious society (Pu & Zhu, 2017; Yang, 2010).

Volunteer motivations at business events

Diverse motivations for volunteering at business events were identified, with individuals driven by different reasons, such as the desire to learn, be part of the event, and networking. The motivational concepts that emerged were categorised into three main aspects: self-development motives, utilitarian reasons, and reciprocal altruism.

1   *Self-development motives.* Self-development was a prime consideration for volunteers at business events. Many volunteers saw volunteering at business events as instrumental for learning that was related to their study, such as "to gain knowledge of the new trends in the industry" (V7), "to apply what I have learned from books" (V8), "to gain pre-job opportunities" (V11), and "to learn about the event industry" (V19). To learn, to enhance soft skills, to prepare for future employment, personal betterment, and transition to paid employment were widely mentioned reasons for individuals to volunteer at business events. Besides the reason to learn knowledge related to the event, participants also saw volunteering as a good way to enhance their soft skills such as teamwork and networking. For many interview participants including A4 and A6, volunteering was a short internship, enabling them to gain real workplace experience and prepare for future employment. Volunteer participants also believed that volunteering at business events was "a good way to get involved in the community" (V11) and "transition from study to work" (V15).

2   *Utilitarian reasons.* Functional and instrumental reasons were common motivations for individuals to volunteer at business events. The volunteers valued the "springboard effect" of their volunteer activities. They saw volunteering at business events enabling them to achieve utilitarian goals, including "building [my] CV" (A8), and "gaining credit as part of the degree requirements" (V7). Some volunteered to get the certificate attesting to their service, which could aid in applications for other honours (e.g. V14). A few interviewees (e.g. V4, V5, and V11) even identified the ability to gain payment for volunteering at business events as a reason for participating; this is further discussed in the next section.

3   *Reciprocal altruism.* Besides the above mentioned self-oriented utilitarian reasons, helping motives were common among interviewees. Participants said they wanted "to help organise the event successfully" (V6), and "to be part of the event" (V12). The participating business event organisers also mentioned volunteers' desire to serve visitors, for example, O4 proposed that:

> They [the volunteers] devote five to seven days' time, do the labour work for organisers, and serve the event attendees.

The research identified that the on-site atmosphere enhanced volunteers' willingness to help. However, this motive was not purely about giving or helping behaviours. Instead, it was based on the expectation that they would benefit from the behaviour, for example to gain honours (e.g. A1 and A3), practical experience (e.g. V8 and V12), and credit (e.g. V7 and V11). In this sense, volunteering at business events was a reciprocal choice, aiming to achieve a win–win situation. This finding is in accord with Trivers' (1971) concept of reciprocal altruism, which refers to a beneficial behaviour involving two actors in the context of symbiosis, yet "with the expectation of a return favour" (Fennell, 2006; Paraskevaidis & Andriotis, 2017).

The identified motivations shared many overlaps with existing literature. Motivations such as networking and being part of the event are consistent with those at sports events (e.g., Giannoulakis, Wang & Gray, 2007; Kim, Fredline & Cuskelly, 2018). However, business events and the Chinese context highlight several elements regarding volunteer motivations at events. Self-development motives have been among volunteers at other types of events, but were dominant reasons for business event volunteers, related to the professional and commercial atmosphere at these events. In addition, the importance of reciprocal altruism (expectation of returns while helping others) in volunteering at business events in China exhibits the exchange nature of volunteering, which has been explored in other contexts (e.g., Paraskevaidis & Andriotis, 2017; Toraldo, Contu & Mangia, 2016).

Monetary rewards for volunteers are common

The research established that it was a common practice for volunteers to receive monetary payment at business events in China, as reflected in the researcher's auto-ethnographic journal:

> Volunteers usually gain a certain amount of payment as returns for their effort, ranging from ¥50 to ¥200 per day (£6- £22). The payment level is diverse in different cities and among different organisations.
>
> *(Research journal, 18 March 2016)*

The three groups of interviewees in the study – student volunteers, business event organisers, and educational institution administrators – agreed that the payment for volunteers was low and specifically that it was lower than the local wage. However, individuals in the different groups had different understandings of the payment. Many business event organisers (e.g. O2, O7, and O9) understood the payment as "a reimbursement to volunteers for their transportation expenses and lunch costs" (O7). However, some volunteers believed the payment was a recognition for their time and help: "I think it [the payment] is a recognition of our work… In fact, I do not care about this [the payment] and it is optional" (V5), while others (e.g. V6 and V9) acknowledged that the monetary rewards blurred the boundaries of volunteering and a part-time job by proposing that "it [the payment] makes it hard to say it is still the traditional volunteering or a part-time job" (V6). The educational institution administrators also had different perceptions of payments and what they mean. Some (e.g. A1, A4, A7, and A9) had a relatively tolerant attitude towards payments to volunteers involved in business events. For example, A7 proposed that:

> When talking with organisers, we reach the agreement that the payment obviously has not reached the local salary level. The money students [volunteers] received is not proportional to their hard work.

A2 also shared a similar opinion:

> Money is not the determinant for volunteers' participation, that is, it is not the money that influences their involvement or not.

However, some participating administrators had different opinions about the payment and claimed that "it [the payment] is way to 'buy' students' time and labour" (A3). Three participants (i.e., A2, A3, and A6) believed that "volunteering is losing its soul", and A6 further commented that "it [volunteering] is no longer the traditional volunteering" due to the monetary element.

Lack of monetary rewards is a core concept within Western conceptualisations of volunteering (e.g., Cnaan, Handy & Wadsworth, 1996). However, monetary rewards for volunteers at business events are a common phenomenon in China, and these activities are still perceived as volunteering. The normalisation of payment has led to the classification of volunteers with payment and volunteers without payment (Tian, 2007). The existence of monetary rewards is one of the features that distinguish volunteering at business events from that in other areas, particularly in non-profit organisations, yet it is not without debate and its legality is becoming an issue. While previous research has demonstrated that volunteer work is not just volunteers 'giving', but that they may also expect rewards (e.g., Kumar, Kallen & Mathew, 2002), in the Western context this tends to relate to reimbursement of expenses, or giving volunteers gift cards or vouchers. In contrast, a monetary reward in the form of a daily payment is a feature in these Chinese business events.

Collective volunteering phenomenon

From the auto-ethnography and interviews, it was identified that most of the volunteers were organised collectively to do volunteer work at business events. As youths or students are the main force of volunteers at business events in China, it is typically colleges (or other educational institutions) who organise whole classes to volunteer collectively as a way to gain practical experiences. Some education institution administrators (e.g. A3, A4, and A6) tended to understand this collective volunteering as way to enhance graduates' capacities of being innovative, productive, and collaborative employees. One of the typical examples was from A3:

> Volunteering at business events was an enlightening process. Through providing the service in a real work environment, the students could see their own strengths and weaknesses, and identify the skills that were needed in the work so they would have directions of learning new knowledge that was necessary for future development.

From the event organisers' perspective, they preferred the collectively organised volunteers, seeing them as easier to manage than individual volunteers. For such collective volunteering, the level of free choice for volunteering among individuals becomes a discussion. Nearly one-third of the volunteer interviewees said they volunteered because they were asked to do so, or they were organised by their college. Other volunteers said that their college had encouraged them to volunteer, but they also felt they had little choice and were unable to "say no" to the opportunity (e.g. V19). The educational institution administrators in the study outlined that, in most cases, the colleges required students to volunteer a few (usually around three to five) times as a compulsory part of the three-year degree, with the aim to enhance their practical skills. They positioned the choice element as the colleges offer differ-ent event volunteering opportunities, so students can choose the ones they are interested in. In Western literature, one's own free will has been one of the most important dimensions of volunteering (Cnaan et al., 1996; Hustinx et al., 2010). The external pressures for volunteer-ing at business events in China seems contradictory to traditional volunteering, making the phenomenon share similarities with compulsory volunteering (Warburton & Smith, 2003; Yang, 2017). The dominant role of government, top-down volunteer initiatives, and the strong collective culture in China can help explain this.

The commercialisation trends of volunteering at business events

Several aspects of the commercialisation of volunteering at business events in China were identified in this research. Besides the widely existing monetary payment for volunteers, the outsourcing of the volunteering program was a common choice for business event organ-isers. Instead of recruiting, training, and managing volunteers themselves, event organisers tended to outsource it to the other HR agents due to the challenges such as finding a large number of volunteers working for only a few days and the high costs of training and manag-ing the volunteers. Outsourcing was seen as an efficient way for business event organisers to recruit and manage volunteers. During the interviews, the organiser participants identified that there has been a growth in these HR agents in recent years and they typically cover the recruitment and management of both volunteers and other on-site event staff. The inter-viewees (e.g. O1 and O3) largely used "volunteers" and "on-site event staff" interchangeably, and believed they perform similar roles. The outsourcing, monetary rewards, and the emer-gence of HR agents demonstrate trends in the commercialisation of volunteering at business events in China.

Blurred boundaries of volunteering at business events with other activities

Several interviewees identified features of volunteering behaviour at business events that indicate blurred boundaries between volunteering and other social activities. Volunteer roles at business events were diverse, including registration, food and beverage, transportation co-ordination, on-site guidance, and translation, which were usually determined by the needs of the event organisers. These volunteer roles were similar to those undertaken by other staff at the events. Many volunteer and organiser interviewees (e.g. V10, V12, V17, O2, and O5) mentioned that the role ambiguity and the wide existence payment for volunteers made it hard to differentiate volunteering from part-time and casual jobs:

> Usually there are no job descriptions or written guidelines to describe the roles of volunteers. The roles played by volunteers are diverse and are often determined by the needs of the event organiser.
>
> *(O2)*

In China, the main participants as volunteers at business events – students – were often or-ganised collectively by their college as a way to gain professional and practical skills. From the higher educational institution administrators' perspective, the main purpose of sending students to the events was to provide them the opportunity to learn from practice and prepare them for future employment. The event organisers expressed a similar opinion that the main purpose for volunteers was service learning. Hence, both groups of interviewees saw volunteering to be like an internship and work integrated learning (WIL) as the students needed to volunteer at a certain number of events to meet the requirements of their degree. Learning and practicing were common themes when volunteers talked about their motivations for volunteering at business events. In this sense, volunteering shared commonalities with compulsory educational service learning.

Discussion and conclusions

This chapter has presented an exploratory investigation of the volunteering phenomenon at business events in China. With the growth of the global business event industry, an increasing number of volunteers are involved at business events; however, they have been largely ignored by researchers. It is therefore vital to pay attention to this growing group of individuals who are valuable to the business events industry. The investigation of this phenomenon is a timely contribution to the literature and will hopefully act as a stepping-stone to further investigation in this field.

In terms of volunteer motivations, this research identifies various motives for volunteering at business events, which confirms that volunteer motivations are complex and multidimensional (Hustinx et al., 2010). The literature on volunteer motivations at cultural and sporting events has demonstrated that volunteer motivations can be grouped into several dimensions: for example, solidary, purposive, egoistic, external factors, and leisure (e.g., Allen & Shaw, 2009; MacLean & Hamm, 2007; Twynam, Farrell & Johnston, 2002). Compared to this, volunteer motivations at business events generally tend to be more egoistic and less purposive; the intrinsic motivations of enjoyment that are common in sports events are not evident at business events, while external factors play an important role. Traditionally, it is believed that volunteers are motivated by non-monetary factors, among which social recognition and group need are variables that have significant impacts on volunteering (MacLean & Hamm, 2007). In contrast, the current research identifies that monetary rewards are not only common in volunteering at business events but also play a role in attracting volunteers. In other contexts, this payment for volunteers could be controversial but brings a new direction to event volunteering literature. In this sense, this project confirms the school of opinion that understands volunteering as exchange (e.g., Paraskevaidis & Andriotis, 2017).

Scholars have proposed that the nature of volunteering is undergoing radical change as a result of broader social transformations, and they have identified many transitions in volunteering, such as from 'traditional' to 'new' and from 'collectivistic' to 'individualistic' (Hustinx & Lammertyn, 2003). Although volunteer activities have been extensively studied, there are different perspectives on the nature of volunteering and the descriptions of this kind of activity are varied, depending on various factors such as culture, participants, and ongoing/episodic participation (Dunn, Chambers & Hyde, 2016; Hustinx et al., 2010). The volunteering experiences identified in this research share several similarities with those in existing literature. Business events volunteers' self-development motives and utilitarian reasons demonstrate individuals' expectations for personal benefits through volunteering, which reflect the reciprocal altruistic nature of volunteer behaviour (Paraskevaidis & Andriotis, 2017). This research also presents confirmation of business event volunteering as an exchange. Volunteering and non-profit literatures have identified the commercialisation trend in volunteering (e.g., Enjolras, 2002; Vaceková, Valentinov & Nemec, 2017). In the tourism area, discussions about the commercialisation of volunteering have focused on volunteer tourism activities (e.g., Coghlan & Noakes, 2012; Godfrey, Wearing, Schulenkorf & Grabowski, 2019). There remains a paucity of research that attempts to explore whether this trend also occurs in event volunteering. The present research addresses this gap and finds that there are several commercialised features in the volunteering activities at business events: the widely existing monetary payment for volunteers, outsourcing, and the emergence of HR agents.

As a culturally specific concept, the understanding of volunteering varies in different contexts. The Chinese context of this research brings several new and different perspectives on the phenomenon of volunteering at business events, which is believed to be a good complement to the Western focus in the existing literature. On the one hand, youths or students are the main force of volunteers at business events in China. This reflects that youths are targeted and encouraged to volunteer, and the Chinese government is trying to institutionalise and normalise university student volunteering as a way for public participation in building a harmonious society, even as volunteering is used as a tool achieve political goals (Huang, 2012; Sun, 2008). On the other hand, this research demonstrates that individuals are organised collectively to volunteer. This can be explained by the collectivistic Chinese cultures, which emphasise collectivism and highlight individuals' obligation to the community (Oyserman, Coon & Kemmelmeier, 2002). However, several volunteer participants in this research proposed that their volunteering decision was not a pure free choice. Free choice or voluntary giving is identified as important for understanding volunteering in Western literature (e.g., Cnaan et al., 1996; Hustinx et al., 2010). But in the Chinese context, individuals seem to be more tolerant of external pressures to volunteer. It is not the intent of this research to debate the extent to which volunteering in China is voluntary, but this finding provides an interesting perspective to reflect on the applicability of the conceptualisation of volunteering in Western countries to other contexts.

As highlighted earlier, the data for this chapter were collected as part of a project that explores student volunteering at business events in China. The discussion need not stop at student groups but could include other volunteer groups. This research is culturally bound, and caution should be exercised in attempting to adopt the findings beyond the specific context – business events in China. Further studies may be conducted to explore the phenomenon of business events volunteering in Western contexts. As another allied research direction, cross-cultural comparison studies may also investigate the similarities and differences of volunteering at business events across countries.

References

Allen, J. B., & Shaw, S. (2009). "Everyone rolls up their sleeves and mucks in": Exploring volunteers' motivation and experiences of the motivational climate of a sporting event. *Sport Management Review, 12*(2), 79–90. http://doi.org/10.1016/j.smr.2008.12.002

Cai, Y. (2010). An analysis of the relationship between volunteer spirit and socialist core value system in China. *Academic Search for Truth and Reality, 192*(2), 66–70.

Cain, L., Orlowski, M., & Kitterlin-Lynch, M. (2021). A holistic investigation of special event volunteer motivation. *Event Management*. http://doi.org /10.3727/152599521X16106577965198.

Cnaan, R. A., Handy, F., & Wadsworth, M. (1996). Defining who is a volunteer: Conceptual and empirical considerations. *Nonprofit and Voluntary Sector Quarterly, 25*(3), 364–383. https://doi.org/10.1177/0899764096253006

Coghlan, A., & Noakes, S. (2012). Towards an understanding of the drivers of commercialization in the volunteer tourism sector. *Tourism Recreation Research, 37*(2), 123–131. https://doi.org/10.1080/02508281.2012.11081697

Dickson, T. J., Darcy, S., & Benson, A. (2017). Volunteers with disabilities at the London 2012 Olympic and Paralympic Games: Who, why, and will they do it again? *Event Management, 21*(3), 301–318. http://doi/org/10.3727/152599517X14942648527527

Dunn, J., Chambers, S. K., & Hyde, M. K. (2016). Systematic review of motives for episodic volunteering. *VOLUNTAS: International Journal of Voluntary and Nonprofit Organizations, 27*(1), 425–464. http://doi.org/10.1007%2Fs11266-015-9548-4

Ellis, C., & Bochner, A. (2000). Autoethnography, personal narrative, reflexivity: Researcher as subject. In N. K. Denzin & Y. S. Lincoln (Eds.), *Handbook of qualitative research* (2nd ed., pp. 733–768). Thousand Oaks, CA: Sage.

Enjolras, B. (2002). The commercialization of voluntary sport organizations in Norway. *Nonprofit and Voluntary Sector Quarterly, 31*(3), 352–376. https://doi.org/10.1177/0899764002313003

Fennell, D. (2006). Evolution in tourism: The theory of reciprocal altruism and tourist-host interactions. *Current Issues in Tourism, 9*(2), 105–124. https://doi.org/10.1080/13683500608668241

Fleischer, F. (2011). Technology of self, technology of power. Volunteering as encounter in Guangzhou, China. *Ethnos, 76*(3), 300–325. https://doi.org/10.1080/00141844.2011.565126

Getz, D. (2008). Event tourism: Definition, evolution, and research. *Tourism Management, 29*(3), 403–428. https://doi.org/10.1016/j.tourman.2007.07.017

Giannoulakis, C., Wang, C. H., & Gray, D. (2007). Measuring volunteer motivation in mega-sporting events. *Event Management, 11*(4), 191–200. http://doi.org/10.3727/152599508785899884

Godfrey, J., Wearing, S. L., Schulenkorf, N., & Grabowski, S. (2019). The 'volunteer tourist gaze': Commercial volunteer tourists' interactions with, and perceptions of, the host community in Cusco, Peru. *Current Issues in Tourism, 23*(20), 2555–2571. https://doi.org/10.1080/13683500.2019.1657811

Hallmann, K., & Harms, G. (2012). Determinants of volunteer motivation and their impact on future voluntary engagement: A comparison of volunteer's motivation at sport events in equestrian and handball. *International Journal of Event and Festival Management, 3*(3), 272–291. https://doi.org/10.1080/13683500.2019.1657811

Huang, Q. (2012). Study on the cultivation and development of voluntary spirit among college students. *Contemporary Youth Studies, 3*, 49–53.

Hustinx, L., Cnaan, R. A., & Handy, F. (2010). Navigating theories of volunteering: A hybrid map for a complex phenomenon. *Journal for the Theory of Social Behaviour, 40*(4), 410–434. http://doi.org/10.1111/j.1468-5914.2010.00439.x

Hustinx, L., & Lammertyn, F. (2003). Collective and reflexive styles of volunteering: A sociological modernization perspective. *VOLUNTAS: International Journal of Voluntary and Nonprofit Organizations, 14*(2), 167–187. http://doi.org/10.1177/0268580909360297

Kim, E., Fredline, L., & Cuskelly, G. (2018). Heterogeneity of sport event volunteer motivations: A segmentation approach. *Tourism Management, 68*, 375–386. https://doi.org/10.1016/j.tourman.2018.04.004

Kumar, A., Kallen, D. J., & Mathew, T. (2002). Volunteer faculty: What rewards or incentives do they prefer? *Teaching and Learning in Medicine, 14*(2), 119–124. https://doi.org/10.1207/S15328015TLM1402_09

MacLean, J., & Hamm, S. (2007). Motivation, commitment, and intentions of volunteers at a large Canadian sporting event. *Leisure/Loisir, 31*(2), 523–556. https://doi.org/10.1080/14927713.2007.9651394

Nwobodo, S., Ngui, K. S., & Voon, M. L. (2019). Business event destination determinants: Malaysia event organisers' perspective. *Event Management, 23*(4–5), 4–5. https://doi.org/10.3727/152599519X15506259855931

Oyserman, D., Coon, H. M., & Kemmelmeier, M. (2002). Rethinking individualism and collectivism: Evaluation of theoretical assumptions and meta-analysis. *Psychological Bulletin, 128*(1), 3–72. https://doi.org/10.1037/0033-2909.128.1.3

Paraskevaidis, P., & Andriotis, K. (2017). Altruism in tourism: Social exchange theory vs altruistic surplus phenomenon in host volunteering. *Annals of Tourism Research, 62*, 26–37. https://doi.org/10.1016/j.annals.2016.11.002

Parry, D. C., & Johnson, C. W. (2007). Contextualizing leisure research to encompass complexity in lived leisure experience: The need for creative analytic practice. *Leisure Sciences, 29*(2), 119–130. https://doi.org/10.1080/01490400601160721

Pu, Q., & Zhu, L. (2017). Research on the influence of volunteer service on volunteers' mainstream ideology. *China Youth Research, 57*(3), 49–54.

Qi, H., Smith, K. A., & Yeoman, I. (2018). What motivates volunteers to help at business events? Reciprocal altruism and reflexivity. *Asia Pacific Journal of Tourism Research, 23*(10), 989–999. https://doi.org/10.1080/10941665.2018.1513050

Qi, H., Smith, K. A., & Yeoman, I. (2019). An exploratory study of volunteer motivation at conferences: A case study of the First World Conference on Tourism for Development. *Asia Pacific Journal of Tourism Research, 24*(6), 574–583. https://doi.org/10.1080/10941665.2019.1610000

Shipway, R., Lockstone–Binney, L., Holmes, K., & Smith, K. A. (2019). Perspectives on the volunteering legacy of the London 2012 Olympic Games: The development of an event legacy stakeholder engagement matrix. *Event Management, 23*(4–5), 4–5. https://doi.org/10.3727/152599519X15506259856327

Smith, K. A., Lockstone-Binney, L., Holmes, K., & Baum, T. (Eds.). (2014). *Event volunteering: International perspectives on the event volunteering experience.* London: Routledge.

Smith, K. A., Wolf, N., & Lockstone-Binney, L. (2014). Volunteer experiences in the build up to the Rugby World Cup. In K. A. Smith, L. Lockstone-Binney, K. Holmes, & T. Baum (Eds.), *Event volunteering: International perspectives on the event volunteering experience* (pp.111–125). London: Routledge.

Stunkel, L., & Grady, C. (2011). More than the money: A review of the literature examining healthy volunteer motivations. *Contemporary Clinical Trials, 32*(3), 342–352. http://doi.org/10.1016/j.cct.2010.12.003

Sun, Y. (2008). Suggestions on institutionalized college student volunteering at community service. *Youth Studies, 1,* 61–64.

Tang, Y. (2007). Research on volunteer organizations and training of Harbin 2009 Winter Universiade Games. *Journal of Harbin Institute of Physical Education, 25*(2), 15–17.

Tian. (2007). *The worker nature of paid volunteers* (Unpublished doctoral thesis). Nanjing University of Information Technology, Nanjing, China.

Toraldo, M. L., Contu, A., & Mangia, G. (2016). The hybrid nature of volunteering: Exploring its voluntary exchange nature at music festivals. *Nonprofit and Voluntary Sector Quarterly, 45*(6), 1130–1149. https://doi.org/10.1177/0899764016649688

Trivers, R. L. (1971). The evolution of reciprocal altruism. *The Quarterly Review of Biology, 46*(1), 35–57.

Twynam, G. D., Farrell, J. M., & Johnston, M. E. (2002). Leisure and volunteer motivation at a special sporting event. *Leisure/Loisir, 27*(3–4), 363–377. https://doi.org/10.1080/14927713.2002.9651310

UFI. (2019). Global economic impact of exhibitions. Retrieved from: https://www.ufi.org/wp-content/uploads/2019/12/Global_Economic_Impact_of_Exhibitions_Dec2019.pdf.

Vaceková, G., Valentinov, V., & Nemec, J. (2017). Rethinking nonprofit commercialization: The case of the Czech Republic. *VOLUNTAS: International Journal of Voluntary and Nonprofit Organizations, 28*(5), 2103–2123. http://dx.doi.org/10.1007/s11266-016-9772-6

Warburton, J., & Smith, J. (2003). Out of the generosity of your heart: Are we creating active citizens through compulsory volunteer programmes for young people in Australia?. *Social Policy & Administration, 37*(7), 772–786. https://doi.org/10.1046/j.1467-9515.2003.00371.x

Xu, Y. (2017). Volunteerism and the state: Understanding the development of volunteering in China. In B. Jacqueline & J. Christopher (Eds.), *Perspectives on volunteering* (pp. 213–226). Chicago: Springer International Publishing.

Xu, Y., & Ngai, N. P. (2011). Moral resources and political capital: Theorizing the relationship between voluntary service organizations and the development of civil society in China. *Nonprofit and Voluntary Sector Quarterly, 40*(2), 247–269. http://doi.org/10.1177/0899764009340229

Yang, J. (2010). Studies on how to improve university students' social practice. *Social Sciences in Chinese Higher Education Institutions, 2*(7), 49–52.

Yang, W. (2017). Does 'compulsory volunteering' affect subsequent behavior? Evidence from a natural experiment in Canada. *Education Economics, 25*(4), 394–405. https://doi.org/10.1080/09645292.2016.1182622

Zhang, T. (2008). *Over 74,000 student volunteers serve Beijing Olympics.* Retrieved from http://news.xinhuanet.com/english/2008-08/15/content_9362945.htm.

PART 4

Managing volunteers

19

DESIGNING A VOLUNTEER PROGRAM

Graham Cuskelly and Michelle Hayes

Introduction

Volunteers are important to the development and delivery of services and programs across varying levels and sectors within events, sport and tourism (EST). For instance, volunteer involvement in tourism includes volunteer tourists delivering community programs in developing countries, working in visitor centres and engaging with tourists. In sport, volunteers are predominantly responsible for running community clubs, while events require volunteers across all levels from local community to major international events such as world cups or the Olympic Games. Large events require a significant number of volunteers and would not be successful without the countless hours they contribute (Dickson, Terwiel & Buick, 2017). Event volunteers are so important that volunteering legacies have become a necessary component throughout the bidding process (Dickson, Darcy & Gadd, 2020). Thus, EST industries depend on volunteers to deliver key services to the community and their stakeholders. Volunteer roles in many sport, event and tourism settings are integral to the successful management and operation of many EST organisations.

To harness the power of volunteers to benefit the industry, organised volunteer programs are a necessity. Volunteer programs conventionally refer to "the organisation and management of service volunteers for best results" (Brudney, 2016, p. 690). A volunteer program provides structure to organisations on how to recruit volunteers, how to conduct screening and induct volunteers into the organisation, the positions that are assigned, what training is appropriate and effective to perform their duties, supervision requirements, how they are afforded recognition to keep them motivated, and how they and the program should be evaluated to continue to progress toward mutually beneficial outcomes. A volunteer program serves as a structure for facilitating the efforts of volunteer and paid staff to ensure the organisational goals are attained. Design and planning are essential factors in the development of a volunteer program (Holmes & Smith, 2009).

This chapter examines the various components of designing a volunteer program within the context of EST organisations including establishing a rationale for volunteer involvement, program leadership, integrating the program, preparing job or position descriptions, training and preparing volunteers, meeting volunteer needs, recruitment and retention, recognition and evaluation of both volunteers and the volunteer program itself. To develop a

DOI: 10.4324/9780367815875-23

volunteer program, organisations must first establish their rationale for involving volunteers and how they plan to integrate them into the organisation.

Establishing the rationale for volunteer involvement

EST organisations require volunteers to perform a variety of functions. However, before developing a volunteer program, organisations must first establish a rationale for involving volunteers in their organisation. Contrary to common belief, incorporating volunteers into an organisation should not begin with recruitment. This important first step of establishing a rationale for volunteer involvement will determine and inform the subsequent stages for the design of the program, including recruitment strategies. When establishing a rationale for volunteer involvement, EST organisations should determine why volunteers are needed. This, in turn, will develop the groundwork to sustain the volunteers eventually recruited. By developing a rationale, organisations can also prevent over-recruitment. Leaders of the organisation should agree on a statement of goals for the volunteer program in the context of the organisation's strategic goals before defining the volunteer positions required and the number of volunteers needed to fill such roles. In a community sport context, this responsibility may fall on a particular committee or board member with the organisation. This may be difficult, however, as the committee or board positions themselves are often voluntary. Policies and procedures for a volunteer program also need to be established and communicated to not only volunteers but also paid staff within the organisation, if applicable (Holmes & Smith, 2009).

In the sport, event and arguably, tourism organisations, differing levels of volunteer involvement and commitment are often evident and have been described as core and peripheral volunteers. Core volunteers are likely to undertake a leadership or policy role (e.g. president, chair or secretary), while peripheral volunteers are more inclined to hold operational or helping roles (e.g. team manager, trainer, instructor, teacher or coach) (Ringuet-Riot, Cuskelly, Auld & Zakus, 2014). Core volunteers make greater contributions to planning, decision-making and hands on work within their clubs compared to peripheral volunteers. Differences also exist in the hours contributed with core volunteers likely to contribute more hours. One of the key issues for sport organisations is how to better engage their volunteers so that more peripheral volunteers can be converted into core volunteers (Ringuet-Riot et al., 2014). Importantly, organisations should define the level of involvement and commitment required from volunteers for roles before engaging in other steps in the volunteer program such as recruitment.

Volunteer program leadership

A successful volunteer program requires leadership from the initial design and implementation through to the evaluation stage. A volunteer program leader assumes the responsibilities of all aspects of the program including developing a rationale, designing the program, the development of job descriptions, engaging in recruitment, and conducting inductions and training. Such a role has been given a variety of names such as 'volunteer coordinator' or 'volunteer manager'. These positions are evident in mega-sport events (e.g. Olympic Games) and their organising committees. Mega-sport event volunteer managers are often tasked with the difficult challenge of realising volunteer legacies (Doherty, 2009; Fairley, Gardiner & Filo, 2016) in addition to running the volunteer program at the event itself. However, other EST organisations may struggle to designate a volunteer program leader if under-resourced or under-funded, or in the case of community sport clubs and local museums, those occupying administrator positions are often volunteers.

An important consideration in the leadership of volunteer program design is the application of volunteer management standards. For example, the Volunteering Australia (the peak body for volunteering in Australia) standards recognise the benefits of a two-way relationship in "providing an opportunity for organisations to achieve their goals by involving volunteers in their activities, and for volunteers to make meaningful use of their time and skills, contributing to social and community outcomes" (Volunteering Australia, 2015, p. 3). The Volunteering Australia National Standards for Volunteer Involvement include standards for leadership and management, recruitment and selection, support and development, workplace safety and well-being, volunteer recognition, quality management and continuous improvement. Other national peak bodies have similar standards or guidelines, such as the Canadian Code for Volunteer Involvement (Volunteer Canada, 2020). EST organisations should note that managing their volunteers requires a different set of processes than managing employees, despite management practices being largely predicated on human resource management (HRM) strategies. The management of volunteers is explored in more depth in Chapter 20.

Integrating the volunteer program into the organisation

Volunteer programs are largely based on an HRM approach. HRM provides a framework for organisations to establish, maintain, and develop long-term and good quality relationships between the organisation and volunteers. Volunteer programs typically follow a similar path by including key components such as planning, the development of job descriptions, recruitment strategies, induction and training, and importantly, recognition and retention. Despite criticisms of HRM's applicability in volunteer management and programs (Hoye, Cuskelly, Auld, Kappelides & Misener, 2020), the approach has been advocated by government agencies, volunteer bodies such as Volunteering Australia, and national sport organisations in the elite and community sport and event contexts. This may be because performance, commitment, satisfaction and ultimately the retention of volunteers are logical outcomes of HRM practices. Put simply, HRM is a collective term and can be described as "a range of practices associated with managing work and employment relations" (Collings & Wood, 2009, p. 5).

By following the path of an HRM framework, an important part of the volunteer program is developing appropriate roles and tasks to be completed by the prospective volunteers, which is essentially human resources (HR) planning. Weerakoon (2016) noted that HR planning consists of planning for factors such as recruitment, selection, induction and training, and rewards to survive while facing uncertainty and changes. An important function of HR planning is to estimate the type and number of volunteer roles to be filled in order to predict the demand for volunteer labour. Once roles are established, it is important for volunteer managers to create job descriptions.

Preparing job descriptions for volunteer involvement

Job descriptions, also referred to as position or role descriptions, are an important aspect in the recruitment of volunteers. Organisations across the EST industries need to design roles that are meaningful to both the organisation and the volunteer. If a rationale for volunteer involvement has been documented, designing volunteer roles and preparing job descriptions should be an easier task. Job descriptions should always be provided and outline what the role entails before volunteers are asked to commit their skills, time and effort (Taylor, Doherty &

McGraw, 2015). Similar to paid roles, the expectations and scope of the volunteer roles need to be clearly communicated to volunteers, so they are able to identify whether they have a preference for the role and whether it relates to their skills and motivations (Holmes & Smith, 2009). Whether the organisation is open to allowing flexibility across roles and hours should be noted. Lockstone, Smith and Baum (2010) noted that flexibility in terms of the type of work (jobs/tasks performed) and rostering allocations (days, hours and start and finish times) was linked to higher satisfaction among tourism volunteers.

There are several volunteer initiatives or peak bodies that can assist EST organisations in the development of job descriptions. Volunteering Australia provides a toolkit for designing volunteer roles and an adaptable template for job descriptions (Volunteering Australia, n.d.). The template consists of essential information including position title, start date, hours required per week, supervisor or who the role reports to, role overview and purpose, and how the role relates to the organisation's mission and other projects. Other information includes key responsibilities, training requirements, the expected benefits to both volunteer and organisation, and a list of other relevant requirements (e.g. police check or medical check where required due to the nature of the role or client group being served). In terms of volunteer tourism, the United Nations (UN) provide descriptions of assignments for their volunteer programs. These descriptions contain important information regarding host cities and agencies, project contexts, key functions (duties), competencies and selection criteria, living conditions and service conditions (United Nations, n.d.a).

For positions that require contact with vulnerable groups such as children, additional requirements need to be clearly communicated. Reference or background checks may be required in order to be compliant with relevant laws. For example, EST volunteers working with children are required to obtain a Working with Children check in Australia. Different jurisdictions have similar or additional legal requirements and organisations should disseminate this information to volunteers through job descriptions. If volunteers decide to accept a position, they should be presented with a well-designed induction and training program that is relevant to the role and the organisation.

Inducting and training volunteers

The transition that occurs when a volunteer takes up their first role presents a significant event in the HRM process and the design of volunteer programs. Inducting and training volunteers is an important strategy to safeguard the success of volunteers in their roles and to ensure their contribution to the organisation is maximised. Depending on the organisation and role, volunteers should be provided with an induction. The induction will familiarise the volunteers with the organisation, while activities could include detailing the organisation's mission and objectives, the provision of operating rules and procedures, health and safety, and an overview of the volunteer program (Brudney, 2016). Induction procedures could minimise stress on new volunteers, enhance progress and productivity, reduce turnover, develop positive attitudes toward the organisation and the organisation's values.

Training should be provided to volunteers to ensure they are equipped with the necessary skills to perform their roles (Hoye et al., 2020). The design of volunteer training in EST organisations will be influenced by a variety of factors including timing, costs, delivery mode, availability of volunteers and specificity. In terms of delivery mode, training technologies and the internet can enable volunteers to complete training in their own time and at their own pace. Good quality online training resources also frees up staff time to focus on other aspects of the volunteer program such as leadership.

In the context of mega-sport events, multiple training opportunities may be needed due to the sheer scale of volunteer numbers. However, researchers have cautioned mega-event organisers about conducting training well in advance of events as key messages may be lost or volunteers may perceive it to be a waste of time which would render the training useless (Benson, Dickson, Terwiel & Blackman, 2014). Instead, training closer to an event and/or on the job training may be better received. Program leaders should also acknowledge the prior experience volunteers may possess to avoid repetition and ensuring their time and already established skills are maximised. In the case of the 2018 Gold Coast Commonwealth Games, the organising committee created the 'Games Shapers' volunteer program. Volunteers were provided with online training, role specific training, venue specific training and event leadership training (Gold Coast 2018 Commonwealth Games Corporation, n.d).

Volunteer tourism presents more complex issues for organisations in the design of volunteer programs. Volunteers are often coordinated from one country while the volunteering itself often takes place in another country (Holmes & Smith, 2009). Although the main focus for volunteer tourism organisations appears to be on the benefits their programs provide to communities (Ong, Pearlman & Lockstone-Binney, 2011), organisations need to ensure that volunteers are prepared before they venture to their destination to begin their volunteering journey. Important areas for consideration include trip-related information such as trip preparation services (i.e., packing lists and cultural information) (Andereck, McGehee, Lee & Clemmons, 2012).

Training presents an opportunity to nurture the volunteer experience and could lead to volunteer retention (Costa, Chalip, Green & Simes, 2006). Cuskelly, Taylor, Hoye and Darcy (2006b) examined the efficacy of volunteer management practices in predicting perceived problems in volunteer retention in community sport organisations. Using an HRM approach, they found that sports clubs that reported extensive use of planning practices, training and support practices were likely to have significantly fewer perceived problems in retaining volunteers.

New forms of volunteer involvement: virtual and episodic volunteering

Advances in information and communication technologies have enabled the design and development of virtual volunteer programs. Such programs enable volunteers to contribute their skills, experience and time to organisations irrespective of physical location. A recently established online volunteering service initiated by the UN allows volunteers to connect with organisations to address challenges anywhere in the world, from any device through the United Nations Volunteers (UNV) program. Organisations can advertise positions and/or tasks that require volunteers through the UN online volunteering website. For example, the International Paralympic Committee sought an online volunteer to conduct social media promotion of Paralympic sports (United Nations, n.d.b). Similar to traditional job descriptions, online volunteering advertisements detail information regarding the task, background and objectives, requirements of the volunteer, type of experience (e.g. writing or communication), and the expected hours and duration of engagement.

Meeting the needs of volunteers

Volunteer program design needs to ensure that volunteer roles are motivating in order to attract the right person to a role, ensure they perform and retain them.

Ability-Motivation-Opportunity (AMO) theory (Boxall & Purcell, 2003) posits that three independent factors explain job performance. The ability of a volunteer, their motivation and an opportunity to contribute must all be present for volunteers to perform their role. A generic volunteer program or management model cannot be applied across all volunteering contexts, especially within the EST industries. Instead, the management of volunteers should be adapted to different situations due to the differences between organisations. For example, some organisations such as local sport clubs are membership oriented, whereas volunteer tourism organisations are often focused on direct service delivery. Volunteer program designers should not only ensure that the needs of the organisation are met, but also those of the volunteers, which can be done by identifying and addressing their motives.

Extensive research focusing on volunteer satisfaction and motivations can be used to inform recommendations for managers working with volunteers to enhance both their retention and performance within the organisation. Engaging in the 'matching strategy' is a consistent recommendation made to volunteer managers (see Clary & Snyder, 1999; Meijs & Brudney, 2007). Specifically, adapting the HRM processes to match tasks with volunteer motives to continue to facilitate motivation and satisfaction enhances performance and retention. The strategy of matching is based on traditional HRM processes and the assumption that effective matching can be made between the organisation's operational and strategic requirements and volunteers' interests, ability, skills and motives (Cuskelly, Hoye & Auld, 2006a; Meijs & Brudney, 2007).

The motives of volunteers across the EST sectors may differ. In tourism, matching the needs of destination and host communities with the needs of the volunteers can ensure that the program is worthwhile for both volunteers and the local community being served. Volunteer tourists appear to be motivated by altruism, self-development, giving back to the host community, participating in community development and cultural understanding (Wearing & McGehee, 2013). The size and scope of volunteer tourism organisations has grown rapidly to accommodate the growing numbers of those wanting to become volunteer tourists. The non-profit British Trust Conservation Volunteers was one of the earliest organisations to develop programs to accommodate volunteer tourists (Wearing & McGehee, 2013). Since then, many more organisations have capitalised on this area of tourism. These programs can be best managed by focusing on volunteer selection, pre-departure preparation, induction and debriefings to ensure that volunteers are best prepared for their journey (Raymond & Hall, 2008).

In other contexts, research on the motivations of sport volunteers has received a large amount of attention. Many volunteers within community sport organisations are parents or guardians of junior-aged participants and engage with community clubs in volunteering roles for a range of reasons which can be conceptualised by altruistic value, personal development, community concern and social adjustment (Hoye, Cuskelly, Taylor & Darcy, 2008). The event sector also represents differences between community level and mega-events such as the Olympic Games. Mega-events attract substantially more volunteers than other sectors with people being motivated to make the event a success and wanting to be part of the international status of the event (Hallmann, Downward & Dickson, 2018).

Reducing barriers to volunteering

An effective program design could reduce the barriers to volunteering by addressing and accommodating the motives for volunteering particularly for underrepresented groups. Culturally and linguistically diverse (CALD) groups present a promising pool of volunteers as they can make valuable contributions in various areas. The engagement of CALD groups as volunteers is an under-researched area in EST contexts. However, research conducted in Western contexts suggests that CALD groups are less likely to engage in volunteer work in general. Spaaij (2013) noted that cultural differences, lack of awareness and attitudes, knowledge and accessibility restraints are issues that lead to under-representation of CALD groups in sport, despite the industry being a platform to promote inclusivity. CALD volunteers involved in sport reported feeling that they lacked the competencies required to perform complex administrative tasks, feeling insufficiently supported or skilled to contribute to building a sustainable sport organisation that is connected to other community services as areas that negatively impacted their experience. It is important for organisations to design volunteer programs in ways that enhance their organisational capacity by recruiting and retaining volunteers from diverse cultural backgrounds.

Effectively designed volunteer programs can also incorporate opportunities for those with disabilities and be used as a vehicle to alter public perceptions of these groups. For example, the 2012 London Olympic and Paralympic Games were used for a strategic push within the United Kingdom to create a long term change in the attitudes and behaviour affecting the people with disabilities (Darcy, Dickson & Benson, 2014; Dickson, Darcy & Benson, 2017). The organising committee was one of the first major event organisers to strategically recruit, train and support volunteers with disabilities. The program highlighted important practical implications for future event organisers engaging volunteers with disabilities including implementing detailed knowledge management systems, effective access and disability strategies and targets, logistics systems and accessible environments.

Recruiting and retaining volunteers

There are several types of recruitment strategies that EST organisations may consider in designing programs for involving volunteers. These informal and formal recruitment strategies are not discussed in depth in this chapter as they are given detailed attention in Chapter 22. Strategies designed to attract and recruit volunteers are varied. For instance, major sport events attract large amounts of volunteers for many reasons, such as the international reputation of the event. The recruitment of volunteers is typically conducted on a global scale. Chanavat and Ferrand (2010) examined the volunteer program employed by organisers of the 2006 Winter Olympic Games and found the program consisted of adopting a global strategy, pre-development of promotional guidelines and identification of the means of communication.

Other organisations direct their recruitment strategies at a more local level. For instance, many of the volunteers in community sport organisations have a variety of roles to fill from leadership or policy roles (e.g. president, secretary or chair) to operational or helping roles (e.g. team manager, trainer, instructor, teacher, coach or other) (Ringuet-Riot et al., 2014). The volunteers who typically engage in these positions are parents or guardians of junior-aged participants or previous players or athletes involved in the club (Cuskelly, 2004; Hoye et al., 2008). However, retaining volunteers long-term can present challenges to EST organisations. For organisations that rely on volunteers, those who have a positive experience are also more likely to return (Bang, Bravo, Mello Figuerôa & Mezzadri, 2019).

Mega-events are unique in that they do not typically require the retention of volunteers in the host city once the event has concluded. However, the experience that these volunteers gained could benefit other EST organisations in their host city. Benson et al. (2014) reflected upon the assertion that the training of event volunteers could contribute to the creation of a social legacy via the transfer of learning to other volunteer contexts. The researchers concluded that the training offered to volunteers at Vancouver 2010 was a missed opportunity in achieving legacy for several reasons. These included a lack of training transfer planning, little recognition of prior learning, focus on event delivery rather than event legacy and insufficient evaluation processes. Benson et al. further argued that a lasting volunteering legacy will occur when long-term learning outcomes are identified, developed into a training plan and delivered in partnership with relevant organisations who may later benefit from the outcomes of the program.

Recognising volunteer effort

One of the factors influencing retention and satisfaction among volunteers is recognition (Farrell, Johnston & Twynam, 1998). Effective volunteer program design plans for the recognition of volunteers, which is both appropriate to the setting and the expectations of volunteers. Although not all volunteers expect some form of recognition or reward to influence their motivation to continue volunteering (Allen & Shaw, 2009), the efforts of organisations to provide recognition are often appreciated. Researchers have argued the importance of recognising and rewarding volunteers for their valued efforts within organisations (Chanavat & Ferrand, 2010; Farrell et al., 1998). In their examination of volunteer retention issues in German Sports Clubs, Breuer, Wicker and Von Hanau (2012) argued that sports clubs should increase the recognition of volunteers by highlighting their significance within organisations. Recognition may vary between organisations and ideally should be tailored to the expectations of individual volunteers.

Mega-event volunteer programs present many examples of volunteer reward and recognition. Although the majority of EST organisations do not have the same resources as mega-events such as the Olympic Games, they can learn from these programs, which manage to design and deliver volunteer programs involving up to tens of thousands of volunteers. Chanavat and Ferrand (2010) examined the essential strategic and operational success factors of a volunteer program through a case study of the 2006 Torino Winter Olympic Games and identified that volunteers for the event were rewarded across three periods: before the games, during the games and after the games. Volunteers were provided with a uniform, gifts from sponsors and invitations to rehearsals for ceremonies prior to the event. Free transport and meals were provided during work times, while some received free entry to the venues during the event. Volunteers were provided with an official participation certificate and a final thank you party where they were given an opportunity to celebrate their experience with their peers, which was highly regarded by volunteers.

Some volunteers may become emotionally attached to their volunteer role and experience sadness and loss and other transitioning emotions when their role comes to end after dominating a certain period of their life (Gellweiler, Fletcher & Wise, 2019). Volunteer managers or coordinators may be able to combat these feelings through their ongoing recognition of volunteers and their importance to the success of an organisation or its programs. For instance, in addition to the strategies already outlined in this section, volunteer reunions provide an opportunity for volunteers to reconnect with those they met during their volunteering experience (Fairley et al., 2016).

Evaluation of volunteers

The evaluation of volunteers is an area that is carried out less frequently and thoroughly as other components of volunteer program design (Brudney, 2016). This could be explained by the more pressing challenges encountered in identifying, recruiting and retaining volunteers. Organisations may be reluctant to appear questioning the performance of the volunteers they heavily rely on. Other reasons could include a lack of time and resources being available for the volunteer program (Steele, Dredge & Scherrer, 2017). The evaluation of volunteers is linked to the concept of performance management. Nel et al. (2016) described performance management as "a process that consolidates goal setting, performance appraisal and employee development into a unified system with the aim of ensuring that the employee's performance is aligned with the company's strategic aims" (p. 315). Volunteer evaluations are one aspect to ensuring the organisation's goals and volunteer program goals are achieved.

While some volunteer managers may be apprehensive about evaluating their volunteers, the feedback may be crucial in meeting volunteer expectations and motives for volunteering. For instance, volunteers may have engaged in their role to gain valuable skills that could support their career progression or begin or rekindle a volunteering career (Fairley et al., 2016; Koutrou & Pappous, 2016). Volunteers also bring a sense of dedication to their roles through wanting to make a difference or contribute to organisations. Engaging in evaluations will enable them to continue to improve their work and outcomes for themselves and for the organisation.

Performance evaluations may also be important for the success of some events. Lee, Kim, Koo and Won (2019) noted that event satisfaction among attendees was significantly linked to volunteer service performance, highlighting that sport event volunteer performance in one of the key aspects of service delivery process for sport events. In the same study, Lee et al. (2019) predicted that event satisfaction could lead to repeat visitors. Their findings emphasise that managers need to effectively manage volunteer service performance to ensure a successful event and promote a positive experience for spectators.

Evaluation of the volunteer program

The final stage of designing a volunteer program is incorporating an evaluation component of the whole program. How the volunteer program will be evaluated should be discussed during the early stages of designing the program rather than as an afterthought. It is important to evaluate and regularly review the volunteer program in order to ensure success and continuous improvement. Reviewing the program will help identify the extent to which it is meeting its objectives, and if not, will identify the areas in need of improvement or further development. Any potential problems inherent with the program will also be identified through evaluations and can be mitigated before they manifest. Volunteer programs should be evaluated in terms of their operational efficiency, perceived quality and primary stakeholder satisfaction (Bremer & Graeff, 2007; Chanavat & Ferrand, 2010).

Evaluation should involve a range of stakeholders responsible for the management of the program and importantly, the volunteers themselves. Determining whether volunteers involved in EST organisations are satisfied represents a key element of program evaluation. Collecting data and feedback from volunteers and stakeholders represents a fruitful way to evaluate the program. Obtaining qualitative and quantitative data can assist in gathering a bigger picture of how the program is performing (Bremer & Graeff, 2007). Organisations should retain accurate records of their volunteer activities such as the number of volunteers within the year and volunteer hours (Holmes & Smith, 2009). These data can assist the evaluation of the program.

Volunteer tourism programs present unique challenges due to their presence across global locations and require sustainable and responsible tourism planning and management.

Therefore, monitoring and evaluation practices are crucial to their continued success. Steele et al. (2017) noted that the practices employed to monitor and evaluate volunteer tourism programs vary greatly among organisations and consist of both informal and formal strategies. Of the organisations canvassed, a small number of organisations engaged in in-depth approaches to host partner organisations and host community focused monitoring and evaluation.

Conclusion

This chapter has examined the design of volunteer programs within the context of EST organisations. Effective program design and planning is essential in the development of a volunteer program and will benefit organisations and volunteers. Organisations should begin with a rationale of volunteer involvement, as this will inform other aspects of the volunteer program including the preparation of job descriptions, recruitment and retention strategies, induction and training, and how volunteers will be recognised for their work. As each entity within the EST environment may differ, it is important for organisations to adapt their practices accordingly. Finally, evaluation of volunteers and the volunteer program itself should be carried out to ensure the continued success of volunteer involvement in EST organisations.

References

Allen, J. B., & Shaw, S. (2009). "Everyone rolls up their sleeves and mucks in": Exploring volunteers' motivation and experiences of the motivational climate of a sporting event. *Sport Management Review*, *12*(2), 79–90. https://doi.org/10.1016/j.smr.2008.12.002

Andereck, K., McGehee, N. G., Lee, S., & Clemmons, D. (2012). Experience expectations of prospective volunteer tourists. *Journal of Travel Research*, *51*(2), 130–141. https://doi.org/10.1177/0047287511400610

Bang, H., Bravo, G. A., Mello Figuerôa, K., & Mezzadri, F. M. (2019). The impact of volunteer experience at sport mega-events on intention to continue volunteering: Multigroup path analysis. *Journal of Community Psychology*, *47*(4), 727–742. https://doi.org/10.1002/jcop.22149

Benson, A. M., Dickson, T. J., Terwiel, F. A., & Blackman, D. A. (2014). Training of Vancouver 2010 volunteers: A legacy opportunity? *Contemporary Social Science*, *9*(2), 210–226. https://doi.org/10.1080/21582041.2013.838296

Boxall, P., & Purcell, J. (2003). *Strategy and human resource management*. Oxford, UK: Blackwell.

Bremer, S., & Graeff, P. (2007). Volunteer management in German national parks—from random action toward a volunteer program. *Human Ecology*, *35*(4), 489–496. https://doi.org/10.1007/s10745-006-9070-9

Breuer, C., Wicker, P., & Von Hanau, T. (2012). Consequences of the decrease in volunteers among German sports clubs: Is there a substitute for voluntary work? *International Journal of Sport Policy and Politics*, *4*(2), 173–186. https://doi.org/10.1080/19406940.2012.656681

Brudney, J. L. (2016). Designing and managing volunteer programs. In D. Renz & R. Herman (Eds.), *The Jossey-Bass Handbook of Nonprofit Leadership and Management* (pp. 688–733). Hoboken, NJ: John Wiley & Sons.

Chanavat, N., & Ferrand, A. (2010). Volunteer programme in mega sport events: The case of the Olympic Winter Games, Torino 2006. *International Journal of Sport Management and Marketing*, *7*(3–4), 241–266. https://doi.org/10.1504/IJSMM.2010.032553

Clary, E. G., & Snyder, M. (1999). The motivations to volunteer: Theoretical and practical considerations. *Current Directions in Psychological Science*, *8*(5), 156–159. https://doi.org/10.1111/1467-8721.00037

Collings, D. G., & Wood, G. (2009). Human resource management: a critical approach. In Collings, D.G. & G Wood (eds). *Human Resource Management: A Critical Approach* (pp. 1–18).

Costa, C. A., Chalip, L., Green, B. C., & Simes, C. (2006). Reconsidering the role of training in event volunteers' satisfaction. *Sport Management Review, 9*(2), 165–182. https://doi.org/10.1016/S1441-3523(06)70024-9

Cuskelly, G. (2004). Volunteer retention in community sport organisations. *European Sport Management Quarterly, 4*(2), 59–76. https://doi.org/10.1080/16184740408737469

Cuskelly, G., Hoye, R., & Auld, C. (2006a). *Working with Volunteers in Sport: Theory and Practice,* 1–180. London: Routledge.

Cuskelly, G., Taylor, T., Hoye, R., & Darcy, S. (2006b). Volunteer management practices and volunteer retention: A human resource management approach. *Sport Management Review, 9*(2), 141–163. https://doi.org/10.1016/S1441-3523(06)70023-7

Darcy, S., Dickson, T. J., & Benson, A. M. (2014). London 2012 Olympic and Paralympic Games: Including volunteers with disabilities—A podium performance? *Event Management, 18*(4), 431–446. http://dx.doi.org/10.3727/152599514X14143427352157

Dickson, T. J., Darcy, S., & Benson, A. (2017). Volunteers with disabilities at the London 2012 Olympic and Paralympic Games: Who, why, and will they do it again? *Event Management, 21*(3), 301–318. https://doi.org/10.3727/152599517X14942648527527

Dickson, T. J., Darcy, S., & Gadd, C. P. (2020). Ensuring volunteer impacts, legacy and leveraging is not "fake news". *International Journal of Contemporary Hospitality Management, 32*(2), 683–705. https://doi.org/10.1108/IJCHM-04-2019-0370

Dickson, T. J., Terwiel, F. A., & Buick, F. (2017). Volunteer management at the Paralympic Games. In S. Darcy, S. Frawley, & D. Adair (Eds.), *Managing the Paralympics* (pp. 193–216). London: Palgrave Macmillan.

Doherty, A. J. (2009). The volunteer legacy of a major sport event. *Journal of Policy Research in Tourism, Leisure and Events, 1*(3), 185–207. https://doi.org/10.1080/19407960903204356

Fairley, S., Gardiner, S., & Filo, K. (2016). The spirit lives on: The legacy of volunteering at the Sydney 2000 Olympic Games. *Event Management, 20*(2), 201–215. https://doi.org/10.3727/152599516X14610017108747

Farrell, J. M., Johnston, M. E., & Twynam, G. D. (1998). Volunteer motivation, satisfaction, and management at an elite sporting competition. *Journal of Sport Management, 12*(4), 288–300. https://doi.org/10.1123/jsm.12.4.288

Gellweiler, S., Fletcher, T., & Wise, N. (2019). Exploring experiences and emotions sport event volunteers associate with 'role exit'. *International Review for the Sociology of Sport, 54*(4), 495–511. https://doi.org/10.1177/1012690217732533

Gold Coast 2018 Commonwealth Games Corporation. (n.d). Games Shapers FAQs. *GC2018.* Retrieved from https://gc2018.com/volunteer/faq#elt

Hallmann, K., Downward, P., & Dickson, G. (2018). Factors influencing time allocation of sport event volunteers. *International Journal of Event and Festival Management, 9*(3), 316–331. https://doi.org/10.1108/IJEFM-01-2018-0004

Holmes, K., & Smith, K. (2009). *Managing volunteers in tourism.* Oxford, UK: Routledge.

Hoye, R., Cuskelly, G., Auld, C., Kappelides, P., & Misener, K. (2020). *Sport volunteering.* London, UK: Routledge.

Hoye, R., Cuskelly, G., Taylor, T., & Darcy, S. (2008). Volunteer motives and retention in community sport: A study of Australian rugby clubs. *Australian Journal on Volunteering, 13*(2), 40–48.

Koutrou, N., & Pappous, A. S. (2016). Towards an Olympic volunteering legacy: Motivating volunteers to serve and remain–a case study of London 2012 Olympic Games volunteers. *Voluntary Sector Review, 7*(3), 269–291. http://dx.doi.org/10.1332/096278916X14767760874050

Lee, Y., Kim, M. L., Koo, J., & Won, H. J. (2019). Sport volunteer service performance, image formation, and service encounters. *International Journal of Sports Marketing and Sponsorship, 20*(2), 307–320. https://doi.org/10.1108/IJSMS-05-2018-0047

Lockstone, L., Smith, K., & Baum, T. (2010). Volunteering flexibility across the tourism sector. *Managing Leisure, 15*(1–2), 111–127. https://doi.org/10.1080/13606710903448202

Meijs, L. C. P. M., & Brudney, J. L. (2007). Winning volunteer scenarios: The soul of a new machine. *International Journal of Volunteer Administration, 24*(6), 68–79.

Nel, P., Werner, A., Fazey, M., Pillay, S., Wordsworth, R., Du Plessi, A., & Suseno, Y. (2016). *Human resource management in Australia.* Retrieved from https://ebookcentral-proquest-com.libraryproxy.griffith.edu.au/lib/griffith/detail.action?docID=4787577

Ong, F., Pearlman, M., & Lockstone-Binney, L. (2011). An examination of not-for-profit volunteer tourism sending organisations' guiding considerations that influence volunteer tourism programmes. *World Leisure Journal*, *53*(4), 296–311. https://doi.org/10.1080/04419057.2011.630787

Raymond, E., & Hall, C. (2008). The development of cross-cultural (mis)understanding through volunteer tourism. *Journal of Sustainable Tourism*, *16*(5), 530–543. https://doi.org/10.1080/09669580802159610

Ringuet-Riot, C., Cuskelly, G., Auld, C., & Zakus, D. H. (2014). Volunteer roles, involvement and commitment in voluntary sport organizations: Evidence of core and peripheral volunteers. *Sport in Society*, *17*(1), 116–133. https://doi.org/10.1080/17430437.2013.828902

Spaaij, R. (2013). Cultural diversity in community sport: An ethnographic inquiry of Somali Australians' experiences. *Sport Management Review*, *16*(1), 29–40. https://doi.org/10.1016/j.smr.2012.06.003

Steele, J., Dredge, D., & Scherrer, P. (2017). Monitoring and evaluation practices of volunteer tourism organisations. *Journal of Sustainable Tourism*, *25*(11), 1674–1690. https://doi.org/10.1080/09669582.2017.1306067

Taylor, T., Doherty, A., & McGraw, P. (2015). *Managing people in sport organizations: A strategic human resource management perspective*. New York: Routledge.

United Nations. (n.d.a). Description of Assignment. *United Nations*. Retrieved from https://www.unv.org/sites/default/files/UNV_PO_DOA_SRE_Pool_February_2017.pdf

United Nations. (n.d.b). Social media promotion of Paralympic sports. *UN Volunteers Online Volunteering*. Retrieved from https://www.onlinevolunteering.org/en/international-paralympic-committee/social-media-promotion-paralympic-sports

Volunteering Australia. (2015). *The National Standards for Volunteer Involvement*. Canberra: Author.

Volunteering Australia (n.d.). Designing volunteer roles and position descriptions. *Volunteering Australia*. Retrieved from https://www.volunteeringaustralia.org/wp-content/uploads/Volunteering_Australia_Volunteer_Roles_Toolkit+1-1.pdf

Volunteer Canada (2020). *Canadian Code for Volunteer Involvement*. Retrieved from https://volunteer.ca/ccvi

Wearing, S., & McGehee, N. G. (2013). Volunteer tourism: A review. *Tourism Management*, *38*, 120–130. https://doi.org/10.1016/j.tourman.2013.03.002

Weerakoon, R. K. (2016). Human resource management in sports: A critical review of its importance and pertaining issues. *Physical Culture and Sport. Studies and Research*, *69*(1), 15–21. https://doi.org/10.1515/pcssr-2016-0005

20

VOLUNTEER STEWARDSHIP MANAGEMENT MODELS FOR VOLUNTEER PROGRAMS

Lucas C.P.M. Meijs

Introduction

Although in the late 1960s and early 1970s volunteer management was already attracting attention (Brudney et al., 2016), volunteer administration and management still adopt a Human Resource Management (HRM) (Studer & von Schnurbein, 2013) approach based on the metaphor of the workplace (see also Safrit & Schmiesing, 2012). This HRM perspective is being supplemented with attention to paid staff-volunteer relations, the development of general management support from nonprofit organisations, and the perspective of community involvement in general (Brudney, Meijs & van Overbeeke, 2019). This has led to the development of a contingency approach in which it is understood that the management of volunteers should differ between contexts (Rochester, 1999). Brudney and Meijs (2014) show that there is indeed a large collection of contingency models based upon the characteristics of either the volunteer, or the programme and organisation. Volunteer-focused criteria relate to such factors as the motivations of volunteers, their willingness to commit time, and their connection to the organisation. Programme/organisation criteria are, for example, the structure, type, and mission of the organisation. Combining volunteer and organisational factors leads to a creative perspective that combines HRM principles with citizen participation and engagement that drive volunteerism: the 'ratchet model' (Brudney & Sink, 2017). They claim that volunteer managers, depending on the situation, should or could tighten (more HRM) or loosen up (a more informal, participative approach) (Brudney & Sink, 2017). The underlying idea for this chapter is that in mega events volunteer management in many cases can be rather tight but that in smaller local events the systems ratchet must be loosened. Likewise, there might be some external developments asking for some loosening up.

For understanding external developments and the balancing of tightening and loosening the volunteer management systems, the recently developed volunteer stewardship model (Brudney et al., 2019) will be used. This model recognises that the value chain of volunteering has two steps. In the first step, volunteer involving organisations access volunteer energy. Volunteer energy is the resource underlying the potential to volunteer (Brudney & Meijs, 2009). In the second step, this potential is guided into effective volunteering. According to Brudney et al. (2019) access to volunteer energy can be typified as a private resource or a common pool. Private resource access means that the potential volunteer is previously

DOI: 10.4324/9780367815875-24

connected to the recruiting volunteer organisation itself such as being a member in a membership organisation (see Tschirhart, 2006) or connected to a sending third party (home) organisation (Haski-Leventhal, Meijs & Hustinx, 2010), for example, community and/or service learning by educational institutes or corporate volunteering by companies. Private access starts with a list of people which the organisation knows how to contact. Common pool access means that a potential volunteer has weak ties with or even has no prior knowledge of the organisation. Common pool access starts with some general communication to unknown audiences. Guidance provided to volunteers is either unitary, when home and host organisation are the same, or shared when the home organisation is, for example, a company while the host organisation is, for example, an event using volunteers. Mega events in many cases already have volunteers sent to them and operate implicitly on shared systems, while smaller local events might be based on one local organisation that uses both regular organisational volunteers and occasional episodic volunteers that participate in every event again (Macduff, 2005).

Combining access and guidance, Brudney et al. (2019) present a 2×2 matrix for volunteer management or stewardship (Table 20.1). The first cell can be characterised as 'membership management' (private resource access, guidance provided by the host membership organisation). A second model can be characterised as 'service delivery or programme management' (common pool access, guidance by the host service organisation). The two other models incorporate new forms in which two organisations and two managers share the volunteers. The third, 'secondary management model' is based on non-volunteer involving third parties (see Haski-Leventhal et al., 2010) where access to the volunteers is restricted (to company employees or students), but two organisations provide guidance. In the last, i.e., 'intermediary management model', volunteers are accessed from throughout the broader community, for example, as in a public media campaign for an event like a National Day of Service (see, for example, Compion et al., 2020). Seen from the four different volunteer stewardship models of Brudney et al. (2019), event volunteering might involve all four models; these will be discussed below.

The first section of this chapter deals with the two traditional unitary guidance approaches to membership versus programme/service delivery management of volunteers. This discussion will be placed in the perspective of the tightening and loosening of the 'ratchet' (Brudney & Sink, 2017). The second section will shed some light on the role of event volunteer managers in the two shared guidance approaches. Given the need for large groups of episodic volunteers, volunteer managers of events will make use of the intermediary model

Table 20.1 Volunteer Stewardship Framework applied to events, sport, and tourism

		Access to Volunteer Energy	
		Common pool	
Guidance of Volunteers	Unitary	Membership Model Examples: local historical society, community sports club	Service Model Examples: airport meet and greet program, zoo docent program
	Shared	Secondary model Examples: hotel's corporate volunteer programme, university sports club	Intermediary Model Examples: events volunteer agency, volunteer tourism sending organisation

Adapted from Brudney et al. (2019, p. 73).

and secondary to be able to contact potential volunteers leading to additional challenges and tasks to do. But, maybe secondary organisations can be very important in providing more skill-based volunteers such as treasurers provided by accountancy firms. The chapter finishes with an outlook of the possibilities for the future.

Membership management and programme management

Handy (1988) and Meijs (1997) show that organizational goal, in the simplest form of service delivery, mutual benefit/support or campaigning, is an important contingency factor for volunteer management. Based on mission, Meijs and Hoogstad (2001) (see, also, Meijs & Karr, 2004) developed two different styles of management of volunteers: membership management and programme management. In this typology, management systems focus either on the volunteers themselves (membership management) or on specific operational tasks (programme management). Membership management is loose, while in programme management volunteer systems are tightened.

For mega events, most volunteer management approaches can be seen as rather focused on the organisational perspective applying a programme management system. First, almost all events attract episodic volunteers, individuals who engage in one-time or short-term volunteer opportunities (Cnaan & Handy, 2005; Macduff, 1990) which is also a global trend (Hyde et al., 2014). Indeed, episodic volunteering is quite common in sporting events (Fairley, Kellett & Green, 2007; Filo, Funk & O'Brien, 2008a, 2008b; Hamm, MacLean & Misener, 2008; Kodama, Doherty & Popovic 2013; Koutrou & Pappous, 2016; Vetitnev, Bobina & Terwiel, 2018) and fundraising events (Beder & Fast, 2008; Wood, Snelgrove & Danylchuk, 2010) but also in religion (see, for example, Cnaan, Heist & Storti, 2017). Cnaan and colleagues recently published a literature review covering episodic volunteering in events (Cnaan et al., 2021).

Mostly episodic volunteers want to be managed in a programme management approach, which sometimes becomes extreme or very tight when the volunteer accept less autonomy in their volunteering than usually ongoing volunteers would (Maas, Meijs, & Brudney, 2021). This is the organisational field of mega events that are large scale one-time events organised by a special organisation or authority attracting visitors and mass media attention. Often, such as the Olympic Games, these mega events change location every time. Mega events can be seen as similar to national days of service (NDS) (Compion et al., 2020; Maas et al., 2021), an example of the intermediary management model to be discussed in the next section.

Second, in contrast, many (smaller) events (non-mega events, see Taks, Chalip & Green, 2015) are organised by an ongoing local organisation that organises the same event every year. Sometimes the local event organisation is part of an organisation that runs activities on a weekly basis, such as when the local athletic association organises the yearly local marathon. In this case volunteers might see themselves more as volunteer-members as compared to mega events that might move locations. These organisations likely will and must apply the membership approach, as some volunteers are regular volunteers within the organisation or the volunteers are occasional volunteers that participate every year in the same event (Macduff, 2005). Occasional volunteers are known to the event organisation from previous years, which makes recruitment easier but also might pose other challenges in management as the volunteers might have their own opinions on how to run things.

It is clear that the two forms of volunteer management are likely combined in events as Rochester (2018, p. 36) argued that many projects always have a core of "highly committed serious leisure volunteers who formed the 'inner group of willing people'" being assisted by a host of episodic volunteers (see also Meijs (2004) for a description of the two systems in a political party). Again, in mega events the core is more detached from the (potential) volunteers than in small local events.[1] So, membership management starts with the possibilities, wants, and needs of the volunteers. The idea of membership management is to start with the preferences of the volunteers by asking each member what he or she wants to do. It resembles a team approach to building a car in which team members can perform all tasks. In this membership approach, management is based upon strong personal links between the manager and the volunteers, leading to accepting management based upon authority instead of power. This yields a strong organisational culture with shared norms and values, which helps to establish organisational control (Pearce, 1993). At the same time, this management approach does not support the idea that volunteers can be disciplined or 'fired' if they do not perform. Recognition comes from peers, not from external forces. According to Meijs and Karr (2004, p. 178) the strong point of membership management is its capability "of generating broad, multifaceted involvement of volunteers, leading perhaps to a greater overall satisfaction with the volunteer experience". In the membership approach, the management systems are loose instead of tightened (Brudney & Sink, 2017).

By contrast, the programme management model operates much like an assembly line for building a car or the classical workplace approach to volunteer management as described above. The model begins with needs assessment from the organisation. These needs are translated into tasks for the volunteers to perform. Because the organisational perspective is the starting point, it becomes much more feasible to control or reject volunteers. Although programme management is unlikely to yield great loyalty on the part of volunteers, it can attract many volunteers based on a volunteer scenario approach, matching the needed availability and assets to what volunteers are willing to bring (Meijs & Brudney, 2007).

Membership management might generate broad, multi-faceted involvement by volunteers. By focusing first on the volunteers (who are treated as members and have a large sense of belonging to the organisation) and their goals, the membership-managed organisation shapes itself to the needs and desires of its volunteers. Through careful attention from a social perspective to who is to be admitted to membership or volunteering, it guards against the introduction of members whose goals may be contrary to those of the existing membership. This leads to a very 'our breed of volunteers' and a difficulty in working with diversity. Because it is tailor-made to the specifications of their own ideas, it would be difficult for a member or volunteer to find such a good fit with any other organisation. Because the costs of both entry and exit are high, the membership-managed organisation may cultivate considerable loyalty among its individual members. Entry costs are high because people need to develop social ties and trust with the organisation (typically this is done by engaging in all kinds of social activities with existing volunteers). Exit costs are high because people lose long-time friendships while leaving. By these means, a strong organisational culture is developed. For events this leads to a reduced need for formal training and introduction. But also, former event-volunteers might still be seen as special guests of the event (part of the 'family') or, in the case of an ongoing organisation that also organises an event, be regular volunteers with the core organisation. Organising an event in a membership approach is a repetitive action for almost all volunteers, not only the organisers.

However, membership management does not always provide a stable basis for the continuity of an event. While individual volunteers may indeed remain loyal to the event for long periods of time, the events and organisation itself risks stagnation and eventually extinction. While the extensive and prolonged involvement of all volunteers, both the core organisers and the occasional episodic, provides continuity to the organisation, it makes it very difficult to adapt to environmental changes, or even demographic shifts in the people who want to participate in the event. In some cases, the core organising volunteers are even more 'old fashioned' or traditional than the occasional volunteers while the occasional volunteer is outdated compared to the diversity in the population and the changes in the event that need to be made. Because of this, the membership-managed organisation may eventually face a slow and painful death! Consider the example of traditional sport organisations that continue to organise tournaments during holidays that non-core volunteers and non-members see as really outdated.

Programme management, on the other hand, has a clear eye toward continuity for the event. The general focus on carefully specified tasks already guards against any one volunteer becoming indispensable. The limited scope of involvement expected of any volunteer facilitates both the entry and exit of volunteers, who may affiliate with the event organisation only for the purpose of performing one specific, time-limited task. This is of course extremely evident when the event moves geographically. Because the tasks to be accomplished take priority over the aims of the volunteers performing them, the programme-managed organisation is capable of maintaining smooth, consistent operations, also in different locations. Because each task is, for the most part, a self-contained unit, changes in response to new developments in the event involves only the reworking of single components rather than an overall shift in ideology or traditions. The programme-managed organisation is resilient and flexible.

Programme management will not cultivate loyalty on the part of volunteers. People who join an event organisation in order to participate in just the event programme or those focused on specific activities are less likely to identify themselves as members of the organisation than are those whose involvement is broader (see Karr, 2001). A programme-managed organisation is dependent on the availability of fresh supplies of volunteers, thus risking high turnover, impersonality, and co-optation. This is, again, no problem at all for the mega events that move location every time and are fashionable to volunteer for. It might even make their volunteer management easier as volunteers indeed will expect to be instructed (see Maas et al., 2021). But it also will lead to higher recruitment and coordination costs that might be difficult to carry for small, local event organisers.

Connecting to the shared management models: intermediary and secondary

The intermediary and secondary models are those in which the volunteer management process is shared between two organisations. The first manager is located in a home, sending thematic organisation such as, in the case of the intermediary model, a volunteer centre, thematic organisations such as single volunteers[2] or family volunteering,[3] or national days of service (see, for example, Compion et al., 2020, Maas et al., 2021). In the secondary model, the home organisation is a third party like companies and educational institutes (Haski-Leventhal et al., 2010). The difference between intermediary and secondary is that in the latter, the volunteers are organisational members of this third party (for example, employees or students). The second manager is located in a host, receiving, and placing organisation such as an event organiser or a regular nonprofit agency. For the host organisations, such as an event organisation, these sending organisations form an additional or even new entrance to volunteer energy (Brudney & Meijs, 2009) and support recruitability. Compion et al. (2020) describe how Mandela Day attracts people that have never volunteered before. Krasnopolskaya, Roza and Meijs (2016) show that in Russia, corporate volunteering is a very prominent way to attract volunteers. According to Brudney et al. (2019) there is limited research on volunteer management in the shared models in leading handbooks or review articles. However they do find some literature applying the volunteer management perspective to corporate volunteering (for example, Roza et al., 2017; Tschirhart, 2005) or service learning and court-referred volunteering (Haski-Leventhal et al., 2010), and volunteer centres (Bos, 2014; Osborne, 1999) and a more specific study (Follman, Cseh & Brudney, 2016) on volunteer programmes in several national parks in the United States.

According to Brudney et al. (2019), the shared models are in many cases based on a, sometimes implicit, 'hyphen' approach. This approach is based on combining volunteering with another activity in the busy schedules/agendas of prospective volunteers to enable and pressure them to volunteer (Hustinx & Meijs, 2011). Indeed, most shared models that 'hyphen' two activities, e.g., dating and volunteering (single-volunteers), learning and volunteering (service learning), and holidaying and volunteering (volunteer tourism), are clear examples of the two strategies, enablement and pressure, used by communities and organisations to re-embed volunteering (Hustinx & Meijs, 2011). Enablement is aimed at improving and enlarging the availability of potential volunteers by creating a 'if you can't beat them, join them strategy'. Pressure is aimed at creating an additional reason, mostly instrumental, for organisations to access their members, employees, or students to ask them to volunteer. An interesting example is corporate volunteering in which companies can decide that they simply facilitate the individual volunteering of employees by allowing some rescheduling or enforce the team building societal volunteering projects and see the time as worktime, but companies can decide to publish or not publish about this to create more or less instrumental value for the company (Meijs et al., 2009).

The managers of the event volunteers in the shared models not only have management issues of working with volunteers in their home (event) organisation but also need to collaborate and develop partnerships with the host organisations or develop themes themselves. In case of the secondary model, there will be a relationship, maybe even a contract, in which the home and host organisations define who will volunteer and under what conditions. Sometimes nonprofit organisations face difficulties in negotiating this contract as, for example, there are (perceived) power imbalances between the home and host organisations such as in corporate volunteering (Roza et al., 2017). For the intermediary model it might be that the event organiser creates assignments that are good for family volunteering, for example, giving water bottles to athletes or cleaning up an area, or that are specific attraction for singles, like cooking together and having a party afterwards. But having said this, the shared models are a promising reality for volunteer managers in events as they give easy access to more and different volunteers. Haski-Leventhal et al. (2010) call this recruitability.

In order to achieve the full benefits of the shared models, the managers have to combine the instrumental use of volunteers for two organisations. For the event organisation the instrumental benefit is clear: without the volunteers there is no event or at least it would be much more expensive or less embedded in society. But for the home organisation or theme this is more diverse although for every 'hyphen' it is clear. Obviously, the intended instrumental result for a single-volunteers organisation are happy couples afterwards, for family volunteering quality time and the transfer of family habits, and for service learning the achievement of learning objectives. But in the case of, for example, corporate volunteering this might be different as corporate volunteering programmes can have multiple goals that might differ between volunteering opportunities even (Roza, 2016). Clearly the volunteer jobs will be different if the corporate goal is to achieve teambuilding, a positive image, or individual development for employees. The volunteer manager of the event saves time and effort on recruiting volunteers but maybe spends more time on creating the instrumental goals.

Conclusion

Generally speaking, volunteer management in events is very straightforward. Events are one of the organisational contexts in which an organisational focused programme management approach (Meijs & Hoogstad, 2001) is very applicable. This programme management can even be tightened more (Brudney & Sink, 2017) in the case of mega scale events that have no problem attracting plenty of volunteers. This is even more so when these events move location every time, such as with the Olympic Games. However, (yearly) recurring local events organised by ongoing local (volunteer) organisations might have a different relationship with their volunteers. As these occasional volunteers (Macduff, 2005) have a history with the event and the organisation, they might have ideas about how to do their work themselves. This creates a reason to loosen the management approach and introduce more membership elements.

Next to this, the emergence of the dual or shared volunteer stewardship models create new challenges for the event volunteer manager. On the one hand these organisations (secondary models) or themes (intermediary) 'hyphen' the volunteering to another obligation in the schedule of the potential volunteer and make recruitment easier. But at the same time, they add another layer of instrumental goals to volunteer involvement. It is not only the volunteer that might have an instrumental goal such as creating a curriculum vitae item; there is also a third party like an educational institute or a company having objectives. For example, in order to achieve service learning goals of a university course, the student-volunteers actually have to learn something, and needing to learn implies that the students are not yet capable of performing at a good enough level. Likewise, if corporate volunteering is meant to support teambuilding, the social aspects might intrude on the volunteer activities.

Notes

1 The sections on membership and programme management are based upon Meijs and Hoogstad (2001) and Meijs and Karr (2004).
2 https://www.singlevolunteers.org/.
3 https://www.doinggoodtogether.org/volunteer-together-local.

References

Beder, J., & Fast, J. (2008). Episodic volunteering: Why people walk/run for charity. *The International Journal of Volunteer Administration, 25*(3), 3–13.
Bos, C.M. van den (2014, Maart 06). *Using Volunteering Infrastructure to Build Civil Society.* Erasmus University Rotterdam (250 pag.) (Arnhem: Stichting Rijnstad).
Brudney, J.L., Lee, Y.J., Bin Afif, S.A., Ockenden, N., and Sillah, A. (2016). Formal volunteer service programs. In D. Horton Smith, R.A. Stebbins, & J. Grotz (Eds.) *The Palgrave Handbook of Volunteering, Civic Participation, and Nonprofit Associations* (pp. 330–348). Palgrave Macmillan.
Brudney, J.L., & Meijs, L.C.P.M. (2009). It ain't natural: Toward a new (natural) resource conceptualization for volunteer management. *Nonprofit and Voluntary Sector Quarterly, 38*(4), 564–581. https://doi.org/10.1177/0899764009333828

Brudney, J.L., & Meijs, L.C.P.M. (2014). Models of volunteer management: Professional volunteer program management in social work. *Human Service Organizations Management, Leadership & Governance, 38*(3), 297–309. https://doi.org/10.1080/23303131.2014.899281

Brudney, J.L., Meijs, L.C.P.M., & van Overbeeke, P.S. (2019). More is less? The volunteer stewardship framework and models. *Nonprofit Management and Leadership, 30*(1), 69–87. https://doi.org/10.1002/nml.21358

Brudney, J.L., & Sink, H.K. (2017). Volunteer management: It all depends. In J.K.A. Word & J.E. Sowa (Eds.) *The Nonprofit Resource Management Handbook: From Theory to Practice.* (pp. 204–222). Routledge.

Cnaan, R.A., & Handy, F. (2005). Towards understanding episodic volunteering. *Vrijwillige Inzet Onderzocht [Volunteering Researched], 2*(1), 29–35.

Cnaan, R.A., Heist, H.D., & Storti, M.H. (2017). Episodic volunteering at a religious megaevent: Pope Francis's visit to Philadelphia. *Nonprofit Management & Leadership, 28*(1), 85–104. https://doi.org/10.1002/nml.21268

Cnaan, R.A., Meijs, L., Brudney, J.L., Hersberger-Langloh, S., Okada, A., & Abu-Rumman, S. (2021). You thought that this would be easy? Seeking an understanding of episodic volunteering. *VOLUNTAS: International Journal of Voluntary and Nonprofit Organizations,* 1–13. https://doi.org/10.1007/s11266-021-00329-7

Compion, S., Jeong, B.G., Cnaan, R., & Meijs, L. (2020). Mobilising episodic volunteers for Mandela Day. *Voluntary Sector Review.* https://doi.org/10.1332/204080520X16000978324405

Fairley, S., Kellett, F., & Green, C. (2007). Volunteering abroad: Motives for travel to volunteer at the Athens Olympic Games. *Journal of Sport Management, 21*(1), 41–57. https://doi.org/10.1123/jsm.21.1.41

Filo, K.R., Funk, D.C., & O'Brien, D. (2008a). It's really not about the bike: Exploring attraction and attachment to the events of the Lance Armstrong Foundations. *Journal of Sport Management, 22*(5), 501–525. https://doi.org/10.1123/jsm.22.5.501

Filo, K.R., Funk, D.C., & O'Brien, D. (2008b). The meaning behind attachment: Exploring camaraderie, cause, and competency at a charity sport event. *Journal of Sport Management, 23*(3), 361–387. https://doi.org/10.1123/jsm.23.3.361

Follman, J., Cseh, M., & Brudney, J.L. (2016). Structures, challenges, and successes of volunteer programs co-managed by nonprofit and public organizations. *Nonprofit Management and Leadership, 26*(4), 453–470. https://doi.org/10.1002/nml.21206

Hamm, S., MacLean, J., & Misener, K. (2008). Understanding the commitment and motivation of large sporting event volunteers. *International Journal of Volunteer Administration, 25*(3), 26–38.

Handy, C. (1988). *Understanding Voluntary Organizations: How to Make Them Function Effectively.* Penguin Books.

Haski-Leventhal, D., Meijs, L.C.P.M., & Hustinx, L. (2010). The third party model: Enhancing volunteering through governments, corporations and educational institutes. *Journal of Social Policy, 39*(1), 139–158. https://doi.org/10.1017/S0047279409990377

Hustinx, L., & Meijs, L.C.P.M. (2011). Re-embedding volunteerism: in search of new collective ground. *Voluntary Sector Review, 2*(1), 5–21. https://doi.org/10.1332/204080511X560594

Hyde, M.K., Dunn, J., Scuffham, P.A., & Chamber, S.K. (2014). A systematic review of episodic volunteering in public health and other contexts. *BMC Public Health, 14*(992). https://doi.org/10.1186/1471-2458-14-992

Karr, L.B. (2001). *Organization and Association: An Examination of Issues Relating to Cooperation in the Context of a National Volunteer-Run Membership Organization.* Unpublished doctoral dissertation, University of South Carolina.

Kodama, E., Doherty, A., & Popovic, M. (2013). Front line insight: An autoethnography of the Vancouver 2010 volunteer experience. *European Sport Management Quarterly, 13*(1), 76–93. https://doi.org/10.1080/16184742.2012.742123

Koutrou, N., & Pappous, A.S. (2016). Towards an Olympic volunteering legacy: Motivating volunteers to serve and remain – a case study of London 2012 Olympic Games volunteers. *Voluntary Sector Review, 7*(3), 269–291. https://doi.org/10.1332/096278916X14767760874050

Krasnopolskaya, I., Roza, L., & Meijs, L.C.P.M. (2016). The relationship between corporate volunteering and employee civic engagement outside the workplace in Russia. *VOLUNTAS: International Journal of Voluntary and Nonprofit Organizations, 27*(2), 640–672. https://doi.org/10.1007/s11266-015-9599-6

Macduff, N. (1990). Episodic volunteers: Reality for the future. *Voluntary Action Leadership*, Spring, 15–17. https://eric.ed.gov/?id=EJ417756

Macduff, N. (2005). *Episodic Volunteering: Organizing and Managing the Short-Term Volunteer Program*. MBA Publishing.

Maas, S.A., Meijs, L.C., & Brudney, J.L. (2021). Designing 'National Day of Service' projects to promote volunteer job satisfaction. *Nonprofit and Voluntary Sector Quarterly*, https://doi.org/10.1177/0899764020982664

Meijs, L.C.P.M. (1997). *Management van vrijwilligersorganisaties*. NOV Publikaties.

Meijs, L.C.P.M. (2004). Campaigning organisaties in verandering. *Vrijwillige Inzet Onderzocht*, *1*(1), 34–44.

Meijs, L.C.P.M., & Brudney, J.L. (2007). Winning volunteer scenarios: The soul of a new machine. *International Journal of Volunteer Administration*, *XXIV*(6), 68–79.

Meijs, L.C.P.M., & Hoogstad, E. (2001). New ways of managing volunteers: Combining membership management and programme management. *Voluntary Action*, *3*(3), 41–61.

Meijs, L.C.P.M., & Karr, L.B. (2004). Managing volunteers in different settings: Membership and programme management. In R.A. Stebbins & M. Graham (Eds.) *Volunteering as Leisure/Leisure as Volunteering* (pp. 177–193). CABI.

Meijs, L.C.P.M., Tschirhart, M., Ten Hoorn, E.M., & Brudney, J.L. (2009). The effect of design elements for corporate volunteer programs on volunteerability. *The International Journal of Volunteer Administration*, *26*, 23–32.

Osborne, S.P. (1999). Volunteer Bureaux and the promotion and support of volunteering in local communities in England. London. *Voluntary Action Institute for Volunteering Research*, *1*, 67–84.

Pearce, J.L. (1993). *Volunteers: The organizational behavior of unpaid workers*. Routledge.

Rochester, C. (1999). One size does not fit all: Four models of involving volunteers in voluntary organizations. *Voluntary Action*, *1*(2), 47–59.

Rochester, C. (2018). *Trends in volunteering*. Volunteer Now.

Roza, L. (2016). *Employee Engagement in Corporate Social Responsibility*. ERIM/Erasmus University, Rotterdam, The Netherlands (No. EPS-2016-396-ORG).

Roza, L., Shachar, I., Meijs, L., & Hustinx, L. (2017). The nonprofit case for corporate volunteering: A multi-level perspective. *The Service Industries Journal*, *37*(11–12), 746–765. https://doi.org/10.1080/02642069.2017.1347158

Safrit, R.D., & Schmiesing, R. (2012). Volunteer models and management. In T.D. Connors (Ed.) *The volunteer management handbook* (2nd ed., pp. 3–30). Wiley.

Studer, S., & Von Schnurbein, G. (2013). Organizational factors affecting volunteers: A literature review on volunteer coordination. *VOLUNTAS: International Journal of Voluntary and Nonprofit Organizations*, *24*(2), 403–440. https://doi.org/10.1007/s11266-012-9268-y

Taks, M., Chalip, L., & Green, B.C. (2015). Impacts and strategic outcomes from non-mega sport events for local communities. *European Sport Management Quarterly*, *15*(1), 1–6. https://doi.org/10.1080/16184742.2014.995116

Tschirhart, M. (2005). Employee volunteer programs. In J.L. Brudney (Ed.) *Emerging areas of volunteering*. Association for Research on Nonprofit Organizations and Voluntary Action.

Tschirhart, M. (2006). Nonprofit membership associations. In W.W. Powell & R.S. Steinberg (Eds.) *The nonprofit sector: A research handbook* (2nd ed., pp. 523–541). Yale University Press.

Vetitnev, A., Bobina, N., & Terwiel, F.A. (2018). The influence of host volunteer motivation on satisfaction and attitudes toward Sochi 2014 Olympic Games. *Event Management*, *22*(3), 333–352. https://doi.org/10.3727/152599518X15239930463145

Wood, L., Snelgrove, R., & Danylchuk, K. (2010). Segmenting volunteer fundraisers at a charity sport event. *Journal of Nonprofit Public Sector Marketing*, *22*, 38–54. https://doi.org/10.1080/10495140903190408

21

VOLUNTEER MOTIVATION

Katja Petrovic and Arthur A. Stukas

Introduction

Why do volunteers undertake the important work that they do? Motivational inquiry aims to understand the reasons why individuals initiate, commit to, or leave, voluntary organisations. By understanding and appealing to the motivations of their volunteers, volunteer managers and organisations can apply strategies that attract more volunteers for recruitment, and boost retention of existing volunteers. In this chapter, we present two central theoretical approaches which consider the motivations that drive individuals to volunteer: the functional approach and self-determination theory. We discuss how an understanding of volunteers' motivations can inform and enhance the decision-making processes of volunteer organisations.

The functional approach: identifying and matching motives

Functionalist theorising began with the consideration that the same attitude may serve different needs for different people (Katz, 1960; Smith et al., 1956). Applied to the field of volunteerism, this approach proposes that people volunteer to satisfy goals and needs which are important to them (Clary & Snyder, 1991). Once we understand which psychological functions are served by volunteer behaviour, a number of questions emerge: should volunteer managers consider individuals' motivations for volunteering when recruiting, and what sort of motivations should they be looking for? Which motivations are likely to lead to the most sustained volunteering behaviour? And how can these considerations be applied to the events, sport, and tourism fields?

The Volunteer Functions Inventory (VFI)

Guided by the functional approach, Clary, Snyder, Ridge et al. (1998) identified six major motivations for volunteering, as measured by their 30-item Volunteer Functions Inventory (VFI). These are: to meet social expectations (Social), to advance career-related goals (Career), to gain knowledge about oneself and others (Understanding), to boost positive affect or self-esteem (Enhancement), to reduce negative affect such as guilt (Protective), and to express altruistic

DOI: 10.4324/9780367815875-25

or humanitarian values (Values). The six-factor structure of this measure has been validated (Clary, Snyder, Ridge, et al., 1998; Okun et al., 1998) and the scale has demonstrated excellent internal consistency (Clary, Snyder, Ridge, et al., 1998; Stukas et al., 2016).

A basic principle of the functional approach is that volunteers may come to the same activities with different (and multiple) motivations but also that different types of activities may appeal to (and fulfil) only certain motivations (e.g., Clary, Snyder & Stukas, 1996; Stukas et al., 2016). In general volunteer samples, the Values motive is typically rated as most important (Clary et al., 1996; Stukas et al., 2016). Similarly, values-based reasons are often the most highly rated by volunteers in events, sport, and tourism contexts (Bang et al., 2008; Busser & Carruthers, 2010; Filo et al., 2014; Hyde et al., 2016; Kim et al., 2010). However, in a sample of nearly 4,000 Australian volunteers, Stukas et al. (2016) reported that sports volunteers had higher Social and Enhancement motivation but lower Values, Protective, and Career motivation relative to volunteers in other activities (e.g. health, education, social services). Moreover, Güntert et al. (2015) uncovered two additional motivations specific to volunteers at the 2008 European football championship: Excitement (having an exciting experience) and Citizenship (representing one's country/city well). These two motivations were rated more highly by participants than any of the original VFI motives, including the Values motive. In contrast, Johnson et al.'s (2017) study of volunteers in a sport management program found that another new motive (Love of Sport) and the Career VFI function were the most highly rated motivations.

The six VFI motives have also been shown to predict a range of volunteering outcomes. In the broader volunteering literature, studies find that the Values motive is often the best predictor of satisfaction (Dwyer et al., 2013; Finkelstein, 2011; Güntert et al., 2016; Stukas et al., 2016). However, specific contexts may reveal that different important motives predict outcomes. For example, in a study of volunteer tourists in China, Wu et al. (2018) found that the Enhancement and Social motives were better predictors of satisfaction than the Values motive and a newly added motivation, Desire to Travel, was the best predictor of satisfaction and, subsequently, intentions to volunteer again in the future. For Johnson et al.'s (2017) sport management volunteers, the Career function predicted both satisfaction and intention to remain in the program, whereas the Values function was a non-significant predictor of either outcome. Sometimes, too, a variety of different motivations may all lead to success. Bang et al. (2013) found that the Values, Understanding, Social, and Enhancement motives (the Career and Protective motives were not examined) each predicted organisational commitment and job satisfaction in a sample of volunteers working for non-profit sports organisations.

Taken together, these results suggest that measures developed with general volunteer samples may not always capture the key drivers of volunteering in the events, sport, and tourism contexts. Fortunately, there is now a burgeoning set of studies examining motivation specific to these contexts.

Motives specific to events, sport, and tourism volunteering

A literature search was undertaken to identify research investigating the motivations of events, sport, and tourism volunteers. A search of Google Scholar in January of 2020 (with no specified time frame) used combinations of the keywords 'volunteer', 'motives', 'motivation', 'event', 'episodic', 'sport', and 'tourism'. Studies mentioning event, episodic, sport, and/or tourism volunteer motivations in the title were then further scrutinised; qualitative research and research that did not mention factor analysis were excluded. Validations of

Table 21.1 Motivations to volunteer identified in the events, sport, and tourism fields

Source/s	Name of scale (if applicable)	Motive 1	Motive 2	Motive 3	Motive 4	Motive 5	Motive 6	Motive 7
Large sporting events								
Bang and Chelladurai (2009) / Bang and Ross (2009)	Volunteer Motivations Scale for International Sporting Events (VMS–ISE)	Expression of Values*	Interpersonal Contacts	Career Orientation	Extrinsic Rewards	Patriotism / Community Involvement	Personal Growth	Love of Sport
Strigas and Jackson (2003)		Purposive	Leisure	Material	Egoistic*	External Influences		
Giannoulakis et al. (2007)	Olympic Volunteer Motivation Scale (OVMS)	Olympic-related*	Egoistic	Purposive				
Downward and Ralston (2005)		Community	Personal Development	Business Opportunities	Volunteer Traditions	Esteem	Egoistic	
Non-specific events								
Farrell, Johnston, and Twynam (1998)	Special Event Volunteer Motivation Scale (SEVMS)	Purposive*	Solidarity	External Traditions	Commitments			
Monga (2006)		Affiliatory*	Fulfilling Experience	Solidarity	Career Development	Personal Rewards		
Hyde et al. (2016)		Socialising / Enjoyment	Celebrating / Remembering / Fighting Back*	Wanting to Support the Organisation	Benefits	Financial Support		
Sporting programs								
Filo et al. (2014)		Learning	Helping*	Obligation	Activity	Philanthropy	Esteem	
Tourism								
Weaver (2015)		Altruism	Personal Well-Being	Personal Status				

Note ★ = Most highly rated motivation (where this information was provided).

existing measures were also excluded, so that only studies containing original categorisations were included – although where a study combined items from multiple scales to derive categories, these were included. The remaining studies are summarised in Table 21.1.

A number of interesting points emerge from a review of the events, sport, and tourism literature. The motivations of episodic sports volunteers may differ from those who volunteer regularly for local sporting events (e.g. coaching and ongoing exercise programs), and even from non-sporting event volunteers. In particular, it has been suggested that, due to the often fun and celebratory nature of episodic events, volunteers are more likely to be motivated by self-serving than other-serving motives (Handy et al., 2000; Monga, 2006). For instance, volunteers for a mega international sporting event may be particularly driven by a desire to associate themselves with a prestigious and well-known event and/or by national pride or patriotism (although this may only be relevant for natives or long-time residents of hosting countries; Bang & Chelladurai, 2009). Moreover, compared to continuous volunteers and episodic non-sports volunteers, episodic sports volunteers may be less likely to be motivated by making a contribution to society and the organisation (Warner et al., 2011). Episodic volunteers may also find experiential aspects (variety, excitement, challenge) more attractive than continuous volunteers (Warner et al., 2011).

For regular or continuous sporting events, especially those in which the volunteer is a participant in the activity (i.e., athlete), motivations related to the benefits gained from physical activity (e.g., fitness, stress relief) may be more applicable. Warner et al. (2011) also found that sport volunteers considered tangible rewards (material goods such as merchandise or free food) more appealing than non-sport volunteers. Hallmann and Harms (2012), after surveying volunteers at handball and equestrian events, suggested that motive profiles may even differ depending on the sport. In support of this, Kim et al. (2010) found that volunteers working at international and special-needs sporting events reported higher motivations across all six VFI domains than volunteers working for national and local sports organisations.

In sum, we note that the literature currently presents a patchwork of results revealing the motivations of specific volunteers in specific contexts and it may be hard to generalise from these particular studies. We encourage organisations to survey their own current and potential volunteers, using the VFI or purpose-built measures, to uncover what drives them to serve.

Motive fulfilment and matching

The functional approach to volunteerism bears a family resemblance to 'person environment fit' models (Judge & Cable, 1997), commonly used in organisational psychology, in its focus on what makes for a successful and committed volunteer. This approach states that there is likely no one 'right' type of volunteer across all organisations and roles. Rather, emphasis should be placed on the extent to which there is a good fit between a volunteer's motives and the volunteer role, activity, or environment. As such, knowing the motivations of volunteers is only the first step in applying the functional approach to improve an organisation's outcomes and an equivalent amount of attention needs to be placed on the environment, which may involve placing volunteers into particular activities or tailoring tasks to suit particular volunteers. This framework has many implications for both recruitment and retention.

Recruitment

The functional approach provides a framework for creating persuasive communications to convince individuals to take up volunteering. It stands to reason that people will be more likely to volunteer if they believe that the activity will satisfy their motivations – this has been called the 'matching hypothesis' (Snyder et al., 2000). Therefore, recruitment messages which appeal to an individual's primary motivations for volunteering should be more effective and persuasive than those appealing to unimportant motives. Research to date has provided support for this hypothesis. Studies using the VFI have demonstrated that participants who view a volunteer recruitment advertisement that appeals to their primary motive (as opposed to a mismatched motive) rate the advertisement as more persuasive (Clary, Snyder, Ridge, et al., 1998; Ridge, 2000), report greater positive emotion regarding the volunteer opportunity (Clary et al., 1994), and have greater anticipated satisfaction and intention to volunteer in future (Clary et al., 1994). Following from this matching principle, websites of volunteer involving organisations often appeal to the motivations and expected benefits of volunteers on their recruitment pages; for example, the Multiple Sclerosis (MS) Society of Australia indicates that working with them allows volunteers to gain new skills (Understanding, Career), make new friends (Enhancement, Social), have fun, enjoy a sense of reward (Enhancement), and change the lives of people living with MS (Values, Protective) (see https://www.ms.org.au/get-involved/volunteer/about-volunteering-for-ms.aspx).

Retention

The functional approach also allows us to measure the extent to which a volunteer's motives are fulfilled by the opportunities—or 'affordances'—of the volunteer role, with the expectation that a volunteer will be more satisfied and committed if placed in a role that fulfils their primary motivation(s) for volunteering. Indeed, volunteers who indicate that their motivations are being fulfilled by their current volunteer activities report greater satisfaction (Caldarella et al., 2010; Davis et al., 2003; Finkelstein, 2008) and future intentions to continue (Stukas et al., 2005). Furthermore, Clary, Snyder, Ridge et al. (1998) found that both elderly and student volunteers who subsequently received benefits relevant to their primary motivations reported greater satisfaction than those receiving mismatched benefits. Student volunteers receiving functionally matched benefits also had greater short and long-term intentions to continue in the volunteer role.

Kim et al. (2019) applied the matching hypothesis to the sporting event volunteer context in their survey of volunteers at the 2018 PyeongChang Winter Olympics. They assessed volunteers' scores on the Values and Enhancement VFI functions. They did not explicitly assess affordances, but instead determined that this event would largely fulfil Enhancement rather than Values motives, thereby providing a better match with the Enhancement motive. In support of their predictions, they found that the Values motive was negatively related to the degree of volunteer involvement at the event, whereas the Enhancement motive was positively related to involvement.

Although the aforementioned studies focus on whether a volunteer's primary motive was satisfied, volunteers may have multiple strongly held motivations. In consideration of this, Stukas et al. (2009) devised a way to calculate overall fulfilment across the set of six VFI motives (the Total Match Index) by multiplying each motive's importance with the degree to which that motive was fulfilled. Using this match index, they demonstrated that the degree of motive fulfilment predicts greater volunteer satisfaction and intention to continue in the volunteer role, as well as more positive emotion and less negative emotion in relation to the volunteering activity. Applying this approach to a sample of event volunteers at the UEFA 2008 European Football Championship, Güntert et al. (2015) found that the Total Match Index predicted satisfaction and future intentions to volunteer, above and beyond the variance explained by other variables such as motives and affordances alone.

Practical implications

Relatively common volunteer motives identified by the events, sport, and tourism literature include caring about the cause, meeting people and belonging to a community, growing personal skills and knowledge, and furthering one's career. Therefore, organisations may wish to ask volunteers to re-affirm why they support this particular cause, provide ample opportunity for socialising, encourage personal development (such as by having volunteers reflect on what they would like to learn), and emphasise career-related benefits.

The matching hypothesis suggests that recruitment efforts can be improved by tailoring messages to target the motivations of the audience. Although the motivations of individuals may not be known, existing research affords educated guesses. For example, organisations working with event or tourism volunteers may offer fun and excitement and a boost in social status or recognition; tangible rewards may also appeal. At international events or competitions, it may be effective to appeal to national pride – appealing to state or regional pride may work for smaller-scale events (Bang & Chelladurai, 2009).

Motivations may also be inferred based on the demographics of the target group (see Clary et al., 1996, or Stukas et al., 2016 for tables). For instance, young people tend to be motivated by career-related goals more so than older individuals (Clary, Snyder, Ridge, et al., 1998), whereas older people may be appealed to more effectively by highlighting boosts to positive affect or a sense of belonging (Okun & Schultz, 2003). Research suggests that young sport leaders may be highly motivated by learning new skills and gaining new perspectives, as well as career considerations (Eley & Kirk, 2002), and younger event volunteers may be more likely to volunteer to have an exciting experience (Güntert et al., 2015). Among sporting event volunteers, women have expressed greater desire for personal growth and development (Bang et al., 2008; Downward et al., 2005) and community involvement (VanSickle et al., 2015) than men, who may be more motivated by extrinsic rewards and a love for the sport (Bang et al., 2008; Coyne & Coyne, 2001; VanSickle et al., 2015). Women volunteering in sports organisations also score higher on the Values and Understanding VFI motives than men (M. Kim et al., 2010). A study of potential volunteer tourists suggests that women may be more motivated to volunteer by altruistic and well-being concerns, whereas men may be more motivated by social status (Weaver, 2015).

Motives may also change in importance over time, and it may be pertinent to appeal to different motives depending on whether the goal is recruitment or retention (Tschirhart et al., 2001). For example, a volunteer who has been engaged in an activity for a prolonged period may reach a point at which they are no longer fulfilling the goal of gaining new knowledge, or growing career-relevant skills. This may necessitate a switch to a different activity for the volunteer to maintain a sense of fulfilment. In their study of youth sports coaches, Busser and Carruthers (2010) showed that personal growth (learning and developing skills) motivation was stronger in new volunteer coaches than returning coaches. Hyde et al.'s (2016) study of participants in cancer charity sporting events further revealed that novices (first timers) who were motivated by the self-oriented motive of 'socialising/enjoyment' were better retained whereas for volunteers with two or more years of experience, the other-oriented motive of 'financial support' (seeking to raise funds for the charity) positively predicted retention. Eley and Kirk (2002) similarly found changes in motivation across a nine-month sports volunteer program with Values, Social, and Enhancement motives all increasing after the program, while the Protective motive decreased. As such, opportunities for personal development, acting on one's values, making and strengthening friendships, and feeling good about oneself may continue to be attractive incentives for volunteers in the sporting domains after the initial recruitment period has passed.

Other motivations are likely to be relatively short-lived. Offering extrinsic rewards (such as free goods or experiences) or appealing to egoistic motives (such as the opportunity to alleviate negative feelings or gain social status) may only be effective in the early stages of recruitment. Although volunteers at large or famous events may initially be drawn in by the 'prestige' factor (Bang et al., 2013) or the excitement of experiencing a once-in-a-lifetime event (Dickson et al., 2014; Downward & Ralston, 2005), this initial excitement is likely to wane – although it may be sustained by travelling from event to event, which a substantial number of mega event volunteers do (Fairley, Kellett & Green, 2007). Appealing to these extrinsic motivations may nonetheless be a more effective way to attract new volunteers (perhaps before a sense of organisational commitment has been able to be established) than to retain existing ones. This is similar to the action–reflection model applied in service-learning programs (see Clary, Snyder & Stukas, 1998) that suggests that self-oriented rewards and motivations may spur volunteers to action but reflecting on how such actions link to important values (i.e., internalising other-oriented motivations) will lead volunteers to continue beyond the availability of initial rewards. Considering that motivations for volunteering are fluid, an ongoing assessment of volunteers' needs and goals, and the extent to which their current role is fulfilling those needs, is warranted.

Self-determination theory: autonomy, incentives, and requirements

Self-determination theory states that individuals will be more satisfied when they engage in behaviour that fulfils fundamental desires to feel autonomous, competent, and related to others (Deci & Ryan, 1987). Thus, volunteer work that offers affordances to meet these three needs should result in volunteers that are more satisfied and successful. Although volunteer organisations commonly aim to support volunteers' competence and relatedness and doing so should increase volunteers' satisfaction and intentions to remain, research on autonomy has been more clearly linked to motivation. Research in sports volunteering, for example, identifies the need to express one's agency and be free from external control as a paramount concern to many volunteers in sporting clubs (Adams & Deane, 2009).

Needs for autonomy are particularly important when considering the growth in programs that involve requirements or incentives to engage in community service activities that are also performed by 'true' volunteers, as these external factors may interfere with need fulfilment. Many school, government, and employment programs offer incentives (such as course credit or monetary payments), and some mandate community service (e.g. school requirements, Stukas et al., 2015; Stukas, Snyder & Clary, 1999). Although volunteerism is, by definition, actions that are freely chosen, rewards and requirements can remove some or all of this freedom. In the literature, autonomous motivation has often been seen as equivalent to intrinsic motivation, choosing activities because of their own merits rather than as a means to some other end (e.g., Deci & Ryan, 1987). Research has consistently found that prosocial activities which are motivated by intrinsic, as opposed to extrinsic (external rewards or gains) reasons, result in greater life satisfaction, positive affect, self-esteem, and self-actualisation (Gebauer et al., 2008). When individuals decide to help another person freely and autonomously, the result is increased positive affect and self-esteem for both the helper and the recipient of help (Weinstein & Ryan, 2010). Autonomous motivation positively predicts satisfaction (Güntert et al., 2016), work engagement (Van Schie et al., 2015), and effort in the volunteer role (Bidee et al., 2013). Among event volunteers, perceived autonomy is positively correlated with satisfaction and intention to volunteer again (Güntert et al., 2015). Conversely, external rewards or coercion undermine the critically important sense of autonomy and reduce intrinsic interest in that activity, turning 'pleasure' into 'pressure' (Deci et al., 1999; Gebauer et al., 2008).

Insofar as requirements undermine intrinsic motivation and interest, future intentions to volunteer may be reduced. Indeed, students in one mandatory university program who felt particularly controlled by the community service requirement had lower intentions to volunteer subsequently, compared with those who retained a feeling of autonomy despite the requirement (Stukas, Snyder & Clary, 1999). Similarly, high schoolers who said they would have volunteered even without the requirement had greater volunteering rates eight years later compared to those who volunteered only because of the requirement (Planty et al., 2006). Moreover, experimental manipulations which reduce volunteers' autonomy by telling them they have no choice about which activity to participate in also reduce future intentions to volunteer freely, but again only in those who were not originally inclined to volunteer (Stukas, Snyder & Clary, 1999).

Requirements may be the most obvious representation of external control, however certain motivations identified by the functional approach also invoke more extrinsic or instrumental benefits (e.g. social status, free goods) whereas others imply an intrinsic enjoyment and valuing of the activity (e.g. desire to learn, a sense of fun and challenge, caring about the cause). Whereas self-determination theory suggests that extrinsic rewards are to be avoided to maintain intrinsic motivation, the functional matching hypothesis proposes that those primarily motivated by instrumental goals should have those motivations appealed to and matched in activities – at least, in the initial recruitment stage – in order to increase their satisfaction.

Research is consistent, however, that intrinsic motivations are most likely to lead to increased volunteer commitment and retention (Güntert et al., 2016). Moreover, research using the VFI has also revealed that motivations highlighting self-benefits (Enhancement, Protective, Career) are associated with lower levels of satisfaction, intentions, and even well-being than so-called other-oriented motivations (Values, Social, Understanding; Stukas et al., 2016). Indeed, new evidence suggests that encouraging volunteers to see tasks as reflecting other-oriented rather than self-oriented motivations may even overcome the negative effects of requirements on future intentions to volunteer (Stukas, Astbury & Petrovic, 2019). Such results align with self-determination theory's instruction that, for volunteer activities to be most satisfying and to boost well-being, they need to ensure volunteers' feelings of competence, relatedness to others, and (to ensure sustained behaviour) autonomy.

Practical implications

To mitigate any negative effects on future intentions, volunteer organisations must be careful that the provision of incentives does not undermine volunteers' sense of having chosen to participate freely. If volunteer organisations find themselves with volunteers who have been coerced or mandated to participate, they should take steps to mitigate the unfortunate consequences of feeling like one's autonomy has been compromised by fulfilling volunteers' needs for autonomy, competence, and relatedness in other ways.

Researchers have suggested that providing autonomy support within a volunteer role can increase volunteers' sense of need fulfilment. This involves acknowledging the volunteers' perspectives and feelings about the role, providing opportunities for choice, supporting their competencies, and encouraging personal initiative (Deci et al., 2001). For instance, volunteers can be provided with autonomy to choose the details of their service activities (Stukas, Clary & Snyder, 1999). Gagné (2003) showed that the degree of perceived autonomy support in a volunteer organisation was related positively to need satisfaction, which was in turn positively related to greater involvement in the organisation and lower likelihood of attrition. Furthermore, autonomy supportive leadership has been found to positively predict greater autonomous motivation in volunteers, in turn predicting greater work engagement (Van Schie et al., 2015). Research has also concluded that providing autonomy support to volunteers has a flow-on effect in fulfilling competence and relatedness needs (Coatsworth & Conroy, 2009; Haivas et al., 2012).

A number of other strategies can be used to increase volunteers' autonomy fulfilment. Their work can be explicitly linked to their own values to strengthen the sense of value congruence, or 'match', between volunteers' and organisational goals (Dwyer et al., 2013; Kim et al., 2019). Value congruence has been shown to be positively related to work engagement in volunteers (Van Schie et al., 2015). Whenever possible, volunteer training should be delivered in a way that meets the expressed needs of volunteers, avoiding the sense that the bureaucracy is imposing unnecessary 'rules and regulations' that reduce perceptions of autonomy (Adams & Deane, 2009). Directly increasing volunteers' sense of relatedness and competence could also potentially mitigate the effects of lost autonomy. For instance, volunteers report being more satisfied when they have relationships that they value with other members of the volunteer team (Dwyer et al., 2013). Competence can be strengthened by providing activities which are optimally challenging, and providing feedback about achievements (Gagné & Deci, 2005). As such, paying attention to how the volunteer environment (roles and tasks) can be adjusted by organisations to better offer affordances for important needs and goals is a key lesson of both self-determination theory and the functional approach to volunteerism.

Conclusions and future directions

Events, sport, and tourism volunteering organisations can benefit in many ways from considering the motivations of their volunteers. The functional approach provides a way for organisations to match volunteers' motivations with the affordances of the volunteer role. Motivations such as love of sport, fun or excitement, patriotism, and a desire for travel – not commonly observed in other volunteer samples – may be key drivers of event-based, sports, and/or tourism volunteering. Future research may identify additional motivations which are important to appeal to in recruitment messaging and to fulfil within a volunteer role, particularly in the under-researched fields of continuous sport volunteering and volunteer tourism. Although self-determination theory presents important considerations for volunteer engagement and retention, it has not generally been applied to the events, sport, and tourism contexts. However, considering that, self-expression has been observed as one potential motivation among these volunteers, it is apparent how this could be undermined by any removal of choice and freedom.

In this chapter, we have chosen to focus on two central approaches to volunteer motivation; however, there are myriad ways to approach this construct. Theories that have not been considered here include expectancy-value theory (Wigfield & Eccles, 1992), the theory of planned behaviour (Ajzen, 2005), self-efficacy theory (Bandura, 1986), goal setting theory (Locke & Latham, 1990), task-specific motivation theory (Kanfer, 1987), and job characteristics theory (Hackman & Oldham, 1980). These all have points of convergence with the approaches discussed here, but a discussion of their unique merits is beyond the scope of this chapter. Nonetheless, the functional approach and self-determination theory offer useful and well-established frameworks for events, sport, and tourism volunteer organisations to draw upon in their recruitment and retention strategies. We are confident that volunteer managers will find value in considering the motivations of their volunteers, with the aim of maximising congruence between motivation and volunteer role, and fulfilling the basic needs of autonomy, relatedness, and competence.

References

Adams, A. & Deane, J. (2009). Exploring formal and informal dimensions of sports volunteering in England. *European Sport Management Quarterly*, *9*(2), 119–140. https://doi.org/10.1080/16184740802571401

Ajzen, I. (2005). *Attitudes, personality, and behavior*. Dorsey.

Bandura, A. (1986). The explanatory and predictive scope of self-efficacy theory. *Journal of Social and Clinical Psychology*, *4*(3), 359–373. https://doi.org/10.1521/jscp.1986.4.3.359

Bang, H., Alexandris, K. & Ross, S. D. (2008). Validation of the revised volunteer motivations scale for international sporting events (VMS-ISE) at the Athens 2004 Olympic Games. *Event Management*, *12*(3–4), 119–131. https://doi.org/10.3727/152599509789659759

Bang, H. & Chelladurai, P. (2009). Development and validation of the volunteer motivations scale for international sporting events (VMS-ISE). *International Journal of Sport Management and Marketing*, *6*(4), 332–350. https://doi.org/10.1504/IJSMM.2009.030064

Bang, H. & Ross, S. D. (2009). Volunteer motivation and satisfaction. *Journal of Venue and Event Management*, *1*(1), 61–77.

Bang, H., Ross, S. & Reio, T. G. (2013). From motivation to organizational commitment of volunteers in non-profit sport organizations. *Journal of Management Development*, *32*(1), 96–112. https://doi.org/10.1108/02621711311287044

Bidee, J., Vantilborgh, T., Pepermans, R., Huybrechts, G., Willems, J., Jegers, M. & Hofmans, J. (2013). Autonomous motivation stimulates volunteers' work effort: A self-determination theory approach to volunteerism. *Voluntas: International Journal of Voluntary and Nonprofit Organizations*, *24*(1), 32–47. https://doi.org/10.1007/s11266-012-9269-x

Busser, J. A. & Carruthers, C. P. (2010). Youth sport volunteer coach motivation. *Managing Leisure*, *15*(1–2), 128–139. https://doi.org/10.1080/13606710903448210

Caldarella, P., Gomm, R. J., Shatzer, R. H. & Wall, D. G. (2010). School-based mentoring: A study of volunteer motivations and benefits. *International Electronic Journal of Elementary Education*, *2*(2), 199–216.

Clary, E. G. & Snyder, M. (1991). A functional analysis of altruism and prosocial behavior: The case of volunteerism. In M. Clark (Ed.), *Review of personality and social psychology* (Vol. 12, pp. 119–148). Sage.

Clary, E. G., Snyder, M., Ridge, R. D., Copeland, J., Stukas, A. A., Haugen, J. & Miene, P. (1998). Understanding and assessing the motivations of volunteers: A functional approach. *Journal of Personality and Social Psychology*, *74*, 1516–1530. https://doi.org/10.1037/0022-3514.74.6.1516

Clary, E. G., Snyder, M., Ridge, R. D., Miene, P. & Haugen, J. (1994). Matching messages to motives in persuasion: A functional approach to promoting volunteerism. *Journal of Applied Social Psychology*, *24*(13), 1129–1146. https://doi.org/10.1111/j.1559-1816.1994.tb01548.x

Clary, E. G., Snyder, M. & Stukas, A. A. (1996). Volunteers' motivations: Findings from a national survey. *Nonprofit and Voluntary Sector Quarterly*, *25*(4), 485–505. https://doi.org/10.1177/0899764096254006

Clary, E. G., Snyder, M. & Stukas, A. A. (1998). Service-learning and psychology: Lessons from the psychology of volunteers' motivations. In R. G. Bringle & D. K. Duffy (Eds.), *With service in mind: Concepts and models for service-learning in psychology* (pp. 35–50). American Association of Higher Education.

Coatsworth, J. D. & Conroy, D. E. (2009). The effects of autonomy-supportive coaching, need satisfaction, and self-perceptions on initiative and identity in youth swimmers. *Developmental Psychology, 45*(2), 320. https://doi.org/10.1037/a0014027

Coyne, B. S. & Coyne, E. J. (2001). Getting, keeping and caring for unpaid volunteers for professional golf tournament events. *Human Resource Development International, 4*(2), 199–216. https://doi.org/10.1080/13678860121999

Davis, M. H., Hall, J. A. & Meyer, M. (2003). The first year: Influences on the satisfaction, involvement, and persistence of new community volunteers. *Personality and Social Psychology Bulletin, 29*(2), 248–260. https://doi.org/10.1177/0146167202239050

Deci, E. L., Koestner, R. & Ryan, R. M. (1999). A meta-analytic review of experiments examining the effects of extrinsic rewards on intrinsic motivation. *Psychological Bulletin, 125*(6), 627. DOI: 10.1037/0033-2909.125.6.62

Deci, E. L. & Ryan, R. M. (1987). The support of autonomy and the control of behavior. *Journal of Personality and Social Psychology, 53*(6), 1024. https://doi.org/10.1037/0022-3514.53.6.1024

Deci, E. L., Ryan, R. M., Gagné, M., Leone, D. R., Usunov, J. & Kornazheva, B. P. (2001). Need satisfaction, motivation, and well-being in the work organizations of a former eastern bloc country: A cross-cultural study of self-determination. *Personality and Social Psychology Bulletin, 27*(8), 930–942. https://doi.org/10.1177/0146167201278002

Dickson, T. J., Benson, A. M. & Terwiel, F. A. (2014). Mega-event volunteers, similar or different? Vancouver 2010 vs London 2012. *International Journal of Event and Festival Management, 5*(2), 164–179. https://doi.org/10.1108/IJEFM-07-2013-0019

Downward, P., Lumsdon, L. & Ralston, R. (2005). Gender differences in sports event volunteering: Insights from Crew 2002 at the XVII Commonwealth Games. *Managing Leisure, 10*(4), 219–236. https://doi.org/10.1080/13606710500348086

Downward, P. & Ralston, R. (2005). Volunteer motivation and expectations prior to the XV Commonwealth Games in Manchester, UK. *Tourism and Hospitality Planning & Development, 2*(1), 17–26. https://doi.org/10.1080/14790530500072310

Dwyer, P. C., Bono, J. E., Snyder, M., Nov, O. & Berson, Y. (2013). Sources of volunteer motivation: Transformational leadership and personal motives influence volunteer outcomes. *Nonprofit Management and Leadership, 24*(2), 181–205. https://doi.org/10.1002/nml.21084

Eley, D. & Kirk, D. (2002). Developing citizenship through sport: The impact of a sport-based volunteer programme on young sport leaders. *Sport, Education and Society, 7*(2), 151–166. https://doi.org/10.1080/1357332022000018841

Fairley, S., Kellett, P. & Green, B. C. (2007). Volunteering abroad: Motives for travel to volunteer at the Athens Olympic Games. *Journal of Sport Management, 21*(1), 41–57. https://doi.org/10.1123/jsm.21.1.41

Farrell, J. M., Johnston, M. E. & Twynam, G. D. (1998). Volunteer motivation, satisfaction, and management at an elite sporting competition. *Journal of Sport Management, 12*(4), 288–300. https://doi.org/10.1123/jsm.12.4.288

Filo, K., Funk, D. & Jordan, J. (2014). Exploring activity-contingent volunteerism: A preliminary investigation of Back on My Feet volunteers. *European Sport Management Quarterly, 14*(4), 397–421. https://doi.org/10.1080/16184742.2014.929158

Finkelstein, M. A. (2008). Volunteer satisfaction and volunteer action: A functional approach. *Social Behavior and Personality: An International Journal, 36*(1), 9–18. https://doi.org/10.2224/sbp.2008.36.10.1353

Finkelstein, M. A. (2011). Intrinsic and extrinsic motivation and organizational citizenship behavior: A functional approach to organizational citizenship behavior. *Journal of Psychological Issues in Organizational Culture, 2*(1), 19–34. https://doi.org/10.1002/jpoc.20054

Gagné, M. (2003). The role of autonomy support and autonomy orientation in prosocial behavior engagement. *Motivation and Emotion, 27*(3), 199–223. https://doi.org/10.1023/A:1025007614869

Gagné, M. & Deci, E. L. (2005). Self-determination theory and work motivation. *Journal of Organizational Behavior, 26*(4), 331–362. https://doi.org/10.1002/job.322

Gebauer, J. E., Riketta, M., Broemer, P. & Maio, G. R. (2008). Pleasure and pressure based prosocial motivation: Divergent relations to subjective well-being. *Journal of Research in Personality, 42*(2), 399–420. https://doi.org/10.1016/j.jrp.2007.07.002

Giannoulakis, C., Wang, C.-H. & Gray, D. (2007). Measuring volunteer motivation in mega-sporting events. *Event Management, 11*(4), 191–200. https://doi.org/10.3727/152599508785899884

Güntert, S. T., Neufeind, M. & Wehner, T. (2015). Motives for event volunteering: Extending the functional approach. *Nonprofit and Voluntary Sector Quarterly*, *44*(4), 686–707. https://doi.org/10.1177/0899764014527797

Güntert, S. T., Strubel, I. T., Kals, E. & Wehner, T. (2016). The quality of volunteers' motives: Integrating the functional approach and self-determination theory. *Journal of Social Psychology*, *156*(3), 310–327. https://doi.org/10.1080/00224545.2015.1135864

Hackman, J. R. & Oldham, G. R. (1980). *Work redesign*. Addison-Wesley.

Haivas, S., Hofmans, J. & Pepermans, R. (2012). Self-determination theory as a framework for exploring the impact of the organizational context on volunteer motivation: A study of Romanian volunteers. *Nonprofit and Voluntary Sector Quarterly*, *41*(6), 1195–1214. https://doi.org/10.1177/0899764011433041

Hallmann, K. & Harms, G. (2012). Determinants of volunteer motivation and their impact on future voluntary engagement: A comparison of volunteer's motivation at sport events in equestrian and handball. *International Journal of Event and Festival Management*, *3*(3), 272–291. https://doi.org/10.1108/17582951211262701

Handy, F., Cnaan, R. A., Brudney, J. L., Ascoli, U., Meijs, L. C. & Ranade, S. (2000). Public perception of "who is a volunteer": An examination of the net-cost approach from a cross-cultural perspective. *Voluntas: International Journal of Voluntary and Nonprofit Organizations*, *11*(1), 45–65. https://doi.org/10.1023/A:1008903032393

Hyde, M. K., Dunn, J., Bax, C. & Chambers, S. K. (2016). Episodic volunteering and retention: An integrated theoretical approach. *Nonprofit and Voluntary Sector Quarterly*, *45*(1), 45–63. https://doi.org/10.1177/0899764014558934

Johnson, J. E., Giannoulakis, C., Felver, N., Judge, L. W., David, P. A. & Scott, B. F. (2017). Motivation, satisfaction, and retention of sport management student volunteers. *Journal of Applied Sport Management; Urbana*, *9*(1), 3–55.

Judge, T. A. & Cable, D. M. (1997). Applicant personality, organizational culture, and organization attraction. *Personnel Psychology*, *50*(2), 359–394. https://doi.org/10.1111/j.1744-6570.1997.tb00912.x

Kanfer, R. (1987). Task-specific motivation: An integrative approach to issues of measurement, mechanisms, processes, and determinants. *Journal of Social and Clinical Psychology*, *5*(2), 237–264. https://doi.org/10.1521/jscp.1987.5.2.237

Katz, D. (1960). The functional approach to the study of attitudes. *Public Opinion Quarterly*, *24*(2), 163–204. https://doi.org/10.1086/266945

Kim, B. J., Kim, M. H. & Lee, J. (2019). Congruence matters: Volunteer motivation, value internalization, and retention. *Journal of Organizational Psychology*, *19*(5). https://doi.org/10.33423/jop.v19i5.2510

Kim, M., Zhang, J. J. & Connaughton, D. P. (2010). Comparison of volunteer motivations in different youth sport organizations. *European Sport Management Quarterly*, *10*(3), 343–365. https://doi.org/10.1080/16184741003770198

Locke, E. A. & Latham, G. P. (1990). *A theory of goal setting and task performance*. Prentice-Hall.

Monga, M. (2006). Measuring motivation to volunteer for special events. *Event Management*, *10*(1), 47–61. https://doi.org/10.3727/152599506779364633

Okun, M. A., Barr, A. & Herzog, A. R. (1998). Motivation to volunteer by older adults: A test of competing measurement models. *Psychology and Aging*, *13*(4), 608. https://doi.org/10.1037/0882-7974.13.4.608

Okun, M. A. & Schultz, A. (2003). Age and motives for volunteering: Testing hypotheses derived from socioemotional selectivity theory. *Psychology and Aging*, *18*(2), 231. https://doi.org/10.1037/0882-7974.18.2.231

Planty, M., Bozick, R. & Regnier, M. (2006). Helping because you have to or helping because you want to? Sustaining participation in service work from adolescence through young adulthood. *Youth & Society*, *38*(2), 177–202. https://doi.org/10.1177/0044118X06287961

Ridge, R. D. (2000). Targeting egoistic motivations: A functional strategy for recruiting volunteers. *Contemporary Social Psychology*, *19*, 12–23.

Smith, M. B., Bruner, J. S. & White, R. W. (1956). *Opinions and personality*. Wiley.

Snyder, M., Clary, E. G. & Stukas, A. A. (2000). The functional approach to volunteerism. In G. R. Maio & J. M. Olson (Eds.), *Why we evaluate: Functions of attitudes* (pp. 365–393). Erlbaum.

Strigas, A. D. & Jackson, E. N. (2003). Motivating volunteers to serve and succeed: Design and results of a pilot study that explores demographics and motivational factors in sport volunteerism. *International Sports Journal*, *7*(1), 111–123.

Stukas, A. A., Astbury, M. & Petrovic, K. (June 2019). *Understanding and reducing the negative effects of "mandatory volunteerism".* Presented at the annual meeting of the Society for the Psychological Study of Social Issues, San Diego, CA, USA.

Stukas, A. A., Clary, E. G. & Snyder, M. (1999). Service learning: Who benefits and why? *Social Policy Report, 13*(4), 1–23.

Stukas, A. A., Daly, M. & Cowling, M. J. (2005). Volunteerism and social capital: A functional approach. *Australian Journal on Volunteering, 10*(2), 35–44.

Stukas, A. A., Hoye, R., Nicholson, M., Brown, K. M. & Aisbett, L. (2016). Motivations to volunteer and their associations with volunteers' well-being. *Nonprofit and Voluntary Sector Quarterly, 45*(1), 112–132. https://doi.org/10.1177/0899764014561122

Stukas, A. A., Snyder, M. & Clary, E. G. (1999). The effects of "mandatory volunteerism" on intentions to volunteer. *Psychological Science, 10*(1), 59–64. https://doi.org/10.1111/1467-9280.00107

Stukas, A. A., Snyder, M. & Clary, E. G. (2015). Volunteerism and community involvement: Antecedents, experiences, and consequences for the person and the situation. In D. A. Schroeder & W. Graziano (Eds.), *The Oxford handbook of prosocial behavior* (pp. 459–493). Oxford University Press. https://doi.org/10.1093/oxfordhb/9780195399813.013.012

Stukas, A. A., Worth, K. A., Clary, E. G. & Snyder, M. (2009). The matching of motivations to affordances in the volunteer environment. *Nonprofit and Voluntary Sector Quarterly, 38*, 5–28. https://doi.org/10.1177/0899764008314810

Tschirhart, M., Mesch, D. J., Perry, J. L., Miller, T. K. & Lee, G. (2001). Stipended volunteers: Their goals, experiences, satisfaction, and likelihood of future service. *Nonprofit and Voluntary Sector Quarterly, 30*(3), 422–443. https://doi.org/10.1177/0899764001303002

Van Schie, S., Güntert, S. T., Oostlander, J. & Wehner, T. (2015). How the organizational context impacts volunteers: A differentiated perspective on self-determined motivation. *VOLUNTAS: International Journal of Voluntary and Nonprofit Organizations, 26*(4), 1570–1590. https://doi.org/10.1007/s11266-014-9472-z

VanSickle, J. L., Pierce, D. A. & Diacin, M. (2015). Volunteer motivations at the 2012 Super Bowl. *International Journal of Event and Festival Management, 6*(3), 166–181. https://doi.org/10.1108/IJEFM-12-2014-0029

Warner, S., Newland, B. L. & Green, B. C. (2011). More than motivation: Reconsidering volunteer management tools. *Journal of Sport Management, 25*(5), 391–407. https://doi.org/10.1123/jsm.25.5.391

Weaver, D. (2015). Volunteer tourism and beyond: Motivations and barriers to participation in protected area enhancement. *Journal of Sustainable Tourism, 23*(5), 683–705. https://doi.org/10.1080/09669582.2014.992901

Weinstein, N. & Ryan, R. M. (2010). When helping helps: Autonomous motivation for prosocial behavior and its influence on well-being for the helper and recipient. *Journal of Personality and Social Psychology, 98*(2), 222. https://doi.org/10.1037/a0016984

Wigfield, A. & Eccles, J. S. (1992). The development of achievement task values: A theoretical analysis. *Developmental Review, 12*(3), 265–310. https://doi.org/10.1016/0273-2297(92)90011-P

Wu, D. C., Fu, H., & Kang, M. (2018). Why volunteer teaching tourism? Empirical evidence from China. *Asia Pacific Journal of Tourism Research, 23*(2), 109–120. https://doi.org/10.1080/10941665.2017.1410191

22

VOLUNTEER RECRUITMENT AND SELECTION

Evidence from the visitor attraction sector

Giancarlo Fedeli and Linda Cigurova

Introduction

It is widely accepted in both practice and academia that visitor attractions (VAs) carry out an important role in the management, development, and overall success of destinations (Weidenfeld & Leask, 2013). VAs constitute a highly varied sector as they may range from providing entertainment experiences to focusing on conservation. Leask (2010) suggested the following VA categories: visitor centres, heritage, religious sites, animal sites, theme parks, natural sites as well as museums and galleries. Hence, VAs can be extremely diverse in terms of purpose, facilities provision, as well as vision and mission statements. While VAs employ a core permanent staff, the sector is heavily dependent on temporary staff and volunteers (Leask et al., 2013). To some extent, this may be explained by the strong seasonality patterns some tourism destinations are characterised by as in the UK case of Scotland, where tourism demand can be highly seasonal (Connell et al., 2015). Data from a 2017 study suggested that unpaid volunteers constituted 51% of the total workforce of Scottish VAs, while over one-third of the paid workforce was employed on a seasonal basis (Moffat Centre, 2018). This evidence suggests volunteers may represent a significant resource for the VA sector.

Volunteers enable organisations to provide services that they could not otherwise deliver, by improving the organisation's capacity to engage with communities or even providing financial benefits to VAs such as reducing personnel expenses (Cordery et al., 2015). Conversely, the management of volunteers may require further resources or investment (e.g. training) as opposed to experienced paid staff. Overall, Connell et al. (2015) and Leask (2010) pointed out a degree of paucity in VA research. Although Leask (2016) recognised a significant increase in studies contributing to the understanding of VA management, a call for more empirical work as opposed to descriptive research and case studies has also been made to aid the triangulation of qualitative and quantitative methods. This observation is reinforced by the scant volume of enquiry specifically on VA volunteer management as highlighted in the course of conducting the current study. Furthermore, volunteer recruitment and selection is a research area constrained by an overarching focus on the volunteers' perspective (Johnson, 2012).

By undertaking a literature review on the researched subject and applying the specific context of the Scottish VA sector, this paper adopts an organisational perspective. It should

DOI: 10.4324/9780367815875-26

be noted that the authors expanded the review of the literature on volunteer recruitment and selection from VA-specific to a broader scope to include the wider organisational literature. This was due to the scarcity of research available on VA's volunteer practices. Furthermore, the majority of the studies from the nonprofit sector literature suggest the significance of volunteer and non-paid positions for the survival of the sector. This research finally aims to identify and critically examine the extent of engagement of VAs with volunteer management, specifically, recruitment and selection issues and practices.

Volunteer recruitment

Given the advantages associated with the participation of volunteers in the operations of VAs, as well as the anticipated large reliance of VAs on the volunteer workforce, effective volunteer recruitment strategies have been deemed as pivotal for the success of organisations (Karl et al., 2008). As such, recruiting volunteers should be one of the crucial tasks for organisations relying on a large number of volunteers. However, it was identified that factors such as lack of resources and time often limit the ability of nonprofit organisations to prioritise the recruitment process in a systematic way (Kappelides et al., 2019). Thus, recruitment is often an informal process performed on an as-needed basis, with word-of-mouth used as the most common recruitment method (Einolf, 2018). Examples of good practices of other recruitment methods include posters and leaflets, notice boards, speculative applications, recruitment via membership, advertisements, open days, as well as specialist external assistance (Lynch & Smith, 2009).

An increasing number of VA organisations are employing more digital technology in an attempt to enhance their services and operations (Fedeli, 2017a). In volunteer recruitment specifically, the Internet represents a valuable tool as it allows fast and effective communication at a minimal cost to the organisation (Dighe, 2012). However, Piatak et al. (2019) argue that while the Internet may appear an appealing volunteer recruitment tool for reaching an extensive number of people, it may also fail to include other segments of the population that could potentially include some of the more committed volunteers. For example, it is estimated that while UK digital recruitment strategies exclude only 10% of the country's population, in the USA this number amounts to a quarter of the whole population (Piatak et al., 2019). Consequently, organisations should consider wide-ranging recruitment strategies in order to extend their reach beyond those who are digitally accessible. The difficulty of recruiting volunteers is identified amongst one of the most frequent challenges faced by organisations (Hotchkiss et al., 2014). In particular, organisations relying on a large number of volunteers are concerned with several aspects of the volunteer recruitment process. These include: recruiting an adequate and diverse pool of volunteers (i.e., equally representative of gender); recruiting different age groups of volunteers; attracting qualified and professional volunteers whose skills and interests match the VA requirements; as well as concerns regarding episodic forms of volunteering hindering more regular and ongoing volunteers' support.

McCurley (2005) noted that with the expansion of the nonprofit sector, increasingly more organisations seek to recruit applicants with specific backgrounds and skill-sets. Furthermore, recent evidence from Scotland has shown signs of deterioration of formal volunteering. Results from the Scottish Household Survey indicate a decline over time in people formally volunteering, from 31% in 2010 to 26% in 2018 (Volunteer Scotland, 2019). Such a decrease has resulted in a restricted number of qualified people willing to volunteer (Cuskelly et al., 2006; Rodell, 2013). Thus, a large number of nonprofit organisations find themselves competing for limited resources therefore facing the challenge of recruiting volunteers in a highly competitive environment (Vantilborgh & Van Puyvelde, 2018). On the other hand, potential volunteers have a vast pool of opportunities to choose from and can afford to be more selective in their choices.

Several studies offer an indication of practices organisations may consider. For instance, Einolf (2018) suggests that organisations should acknowledge and emphasise the value of diversity in their recruitment strategies. Empirical findings by Boezeman and Ellemers (2014) indicated that students were considerably more interested in volunteering when the recruitment materials highlighted the necessity for young volunteers to act as role models for children. Another option to diversify the volunteer workforce in nonprofit organisations is to recruit people who volunteer informally, i.e., in a non-coordinated form. Lee and Brudney's (2012) study explored motivational factors of formal as opposed to informal volunteering, and the relationship between the two categories. The findings of their study demonstrated a positive relationship between formal and informal volunteering, i.e., both activities shared similar characteristics among volunteers such as self-confidence and empathy. Consequently, Lee and Brudney (2012) suggest that organisations should consider targeting informal volunteers as a cost-effective way of recruiting compared to targeting people indiscriminately (Lee & Brudney, 2012).

The literature suggests that the changing demographics of the volunteer workforce (i.e., aging individuals) also represents an issue for organisations seeking volunteers (Rogers et al., 2013; Warburton et al., 2018). The results of the 'Community Life' survey conducted by the Digital, Culture, Media and Sport (DCMS) Department (2018) in the UK found that the largest group of volunteers in 2017–2018 was aged between 65 and 74 years old, with 42% volunteering at least once a year, while 29% volunteered regularly. Those who were less likely to be involved in volunteering activities were individuals aged 25–34, with only 15% volunteering once a month (DCMS, 2018). Hager and Brudney (2011) and Warburton et al. (2018) argue that difficulties in recruiting younger people and the higher turnover associated with this category are mainly due to lack of interest or time and the eagerness of younger people to try out various experiences as well as the greater volubility associated with this life stage. Shields (2009) also points out that unless young volunteers develop a sense of commitment and rapidly engage in their roles, they tend to quickly lose interest thus becoming susceptible to discontinuing volunteering. Furthermore, those who are willing to offer their time at no cost are often more concerned with personal development (e.g. work experience, the fulfilment of degree requirements, advertised position's associated career benefits) instead of genuinely wishing to help out (Briggs et al., 2010; Rogers et al., 2013).

To increase recruitment rates among younger volunteers, Tiraieyari et al. (2019) recommended raising awareness of volunteering and developing ad hoc roles that overcome potential barriers to involvement. As previously touched upon, the use of digital applications such as social network sites could also be utilised as a possible means for engaging with younger volunteers. Young-Joo (2020, p. 212) points out that while social media might not represent the most effective tool for recruiting long-term volunteers, it could be used for "getting the word out" in an attempt to attract occasional or seasonal volunteers. Furthermore, those organisations with limited resources for paid advertising should focus on targeting volunteers whose interests or study area relate to the organisation's field of work (Tiraieyari et al., 2019).

Finally, recruitment difficulties can also be associated with the mission of the individual organisation. For example, Leviton et al. (2006) point out that it can be particularly difficult to recruit volunteers for social service organisations that assist individuals with long-lasting illnesses. Generally, as Hager and Brudney (2011) note, organisations that are defined by a specific mission or that deal with a specific population face the challenge associated with the specificity of their operations and the associated limitations to recruit suitable volunteers. Consequently, greater emphasis should be placed on the organisational nature of volunteering when developing recruitment strategies. It should be noted that as the discussion relates to the broader literature on volunteer recruitment, some of the issues highlighted thus far may not necessarily apply to the given context concerning VAs. While some of the elements presented above may have relevance to a range of VA organisations involving volunteers, their wider applicability must be treated with caution. Nevertheless, it is worth considering the elements presented above that served as an important basis for the primary research and analysis conducted for this study as presented in the following sections.

Volunteer selection

One of the most significant human resources management practices crucial to any organisation's long-term success is the selection of both paid and unpaid employees. Specifically, some potential negative outcomes deriving from unsuitable selection practices were highlighted by Lynch and Smith (2009) in their study applied to heritage VAs. These included problems in the working relationship associated with volunteers' motivations and expectations and the overall performance of volunteers. Past research has identified two distinct types of selection practices that can be employed to perform an effective recruitment procedure, namely, standard-conventional and unconventional-alternative practices. Standard practices include: the collation of a curriculum vitae (CV) and the qualification documents of the applicant; an informal interview; written applications; reference checking; as well as case and psychological tests (Cvetkoska et al., 2011; Lynch & Smith, 2009). Moreover, unconventional volunteer selection practices include: graph analysis; inspections of drug use; polygraph examinations, etc. With regard to the interview process, although informal in nature, the interview should be properly planned and structured to allow the interviewer to cover all relevant information and enable a clear comparison of the candidates. Mullins (1999) recommends using a checklist during the volunteer interviewing process. This should seek answers to the applicants' motivations for wanting to volunteer for a particular organisation/event and their understanding of the requirements and demands of the position. It should also include questions regarding the volunteer's background as well as his/her physical or medical condition that might affect their ability to perform in the position (Nassar & Talaat, 2008).

Another conventional method used to select suitable applicants is volunteer screening. Kreutzer and Jäger (2011) and Lynch and Smith (2009) point out that this method is more frequently employed in the case of paid positions. While organisations that employ mostly low-skilled or occasional volunteers may not find it convenient or affordable to screen volunteers, other nonprofits that depend largely on a volunteer workforce or serve vulnerable individuals should consider implementing such processes as trustworthy selection methods (Johnson, 2012). Meanwhile, Carvalho and Sampaio (2017) and Holmes and Smith (2009) note that the lack of volunteer screening within organisations may be motivated by their inherent hesitation to reject people who are willing to volunteer. Rejecting willing volunteers is often refrained from even if candidates are not suitable due to the fear of missing recruitment opportunities (Lynch & Smith, 2009). However, Warburton et al. (2018) point out that merely accepting anyone willing to volunteer can often be counterproductive, leading to unsuitable recruits who can negatively affect the organisation.

In some cases, an additional volunteer selection method called the analytic hierarchy process method (AHP) can be employed. AHP is a flexible and powerful multicriteria decision-making tool that is most frequently used when the decision is based on several criteria and sub-criteria. The method is used to solve complex decisions and entails the evaluation of given alternatives based on their relevance (Cvetkoska et al., 2011). An example of its application is given by the University Career Center in Skopje, North Macedonia, that applied this method in the selection process of student volunteers to develop candidates' rankings. The determining criteria included: the applicant's motivation to volunteer at the institution; her/his initiative and creativity; CV structure and the candidate's features including knowledge of foreign languages, IT skills, and quality of communication skills. The sub-criteria for each of these aspects cited ranged thus: excellent, very good, good, average, and poor.

Newell and Shackleton (2000) argue that every organisation should have specific criteria based on the job description and profile specification, against which volunteers are evaluated to enable consistent selection decisions. However, Carvalho and Sampaio's (2017) study of volunteer management practices in Portuguese nonprofits found out that, while some large scale organisations adopt more formalised approaches of volunteer selection (e.g. specified selection criteria), the majority of nonprofits follow rather informal volunteer selection processes with no pre-established criteria. Similarly, Allen (1987) noted that volunteer selection practices used by a number of social, medical, and educational organisations are rarely elaborate, with decisive factors often including little more than the availability and eagerness of the volunteer. As such, volunteers are not expected to demonstrate particular credentials, skills, or previous experience for the position sought (Lee Ashcraft & Kedrowicz, 2002). Research applied to the context of heritage VAs by Lynch and Smith (2009) revealed that the effectiveness of recruitment practices and selection methods can be compromised by the scarcity of supporting resources and excessive formality. In contrast, divergent findings (see, e.g., Hager & Brudney, 2015; Stirling & Bull, 2011) indicate the insignificance of the relationship between formal policies in volunteer recruitment and selection, and the ability of organisations to successfully recruit.

The review of the extant literature on volunteer recruitment and selection practices among VA organisations revealed that such themes are scarcely researched. Extant research mostly focuses on the volunteers' perspective and it is limited to cultural and heritage attractions (e.g., see Edwards, 2008; Holmes, 2003). Further, authors are generally more engaged in discussions of other human resource management practices such as orientation, supervision, recognition, and retention (Johnson, 2012). Consequently, our empirical investigation focuses on exploring the recruitment and selection practices amongst VAs given their close relationship and relevance for the sector, by applying the case of Scotland.

Methodology

In order to further explore the volunteer recruitment and selection practices within Scottish VAs, this study adopts a mixed-methods approach that involves data collection via questionnaire and semi-structured interviews. The key assumptions of the mixed-methods approach is that the combination of qualitative and quantitative data provides further insights beyond the information acquired through one method alone (Creswell & Creswell, 2018) and compensates for the weaknesses of either method (Lindsay, 2013; Punch, 2014). Thus, a sequential explanatory design was applied for the study, a strategy that involves a two-phase project in which the researcher first collects quantitative data and then follows up with a second qualitative data collection and analysis (Creswell, 2014).

Firstly, the quantitative phase of the study used self-completed questionnaires to collect information from a number of VA representatives. The questionnaire was distributed online with the aid of the Moffat Centre, the travel and tourism research centre at Glasgow

Caledonian University. The Centre regularly conducts VA research, deemed as the largest source of VA industry data at present in the UK (Moffat Centre, 2019). This trusted status facilitated the collection of the data and increased the likelihood of a satisfactory response rate. As each VA representative responded to the same set of questions, the self-completed questionnaire provided a systematic way of gathering data from a large sample (Saunders et al., 2016).

Secondly, a semi-structured interview protocol was designed and used for the qualitative data collection. Although the interview design consisted of a specific set of questions, the semi-structured interview form allowed the interviewer a great deal of flexibility in obtaining information (Bryman, 2016). Interviews were conducted by phone with an average length of 16 minutes. The interviews allowed the researcher to achieve depth and richness of data. Furthermore, they served as part of the mixed-methods design to explore and validate themes that emerged from the initial questionnaire (Teddlie & Tashakkori, 2009). Purposive sampling, a non-probability sampling technique, where researchers chose the population to sample, best suited the exploratory nature of the study and was employed for the collection of quantitative data (Bell et al., 2019). The population sample ($n = 530$) corresponded to the number of VAs participating in monthly Moffat Centre research at the time the study was conducted. Such a figure has also been estimated to reach out to over 70% of the presumed Scottish VA population (Fedeli, 2017b; Fyall et al., 2001). The sampling strategy adopted for the qualitative data was self-selection sampling, whereby the respondents for the qualitative research phase were drawn from the pool of participants of the quantitative sample, based on their availability to participate.

With regard to data analysis, the quantitative data from the questionnaire were analysed through descriptive analysis on a variable-by-variable basis using Microsoft Excel software. This allowed the researcher to understand the distribution of each variable across the participating VAs (Punch, 2014). The data analysis technique adopted for the qualitative semi-structured interviews was thematic analysis, referred to by Braun and Clarke (2006, p. 78) as a "foundational method for qualitative analysis". The purpose of this technique was to search for emerging patterns or themes elicited from the collected data set (Saunders et al., 2016). Finally, in terms of limitations, it is important to mention that as the results of the primary data consisted of only those VA operators participating in Moffat Centre research, a degree of bias might exist due to the partial representativeness of the population sample being studied (Bell et al., 2019).

Results and discussion

The questionnaire was distributed via email with the support of the Moffat Centre in February 2019. Several techniques to increase the response rate such as email reminders and incentives were also employed following Denscombe's (2010) guidelines. Eighty-six complete entries were gathered from the 530 invitations corresponding to a response rate of 16%. Given the exploratory aim of this research, the level of participation was deemed satisfactory in line with previous research on VAs (Benckendorff et al., 2005). Out of 17 survey respondents that participated in the qualitative interviews, 9 eventually further agreed to take part in the second phase of the study. Finally, seven VAs were purposely selected to undertake the interviews, based on the criteria of representation of diverse levels of reliance upon volunteers, and ownership type. For simplicity, based on a dichotomous measure of size – 'large/small' – three of the selected VAs were considered large-scale while four were small-scale. The selection criteria allowed for tentative comparisons to be drawn among the range of VAs with regard to volunteer recruitment and selection processes. Table 22.1 outlines the profiles of the participating interviewees.

Table 22.1 Interview respondents' profile

Ownership	Name	Position	No. of current volunteers	Large/ small scale
Religious Organisation	SM	Treasurer and Volunteer Coordinator	20	small
Public Body	RW	National Tourism and Destination Development Manager	405	large
Charity No.1	FE	Evaluation Coordinator	30	small
Charity No.2	FC	Project Development Officer	65	small
Charity No.3	RF	Student Engagement Officer	50	small
Charity No.4	KM	Volunteer Program Coordinator	300	large
Charity No.5	YB	Volunteer Emplacement Coordinator	180	large

Volunteer recruitment

Considering the vast reliance on the volunteer workforce amongst VAs in Scotland, it was important to investigate the current practices in volunteer recruitment and selection across the sector. With regard to volunteer recruitment, the survey results revealed that several channels of recruitment were employed by Scottish VAs (Figure 22.1).

Word-of-mouth was prevalent with 93% of respondents using this method to recruit volunteers. This finding is in line with the current literature (Einolf, 2018; Holmes & Smith, 2009). Other methods regularly used included posters and leaflets (48%), notice boards (37%), and advertisements (35%). Nevertheless, only 15% of the surveyed

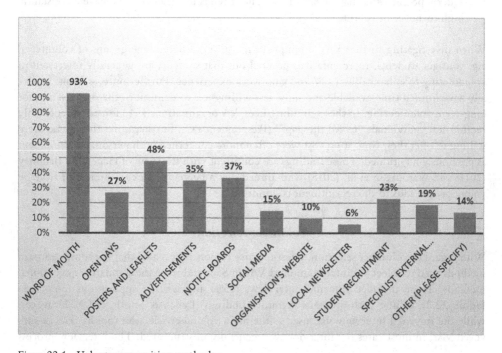

Figure 22.1 Volunteer recruiting methods

organisations adopted social media platforms. This is rather surprising given the relevance and potential of social media and other digital platforms for volunteer recruitment, and as enablers of rapid communication at a low or minimal cost to the organisation (Kappelides et al., 2019).

The results of the online questionnaire also revealed that volunteer recruitment emerged as the second most prevalent volunteer management challenge amongst VA operators in Scotland. Consequently, the interviews were used to gain further insight into the specific issues VAs face in volunteer recruitment. The interview findings highlighted that larger organisations found it particularly challenging to recruit volunteers in specific areas of the city/country. For example, the Public Body respondent (RW) highlighted barriers to volunteer recruitment due to the rural and remote location of the organisation's areas of operation.

> A lot of our volunteering is based out rurally and often these sites do not have a large selection of individuals for volunteering, as opposed to larger cities where there are much better opportunities for recruitment. So, often our volunteer recruitment campaigns in these areas result in recruitment of only 2–3 people.

Another challenge faced by smaller-scale VAs appeared to be the difficulty of attracting different volunteer demographics. As SM pointed out:

> It is mainly people who are retired that have the time to volunteer.

FC, whose VA also received a large number of senior volunteers added:

> Elderly people often have health issues and it tends to mean that we have a constantly high turnover of volunteers.

When investigating further VAs' attempts of recruiting different age groups of volunteers, e.g. younger students, representatives pointed out that students are generally interested in volunteering to enhance their CV and gain work experience. Furthermore, students generally have limited time available and show less willingness to commit to the organisation for long-term volunteering. In these circumstances, VA organisations were forced to repeatedly recruit new individuals "to fill the gaps" (Respondent FC). Furthermore, those who were willing to offer their time at no cost were often more concerned with personal development as previously mentioned. These findings are consistent with the view of Hager and Brudney (2011) and Warburton et al. (2018) who argued that a perceived lack of interest or time by young people adds to the recruitment conundrum.

Volunteer selection

With regard to volunteer selection, questionnaire responses revealed that the most common methods used to select volunteers amongst VAs in Scotland were the standard-conventional methods. These included informal interviews (85%) and written applications (36%) (see Figure 22.2), in line with previous literature findings (Lynch & Smith, 2009). However, while the informal interview was used as the main volunteer selection tool by 85% of surveyed VAs, in most cases the interview was generally unstructured. The interview process

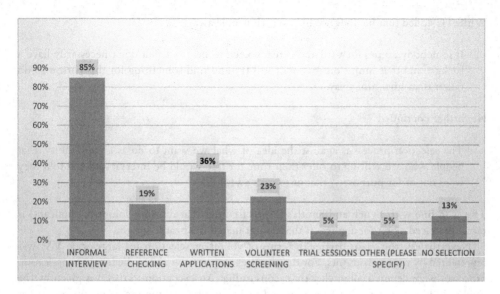

Figure 22.2   Volunteer selection methods

was therefore comparable to a casual conversation between recruiter and volunteer rather than following a planned set of steps to review the candidate's skills and experience. This is in contrast with Nassar and Talaat's (2008) suggestion that the interview process, although informal in nature, should be rather planned and structured to allow for direct comparisons between potential candidates. Nevertheless, such a scenario implies the presence of more than one candidate involved in the selection process and that a defined number of volunteers is sought by the organisation.

With regard to other volunteer selection methods, practical findings elicited from the survey diverged yet again from the literature (e.g. Kreutzer & Jäger, 2011; Lynch & Smith, 2009). While previous studies noted that the screening of volunteers is less frequently used, 23% of VAs indicated the use of this method which was more frequent than the use of reference checking (19%) and trial sessions (5%). Moreover, volunteer screening was found to be used mostly by organisations that depended largely on a volunteer workforce and was part of the organisation's policy. As RW notes:

> Basic disclosure checks are still carried out as well a photographic ID and visa checks, as they are a part of our policy.

Unconventional-alternative volunteer selection methods such as graph analysis or polygraph examinations were not found among the practices of any of the VAs surveyed. It is also important to point out that 13% of the VAs noted that they have no volunteer selection processes in place as they accept anyone willing to volunteer. While Warburton et al. (2018) argued that merely accepting everyone willing to volunteer can often be counterproductive, several organisations were in constant need of volunteers and could not afford selective behaviours. This was a regular theme amongst the small-scale VAs. As SM notes:

> We don't have enough volunteers to be selective, so we accept anyone who wishes to volunteer.

While FC added that he does not like to turn people away:

> If somebody comes forward and is really keen to help out, but don't necessarily have a background that jumps out, we will still try and find something for this person to do rather than turn him away.

He further continued:

> The selection process is against the idea of what we want to do as a community, that people who are willing to offer their time for free would be interviewed and told they were not fit for purpose... that just seems awful.

This is in line with Lynch and Smith's (2009) findings that refusing volunteer applicants is rarely practiced albeit for applicants that do not match the profile sought.

Nevertheless, the main barrier in terms of volunteer selection for large-scale VAs was represented by time constraints. For the charities numbered 4 and 5, the lengthy application processes were deemed somewhat time-consuming. An exception to this was given by the Public Body respondent that had addressed such issues by making the selection process "as much inclusive as possible" (RW). RW explains the refinement of the selection process:

> Instead of having a long, chunky application form, we now run volunteer taster sessions to allow for 'self-sifting'. This way the potential volunteers can meet the site teams, learn more about the volunteer role and decide whether they would like to join the organisation. The taster sessions are then followed up by an informal interview where we ask for examples of three competencies based on communications, teamwork and delivering a personal achievement.

Level of formality of volunteer recruitment and selection

Finally, the research also investigated the level of formality of volunteer recruitment and selection amongst VAs. The impulse to this was given by the findings from the literature review revealing that managing volunteers more formally is increasingly viewed as essential (Baillie Smith & Laurie, 2011; Carvalho & Sampaio, 2017). However, there appears to be a lack of consensus on whether volunteers should be recruited and selected similarly to paid staff, or whether organisations should rather follow alternative, more flexible approaches that take into account the uniqueness of volunteers. The results revealed that the extent to which volunteer management practices were formalised into the completion of official documents, forms, and checklists varied greatly across organisations. Within small-scale VAs, the informal nature of volunteer management emerged as a recurring theme. VA representatives explained that their volunteer recruitment and selection processes were not formalised, noting that they did not have any specific forms to complete or standardised formats to gather information. FC, project development officer for Charity No. 2, described the informal approach to volunteer selection and the reasons for the lack of more formal processes:

> Often people are in volunteering because they are not in employment or they lack confidence so, by over formalising things, I think, it can sometimes put people off. Therefore, we are trying to keep the selection process of our volunteers as informal as possible to be honest.

Similarly, SM reflected:

> Our approach to volunteer management is very informal as we don't want to put any undue pressure on our volunteers. They are aware that there is always someone to ask advice from, if they feel that they need it.

Yet, approaches to volunteer recruitment and selection within large-scale VAs ranged from formal and structured processes to a combination of both formal and informal processes. As such, in the context of VAs in Scotland, it tentatively appears that the level of formalisation adopted is based on the individual organisation's environment, and the characteristics of volunteers.

Conclusion

This study aimed to identify and critically examine the extent to which VAs in Scotland engage with volunteer management, specifically – recruitment and selection practices, and highlight modes and key issues. Firstly, the discussion highlights the differences identified in both small and large-scale VAs, albeit based on a small number of interviews. The extent to which volunteer recruitment and selection practices were formalised into the completion of official forms and documents varied greatly across organisations. Within large-scale VAs, volunteer recruitment and selection ranged from formal and structured processes to a combination of both formal and informal processes, while in small-scale VAs these processes were found to be mainly informal. Secondly, our research found out that although various recruitment channels were used across VA organisations in Scotland, word-of-mouth was the most used means employed, with 93% of respondents claiming to use this method. Social media platforms were only used by 15% of the surveyed organisations. Furthermore, while for large-scale organisations it was particularly difficult to attract volunteers in certain regions (e.g. remote areas or city districts), the challenge for smaller-scale VAs lay in the difficulty of attracting heterogeneity across volunteer demographics, particularly students.

Thirdly, the research revealed that the most common methods used to select volunteers amongst VAs are standard-conventional methods, such as informal interviews and written applications. Interestingly, while the interview process was usually informal, in many cases it was also completely unstructured. This makes it problematic for the interviewer to gather consistent information about the candidate and, in the case of competing candidates, draw fair comparisons among the applicants. Furthermore, a regular theme amongst small-scale VAs in particular, was the absence of recruitment and selection practices mainly dictated by the sheer need for volunteers combined with the difficulties in recruiting them. On the other hand, for large-scale visitor attractions, time-constraints emerged as a major issue in terms of volunteer selection.

This study also offers recommendations for practical application to VAs. It recommends the intensification of the use of social media as a recruitment method. Social media platforms are popular amongst all age groups (Özdemir & Çelebi, 2017). Not only might advertising volunteer positions via social media help VAs reach out potential applicants, but social media platforms have been found to be instrumental in building strong and lasting relationships and harnessing the volunteering efforts of organisations (Boulianne, 2015; Briones et al., 2011). Furthermore, the extent to which volunteer recruitment and selection is formalised into the completion of official documents, forms, and checklists should be adapted to the characteristics of each VA and the uniqueness of its volunteers, rather than the size of the organisation or the number of volunteers it seeks to recruit. As Kreutzer and Jäger (2011) note, the risk of over formalisation of volunteer management processes may conflict with the values and spirit of volunteering and consequently alienate volunteers.

While considering the limitations of this study, several theoretical considerations and potential avenues for future research are finally drawn. Given the exploratory nature of this research, the study aimed to achieve an overview of the whole VA sector in Scotland as all VAs were included in the online survey phase without distinction, for instance, of category or size. Significant differences were identified across the sector in terms of recruitment and selection practices, as well as the challenges faced by VA organisations. Further research may therefore focus on specific VA categories (e.g. natural attractions, religious organisations etc.) as well as concentrate the examination based on features such as size and ownership type in order to provide insights on the possible causes and associations of factors determining the heterogeneity of the data. Another limitation of this study was given by the limited number of questionnaire responses and interviews obtained that may restrict the generalisation of the findings. Therefore, it is also recommended that further research should be undertaken that considers larger samples and compares several geographical references of VAs. Furthermore, given the focus of this study taking an organisational perspective, there is need for further research that considers the volunteers' point of view concerning VA recruitment and selection practices. For instance, it may be relevant to investigate differences and similarities between paid staff and volunteer practices of recruitment and selection.

To conclude, although VAs represent a unique sector that lends itself to creating and offering volunteering opportunities in tourism, new research may benefit from seeking potential linkages between the wider tourism literature on volunteer management (in particular sport and events) and human resource management, in order to draw comparisons and build theoretical advances in the field. Given the high reliance of VA organisations on volunteers and the widely acknowledged importance of the VA sector in serving a wide range of cultural and leisure-related opportunities, as well as the socio-economic role that the sector plays for many destinations, a call for further research into the recruitment and selection practices of VAs is made here. Overall, it is deemed that a better understanding of such practices would benefit both organisations and aspiring volunteers. It is hoped that such an enhanced understanding may enable more efficient practices to ensure suitable candidates fulfil the positions offered, while aiding the alignment of personal aspirations and goals of candidates with the organisations' objectives.

References

Allen, N. J. (1987). The role of social and organizational factors in the evaluation of volunteer programs. *Evaluation and Program Planning, 10*(3), 257–262. https://doi.org/10.1016/0149-7189(87)90037-1

Baillie Smith, M., & Laurie, N. (2011). International volunteering and development: global citizenship and neoliberal professionalisation today. *Transactions of the Institute of British Geographers, 36*(4), 545–559. https://www.jstor.org/stable/23020828

Bell, E., Bryman, A., & Harley, B. (2019). *Business research methods.* 5th ed. New York: Oxford University Press.

Benckendorff, P., Moscardo, G., & Murphy, L. (2005). High tech versus high touch: Visitor responses to the use of technology in tourist attractions. *Tourism Recreation Research, 30*(3), 37–47. https://doi.org/10.1080/02508281.2005.11081485

Boezeman, E., & Ellemers, N. (2014). Volunteer recruitment. In: K. Yu & D. Cable (Eds.). *The Oxford handbook of recruitment* (pp. 73–87). Oxford: Oxford University Press.

Boulianne, S. (2015). Social media use and participation: A meta-analysis of current research. *Information Communication and Society, 18*(5), 524–538. https://doi.org/10.1080/1369118X.2015.1008542

Braun, V., & Clarke, V. (2006). Using thematic analysis in psychology. *Qualitative Research in Psychology*, *3*(2), 77–101.

Briggs, E., Peterson, M., & Gregory, G. (2010). Toward a better under-standing of volunteering for nonprofit organizations: Explaining volunteers' pro-social attitudes. *Journal of Macromarketing*, *30*(1), 61–76. https://doi.org/10.1177/0276146709352220

Briones, R. L., Kuch, B., Liu, B. F., & Jin, Y. (2011). Keeping up with the digital age: How the American Red Cross uses social media to build relationships. *Public Relations Review*, *37*(1), 37–43. https://doi.org/10.1016/j.pubrev.2010.12.006

Bryman, A. (2016). *Social research methods*. 5th ed. New York: Oxford University Press.

Carvalho, A., & Sampaio, M. (2017). Volunteer management beyond prescribed best practice: A case study of Portuguese non-profits. *Personnel Review*, *46*(2), 410–428. https://doi.org/10.1108/PR-04-2014-0081

Connell, J., Page, S. J. and Meyer, D. (2015). 'Visitor attractions and events: Responding to seasonality', *Tourism Management*. E, *46*, 283–298.

Cordery, C., Smith, K., & Proctor-Thomson, S. (2015). Staff and volunteers' perceptions of the volunteer programme: An alternative use of the net benefits index. *Voluntary Sector Review*, *6*(2), 173–192. https://doi.org/10.1332/204080515X14291983096544

Creswell, J. (2014). *Research design: Qualitative, quantitative, and mixed methods approaches* 4th ed. Los Angeles: SAGE Publications.

Creswell, J. W., & Creswell, J. D. (2018). *Research design: Qualitative, quantitative, and mixed methods approaches*. 5th ed. SAGE Publications.

Cuskelly, G., Hoye, R., & Auld, C. (2006). *Working with volunteers in sport*. New York: Routledge.

Cvetkoska, V., Sekulovska, G. B., & Sekulovska, M. (2011). Recruitment and selection of student–volunteers: A multicriteria methodology. *Management*, *61*, 139–146.

Denscombe, M. (2010). *The good research guide: For small-scale social research projects*. Maidenhead: McGraw-Hill/Open University Press.

Department for Digital, Culture, Media & Sport. (2018). *Community life survey 2017-18*. London: Department for Digital, Culture, Media & Sport.

Dighe, A. (2012). Demographic and technological imperatives. In: L. M. Salamon (Ed.). *The state of nonprofit America* (pp. 616–638). Washington, DC: Brookings Institution Press.

Edwards, D. (2008). It's mostly about me: Reasons why volunteers contribute their time to museums and art museums. *Tourism Review International*, *9*(1), 21–31.

Einolf, C. (2018). Evidence-based volunteer management: A review of the literature. *Voluntary Sector Review*, *9*(2), 153–176. https://doi.org/10.1332/204080518X15299334470348

Fedeli, G. (2017a). ICTs, disruptive forces and the production paradox in tourism: Present and future issues in the visitor attraction sector. *Mediterranean Journal of Communication*, *10*(1), 113–121.

Fedeli, G. (2017b). The role and potential of ICT in the visitor attractions sector: The case of Scotland's tourism industry. In *ENTER2017 eTourism Conference PhD Workshop Research Proposals*. Università della Svizzera italiana.

Fyall, A., Leask, A., & Garrod, B. (2001). Scottish visitor attractions – A collaborative future? *International Journal of Tourism Research*, *228*(3), 211–228. https://doi.org/10.1002/jtr.313

Hager, M. A., & Brudney, J. L. (2011). Problems recruiting volunteers: Nature versus nurture. *Nonprofit Management and Leadership*, *22*(2), 137–157.

Hager, M. A., & Brudney, J. L. (2015). In search of strategy universalistic, contingent, and configurational adoption of volunteer management practices. *Nonprofit Management and Leadership*, *25*(3), 235–254. https://doi.org/10.1002/nml.20046

Holmes, K. (2003). Volunteers in the heritage sector: A neglected audience? *International Journal of Heritage Studies*, *9*(4), 341–355. https://doi.org/10.1080/1352725022000155072

Holmes, K., & Smith, K. (2009). *Managing volunteers in tourism: Destinations, attractions and events*. Wallingford: Elsevier Butterworth-Heinemann.

Hotchkiss, R. B., Unruh, L., & Fottler, M. D. (2014). The role, measurement, and impact of volunteerism in hospitals. *Nonprofit and Voluntary Sector Quarterly*, *43*(6), 111–1128. https://doi.org/10.1177/0899764014549057

Johnson, K. A. (2012). *Implementing human resources best practices in volunteer selection*. Arizona: The University of Arizona.

Kappelides, P., Cuskelly, G., & Hoye, R. (2019). The influence of volunteer recruitment practices and expectations on the development of volunteers' psychological contracts. *Voluntas*, *30*(1), 259–271. https://doi.org/10.1007/s11266-018-9986-x

Karl, K. A., Peluchette, J. V., & Hall, L. M. (2008). Give them something to smile about: A marketing strategy for recruiting and retaining volunteers. *Journal of Nonprofit & Public Sector Marketing, 20*(1), 71–96. https://doi.org/10.1080/10495140802165360

Kreutzer, K., & Jäger, U. (2011). Volunteering versus managerialism: Conflict over organizational identity in voluntary associations. *Nonprofit and Voluntary Sector Quarterly, 40*(4), 634–661. https://doi.org/10.1177/0899764010369386

Leask, A. (2010). 'Progress in visitor attraction research: Towards more effective management', *Tourism Management, 31*(2), pp. 155–166.

Leask, A. (2016). 'Visitor attraction management: A critical review of research 2009–2014', *Tourism Management.* Elsevier Ltd, 57, pp. 334–361.

Leask, A., Fyall, A. and Garrod, B. (2013). 'Managing revenue in Scottish visitor attractions', *Current Issues in Tourism, 16*(3), pp. 240–265.

Lee, Y., & Brudney, J. L. (2012). Participation in formal and informal volunteering: Implications for volunteer recruitment. *Nonprofit Management and Leadership, 23*(2), 159–180. https://doi.org/10.1002/nml.21060

Lee Ashcraft, K., & Kedrowicz, A. (2002). Self-direction or social support? Nonprofit empowerment and the tacit employment contract of organizational communication studies. *Communication Monographs, 69*(1), 88–110. https://doi.org/10.1080/03637750216538

Leviton, L. C., Herrera, C., Pepper, S. K., Fishman, N., & Racine, D. P. (2006). Faith in Action: Capacity and sustainability of volunteer organizations. *Evaluation and Program Planning, 29*(2), 201–207. https://doi.org/10.1016/j.evalprogplan.2006.01.011

Lindsay, G. (2013). The benefits of combined (mixed) methods research. *Social Work and Social Sciences Review, 16*(2), 76–87. https://doi.org/10.1921/swssr.v16i2.532

Lynch, S., & Smith, K. (2009). The dilemma of judging unpaid workers. *Personnel Review, 39*(1), 80–95. https://doi.org/10.1108/00483481011007878

McCurley, S. (2005). Keeping the community involved: Recruiting and retaining volunteers. In: R. D. Herman (Ed.). *The Jossey-Bass handbook of nonprofit leadership and management* (pp. 587–622). San Francisco: Jossey-Bass.

Moffat Centre (2018). *Scottish visitor attraction monitor 2017.* Glasgow: Glasgow Caledonian University.

Moffat Centre (2019). *Scottish visitor attraction monitor 2018.* Glasgow: Glasgow Caledonian University.

Mullins, L. (1999). *Management and organizational behaviour.* 5th ed. London: Financial Times/Pitman Publishing.

Nassar, N., & Talaat, N. (2008). Motivations of young volunteers in special events. *TOURISMOS: An International Multidisciplinary Journal of Tourism, 4*(1), 145–152.

Newell, S., & Shackleton, V. (2000). Recruitment and selection. In: S. Bach & K. Sisson (Eds.). *Personnel management: A comprehensive guide to theory and practice* (pp. 111–136). Oxford: Blackwell.

Özdemir, G., & Çelebi, D. (2017). A social media framework of cultural museums. *Advances in Hospitality and Tourism Research (AHTR), 5*(2), 101–119.

Piatak, J., Dietz, N., & McKeeveret, B. (2019). Bridging or deepening the digital divide: Influence of household internet access on formal and informal volunteering. *Nonprofit and Voluntary Sector Quarterly, 48*(2), 123–150. https://doi.org/10.1177/0899764018794907

Punch, K. F. (2014). *Introduction to social research: Quantitative and qualitative approaches.* 3rd ed. London: SAGE Publications.

Rodell, J. (2013). Finding meaning through volunteering: Why do employees volunteer and what does it mean for their jobs? *Academy of Management Journal, 56*(5), 1274–1294. https://doi.org/10.5465/amj.2012.0611

Rogers, S. E., Rogers, C. M., & Boyd, K. D. (2013). Challenges and opportunities in healthcare volunteer management: Insights from volunteer administrators. *Hospital Topics, 91*(2), 43–51. https://doi.org/10.1080/00185868.2013.806012

Saunders, M. N. K., Lewis, P., & Thornhill, A. (2016). *Research methods for business students.* 7th ed. London: Pearson Education.

Shields, P. O. (2009). Young adult volunteers: Recruitment appeals and other marketing considerations. *Journal of Nonprofit & Public Sector Marketing, 21*(2), 139–159. https://doi.org/10.1080/10495140802528658

Stirling, C., & Bull, R. (2011). Collective agency for service volunteers: A critical realist study of identity representation. *Administration & Society, 43*(2), 193–215. https://doi.org/10.1177/0095399711400046

Teddlie, C., & Tashakkori, A. (2009). *Foundations of mixed methods research: Integrating quantitative and qualitative approaches in the social and behavioural sciences.* Thousand Oaks, CA: Sage.

Tiraieyari, N., Ricard, R. M., & Mclean, G. N. (2019). Factors influencing volunteering in urban agriculture: Implications for recruiting volunteers. *Urban Forestry & Urban Greening, 45,* 18–27. https://doi.org/10.1016/j.ufug.2019.126372

Vantilborgh, T., & Van Puyvelde, S. (2018). Volunteer reliability in nonprofit organizations: A theoretical model. *Voluntas: International Journal of Voluntary and Nonprofit Organizations, 29*(1), 29–42. https://doi.org/10.1007/s11266-017-9909-2

Volunteer Scotland (2019). *Volunteering in Scotland: Scottish household survey 2007 - 2017 Summary* Report. Stirling: Volunteer Scotland.

Warburton, J., Moore, M., & Oppenheimer, M. (2018). Challenges to the recruitment and retention of volunteers in traditional nonprofit organizations: A case study of Australian meals on wheels. *International Journal of Public Administration, 41*(16), 1361–1373. https://doi.org/10.1080/01900692.2017.1390581

Weidenfeld, A., & Leask, A. (2013). Exploring the relationship between visitor attractions and events: Definitions and management factors. *Current Issues in Tourism, 16*(6), 552–569. https://doi.org/10.1080/13683500.2012.702736

Young-Joo, L. (2020). Facebooking alone? Millennials' use of social network sites and volunteering. *Nonprofit and Voluntary Sector Quarterly, 49*(1), 203–217. https://doi.org/10.1177/0899764019868844

23

EXPLORING RETENTION AND REWARDS IN COMMUNITY SPORT VOLUNTEERING

Nadina Ayer and John R. Cooper

Introduction

The very nature of volunteering suggests motives and behaviours to differ from those of paid employees (Alfes & Langner, 2017). Sport volunteers tend to be motivated by common interests, building friendships, and career-related opportunities (Johnson et al., 2017). Volunteering can be viewed as a leisure activity, performed during one's free time for the benefits of others (see Cnaan et al., 1996) and thus, opportunities for positive experiences and growth seem necessary. Opportunities for development and learning seem important for volunteer retention and intention to stay (see Newton, Becker & Bell, 2014; Henderson & Sowa, 2018). Similarly, support including assistance, responsibility, and respect increased volunteer satisfaction (Farrell, Johnston & Twynam, 1998; see also Schlesinger, Egli & Nagel, 2019; Sharpe, 2006), playing a role in retention (see Nagel et al., 2020; Sharpe, 2006).

Recognition, also known as acknowledgement, honour, and appreciation of one's contributions, is seen as one of the best influencers of volunteer satisfaction (Dwiggins-Beeler, Spitzberg & Roesch, 2011; Farrell et al., 1998). Hence, recognition has also been viewed and recommended as a way to help clubs of any size and context ensure volunteer retention (Nagel et al., 2020). Awards can help recognize volunteers through thank you notes, annual dinners, newsletters, etc. As a leisure activity, volunteering, at times, can have a different set of rewards with material incentives (minor payments) and 'fringe benefits' being positively perceived (Nichols, 2017; see also Nagel et al., 2020). Using awards as incentives for volunteering can have several benefits such as increased performance and efforts (Frey & Gallus, 2017, 2018) and long-term commitment (Smith & Grove, 2017). While awards can positively influence volunteer retention (e.g., see discretionary awards in Gallus, 2016) they may also negatively impact the non-recipients (Frey & Gallus, 2017).

Overall, if dissatisfied volunteers tend to leave organizations (Pearce, 1983), then those whose expectations are met are expected to stay (Bang, 2015; Green & Chalip, 2004; see also Doherty, 2005; Kim, Chelladurai & Trail, 2007). Recognition (awards), satisfaction, motivation, development opportunities, and perceived organizational support have all been related to volunteer retention, commitment, and intentions (Cuskelly & Hoye, 2013; Giel & Breuer, 2020; Hoye et al., 2008; Livingston & Forbes, 2016; Nagel et al., 2020; Newton et al., 2014;

DOI: 10.4324/9780367815875-27

Schlesinger et al., 2019). The many factors demonstrate the complex nature of volunteering in sport. Research on recognition and retention is often conducted from an institutional perspective (see Wicker, 2017). To our knowledge, the majority of research concerning sport volunteer recognition and retention is quantitative. Our study qualitatively approaches the topic, looking at the experiences of sport volunteers in various roles, responsibilities, and lengths of involvement. Further to perceptions of recognition, we explore experiences of resignation (own and that of others), providing additional insight into values and challenges.

Our study

Regardless of turnover challenges, volunteering remains a popular activity. In 2018, 12.7 million Canadians over the age of 15 were involved in formal volunteering, donating 1.6 billion hours, 106 hours per individual to sport organizations (Statistics Canada, 2020). We were interested in exploring Canadian sport volunteers' motives, perception of rewards, and experiences of resignation. We utilized email to conduct semi-structured interviews with eight volunteers from different community sport clubs. Some disadvantages of email interviews can include being time-consuming, lacking social cues, and resulting in potentially short responses (see Fritz & Vandermause, 2017). The asynchronous nature and participants' ability to control their level of participation in email interviews (see Mason & Ide, 2014) were deemed appropriate during the uncertainty of a national lockdown when the study took place. Like others (see Gibson, 2010), our participants also used written cues and symbols such as smiley faces to depict emotions and moods. Overall, the advantages of email interviews include clear, concise, better topic-focused responses, and in turn, more coherent transcripts (Fritz & Vandermause, 2017, see also Bowden & Galindo-Gonzalez, 2015; Synnot et al., 2014).

In this chapter, we report on the experiences of Canadian community sport volunteers who have been or currently are involved in supervisory, administrative, and/or coaching roles. A six-phase thematic analysis approach (see Braun & Clarke, 2006) was performed. The findings are organized into three major themes: reasons for continuing volunteering, rewards and recognition, and resignation. Each theme consists of key sub-themes representing an important aspect of volunteers' involvement. We use direct quotes to describe experiences and offer interpretations within a broader concept of volunteer retention. We consider the importance of support and conclude the chapter with implications for practice and future research.

Reasons for continuing volunteering

Volunteers can continue with an activity for several reasons. In particular, the role of others, good fit, and ability to reach personal goals seemed important.

The role of others

Community sport volunteers seem to start volunteering because of others. They may do so for and because of family, for example: "to support my cousin diagnosed with Down Syndrome" and "my kids started cross country ski lessons and I got involved". Others got recruited, "the Manager... asked me to form a new chapter...which I did". In this way, volunteers may have had the required skills for recruitment to the leadership role. More often though, volunteers got recruited into start-up positions and gradually moved onto more demanding roles. As one volunteer explained:

> My son's soccer coach asked me to be on the committee with him…to be the secretary and take the minutes. When the games were finished…I was put on the fundraising committee. I ended up in charge of all the funds… After the 2000 tour, Special Olympics restructured the chapter, and I was asked to help build it…the rest is history.

Community sport volunteers seem to also continue volunteering because of others, enjoying the impact of the program. This could be their very best volunteering experience:

> Running the program was certainly the best experience…We could see the benefits for kids as they learned to participate in sport, … as well for parents as they saw their children's enjoyment and gained some respite time each week…We had lots of volunteers… making my role…simpler.

Thus, everything came together to make the program successful.

While some volunteered "to give back to a way of life that helped define" them, most appreciated the role of others. As one volunteer explained, "…other volunteers were very enthusiastic, and it felt good to be with that group of people. We kind of fed on each other's energy…a lot of support …very rewarding". The opportunity to socialize can make mundane activities special, "I was placed on a team of six…who were amazing. We bonded like a family. Today, I am still in touch with one of the young girls that was on the team". Here, volunteering is more than just necessary tasks; it is developing long-lasting friendships. Friendships and camaraderie have been long recognized as motivating factors for volunteering (see Farrell et al., 1998).

Others seemed important in decision-making, as volunteers sought opportunities to share their vision and goals, "…coaching the provincial team with like-minded coaches…allowing our athletes to do the best they can". They also sought "to collaborate with young people…interested in learning", describing the opportunity as "an ideal volunteering practice". As shown, volunteers emphasized the team unit. Social relationships and a shared passion for sport can drive volunteers in their roles (Johnson et al., 2017; Welty Peachey et al., 2014).

Good role fit

What seems to help community sport volunteers continue volunteering is their satisfaction and enjoyment of the activities, roles, and those involved. Some suggest an ideal volunteering experience to include an appropriate fit between their goals and the organization, for example:

> …one that allowed me to volunteer for something I really believe in, doing work that I am good at and enjoy…something that also fits in well with my schedule, so that…I can dedicate the appropriate amount of time to…Ideally, I would get along well with the people I interact with.

Entrusting volunteers and good organizational fit can contribute to continued volunteering (see Kim et al., 2007).

Volunteering can help one reach goals and volunteers understand this potential. As one volunteer explained,

Volunteering in sport provides an opportunity to enhance or learn new skills, engage in co-operative efforts with other people to achieve goals and to increase self-confidence. It opens doors to participation in other community, professional or trade organizations, and possibly to increased responsibilities with a person's employment.

In this way, volunteers tend to understand the responsibilities and commitment necessary for a successful experience. Commitment can also influence continued volunteering (see Cuskelly & Hoye, 2013).

Reaching personal goals

Community sport volunteers seem to be very much in tune with their roles. They understand who they are, describing themselves as "…a committed, passionate volunteer who enjoys a challenge and achieving a goal that enables other people". They actively reflect and evaluate:

As a volunteer today, I have a passion for the role and organization…I like to volunteer with an organization that I have a chance to grow. In the future I see myself as a more experienced volunteer, better relating to people…up with the trends, better use of technology, and more as a facilitator guiding participants and organization to reach their goals. I would see myself listening more to people, role modeling more kindness, and caring for other people. Changing with the times.

When community sport volunteers want to retire, some decide to "…be more of a resource and mentor". Their plan can have a timeline, "In the next 2 years…I hope to retire from my intense volunteer roles…" and "Sorry to say but in 10 years I will have probably hung up my volunteer hat". They may suggest, "To accomplish this, I must mentor other volunteers to develop the necessary skills and knowledge or find volunteers who possess these attributes to replace me…". Volunteers seem committed, showing responsibility. Their passion to help is evident, leaving them feeling obligated and even apologetic. They identified training of recruits as an essential step to ensure a successful transition, relating to the importance of learning opportunities and skill development (see Newton et al., 2014).

Rewards and recognition

Volunteers may feel rewarded and be recognized, which sometimes led to talks of credibility and reflection on their meaning.

Feeling rewarded

Community sport volunteers seem to feel rewarded when they are supported and meet others' needs. As one volunteer reflected:

My sister and I volunteered together along the marathon path and we provided snacks, drinks, and words of encouragement to the participants. It was during October…we didn't properly predict the weather…near the waterfront. It was very cold and several times I got angry with myself for signing up… However, every time I encouraged someone or gave them a snack/drink, my heart swelled, and I felt very rewarded. It was a moment where I knew that I was truly appreciated and thanked for what I was doing. It was very memorable…being very happy and fulfilled.

In this case, the presence of others and the act of volunteering changed the initial sense of regret and anger, resulting in feelings of appreciation and thanks, making the event a memorable experience. Others have found appreciation to be related to volunteer satisfaction in general (see Nagel et al., 2020) making rewards and in turn, recognition necessary in volunteer retention (see Walk, Zhang & Littlepage, 2019; Hager & Brudney, 2008).

Being recognized

Organizations may regularly recognize their volunteers for various reasons, resulting in experiences of formal and/or informal acknowledgement. Formally volunteers may be acknowledged for supervisory contributions, "I was recognized for mentoring a group of students…three years…providing a series of fun, creative, innovative workshops… at the camp". Some were rewarded for long-term service, "I received an award for volunteering with the kid's programs and being on the Board". Others received monetary awards; as one coach explained, "…parents recognized countless hours… excellence, detail, empathetic and caring culture – not my words-…received a $1,000 bursary". Sometimes volunteers were recognized collectively, "Our committee was recently nominated for an annual award to recognize our contributions". Often recognition included a selection process where a volunteer "…was selected by the Awards Committee", and formally celebrated at "the awards banquet… receiving a standing ovation and the seal of approval", for instance.

Community sport volunteers seemed to experience small tokens of recognition regularly, "From the athletes, I am always receiving letters/cards" and "a small gift card from the chairs of the committee". Such tokens can accompany formal awards,

> …at the season's end banquet, I got the adult racer of the year award. In recognition I got a brush to help with waxing skis, which I thought was great and very useful. It was also mentioned in the newsletter.

Small appreciations were cherished and well perceived.

Understanding recognition

Community sport volunteers believed recognition to be important as "…publicly recognizing long-time volunteers brings recognition in the community to the organization and makes other people want to join". Some believed that "…without it, I am not always sure my efforts are appreciated. I have always been acknowledged…which is perhaps why I have been a volunteer for so long". Volunteers tend to seek some acknowledgement showing their efforts are valued (see Sheptak & Menaker, 2016). While these volunteers viewed recognition as an imperative action, others have rejected the idea, suggesting a more intrinsic need for volunteering. As one explained, "I did not do the job for recognition, we do it for love of sport". At times some refused the praise altogether, "…players nominated me for coach of the year, I declined to be nominated. Awards are not why we coach". Being at odds about recognition in volunteering, in general, suggests the complexity of how volunteers may be acknowledged.

Community sport volunteers seemed to emphasize how they were recognized. Some felt not worthy of the nomination, as one explained, "I believe I was nominated by friends...I don't think I deserved the nomination as I often volunteer sporadically". Another experienced frustration about the recognition they received:

> ...after the Games, I received a note of thanks and a picture on a plaque of 4 athletes from the Rhythmic Gymnastics team...My partner did not receive any recognition...I was not impressed...if you are going to say thank you, at least have the correct sport, Athletics, and do not forget other individuals who worked to make the team successful.

The community sport volunteers questioned the credibility of recognition.

Although community sport volunteers may experience some form of recognition, as an individual or a team member, they do take them as non-guaranteed outcomes. As one volunteer suggested, "...one usually does not get anything tangible from volunteering, there are benefits including fulfillment and networking". While efforts to acknowledge are valued, volunteers seem to look for other benefits associated with their role. A volunteer in a leadership role explained, "While most volunteers do not expect any reward, they do appreciate simple appreciations and a sense of accomplishment and self-worth". The personal benefits seem to be some of the very reasons for continued involvement. We discuss such involvement concerning experiences of resignation.

Resignation

Volunteers seemed to experience resignation in two ways, as their own and that of others. In doing so, they discussed ways of dealing with and preventing resignation.

Resigning from volunteering

Volunteers can resign for different reasons and at various stages, for example:

> The plan was to get girls out to ski...with no pressure to perform... There were other volunteers that we had asked to help, ...one group of experienced skiers ended up doing a bit more...the volunteer who left halfway through felt that...it was getting too competitive. We did talk...and tried to find a way to continue, which didn't lead to a solution.

Some resigned due to others' involvement and a lack of policy enforcement, "Parents wanted to control the financial side of the team...looking to contribute to allow their child to get ahead. The President wouldn't get involved even though they contradicted the [governing body's] Code of Ethics". The self-interest of other volunteers has previously been noted as a reason for resignation (see Spallanzani, 1988). Others resigned for personal reasons, "I had to resign when I went to Japan to work. It was not possible to perform my volunteer duties away from Canada".

In general, community sport volunteers seemed to seek benefits, valuing met expectations, personal goals, and a good fit. One volunteer summarized multiple reasons:

> I had volunteered with the organization for sixteen years. I resigned, finding myself going stagnant, no room to grow, and the organization going in a direction, I felt

I did not fit. Evidence of this was through our monthly meetings. A few people always getting their way to meet their needs and deciding who was going to present workshops amongst the executive without going to the membership to get their involvement. I must say, I left well respected when I resigned without burning any bridges.

This experience also outlines the importance of the way one resigns, and how one resigns from their role is noteworthy:

> I talked...to explain that I am not achieving my goals. We had to re-evaluate...I had to take on a different role... I feel you need to be flexible and willing to listen and have alternatives... With the experiences I have had, this concept has worked. The coordinator listened to my concerns... She was most helpful by being kind and showing she cared.

Seeking support allowed for continued participation, reiterating the importance of the driving motivation factors. Others have also found sport volunteers to be motivated by values, understanding and career, social, and self-enhancement factors (see Welty Peachey et al., 2014). These factors can serve two purposes, as a driver to continuing volunteering and as a reason to resign. Some volunteers resigned because their values and priorities were not met. Others continued by taking on a role more aligned with their needs and skills.

How one approaches those in supervisory roles seems imperative to continued participation. One volunteer advised, "I would approach the Board and ask for support, it always helps to have a detailed plan before". Some give plenty of notice, offering to help:

> Last year I decided to resign from the position of Head Coach for snowshoeing. I decided I would focus on Athletics. I gave our council a year to find a new Head Coach. I was willing to train the person. The volunteer did not work out...didn't even show up. As the National Games approached, 4 of my athletes did not have a coach so I ended up returning until they went to the Games. There were other athletes in the club that I also had to coach. The question is will they find a replacement for next year?

Volunteers can display continued dedication by being cooperative and helpful, demonstrating that a decision to resign can come with continued worry about the role and its overall effect on the program and its participants. It can also result in the need to delay resignation and remain in the role. While filling the role takes time, some believed that lack of interest makes recruiting difficult, "people are not banging down doors to volunteer".

Volunteer concerns about the negative impacts of resignation are meaningful. As one volunteer disclosed,

> I resigned after running the program for three years because I moved...there was no one to take my place and...the program ended. I fear that is what will happen with our inclusive sports program this fall, which makes me want to keep running it myself....

Schlesinger, Egli, and Nagel (2013) viewed this as a "sense of obligation" where sport club volunteers would not terminate their volunteering when they felt an obligation to solidarity and attachment to the club. They found if interests changed and conflicts occurred within a club such as finding subs, then the risk of termination seemed present.

Dealing with resignation

Community sport volunteers experienced resignation as part of their role performance, which can be their own or by another volunteer. Resignation, in general, suggests having negative effects on others, taking on "their responsibilities", "to make more phone calls to find another". The resignation also tends to negatively impact the organization, "We often saw poor fidelity around the mid-term season, and purposefully ended our program...to prevent issues of volunteers not showing up and not being able to find substitutes".

The challenge of resignation lies in increased duties and time-consuming recruitments, "It is not easy to face and overcome these challenges because of the additional workload for me, and it takes several weeks or months to recruit and involve a new volunteer". Those left behind helped finish the program, finding it "a bit stressful to do on short notice", emphasizing that "...it can be overwhelming to have so much work on one plate". Others have found similar results of increased workload assignment for those remaining to compensate for the loss of a volunteer (see Wicker & Breuer, 2011).

Volunteers' understanding of resignation outcomes has prompted a utilization of recruitment strategies, seeking help from trusted parties, "Go to the parent you know can help". Some believed that "...in many organizations it's generally friends and family that we talk into volunteering to help out". Many admitted such parties to be good resources, outlining, "we receive some of our best volunteers that way... parents...turned out to be...terrific". Parents whose children belong to the club may be more committed to volunteering because of the lower opportunity cost that exists for them (see Schlesinger et al., 2013).

Others, however, cautioned against heavy reliance on such parties, explaining in detail the alternative options in recruitment and why they may be a better fit:

> Many sports clubs require parents to conduct fundraising, become coaches, members of the Board of Directors, and volunteers at competitions because of the potential interest they might have in their child's participation and success...This is not necessarily the best approach to recruiting volunteers. Parents do not have excess time to perform these roles adequately. Those serving on the Board of Directors or coach selection committees are exposed to a conflict of interest...particularly in making decisions that benefit their own children. Recruiting young adults, professionals, and retired people as coaches and Directors is a more appropriate approach. Directors have a fiduciary duty to the organization. Most people are not aware of the implications of this legal requirement, and consequently, poor decisions with disastrous results for the organization are made.

In general, community sport volunteers believed that more is needed to ensure a good fit, suggesting the recruitment can be convoluted,

> Constantly advertise for and train potential volunteers using various methods...Write clear and simple job descriptions with expected time commitment and make the roles simple... Utilize support from other organizations and know which of these can help find new people to fill vacant roles.

This reiterates the complexity and variety of volunteer recruitment approaches in sport organizations (see Schlesinger, Klenk & Nagel, 2015). In this way, understanding the recruitment practice, evaluating and identifying its strengths, potential challenges, and areas for improvement seems crucial.

Preventing resignation

Community sport volunteers believed that resignation could, in some instances, be prevented. To them, the prevention rests on volunteers and the organization, concluding that volunteers could do things that make them happy and successful. Some "recommend that sport volunteers take the time to seriously consider their personal commitments and schedule, as well as the requirements of the position before making the commitment to ensure they have the necessary time". The role compatibility with volunteers' other responsibilities has been linked to the intention to continue (see Giel & Breuer, 2020). Others advised that volunteers be cognizant of motivations, to "keep reminding themselves of why they are choosing to volunteer", remembering "what the sport is doing for the child or the child for the sport". Some suggested that volunteers need to "communicate well at all levels". They recommend to "try to look for sports organizations that can help you fulfill your...idea", to "never burn bridges", and to "leave on a positive note". They also suggest to "be open, flexible and reflective", to "learn from your experience", calling for balance. As one put, "do not take on too many tasks. You will burn out and be of no value to anyone".

Efforts to prevent resignation and subsequently its negative impacts can also be the responsibility of the organization and those in leadership roles, to "focus on building a strong team of volunteers to develop trust and dedication". Volunteers highlighted the need to have adequate assistance, to "train properly", and "financial support...to take on extra training". Organizational support and training practices were found effective in volunteer retention in the past (Cuskelly et al., 2006; see also Walker, Accadia & Costa, 2016). Others believed that "volunteers should have...mentors" and a reasonable workload, "Do not overload or overwhelm the new volunteer with work. Ease them into the position".

Volunteers concluded that organizations should recognize efforts, "...dinners or BBQ with healthy food options...skiers are food motivated ☺". Workload and volunteering conditions such as support can play a role in satisfaction, being important for retention (see Nagel et al., 2020). The importance of a reasonable workload in preventing resignation was suggested but not listed as a reason for resigning. Instead, an overwhelming and stressful workload was the result of resignation, prompting a need to balance equal assignments.

Volunteers may leave for a myriad of reasons and there are times when resignation is unavoidable. Whatever the reason, how resignation is handled seemed important:

> I feel it should be dealt with in a positive way so that both sides grow from the situation. I would see [it] as problem-solving and working together to come up with a solution. Nothing is gained by a person leaving... If the situation isn't dealt with in a reasonable, positive way, negativity spreads like wildfire.

If managed inadequately, conditions can become undesirable, further risking volunteer exodus.

Conclusion

Many aspects of volunteers' environment can contribute to their continuation and resignation, which can pose challenges to using rewards as a volunteer retention tool. Awards can entice achievement (Frey & Gallus, 2018) and keep volunteers (Gallus, 2016; Hager & Brudney, 2008; Walk et al., 2019). Awards can also discourage the non-recipients (see Frey & Gallus, 2017). Interestingly, none of the volunteers in our study expressed recognition as a way to prevent resignation. Our findings revealed that sport volunteers are at odds about recognition and rewards as some refused nominations altogether and others relied on them for self-assessment. While rewards were often appreciated, disappointment was also experienced (e.g. wrong sport on the plaque and lack of partner recognition), suggesting concerns over accuracy and fairness. This underlines the need for organizations having the resources to recognize volunteers to also consider awards' potential impact on recipients and non-recipients and decide accordingly (see also Frey & Gallus, 2017; Gubler, Larkin & Pierce, 2016).

This study included the perceptions of volunteers who have quit in the past. The findings highlight the complexity of resignation as a process filled with difficult decisions. Often, abrupt disruption was experienced as a result of a fellow volunteer's resignation. Otherwise, some were unable to resign because of the lack of support available (e.g. replacement). Most believed that resignation rests on both, the volunteer and the organization. To them, these parties need to consider the motivational factors, time commitment, role fit, support, and being professional. While some of these rest solely with the individual, organizations can focus on providing adequate support, which has been linked to continued volunteering (Cuskelly et al., 2006; Giel & Breuer, 2020; Nagel et al., 2020; Walker et al., 2016). Indeed, at times, the resignation was inevitable (e.g. relocation), indicating the need for a strategy. Lack of organizational support such as protocol can lead to frustrations (see Sheptak & Menaker, 2016). More research into the process, the impact of resignation (e.g. the workload in Wicker & Breuer, 2011), and how to effectively recover from it is needed.

As this chapter is written, COVID-19 continues to affect local communities and nations globally. In Canada, a decrease of 40% in volunteering was noted (Volunteer Canada, 2020). While the chapter's focus was not the pandemic's impact, experiences seem noteworthy as some "had to stop" because "all volunteering opportunities were put on hold", facing challenges, "we had our spring provincial games postponed", and attending modified events, "the awards banquet will happen remotely". There was uncertainty, "I assume they are going to happen". Plans were questioned, "I will likely wait as participants living with disabilities may be more susceptible". Sometimes opportunities emerged, "During the period of social isolation…saw an organization looking for a Social Media Writer". Discussions about alternative volunteering have started (see Lachance, 2020). We plan to explore the continued volunteering amid COVID-19 as volunteers strive to keep "volunteer spirit" and to do "whatever it takes".

References

Alfes, K., & Langner, N. (2017). Paradoxical leadership: Understanding and managing conflicting tensions to foster volunteer engagement. *Organizational Dynamics, 46*(2), 96–103. https://doi.org/10.1016/j.orgdyn.2017.04.005

Bang, H. (2015). Volunteer age, job satisfaction, and intention to stay. *Leadership & Organization Development Journal, 36*(2), 161–176. https://doi.org/10.1108/LODJ-04-2013-0052

Bowden, C., & Galindo-Gonzalez, S. (2015). Interviewing when you're not face-to-face: The use of email interviews in a phenomenological study. *International Journal of Doctoral Studies, 10*, 79–92. http://ijds.org/Volume10/IJDSv10p079-092Bowden0684.pdf

Braun, V., & Clarke, V. (2006). Using thematic analysis in psychology. *Qualitative Research in Psychology, 3*, 77–101. https://doi.org/10.1191/1478088706qp063oa

Cnaan, R. A., Handy, F., & Wadsworth, M. (1996). Defining who is a volunteer: Conceptual and empirical considerations. *Nonprofit and Voluntary Sector Quarterly, 25*(3), 364–383. https://doi.org/10.1177/0899764096253006

Cuskelly, G., & Hoye, R. (2013). Sports officials' intention to continue. *Sport Management Review, 16*, 451–464. https://doi.org/10.1016/j.smr.2013.01.003

Cuskelly, G., Taylor, T., Hoye, R., & Darcy, S. (2006). Volunteer management practices and volunteer retention: A human resource management approach. *Sport Management Review, 9*, 141–163. https://doi.org/10.1016/S1441-3523(06)70023-7

Doherty, A. (2005). *Volunteer management in community sport clubs: A study of volunteers' perception.* Parks and Recreation Ontario and the Sport Alliance of Ontario.

Dwiggins-Beeler, R., Spitzberg, B., & Roesch, S. (2011). Vectors of volunteerism: Correlates of volunteer retention, recruitment, and job satisfaction. *Journal of Psychological Issues in Organizational Culture, 2*(3), 22–43. https://doi.org/10.1002/jpoc.20074

Farrell, J. M., Johnston, M. E., & Twynam, G. D. (1998). Volunteer motivation, satisfaction, and management at an elite sporting competition. *Journal of Sport Management, 12*, 288–300. https://doi.org/10.1123/jsm.12.4.288

Frey, B. S., & Gallus, J. (2017). Towards an economics of awards. *Journal of Economic Surveys, 31*(1), 190–200. https://doi.org/10.1111/joes.12127

Frey, B. S., & Gallus, J. (2018). Volunteer organizations: Motivating with awards. In R. Ranyard (Ed.), *Economic psychology* (pp. 273–286). Wiley.

Fritz, R. L., & Vandermause, R. (2017). Data collection via in-depth email interviewing: Lessons from the field. *Qualitative Health Research, 28*(10), 1640–1649. https://doi.org/10.1177/1049732316689067

Gallus, J. (2016). Fostering public good contributions with symbolic awards: A large-scale natural field experiment at Wikipedia. *Management Science, 63*(12), 3999–4015. https://doi.org/10.1111/joes.12127

Gibson, L. (2010). Realities toolkit: Using email interviews. *ERSC National Center for Research Methods*, 1–7. http://eprints.ncrm.ac.uk/1303/1/09-toolkitemail-interviews.pdf

Giel, T., & Breuer, C. (2020). The determinants of the intention to continue voluntary football refereeing. *Sport Management Review, 23*(2), 242–255. https://doi.org/10.1016/j.smr.2019.01.005

Green, B. C., & Chalip, L. (2004). Paths to volunteer commitment: Lessons from the Sydney Olympic Games. In R. A. Stebbins & M. Graham (Eds.), *Volunteering as leisure/leisure as volunteering: An international assessment* (pp. 49–68). CAB International.

Gubler, T., Larkin, I., & Pierce, L. (2016). Motivational spillovers from awards: Crowding out in a multitasking environment. *Organization Science, 27*(2), 286–303. https://doi.org/10.1287/orsc.2016.1047

Hager, M., & Brudney, J. (2008). Management capacity and retention of volunteers. In M. Liao-Troth (Ed.), *Challenges in volunteer management* (pp. 9–27). Information Age Publishing.

Henderson, A. C., & Sowa, J. E. (2018). Retaining critical human capital: Volunteer firefighters in the commonwealth of Pennsylvania. *Voluntas: International Journal of Voluntary and Nonprofit Organizations, 29*(1), 43–58. https://doi.org/10.1007/s11266-017-9831-7

Hoye, R., Cuskelly, G., Taylor, T., & Darcy, S. (2008). Volunteer motives and retention in community sport: A study of Australian rugby clubs. *Australian Journal on Volunteering, 13*(2), 40–48. https://doi.org//10.3316/IELAPA.5867646189150

Johnson, J. E., Giannoulakis C., Felver N., Judge, L. W., Piece, D. A., & Scott, B. F. (2017). Motivation, satisfaction, and retention of sport management student volunteers. *Journal of Applied Sport Management, 9*(1), 1–27. https://doi.org/10.18666/JASM-2017-V9-I1-7450

Kim, M., Chelladurai, P., & Trail, G. T. (2007). A model of volunteer retention in youth sport. *Journal of Sport Management, 21*(2), 151–171. https://doi.org/10.1123/jsm.21.2.151

Lachance, E. L. (2020). COVID-19 and its impact on volunteering: Moving towards virtual volunteering. *Leisure Sciences*, 1–7. https://doi.org/10.1080/01490400.2020.1773990

Livingston, L. A., & Forbes, S. L. (2016). Factors contributing to the retention of Canadian amateur sport officials: Motivations, perceived organizational support, and resilience. *International Journal of Sports Science & Coaching, 11*(3), 342–355. https://doi.org/10.1177/1747954116644061

Mason, D. M., & Ide, B. (2014). Adapting qualitative research strategies to technology savvy adolescents. *Nurse Researcher, 21*(5), 40–45. https://doi.org/10.7748/nr.21.5.40.e1241

Nagel, S., Seippel, Ø., Breuer, C., Feiler, S., Elmose-Østerlund, K., Llopis-Goig, R., Nichols, G., Perényi, S., Piątkowska, M., & Scheerder, J. (2020). Volunteer satisfaction in sports clubs: A multilevel analysis in 10 European countries. *International Review of Sociology of Sport, 55*(8), 1074–1093. https://doi.org/10.1177/1012690219880419

Newton, C., Becker, K., & Bell, S. (2014). Learning and development opportunities as a tool for the retention of volunteers: A motivational perspective. *Human Resource Management Journal, 24*(4), 514–530. https://doi.org/10.1111/1748-8583.12040

Nichols, G. (2017). *Volunteering in community sports associations: A literature review.* Brill.

Pearce, J. L. (1983). Job attitude and motivation differences between volunteers and employees from comparable organizations. *Journal of Applied Psychology, 68*(4), 646–652. https://doi.org/10.1037/0021-9010.68.4.646

Schlesinger, T., Egli, B., & Nagel, S. (2013). 'Continue or terminate?' Determinants of long-term volunteering in sports clubs. *European Sport Management Quarterly, 13*(1), 32–53. https://doi.org/10.1080/16184742.2012.744766

Schlesinger, T., Egli, B., & Nagel, S. (2019). Determinants of stable volunteering in Swiss soccer clubs. *Soccer & Society, 20*(3), 543–559. https://doi.org/10.1080/14660970.2017.1355789

Schlesinger, T., Klenk, C., & Nagel, S. (2015). How do sport clubs recruit volunteers? Analyzing and developing a typology of decision-making processes on recruiting volunteers in sport clubs. *Sport Management Review, 18*, 193–206. https://doi.org/10.1016/j.smr.2014.04.003

Sharpe, E. K. (2006) Resources at the grassroots of recreation: Organizational capacity and quality of experience in a community sport organization. *Leisure Sciences, 28*(4), 385–401. https://doi.org/10.1080/01490400600745894

Sheptak, R. D., & Menaker, B. E. (2016). The frustration factor: Volunteer perspectives of frustration in a sport setting. *Voluntas: International Journal of Voluntary and Nonprofit Organizations, 27*(2), 831–852. https://doi.org/10.1007/s11266-015-9635-6

Smith, S. L., & Grove, C. J. (2017). Bittersweet and paradoxical: Disaster response volunteering with the American red Cross. *Non-profit Management and Leadership, 27*(3), 353–369.

Spallanzani, C. (1988). A profile of junior level hockey coaches and their motives for involvement and resignation. *Canadian Journal of Applied Sport Sciences, 13*(2), 157–165.

Statistics Canada (2020). *Study: Volunteering in Canada: Challenges and opportunities during the COVID-19 pandemic.* https://www150.statcan.gc.ca/n1/daily-quotidien/200626/dq200626c-eng.htm

Synnot, A., Hill, S., Summers, M., & Taylor, M. (2014). Comparing face-to-face and online qualitative research with people with multiple sclerosis. *Qualitative Health Research, 24*(3), 431–438. https://doi.org/10.1177/1049732314523840

Volunteer Canada (2020). *The volunteering lens of COVID-19: Data highlights.* https://volunteer.ca/index.php?MenuItemID=364

Walk, M., Zhang, R., & Littlepage, L. (2019). "Don't you want to stay? The impact of training and recognition as human resource practices on volunteer turnover. *Nonprofit Management and Leadership, 29*, 509–527. https://doi.org/10.1002/nml.21344

Walker, A., Accadia, R., & Costa, B. M. (2016). Volunteer retention: The importance of organisational support and psychological contract breach. *Journal of Community Psychology, 44*(8), 1059–1069. https://doi.org/10.1002/jcop.21827

Welty Peachey, J., Lyras, A., Cohen, A., et al. (2014). Exploring the motives and retention factors of sport-for-development volunteers. *Nonprofit and Voluntary Sector Quarterly, 43*(6), 1052–169. https://doi.org/10.1177/0899764013501579

Wicker, P. (2017). Volunteerism and volunteer management in sport. *Sport Management Review, 20*(4), 325–337. https://doi.org/10.1016/j.smr.2017.01.001

Wicker, P., & Breuer, C. (2011). Scarcity of resources in German non-profit sport clubs. *Sport Management Review, 14*, 188–201. https://doi.org/10.1016/j.smr.2010.09.001

24

THE ROLE OF ORGANISATIONAL CULTURE IN SUSTAINING VOLUNTEERS IN HERITAGE ATTRACTIONS

The case of Puffing Billy Railway

Josephine Pryce

Introduction

While research on volunteers is extensive, work presenting a holistic view of the influence of management practices on volunteers is slowly emerging. Specifically, the contribution of the role played by organisational culture (OC) in sustaining volunteers is scant. This project addresses this paucity by drawing on participant observation, interviews, and archival materials in seeking to identify and understand the dimensions of OC that impact on volunteers in heritage attractions. It aims to highlight the importance of these organisational factors in sustaining a viable volunteer workforce for such enterprises. It also acknowledges that work and/or occupation is important as a source of identity, meaning, and social affiliation (Ashforth & Mael, 1989; Kenyon, Thurston & Sweet, 2017; Pryce, 2013).

As visitation to industrial heritage attractions is gaining momentum and interest, heritage railway attractions have assumed a significant place in this arena (Conlin & Bird, 2014). Subsequently, staffing of these operations has in some cases drawn attention to the sustainability of volunteer workforces (Holmes & Smith, 2009). The case of Puffing Billy Railway (PBR) in the Dandenong Ranges of Victoria in Australia affords a unique opportunity to address the issue of sustainability of volunteer workforces and lend insight into how engaging people in volunteer work can add meaning and purpose to people's lives while assist in achieving organisational goals. This chapter captures PBR's OC to highlight the organisational values, commitment, and challenges in attracting, engaging, and maintaining volunteers at heritage attractions. In so doing, it adds to the understanding of the value of volunteers in the development and maintenance of a sustainable workforce in the leisure industry.

Puffing Billy Railway

PBR is an iconic Australian railway heritage attraction. It is one of Australia's most recognised travel experiences, much loved by both locals and visitors. Equally, it is internationally recognised as "one of the largest narrow-gauge steam and heritage railways in the

DOI: 10.4324/9780367815875-28

world" (ETRB, 2019). PBR began operation in 1900 with operations controlled by Victorian Railways (PBR, 2019). By its 50th anniversary, continued financial losses at PBR forced the Victorian Government to rethink the enterprise and a landslide in 1953 forced the line's closure. In June 1955, the Puffing Billy Preservation Society (PBPS) was formed to provide financial assurance against losses to Victorian Railways and to provide the workforce needed for operation of PBR. As part of PBPS's remit, volunteers became active as 'safety officers' and in undertaking fundraising and promotional work, with some volunteers working under the supervision of Victorian Railways to assist with the physical work of track reconstruction.

On 1 October 1977, Victorian Railways surrendered ownership and operation of PBR to the Emerald Tourist Railway Board (ETRB), which became responsible for "preservation, development, promotion, and maintenance of the historical narrow-gauge steam railway [known as Puffing Billy]" (Victorian Government, 2019, p. 2). ETRB remains interconnected with the PBPS in assuming responsibility of overseeing the overall management of PBR and its corporate governance. In July 1992, PBR reopened as a not-for-profit visitor attraction and in that year welcomed 108,841 visitors (ETRB, 2016). Annual patronage has steadily increased, with visitor numbers recorded at 417,155 for 2016 (ETRB, 2016). Parallel to visitor growth, volunteer numbers at PBR have consistently been substantial, with 81.5% (441) of the workforce in 2019 being volunteers (ETRB, 2020). ETRB's 2019 Annual Report stated that:

> [v]olunteers are involved in every aspect – administrative support, special events, driving the trains, restoring the heritage carriages, maintaining buildings and infrastructure along the Railway and selling the Railway's commercial retail offering at smaller stations to patrons. Without these key people, the Railway would not function. The value of Volunteer Contribution over the last Financial was estimated at over $6.5m.
>
> *(p. 17)*

ETRB's 2016 Annual Report specifically acknowledged the contribution made by volunteers during what was "an exceptionally lengthy fire season" (p. 1). However, by 2016, there was growing recognition that PBR's extraordinary growth was creating various issues and constraints and a Strategic Master Plan was designed and advanced by ETRB. Financial support was promised by a Federal Government Grant ($5.5 million) and funds from the Victorian State Government ($8.2 million) to assist with major projects, such as a Discovery Centre (ETRB, 2018). Subsequent critical events impacted unduly on PBR: (1) the Victorian Ombudsman's Report into activities of a convicted child sex offender who was associated with PBR (Victorian Government, 2018); (2) associated resignation of the Board and CEO in June 2018; (3) appointment of new members to ETRB, committed to reviewing and restoring the OC at PBR; (4) a level crossing accident where the long-term practice of 'dangling legs' on the sides of carriages was suspended; (5) severe weather conditions and total fire bans in summer 2019–2020; and (6) COVID-19.

The 2017–2018 Annual Report talks of 2018 as being 'The Year of Transition', and refers to the change of leadership and governance at PBR, and mentions a new focus on 'openness' across all levels of the organisation, for example, in relationships between Board/Management and PBPS, staff, and volunteers. The research presented here draws on various sources of data to highlight the ways in which PBR have tried to transform their OC to regain integrity and rebuild trust, both internally and externally to the organisation.

When I visited PBR in 2016, I was surprised to learn that 92% of the workforce (just over 900 people) were volunteers and that there were 22 volunteer positions, covering various roles, including administrative, conductors, train drivers, organising special events, restoration of heritage carriages, retail, and maintenance of buildings, infrastructure, and railway corridor lines. Of the paid staff, almost 90% also volunteered. This focus on volunteering by many of the people involved with PBR shows the way in which volunteering is woven into the fabric of the organisation and is evident through one person's comment, "volunteers are so much a part of the ethos of this railway". Similarly, ETRB Annual Reports acknowledge the importance of volunteers to the sustainable operations of PBR. This was evident in the 2020 Chairman's Report, "Our dedicated and passionate volunteers continue to support the operations for the Railway, the work they perform is invaluable" (ETRB, 2020, p. 11). Data from the 2016 Volunteer Satisfaction Survey (VSS) – mentioned in detail below – showed that tenure of volunteers was long-term, with just under 40% of volunteers having been at PBR for less than five years; 17% had been there for 30 plus years, 11% for 15–19 years, and 11% for 8–10 years. ETRB's Annual Report (2020, p. 34) presented workforce data which showed that, as of 30 June, for 2019 and 2020, 441 (81.5%) and 479 (86.5%), respectively, of workers were volunteers. Hence, PBR continues to sustain a high percentage of volunteers as its workforce. This predominance of volunteers in the organisation provides a unique situation for exploring the nature of OC.

Journeying with volunteers

This chapter focuses on my keen interest in PBR and draws in part on field work during an extended and memorable visit to PBR. The visit began on 31 August 2016, when I arrived at PBR to commence a five-day stay at the heritage railway complex in Belgrave, Victoria. During this time, I was permitted by management to venture through areas of the complex, particularly in Belgrave but also at other points along the Puffing Billy route. For the first two days, I was guided through the complex by a long-term volunteer. The first day was spent in the Belgrave station area but on the second day, the assigned volunteer and I travelled the PBR journey from Belgrave to Gembrook (see Figure 24.1), stopping at different points to meet other volunteers stationed in those areas. Following this introduction to the front- and back-of-house operations, I was left to explore the happenings at PBR, predominantly from the front-of-house perspective. I utilised one day to take the PBR journey as an independent traveller, having done so many times before but this time with a more targeted purpose, i.e., through the eyes of a researcher and participant observer.

Through various ethnographic interactions, this visit allowed me to gain deep insights into the OC of PBR, and has been the inspiration and foundation for this chapter. The chapter continues with an overview of the literature relating to volunteers, with consideration to those in heritage railway attractions. This section is followed by a synopsis of OC, focusing on research to date that explores the nexus between OC and volunteerism. The chapter then moves on to the methodology, findings, and discussion, before ending with conclusions from this current research.

Volunteers in railway heritage attractions

The role that volunteers play in visitor attractions and more specifically, heritage attractions has witnessed a growing interest in academic literature in the last two decades. Of particular interest here, is growing recognition of the key role that volunteers play in sustaining operations for heritage railway attractions. Prominent in the literature in this space, is the work of Rhoden, Ineson and Ralston (2009), Bhati, Pryce and Chaiechi (2014), and Carnicelli, Drummond and Anderson (2020), but we begin with the seminal work of Holmes (2003).

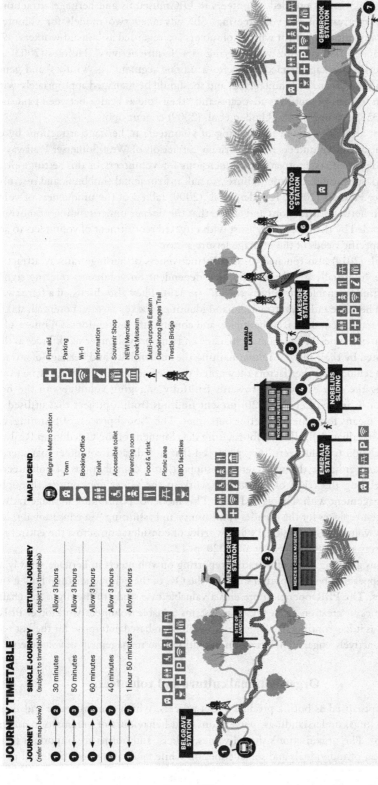

Figure 24.1   The Puffing Billy Railway journey from Belgrave to Gembrook

Holmes' (2003) study profiled volunteers in UK museums and heritage attractions, exploring their motivations for volunteering. She advanced two models for volunteering: (1) the economic model, within which volunteers are regarded as 'unpaid workers'; (2) and, the leisure model, that captures volunteering as a 'leisure activity'. Holmes (2003) argued that volunteers in heritage attractions were "a unique segment" of 'visitors' and generally, distinct from other forms of volunteering, and so, should be managed appropriately with due consideration to their potential as advocates and "their role as bridge between paid staff and visitors" (p. 355), a point which Rhoden et al. (2009) concur upon.

Rhoden et al. (2009) added to profiling of volunteers in heritage attractions by examining motivations of volunteers in the heritage attraction of West Somerset Railway in the UK. They identified six motivational dimensions for volunteers in this setting: altruistic, egoistic (work substitute), egoistic (leisure), social, instrumental (hobbies), and instrumental (skills). As per Holmes (2003), Rhoden et al. (2009) talked of the uniqueness of volunteer workforces in heritage attractions and added that the deeper understanding of motivational factors as afforded by their study can assist with targeted recruitment of volunteers to accommodate the specific needs of the heritage leisure sector.

Bhati et al. (2014) also touched on the distinctiveness of heritage railway attractions in that they are "unusually ... likely to be very dependent on volunteers offering significant amounts of time to enable the railway to run" (p. 119). They also discussed a framework for evaluation of heritage railways attractions and identified six key factors: potential, stakeholders, adaptive reuse, economics, authenticity, and community perceptions. Of interest here, is their mention of the need to adequately manage and support volunteer workforces as they are often motivated by their interest in maintaining the authenticity and heritage of attractions, which can preclude the other factors they noted that define heritage railway attractions.

Advancing the idea of working towards fruitfully engaging volunteers in the heritage railway sector, Carnicelli et al. (2020) present findings from a project that utilised action research as a means for achieving better outcomes. The "spiral process of planning, acting, observing (or evaluating)" allowed for revising development of the Caledonian Railway activities. In relation to volunteers, they proposed that 'a dedicated volunteer manager' could consolidate and enhance the management, support, and contributions of volunteers, and possibly extending the reach of volunteers' work to the wider community through such things as engagement with schools and fairs. This model of positioning heritage railway attractions as centrepieces for the broader community and assuming "an educational role ... to seek out new volunteers" is visionary and worthy of consideration across the entirety of the heritage railway sector (Carnicelli et al., 2020, p. 12).

Despite this growing body of literature reporting on volunteers in heritage railway attractions, there appears to be no reported study on the OC of these attractions and how it impacts on volunteers. The PBR operation presents a valuable case study to highlight the challenges and possibilities in creation of an OC that sustains a viable volunteer workforce. PBR is of interest here as it has continued to operate as a volunteer-based enterprise for the last 65 years (1955–2020), actively engaged in attraction, retention, and management of volunteers.

Organisational culture and volunteers

OC is conceptualised as both a product and a process, which can influence and shape the thoughts, feelings, understandings, perceptions, and behaviours of organisational members (Evans, 1996). The organisation's shared values, beliefs, and norms are important to fostering motivation of individuals and social cohesion while facilitating organisational processes and practices (Flint, 2000). Seminal authors in the study of OC, conceptualise culture as consisting of multiple layers, where values and 'basic underlying assumptions' are not visible but are at the core of OC; and aspects such as rituals, stories, routines, heroes, and symbols evidence tangible aspects of OC (for example, Hofstede, 2001; Schein, 1985). Johnson (1992) describes the core of OC as 'the paradigm' with "a set of core beliefs and assumptions which are specific and relevant to the organization" (p. 29). He explains that individuals have their own personal values and beliefs of their world, including their organisational environment. Equally, organisations are driven by 'a web' of assumptions that enable them to exist and to function. It is within this web that workers become entrained and that organisational life thrives. Hence, Johnson (2000) maintains that culture is the underlying paradigm that drives peoples' thoughts, feelings, perceptions, and behaviours.

The elements of culture that are invisible make it difficult to study culture directly and so, it is studied through inferences. The three levels of culture presented by Schein (1985) provide a framework for studying the inferences: artefacts and creations, espoused values, and basic assumptions. The 'artefacts and creations' level is the most observed because of its visible and tangible elements, such as visible behaviour, policies, rituals, customs, language, technology, and uniform (style of dress).

The literature presents some consensus on what are the main elements and layers that constitute OC, and these are often referred to as 'the dimensions of OC'. However, there is variation in the literature on how these dimensions are brought together. In her study on hospitality workers, Pryce (2004) built on the work of previous scholars to identify dimensions that define OC. In particular, she utilised the framework presented by Maull, Brown and Cliffe (2001) that identified four broad factors, which are here referred to as: organisational culture core, personal outcomes, customer orientation/context, and organisational structures and processes (Table 24.1). Pryce (2004) adapted the work of Maull et al. (2001) and other OC scholars to present 12 dimensions that aligned with the four factors. This framework is further adapted for this study to accommodate the literature exploring OC and volunteers, resulting in 18 dimensions.

The literature on OC is extensive and continues to grow. The emerging number of reviews (systematic reviews, scoping reviews, and meta-analyses) are indicative of the body of established literature on the nature of OC. By contrast, a review of the literature on the nexus between OC and volunteers highlights a paucity of research in this space. Dwiggins-Beeler, Spitzberg and Roesch (2012) point out that understanding the impact of organisational factors on volunteers needs further investigation. A search of the literature found some articles that relate to research that examines the importance of OC in relation to volunteers, but none could be found in the context of heritage railway attractions. Examples of these articles include two that were conceptual (Ciucescu, 2012; Smith, 2011) and others that discussed OC in relation to volunteers in the context of social workers (Caduri & Weiss-Gal, 2015), non-profit service organisations (Dwiggins-Beeler et al., 2012), university students (Friedman, 2015), hospital settings (Jordan, 2009), sport (Kenyon et al., 2017), and corporate volunteering (Nueangjamnong & Sthapitanonda, 2019).

This previous research presents valuable insights into the notion of OC and highlights its impact on volunteers. It showcases dimensions of OC that need to be considered and inform evaluations of OC at PBR. These articles were reviewed and analysed to identify the dimensions of OC that were relevant to volunteers and so, assisted in adapting the work of Pryce (2004) to suit this research (Table 24.1).

Of the articles found, Smith (2011) presents a comprehensive overview of OC and its history. Her paper focused on employee and volunteer commitment and sought to understand

Table 24.1 Dimensions of organisational culture as used in this study

Factors	Dimensions
Organisational culture core	1. Values, Organisational philosophies,
	2. Rituals, The Social Club, Group membership, Socialisation/Orientation
	3. Heroes, Owner-Heroes, Leaders
	4. Symbols, Artefacts (e.g. uniform, décor, amenities, parking)
	5. Behaviours
	6. Values-Congruence, Person-Organisation-Fit
Personal Outcomes	7. Work / Job Satisfaction – Importance of job, role ambiguity, role identity, promotional opportunities, job variety, empowerment, motivation, professional development, stress, well-being
	8. Team Spirit, Workgroup conflict, Relationships, Silos, Organisational Politics
	9. Getting-job-done, Training, experience, problem-solving, resources, skills, performance management
	10. Commitment – loyalty, acceptance or organisational values, work effort
	11. 'Being valued', Recognition, Reward, Being equal
Customer Orientation / Context	12. Service delivery to internal and external customers; Heritage/Authenticity
Organisational Structures & Processes	13. Communications, Grapevine, Stories
	14. Power Structure, Leadership Structure & Politics
	15. Processes, Safety
	16. Planning, Decision-making, Strategies, Governance
	17. Organisational support
	18. Effectiveness, Efficiencies, & Change

Source: Adapted from Pryce (2004, pp. 187–188, Table 5.6).

how OC could be 'shaped' to engender long-term commitment. Smith (2011) argues that while organisations are dynamic and constantly evolving and responding to external factors, they inevitably rely on the commitment of their workers to sustain effective and successful performance. Such viability means that managers need to build and nurture an OC that supports and maintains workers' commitment. Smith's work suggests that commitment is an important dimension for OC. This perspective is consistent with the organisational behaviour literature, where commitment is considered to parallel job satisfaction as an employee attitude relating to work (for example, Bartol, 1979; Robbins & Judge, 2017).

Beyond Smith's (2011) focus on commitment, Dwiggins-Beeler et al. (2012) examined structural dimensions in organisations that impact on 'job satisfaction' of volunteers. Dwiggins-Beeler et al. (2012) argue that when volunteers evaluate their overall satisfaction with an organisation, they most probably consider factors that motivate them, assessing these factors against the organisational environment. As an example, they point out a key finding from their research that showed volunteer's motivation aligned with the organisation's communication aspects.

Dwiggins-Beeler et al. (2012) also touch on evidence of the importance to volunteers of 'being valued'. Jordan (2009) also picks up on the term 'valued' and its importance to volunteers. In a study that explores volunteers in hospitals by focusing on socialisation, person-organisation fit, organisational commitment, and job satisfaction, Jordan (2009) addresses these elements as "valued organization and individual outcomes" (p. 67). Her research extended over six different Western Kentucky Hospitals. She found that these outcomes were possible where socialisation experiences for new volunteers were engineered.

Ciucescu (2012) parallels Jordan's (2009) focus on socialisation and highlights the importance of orientation of volunteers as a first step in integrating volunteers into organisations. She contends that through orientation, volunteers are trained to learn about the organisation, its operational activities, standards, procedures, and values. Ongoing training, including a staged formal program, can work toward minimising problems. An important aspect of the process is that volunteers determine the compatibility of the OC with their own individual 'culture' (Ciucescu, 2012) because ultimately, it is the enmeshing and acceptance of values between organisation and volunteers that determines the success of volunteerism for both parties.

Similarly, Caduri and Weiss–Gal (2015) found that the key factor in successful engagement of volunteers was to develop an OC that is supportive of working with volunteers. Other notable findings from Caduri and Weiss-Gal's (2015) work was that paid social workers thought the following: that volunteers make important contributions; volunteering should not be valued any less than salaried work; and, that most had volunteering experience themselves. From these studies, it would seem that 'recognition and reward' should be positive aspects of OC that can engender 'being valued'.

Friedman's (2015) research supports this contention. She investigated the impact of recognition on volunteers and more particularly, on their intention to volunteer in the future. Her findings suggest that recognition is important, but it needs to be administered purposefully and in a timely manner. She also found that positive feedback can contribute to strengthening the commitment of volunteers and cautions that negative feedback should be reserved for experienced and longer tenured volunteers, who have already established their commitment to the organisation. The key ultimately is that recognition, either positive or negative, can improve intentions to volunteer but it does need to be tailored to the characteristics of the individual or dynamics of the group.

A further point to consider is that the nature of the organisation can impact on formation of its OC. To illustrate, Kenyon et al. (2017) found that the sport of sailing defined the OC of the club. Similarly, Pryce (2009) found that the OC of hotels was determined by the hospitality occupational culture of the hospitality industry. In a similar vein, the idea of corporate volunteering is a phenomenon that reflects an organisation's culture where both "commercial and social benefits" are pursued (Nueangjamnong & Sthapitanonda, 2019). Corporate volunteering has been found to tap into individuals' altruism and strengthens their intrinsic motivation. It also influences employees' engagement with work and commitment to an organisation that supports corporate volunteering and highlights the importance of the congruence of values between volunteers and the organisation (Nueangjamnong & Sthapitanonda, 2019).

Smith (2011) referred to 'value congruence' and emphasised the importance of 'on-boarding' or 'acculturation' of employees into the organisation's culture. She sums up the process of organisational enculturation by saying that "The order in which one would typically progress … would be from the physical to the intellectual; from the intellectual to the emotional; and, finally, to the deepest level of enculturation, the spiritual level" (p. 90). She makes note of the work of Edgar Schein who emphasised that the stable elements of OC are "learning, adaptation, innovation, and perpetual change" and that OC and leadership "are two sides of the same coin" (Smith, 2011, p. 90). It is incumbent on managers and leaders to understand OC and its influence and power. Equally, it is the responsibility of the organisation's leadership to develop and maintain a positive, thriving, and efficacious culture; to moderate and adjust the OC as is needed; and to effect transformational change if required.

The story of PBR is one such case where in recent years transformational change of its OC is being sought. The impact on staff and volunteers is still evolving but this chapter presents some insights into the various layers of OC at PBR.

Methodological approach

A triangulation of approaches has enabled collection of data that contributed to building a profile of PBR's OC, especially as it relates to the volunteer workforce. This process involved collecting data in two ways: (1) by being in the field, and (2) from archival material. Initial data collection was through fieldwork, which began during initial visits in 2012 to PBR as observations that were framed by my own experiences as a visitor to PBR and as a researcher. A period of intense immersion at PBR occurred in September 2016, which allowed for a week-long engagement with volunteers and staff during which further observations were enhanced by listening to volunteers' stories through conversational interviews. Observations were captured through photos and written and digital fieldnotes.

Archival documents consisted of data from: (1) a '2016 Volunteers' Satisfaction Survey (VSS)', which was administered online by PBR as a SurveyMonkey questionnaire and returned 239 valid responses; and (2) a 2018 Consultancy Document from a facilitator external to PBR who conducted conversational interviews with staff and volunteers to examine the OC of PBR. Both these documents contained raw data from open-ended questions, which was analysed in NVivo 12 (Version 12.6). These archival documents and associated data, and its analysis, presented valuable insights into the OC of PBR. This data was supplemented by ETRB Annual Reports from 2016 to 2020, inclusive. All the data was collated and examined and analysed both manually and in NVivo. The qualitative analysis of the data was inductive to determine the story emerging about the OC at PBR from the data, but as part of an iterative process, backwards and forwards between data and themes, it sought to find themes that were relevant to OC and its related dimensions, especially those noted in Table 24.1.

Organisational culture and volunteerism at Puffing Billy Railway

A first glance into the OC at PBR

While in the field at PBR, it was evident that volunteers enjoyed their work. One mentioned that, "the really nice thing about being here is because we want to be here". Another added, "we just love being here" and from my fieldnotes, one observation that I made details that, "the train crew seems to be very hard working, very devoted, conscientious but quite friendly and cheerful. It is like they really want to be here". This last comment highlights that volunteers were passionate about their work and welcomed opportunities to be part of the PBR organisation. My fieldnotes add to this cameo of the 'way things are' at PBR by the observation that, "It seems that the volunteers are inspired, motivated, and energised by the knowledge and understanding that they are in some way contributing to the preservation of this living cultural heritage". Everyone seemed to take their role seriously, combining an attention to service with an awareness to safety. These comments build a picture of PBR's OC and suggest that the culture at PBR is multifaceted and complex and that it is the motivating influence at the heart of PBR.

Thematic analysis of the 2016 VSS qualitative data highlighted that volunteers 'enjoyed' working for PBR for a myriad of reasons, including opportunities to interact with 'people' and their love of 'trains', and that they drew 'satisfaction' from their 'experiences' at PBR.

However, further analysis of the 2016 VSS showed that there were also areas of concern. Similarly, thematic analysis of the qualitative data from the 2018 Consultancy Document also emphasised 'the clear passion', 'genuine care', and 'commitment' that volunteers have to PBR but more importantly, it revealed an organisation in trouble, with workers' discontent at breaking point and with staff choosing to leave the organisation 'to preserve their health and well-being', despite their 'love of Puffing Billy', as some said. Interestingly, observations from the field painted a much rosier picture of these issues than highlighted by the 2016 VSS. The impression was of "enlightened management that engages volunteers and cares for them", as my fieldnotes read. Reflecting on the data beyond the fieldwork, it seems that the 'spirit of volunteering' was evident at PBR but equally, there was a growing unrest that permeated the fabric of PBR. Triangulation of data (from the field, the 2016 VSS, and the 2018 Consultancy Document) revealed the depth of discontent.

Delving deeper

As part of the 2016 VSS, volunteers were asked to comment on two key open-ended questions: (1) 'What is the single most important issue that needs to be addressed', for which 59 responses were documented; and (2) 'What can PBR improve upon', for which 199 responses were returned. These 258 responses were initially analysed inductively, as was the 2018 Consultancy Document data. As sub-themes emerged from the various sources of data, the analysis was iterative in that data from the various sources was revisited repeatedly to search for emerging broad themes and ultimately, sub-themes were collated where possible, into themes that aligned with the dimensions of OC from the adapted Pryce (2004) framework above. The resultant main themes were (Table 24.2): Getting-job-done,

Table 24.2 Themes from the analysis of the raw secondary data from 2016 VSS and 2018 Consultancy Document

Dimension (Factor)	Main specific element of dimension	Number of responses
Getting-job-done (Personal Outcomes = PO)	Training (29), Resources (31), Performance Management (11), Other (7)	78
Planning & Decision-making (Organisational Structures & Processes = OSP)	Planning (26), Decision-making (3), Consultation (10), Direction (8), Strategy (4)	43
Communication (OSP)	Grapevine (1) and Honesty (1)	39
Being Valued(PO)	Equity (9), Recognition (6), Rewards (5), Respect (4)	35
Working Conditions (Organisational Core Culture)	Amenities (13)	27
Leadership Structure (OSP)	Lack of leadership (14), Senior Managers (7)	25
Processes (OSP)	Safety (19)	23
Relationships (PO)	Relationships between volunteers and management/paid staff (9), Silos (4), conflict/tensions (3)	18
Professional Development (PO)	Opportunities (13)	13
Heritage/Authenticity (Context)		10
Change/Effectiveness (OSP)		10

Planning & Decision-making, Communication, Being Valued, Working conditions Leadership Structures, Processes, Relationships, Professional Development, Change/Effectiveness, and Heritage/Authenticity.

Adding to the story of OC at PBR

The results show that organisations that engage with volunteers need to be mindful that their OC supports the work of volunteers, alongside that of paid staff. This finding is consistent with the work of previous researchers who have examined volunteers (for example, Holmes, 2003) and OC in relation to volunteers (for example, Caduri & Weiss-Gal, 2015). Each previous study added to the understanding of OC and its impact on volunteers. This study has extended that knowledge by seeking to capture a holistic, multi-dimensional view of OC. To add to the discussion, some of the main elements of the dimensions are discussed further in the next section and supported with comments from the 2016 VSS.

Planning & leadership

Planning and leadership go hand-in-hand and the results show how the two are intertwined. Volunteers highlighted "lack of and distrust of leadership", "lack of clarity on the direction of the organisation", and "increasing disconnection between management and volunteers". They noted that leaders were "promoting a culture of avoidance", "playing politics", and had a "lack of understanding and awareness of issues". Jordan (2009) talked of 'management responsiveness' as being integral to volunteers' commitment to an organisation. Equally, Cohen-Callow (2008) emphasised the need to prepare managers on all aspects of managing and leading volunteers. She also highlighted the imperative for managers to create organisational environments that are welcoming, inclusive, supportive, and valuing of volunteers. Some of these points are evident in comments from participants. As one volunteer said, "We need clearer and more defined direction from senior management". Another added, "There is no business plan or strategic plan, little or no transparent frank communication, no strong governance or direction – all which needs to come from strong leadership". Yet another volunteer noted, "Most management have very little or poor people skills with an aversion to being truthful and facing problems with a bit of backbone and consistency". These comments highlight the need to build capacity and capability in management so that managers are well equipped to model appropriate behaviours, build trust, and deal with issues. They emphasise the need for governance that incorporates awareness and understanding of all workers, paid staff, and volunteers.

In 1987, Allen maintained that "volunteer-staffed programs have implications for their planning, administration, and especially, evaluation" (p. 261). As was the case then, today it is equally imperative that in order to retain volunteers, organisations need to plan, implement, monitor, and assess their OC to build and foster positive and strong volunteering cultures. As a way forward, there are lessons to be learnt from the work of Carnicelli et al. (2020) and their progressive thinking for heritage railway attractions to plan and act for the present volunteer workforce and provide opportunities "to gain a sense of achievement, feel valued, and engage with a community" (p.12) and, with the future in mind, especially in terms of succession of volunteers and reaching out to schools to recruit prospective volunteers.

Communication

One of the most frequently mentioned dimensions was communication. In both the 2016 and 2018 surveys, volunteers talked of the 'lack of feedback to volunteers', 'lack of transparent communication and shared information', 'channels for dissemination of information to volunteers lacking', and 'not listening to volunteers'. The findings are consistent with the work of Dwiggins-Beer et al. (2012) who identified that communication context and content is important to volunteers' motivation and job satisfaction. She found that communication was pivotal to multiple dimensions of OC. Hence, it is not surprising that in this study, communication was at the forefront of volunteers' perceptions of the PBR's OC. Observations in the field and comments in the 2016 VSS indicated that the most frequently recurring aspect was the poor communication from management to volunteers. As one respondent said, "Very little information is passed on from my supervisor". Someone suggested the need for "proper toolbox meetings that provide workers with all that is needed to know for day-to-day safety and jobs". Stukey's (2016) study on the role of organisational support and communication on retention of volunteers, concluded with the need for development of policies and procedures that promote communication, especially face-to-face communication. These comments indicate that management need to open the channels of communication and allow dissemination of information across all levels and in various directions. Giving volunteers opportunities to provide feedback could also ameliorate this situation.

Being valued

An almost equally contentious aspect for volunteers was the notion of 'being valued'. Respondents talked of 'lack of respect, recognition and reward', the 'need for genuine care and concern', and an urgency to 'affirm trust', especially in relation to management. The notion of 'being valued' is a part of the OC literature and refers to organisational members being valued for their work and contributions (Pryce, 2004). Various respondents commented on this point, with one volunteer saying in relation to management, "Allowing the volunteers to think that they are a greater part of the overall running and management of the railway!!".

It was clear that PBR presented opportunities for a diversity of people who could work there, be valued, and flourish. The range of volunteering positions available are further testimony to the tapestry of skills, knowledge, and expertise needed to sustain PBR's operations and which were filled by volunteers. Above all, the attitudes of the people involved, whether they be volunteers, paid staff, management, ETRB members, or community residents and businesses, play a key role in ensuring that the volunteer workforce is satisfied and sustained. For an organisation such as PBR which relies heavily on volunteers, the value that each volunteer brings to the organisation needs to be considered and where necessary, recognised and rewarded.

Dwiggins-Beeler et al. (2012) also found that volunteers' feelings of being valued are intrinsically connected to their role identity. Caduri and Weiss-Gal (2015) noted that perceptions of volunteers' status, especially by paid staff, can influence attitudes and behaviours towards volunteers and discussed how OC can impact on creating positive normative practices that value the contributions of volunteers to occupations and workplaces. PBR can learn from these findings and develop policies and practices that foster an OC that supports and values the work of volunteers.

Relationships and work satisfaction

Occasionally, comments were made that alluded to the underlying issues dividing the work-force and created dissatisfaction. For example, on one occasion a volunteer was beginning to describe to me the poorer aspects of PBR's OC when he was interrupted by another volunteer who made light of the complaints. The volunteer was talking about tensions between paid staff (clarifying, "I am referring to management") and volunteers. He said, "They don't recognise the volunteers! They can't even say 'hello' to us! It's shameful!" At this point, the other volunteer hurried me along and said, "He's always disgruntled. His glass is half empty". In conversation with another volunteer who was commenting on the divide between management and volunteers, the volunteer emphasised that, "Everyone is equally important – whether volunteer or paid staff. We are all given autonomy, responsibility and accountability and we should act accordingly and appropriately". In probing further, it became evident that reference to 'paid staff' was often in relation to 'management' and those who worked in various roles such as administration and did not volunteer. So, it seemed that volunteering added to 'role identity' and 'status', points which Cohen-Callow (2008) examines in more detail. Such interactions with volunteers highlighted that the management of PBR has espoused OC values that promote the importance of volunteers to the organisation but there were people who were actively preventing PBR's OC to be actioned and for the associated issues to be addressed. The implications of these observations became evident in due course, especially with the precipitation of events described earlier and documents, such as the 2018 Consultancy Document and the 2019 and 2020 ETRB Annual Reports.

A time for change

ETRB's 2018 Annual Report states that, "Puffing Billy offers a unique volunteer experience. It is recognised throughout the country for its quality, dedication and diversity of community minded people who operate this iconic railway through the scenic Dandenong Ranges" (p. 3). In terms of volunteers, ETRB's 2019 Annual Report stated that "[f]or many of these individuals [volunteers], Puffing Billy is a community, a place to come and share positive experiences with many people from varying backgrounds, all with the common love of trains, or the district it represents" (p.17). These statements provide interesting insights into PBR as an integral part of the community of the Dandenong Ranges and yet, as community itself that affords 'a place' for volunteers to spend time working on heritage trains (for example, as engineers, engine cleaners), or as part of the crew (for example, as conductors), or as part of associated teams (for example, environmental and events teams). It parallels an encounter that I had with one of the gardeners at Belgrave Railway Station during my 2016 field trip. I asked her if she was volunteering with PBR because of an affinity to trains. She laughed bemusedly and then said, "No, I love gardening. I'm not interested in the trains, but I like to keep the Puffing Billy gardens lovely for the visitors and the Belgrave community". Her comments made me think that the intrinsic values brought by working as a volunteer for PBR may be variable and motivations can be drawn from interests beyond heritage, steam, and/or trains.

Both ETRB 2018 and 2019 Annual Reports identify 'Organisational Culture' as one of the eight key elements of the PBR Strategic Plan. While noted as a separate aspect of the Strategic Plan, promotion of a safety culture is recognised at PBR as an important part of continued improvement. As part of the 2018 changes in leadership, PBR sought to capture

Table 24.3 Strategic Initiatives from 2019 PBR Business Plan, aligned to OC dimensions

Project No.	Strategic Initiative	Priority Actions 2019–2020
54	Ensuring we have diverse, solid, and significant volunteer base; and they are valued & feel engaged, supported & have fun doing it – **BEING VALUED**	Develop & implement a strategy to diversify our volunteer base, reduce shift length, provide more flexibility, enhance and utilize their volunteer skills, and make it a fun experience and place they want to be – **WORKING CONDITIONS, RECOGNITION, LEADERSHIP**
55		Partner with other institutions to access volunteers (e.g. universities) – **GETTING JOB DONE**
56		Establish a clear business model to outline volunteer roles, distinct from paid staff positions – **GETTING JOB DONE**
57		Provide improved amenities for volunteers – **WORKING CONDITIONS**
58		Establish and engage volunteer representative group – **COMMUNICATION**
59		Introduce and action cyclic volunteer staff satisfaction and engagement surveys – **COMMUNICATION**
60		Promote support services available to volunteers and staff – **COMMUNICATION**
61	Create an organisation of choice and improved value proposition – **PLANNING & LEADERSHIP**	Implement program for establishing missing employment contracts and position descriptions – **LEADERSHIP (GOVERNANCE)**
62		Prepare and implement a program for reward and recognition of staff and volunteers – **BEING VALUED**
63		Develop & implement personal development and Appraisal Program – **BEING VALUED, MANAGING PERFORMANCE**
64		Prepare and implement learning and development plan for staff – **GETTING JOB DONE**
65		Develop program for increased networking and social activities – **COMMUNICATION**
66		Ensure fair, transparent, and universal terms and conditions for workforce through establishment of an Enterprise Agreement – **COMMUNICATION**
67		Establish Workforce & Succession Plan – **PLANNING**
68	Ensure recruitment is in line with our values and cultural directions.	Align recruitment with PBR values & the right type of people – **PROCESSES**
69		Promote PBR values & hold each other accountable for acceptable, matching behaviour – **COMMUNICATION, MANAGING PERFORMANCE**
70	ETRB succession planning	Work with Department of Jobs Precincts and Regions to develop Board succession plan – **PLANNING & LEADERSHIP**

the voice of "all staff, society members and volunteers" (ETRB, 2018, p. 8). Appointment of a new CEO in 2019 heralded the 'Year of Stabilisation' (ETRB, 2018, p. 8) and subsequent development of a Business Plan in late 2019. This deliberate shift in OC at PBR was confirmed in more recent conversations with PBR management and in the documents made available for this research. The onset of COVID-19 has meant that implementation of those plans has been stalled but it is worthwhile here to examine the proposed initiatives relating to volunteers. The 2019 PBR Busines Plan as provided by the CEO for this research identifies several 'Strategic Initiatives' that relate to volunteers; these are aligned with dimensions of OC from Table 24.1 and presented in Table 24.3.

Fair et al. (2018) reminds us that, "The culture of an organization is reflected in how an organization responds to challenges", an idea originally presented by Schein in 1985. Fair et al. (2018) identified 'organisational behaviour in response to limited resources' as a theme in their exploration of school culture. Other themes they found were organisational values, internal support, value placed on staff training and professional development, and school climate. The case study of PBR shows that management are attempting to address the issues raised and, in the process, PBR has given due consideration to elements of OC, for example, leadership, working conditions, recognition, being valued, managing performance, planning, and communication. However, it remains to be seen whether PBR's OC will change for the better. It would be worthwhile for future research to identify if improvements have been able to be achieved.

The research has highlighted the early rumblings in 2016 of a toxic OC at PBR that was in deep need of urgent change. The field trip of 2016 uncovered some dissatisfaction amongst the volunteers. Their comments revealed that they were largely satisfied with working for PBR but there were some indications of discontent with Management and with ETRB members. This finding was evident in the 2016 survey conducted by PBR and later supported in the Consultancy Document of 2018. There were members of PBR workforce (paid staff and volunteers) who had compelling concerns about aspects that related to PBR's OC and about the impact of those issues on the welfare and well-being of workers. The chapter has presented dimensions of OC that dominated the feedback from volunteers. The health of PBR's OC and the demands of multiple stakeholders (of which the volunteers are one) highlights the mammoth task ahead for PBR. Yet, the concerted intent and proposed strategic initiatives indicate that Management at PBR have laid the foundations for cultivating a revitalised culture at PBR that should better meet the needs of all its stakeholders and ensure the ongoing sustainability of this unique heritage railway attraction.

Conclusion

Growing participation in heritage railway attractions presents many benefits to regions, including economic, social, and educational. Volunteers play a key role in sustaining these operations, as is noted in other visitor attractions, such as museums. The research and literature relating to the experience, worth, and sustainability of volunteer workforces for heritage railway attractions continues to be scant. This research project has afforded opportunity to contribute to understanding and knowledge of this workforce and to facilitate informing heritage railway attractions in continuing to preserve their legacy. It has sought to understand how OC impacts on volunteers, using the case of PBR.

Previous research has made important contributions to the study of aspects of OC that influence volunteers, with each study examining different OC factors. This study has taken a holistic, multi-dimensional approach, with a view to considering all dimensions of OC, across the visible and invisible layers as described in the seminal work of Schein and later advanced by researchers such as Maull et al. (2001) and Pryce (2004). PBR with its unique focus on railway heritage and a workforce that is predominantly made up of volunteers has afforded an opportunity to explore OC as an overarching, holistic phenomenon that impacts on volunteers.

The study has highlighted the need to understand that volunteers are part of the fabric of organisations and so, are affected by the environment in which their work is carried out. This means that they are impacted by the organisation's culture and that managers, at all levels, need to be mindful of developing and fostering an OC that supports and sustains the work of volunteers. This task is a mammoth but important one as it encompasses a range of elements such as personal outcomes for volunteers (including motivation, job satisfaction, and commitment), organisational issues (such as communication, leadership, and relationships), and core values (for example, rituals, socialisation, and mission statements).

On a final note, this study has added to the understanding of OC by revealing a deeper understanding of the characteristics of OC's dimensions. In addition, it has shown that organisations that engage volunteers need to be mindful of how the OC impacts and influences the attitudes, behaviours, and performance of volunteers. To date, the limited literature in examining the nexus of OC and volunteers has exposed the fragmented approach in studying aspects of OC in relation to volunteers and highlighted the need for further research in this space. This research has contributed to that void by exploring a holistic perspective of OC and sought to capture the multifaceted dimensionality of OC and emphasise the interplay of these on volunteers' commitment and satisfaction.

References

Allen, N. J. (1987). The role of social and organizational factors in the evaluation of volunteer programs. *Evaluation and Program Planning, 10*(3), 257–262. https://doi.org/10.1016/0149-7189(87)90037-1

Ashforth, E., & Mael, F. (1989). Social identity theory and the organization. *Academy of Management Review, 14*(1), 20–39. https://doi.org/10.2307/258189

Bartol, K. (1979). Professionalism as a predictor of organizational commitment, role stress, and turnover: A multidimensional approach. *Academy of Management Journal, 22*, 815–821. https://doi.org/10.5465/255817

Bhati, A., Pryce, J., & Chaiechi, T. (2014). Industrial railway heritage trains: The evolution of a heritage tourism genre and its attributes. *Journal of Heritage Tourism, 9*(2), 114–133. https://doi.org/10.1080/1743873X.2013.867963

Caduri, A., & Weiss-Gal, I. (2015). Social workers who work with and without volunteers: Comparison of perceptions, organisational culture, training and experience. *British Journal of Social Work, 45*, 2458–2475. https://doi.org/10.1093/bjsw/bcu028

Carnicelli, S., Drummond, S., & Anderson, H. (2020). Making the connection using action research: serious leisure and the Caledonian Railway. *Journal of Heritage Tourism*, 1–17. https://doi.org/10.1080/1743873X.2020.1820015

Cohen-Callow, A. (2008). *Factors associated with older adult volunteers' organizational withdrawal: Testing a model of volunteer behavior.* PhD Thesis, University of Maryland. http://hdl.handle.net/10713/995

Conlin, M. V., & Bird, G. R. (2014). Railway heritage and tourism: Themes, issues and trends. In M. V. Conlin & G. R. Bird (Eds.), *Railway heritage and tourism: Global perspectives* (pp. 3–16). Channel View Publications.

Ciucescu, N. (2012). Orientation and integration of volunteers in organizational culture. *Economic Sciences Series, 12*(1), 856–860.

Dwiggins-Beeler, R., Spitzberg, B., & Roesch, S. (2012). Vectors of volunteerism: Correlates of volunteer retention, recruitment, and job satisfaction. *Journal of Psychological Issues in Organizational Culture, 2*(3), 22–43. https://doi.org/10.1002/jpoc.20074

ETRB, Emerald Tourist Railway Board (2016). *Annual Report 2016*. https://www.parliament.vic.gov.au/file_uploads/Emerald_Tourist_Railway_Board_Report_2015-16_RLJ5WKxt.pdf

ETRB, Emerald Tourist Railway Board (2018). *Annual Report 2017–2018*. https://puffingbilly.com.au/wp-content/uploads/PB-ANNUAL-REPORT-17-18-HR.pdf

ETRB, Emerald Tourist Railway Board (2019). *Annual Report 2019*. https://puffingbilly.com.au/wp-content/uploads/Annual-Report-Puffing-Billy_27-October-Final.pdf

ETRB, Emerald Tourist Railway Board (2020). *Annual Report 2020*. https://puffingbilly.com.au/wp-content/uploads/PUFFING-BILLY-ANNUAL-REPORT-2020.pdf

Evans, R. (1996). *The human side of school change: Reform, resistance, and the real-life problems of innovation*. Jossey-Bass.

Fair, K., Williams, K., Warren, J., McKyer, L., & Ory, M. (2018). The influence of organizational culture on school-based obesity prevention interventions: A systematic review of the literature. *Journal of School Health, 88*(6), 462–473. https://doi.org/10.1111/josh.12626

Flint, N. (2000). *Culture club: An investigation of organisational culture*. Paper presented at the Annual Meeting of the Australian Association for Research in Education, Sydney, Australia. http://www.academia.edu/3536075/Organizational_Culture_in_a_Successful_Primary_School_An_Ethnographic_Case_Study

Friedman, A. (2015). *The volunteer dilemma: Apathy in organizational culture*. Honours dissertation, University of Arizona. http://hdl.handle.net/10150/579243

Hofstede, G. (2001). *Culture's consequences* (2nd Ed.). Sage.

Holmes, K. (2003). Volunteers in the heritage sector: A neglected audience? *International Journal of Heritage Studies, 9*(4), 341–355. https://doi.org/10.1080/1352725022000155072

Holmes, K., & Smith, K. (2009). *Managing volunteers in tourism*. Butterworth-Heinemann.

Johnson, G. (1992). Managing strategic change—strategy, culture and action. *Long Range Planning, 25*(1), 28–36. https://doi.org/10.1016/0024-6301(92)90307-N

Johnson, G. (2000). Strategy through a cultural lens: Learning from managers' experience. *Management Learning, 31*(4), 403–426. https://doi.org/10.1177/1350507600314001

Jordan, T. A. (2009). *Volunteer entry into hospital culture: Relationships among socialization, P-O fit, organizational commitment, and job satisfaction*. Doctoral dissertation, University of Louisville. https://doi.org/10.18297/etd/713

Kenyon, J. A., Thurston, A. J., & Sweet, J. (2017). *Organisational culture in the volunteer sport sector: A case study of sailing*. In 25th European Association for Sport Management (EASM) Conference, Bern and Magglingen, Switzerland. European Association for Sport Management.

Maull, R., Brown, P., & Cliffe, R. (2001). Organisational culture and quality improvement. *International Journal of Operations & Production Management, 21*(3), 302–313. https://doi.org/10.1108/01443570110364614

Nueangjamnong, P., & Sthapitanonda, P. (2019). Engaging happy employee: Perspectives of CSR organizational culture, Volunteer work motivation, and corporate volunteering. In M. Morsing, U. Golob, & K. Podnar (Eds.), *CSR Communication Conference* (pp. 21–30). Stockholm School of Economics. http://csr-com.org/img/upload/final_CSRCOMproceedings2019_web.pdf

Pryce, J. (2004). *An examination of the influence of organisational culture on the service predispositions of hospitality workers in tropical North Queensland*. PhD thesis, James Cook University.

Pryce, J. (2009). Toward a theoretical understanding of occupational culture: Meanings from the hospitality industry. *International Journal of Knowledge, Culture & Change Management, 9*, 141–154. https://doi.org/10.18848/1447-9524/CGP/v09i03/49712

Pryce, J. (2013). An evaluation of 'work' for people with a severe persistent mental illness. *Employee Responsibilities and Rights Journal, 25*(4), 239–255. https://doi.org/10.1007/s10672-013-9229-7

PBR, Puffing Billy Railway. (2019). *History and heritage*. https://puffingbilly.com.au/about/history-heritage/

Rhoden, S., Ineson, E. M., & Ralston, R. (2009). Volunteer motivation in heritage railways: A study of the West Somerset Railway volunteers. *Journal of Heritage Tourism, 4*(1), 19–36. https://doi.org/10.1080/17438730802233864

Robbins, S. P., & Judge, T. A. (2017). *Organizational behavior* (17th edition), Pearson Education Limited.

Schein, E. (1985). *Organizational culture and leadership*. Jossey-Bass.

Smith, J. A. (2011). Shaping an organizational culture of employee and volunteer commitment. In T. Connors (Ed.), *The volunteer management handbook: leadership strategies for success* (2nd ed., pp. 81–101). John Wiley & Sons, Inc.

Stukey, J. (2016). *Predictive factors of organizational support communication in volunteer mentor retention.* PhD Thesis, Walden University. https://scholarworks.waldenu.edu/dissertations/1868

Victorian Government. (2018). *Investigation into child sex offender Robert Whitehead's involvement with Puffing Billy and other railway bodies.* https://www.ombudsman.vic.gov.au/our-impact/investigation-reports/investigation-into-child-sex-offender-robert-whiteheads-involvement-with-puffing-billy-and-other-railway-bodies/

Victorian Government. (2019). *Emerald Tourist Railway Act 1977.* Version No. 027. Emerald Tourist Railway Act 1977 (legislation.vic.gov.au)

PART 5

Impacts and legacies of volunteering

25

UNDERSTANDING VOLUNTEERING IMPACT AND LEGACY, A SUSTAINABILITY APPROACH

Andrew Adams and John Deane

Introduction

Volunteering has not always concerned itself with the issues of legacy and impact. Located predominantly in the domain of leisure, volunteering has perhaps been dominated by the pragmatic business of understanding and managing human activity based on 'organising around enthusiasms' (Bishop & Hoggett, 1986). Taken from a serious leisure perspective (see Chapter 33 for a brief overview), volunteering is often viewed as akin to unpaid work (Stebbins, 1996, 2013) and is subsequently determined by the potential for an individual to persist with their enthusiasm building and developing the necessary skills and/or knowledge to be able to build an enduring engagement in a chosen volunteer activity, often referred to as a 'career' (Stebbins 1992, 1996). In taking a lead from Dean (2015), we focus on volunteering as primarily an individual activity that is often collectively organised. We do not seek to examine particular voluntary organisational contexts other than to locate them in the ongoing "marketisation and individualisation" (Dean, 2015, p. 140) that tempers considerations of volunteering. This chapter examines legacy and impact of volunteering and in so doing locates altruism and instrumentality as competing contexts that underpin the potential of volunteering to be sustainable. Critically, for this analysis we argue that whilst altruism and instrumentality compete, legacy and impact appear to exist in a state of 'coopetition' (Bengtsson & Kock, 2000).

Coopetition can exist where two competing entities or ideas compete and cooperate at the same time and can account for a complex but advantageous relationship (Bengtsson & Kock, 2000). This may be a bold statement, but an indication from volunteer research across a range of disciplines and in different contexts (e.g. Alfes, Antunes & Shantz, 2017; Brockner, Senior & Welch, 2014; Caligiuri, Mencin & Jiang, 2013; MacAloon, 2008; McDonald, Fielding & Louis, 2014) is that legacy and impact 'coopete' at the philosophical, outcome and output levels. This occurs none more so than in relation to the competition between altruism – the giving freely of oneself for others (not family) to benefit – and instrumentalism – taking part for the benefit that will accrue to the individual from taking part. In many instances, these competing aspects of volunteering are in balance (Adams, 2011). However, volunteering contexts have become prone to neoliberal predilections for measurement, evidence, efficiency and effectiveness (Dean, 2015; Georgeou & Engel, 2011). Subsequently, volunteering

DOI: 10.4324/9780367815875-30

has become more formalised and structured (Carvalho & Sampaio, 2017; Hill & Stevens, 2011) and incorporated into government strategy (Taylor, Panagouleas & Nichols, 2012; Zimmeck, 2010). The outcome of this topographical shift has become manifest in the increase in coopetition between impact and legacy.

In addition to the above description of volunteering contexts related to impact and legacy, it is important to clarify that for volunteering to endure as a serious leisure activity (Stebbins, 1996), then it is sustainability that is being referred to. The adoption of the 17 Sustainable Development Goals (SDGs) as part of the 2030 Sustainable Development Agenda (United Nations General Assembly, 2015) has ensured that sustainability of human activity has become a premium concern for governments, policymakers and stakeholders worldwide. It is in considering sustainability that the cooperative aspects of impact and legacy first diverge. To establish legacy and legacy strategies, sustainability becomes the predominant driving force (Kellet, Hede & Chalip, 2008) with the necessity to build sustainability into the programme design from the outset (Attwell, Morgan & Parker, 2019). Sport legacy projects, for example, which are often embedded in mega or large-scale sport events (Roche, 2000), are often recipients of public funds and subject to the international public gaze and scrutiny, and must incorporate sustainability into project design from the outset (Lindsey 2008; Pluye, Potvin & Denis, 2004; Schulenkorf & Adair, 2014; Shediac-Rizkallah & Bone, 1998). Furthermore, to achieve sustainable development the local delivery context must be accounted for, as must a cooperative agreement with local sports agency stakeholders (Jamal, Rashid & Drira, 2014; Thomas & Dyall 1999). In short, legacy is fundamentally altruistic. It necessitates design and planning and is reliant on the capacity of the constitutive local context to determine cooperation and engage.

Impact, conversely, focuses on the individual and how the individual can benefit from volunteering activity. The critical context to make sense of the language of impact is that of neoliberalism (Dean, 2015). Neoliberalism has come to be viewed as the predominant political, cultural and philosophical context within which social action takes place. Famously for Fukuyama (1992), neoliberalism represented the 'end of history'. Fukuyama's thesis was that in the realm of ideas liberalism had become the dominant position with liberal democracy and market economies accepted ideologically as the winners for global consumption. Accordingly, neoliberalism has been subject to rigorous scrutiny by many authors, from many academic disciplines. It has been characterised differently as a philosophical project (Foucault, 2008; Giroux, 2008; Harvey, 2005), an ideology (Peck & Tickell, 2007) and a culture (Giroux, 2005). It is of course all of these. Neoliberalism is the dominant contextual factor that has impinged on all aspects of public and private life as 'the spirit of the time' (Giroux, 2005), and in this regard volunteering and how volunteering is perceived, understood and undertaken has become susceptible to the language and processes of neoliberal managerialism. The emergence of 'New Public management', which promotes economic efficiency, increasing productivity, the incorporation of neoliberal operational and governance systems within the neoliberal agenda of small government, privatisation, deregulation and liberalisation has contextualised how volunteering outputs may serve to enable the consumption of impact as a quasi-market outcome (Lyons 1998; Roberts, Jones & Fröhling, 2005). It is in this regard that the encouragement and promotion of volunteering is often couched in the language of impact, skills and benefits that can accrue to the individual for individual betterment rather than a social good. This movement from a collective social focus approach, involving an almost Keynesian approach to public management, to an approach based on individualisation and marketisation (the neoliberal context), seriously challenges the balance of altruism and instrumentalism (Adams, 2011; Dean, 2015).

Volunteering has become yet another front in the colonisation of public management by neoliberal culture (Springer, 2020), so that 'modernised' volunteering must demonstrate both impact for individuals and legacy for communities/groups/organisations. However, planned legacy as a collective outcome is never usually met. Perhaps because legacy is never a fixed thing (it evolves over time) or because legacy targets are simply over-ambitious or simply because aggregating individual benefit to the societal level to account for legacy fulfilment is unsatisfactory. This chapter locates neoliberalism in the guise of "market individualism and flexible capitalism" (Dean, 2015, p. 139) as a backdrop to the volunteering landscape and the potential creation of impact and legacy. More specifically, we seek to argue that this conceptual analysis of volunteering output only really makes sense in the context of achieving sustainability.

This chapter adapts a multilevel sustainability framework, synthesised by Lindsey (2008), to examine two levels of sustainability: individual and community; and organisational and institutional. We also take this position against a backdrop of hegemonic neoliberal processes which enables us to ask whether volunteering impact and legacy can be more than mere rhetorical devices when considering the value and meaning of volunteering. This chapter thus aims for a critical examination of a facet of volunteering that has received too little critical attention to date (Rochester, 2015), and asks whether impact and legacy can continue to *coopete* given "the infiltration of the culture and behaviours of the market into the non-market parts of our society" (Rochester, 2015).

Individual and community sustainability

Lindsey (2008) notes that the concept of sustainability is fragmented within and across the particular confines of academic disciplines and, whilst accepting this limitation, argues that synthesising and transposing sustainability across academic boundaries can help to clarify this somewhat nebulous concept. Lindsey translates sustainability from a health context to a sport context and in doing so offers some promise in clarifying sustainability from an "amorphous concept" (Lindsey, 2008, p. 280) to a process that allows for "an enhanced understanding of the processes that affect sustainability" (Lindsey, 2008, p. 292). We abstract a stage further to argue that individual and community sustainability in sport volunteering is (a) captured in the term 'volunteer impact', and (b) that it reflects understandings of outcomes across a broad spectrum of volunteering activity. Of central importance in making sense of the idea of volunteer impact is the dominant context of neoliberalism, which has provided the lens, language and rhetorical tools that volunteering has had to contend with as it has sought to become a modernised activity (Studer, 2015; Wicker, 2017).

Given our focus on volunteering we seek here to merely describe the relevant contextual architecture of neoliberalism; there is plenty of further reading that extensively eviscerates neoliberalism. For Giroux (2008) it is the subjugation by economics of the political sphere that has enabled neoliberal market rationalities to dominate, organise, regulate and define the basic principles and workings of the state. Giroux went further to argue that neoliberalism has become "weaponised", producing a "low-intensity warfare at home" (Giroux, 2008, p. 58). The organising 'logics' of neoliberalism, which are largely framed through the language of modernisation (Finlayson, 2003), have become increasingly embedded in social, political, economic and cultural systems. The result of this process has been a hollowing out of the state and the death of the public sphere, a decay in politics, an acceptance of a surveillance culture, and a general dislike for all things public, social and collective (Silk & Pullen, 2020). The importance of modernisation for individual and community volunteering involves the embracing of the core tenets of the New Public Management, which arising from the neoliberal dominance as a spoil of war includes a commitment to professional management, auditing and performance management as standard bearers, and an embracing of contractualisation in relation to inter-organisational governance (McLaughlin, Ferlie & Osborne, 2002).

Impact, as used in literatures that discuss volunteering output, is most often cited in the context of (sport) events, with economic impact the dominant style (Dawson & Downward, 2013), but there are also health impacts (Yeung et al., 2018), participation impacts (Smith et al., 2016) and community impacts (Mohan & Bennett, 2019 and classically De Tocqueville's *Democracy in America* [1835] 2003). What unites all of these understandings of impacts (except De Tocqueville), and this is where the neoliberal infrastructure has a grip, is in the language used to describe the intended outcomes, expectations and values for volunteers. Georgeou and Engel (2011) in discussing the Australian context of development volunteering note how neoliberal managerialism has had a streamlining effect which, whilst appearing positive, has ensured that job descriptions, targeted recruitment of volunteers and reduced flexibility have resulted in less sensitisation and effect in relation to local needs and hence outcomes. Georgeou and Engel (2011) note how the vocationalisation of development volunteering in Australia has reflected government recruitment practices, which, based on technical practices, moves "volunteering away from concepts of exchange and the development of the capacities and skills of local people" (Georgeou & Engel, 2011, p. 308), towards individual upskilling and readiness for career enhancement in the development industry.

It is almost without exception that it is the individual volunteer who receives an almost contractual promise to benefit from their volunteering output (Allen & Bartle, 2014; Benson et al., 2014). To be sure, neoliberal and managerialist approaches in examining dimensions of operational volunteer management dominate practice. Wisner et al. (2005) proposed seven dimensions relevant to volunteer management: schedule flexibility, orientation and training, empowerment, social interaction, reflection, and rewards. Critically, Wisner et al. (2005) approached volunteering as a work orientated instrumental activity, where the language of the market and individual improvement dominate the potential impact potential. This overriding situation consigns the notion of altruistic reward to an almost afterthought as a motivational factor rather than as an implicit and complex altruistic emotional state that perhaps situates one's volunteering activity in the first instance. Similarly, Aisbett and Hoye (2015) have argued that volunteers' satisfaction and sustained volunteering are determined by volunteer management practices that can enhance volunteers' abilities, motivations and opportunities. It is not so much that we should not aim to manage volunteers, but that the focus of management should be on the individual and is more concerned with individual volunteer satisfaction with his/her experience rather than the output of any volunteering activity.

Impact, when used and understood within a dominant neoliberal narrative is thus akin to individual sustainability to maintain particular outcomes for the individual volunteers themselves, and for the individual recipients of volunteer action. Certainly, in the sport domain, outcomes of volunteering, for volunteers and recipients alike, have become dominated by issues of personal development and success to the detriment of social issues and "the need for progressive change at a collective or community level" (Coakley, 2011, p. 309). The neoliberal concern for personal development and individual life enhancement is thus at the heart of individual sustainability, and in so doing becomes the 'weapon' of volunteering impact. The long-term goal of impact as viewed through a lens of neoliberal trickle-down economics is arguably to enable community sustainability. This secondary outcome is largely unproven based on a loose appreciation of methodological individualism, where individual traits, benefits and developments are rounded upwards for community benefit. The logical inference of this process is that individual volunteer impacts lead to individual sustainability and consequently this leads to community level sustainability. In this way, the language and practice of neoliberal culture is reproduced and reaffirmed as the dominant hegemony for understanding the relationship between the individual, the idea of community and society. Volunteering impact thus becomes incorporated as a logical and coherent individual outcome that can meet community sustainability goals. This drive for sustainability is also specified in the United Nations' (UN) Secretary-General's plan of action for volunteering to contribute to lasting development. Neoliberal language once again frames how volunteering can be understood. The Secretary-General's report states that to "fully and systematically leverage the potential of volunteerism, evidence of its contribution to peace and development needs to be strengthened" (United Nations General Assembly, 2015, p. 24).

In flagging the clear link between individual and community sustainability as an outcome of volunteer impact we find the ground strewn with conceptual potholes into which it is possible to fall, and never to recover. Not least here is the problematic notion of community action, which can be understood descriptively, to describe common interests which individuals might share; normatively, as a school of thought in making assumptions about the way individuals should live; and instrumentally, where community becomes a proactive arm of policy implementation (Taylor, 2003). Community also comes in many guises, from the imagined (Anderson, 1991) to the geographical (East, 2002) to the product of civil culture (Giddens, 2000). Similarly, when discussing volunteering activity and community impact it is necessary to refer to social capital. Social capital was arguably the dominant social science concept of the 2000s and like community it has many meanings, interpretations and applications, with a wealth of literature that explains and explores its varied use. Social capital can be conceived as a shorthand term for the networks and relationships that individuals build as part of their community development, and is predicated on the work of Robert Putnam, Pierre Bourdieu and James Coleman. Putnam famously attributed the value of volunteering (in associations) for democracy based on norms of reciprocity, mutual support and trustworthiness (Feldstein and Putnam, 2003; Putnam, 2000). Whereas both Bourdieu and Coleman have very differently taken an individual, micro-level approach. The former understood social capital as power derived from one's social class as applied within a group, whilst the latter focused on the interdependencies between people as a functional and productive multi-entity (Coleman, 1988).

The significance for volunteering impact arguably lies in the way in which "networks and shared values function as a resource for people and organisations" (Field, 2003, p. 43). Individual volunteers can and do form communities of practice that can be seen to serve the 'true' aims of neoliberal social policy by creating economic growth and privatisation. Thus, the impact of volunteering at the community level can be to privatise individual impacts upwards, ensuring that the consumption of volunteer impacts is in line with the neoliberal enterprise from within the social body. For Foucault, this is the key for nothing less than the survival of neoliberalism by inciting marketisation throughout the social body and constituting the "formative power of society" (Foucault, 2008, p. 148). Whilst this all sounds rather negative, the positive use value is in the detail and perhaps in how coopetition between impact and legacy can be better understood as a drive towards the sociability of volunteering and mutual exchange (Morris, 2018). This logic announces two questions for making sense of volunteering impact for sustainable practice. First, when considering community volunteering impact normatively and instrumentally, we can question how and why a community can and does form and then, whether it has the capital to be sustainable. Second, using the notions of volunteering impact and sustainability as a thinking tool we can ask whether volunteers, as they become upskilled through volunteering activity, can begin to see beyond the neoliberal smokescreen of individualistic and instrumental development. For Springer (2020), the COVID-19 pandemic has reignited desires for mutual aid and reciprocity within communities across the globe, challenging capitalism's hegemony. Volunteering as the base-metal of mutual aid is part of what makes humans human, and it is part of our DNA (Bowles & Gintis, 2011). If it is possible to reimagine individual and community volunteer impact as sustainable progress, then we should perhaps accept that mutual aid "is the glue that keeps human societies together" and that, perhaps, the "silver lining to this virus, then, is that we are reawakening to the possibilities of our fundamental connection to one another" (Springer, 2020, p. 3).

Organisational and institutional sustainability

Lindsey (2008) focuses on 'capacity and viability' as two separate and overlapping areas of organisational sustainability (OS), with 'capacity' being the ability of an organisation to continue to deliver a service, and 'viability' as the financial and other resources required to do so. Institutional sustainability (Lindsey, 2008) is about the longer-term changes that are able to be made to the areas of how equitably resources allocated, the policy context within which sports organisations operate, and the ability to lobby to bring about policy and regulatory change.

In the case of volunteering and mega events such as the Olympics, the idea of delivering a volunteer service until the end of the event and beyond as a legacy is often promoted as an intention. The critical test for events such as these is to have the resources to maintain 'viability' to enable this legacy to occur once the Games have ended, and not to serve as a mere rhetoric device. Lindsey (2008, p. 13) defines organisational sustainability as "the maintenance or expansion of sports development programmes by the organisation responsible for their delivery". As we argue above, volunteering and mega events that take place in neoliberal contexts consequently need a legacy strategy that should focus pre-event on building a funding model with government and key stakeholders to establish a financial support package for an existing, or a new agency, to maintain the engagement of volunteers in the local geographic community after the event. For an event such as the Olympic Games, this volunteer agency could form the existing arm of the Local Organising Committee that would be responsible for the volunteer programme morphing into the new volunteering agency or the expansion of the existing volunteer agency infrastructure to support sporting and cultural volunteers. The key issue here as argued by Shipway, Ritchie and Chien (2020) is a lack of coordination and communication between event organising committees and the existing volunteer infrastructure that exists in local communities that host the staging of the Games. The weight of the research from an extensive literature review on volunteering and mega sports events by Woodall et al. (2016) suggests that there is still an issue in being able to claim that there are any real long-term outcomes for either communities or individuals.

At the heart of this discourse on legacy is the issue of neoliberalism. As identified in the first section of this chapter this 'new managerial discourse' is all pervasive in terms of volunteer legacy. This dominance of the new discourse is played out by the International Olympic Committee (IOC) and the cities that bid to host the Games through both the prioritisation of volunteer legacy planning and in the language and focus on the market (MacAloon, 2008). Cities are seen as building on the Olympic brand and not focusing and adding to the heritage and history of legacy. This heritage and history are about the community and social legacy of volunteering based in altruism. In essence, we can see the coopetition between impact and legacy playing out in the context of neoliberalism where altruism and instrumentalism are forced to compete. The dominant IOC discourse concerning bid structure/content and the response of bid cities to this is visible in legacy planning. This issue of neo-liberalism and instrumentalism being the dominant discourse in legacy volunteer planning was exemplified by the set-up of the London 2012 Games as a private company in the form of the London Organising Committee for the Olympic and Paralympic Games (LOCOG). LOCOG could have been established as a not for profit or third sector agency with long-term legacy in its many forms central to its mission. This agency could have established in terms of its governance structures key representatives from the key community agencies in the East end of London.

This development has been termed a form of 'regulatory capitalism' that has had a significant but hidden impact on the ability of a mega event, in this case the Olympic Games, to deliver on particular legacy aspirations (Nichols & Ralston, 2015). The primary focus of LOCOG was the 'bottom line' and delivering short term goals that meet the demands of the political paymasters. The key drivers of the LOCOG senior management team were establishing a managerial efficiency culture that does not allow any focus on long-term volunteer legacy planning. Long-term legacy planning that might be achieved through volunteering was not one of the key performance indicators upon which LOCOG in this instance was being judged. This is further evidence of the structure of agencies established to run sport mega events such as the Olympic Games delivering on the neoliberalism agenda as already identified by Giroux (2005). It could be argued that since neoliberalism has been the dominant public policy agenda for the last 40 years, the organisers of sport mega events have little choice but to understand and attempt to develop legacy through a neoliberal lens or it is likely that these developing organisations would not be sustainable entities themselves in the long-term. The view of legacy as being about instrumentalism rather than altruism is the dominant narrative driven by short-term financial rather than social and community goals.

Lindsey (2008) argues that the focus on securing organisational sustainability as the dominant factor is desirable to ensure that individual, community and institutional outcomes are sustainable. This focus on the community aspects of legacy is central to the notion that ideally volunteer impacts are concerned with social capital and there is some evidence that it can deliver this development of a shared identity amongst volunteers who are invested in an altruistic experience that is focused on a common purpose (Allen & Shaw, 2009; Weed et al., 2008; Wicker & Hallmann, 2013).

It is the design and set-up of legacy plans at the outset that is the dominant factor in ensuring organisational sustainability and the delivery of other forms of sustainability. It is the absence of a specific focus on the establishment of post-event agency; a lack of long-term sustainable funding, and the lack of established stakeholder networks that mean that there is no sustainable long-term volunteer legacy (Dickson, Darcy & Pentifallo Gadd, 2020). Koutrou, Pappous and Johnson (2016) identified this issue in a post-event study of London 2012 volunteers four years after the Olympic Games, which also highlighted that volunteers were not sure how to get involved in volunteering in their local area. They were also critical in pointing out that to sustain volunteering after the London Olympic Games, the post-event structures such as 'Join In' were set up too late. 'Join In' was established by LOCOG during 2012 as the national agency for local sports volunteering, to help sport clubs and those who need volunteers. 'Join In' also provided opportunities for those who wanted to get involved, and promoted the social value created by volunteers. It could be argued that this agency should have been established well before 2012 to allow it to work more closely with existing volunteer agencies to plan a volunteer legacy. Koutrou et al. (2016) in their research showed that not enough was done to engage and work with the existing volunteer infrastructure which existed in the local area (Koutrou et al., 2016). This again suggests that the London 2012 volunteer legacy was left to the private structures of LOCOG, and in this instance impact rather than legacy was delivered, largely at the expense of engaging community volunteer agencies that are embedded in their local geographic and imagined communities.

The academic literature is clear in arguing that engaging volunteers for sports mega events does not lead to a lasting engagement and hence a legacy for volunteering (Benson et al., 2014; Koutrou et al., 2016). The argument has been made for some time now that all sports mega events from the planning stage need to establish longitudinal studies that track volunteers' ongoing engagement in volunteering post the games (Gratton & Jones, 2004). As we point out when discussing impact there may well be individual impact in terms of volunteers upskilling themselves, but we should not rely on assuming a societal impact from individual benefit to have a sustainable impact on communities or community organisations. This point about the need to conduct research over a longer period of time to understand the social and community or altruistic benefits of volunteer legacy is a key recommendation of the extensive review of the volunteering of the 2014 Glasgow Commonwealth Games undertaken by Woodall et al. (2016).

The Volunteer Strategy for Olympic and Paralympic Games Tokyo 2020 describes the establishment of a system to allow the continuation of volunteering post Games:

> We will establish a system by 2020 that enables the volunteers involved with the Tokyo 2020 Games to also play an active role after the Games, aiming to firmly establish a culture of volunteerism in Japan.
>
> *(Tokyo Organising Committee of the Olympic and Paralympic Games, 2016, p. 25)*

There is no indication of how this will be funded or any indication of how this system will have ongoing monitoring and evaluation. However, the results of the study by Koutrou et al. (2016) suggest that the participants were either not aware or not sure about how to get involved in further volunteering in their area. Clearly, support mechanisms to promote and sustain such opportunities are vital in realising a volunteer legacy following a sport mega event.

The institutional sustainability of any sport mega event is thus dependent on the establishment of long-term change which primarily concerns the policy context within which government and national sport agencies operate. In the UK, government is the principal agent for this context, but is aided by UK Sport, which is the national sport agency with responsibility for ensuring elite sport success. Bound together in a top-down power structure, the government and UK Sport are responsible for setting forth both context and framework, and long-term legacy strategy to promote and enhance volunteering in and through bidding to host mega sport events. It is important to recognise that the current policy context set in the UK by the government has been dominated by neoliberal policy instruments, regardless of political party control for the last 40 years. Perhaps if this national context and framework for legacy was developed with altruism, community and the promotion of the social aspects of volunteering as defining principles, then there would be some push back against the short-term instrumental legacy goals set by international sports rights holders such as the IOC and FIFA. A clear goal of London 2012 for example, was to bring about a lasting change to the volunteering landscape in the UK (UK Sport, 2006). However, there has been limited evidence of significant longer-term policy or structural change in the UK in terms of volunteering and the longer investment and local structures to support such a change. In fact, most research suggests that over the long-term the 2012 Games have had little or no long-term impact on the number of people volunteering either in sport or more generally across English society (Holmes, Nichols & Ralston, 2018; Koutrou et al., 2016; Nichols & Ralston 2015). Research by Koutrou et al. (2016, p. 9) conducted three to four years after 2012 suggested there was limited evidence of a volunteer legacy from the 2012 London Olympics.

It is a moot point, but from an institutional sustainability approach, the privatisation of legacy development via the outsourcing of services to LOCOG directly worked against any changes in volunteering policy or the creation of a volunteer legacy. As Holmes et al. (2018, p. 401) argued "LOCOG's contract was just to deliver the Games, not to also generate a legacy. This contract made LOCOG's work simpler, cheaper, and reduced political interventions". The tensions of neoliberal economic rationalism once again appear to drive the coopetition between legacy and impact and suggest that with spiralling costs of hosting mega sports, leveraging is vital to leave some lasting volunteer legacy to the community. In this instance instrumentalism is driving the legacy planning process to meet necessary outcomes that can be measured through technocratic evaluation to set targets. Altruistic community concerns are thus subsumed by a strict adherence to dominant neoliberal conditions. The tension here between institutional and policy concerns contrasts volunteering impact and legacy with social capital, altruism and serious leisure to highlight that legacy planning is a long-term process that necessitates planning and relationship building with the wider community. This approach to long-term legacy planning is anathema to the neoliberal 'managerial' model. There is a need for some new thinking to put altruism and the social and community aspects of volunteering at the heart of legacy planning.

Organisation and institutional sustainability will only work when the key agencies involved who are the rights holders to mega sports events, such as the IOC and FIFA, change the bidding process fundamentally. It could be argued that in order for legacy planning to be able to deliver long-term lasting outcomes for communities, agencies such as FIFA and the IOC should require clear evidence of a bottom-up local approach from host cities. As argued by Shipway et al. (2020) this would require cities bidding to host having to show evidence of working with the existing volunteer infrastructure in order to bring about structural changes to volunteering. Structural change needs to be further reinforced via the national sporting federations and national governments who are underwriting the cost of the games to commit to long-term funding and staffing to make the volunteer legacy sustainable into the future. The current situation of asking host cities to put forward a volunteer legacy strategy as part of their bid documentation is not working. This is largely because there is no mechanism, post event hosting, for events rights holders, such as the IOC or FIFA, to be able to review and ensure that the volunteer legacy strategies are implemented for the long-term. Unless there is a move away from short-term thinking driven by neoliberal agendas of efficiency, effectiveness and profit we will fail to see the delivery of a sustainable volunteer legacy from any future events. Altruism and the community and social aspects of volunteer legacy planning need to be built into the bidding mechanisms for mega sports events. In their detailed study of the primary and secondary evidence of a volunteer legacy from the Sydney 2000 and London 2012 Games, Lockstone-Binney et al. (2016, p. 67) argue that "our conclusions tentatively propose that greater engagement between OCOGs and the host cities' volunteer infrastructure could better facilitate the realisation of volunteer legacies".

Conclusion

This review of volunteer impact and legacy has argued that volunteering has shifted to become focused on instrumentalism as a means to improve an individual's skills, at the expense of the altruistic benefits from giving of oneself to benefit other people whom you do not necessarily know. We have argued that altruism and instrumentalism are in a constant state of tension as these terms compete semantically and practically as part of an acknowledgement that volunteering has had to accommodate the realities of some 40 years of neoliberalism. This is not a new consideration, but we believe our discussion adds a critical nuance to how the issues of legacy and impact can be considered and understood. Philosophically, if we accept that coopetition between the terms is both a reasonable and logical assertion then we are in a position to understand how operational contexts are both compromised and conditioned by intentions for sustainability. Thus, volunteering as a form of serious leisure is at odds with the instrumental recruitment strategies of organisations that seek volunteers and who tend to focus on the benefit volunteering can bring to an individual. Volunteer impact and legacy are both modernised products of neoliberalism, each of which competes and cooperates, depending upon inputs, outputs and context. We have argued that volunteer impact is almost wholly subsumed by neoliberal culture and the emphasis on developing and expanding individual capital. Conversely, we have also argued that the idea of legacy is fundamentally tied to altruistic notions of social, community and collective benefit. It is this respect that impact and legacy coopete, whilst altruism and instrumentality compete.

In making this argument we should acknowledge our own cultural biases as English academics operating in a western European context. There are many individuals and cultures across the globe who interpret the world outside of this perspective.

References

Adams, A. (2011). Between modernization and mutual aid: The changing perceptions of voluntary sports clubs in England. *International Journal of Sport Policy and Politics, 3*(1), 23–43 https://doi.org/1 0.1080/19406940.2010.544663

Allen, J. B., & Bartle, M. (2014). Sport event volunteers' engagement: Management matters. *Managing Leisure, 19*(1), 36–50 https://doi.org/10.1080/13606719.2013.849502

Allen, J. B., & Shaw, S. (2009). 'Everyone rolls up their sleeves and mucks in': Exploring volunteers' motivation and experiences of the motivational climate of a sporting event. *Sport Management Review, 12*, 79–90 https://doi.org/10.1016/j.smr.2008.12.002

Anderson, B. (1991). *Imagined Communities: Reflections on the origin and spread of nationalism* (Rev. ed.). Verso.

Aisbett, L., & Hoye, R., (2015). Human resource management practices to support sport event volunteers. *Asia Pacific Journal of Human Resources, 53*(3), 351–369. https://doi.org/10.1111/1744-7941.12062

Alfes, K., Antunes, B., & Shantz, D. (2017). The management of volunteers – what can human resources do? A review and research agenda. *International Journal of Human Resource Management, 28*, 62–97. https://doi.org/10.1080/09585192.2016.1242508

Attwell, S., Morgan, H., & Parker, A. (2019). Major sporting events: Achieving an international sport development legacy. *Managing Sport and Leisure, 24*(6), 356–371. https://doi.org/10.1080/2375047 2.2019.1679038

Bengtsson, M., & Kock, S. (2000). 'Coopetition' in business networks—to cooperate and compete simultaneously. *Industrial Marketing Management, 29*, 411–426, https://doi.org/10.1016/ S0019-8501(99)00067-X

Benson, A. M., Dickson, T. J., Terwiel, F. A., & Blackman, D. A. (2014). Training of Vancouver 2010 volunteers: A legacy opportunity? *Contemporary Social Science, 9*, 210–226. https://doi.org/10.1080 /21582041.2013.838296

Bishop, J., & Hoggett, P. (1986). *Organising around enthusiasms: Mutual aid in leisure.* Comedia.

Bowles, S., & Gintis, H. (2011). *A cooperative species: Human reciprocity and its evolution*. Princeton University Press.

Brockner, J., Senior, D., & Welch, W. (2014). Corporate volunteerism, the experience of self-integrity, and organizational commitment: Evidence from the field. *Social Justice Research, 27*, 1–23. https://doi.org/10.1007/s11211-014-0204-8

Caligiuri, P., Mencin, A., & Jiang, K. (2013). Win–win–win: The influence of company-sponsored volunteerism programs on employees, NGOs, and business units. *Personnel Psychology, 66*, 825–860. https://doi.org/10.1111/peps.12019

Carvalho, A., & Sampaio, M. (2017). Volunteer management beyond prescribed best practice: A case study of Portuguese non-profits. *Personnel Review, 46*(2), 410–428. https://doi.org/10.1108/PR-04-2014-0081

Coakley, F. (2011). Youth sports: What counts as positive development? *Journal of Sport and Social Issues, 20*, 1–19. https://doi.org/10.1177/0193723511417311

Coleman, J. S. (1988). Social capital in the creation of human capital. *The American Journal of Sociology, 94*(1) Supplement: Organizations and institutions: Sociological and economic approaches to the analysis of social structure, 95–120. https://www.jstor.org/stable/2780243

Dawson, P., & Downward, P. (2013). The relationship between participation in sport and sport volunteering: An economic analysis. *International Journal of Sports Finance, 8*(1), 75–92 https://EconPapers.repec.org/RePEc:jsf:intjsf:v:8:y:2013:i:1:p:75-92

De Tocqueville, A. ((1835] 2003). *Democracy in America*. Penguin.

Dean, J., (2015). Volunteering, the market, and neoliberalism. *People, Place and Policy, 9*(2), 139–148. https://doi.org/10.3351/ppp.0009.0002.0005

Dickson, T. J., Darcy, S., & Pentifallo Gadd, C. (2020). Ensuring volunteer impacts, legacy and leveraging is not 'fake news': Lessons from the 2015 FIFA Women's World Cup, *International Journal of Contemporary Hospitality Management, 32*(2), 683–705. https://doi.org/10.1108/IJCHM-04-2019-0370

East, L. (2002). Regenerating health communities: Voices from the inner City. *Critical Social Policy, 22*(2), 273–299. https://doi.org/10.1177/02610183020220020101

Feldstein, L., & Putnam, R. (2003). *Better together*. Simon & Schuster.

Field, J. (2003). *Social capital*. Routledge.

Finlayson, A. (2003). *Making sense of new labour*. Lawrence & Wishart, Project MUSE.

Foucault, M. (2008) *Birth of biopolitics: Lectures at the Collège de France, 1978–1979*, Palgrave.

Fukuyama, F. (1992). *The end of history and the last man*. Free Press.

Georgeou, N., & Engel, S. (2011). The impact of neoliberalism and new managerialism on development volunteering: An Australian case study. *Australian Journal of Political Science, 46*(2), 297–311, https://doi.org/10.1080/10361146.2011.567970

Giddens, A. (2000). *The third way and its critics*. Polity Press.

Giroux, H., (2005). The terror of neoliberalism: Rethinking the significance of cultural politics. *College Literature, 32*(1), 1–19 https://www.jstor.org/stable/25115243

Giroux, H. (2008). The militarization of US Higher Education after 9/11. *Theory, Culture & Society, 25*(5), 56–82. https://doi.org/10.1177/0263276408095216

Gratton, C., & Jones, I. (2004). *Research methods for sport studies*. Routledge.

Harvey, D. (2005). *A brief history of neoliberalism*. Oxford University Press.

Hill, M., & Stevens, D. (2011). Volunteers who manage other volunteers and the professionalisation of volunteer management: Implications for practice. *Voluntary Sector Review, 2*(1), 107–114 https://doi.org/10.1332/204080511X560657

Holmes, K., Nichols, G., & Ralston, R. (2018). It's a once-in-a-lifetime experience and opportunity—deal with it! Volunteer perceptions of the management of the volunteer experience at the London 2012 Olympic Games. *Event Management, 22*(3), 389–403. https://doi.org/10.3727/152599518X15252895715050

Jamal, A., Rashid, M., & Drira, M. (2014). Optimal level of participatory approach in an NGO development project. *Journal of Comparative International Management, 17*(1), 14–23, https://id.erudit.org/iderudit/jcim17_1art02

Kellet, P., Hede, A. M., & Chalip, L. (2008). Social policy for sport events: Leveraging (relationships with) teams from other nations for community benefit. *European Sports Management Quarterly, 8*(2), 101–121. https://doi.org/10.1080/16184740802024344

Koutrou, N., Pappous, A., & Johnson, A. (2016). Post-event volunteering legacy: Did the London 2012 Games induce a sustainable volunteer engagement? *Sustainability, 8*, 1221. https://doi.org/10.3390/su8121221

Lindsey, I. (2008). Conceptualising sustainability in sports development. *Leisure Studies*, 27(3), 279–294. https://doi.org/10.1080/02614360802048886

Lockstone-Binney, L., Holmes, K., Shipway, R., & Smith, K. (2016). *Evaluating the volunteer infrastructure legacy of the Olympic Games: Sydney 2000 and London 2012*. Final Report, IOC Olympic Studies Centre. https://library.olympic.org/Default/doc/SYRACUSE/165803/evaluating-the-volunteering-infrastructure-legacy-of-the-olympic-games-sydney-2000-and-london-2012-l

Lyons, M. (1998). The impact of managerialism on social policy. *Public Productivity and Management Review*, 21(4), 419–432. https://doi.org/10.2307/3380549

MacAloon, J. J. (2008). 'Legacy' as managerial/magical discourse in contemporary Olympic affairs. *The International Journal of the History of Sport*, 25(14), 2060–2071, https://doi.org/10.1080/09523360802439221

McDonald, R. I., Fielding, K. S., & Louis, W. R. (2014). Conflicting norms highlight the need for action. *Environment and Behavior*, 46(2): 139–162, https://doi.org/10.1177/0013916512453992

McLaughlin, K., Ferlie, E., & Osborne, S. (Eds.) (2002) *New public management: Current trends and future prospects*. Routledge.

Mohan, J., & Bennett, M. (2019). Community-level impacts of the third sector: Does the local distribution of voluntary organizations influence the likelihood of volunteering? *Economy and Space*, 51(4), 950–979 https://doi.org/10.1177%2F0308518X19831703

Morris, B. (2018). *Kropotkin: The politics of community*. PM Press.

Nichols, G., & Ralston, R. (2015). The legacy costs of delivering the 2012 Olympic and Paralympic Games through regulatory capitalism. *Leisure Studies*, 34(4), 389–404 https://doi.org/10.1080/02614367.2014.923495

Peck, J., & Tickell, A. (2007). *Contesting neoliberalism*: Urban Frontiers.

Pluye, P., Potvin, L., & Denis, J. (2004). Making public health programmes last: Conceptualizing sustainability. *Evaluation and Program Planning*, 28(2), 123–137 https://doi.org/10.1016/j.evalprogplan.2004.01.001

Putnam, R. (2000). Bowling alone: America's declining social capital. *Journal of Democracy*, January, 65–78. https://doi.org/10.1007/978-1-349-62965-7_12

Roberts, S. M., Jones, J. P., & Fröhling, O. (2005). *NGOs and the globalization of managerialism: A research framework*. Elsevier.

Roche, M. (2000). *Mega-events and modernity: Olympics and expos in the growth of global culture*. Routledge.

Rochester, C. (2015). *Critical thinking about voluntary action and its history*. Retrieved July 22, 2020, from. http://www.vahs.org.uk/2015/02/critical-thinking-about-voluntary-action-and-itshistory

Schulenkorf, N., & Adair, D. (2014). *Global sport-for-development: Critical perspectives*. Palgrave Macmillan.

Shediac-Rizkallah, M. C., & Bone, L. R. (1998). Planning for the sustainability of community-based health programmes: Conceptual frameworks and future directions for research, practice and policy. *Health Education Research*, 13(1), 87–108. https://doi.org/10.1093/her/13.1.87

Shipway, R., Ritchie, B. W., & Chien, P. M. (2020). Beyond the glamour: Resident perceptions of Olympic legacies and volunteering intentions. *Leisure Studies*, 39(2), 181–194. https://doi.org/10.1080/02614367.2019.1693612

Silk, M., & Pullen, E. (2020). Disability, masculinity, militarism: The Paralympics and the cultural (re)production of the para-athlete-soldier. *Journal of War & Culture Studies*, 13(4), 444–461. https://doi.org/10.1080/17526272.2020.1829789

Smith, D. H., with Dury, S., Mohan J., & Stebbins, R. A. (2016). Volunteering as related to other leisure activities. In D. H. Smith, R. A. Stebbins & J. Grotz (Eds.) *The Palgrave handbook of volunteering, civic participation, and nonprofit associations*, Volume 1 (pp.145–177). Palgrave.

Springer, S. (2020). Caring geographies: The COVID-19 interregnum and a return to mutual aid. *Dialogues in Human Geography*, 1–4, https://doi.org/10.1177/2043820620931277

Stebbins, R. (1992). *Amateurs, professionals and serious leisure*. McGill-Queen's University Press.

Stebbins, R. A. (1996). Volunteering: A serious leisure perspective. *Nonprofit and Voluntary Sector Quarterly*, 25, 211–224. https://doi.org/10.1177%2F0899764096252005

Stebbins, R. A., (2013). Unpaid work of love: Defining the work–leisure axis of volunteering. *Leisure Studies*, 32(3), 339–345. https://doi.org/10.1080/02614367.2012.667822

Studer, S. (2015). Volunteer management: Responding to the uniqueness of volunteers. *Nonprofit and Voluntary Sector Quarterly*, 45(4), 688–714. https://doi.org/10.1177%2F0899764015597786

Taylor, M. (2003). *Public Policy in the Community*. Palgrave.

Taylor, P. D., Panagouleas, T., & Nichols, G. (2012). Determinants of sports volunteering and sports volunteer time in England. *International Journal of Sport Policy and Politics*, 4(2), 201–220. https://doi.org/10.1080/19406940.2012.656679

Thomas, D. R., & Dyall, L. (1999). Culture, ethnicity, and sport management: A New Zealand perspective. *Sport Management Review*, 2(2), 115–132. https://doi.org/10.1016/S1441-3523(99)70092-6

Tokyo Organising Committee of the Olympic and Paralympic Games (2016). *Volunteer strategy for Olympic and Paralympic Games*. Tokyo 2020.

United Nations General Assembly (2015). *Integrating volunteering in the next decade. Report of the Secretary General*. United Nations.

UK Sport (2006) *Annual Review 2006*. London, UK Sport.

Weed, M., Coren, E., Fiore, J., Mansfield, L., Wellard, I., & Chatziefstathiou, D. (2008). *A systematic review of the evidence base for developing a physical activity and health legacy from the London 2012*. Physical Activity Network West Midlands.

Wicker, P. (2017). Volunteerism and volunteer management in sport. *Sport Management Review*, 20, 325–337. https://doi.org/10.1016/j.smr.2017.01.001

Wicker P., & Hallmann K., (2013). A multi-level framework for investigating the engagement of sport volunteers. *European Sport Management Quarterly*, 13(1), 110–139. https://doi.org/10.1080/16184742.2012.744768

Wisner, P. S., Stringfellow, A., Youngdahl, W. E., & Parker, L. (2005). The service volunteer – loyalty chain: An exploratory study of charitable not-for-profit service organizations. *Journal of Operations Management*, 23(2), 143–161 https://doi.org/10.1016/j.jom.2004.07.003

Woodall, J., Scott, J., Southby, K., May, E., Bagnall, L., & Coan, S. (2016). *Exploring the experiences and impacts of volunteer applicants for the Glasgow 2014 Commonwealth Games*. Leeds Beckett University.

Yeung, J. W. K., Zhang, Z., & Kim, T. Y. (2018). Volunteering and health benefits in general adults: Cumulative effects and forms. *BMC Public Health*, 18(8). https://doi.org/10.1186/s12889-017-4561-8

Zimmeck, M. (2010). Government and volunteering: Towards a history of policy and practice. In C. Rochester, A. Ellis Paine, S. Howlett & M. Zimmeck (Eds.) *Volunteering and society in the 21st century* (pp.84–102). Palgrave Macmillan.

26

"IT'S JUST A FUN DAY OUT REALLY"

Perceptions of volunteering and mega-event volunteer legacy

Ellie May

Introduction

This chapter explores perceptions of volunteering at the Paralympic Games and explores the implications for volunteer legacy. The chapter advocates the four dimensions of volunteering developed by Cnaan, Handy, and Wadsworth (1996), as despite the complexity of defining volunteering, these tend to underpin conceptual frameworks of volunteering. As a result, 'traditional' understandings of volunteering dominate with definitions assuming altruistic motivations, a long term and regular commitment, and dedication to the organisation. Recognising the changing nature of volunteering, these dimensions are then applied to collective and reflective forms of volunteering as outlined by Hustinx and Lammertyn (2003), and applied to the concept of 'volunteerability' (Hustinx & Meijs, 2011). This chapter argues that these frameworks are significant when exploring volunteer legacy as dominant conceptualisations of volunteering can influence public perceptions of volunteering impacting on both willingness to engage and the type of activities undertaken.

As Nichols (2012, p. 215) states, the Olympic and Paralympic Games are the "epitome" of sporting mega-events. The services of large numbers of volunteers are crucial to the staging of mega-events, indeed it is frequently cited that events could not take place without the contributions of volunteers (Alexander, Kim & Kim, 2015). The London 2012 Olympic and Paralympic Games was no exception, with the event utilising the services of 70,000 volunteers (termed Games Makers) and 23,157 specifically at the Paralympic Games (DCMS, 2012). Replicating broader sports volunteering, research relating to volunteering at the Olympic and Paralympic Games has concentrated predominantly on motivations, based on the premise that understanding motivations will lead to enhanced volunteer management and retention. Motivational research stresses the importance of the unique attributes of mega-events in reasons for volunteering, with the experience being constructed as a 'once in a lifetime opportunity' (Alexander et al., 2015; Dickson & Benson, 2013).

The volunteer legacy of the London 2012 Games has received less attention (Doherty & Patil, 2019; Koutrou, Pappous & Johnson, 2016). The research that has been undertaken tends to be descriptive in nature, concentrating on future volunteer intentions rather than

DOI: 10.4324/9780367815875-31

actual behaviour and gives limited attention to the type of volunteering undertaken or barriers faced (with the exception of Koutrou et al., 2016). This chapter addresses this research gap by drawing upon longitudinal research with Games Makers at the London 2012 Games. Using volunteer frameworks, this chapter explores Games Makers' conceptualisations of volunteering prior to the event. The chapter continues by illustrating how these understandings evolved as a result of their experience at the London 2012 Games and how this impacted their future engagement in volunteering. Discussion of the results draws out the wider implications for the volunteer legacy of mega sport events.

Literature review

Conceptualising volunteering

The four dimensions developed by Cnaan et al. (1996) (free will, availability of rewards, formal organisation, and proximity to the beneficiaries) underpin definitions of volunteering and are widely adopted by academics when assessing and classifying who is a volunteer. Each of the dimensions consists of a continuum ranging from those who are perceived to be 'pure' volunteers to those who are less likely to be volunteers. An individual is considered to be a 'pure' volunteer when they undertake volunteering entirely out of free will, receive no reward, and provide a service through a formal organisation (such as a non-profit within the third sector) for the benefit of strangers rather than friends or family. Snyder and Omoto (2008) added two further dimensions. First, that volunteering should include a certain amount of decision making and second, that volunteering should extend over a period of time extending over weeks, months, and years. Taken together, these dimensions result in the popular definition provided by Snyder and Omoto (2008, p. 3) – "freely chosen and deliberate helping activities that extend over time, are engaged in without expectation of reward or other compensation and often through formal organisations, and that are performed on behalf of causes or individuals who desire assistance".

Cnaan et al. (1996) and Snyder and Omoto's (2008) dimensions resonate with the 'dominant' perspective of volunteering (Rochester, Ellis Paine, Howlett & Zimmeck, 2012) and 'collective' forms of volunteering (Hustinx & Lammertyn, 2003). Both these frameworks emphasise altruistic motivations for engaging in volunteering and specify that any reward must be intrinsic to the act of volunteering. Through this lens, motivations for volunteering are underpinned by a strong sense of duty to the local community and a desire to help those 'in need'. However, Wilson (2000) and Manatschal and Freitag (2014) argue that it is misleading to view volunteering as an altruistic act, as individuals can have a combination of altruistic and egoistic reasons for engaging in an activity. Using the norm of reciprocity, Musick and Wilson (2008) argue that volunteering is a reciprocal relationship where both individuals benefit. Manatschal and Freitag (2014) distinguish between strategic and altruistic reciprocity. Strategic reciprocity includes instances where individuals volunteer to help others with the expectation that this kindness will be returned at some point in the future. Rather than being repaid by a specific person, it is believed that the good deed will be repaid in a generalised way in the future (Musick & Wilson, 2008). In contrast, altruistic reciprocity is where an individual will volunteer to 'give back' for services already received, rather than the expectation of future rewards (Manatschal & Freitag, 2014; Musick & Wilson, 2008). Underpinning both concepts is a sense of moral obligation, that it is right to be concerned about others.

Dominant perspectives of volunteering are criticised for failing to consider wider changes in society such as the demise of traditional social structures, longer working hours, dual earner households, and changes in the nature of employment, resulting in both unpredict-able and unstable individual biographies where individuals have more freedom to construct their own identity and life course (Cnaan & Handy, 2005; Handy, Brodeur & Cnaan, 2006; Hustinx & Lammertyn, 2003). This has given way to 'new' forms of volunteering which Hustinx and Lammertyn (2003) refer to as reflexive volunteering. In contrast with 'tradi-tional', 'collective', and 'dominant' forms of volunteering, reflexive volunteering is driven by more individualised motivations associated with pursuing personal interests and exciting experiences. Haski-Leventhal et al. (2019) argue that reflexive volunteering is not adequately captured by existing definitions.

Due to their unpredictable and unstable individual biographies, reflexive volunteers are argued to have less time to volunteer and therefore tend to engage in episodic opportunities where they undertake a well-defined role for a specified time period (Rochester et al., 2012). Rather than comprising one distinct category of volunteer, Handy et al. (2006) separate ep-isodic volunteers into three categories: long-term committed volunteers (LTVs) who engage in episodic volunteering alongside long-term, regular committed volunteering; habitual ep-isodic volunteers (HEV) who volunteer for multiple episodic opportunities (three or more) throughout the year; and genuine episodic volunteers (GEV) who volunteer for two or fewer volunteer episodes in a year. The typology proposed by Handy et al. (2006) recognises that rather than engaging in long-term or episodic volunteering, individuals can engage in a 'portfolio of volunteer activities' (Holmes, 2014). Therefore, volunteers can be engaged in both long-term and episodic volunteering at the same time.

Dominant conceptualisations of volunteering present implications for volunteer legacy as they can influence perceptions of volunteering which can impact upon future engagement and in some instances, lead to individuals deciding against volunteering. By way of illustra-tion, the UK Civil Society Almanac (NCVO, 2020) outlines that one of the main barriers to volunteering was the perception that it would be time consuming and lack flexibility, which is consistent with the view that volunteering involves a long-term and regular commitment, as outlined by Cnaan et al. (1996) and Snyder and Omoto (2008).

Furthermore, Hustinx and Meijs (2011) explain that individualisation and the shift from 'traditional' collective volunteering to 'newer', more reflexive forms can also impact upon constructions of volunteering. This can be illustrated using the concept of 'volunteerabil-ity' which consists of an individual's willingness and ability to volunteer (Hustinx & Meijs, 2011). 'Traditional' or 'collective' volunteers are considered to possess a high level of 'vol-unteerability' as their loyalty and dedication to the organisation results in a willingness to volunteer. In addition, they have the time available and/or the ability to overcome obstacles, enabling them to make a regular volunteer commitment. Conversely, reflexive volunteers are considered to be less willing to volunteer and if they do engage in volunteering it is un-dertaken on a more conditional basis and relates to their personal self-interests (Hustinx & Meijs, 2011). The absence of altruistic motivations, potential for rewards, and short-term nature leads to reflexive, episodic volunteering being perceived as "less pure" and a "low level of volunteering" on Cnaan and Handy's spectrum (2005, p. 31).

Rochester et al. (2012) suggest that in contrast to the commitment and dedication demon-strated by long-term volunteers, reflexive volunteers are deemed to have little or no dedica-tion to the organisation and demonstrate less loyalty, due to the presence of self-orientated motives. However, rather than being constructed as an inferior form of volunteering, find-ings from the (NCVO, 2019) indicate that reflexive volunteering offers the potential to engage individuals, particularly those who have never volunteered. Flexible volunteering opportunities where individuals can "dip in and out of activities" were highlighted as factors that can encourage individuals to get involved in volunteering (NCVO, 2019, p. 78). The attractiveness of "giving time for a one-off activity or event", "opportunities to take part in fun and employable activities", and "opportunities to combine volunteering with existing hobbies or interests" were also highlighted (NCVO, 2019, p. 72).

Volunteer legacy

Due to the shortage and importance of volunteers, sport event volunteering research focuses on volunteer management including the motivation, satisfaction and retention of volunteers (Bang, Bravo, Mello Figueroa & Mezzadri, 2019; Kim, Kim, Kim & Zhang, 2019). The various aspects of volunteer management are interrelated. At the beginning of the volunteer journey it is important to understand motivations and expectations so managers can design or assign roles and tasks accordingly (Khoo & Engelhorn, 2011). The extent to which volunteers believe their needs and goals will be fulfilled through volunteering is argued to impact upon future intention to volunteer (Bang, Won & Kim, 2009) and levels of satisfaction (Ralston, Downward & Lumsdon, 2004; Strigas & Jackson Jr, 2003). These two factors are interrelated, as the more satisfied volunteers are, the more likely they will be to volunteer again in the future. The retention of volunteers is considered to be fundamental to the sustainability of events through the provision of a pool of experienced and skilled volunteers available to contribute at future events (Cuskelly, Auld, Harrington & Coleman, 2004).

In the context of the Olympic and Paralympic Games, volunteer retention is framed as the volunteer legacy of the event. Doherty (2009) outlines that volunteer legacy consists of three aspects: increased positive attitudes, increased levels of volunteering, and enhanced volunteer support for future events. Positive volunteer legacy aspirations were evident in the objectives of the London 2012 Games with claims made around how the "inspirational power" and "Olympic spirit" would inspire more people to take part in volunteering, creating a "new culture of volunteering across the UK" (DCMS, 2012, p. 48). The Games Makers were symbolic of these Government aspirations. The narrative around Government aspirations to increase levels of volunteering after the London 2012 Games tended to be associated with 'pure' forms of volunteering, in that the Games were used as a vehicle to encourage levels of long term volunteering within the local community. However, these ideas are problematic given that empirical research ascertains that Games Makers were motivated predominantly by the unique nature of the event (Dickson & Benson, 2013). Given these motivations and the unique Olympic and Paralympic volunteering experience, it is argued that individuals would be less likely to volunteer within their local community due to the differences in the type of volunteering.

There is a small body of literature concentrating on the volunteer intentions of Games Makers following the London 2012 Games which tends to adopt a quantitative approach (Dickson, 2013; Dickson & Benson, 2013; Kim et al., 2019). This body of literature concentrates on identifying individuals' intentions to volunteer immediately after the event (Dickson & Benson, 2013; Dickson, Benson & Terwiel, 2014). Dickson and Benson (2013) revealed that 45% of Games Makers involved in the London 2012 Games expected to increase their levels of volunteering post-event. Further analysis identified that females, younger people (aged 19–44), and those who had not volunteered in the past 12 months planned to volunteer more post the Games. Fairley, Gardiner, and Filo (2016) and Koutrou et al. (2016) support the assertion that individuals without any previous volunteering experience prior to the London 2012 Games were more likely to be engaged in volunteering after the event.

Although this research is useful in identifying volunteer intentions, the findings could be influenced by the 'afterglow' of the event resulting in participants inflating their desire to volunteer again in the future (Dickson & Benson, 2013). Furthermore, the research does not identify motives for continuing volunteering and the extent to which individuals fulfil their plans to volunteer. Longitudinal studies that track actual engagement in volunteering at different points post-event, are required in order to identify if individuals actually go on to volunteer (Doherty, 2009; Doherty & Patil, 2019; Fairley, Kellett & Green, 2007), to identify what types of volunteering they engage in, and the barriers that exist preventing future volunteering.

Acknowledging this research gap, Koutrou et al. (2016) conducted a survey with volunteers four years after the London 2012 Games. This research found high rates of volunteering amongst participants. For those engaged in volunteering, their experience at the London 2012 Games was an important factor influencing their decision to consider further volunteering both at sport events and general activities (Koutrou et al., 2016). Those not currently engaged in volunteering identified three barriers to engagement in volunteering; time, location, and the perception that no other volunteering opportunities were as inspiring as the London 2012 Games (Koutrou et al., 2016). Consistent with research undertaken by NCVO (2019) 'having more time' and an 'inability to make a regular commitment' to volunteering were highlighted as practical issues preventing continued volunteering. This would indicate volunteering being constructed in accordance with the dimensions outlined by Cnaan et al. (1996) and Snyder and Omoto (2008).

The perception that no volunteering opportunity will be as inspiring as the London 2012 Games, and the centrality of the mega-event context to volunteer motivations, has the potential to limit the volunteer legacy of the Games and may impact the type of volunteering that individuals engage in. Related to this, Fairley et al. (2007) found that volunteer's experience at the Sydney 2000 Olympic Games was fundamental to their motives for applying to volunteer at the Athens 2004 Olympics. Specifically, nostalgia, camaraderie, friendship, and feeling a connection to the Olympic Games were key factors. Both these research studies highlight the importance of the volunteer experience on future intention to volunteer, and therefore the potential volunteer legacy of the Games. However, similar to research undertaken by Dickson et al. (2014), the research fails to explore the type of volunteering engaged in. This is an important consideration as it adds to the narrative around volunteer legacy and the type of volunteering that mega-events can encourage. This chapter contributes to the volunteer legacy literature by drawing upon volunteer frameworks to explore how Games Makers' understandings of volunteering impact upon their engagement in volunteering after the event.

Methodology

Data informing this chapter is taken from a larger study investigating volunteer experiences at the London 2012 Paralympic Games which focused on three main areas. First, Games Makers' reasons for volunteering. Second, their experiences at the event and finally their perceptions of disability, disability sport, and the 'disabled' athlete. In order to address the need for both qualitative and longitudinal research, this study adopted a qualitative longitudinal (QL) approach. This involved a series of in-depth semi-structured interviews held at various stages of the volunteers' journey; before, during, immediately after, and approximately 15 months after the Games. By undertaking QL research, the study presented a 'movie' of the lived experience of being a Games Maker at the London 2012 Games

(Neale & Flowerdew, 2003). QL research provided a number of benefits including capturing how experiences unfolded over time; the opportunity to build on issues discussed in each subsequent interview; and developing the credibility and quality of the research. In terms of ensuring the quality of the research, the series of successive interviews allowed the researcher to revisit and clarify information in subsequent interviews. This allowed information to be checked with the participant at various stages of their volunteer journey and the construction of in-depth individual accounts over time.

Criterion-based purposive sampling was adopted to select participants for the study. Criterion-based sampling involves establishing criteria for the selection of cases and then choosing participants because they possess the relevant feature, attribute, or characteristic (Sparks & Smith, 2014). An obvious criterion for individuals to participate in the research was that they had been successful in their application to be a Games Maker and were due to volunteer at the Paralympic Games. In addition, in order to maximise diversity in the research sample, demographic criteria (gender, disability, and ethnicity) and volunteer role were used to select participants. Participants were recruited to the study using social networking, namely Facebook and Twitter. Messages explaining the focus of the research and what participation would involve were posted on various Facebook pages and in Facebook groups. Those who expressed an interest were then sent a participant information sheet, consent form, and asked to complete a screening questionnaire which was used to select the final sample.

A total of 26 participants were recruited to the study, resulting in 91 interviews being conducted over the course of the research: 26 before the Games, 17 during, 25 immediately after, and 23 fifteen months after. All interviews were recorded and personally transcribed verbatim in order to gain intimate knowledge of the data and emerging themes. Interview data were then analysed thematically informed by both thematic (Clarke & Braun &, 2013) and template analysis (King, 2014). Both approaches to coding involve the process of identifying themes within a data set which relate to the research questions through 'attaching' codes to relevant sections of the text. Consistent with template analysis (King, 2014), coding involved a combination of *a priori* codes identified through the literature review and open coding. Codes included those that related to that particular stage in the volunteer journey and those that pertained to all four stages. Given the longitudinal nature of the research, analysis was completed at a number of different levels. The first wave of data analysis involved exploring the individual volunteer journey before exploring the data both cross-sectionally and longitudinally. This ensured the individual experience was maintained whilst also identifying common and divergent themes across cases and change over time. Throughout these waves of data analysis, the coding template was revised to take into account themes arising from each stage of data analysis.

This chapter focuses on four themes relating to participants' understandings of volunteering and their engagement in volunteering following the London 2012 Games. To illustrate the themes arising from the wider sample, this chapter concentrates on seven individual cases who were interviewed at all four stages of their volunteer journey: Megan and Rita, both in their fifties who volunteered at the Paralympic Games and Penny (twenties), Mackenzie (thirties), Adam (thirties), Dawn (forties), and Freya (forties) who volunteered at both the Olympic and Paralympic Games. These individual stories reflect how their journey at the London 2012 Games impacted upon their volunteering post event and have been chosen as they capture the diverse range of experiences and issues that were highlighted by the wider sample. The cases are used to provide a sketch of how the individual's life stage, personal circumstances, and experiences intertwine to influence their conceptualisations of and engagement in volunteering, demonstrating the complexity of volunteer legacy.

Findings

Previous engagement in volunteering

Comparable to the findings of other research (Alexander et al., 2015; Dickson & Benson, 2013), volunteers interviewed as part of this research had volunteered prior to the London 2012 Games. However, unlike existing studies, this research explores the type of volunteering undertaken. This insight is valuable as it can help inform understandings of volunteer legacy by revealing changes in the type of volunteering undertaken post-event.

The seven individuals had differing levels of engagement prior to the London 2012 Games. Despite having previously volunteered in the past, Dawn, Rita, and Freya were not actively volunteering prior to being Games Makers. These three participants will be referred to as non-volunteers. Using the concept of 'volunteerability' outlined by Hustinx and Meijs (2011), their ability to volunteer was impacted by their personal circumstances. For example, due to caring responsibilities for her sick husband, Rita had not been able to dedicate any time to volunteering despite having the willingness to do so. Similarly, both Dawn and Freya had recently divorced and were adjusting to the change in their circumstances.

Conversely, Adam, Penny, Megan, and Mackenzie were actively volunteering although the type and frequency varied. Penny and Mackenzie could both be described as 'collective volunteers' due to their regular commitment and dedication to the organisation (Hustinx & Lammertyn, 2003). Penny had been a regular volunteer at her local Brownie and Guide unit since she was 14 years old. Similarly, Mackenzie was a volunteer within his local church where he completed a number of roles including managing a development group for young people.

The volunteering trajectories of Megan and Adam were more varied with both individuals involved in a 'portfolio of volunteer activities' (Holmes, 2014). Megan had engaged in a combination of collective and reflexive (Hustinx & Lammertyn, 2003) voluntary activities for the past 30 years. Her engagement started when she was in her early twenties when she provided unpaid support to the Multiple Sclerosis (MS) Society as her mother suffered with the condition. She started as a 'wheelchair pusher' but then increased her involvement to assisting with trips and activities for the beneficiaries of the charity. Her other voluntary roles relate to her personal interest in equestrian. When she was younger, Megan was a nanny at an international show jumping competition. More recently, she has been involved in fundraising and rights of way (a path that everyone has the legal right to use) committees, pony club, and Riding for the Disabled. She was also a driver for her local disability transport service. Alongside his paid employment as a nurse, Adam was also engaged in a 'portfolio of volunteer activities' (Holmes, 2014) including volunteering with St Johns Ambulance, British Red Cross, and his local Lowland Search and Rescue team providing medical services.

Definitions of volunteering prior to the London 2012 Games

The descriptions of volunteering provided by the seven participants highlighted how their understandings were linked to their individual biography and their motivations. Understandings of volunteering prior to the London 2012 Games were similar for both those volunteering on a regular basis and those not actively volunteering. The findings illustrate the prominence of norms of reciprocity (Musick & Wilson, 2008) with volunteering constructed as a way of 'giving back'. The specific nature of 'giving back' varied according to their specific biography and personal circumstances. However, there were no differences relating to their volunteer history and type of volunteering engaged in.

Both Mackenzie and Megan, drew upon life events to explain that volunteering was a way of 'giving back' for the services they have received from others. Mackenzie explained that following his amputation he had increased mobility meaning he was now physically able to volunteer.

> ...when I gained my mobility, you know through the amputation, it spurred me on to sacrifice some of my time into helping others. Plenty of people have sacrificed their time for me during the early stages of my disability and I thought, you know what, I'm able to give this back and that's how I got engaged in volunteering.
>
> *(Mackenzie)*

He described his desire to volunteer with young people in order to 'help those less privileged' and to 'give back' for the services he received in childhood. Similarly, Megan described how following the support her mother received from the MS Society and her local hospital when her daughter was ill following childbirth, she needed to 'give something back'.

In contrast, Penny felt a desire to 'give something back' to her local community and society more broadly which arose from her upbringing and the perception that other people might not be as privileged as she is.

> You have to give something back haven't you because some people aren't as privileged as you are. If you've had opportunities in your life, you've got to give others the opportunity to do something as well.
>
> *(Penny)*

The extract from Penny also indicates a sense of obligation in expressing that she feels she has a duty to help those less privileged. Finally, Adam also expressed the need to 'give something back to the community that you live and work in'. However, in this instance it was related to the skills he has and the need to share these for the benefit of others, which volunteering allows him to do. When explaining their understandings and volunteering history, individuals frequently supplemented their desire to give something back with expressing their 'helping' disposition.

These narratives are consistent with altruistic reciprocity outlined by Manatschal and Freitag (2014). Rather than volunteering in order to be compensated by future reward, participants were 'giving something back' for services already received. This type of reciprocity can be considered to have similarities with the dominant perspective of volunteering which is underpinned by altruism and helping others (Rochester et al., 2012). Furthermore, these examples also illustrate that individuals have high levels of 'volunteerability' as they have the willingness to volunteer and feel they have the ability to volunteer in terms of time, skills, social resources, and physicality (Hustinx & Meijs, 2011).

Understandings of volunteering after the London 2012 Games

The benefit of the longitudinal nature of this research is that understandings of volunteering and levels of engagement could be revisited after the London 2012 Games. These data reveal a shift in understandings of volunteering as a result of volunteer experience. In particular, some participants demonstrated increased awareness of the benefits of episodic forms of volunteering whereas others highlighted the difference between traditional and event volunteering based on the reward dimension (Cnaan et al., 1996).

Linking back to Hustinx and Meijs (2011), after the London 2012 Games Dawn, Freya, Adam, and Rita had limited 'volunteerability'. Despite demonstrating the willingness to volunteer they lacked the ability in terms of their availability. Consistent with NCVO (2019) research, differing personal circumstances presented barriers to making a regular commitment to volunteering. For example, Rita had caring responsibilities for her mother which meant that she could not commit to volunteering at the same time each week. Similarly, after the Paralympics, Adam was unable to volunteer due to family commitments. Finally, Freya indicated how being self-employed prevented her being able to commit to regular forms of volunteering as illustrated in the following extract:

> Yeah, that really is more to do with the way I work, because I'm self-employed I travel a lot for work. I only go to London and back and occasionally abroad but not very often. I just don't know where I'm going to be from one week to the next...say I was volunteering at an animal sanctuary which is probably what I would do if I could do something regular, the amount of times I would have to cancel would be awful and that sort of volunteering they need somebody they can rely on and you can't rely on me not because I'm not reliable but because I don't know where I'm going to be from one day to the next...
>
> *(Freya)*

For this group of individuals, their experience at the London 2012 Games increased their awareness of episodic volunteering. In particular, they understood how this type of volunteering could be organised around their existing commitments and planned for in advance. The flexibility of episodic volunteering increased their 'volunteerability' by enabling them to develop the ability to overcome the barriers faced.

Discussions relating to episodic volunteering led to broader discussions about event volunteering and 'traditional' forms of volunteering. The sentiments expressed by participants relate to the reward dimension of volunteering developed by Cnaan et al. (1996) which stipulates that 'pure' volunteering occurs when individuals receive no rewards. The rewards gained from event volunteering were met with criticism from those individuals who still perceived volunteering an altruistic activity intended to help those in need. Illustrative of this, are the sentiments of Megan. Megan discussed how 'real' volunteering was about helping somebody else resulting in a 'long term good' whereas event volunteering was perceived as a 'fun day out with no end result other than people enjoying a sport event'.

> Real volunteering is getting up every Sunday morning and walking round and round, leading a dull old pony with a person with a disability, riding them year in year out, you know, that's the commitment of volunteering rather than you know sports events.
>
> *(Megan)*

The views expressed by Megan are consistent with dominant understandings of volunteering which emphasise the dedication of volunteers in making a regular commitment in order to help others (Rochester et al., 2012). This resonates with 'pure' forms of volunteering, whereby activity is only considered volunteering if it costs the volunteer. In comparison, event volunteering was considered to lead to the accrual of indirect benefits in the form of unique experiences resulting from the intrinsic nature of events, such as being able to go 'backstage' and 'consuming the event experience' whilst volunteering. The London 2012 Games were considered to be a distinct form of volunteering due to the unique attributes of mega-events including the scale of the event, intensity of the experience, and global attention. The distinction made between 'traditional' and event volunteering is potentially problematic for leveraging the volunteer legacy of the Games, specifically increased levels of volunteering within the local community. The construction of event volunteering as a distinct form of volunteering with different motivations limits the ability of the Games to lead to increased levels of volunteering in 'traditional' contexts.

Engagement in volunteering after the London 2012 Games

A limitation of volunteer legacy research is the lack of longitudinal studies that follow up positive volunteer intentions expressed in the 'afterglow' of events. There are limited studies that follow up these intentions to establish if they manifest into increased levels of engagement. The experiences of these seven individuals highlight the complexity of volunteer legacy and stress the importance of exploring engagement in volunteering in the context of their broader life stage. The findings also indicate differing engagement in volunteering related to their prior experiences.

Examining the experiences of Dawn, Rita, and Freya highlights how their awareness of episodic volunteering, resulted in increased engagement in episodic volunteering at a range of different events. This group of individuals expressed an interest in volunteering at various events immediately after the London 2012 Games. By the time of the final interview, 15 months later, this group of individuals had become 'habitual episodic volunteers' (Handy, Brodeur & Cnaan, 2006) and were engaged in multiple episodic opportunities. Illustrative of this are the experiences of Freya who had volunteered at a number of national and international sport events and cultural festivals. Freya's motives for volunteering appear to be consistent with reflexive volunteering (Hustinx & Lammertyn, 2003). For instance, her decision to volunteer at the World Police and Fire Games was positively influenced by her experience at London 2012, whereas her involvement in regional literature and film festivals was related to her personal interests and her connection to the city where she lives. Similarly, Dawn described how she had become a 'volunteer-acholic' (addict) due to the number of events that she had been involved with which included the Anniversary Games (an event held one year after the London 2012 Games), World Police and Fire Games, Rowing World Cup, and LolliBop (a children's festival).

For this group of individuals, given their unpredictable personal circumstances, episodic opportunities were advantageous as they could be organised around existing commitments and planned for in advance allowing them to overcome barriers preventing regular volunteering. Returning to Freya, she explained that she was able to take holiday in order to volunteer at events;

> I mean the short-term things really fit in well because I know I can say yes I can do those three days; I will block them out. I will call them holiday, I will tell everybody that I'm on my holiday, don't bother me for those three days, as long as I have enough warning for people, then I can do that. However, I can't say, I can't work on a Monday because I would lose so much work and I wouldn't be able to do my job properly.
>
> *(Freya)*

Rita indicated how episodic volunteering allowed her to remain flexible and accommodate caring commitments

> I'm not entirely sure that I want to commit to a regular commitment as my mother is quite elderly. My sister looks after her and when I'm retired, I'll be able to help out more so I thought that it would be better if I kept myself flexible and just carry on going for the one-off events.
>
> *(Rita)*

Rita's example illustrates how the combination of life events, the death of her husband, retirement, and her aging mother resulted in the attractiveness of episodic opportunities which allowed her to maintain flexibility.

This information reveals that for those not actively volunteering, mega-event volunteering leverages repeat episodic volunteering at other events rather than encouraging individuals to engage in regular volunteering within their local community. Labelling this type of volunteering as 'less pure' with individuals lacking the dedication and loyalty of 'traditional' volunteers is clearly inappropriate (Rochester et al., 2012). These individual stories reveal the level of commitment of this group of volunteers demonstrated through the frequency of their engagement and the important role that volunteering played in the individual's life. Although this group of volunteers was engaged in episodic volunteering, they did so on a frequent basis.

Conversely, the volunteering trajectories of Penny and Mackenzie provide an interesting contrast. Both these individuals returned to their existing regular volunteer commitments that they were engaged in prior to the London 2012 Games. Immediately after the Games, Mackenzie expressed an interest in volunteering at the Glasgow Commonwealth Games and Rio 2016 Olympic and Paralympic Games. However, in the final interview, Mackenzie had withdrawn his application due to other commitments and limited annual leave. Favouring regular opportunities, Penny had started volunteering with a group of young people with special needs in order to gain more experience to become a special needs teacher. Penny described how volunteering at the Paralympic Games had made her more willing to volunteer with disabled people. Related to this Mackenzie had also expressed an interest in volunteering within wheelchair tennis based on his enjoyment of the sport at the Paralympic Games. However, he had not found suitable opportunities that fit in alongside his employment commitments.

Conclusion

It is evident from the interview data presented that future engagement was influenced by the complex intersection of conceptualisations of volunteering, prior engagement, individual life circumstances, and experiences at the London 2012 Games. Consequently, instead of exploring volunteering at a particular event in isolation, this research emphasises the importance of situating an individual's experience at a specific event within their wider volunteer career and life course (Nichols, Hogg, Knight & Storr, 2019). Advancing existing research, the QL research approach adopted by this study allowed interpretations of volunteering to evolve over the duration of the research study, and for engagement in volunteering to be tracked 15 months after the Games. In doing so, actual volunteer behaviour could be compared with intentions immediately following the event and further detail provided about the type of volunteering engaged in.

The perceptions and volunteer career of these seven individuals reveal that for those not engaged in volunteering prior to the London 2012 Games, their experience at the event increased their awareness of reflexive, episodic volunteer opportunities. The realisation of the benefits of this form of volunteering allowed them to increase their 'volunteerability' by providing a way to overcome obstacles preventing regular forms of volunteering (Hustinx & Meijs, 2011). This is interesting as it suggests the fluidity of volunteering and how both understandings and engagement can be influenced by volunteer experiences.

For some, particularly those involved in collective forms of volunteering prior to the London 2012 Games, the nature of sport event volunteering led them to question whether this type of volunteering could be considered 'real' volunteering due to the presence of rewards such as being 'backstage', 'consuming the event experience', and general enjoyment. Interestingly, this group of volunteers tended to return to their existing volunteer commitments following the event. Where this group did increase their levels of volunteering, it involved additional collective volunteering involving a regular commitment (Hustinx & Lammertyn, 2003).

The findings of this study present implications for volunteer legacy. Rather than using mega-events to facilitate increased levels of regular volunteering within the local community, this research advocates volunteer stakeholders using such events to promote episodic forms of volunteering which may be more attractive to individuals with personal circumstances preventing them from making a regular commitment. For certain individuals, this could present a route into other forms of volunteering where obstacles/barriers can be surmounted or where changes in personal circumstances allow. Furthermore, recognising diverse individual biographies, volunteering opportunities should be so designed that they can be undertaken around other commitments. In doing so, volunteering could appeal to and engage a diverse range of individuals. In addition, the impact of the volunteer experience on future engagement, in particular those not engaged in volunteering prior to the event, emphasises the need for effective volunteer management. Organising Committees for the Olympic Games and volunteer stakeholders need to ensure that volunteers are allocated tasks that meet their expectations and provide adequate support to undertake their roles.

More broadly, conceptualisations of volunteering need to be extended in order to recognise the value of episodic opportunities. As illustrated by this research, focusing on 'dominant' understandings can deter individuals from engaging in volunteering and limit their awareness of the diverse range of opportunities available. Volunteer stakeholders should invest time in educating individuals about these aspects in order to increase their 'volunteerability' (Hustinx & Meijs, 2011).

This study confirms the value of QL research when exploring volunteer legacy. This approach enables the volunteer journey, including motivations, experiences, and future intention to volunteer, to be revealed over time. However, a limitation of the study, is that it is based on the experiences of a small cohort of volunteers within the unique social context of the London 2012 Games. Therefore, the transferability of findings to other mega-events cannot be claimed. Despite this, the research provides rich and interesting insights into volunteer legacy which can form the basis of future studies to explore whether the themes identified resonate with mega-events held within different social contexts.

References

Alexander, A., Kim, S.-B., & Kim, D.-Y. (2015). Segmenting volunteers by motivation in the 2012 London Olympic Games. *Tourism Management, 47*, 1–10. doi:10.1016/j.tourman.2014.09.002

Bang, H., Bravo, G. A., Mello Figueroa, K., & Mezzadri, F. M. (2019). The impact of volunteer experience at sport mega-events on intention to continue volunteering: Multigroup path analysis. *Journal of Community Psychology, 47*(4), 727–742. doi:10.1002/jcop.22149

Bang, H., Won, D., & Kim, Y. (2009). Motivations, commitment, and intentions to continue volunteering for sporting events. *Event Management, 13*(2), 69–81. doi:10.3727/152599509789686317

Clarke, V., & Braun, V. (2013). *Successful qualitative research: A practical guide for beginners.* London: Sage.

Cnaan, R. A., & Handy, F. (2005). Towards understanding episodic volunteering. *Vrijwillige Inzet Onderzocht, 2*(1), 28–35.

Cnaan, R. A., Handy, F., & Wadsworth, M. (1996). Defining who is a volunteer: Conceptual and empirical considerations. *Nonprofit and Voluntary Sector Quarterly, 25*(3), 364–383.

Cuskelly, G., Auld, C., Harrington, M., & Coleman, D. (2004). Predicting the behavioral dependability of sport event volunteers. *Event Management, 9*(1–2), 73–89. doi:10.3727/1525995042781011

DCMS. (2012). *Beyond 2012: The London 2012 legacy story.* Department for Digital, Culture, Media & Sport (DCMS), London.

Dickson, T. J. (2013, 3rd May). *London 2012 volunteers: Motivations & social legacy potential.* Paper presented at the IPC Vista Conference Bonn.

Dickson, T. J., & Benson, A. (2013). *London 2012 games makers: Towards redefining legacy.* Retrieved from https://www.gov.uk/government/uploads/system/uploads/attachment_data/file/224184/Games_Makers_Annex.pdf

Dickson, T. J., Benson, A., & Terwiel, A. F. (2014). Mega-event volunteers, similar or different? Vancouver 2010 vs London 2012. *International Journal of Event and Festival Management, 5*(2), 164–179. doi:10.1108/IJEFM-07-2013-0019

Doherty, A. (2009). The volunteer legacy of a major sport event. *Journal of Policy Research in Tourism, Leisure and Events, 1*(3), 185–207. doi:10.1080/19407960903204356

Doherty, A., & Patil, S. (2019). Reflections on major sport event volunteer legacy research. *Journal of Policy Research in Tourism, Leisure and Events, 11*(sup1), s34–s42. doi:10.1080/19407963.2019.1569433

Fairley, S., Gardiner, S., & Filo, K. (2016). The spirit lives on: The legacy of volunteering at the Sydney 2000 Olympic Games. *Event Management, 20*(2), 201–215.

Fairley, S., Kellett, P., & Green, B. C. (2007). Volunteering abroad: Motives for travel to volunteer at the Athens Olympic Games. *Journal of Sport Management, 21*, 41–57.

Handy, F., Brodeur, N., & Cnaan, R. A. (2006). Summer on the Island: Episodic volunteering. *Voluntary Action, 7*(3), 31–46.

Haski-Leventhal, D., Oppenheimer, M., Holmes, K., Lockstone-Binney, L., Alony, I., & Ong, F. (2019). The conceptualization of volunteering among nonvolunteers: Using the net-cost approach to expand definitions and dimensions of volunteering. *Nonprofit and Voluntary Sector Quarterly, 48*(2_suppl), 30S–51S. doi:10.1177/0899764018768078

Holmes, K. (2014). 'It fitted in with our lifestyle': An investigation into episodic volunteering in the tourism sector. *Annals of Leisure Research, 17*(4), 443–459. doi:10.1080/11745398.2014.965183

Hustinx, L., & Lammertyn, F. (2003). Collective and reflexive styles of volunteering: A sociological modernization perspective. *VOLUNTAS: International Journal of Voluntary and Nonprofit Organizations, 14*(2), 167.

Hustinx, L., & Meijs, L. C. P. M. (2011). Re-embedding volunteering: In search of a new collective ground. *Voluntary Sector Review, 2*(1), 5–21. doi:10.1332/204080511X560594

Khoo, S., & Engelhorn, R. (2011). Volunteer motivations at a national special Olympics event. *Adapted Physical Activity Quarterly, 28*, 27–39.

Kim, M., Kim, S. S.-K., Kim, M., & Zhang, J. J. (2019). Assessing volunteer satisfaction at the London Olympic Games and its impact on future volunteer behaviour. *Sport in Society, 22*(11), 1864–1881. doi:10.1080/17430437.2019.1616926

King, N. (2004). Using templates in the thematic analysis of text. In C. Cassell & G. Symon (Eds.), *Essential guide to qualitative methods in organizational research* (pp. 11–22). London: Sage Publications.

Koutrou, N., Pappous, A., & Johnson, A. (2016). Post-event volunteering legacy: Did the London 2012 games induce a sustainable volunteer engagement? *Sustainability, 8*(12). doi:10.3390/su8121221

Manatschal, A., & Freitag, M. (2014). Reciprocity and volunteering. *Rationality and Society, 26*(2), 208–235. doi:10.1177/1043463114523715

Musick, M. A., & Wilson, J. (2008). *Volunteers: A social profile.* Bloomington: Indiana University Press.

NCVO. (2019). *Time well spent: A national survey on the volunteer experience.* Retrieved from https://www.ncvo.org.uk/images/documents/policy_and_research/volunteering/Volunteer-experience_Full-Report.pdf

NCVO. (2020). *UK Civil Society Almanac 2020 Data. Trends. Insights.* Retrieved from https://data.ncvo.org.uk/volunteering/motivations-and-barriers/

Neale, B., & Flowerdew, J. (2003). Time, texture and childhood: The contours of longitudinal qualitative research. *International Journal of Social Research Methodology, 6*(3), 189–199.

Nichols, G. (2012). Sports volunteering. *International Journal of Sport Policy and Politics, 4*(2), 155–157. doi:10.1080/19406940.2012.667818

Nichols, G., Hogg, E., Knight, C., & Storr, R. (2019). Selling volunteering or developing volunteers? Approaches to promoting sports volunteering. *Voluntary Sector Review, 10*(1), 3–18. doi:10.1332/20 4080519x15478200125132

Ralston, R., Downward, P., & Lumsdon, L. (2004). The expectations of volunteers prior to the XVII Commonwealth Games 2002: A qualitative study. *Event Management, 9*(1–2), 13–26. doi:10.3727/1525995042781084

Rochester, C., Ellis Paine, A., Howlett, S., & Zimmeck, M. (2012). *Volunteering and society in the 21st century*. Basingstoke: Palgrave Macmillan.

Snyder, M., & Omoto, A. M. (2008). Volunteerism: Social issues perspectives and social policy implications. *Social Issues and Policy Review, 2*(1), 1–36. doi:10.1111/j.1751-2409.2008.00009.x

Sparks, A. C., & Smith, B. (2014). *Qualitative research methods in sport, exercise and health: From process to product*. London: Routledge.

Strigas, A. D., & Jackson Jr, E. N. (2003). Motivating volunteers to serve and succeed: Design and results of a pilot study that explores demographics and motivational factors in sport volunteerism. *International Sports Journal, 7*(1), 111.

Wilson, J. (2000). VOLUNTEERING. *Annual Review of Sociology, 26*, 215–240.

27

CREATING A SOCIAL LEGACY FROM EVENT VOLUNTEERING

Robert Rogerson, Fiona Reid and Rafaelle Nicholson

Introduction

While volunteering has been a consistent feature of most societies over the centuries, in the past few decades there has been a growing expectation in public and social policy that volunteering can contribute to individual development, the social cohesion of communities, and address social needs. From notions of the 'Big Society' in the UK, the European Union's Volunteering Charter, and the annual recognition of volunteering on International Volunteers Day by the United Nations, expectations about the valuable contribution that volunteering can make are at a new high globally (Rochester, 2018).

This awareness has come at a time when research has highlighted that the ways in which people engage with volunteering is changing. Previous models of a small but highly dedicated proportion of the population giving sustained commitment to voluntary groups and causes has given way to a more eclectic mix of forms of commitment in civic society (Hustinx & Lammertyn, 2003). This includes expansions of new forms of episodic volunteering, the focus of this chapter. The rise of more reflexive and individual forms of volunteering has loosened bonds between individuals and voluntary organisations (Eimhjellen et al., 2018), and has profound implications for the operational sustainability of organisations reliant on volunteering (Dunn et al., 2020).

In this context where volunteering commitment is time limited and often task-specific, greater attention has been given to the ways in which event volunteering, and especially major sport event volunteering, can offer insights that have resonance across the wider volunteering landscape. As inherently episodic, event volunteering has underlined the importance of a deeper understanding of how best to recruit, train, and retain volunteers, and how management practices impact on volunteer satisfaction and future behaviour. Although events are by their nature one-off, unique experiences for most volunteers, research has signalled that a positive experience of event volunteering can lead to future, regular volunteering (Doherty, 2009). However, future volunteering is only one expression of how a one-off event volunteering experience might impact on those involved.

The central thrust of this chapter is to explore how event volunteering research can offer insights into whether such volunteering experiences can engender wider social legacies, and if so, how these legacies might be achieved. This focus adds to the considerable corpus

DOI: 10.4324/9780367815875-32

of research into the more direct impacts of events (including volunteering legacies) that encourages event organisers and policy makers to use major events strategically for social, economic, and environmental purposes. Our argument is that events are opportunities to leverage additional, less direct impacts including the generation of social benefits (Chalip, 2017). Such leveraging utilises the experiences and liminoid feelings engendered by events to create social outcomes through strategic and managed approaches. The underlying theory of change is that major sporting events can help to inspire social change, with the experience breaking "down social barriers, thereby enabling behaviours and social interaction that might otherwise be unlikely or impossible during everyday life" (Chalip, 2014, p. 5).

In particular, this chapter seeks to illuminate debate over connections between event volunteering and its social contribution to local communities and society more generally. To open up discussion about achieving such social legacies, it draws on the experience of a dedicated event volunteer program associated with the 2014 Commonwealth Games held in Glasgow. This Host City Volunteer (HCV) initiative was a deliberate attempt to infiltrate a different culture and approach to volunteering from that traditionally found in the 'market place' of event volunteering. Such approaches have been subjected to a mounting critique that pressure to deliver successful events marginalises the production of social legacies. In contrast, the HCV initiative sought explicitly to enhance social connectivity amongst volunteers by using both the event volunteering experience and the wider volunteer development program in order to foster higher levels of social linkages within communities and social networks. Using unique insights from the Host City Volunteers' experiences before the Games, during the event, and in the subsequent three years, this chapter further examines how the management of event volunteering and the social policy context in which such programs are constructed can lead to social legacies.

After exploring this specific initiative, the latter part of the chapter widens the discussion to firstly consider lessons around event volunteering management. These include how the adoption of particular event management and planning tools may increase the likelihood of leveraging social outcomes. This is particularly relevant where such tools acknowledge that the event volunteering role is a new experience for the participant, requiring opportunities to learn about being socially connected, and being agile enough to respond to the consequences of such learning. We also reflect on how generating social and volunteering legacies can be assisted by more fluid legacy planning (Byers et al., 2020), adapting in response to emerging evidence and volunteer experiences ahead of the event, as part of overall event management.

Secondly, we use the HCV experiences, as revealed through detailed interviews and focus groups, to explore how volunteering legacies and social legacies are inter-connected. In particular, we reflect on Doherty and Patil's (2019) call to examine potentially negative volunteer experiences, and Sharp's (2018) analysis of volunteer well-being as a key element of achieving social impacts and legacies.

Thirdly, we extend our discussion of social connectedness as an HCV legacy goal to consider how event volunteering and episodic volunteering relate to the development of social capital. Specifically, we consider networks, norms, and trust that facilitate coordination and cooperation for mutual benefit (Putnam, 1995), and foster cultural values such as kindness, philanthropy, and acceptance (Fukuyama, 1995).

New models of volunteering

Volunteering is continually evolving, with new forms emerging and the nature of existing volunteering activity altering, reflecting wider transformations in society. As a result, its conceptualisation has changed. Whilst there is a broad consensus in academic research on the core characteristics of volunteering, perceptions within wider society have been more fluid (Hustinx et al., 2010; Oppenheimer & Warburton, 2014). This has led McAllum (2014) to suggest that the term remains ambiguous. Traditional notions of volunteering as face-to-face, collectively undertaken and organised, and requiring free (i.e., non-work) time commitments are being reshaped. One clear trend globally has been the emergence and growth of short term episodic volunteering, variously described as a rise in informal voluntary participation (Nichols, 2017), cause-driven volunteering (Evans & Saxton, 2005), and 'revolving door' engagement (Dekker & Halman, 2003).

Importantly, the impact of the growth of such episodic volunteering extends beyond the nature of the volunteering input. First, it has opened up volunteering to a wider cohort of the population, including those who have previously been non-volunteers. The time limited nature of the volunteering activity offers more flexibility to incorporate it into people's life patterns, reinforced by the attractive, often simple and memory-forming activities (Haski-Leventhal et al., 2018). Second, this form of volunteering often involves people with shared values and focuses on purposeful outcomes for a community or cause, which are quickly realised and evident. This makes it appealing to those seeking a focused outcome and benefit from their input. Third, episodic volunteering reinforces a shift towards people increasingly seeking specific experiences and rewards rather than just supporting a cause (Rochester et al., 2016). Finally, in what might be described as a 'gateway', episodic volunteering offers a convenient entry point to begin longer term volunteering contributions to society (Haski-Levenethal et al., 2018).

In this debate, a key element is the degree to which different forms of volunteering contribute to society, and in particular offer societal benefits beyond the direct actions of the volunteer. In exploring one example of episodic volunteering we argue that such time limited and event focused volunteering can provide societal benefits, but this is not a 'given' or achieved without deliberate consideration of how social legacies can be supported. Our contribution here moves the focus to a particular form of episodic volunteering, event volunteering, and within that our lens is on major sporting event volunteering. Such cases resonate with episodic volunteering of other types and settings, and can specifically focus on developing wider societal benefits well beyond the confines of the major sporting event.

Using events to introduce volunteering ethos

As Preuss (2007) contends, a legacy is a consequence of the event. As such, the cohort of event volunteers could be considered one legacy component, having been trained and supported to help deliver the event. For some commentators like Dickson et al. (2013) the presence of this cohort is a latent legacy. Such legacy is only realised if there is either an increase in volunteering from existing volunteers and/or the recruitment of people new to volunteering as a result of their roles at the event.

Conceiving legacy in this way has meant that to date, most research on episodic and event volunteering has examined how these opportunities can act as precursors to widening future volunteering, creating a 'volunteering ethos'. In particular, short term one-off volunteering that dominates event volunteering is viewed as a way to target those who have limited experience, thereby generating new recruits to volunteering. The assumption, based on some evidence, is that there are non-volunteers who, with the right incentives or volunteer roles, could potentially be attracted to volunteer. They have, as Meijs et al. (2006) argue, 'volunteerability', that is, the ability of individuals to become volunteers by overcoming obstacles that impede engagement. Such obstacles include lower levels of motivation, less positive attitudes to volunteering, and less appreciation of values of volunteerism than those already engaged with volunteering (Haski-Leventhal et al., 2019). Further, once they have become engaged in volunteering, individuals are more likely to overcome time constraints to volunteer in the future.

Dunn et al.'s (2016) review of the academic literature on episodic volunteering suggests that emphasis on altruism (helping others) and social interaction can be primary motivators to encourage engagement by new volunteers. However, they admit that research is still in the early stages of development and there is an absence of primary qualitative data to identify salient motives for episodic volunteering. Similar gaps have been identified with sport event volunteering research (Kim, 2018). Kim's research underlines common motivators of altruistic values and social networks, and adds the motivational attraction of links with sport in recruiting volunteers.

One potential key barrier to volunteering is the degree of isolation of individuals. There is no shortage of evidence that people who are isolated are unlikely to look for opportunities for volunteering or to take up those that are offered to them. They are viewed as lacking the confidence and a shared culture of participation that encourages people into volunteering activities (Lim & Laurence, 2015). Mobilising them thus requires providing both self-confidence and experience of the collective ethos of volunteering. In turn, volunteering can play an important role in addressing and overcoming isolation (Volunteer Now, 2017).

There is a deeper question about whether event volunteering offers a logical starting point for wider volunteering, thus generating volunteering legacies. Event volunteering, especially around major sports events, is formalised and organised. In this respect, it mirrors volunteering conducted within a registered organisation where roles are set out, and thus the transfer of experiences into such settings may be easier. However, as noted above, new models of volunteering constructed around looser-knit forms of collective volunteering are becoming more typical of contemporary volunteering (Rochester, 2018). In this context, the transference of event volunteering into other forms may be more challenging, especially where individual motivation, identification of roles and tasks, and networking are all required of the individual volunteer. Thus experiences, knowledge, and skills acquired within event volunteering may not be easily transferred to those contexts (Paine et al., 2014), and may be less pertinent where informal volunteering like 'helping' out a friend or a neighbour is undertaken on an individual basis (Hickman et al., 2014; Woolvin & Harper, 2015).

Generating a wider social legacy

Beyond such issues around volunteering legacies, there are further questions over whether other social impacts and legacies are being constructed and supported through event volunteering. There is a growing recognition that these impacts need to be better understood (Brown et al., 2015, Kim et al., 2015), and there remains a pressing need to explore the wider social benefits, beyond those of a specific event, where emphasis is on assisting event organisers (Wallstam et al., 2020). To this end, more attention is now being given to addressing our understanding of the social legacies associated with events and how to measure their social impact.

In considering these questions, we draw upon Wallstam et al.'s (2020) definition that:

> social impacts encompass everything from the conditions in which people live and their quality of life to their well-being and happiness. The social impact of planned events, therefore, sees the event as the agent affecting change in peoples' lives.
>
> *(Wallstam et al., 2020, p. 4)*

Table 27.1 Social indicators of events

Key indicator	Impact being measured
Community quality of life	The general impact on the perceived conditions under which community residents live.
Community pride	The impact on community residents' sense of pride from living in a locality where a certain event takes place.
Social capital	The impact an event has on community residents' social networks and networking opportunities.
Sense of community	The impact an event has on community residents' perceived sense of cohesion following an event.
Community capacity enhancement	The ways in which an event provides opportunities for community members to somehow build competency.
Facilities impact	The perceived improvement of infrastructure and facilities because of a planned event, as well as the perceived access to these facilities for community members.

Source: Based on Wallstam et al. (2020, pp. 134–136).

Measuring such impact or legacy can be through social impact indicator(s) which assess directly or indirectly the effect of the event on the societal issues. However, in analyses of social legacies, volunteering issues do not feature prominently, and indeed are absent from many (e.g., see Chalip, 2006). This absence is also found in the social impact indicators derived through consensus by Wallstam et al. (2020), as illustrated in Table 27.1, although many of the impacts they identify may be enhanced through event volunteering.

These absences have meant that in practice, the definition and measurement of social impacts and legacies has been left to individual events and event managers. This was the case with the HCV Program, which we will now examine.

The Host City Volunteer programme

As part of the 2014 Commonwealth Games held in Glasgow, a team of 1,100 HCVs was deployed across the city to complement the 12,500 venue-based 'Clyde-sider' volunteers recruited, trained, and managed by the 2014 Organising Committee, Glasgow 2014 Ltd. The HCV program was managed by Glasgow Life on behalf of Glasgow City Council and independent of the Organising Committee. It was designed to run over a period of three years: in advance of the event to recruit and train volunteers; during the event to support the volunteers in undertaking their roles; and for 12 months thereafter, to assist volunteers to reflect on their event experiences and to help identify future roles (Rogerson et al., 2018). Over this extended time period, the program sought to utilise specific event volunteering opportunities at the 2014 Commonwealth Games as a means to encourage people to: overcome barriers to general volunteering; support future volunteering; foster civic pride, and encourage HCVs to help their local communities.

The HCV program was viewed as successful in meeting its primary objectives (SMG, 2016). It supported the delivery of the Commonwealth Games and provided opportunities for local people to feel connected, and have an active part in the event. It was more inclusive, attracting those without prior volunteering experience, and ensured that the volunteers had a positive experience. Research conducted in the period immediately after the Games also highlighted the strong intention amongst the HCVs to continue to volunteer (Rogerson et al., 2015). Since the end of the Commonwealth Games in 2014, further research has been conducted with the HCVs, including a follow-on study three years later by the authors. This highlighted that, although highly motivated by their roles at the event, the HCV's intentions to increase volunteering were not translated into subsequent behaviour. Indeed, most HCVs are continuing with similar levels of volunteering as those prior to the event (Rogerson et al., 2018).

A key feature of the HCV program was that it sought both to focus on social outcomes leveraged through the event volunteering opportunities, and to conceive and manage the event roles to support these goals. As a purposeful initiative, it was unique in recent major sporting events to place social legacies into the planning process. One element of this was the recruitment process. This was designed as a way to enhance links between event volunteering and social equity, without being prescriptive about the profile of the event volunteers. There was an appreciation that the opportunity to have a positive impact on social equity would be absent if the HCV program failed to get interest amongst those groups least connected and networked. The program thus sought to reach into those communities wanting to be part of the event, but least likely to have the knowledge about how to apply, or to have had prior experience of volunteering. A more targeted and personal approach was used, drawing on existing community networks to use word of mouth to encourage applications, and a much-simplified process of application. In so doing, it aimed to reach into communities frequently under-represented in event volunteering, including people with disabilities, asylum seekers, refugees, black and minority ethnic women, and people over the age of 60. In part, this approach reflected the time pressures placed on the scheme for recruitment, but also the difficulties experienced by other events globally in reaching out to those most excluded. The profile of those recruited underscored the value of this approach in achieving more social equity, with 31% reporting that they had never volunteered before, 15% identifying themselves as disabled, and 11% stating they were aged 65 or older (Sly, 2018). Across the group, 38% were considered 'hard pressed', experiencing the most difficult social conditions including struggling families, burdened singles, and those finding hardship in high-rise or inner-city properties.

A second planned legacy was associated with the development of capacity building. Whilst most event volunteering programs include training, they position this as focusing on event delivery (primary), and in some cases learning applicable to future volunteering (secondary). There are increasing questions about whether events should have a role in providing opportunities for education and skills development (Lundberg et al., 2019). The HCV program approach differed from the above foci, seeking to deliver capacity building set within a context of leadership skills (for some), group working and social networking (for all), and citizenship (for all). The main focus was on creating engaged citizens and on strengthening social connections, although in reality the measurable legacy outcome was future volunteering.

A variety of different pathways were provided as part of the HCV program. Using Stebbins' (2005, 2007) schema of leisure, these included:

a   Continued project-based leisure volunteering – offering their services to support future events in the city as part of Glasgow Life's strategy for economic and social change. In this respect, it provided civic benefits as these volunteers brought with them skills and knowledge obtained through previous experiences, and reduced needs for training.

The HCV program mirrored the aim of the Manchester Event Volunteers, Commonwealth Games in Manchester 2002, and the London 2012 Olympics Ambassadors programme (Nichols et al., 2017).

b   Serious leisure volunteering – spurred on by the experience of being an HCV, the hope was that some of the volunteers would become more committed volunteers within their local community organisations (including sport). There is a paucity of research into evaluating residents' future volunteering intentions in a post-event legacy era (Shipway et al., 2019b) although Wilks (2016) deployed the notion of serious leisure to explore volunteering at the London 2012 Olympics through the use of diaries. Examples of serious leisure volunteering included the Facebook-based group, VAMOS2014. The participants of which have migrated from a one-off role as Frontrunners at the 2014 Games to more regular but still leisurely volunteers (i.e., not seeking paid work or career/skills development). VAMOS2014 reinforces Fairley et al.'s (2014) assessment of the importance of the social connections that volunteers create amongst themselves during sport events, making leisure experiences enjoyable while supporting a stronger commitment to the activity.

c   Casual leisure volunteering – adopting Stebbins' (2007) characteristics of play, relaxation, and passivity, the HCV program aimed to generate more sociable and social volunteering to support people within communities, where social connectedness was more important and volunteering called upon on a casual basis as needed.

Analysis three years after the event of the HCV program suggest that whilst volunteering had actually decreased from pre-Games levels (Rogerson et al., 2019), with 61% of respondents (193 people) volunteering in 2017, compared with 72% (219 people) before the Games, there was a growth in levels of social connectedness (Rogerson et al., 2022). More felt connected to their local community (20%), felt more able to influence decisions affecting their local area (22%), met up with other people more than they did before the Games (25%), and talked to their neighbours more than they did before the Games (16%). Additionally, the research also uncovered a number of intangible impacts which respondents associated with being involved in the HCV program. Themes included community involvement as well as increased civic pride and, on a personal level, improved self-confidence and improved psychological wellbeing.

Achieving these social impacts required a different approach to post-event planning, a third strand of legacy planning. Previous research has highlighted the absence of sufficient tactics and strategies being utilised to leverage opportunities arising from an enhanced sense of community amongst residents with both current and future volunteering intentions (Nichols et al., 2017; Shipway et al., 2019a). In part, this can reflect the complexity of post-event legacy planning and delivery, making achievement of such opportunities difficult (Nichols et al., 2017). Often, it is the result of event planning failure to consider and explore the mechanisms or structures by which this can be achieved (Shipway et al., 2019b). In the case of the HCV program, there was a conscious attempt to simplify this by integrating the immediate (one year) post-event delivery of a legacy within the overall planning, and retaining staff in the management team for this period. The smaller scale and the operations team being external to the Organising Committee made this possible.

Lessons from Glasgow 2014

Although the Host City Volunteer initiative may be unique to Glasgow's Commonwealth Games, it does nevertheless resonate with many attempts across sporting and similar events to leverage social benefits through event volunteering. The fact that the HCV program actively sought to place these as part of its legacy planning makes it stand out, and in turn, offers some potentially significant insights of value to other contexts. There are three main points we believe merit more detailed consideration.

First, there are key lessons and implications in terms of event volunteering management in order to increase the likelihood of leveraging social outcomes. Event planning tools need to acknowledge that where the event volunteering role is a new experience for the participant there must be opportunities to learn about being socially connected. Importantly too, event planning needs to be agile enough to respond to the consequences of such learning.

More significant is the need to move away from the traditional viewpoint of event volunteering as an altruistic activity (i.e., the common good of the event and host city), to one where individualism is more significant. In other words, by seeking to alter event volunteers' identity, behaviour, and values through the event, the focus for event managers moves beyond supporting the (event) community. In this respect, it mirrors what Beck (1992) and others have commented more generally about identity. The constructed nature of the event volunteer process is thus of importance, not only in recruiting for a wider purpose (in this case, legacy), but also altering the ways in which event experience is considered (e.g. skills, team working, leadership, social connections), and in turn, how success is being measured. Individualisation can therefore create what Smit and Melissen (2018) see as a socially deflective choice rather than a socially cooperative choice.

One aspect of this is that event volunteer management has to switch away from managing the tangible product of 'a role' in the event, to one seeking to enhance experiences. Event volunteer management is about achieving (or exceeding) volunteers' expectations (key to retention), and providing memorable encounters and even transformative experiences so that longer-term impacts can be achieved. Together, the focus is less on event delivery roles and more on finding ways to meet the different and individual desires of the volunteers. In turn, this alters the ways in which event volunteers have to be catered for, or managed during the event, by being more sensitive to the stimuli that are triggering positive or negative experiences.

However, there are inherent contradictions within this approach. Take, for example, Hawkins and Bonney's (2019) exposition of how event volunteering could be continuously improved through adopting 'lean' approaches. Borrowing the language and insights from the car manufacturing industry, and also widely adopted in other business contexts, the authors argued that the elimination of waste to maximise benefits for people (in this case volunteers) that characterise the lean approach is also applicable to the event industry. Advantageously, such a lean approach could include: systematically and efficiently leveraging the skills and knowledge of volunteers to improve their event experience; addressing under-utilised creativity by freeing up creative personnel to spend more time on the creative aspects and less on the administration side of event planning and management; reducing time spent by volunteers that is unused; and, decreasing occasions where there are excessive numbers of volunteers. To the contrary, and undermining the goal of maximising social legacy objectives, many of the above changes could have undesirable effects. They will, for example, reduce the time for social interactions, for networks to be formed between volunteers, and for them to benefit beyond the skills of event volunteering.

Our second implication relates to the event volunteers and their motivations and expectations of social legacies arising from their involvement in events. Whilst enabling these to occur can be an important part of event management as suggested above, embedded in this is an assumption that the volunteers are seeking such experiences. It presumes that they are looking for legacies/impacts which extend beyond the event itself. Empirical evidence from research conducted at major events suggests that a minority engage with event volunteering for this purpose (Blackman et al., 2017; Doherty, 2009). A consistent picture emerges from surveys conducted on motivations, that being part of the event and giving back time and resources to support the event, and the wider community, are key motivating factors.

One proposed entry point to enhancing our understanding of motivation is to examine more deeply the effect of dissatisfaction amongst event volunteers. To date, little evidence exists on the impact of poor or negative volunteering experiences and their effect on the volunteer's subsequent behaviour (Doherty & Patil, 2019). The assumption is that if the event experience is perceived as not meeting expectations and leaving bad memories, then those involved are unlikely to be repeat event volunteers. It is assumed that this could be extended to other volunteering too. A similar lack of research exists around whether bad volunteering experiences impact on other social legacies. The subsequent social connectedness of the small cohort of HCVs who indicated that they were not satisfied with their experience, statistically only 1% of the 1,100 volunteers, did not vary from those satisfied. This may be a fruitful area for further, in-depth qualitative analysis.

Our third implication relates to the balance of contribution that event volunteering makes between personal, individual benefits and wider societal impacts. Similar to previous research, Hallmann et al. (2020) suggest that volunteers primarily volunteered for personal growth and the focus on personal benefits dominates the approaches used to research legacies. For example, whilst recognising that event volunteers are by nature diverse and are likely to have different motivations to participate, Kim et al.'s (2018) useful attempt to conduct segmentation analysis continues to underscore personal rather than societal or collective benefits. Their cluster analysis builds on six factors, each of which is expressed primarily in terms of what volunteers wanted individually, with only factor 4 (Community Involvement) relating to community. However, even here the factor included 'I am proud of my community for hosting this sport event' and 'I want to express my pride in my community'. Sharp's (2018) recent analysis of volunteer well-being highlights that this can represent a largely under-researched contribution to the social impacts and legacies of an event, and specifically event volunteering. The reported increase in levels of self-confidence, optimism, and a feeling of usefulness in her research acts as a reminder that social benefits can extend beyond future volunteering.

Appreciative that such outcomes can be leveraged through event volunteering, the HCV program sought to utilise the event opportunities to foster the development of social capital and, in particular, networks, norms, and trust that facilitate coordination and cooperation for mutual benefit (Putnam, 1995), as well as foster cultural values such as kindness, philanthropy, and acceptance (Fukuyama, 1995). It sought to enhance the psychic connections between people that can lead to a series of behavioural outcomes, such as civic engagement and social participation, that are beneficial to a community (Misener & Mason, 2006). Whilst there is research indicating involvement in sports events (by volunteers, participants, and other actors) as helping to build social capital, Zhou and Kaplanidou (2018, p. 192) suggest that "there is a missing link between social capital development and community benefits that answer the question: what are the processes through which social capital can benefit the community long term?".

Hallmann et al.'s (2020) research helps to address this missing link. Drawing on a sample of volunteers at the 2014 Special Olympics in Germany, they found that strong interconnections between motivation, commitment, and social capital exist in event volunteering, with the development of social capital significantly mediated by commitment amongst the volunteers. Of course, this could indicate that short term, episodic volunteering, with its associated limited levels of commitment, is less likely to foster social capital. Zhou and Kaplanidou's (2018) analysis of social capital building through participation in local running events is insightful as it underlines that periodic involvement, which creates social bonds, is possible. However, their analysis remains constructed within the context of the event itself rather than wider social capital. They conclude, for example, that "because of the perceived social benefits from sport events, participants became more tolerant toward the inconvenience and costs associated with events, demonstrating cooperative and supportive behaviours towards the events" (Zhou & Kaplanidou, 2018, p. 500).

Concluding thoughts

As part of the increasing importance of non-infrastructural, intangible, or 'soft' legacies arising from major events in justifying the hosting of events, renewed attention is being given to measuring their social impact (Lockstone-Binney et al., 2020; Wallstam et al., 2020). Post-event volunteering forms one important dimension of this, but as we have argued here, event volunteering can also contribute to wider social legacies. The HCV program marks an example of a limited number of attempts in event volunteering programs to build social legacies into their planning. Its conditional success reflects well on the local organising team in Glasgow, but it also underlines the limited attention that has been given to social legacy delivery as part of events, and in volunteering more specifically. As both Thomson et al. (2019) and Byers et al. (2020) note, in connection with sports event legacy more generally, there is a need for a more holistic approach to understand how social legacies can be delivered. Such a model needs to move away from individual event experiences to distinguish between event-specific outcomes and more general conclusions (Koenigstorfer et al., 2019).

There has been excessive focus on the processes of event volunteering delivery, and to a much more limited extent, on legacy delivery. In turn, this has emphasised the role, interests, and experiences of some key stakeholders, especially event rights holders (e.g. International Olympic Committee and Commonwealth Games Federation). In this context, there remains a need to focus more research on how legacies associated with event volunteering are produced (Bocarro et al., 2018).

In asking different questions about how event volunteering can impact on people's behaviour and intentions, the HCV program sought to look beyond an approach to event volunteering which sees the event itself as a solution to the wider issue of enhancing volunteerism in society. Instead, it focused on how more tangential, but nevertheless potentially longer lasting, event volunteering can foster social connectedness – with the city, with communities, and with other people. In this respect, it redefines the event roles as more than an opportunity to experience volunteering.

However, accompanying this is a need for more attention to be given to other perspectives, especially of the participant event volunteers and their 'realities', as part of a critical realist conceptualisation (Byers et al., 2020). As the HCV program has revealed, despite the adoption of the learning and many of the best practices derived from other recent major events (Rogerson et al., 2019), and the success of the program in motivating volunteers, it did not translate into future volunteering behaviour. More attention is required as to which aspects of the volunteer's context impact on such translation processes. This would extend research beyond post-event volunteering towards an understanding of, which characteristics of volunteering opportunities motivate event volunteers, and into the factors which inhibit their engagement with such opportunities.

Byers et al. (2020)'s call for exploring legacies as 'wicked problems' through a critical realist lens is a positive start towards this. However, as event volunteering continues to become a more significant part of events across the world, there is a need to extend our investigations beyond the complex and multifaceted process of legacy delivery to engage with event volunteers. As key stakeholders, and crucial actors in the realisation of social legacies, they have to be placed centre stage.

References

Beck, U. (1992). *Risk society: Towards a new modernity.* London: Sage Publications.

Blackman, D., Benson, A. M., & Dickson, T. J. (2017). Enabling event volunteer legacies: A knowledge management perspective. *Event Management, 21*(3), 233–250. https://doi.org/10.3727/15259 9517X14942648527473

Bocarro, J., Byers, T., & Carter, L. (2018). Legacy of sporting and non-sporting mega event research: What next? In I. Brittain, J. Bocarro, T. Byers & Kamilla Swart (Eds.), *Legacies and mega-events: Facts or fairy tales* (pp. 7–24). Routledge. https://doi.org/10.4324/9781315558981

Brown, S., Getz, D., Pettersson, R., & Wallstam, M. (2015). Event evaluation: Definitions, concepts and a state of the art review. *International Journal of Event and Festival Management, 6*(2), 135–157. http://orcid.org/0000-0001-9322-1299

Byers, T., Hayday, E., & Pappous, A. S. (2020). A new conceptualization of mega sports event legacy delivery: Wicked problems and critical realist solution. *Sport Management Review, 23*(2), 171–182. https://doi.org/10.1016/j.smr.2019.04.001

Chalip, L. (2006). Towards social leverage of sport events. *Journal of Sport & Tourism, 11*(2), 109–127. https://doi.org/10.1080/14775080601155126

Chalip, L. (2014). From legacy to leverage. In J. Grix (Ed.), *Leveraging legacies from sports mega-events: Concepts and cases* (pp. 2–12). Palgrave Pivot. https://doi.org/10.1057/9781137371188

Chalip, L. (2017). Event bidding, legacy, and leverage. In R. Hoye & M. Parent (Eds.,) *The SAGE handbook of sport management* (pp. 401–420). Sage. http://dx.doi.org/10.4135/9781473957961

Dekker, P., & Halman, L. (2003). *The values of volunteering: Cross-cultural perspectives.* Kluwer Academic/ Plenum Publishers. https://doi.org/10.1007/978-1-4615-0145-9

Dickson, T. J., Benson, A. M., Blackman, D. A., & Terwiel, A. F. (2013). It's all about the games! 2010 Vancouver Olympic and Paralympic winter games volunteers. *Event Management, 17*(1), 77–92. https://doi.org/10.3727/152599513X13623342048220

Doherty, A. (2009). The volunteer legacy of a major sport event. *Journal of Policy Research in Tourism, Leisure and Events, 1*(3), 185–207. https://doi.org/10.1080/19407960903204356

Doherty, A., & Patil, S. (2019). Reflections on major sport event volunteer legacy research. *Journal of Policy Research in Tourism, Leisure and Events, 11*(Sup1), S34–S42. https://doi.org/10.1080/1940796 3.2019.1569433

Dunn, J., Chambers, S. K., & Hyde, M. K. (2016). Systematic review of motives for episodic volunteering. *VOLUNTAS: International Journal of Voluntary and Nonprofit Organizations, 27*(1), 425–464. https://doi.org/10.1007/s11266-015-9548-4

Dunn, J., Scuffham, P., Hyde, M. K., Stein, K., Zajdlewicz, L., Savage, A., Heneka, N., Ng, S. K., & Chambers, S. K. (2020). Designing organisational management frameworks to empower episodic volunteering. *VOLUNTAS: International Journal of Voluntary and Nonprofit Organizations.* https://doi. org/10.1007/s11266-020-00226-5

Eimhjellen, I., Steen-Johnsen, K., Folkestad, B., & Ødegård, G. (2018). Changing patterns of volunteering and participation. In B. Enjolras & K. Strømsnes (Eds.), *Scandinavian civil society and social transformations: The case of Norway* (pp. 25–65). Springer, https://doi.org/10.1007/978-3- 319-77264-6

Evans, E., & Saxton, J. (2005). *The 21st century volunteer: A report on the changing face of volunteering in the 21st century.* nfpSynergy.

Fairley, S., Green, B. C., O'Brien, D., & Chalip, L. (2014). Pioneer volunteers: The role identity of continuous volunteers at sport events. *Journal of Sport and Tourism, 19*(3–4), 233–255. https://doi.or g/10.1080/14775085.2015.1111774

Fukuyama, F. (1995). *Trust: The social virtues and the creation of prosperity.* Free Press. https://doi.org/10.2307/20752121

Hallmann, K., Zehrer, A., Fairley, S., & Rossi, L. (2020). Gender and volunteering at the Special Olympics: Interrelationships among motivations, commitment, and social capital. *Journal of Sport Management, 34*(1), 77–90. https://doi.org/10.1123/jsm.2019-0034

Haski-Leventhal, D., Meijs, L. C., Lockstone-Binney, L., Holmes, K., & Oppenheimer, M. (2018). Measuring volunteerability and the capacity to volunteer among non-volunteers: Implications for social policy. *Social Policy & Administration, 52*(5), 1139–1167. https://doi.org/10.1111/spol.12342

Haski-Leventhal, D., Oppenheimer, M., Holmes, K., Lockstone-Binney, L., Alony, I., & Ong, F. (2019). The conceptualization of volunteering among nonvolunteers: Using the net-cost approach to expand definitions and dimensions of volunteering. *Nonprofit and Voluntary Sector Quarterly, 48*(2_suppl), 30S–51S. https://doi.org/10.1177%2F0899764018768078

Hawkins, C. J., & Bonney, M. S. (2019). Lean thinking in leisure: continuously improving event volunteering and management. *Annals of Leisure Research, 22*(3), 362–372. https://doi.org/10.1080/11745398.2019.1568267

Hickman, P., Batty, E., Dayson, C., & Muir, J. (2014). *Understanding higher levels of volunteering; the case of Short Strand and Sion Mills*, Centre for Regional Economic and Social Research, Sheffield Hallam University. https://www.executiveoffice-ni.gov.uk/sites/default/files/understanding-higher-levels-of-volunteering-short-strand-and-sion-mills.pdf

Hustinx, L, Cnaan, R., & Handy, F. (2010) Navigating theories of volunteering: A hybrid map for a complex phenomenon, *Journal for the Theory of Social Behaviour, 40*, 410–434 http://dx.doi.org/10.1111/j.1468-5914.2010.00439.x

Hustinx, L., & Lammertyn, F. (2003). Collective and reflective styles of volunteering: A sociological modernization perspective. *VOLUNTAS: International Journal of Voluntary and Nonprofit Organizations, 4*, 167–187. https://doi.org/10.1023/A:1023948027200

Kim, E. (2018). A systematic review of motivation of sport event volunteers. *World Leisure Journal, 60*(4), 306–329. https://doi.org/10.1080/16078055.2017.1373696

Kim, E., Fredline, L., & Cuskelly, G. (2018). Heterogeneity of sport event volunteer motivations: A segmentation approach. *Tourism Management, 68*, 375–386. https://doi.org/10.1016/j.tourman.2018.04.004

Kim, W., Jun, H. M., Walker, M., & Drane, D. (2015). Evaluating the perceived social impacts of hosting large-scale sport tourism events: Scale development and validation. *Tourism Management, 48*, 21–32. https://doi.org/10.1016/j.tourman.2014.10.015

Koenigstorfer, J., Bocarro, J. N., Byers, T., Edwards, M. B., Jones, G. J., & Preuss, H. (2019). Mapping research on legacy of mega sporting events: Structural changes, consequences, and stakeholder evaluations in empirical studies. *Leisure Studies, 38*(6), 729–745. https://doi.org/10.1080/02470406 7.2019.1669065

Lim, C., & Laurence, J. (2015). Doing good when times are bad: Volunteering behaviour and economic hard times. *British Journal of Sociology, 66*(2): 319–344 https://doi.org/10.1111/1468-4446.12122

Lockstone-Binney, L., Urwin, G., Bingley, S., & Burgess, S. (2020). Identifying social impact from supplemental events: A research framework. *Leisure Studies, 39*(6), 877–892. https://doi.org/10.1080/02614367.2020.1795227

Lundberg, E., Andersson, T., & Armbrecht, J. (2019). Introduction. In J. Armbrecht, E. Lundberg & T. D. Andersson (Eds.), *A research agenda for event management.* Edward Elgar Publishing. https://doi.org/10.4337/9781788114363

McAllum, K. (2014). Meanings of organizational volunteering: Diverse volunteer pathways. *Management Communication Quarterly, 28*, 84–110. https://doi.org/10.1177%2F0893318913517237

Meijs, L. C. P. M., Ten Hoorn, E. M., & Brudney, J. L. (2006). Improving societal use of human resources: From employability to volunteerability. *Voluntary Action, 8*(2), 36–54.

Misener, L., & Mason, D. S. (2006). Creating community networks: Can sporting events offer meaningful sources of social capital? *Managing Leisure, 11*(1), 39–56. https://doi.org/10.1080/13606710500445676

Nichols, G., Ralston, R., & Holmes, K. (2017). The 2012 Olympic Ambassadors and sustainable tourism legacy. *Journal of Sustainable Tourism, 25*(11), 1513–1528. https://doi.org/10.1080/09669582.2017.1291648

Oppenheimer, M., & Warburton, J. (eds.) (2014). Volunteering in Australia, Sydney, Federation Press, ISBN 978186287936, pp. 2–12.

Paine, A., Hill, M., & Rochester C. (2014). 'A rose by any other name': Revisiting the question 'what exactly is volunteering'. Working Paper 1: Institute for Volunteering Research. https://www.ifrc.org/docs/IDRL/Volunteers/a-rose-by-any-other-name-what-exactly-is-volunteering.pdf

Preuss, H. (2007). The conceptualisation and measurement of mega sport event legacies. *Journal of Sport and Tourism*, *12*(3–4), 207–228. https://doi.org/10.1080/09669582.2017.1291648

Putnam, R. D. (1995): Bowling alone: America's declining social capital. *Journal of Democracy*, *6*(1), 65–78. https://doi.org/10.1007/978-1-349-62965-7_12

Rochester, C. (2018). *Trends in volunteering*. Volunteer Now https://www.volunteernow.co.uk/app/uploads/2019/10/Trends-in-Volunteering-Final.pdf

Rochester, C., Paine, A. E., Howlett, S., Zimmeck, M., & Paine, A. E. (2016). *Volunteering and society in the 21st century*. Springer. https://doi.org/10.1057/9780230279438

Rogerson, R., Pavoni, A., & Duncan, T. (2015). *Participating as a host city volunteer: Perspectives from those involved in the Glasgow 2014 Commonwealth Games*. Glasgow Life. https://prodglportalv2.azureedge.net/media/2417/glasgow-2014-participating-as-a-host-city-volunteer-2015.pdf

Rogerson, R., Reid, F., Sly, B., & Nicholson, R. (2018). *Three years on – eh impact of being a host city volunteer at the 2014 Commonwealth Games*. Glasgow Life. https://prodglportalv2.azureedge.net/media/2419/hcv-legacy-2018.pdf

Rogerson, R. J., Nicholson, R., Reid, F., & Sly, B. (2019). Using major events to increase social connections: The case of the Glasgow 2014 Host City Volunteer programme. *Journal of Policy Research in Tourism, Leisure and Events*, 1–13. https://doi.org/10.1080/19407963.2019.1696351

Rogerson, R., Reid, F., & Nicholson, R. (2022). Creating an event volunteering legacy: The 2014 Host City Volunteer initiative. *Event Management.26*(4). https://doi.org/10.3727/1525995 21X16192004803737

SMG (2016). *'Taking volunteering to the people' An evaluation of the Host City Volunteer (HCV) programme*. Social Marketing Gateway. https://prodglportalv2.azureedge.net/media/2421/hcv-partnership-working-co-production-2016.pdf

Sharp, B. (2018). Volunteering and wellbeing: Case study of the Glasgow 2014 Commonwealth Games volunteer programmes. In R. Finkel, B. Sharp & M. Sweeney. (Eds.), *Accessibility, inclusion, and diversity in critical event studies* (pp. 177–192). Routledge. https://doi.org/10.4324/9781351142243-14

Shipway, R., Lockstone–Binney, L., Holmes, K., & Smith, K. A. (2019a). Perspectives on the volunteering legacy of the London 2012 Olympic Games: The development of an event legacy stakeholder engagement matrix. *Event Management*, *23*(4–5), 4–5. https://doi.org/10.3727/1525995 19X15506259856327

Shipway, R., Ritchie, B. W., & Chien, P. M. (2019b). Beyond the glamour: Resident perceptions of Olympic legacies and volunteering intentions. *Leisure Studies*, 1–14. https://doi.org/10.1080/0261 4367.2019.1693612

Sly, B. (2018). *Developing an events legacy*. [Presentation]. Sports Volunteering Research Network, October 2018.

Smit, B., & Melissen, F. (2018). *Sustainable customer experience design: Co-creating experiences in events, tourism and hospitality*. London: Routledge. https://doi.org/10.4324/9781315620749

Stebbins, R. A. (2005). Project-based leisure: Theoretical neglect of a common use of free time. *Leisure Studies*, *24*(1), 1–11. https://doi.org/10.1080/0261436042000180832

Stebbins, R. A. (2007). *Serious leisure: A perspective for our time*. Routledge. https://doi.org/10.4324/9781315129167

Thomson, A., Cuskelly, G., Toohey, K., Kennelly, M., Burton, P., & Fredline, L. (2019). Sport event legacy: A systematic quantitative review of literature. *Sport Management Review*, *22*(3), 295–321. https://doi.org/10.1016/j.smr.2018.06.011

Volunteer Now (2017). *Volunteering and combating social isolation and loneliness: A report of a survey into the link between volunteering and combating social isolation in older people* Volunteer Now. https://www.volunteernow.co.uk/app/uploads/2019/10/Volunteering-Combating-Social-Isolation-Loneliness.pdf

Wallstam, M., Ioannides, D., & Pettersson, R. (2020). Evaluating the social impacts of events: In search of unified indicators for effective policymaking. *Journal of Policy Research in Tourism, Leisure and Events*, *12*(2), 122–141. https://doi.org/10.1080/19407963.2018.1515214

Wilks, L. (2016). The lived experience of London 2012 Olympic and Paralympic Games volunteers: A serious leisure perspective. *Leisure Studies*, *35*(5), 652–667. https://doi.org/10.1080/02614367.2 014.993334

Woolvin, M., & Harper, H. (2015). *Volunteering 'below the radar'? Informal volunteering in deprived urban Scotland: Research summary*. Volunteer Scotland http://epapers.bham.ac.uk/787/1/WP51_BTR_in_a_Big_Society_McCabe_Dec_2010.pdf

Zhou, R., & Kaplanidou, K. (2018). Building social capital from sport event participation: An exploration of the social impacts of participatory sport events on the community. *Sport Management Review*, 21(5), 491–503. https://doi.org/10.1016/j.smr.2017.11.001

28

WIDENING THE SCOPE OF EVALUATING VOLUNTEER TOURISM

Beyond impact measurement

Simone Grabowski, Phoebe Everingham and Tamara Young

Introduction

Volunteer tourism can provide substantial social and economic benefits to host communities but, if poorly planned, it can result in negative consequences. To date, much of the existing academic research has focused on measuring the various impacts on volunteers themselves (e.g., Alexander, 2012; Bailey & Russell, 2010; Matthews, 2008; McBride et al., 2012) and a focus on host communities remains overdue (Griffiths, 2016; Zahra & McGehee, 2013). Measuring the impacts of volunteer tourism on host communities is important to facilitate a more equitable industry; however, it is difficult to quantify certain impacts into universal typologies for several reasons. First, the volunteer tourism industry is diverse. This industry contains heterogeneous organisations that cater to different market segments (Benson, 2015) and require context specific measurements. Indeed, Taplin et al. (2014) suggest that appreciating context is more important than a "methods first approach" (Taplin et al., 2014, p. 882). Supply chains and broader environmental impacts also need to be considered when evaluating volunteer tourism (Eckardt et al., 2020). Second, evaluation measurements are often framed within a Eurocentric development aid model. Such models fail to prioritise the well-being of individuals and communities, and perpetuate and normalise neo-colonial stereotypes of who are 'the helpers' and who should be 'helped' (Everingham, 2015, 2016; Wearing et al., 2017). Third, measurement of impacts is based upon (and also implies) quantitative outcomes. Such measures obscure the context specific lived experiences and alternative narratives of the local community members involved in volunteer tourism programs and the potential for emergent cross-cultural understanding. Relationship building through participatory action should occur before appropriate evaluation methods are sought (Wearing et al., 2017).

The problematisation of these unique circumstances of volunteer tourism leads to our critique of traditional impact measurement models that conceal broader environmental impacts, impacts that arise along supply chains, and alternative narratives and experiences. Further, as one of the key tenets of volunteer tourism is to provide volunteers with cross-cultural, immersive tourism experiences (Wearing & Grabowski, 2011), it is also challenging to quantify the nuanced personal impacts and the myriad of co-constructed relational experiences between

DOI: 10.4324/9780367815875-33

volunteers and host communities. These relational, emotional and affective aspects of the embodied encounters between host community members and volunteers are difficult to capture through measurement and evaluative systems (Everingham, 2015, 2016; Wearing et al., 2017). Without considering these aspects of relational and lived experiences, volunteer tourism impact studies also run the risk of erasing the agency of local communities (Chen, 2018).

In this chapter, we review and critique the various ways that the impacts of volunteer tourism have been traditionally measured. The difficulties of measuring volunteer tourism when broader environmental impacts and supply chains are considered, and the small but salient growing range of alternative approaches to impact measurement are examined. We argue that these alternative approaches provide more insightful and contextual analyses of the intangible outcomes of volunteer tourism that account for host communities, volunteers and volunteer sending organisations. These intangible outcomes are difficult, if not impossible, to quantify into traditional impact measurements in volunteer tourism, particularly when they are driven by development aid outcomes. To this end, we engage with Wearing and McGehee's (2013) analysis of Jafari's (2001) platforms of research and practice that have emerged in volunteer tourism over the past two decades.

Volunteer tourism and its impacts

Volunteer tourists are defined as those who, "for various reasons, volunteer in an organized way to undertake holidays that might involve aiding or alleviating the material poverty of some groups in society, the restoration of certain environments or research into aspects of society or environment" (Wearing, 2001, p. 1). Since Wearing introduced this definition two decades ago, the volunteer tourism industry has exploded and become increasingly commodified, with 'voluntourism' emerging as a term encapsulating this commercialisation.

However, the volunteer tourism industry is extremely diverse, and those individuals who volunteer seek varying levels of engagement and experience with host communities. For example, Brown and Lehto (2005) argue that 'volunteer tourists' should be distinguished from 'voluntourists', with the latter being 'vacation-minded' rather than 'volunteer-minded'. For voluntourists, the volunteering component is often only a small portion of the whole trip. On the other hand, volunteer tourists tend to volunteer for the entire length of the trip, and the length of their trips are usually longer. While these definitions are perhaps arbitrary considering the lines between tourism and volunteering are blurry, and volunteer tourists themselves generally do not identify with the term 'volunteer tourist' (Gray & Campbell, 2007; Lepp, 2008; Mostafanezhad, 2013), This diversity needs to be accounted for when proposing evaluative frameworks.

Wearing and McGehee (2013) trace the 'scientification' of volunteer research using Jafari's (2001) four platforms of tourism research. The first *advocacy phase* positions volunteer tourism as an ideal tourism activity, as an alternative to mass tourism, which benefits local communities. The second *cautionary phase* examines the potential negative impacts of volunteer tourism on local host communities. The third *adaptancy phase* prescribes specific ways for the industry to minimise these negative impacts. The final *scientific phase* calls for challenging and altering our approach to volunteer tourism research through, for example, the utilisation "of structured, interdisciplinary, transdisciplinary, transnational, and mixed method approaches for examining volunteer tourism" (Wearing & McGehee, 2013, p. 122). While these platforms are perhaps too linear, together they provide a useful framework for thinking through the broader context of how tourism scholars have evaluated volunteer tourism to date.

Much of the early literature in the advocacy phase examines the impacts of tourist experiences on the volunteer. For example, researchers focus on the ways by which volunteering in tourism has the ability to facilitate self-development, fulfil altruistic motivations, and provide young people with experiences for their professional and career development (e.g., Bell, 1994; Broad, 2003; L. Brown, 2009; S. Brown & Lehto, 2005; Matthews, 2008). Such research coincided with the increased commercialisation and commodification of the industry, with greater focus on the transformative experiences of the volunteer tourists rather than on the needs and agency of the host communities (Godfrey et al., 2019; Sin, 2009).

As the volunteer tourism research moved into the cautionary phase, the literature increasingly provided evidence of a broader range of volunteer tourism impacts – particularly those that affect host communities and destination environments. Due to the diversity of the global volunteering programs available, and the often intense and immersive experience of volunteer tourism, these impacts can be both positive and negative. For example, in conservation projects, the presence of volunteers can rejuvenate or rehabilitate flora and fauna (e.g., Broad & Jenkins, 2008) or enhance conservation awareness in communities (Rattan et al., 2011) while economically, volunteer projects can increase spending in the community (Hernandez-Maskivker et al., 2018; Sin et al., 2015). Despite such positive impacts, the cautionary phase clearly highlights many negative impacts of volunteer tourism. For instance, Guttentag (2009), observes:

> 'a neglect of locals' desires, a hindering of work progress and completion of unsatisfactory work, a disruption of local economies, a reinforcement of conceptualisations of the 'other' and rationalisations of poverty, and an instigation of cultural changes.
>
> *(Guttentag, 2009, p. 537)*

This quote highlights that serious ethical concerns relating to volunteer tourism exist, particularly in developing countries. Volunteer tourism runs the risk of taking jobs away from local residents, with some commentators suggesting that the money volunteers spend on their trips would be of greater economic benefit if directly channelled into the communities themselves (e.g., Tiessen & Heron, 2012). Others have argued that framing volunteer tourism as 'helping' host communities can reinforce stereotypes of the 'white saviour' and can lead to a reliance on development and aid (Tiessen & Heron, 2012). Zahra and McGehee (2013), for example, found a disruption in the economic operations and opportunities of the community in a community in the Philippines. Volunteers requested food items that were difficult to source or were given tokens of appreciation that would normally be sold to tourists, meaning the community consequently suffered financially.

In line with the adaptancy phase, it could be argued that many of the negative impacts of volunteer tourism can be linked to the framing of volunteer tourism as development aid (Everingham, 2015, 2016; Everingham & Motta, 2020; Wearing et al., 2017). While Wearing's (2001) initial definition of volunteer tourism as "aiding or alleviating the material poverty of some groups in society" (Wearing, 2001, p. 1) came from a place of advocacy in response to the irresponsible practices of the mass tourism industry, the definition has framed this form of tourism within a problematic 'helping' narrative. This discourse works to reinforce binaries between privileged minority world actors as active and generous paternalistic carers, while majority world actors are portrayed as grateful and passive disadvantaged people in need. In these framings of volunteer tourism, binaries become reinforced and naturalised through a geography of need, and poverty becomes the marker of difference (Crossley, 2012; Simpson, 2004). For example, Bargeman et al. (2018) learnt that once volunteers left the schools they were "supporting" in Ghana, the hand over procedures were so poor that local teachers were unable to continue, particularly as "volunteers do not teach in line with the Ghanaian teaching system" (Bargeman et al., 2018, p. 1492). Thus, the primary motivation of the volunteer organisations (and, subsequently the volunteers) was self-serving and not community driven.

On the contrary, when projects are framed beyond and outside a development aid discourse, there is significant scope to focus on mutual intercultural learning and cross-cultural understanding. For example, Everingham (2015) highlights the benefits of volunteering when it is connected to community development, creativity and language exchange rather than development aid. In her research at an interactive children's library in Banos in Ecuador, she finds that when volunteer tourism organisations facilitate meaningful intercultural connections, the typical framings of volunteers as 'experts' and 'white saviours' can be subverted leading to mutual intercultural learning.

Taking this perspective further, in line with the scientific phase, Wearing et al. (2017) call for a rethinking of how volunteer tourism is practiced and evaluated: away from development aid outcomes towards meaningful intercultural exchange and decommodification. They argue that this is a necessary shift away from unequal neo-liberal geographies that stereotype and perpetuate neo-colonial stereotypes and white saviour narratives of the helpers and the helped. Everingham (2015) argues that measuring volunteer tourism impacts within fixed, static and universal models reifies the power of Eurocentric development aid models and undermines the agency of local communities within volunteer tourism encounters. In turn, evaluative measurements can turn invisible the affective, emotional and relational aspects of the volunteering experience that contain possibilities for emergent decolonising connections across cultural difference (Everingham & Motta, 2020).

These studies reveal that for minimal impact to occur, the agency of the local communities is central to volunteer tourism. Benali and Oris (2019) examine the everyday dynamics of volunteers and hosts to demonstrate how "initial power relations can be destabilized and reconstructed" (Benali & Oris, 2019, p. 111). Their research includes the voices and perspectives of several different actors within the volunteer tourism experience: the sending organisations, the volunteers and the local residents. In doing so, Benali and Oris (2019) demonstrate that local people can actually assume a dominant role in these tourism experiences, by engaging or disengaging with volunteers according to the volunteers' willingness to adapt and share in everyday life. In critiquing the impacts of broader structural power dynamics and the related impacts in and upon local communities, the agency of local communities must not be erased and the heterogeneity of host community perspectives must be acknowledged (Young et al., 2020). Thus, in much the same way that the conceptualisation and practice of volunteer tourism is multidimensional, several different approaches have been employed to measure the impacts of volunteer tourism.

Measuring impact in volunteer tourism

The target of impact measurement in volunteer tourism typically focuses on volunteers and host communities (albeit with a deficit of research on the latter) as well as the type of host destination impact (social, cultural, environmental, economic). However, as outlined in this section, there are methodological and epistemological discrepancies in the variables under examination. For example, many studies that explore the impact of volunteer tourism on the volunteering participants typically have a quantitative focus aimed at determining the satisfaction outcomes of the volunteer (Bailey & Russell, 2010; Hallmann & Zehrer, 2016;

Lough et al., 2009). This quantitative approach is evident, for example, in the International Volunteering Impacts Survey (IVIS) (Lough et al., 2009). This survey, aimed at measuring volunteer outcomes and impacts, identifies 11 categories of volunteer outcomes: international contacts, open-mindedness, international understanding, intercultural relations, global identity, social skills, life plans, civic activism, community engagement, media attentiveness and financial contributions (Lough et al., 2009). The IVIS provides insights into the perceived impact of experiences on international volunteers (McBride et al., 2012). As summarised in the previous section, minimal impact requires community agency. Therefore, impact studies must be holistic and inclusive of stakeholders beyond the volunteer tourists who are ostensibly seeking beneficial outcomes through personal relationships with other cultures.

Certainly, as outlined above, the impact of volunteer tourism development on the sociocultural fabric of host communities is an area neglected in much of the early volunteer tourism research (Freidus, 2017; Hernandez-Maskivker et al., 2018; Lupoli & Morse, 2015; Lupoli et al., 2014, 2015). The advocacy approaches to measuring volunteer tourism impact focus on the potential for empowering communities within capacity development models (Wearing & McGehee, 2013). For example, Irvin (2006) employs Alkire's (2002) participatory approach in her research on South African volunteer tourism projects to uncover seven potential development impacts to communities: empowerment, knowledge, excellence in work and play, health/security, relationships, inner peace and religion. As a result of Irvin's (2006) interviews with community members, she finds that volunteer tourism benefits host communities in four distinct ways: "making financial contributions, facilitating cultural exchange, building relationships with children who are project beneficiaries and filling gaps in the organisational needs of project hosts" (Irvin, 2006, p. iii). These categories enable a broader impact measurement perspective by positioning development beyond simply increasing GDP to, instead, centre the capability of volunteer tourism projects to meet the needs of communities. In particular, it would be valuable to elicit whether communities seek and/or see value of the projects in promoting their sense of wellbeing. Irvin's (2006) study, therefore, offers valuable insights into how we measure and evaluate the impacts of volunteer tourism development on host communities.

Development is complex, it should not be imposed from above, and it is not simply about poverty alleviation. To achieve impacts beyond economic benefit, communities need to be engaged in the ownership of the projects that they are involved in, and value these projects for their cultural identity and well-being (Chassagne & Everingham, 2019). Volunteer tourism that negates the freedom of communities to decide if and how they want to participate in development must be critically considered. When volunteer tourism as an "industry" commodifies forms of development there is a risk that problematic forms of development are offered as consumable products centred on the misguided and Eurocentric desires of volunteers who "who want to make a difference" (Wearing et al., 2017).

Taking an adaptancy stance, Lupoli and colleagues (Lupoli & Morse, 2015; Lupoli et al., 2014, 2015) engage participatory research methods to create an assessment tool for local communities to evaluate whether volunteer tourism is beneficial for their communities. Through an online survey of volunteer sending organisations, they propose a list of indicators that seek to understand community impacts. They also facilitated workshops within communities hosting volunteers to further define these indicators, particularly those to be assessed in a sustainability framework. The results of their studies provide a useful framework for assessing community involvement in volunteer tourism, yet they are highly specific to each community. Importantly, education through intercultural exchange was identified as the most significant benefit indicator for communities hosting volunteer tourists (Lupoli & Morse, 2015; Lupoli et al., 2014, 2015). Education as a key outcome for host communities is also a key finding in Dillette et al.'s (2017) study of volunteer tourism in the Bahamas. Social exchange theory informed interviews and surveys with destination residents, and eight major themes arose in examining how community members perceive volunteer tourism to facilitate cross-cultural exchange and their desire to learn about other cultures. Dillette et al. (2017) findings reveal that the positive benefits of hosting volunteers (for example, community involvement, empowerment, sustainability, education and communication) appeared to outweigh the negative impacts (for example, dependency, neglect of community needs and loss of Bahamian culture). Their conclusion indicates that the results may be relevant for other small island destinations but the contextual characteristics need to be similar. Yet, as prior research on island tourism has established, tourism may be at various stages of development and have altered destination communities to such extremes that any form of tourism may be seen as detrimental or unsustainable (Young et al., 2020).

Taplin et al. (2014) also take an adaptancy stance in discussing the use of monitoring and evaluating volunteer tourism. They highlight the importance of social, cultural, historical, economic and political contexts and, in so doing, find that there are far too many variables to establish a consistent method of volunteer tourism evaluation. These variables include, but are not limited to, volunteer tourism markets, stakeholders, organisations and volunteer programme dimensions. Their critical stance leads them to conclude that any form of measurement is value-laden and always "embedded within uneven power relations, agendas and interests" (Taplin et al., 2014, p. 891). Therefore, critical and interpretative approaches can potentially facilitate a far greater understanding of the many nuances in stakeholder voices, and promote dialogue between them.

More recent cautionary approaches to measuring the impacts of volunteer tourism argue that environmental impacts on host destinations must also be considered when evaluating volunteer tourism. While the advocacy platform presents the positive effects volunteer tourism can have on wildlife, the carbon footprint of volunteers from predominantly wealthy minority world countries can negate the positive impacts. By employing a carbon footprint calculator, El Geneidy's (2019) study of volunteer tourism in India finds many significant indirect environmental costs. For instance, while aviation is a prominent contributor to CO_2 emissions, the transportation of products, and the consumption of food and other products in volunteer tourism also contribute to environmental impacts. Liu and Leung (2019) examine impacts of environmental biodiversity in Taiwan, arguing that while the intentions of volunteer programs on conservation projects are commendable, endangered species at the destination may be threatened due to cultural changes to community life.

The impact measurement studies described above demonstrate diverse ways that volunteer tourism impacts have been measured through a range of frameworks. Generally these studies, in much the same way as evaluation initiatives, "can be perceived to come from outside the community's interests and control and based instead on an external agenda" (Price et al., 2012, p. 33). Rather, in order to assess or measure the effectiveness of volunteer tourism, there needs to be understandings of exactly what the programme entails (Lough & Tiessen, 2018; Taplin et al., 2014) and the selection of culturally appropriate methods and indicators that are both community and programme specific (Lupoli et al., 2015). These studies show that quantitative methods may not be the most appropriate way to understand the impacts of volunteer tourism. If such approaches are used, they need to be culturally appropriate and context specific. However, we argue that alternate approaches to volunteer tourism research are needed to understanding nuance and diversity of organisations, communities and local environments.

Alternative understandings of impact measurement

Castañeda (2012) argues that the notion of impact neglects the fact that tourism affects different groups in different ways. Likewise, in the case of volunteer tourism, traditional impact analyses homogenise the volunteer tourism industry and its impacts "without taking into account long term sociohistorical processes or considering the multiple and different consequences and effect that [volunteer] tourism could have" (Castañeda, 2012, p. 47). As noted earlier, the volunteer tourism industry is very diverse. The industry comprises heterogeneous organisations from charities, private companies, social enterprises, brokers, non-governmental organisations and non-profits, catering to different segments of the market (Benson, 2015; Taplin et al., 2014). Homogenous and universal approaches to impact measurement therefore obscure the diversity of experiences, not only for volunteers, but also for host communities.

Alternative approaches to measuring impact in volunteer tourism are emerging, including research that engages methodologies that are more conducive to non-western host community perspectives, and that prioritise the voices of host communities, which may be community-driven. For example, in a study of volunteer tourism in Ghana, Bargeman et al. (2018) employ a practice approach to investigate the effects of interactions between volunteers and local community members. By engaging an alternate approach through practice theory, their findings unpack the ways by which social practices can better account for the embodied, emotional and affective dimensions of volunteer tourism experiences. Relationality between actors is key, as well as their socio-economic and cultural backgrounds, taking account of the context-specific dimensions essential to understand when exploring a phenomenon of practice. Bargeman et al. (2018) argue that interaction is central to immersive volunteering experiences. When positive and negative consequences of interactions are identified, these are relational and dependent on each of the 'guest' and 'host' actors, their backgrounds, routines and other context specific factors.

In line with this context specific approach, Eckardt et al. (2020) argue that "supply chains within the volunteer tourism industry need to be examined in order to explain what works, for whom, under which circumstances" (Eckardt et al., 2020, p. 647). The voices of the supposed beneficiaries of volunteer tourism (that is, the host communities) are often unheard because they are too far down the supply chain, and the root causes of the exploitation of host communities, as well as dissatisfied volunteers, often occurs within the supply chains themselves. The supply chain acts like a black box that nobody truly understands and for sustainable change to occur, project evaluations need to be context sensitive, particularly in relation to "contextual components of supply chain management mechanisms" (Eckardt et al., 2020, p. 650). Traditional linear supply chain models are insufficient in capturing and measuring these collaborative relationships in volunteer tourism supply chains. This is particularly the case in volunteer tourism because it is ultimately an intangible product related to "level of exchanges in knowledge, expertise and resources, and the formation of personal relationships and cultural exchanges" (Eckardt et al., 2020, p. 657) which are significant during the volunteer placement.

In a holistic manner, Zahra and McGehee (2013) examine impact from the perspective of a Filipino host community employing a community capitals framework. They find that while young volunteer tourists affect changes to the financial, human, built, natural, cultural and political environments (or financial, human capitals etc.) through the different projects, these changes were generally perceived in a positive light. For example, the volunteers' persistence in keeping the area clean flows onto the community members who consequently insist that the younger members of the community should do the same.

However, in this discussion of alternative impact measurement we cannot ignore extreme world events which have had devastating effects on communities that rely on tourism. Everingham and Chassagne (2020) argue that the Covid-19 pandemic offers us an opportunity to "rethink the hyper consumption endless growth model" (Everingham & Chassagne, 2020, p. 2) of modern neo-liberal capitalism that is tourism. Their alternative model is based on *Buen Vivir,* a communitarian view of well-being with roots in Latin American Indigenous cosmology. They argue that having a *Buen Vivir* mindset can create growth in well-being, environmentalism and social connection, and that this would lead to degrowth in socially and environmentally damaging tourism sectors. Connecting *Buen Vivir* to the 'slow tourism' movement (which has similarities to volunteer tourism (Heitmann et al., 2011)) challenges our notion of a post-assessment of impact to one in which the potential outcomes of volunteer tourism are embedded in designing community-led programs.

These studies demonstrate the importance of context when measuring impact from a community perspective. Specifically, the studies reviewed indicate that evaluating volunteer tourism is complex and context dependent, connected to relational social systems which include individuals, social structures, organisations and processes. However, there still remains a significant omission in terms of ways to understand the intangible aspects of the volunteer tourism experience. Indeed, this may be one of the most pressing challenges in evaluating the impacts of volunteer tourism, and is discussed below.

The importance of intangible outcomes in volunteer tourism impact measurement

There are contextual factors that present challenges in measuring the impacts of volunteer tourism. These include the large variety of intersecting experiences, in terms of the volunteer organisations (whether they are for profit, not for profit, non-governmental organisations, charity, service learning, religiously orientated etc.) and the volunteers and their various motivations (including their levels of skill and cross-cultural awareness). The broader environmental impacts, the impacts inherent within supply chains and most importantly, the impacts on host communities are also among the contextual factors.

However, as the volunteer tourism experience is packaged and presented as an intangible and experience-orientated product, analysing impacts must also consider on-the-ground practices, positionalities and experiences of volunteers and host communities. The relationalities make measuring impacts highly context specific. Impact assessments of community driven programs are more likely to succeed if the tools are locally specific and designed. In the context of a global pandemic, such as Covid-19 when international tourism halted, there is an opportunity to reset tourism when the borders reopen according to the desires of local communities. For example, research by Scheyvens and Movono (2020) on tourism dependent economies in the South Pacific highlights how during Covid-19, many of those in the tourism industry affected by shutdowns are experiencing the benefits of a less-stressful lifestyle. They have returned to land and found strength in their communities and family life. This reinforces the importance of reframing development aid away from growth models and towards collective well-being, and the importance of being clear about what local communities actually want in terms of tourism and development more generally. Alternative models to growth are required that focus on the welfare and well-being of the collective to work towards sustainable futures. For example, New Zealand is now utilising well-being measurements rather than relying solely on economic indicators such as GDP (Ellsmoor, 2019). *Buen Vivir* is one such model that can be used by the tourism industry to 'reset' and 'rethink', towards the collective well-being of people and nature with an emphasis on plural and culturally contextual pathways. Volunteer tourism needs to (re)consider how development is framed, the broader impacts of well-being more generally and most importantly, to centre the needs and wants of the local communities that are hosting volunteers.

While universal typologies can be useful for assessing broad patterns of behaviours, our concern is that the methodologies that underpin these typologies tend to be Eurocentric. The issue here is that impact measurement studies privilege the frameworks of western understandings of development and do not necessarily account for the cultural differences in values and well-being. When we look beyond tourism research, we find that Indigenous social impact research aims to decolonise the research process. For example, in using a code-signed, community-based participatory research approach in Australia, Denny-Smith et al. (2019) showed that a yarning (Aboriginal cultural conversation) discussion group is culturally appropriate, and emphasises oral histories, knowledges and perspectives of Indigenous people.

When measuring and evaluating volunteer tourism, researchers also need to attend to the actual encounters themselves. Examining such encounters requires specific methodologies that prioritise the relationalities of these encounters, specifically the emotional/affective realms of the experience (Wearing et al., 2017). The intangible aspects of volunteer tourism, such as intercultural learning and mutuality, cannot always be quantified into outcomes that are measured in terms of development. As Everingham (2015) argues, many other experiences occur in volunteer tourism that require analysis and need to be acknowledged and emphasised if they are to be mutually beneficial for both volunteers and the local communities. As an example, Everingham and Motta (2020) illustrate the problems associated with applying singular monological and ethnocentric logics to the embodied intercultural encounters that happen on the ground in volunteer tourism. Whilst 'meaningful' and 'experiential' encounters with host communities is a key selling point within volunteer tourism promotional discourses, much of the academic analysis can ironically skim over the lived experiences of these encounters. How these encounters will play out post Covid-19 is difficult to know. Will the volunteer industry continue with face to face encounters, and to what extent will volunteers be travelling around the globe? During Covid-19, the Australian Volunteer Program, run through the Department of Foreign Affairs and Trade (DFAT), began promoting remote volunteering and Impact Fund initiatives. Remote volunteering allows repatriated volunteers to complete their interrupted assignments and stay connected to their host organisations. An Impact Fund provides eligible partner organisations access to small grants that will help communities respond to and recover from the impacts of Covid-19. A more strategic approach involved exploring new ways of working through an Innovation Fund, which "identifies, develops and pilots new ideas and solutions to increase the impact of the program" (Australian Volunteer Program, 2020). There is scope for the volunteer tourism sector to respond to these challenges in innovative ways. However, considering the importance of the embodied experiential nature of volunteering internationally it remains to be seen how the industry will move forward post Covid-19.

Alternative participatory approaches have been uncovered earlier in this chapter. Although some of the abovementioned studies are alternative in their theoretical frameworks, they continue to employ research designs and methods *prior* to establishing relationships in the host communities. There is a need to take alternative methodological approaches that account for the contingencies and relationalities of various actors within these tourism spaces. In Everingham's (2015, 2016) research in South America, she engages an autoethnographic approach to fieldwork within two volunteer tourism organisations. Autoethnography allowed Everingham to consider her own embodied positionality in these projects, as well as her own attunement to emotional and affective registers. These methodologies provide insightful articulation of the many ambivalences of these encounters that can both perpetuate neo-colonial stereotypes as well as subvert them. When intercultural exchange is deliberately fostered by volunteer tourism organisations, neo-colonial stereotypes of 'the helper' and 'the helped' can be disrupted. Similarly, Zahra and McGehee's (2013) work in the Philippines recognises the importance of embeddedness in community prior to any form of data collection. An obstacle such as Covid-19 therefore should have little effect on the impact evaluation process.

Arguably, the potential for volunteer tourism to delegitimise "geographies of need" (Simpson, 2004) should be fundamental in evaluating the transformative potentials of volunteer tourism. However, particular methodologies that are attentive to these transformative aspects, and occur within the intangible affective realms of the experience, are needed. As Griffiths (2018) argues, much of the critical literature on international volunteering focuses on structural framings of power dynamics and skims over the actual encounters themselves, thereby creating silences around the "body's intersubjective capacities" and the "political potentials of the body in terms of forging positive possibilities" (Griffiths, 2018, p. 117). Following Wearing et al. (2017), we propose that in order for volunteer tourism to be sustainable and decommodified, the agency of volunteers and local communities must be at the centre of the activity. Spaces must be facilitated for the outcomes of deep intercultural exchange and then volunteer tourism research and impact measurement can engage beyond Eurocentric frameworks.

Conclusions and implications

Measuring impacts in volunteer tourism is useful when context specific approaches and methodologies are undertaken. Adhering to the triple bottom line in terms of economic, sociocultural and environmental impacts is useful for ensuring volunteer tourism is beneficial for local communities and the environment, and for volunteers themselves who are often looking for meaningful tourism experiences. However, as we have argued throughout this chapter, the scope of evaluation must be widened to include or be driven by the local community actors, the various contextual aspects of volunteer tourism supply chains and the inequalities (as well as mixed messages) inherent within such international business models. The volunteer tourism experience itself is ultimately intangible and is, therefore, difficult to assess, particularly when non-interpretative methodologies attempt to account for the lived experiences within these programs.

Volunteer tourism impacts would best be evaluated in context-engaging interpretative methodologies focusing on community specific means. If methodologies are not connected to the emotional and affective realms of the concurrent lived experiences of tourists and communities, there is a risk that measuring volunteer tourism impact will erase the agency of local communities and continue to reinforce neo-colonial stereotypes that underpin the geography of need in volunteer tourism. By moving beyond development aid assessment models in ways that account for the heterogeneity and emergent possibilities for decolonising connections across difference, volunteer tourism research can uncover possibilities for intercultural connection. Evaluative measures must, therefore, focus on individual context specific examples that are cognisant of the diversity of organisations, experiences and impacts (Benson, 2015; Wearing et al., 2017). The scientific platform of volunteer tourism research (Wearing & McGehee, 2013) can be further epitomised through ongoing engagement with interdisciplinary and interpretative approaches to impact measurements. In so doing, evaluations of volunteer tourism should emphasise the need for organisations to facilitate programs that foster the importance of intercultural exchange and connections across and through cultural differences.

References

Alexander, Z. (2012). International volunteer tourism experience in South Africa: An investigation into the impact on the tourist. *Journal of Hospitality Marketing & Management, 21*(7), 779–799. https://doi.org/10.1080/19368623.2012.637287

Alkire, S. (2002). *Valuing freedoms: Sen's capability approach and poverty reduction.* Oxford University Press.

Australian Volunteer Program. (2020). *Australian volunteers.* https://www.australianvolunteers.com/how-were-responding-to-covid19/

Bailey, A. W., & Russell, K. C. (2010). Predictors of interpersonal growth in volunteer tourism: A latent curve approach. *Leisure Sciences, 32*(4), 352–368. https://doi.org/10.1080/01490400.2010.488598

Bargeman, B., Richards, G., & Govers, E. (2018). Volunteer tourism impacts in Ghana: A practice approach. *Current Issues in Tourism, 21*(13), 1486–1501. https://doi.org/10.1080/13683500.2015.1137277

Bell, J. (1994). The Australian Volunteers Abroad experience: Impact on career development. *Australian Journal of Career Development, 3*(3), 33–36. https://doi.org/10.1177/103841629400300310

Benali, A., & Oris, M. (2019). Consuming poverty: Volunteer tourism in an orphanage in Nepal. In J. M. Cheer, L. Matthews, K. E. van Doore, & K. Flanagan (Eds.), *Modern day slavery and orphanage tourism* (pp. 110–122). CABI.

Benson, A. (2015). Why and how should the international volunteer tourism experience be improved? *Worldwide Hospitality and Tourism Themes, 7*(2), 208–214. https://doi.org/10.1108/WHATT-01-2015-0002

Broad, S. (2003). Living the Thai life – A case study of volunteer tourism at the Gibbon Rehabilitation Project, Thailand. *Tourism Recreation Research, 28*(3), 63–72. https://doi.org/10.1080/02508281.2003.11081418

Broad, S., & Jenkins, J. (2008). Gibbons in their midst? Conservation volunteers' motivations at the Gibbon Rehabilitation Project, Phuket, Thailand. In K. Lyons & S. Wearing (Eds.), *Journeys of discovery in volunteer tourism: International case study perspectives* (pp. 72–85). CABI.

Brown, L. (2009). The transformative power of the international sojourn: An ethnographic study of the international student experience. *Annals of Tourism Research, 36*(3), 502–521. https://doi.org/10.1016/j.annals.2009.03.002

Brown, S., & Lehto, X. (2005). Travelling with a purpose: Understanding the motives and benefits of volunteer vacationers. *Current Issues in Tourism, 8*(6), 479–496. https://doi.org/10.1080/13683500508668232

Castañeda, Q. (2012). The neoliberal imperative of tourism: Rights and legitimization in the UN-WTO global code of ethics for tourism. *Practicing Anthropology, 34*(3), 47–51.

Chassagne, N., & Everingham, P. (2019). Buen Vivir: Degrowing extractivism and growing wellbeing through tourism. *Journal of Sustainable Tourism, 27*(12), 1909–1925.

Chen, J. (2018). Understanding development impact in international development volunteering: A relational approach. *The Geographical Journal, 184*(2), 138–147. https://doi.org/10.1111/geoj.12208

Crossley, É. (2012). Poor but happy: Volunteer tourists' encounters with poverty. *Tourism Geographies: An International Journal of Tourism Space, Place and Environment, 14*(2), 235–253. https://doi.org/10.1080/14616688.2011.611165

Denny-Smith, G., Loosemore, M., Barwick, D., Sunindijo, R., & Piggott, L. (2019, 2–4 September). *Decolonising Indigenous Social Impact Research Using Community-Based Methods* [Paper presentation]. 35th Annual ARCOM Conference, Leeds, UK.

Dillette, A. K., Douglas, A. C., Martin, D. S., & O'Neill, M. (2017). Resident perceptions on cross-cultural understanding as an outcome of volunteer tourism programs: The Bahamian Family Island perspective. *Journal of Sustainable Tourism, 25*(9), 1222–1239. https://doi.org/10.1080/09669582.2016.1257631

Eckardt, C., Font, X., & Kimbu, A. (2020). Realistic evaluation as a volunteer tourism supply chain methodology. *Journal of Sustainable Tourism, 28*(5), 647–662. https://doi.org/10.1080/09669582.2019.1696350

El Geneidy, S. (2019). *Does the end justify the means?: carbon footprint of volunteer tourism in an Indian NGO.* [Master's thesis, School of Business and Economics, Jyväskylä University]. JYX Digital Repository. https://jyx.jyu.fi/handle/123456789/63267

Ellsmoor, J. (2019, 11 July). New Zealand ditches GDP for happiness and wellbeing. *Forbes.* https://www.forbes.com/sites/jamesellsmoor/2019/07/11/new-zealand-ditches-gdp-for-happiness-and-wellbeing/?sh=a7d9c0c19420

Everingham, P. (2015). Intercultural exchange and mutuality in volunteer tourism: The case of intercambio in Ecuador. *Tourist Studies, 15*(2), 175–190. https://doi.org/10.1177/1468797614563435

Everingham, P. (2016). Hopeful possibilities in spaces of 'the-not-yet-become': Relational encounters in volunteer tourism. *Tourism Geographies, 18*(5), 520–538. https://doi.org/10.1080/14616688.2016.1220974

Everingham, P., & Chassagne, N. (2020). Post COVID-19 ecological and social reset: moving away from capitalist growth models towards tourism as Buen Vivir. *Tourism Geographies,* 1–12. https://doi.org/10.1080/14616688.2020.1762119

Everingham, P., & Motta, S. C. (2020). Decolonising the 'autonomy of affect' in volunteer tourism encounters. *Tourism Geographies,* 1–21. https://doi.org/10.1080/14616688.2020.1713879

Freidus, A. L. (2017). Unanticipated outcomes of voluntourism among Malawi's orphans. *Journal of Sustainable Tourism, 25*(9), 1306–1321. https://doi.org/10.1080/09669582.2016.1263308

Godfrey, J., Wearing, S. L., Schulenkorf, N., & Grabowski, S. (2019). The 'volunteer tourist gaze': Commercial volunteer tourists' interactions with, and perceptions of, the host community in Cusco, Peru. *Current Issues in Tourism,* 1–17. https://doi.org/10.1080/13683500.2019.1657811

Gray, N. J., & Campbell, L. M. (2007). A decommodified experience? Exploring aesthetic, economic and ethical values for volunteer ecotourism in Costa Rica. *Journal of Sustainable Tourism, 15*(5), 463–482. https://doi.org/10.2167/jost725.0

Griffiths, M. (2016). An opinion piece. A response to the Special Issue on volunteer tourism: The performative absence of volunteers. *Journal of Sustainable Tourism, 24*(2), 169–176. https://doi.org/10.1080/09669582.2015.1071382

Griffiths, M. (2018). Writing the body, writing others: A story of transcendence and potential in volunteering for development. *The Geographical Journal, 184*(2), 115–124. https://doi.org/10.1111/geoj.12200

Guttentag, D. (2009). The possible negative impacts of volunteer tourism. *International Journal of Tourism Research, 11*(6), 537–551. https://doi.org/10.1002/jtr.727

Hallmann, K., & Zehrer, A. (2016). How do perceived benefits and costs predict volunteers' satisfaction? *VOLUNTAS: International Journal of Voluntary Nonprofit Organizations, 27*(2), 746–767.

Heitmann, S., Robinson, P., & Povey, G. (2011). Slow food, slow cities and slow tourism. In P. Robinson, S. Heitmann, & P. Dieke (Eds.), *Research themes for tourism* (pp. 114–127). CABI.

Hernandez-Maskivker, G., Lapointe, D., & Aquino, R. (2018). The impact of volunteer tourism on local communities: A managerial perspective. *International Journal of Tourism Research, 20*(5), 650–659. https://doi.org/10.1002/jtr.2213

Irvin, K. (2006). *Volunteer tourism and development: An impact assessment of volunteer tourists from two organisations in Cape Town.* [Master's thesis, University of Cape Town]. https://open.uct.ac.za/bitstream/handle/11427/3834/thesis_hsf_2006_irvin_k.pdf?sequence=1

Jafari, J. (2001). The scientification of tourism. In V. L. Smith & M. Brent (Eds.), *Hostsand guests revisited: Issues of the 21st century* (pp. 28–41). Cognizant.

Lepp, A. (2008). Discovering self and discovering others through the Taita Discovery Centre Volunteer Tourism Programme, Kenya. In K. Lyons & S. Wearing (Eds.), *Journeys of discovery in volunteer tourism: International case study perspectives* (pp. 86–100). CABI.

Liu, T.-M., & Leung, K.-K. (2019). Volunteer tourism, endangered species conservation, and aboriginal culture shock. *Biodiversity Conservation, 28*(1), 115–129.

Lough, B., McBride, A., & Sherraden, M. (2009). *Measuring volunteer outcomes: Development of the international volunteer impacts survey* (CSD Working Papers, No. 09-31). Washington University in St. Louis. https://openscholarship.wustl.edu/cgi/viewcontent.cgi?article=1509&context=csd_research

Lough, B., & Tiessen, R. (2018). How do international volunteering characteristics influence outcomes? Perspectives from partner organizations. *VOLUNTAS: International Journal of Voluntary Nonprofit Organizations, 29*(1), 104–118. https://doi.org/10.1007/s11266-017-9902-9

Lupoli, C. A., & Morse, W. C. (2015). Assessing the local impacts of volunteer tourism: Comparing two unique approaches to indicator development. *Social Indicators Research, 120*(2), 577–600.

Lupoli, C. A., Morse, W. C., Bailey, C., & Schelhas, J. (2014). Assessing the impacts of international volunteer tourism in host communities: A new approach to organizing and prioritizing indicators. *Journal of Sustainable Tourism, 22*(6), 898–921. hppts://doi.org/10.1080/09669582.2013.879310

Lupoli, C. A., Morse, W. C., Bailey, C., & Schelhas, J. (2015). Indicator development methodology for volunteer tourism in host communities: creating a low-cost, locally applicable, rapid assessment tool. *Journal of Sustainable Tourism, 23*(5), 726–747. https://doi.org/10.1080/09669582.2015.1008498

Matthews, A. (2008). Negotiated selves: Exploring the impact of local-global interactions on young volunteer travellers. In K. Lyons & S. Wearing (Eds.), *Journeys of discovery in volunteer tourism: International case study perspectives* (pp. 101–117). CABI.

McBride, A. M., Lough, B. J., & Sherraden, M. S. (2012). International service and the perceived impacts on volunteers. *Nonprofit Voluntary Sector Quarterly, 41*(6), 969–990. https://doi.org/10.1177/0899764011421530

Mostafanezhad, M. (2013). Locating the tourist in volunteer tourism. *Current Issues in Tourism, 17*(4), 381–384. https://doi.org/10.1080/13683500.2013.793301

Price, M., McCoy, B., & Mafi, S. (2012). Progressing the dialogue about a framework for Aboriginal evaluations: Sharing methods and key learnings. *Evaluation Journal of Australasia, 12*(1), 32–37. https://doi.org/10.1177/1035719x1201200105

Rattan, J. K., Eagles, P. F. J., & Mair, H. L. (2011). Volunteer tourism: Its role in creating conservation awareness. *Journal of Ecotourism, 11*(1), 1–15. https://doi.org/10.1080/14724049.2011.604129

Scheyvens, R., & Movono, A. (2020). *Development in a world of disorder: Tourism, COVID-19 and the adaptivity of South Pacific people.* Institute of Development Studies Working Paper Series, Massey University. https://mro.massey.ac.nz/handle/10179/15742

Simpson, K. (2004). 'Doing development': The gap year, volunteer-tourists and a popular practice of development. *Journal of International Development, 16*(5), 681–692. https://doi.org/10.1002/jid.1120

Sin, H. L. (2009). Volunteer tourism: "Involve me and I will learn"? *Annals of Tourism Research, 36*(3), 480–501. https://doi.org/10.1016/j.annals.2009.03.001

Sin, H. L., Oakes, T., & Mostafanezhad, M. (2015). Traveling for a cause: Critical examinations of volunteer tourism and social justice. *Tourist Studies, 15*(2), 119–131. https://doi.org/10.1177/1468797614563380

Taplin, J., Dredge, D., & Scherrer, P. (2014). Monitoring and evaluating volunteer tourism: a review and analytical framework. *Journal of Sustainable Tourism, 22*(6), 874–897. https://doi.org/10.1080/09669582.2013.871022

Tiessen, R., & Heron, B. (2012). Volunteering in the developing world: The perceived impacts of Canadian youth. *Development in Practice, 22*(1), 44–56. https://doi.org/10.1080/09614524.2012.630982

Wearing, S. (2001). *Volunteer tourism: Experiences that make a difference.* CABI.

Wearing, S., & Grabowski, S. (2011). Volunteer tourism and intercultural exchange: Exploring the 'Other' in this experience. In A. M. Benson (Ed.), *Volunteer tourism: Theoretical frameworks and practical application* (pp. 193–210). Routledge.

Wearing, S., & McGehee, N. G. (2013). Volunteer tourism: A review. *Tourism Management, 38*, 120–130. https://doi.org/10.1016/j.tourman.2013.03.002

Wearing, S., Young, T., & Everingham, P. (2017). Evaluating volunteer tourism: has it made a difference? *Tourism Recreation Research, 42*(4), 512–521. https://doi.org/10.1080/02508281.2017.1345470

Young, T., Reindrawati, D., Lyons, K., & Johnson, P. (2020). Host gazes from an Islamic island: Challenging homogenous resident perception orthodoxies. *Tourism Geographies, 23*(3), 599–622. https://doi.org/10.1080/14616688.2020.1733067

Zahra, A., & McGehee, N. G. (2013). Volunteer tourism: A host community capital perspective. *Annals of Tourism Research, 42*(0), 22–45. https://doi.org/10.1016/j.annals.2013.01.008

PART 6

Critical issues in volunteering

29
ETHICS OF VOLUNTEERING IN TOURISM
Ethics of the heart

Konstantinos Tomazos

Introduction

The quote "the world is a book and those who do not travel, read only one page", usually attributed to St Augustine (Fielding, 1824, p. 203) precisely reflects the significance of tourism and taking on the role of the tourist. On the road to becoming the world's largest industry, tourism has gone through various stages, and phases in its development and it is in constant flux as new niche tourism products emerge that challenge our understanding of what tourism is and what tourists do (Tomazos, 2020). As tourism develops almost organically, it serves as an umbrella term that has come to mean different things to different people. Meanwhile, in this environment, volunteering in tourism has evolved and changed due to the commodification of good intentions and helping others (Godfrey, 2018).

As we will see in this chapter, not all volunteering is good by nature; if good volunteering necessitates an individual to principally act on their aspiration to help others or a good cause, there might also be some obvious way of failing to be a good volunteer. Our common understanding of what volunteering means is shifting along with the spatial scope of volunteering to a universal plane, where people exercise their good intentions at a global scale (Silk, 2000). This virtuous cosmopolitan line of thinking (Salazar, 2015) has become fashionable in contemporary culture as we try to reconfigure ethics in a "post moral society and humanity" (Bilasová, 2008, p. 8). It has spawned new paradigms of green management, ethical consumption and human rights groups and movements (Barnett et al, 2005). While this is encouraging, the fact remains that ethics and ethical behaviour have become fashionable as virtue signalling, raising some moral and ethical dilemmas (Komenská, 2017). If fashion and trends can influence moral choices, they may do so in an unethical way, especially if decisions are based on social expectations instead of moral values and ethical considerations.

This trend is not surprising as it reflects that different people perceive right and wrong differently, and they vary in the way they analyse complex moral issues (Kohlberg, 1984). Kohlberg's work classifies moral reasoning in three distinct levels: pre-conventional (motivated by self-interest), conventional (motivated by maintaining social order, rules and laws), and post-conventional (motivated by social contract and universal ethical principles). Inevitably, good intentions are becoming increasingly commodified to the extent that Ryška argues that these days, volunteering has become "a historically unique and popular face of

DOI: 10.4324/9780367815875-35

humanism" (2014, p. 82). It has become a product that tourists can pay for in many cases, leading to humanitarian or cause-driven tourism and other volunteering forms in a tourism context.

However, the involvement of volunteers is not homogenous. When not humanitarian and ideologically driven, it can be practical and operational. When not episodic, it could become part of someone's routine or serious leisure (Stebbins, 2020). While there are overlaps, and the lines between the two are increasingly blurred (Holmes & Smith, 2009; Qi, 2020), we can divide volunteering into volunteering as hosts and volunteering as a guest. The former has been examined in the context of local volunteers supporting tourism attractions' operations or providing vital assistance to one-off events and mega-events. While volunteering as a host is important, this chapter examines international volunteering as a guest, and it draws on ethical theory to discuss the increasing commoditisation of good intentions in a tourism context.

Volunteers as guests: international volunteering

Although the motivations behind human attempts to assist other humans are disputed, there is little doubt that we do try to help each other. Much of the discussion on volunteers' ethical values has typically turned to the polarities of altruism and egoism (Clary et al., 1996; Lohmann & Van Til, 1992). Not surprisingly, the pure unconditional sacrifice of altruism is set against ethical egoism and the pragmatic self-serving of volunteers seeking to meet their needs (Tomazos & Luke, 2015). Under the prism of enlightened self-interest, there has been a shift from collective to individualised reflexive volunteerism suggesting a swing from selflessness to a more self-interest-centred form of moral serving to create oneself into a more virtuous and often spiritual person (Allahyari, 2000; Eimhjellen et al., 2018). However, over time, the international volunteer profile has evolved to reflect host countries' changing demands and changing volunteers. Developing countries are no longer in need of low-skilled volunteers from developed countries. Instead, they require highly-skilled professionals with tangible, transferable skills that can make a difference by contributing to an existing need and training the locals (Lough et al., 2018).

From the volunteers' perspective, volunteering as a concept has also been subject to change as it has been re-invented to meet the needs of the volunteers as 'revolving-door', 'drop-by', or 'plug-in' volunteering (Dekker & Halman, 2003; Eliasoph, 1998). This new trend has been captured as 'new volunteerism' (Hustinx, 2001, 2010; Wollebaek & Selle, 2002), which proclaims volunteers as autonomous and self-conscious actors challenging the boundaries between altruism and self-interest as "reflexive volunteering", fundamentally entrenched in the active (re)design of individualised biographies and lifestyles (Hustinx & Lammertyn, 2003, p. 238). Subsequently, contingent on specific biographical needs and conditions, reflexive volunteers devote a restricted amount of time and perform a restricted set of activities (Hustinx et al., 2010).

In this context, international volunteering, while often seen as an unqualified good, has faced criticism based on its impacts (Lewis, 2005; Mutchnick et al., 2003; Sherraden et al., 2008). Most studies of the effects of international volunteers come from medical volunteering, and the tone used to describe this type of volunteering is rather critical. Short-term placements are deemed ineffective and insignificant (Green et al., 2009) at best, viewed as self-serving colonialists' efforts (Bezruchka, 2000) at worst. In particular, international volunteering ignores local needs and in many cases, undermines existing services (Green et al., 2009; Montgomery, 1993; Pyott, 2008), while also allowing external organisations to acquire disproportionate political influence over local health policies (Anheier & Salamon, 1999). The worst accusation levelled at international volunteering is being guilty of what has been described as a form of humanitarian neocolonialism (Dupuis, 2004) that exploits local communities.

In some cases, international volunteers use local poor people as experimental fodder to improve their limited or non-existent technical skills (Roberts, 2006). Young volunteers are allowed to wear stethoscopes, take blood pressures and hand out vitamins conveying the message of medical expertise, when there is none (Loiseau et al., 2016). Even when they have the best intentions, if such volunteers give medical care, there is a higher likelihood of harm to local communities (Boetzkes & Waluchow, 2000) as the untrained volunteers are poten-tial security, health and political hazards (Pinto & Upshur, 2009). If volunteers do not bring added value from their expertise, they become a drain to the community's already scarce resources. However, can it be that simple? Are volunteers that bad? The answer is yes, and no. The presence of volunteers allows for the development of new markets and businesses. Whether they like it or not, short-term international volunteers are also tourists, and here is where the overlaps between international volunteering and volunteer tourism become very pronounced.

Volunteer tourists

Tourists yearn for something that transcends mere photo-taking and souvenir buying. In the context of volunteer tourism, they strive for extraordinary experiences of making a differ-ence and contributing to the life of others working on a variety of projects around the world (Han et al., 2019; McGeehee, 2014; Tomazos & Cooper, 2012) (see Figure 29.1). The scale of growth in volunteer tourism from its early days until now is astonishing as it harnessed the power of simple messages of the ethical, social or environmental ilk to energise tourists. This duality of tourism and citizenship means that participation is charged and galvanised with political or ethical meanings (Smith, 2014). Tourists are allowed to be tourists while also sending a political message through their choices, and this signals to producers and businesses that there is potential for economic gain through the trading of such powerful and meaning-ful tourism products. The ensuing gold-rush inevitably leads to replication and standardisa-tion due to economies of scale, and the initial magic is gone. In many respects, the once new, different, unique product becomes a victim of its success, and that is one paradox of volun-teer tourism. As its audience grew, volunteer tourism became 'visible' and thus vulnerable to the irresistible product-shaping-forces of the market (Tomazos, 2020). Everyone was eager to jump on the volunteer tourism bandwagon, codify and package good intentions, charity, and make a difference in one easily-replicated, homogenised, bright package (Brown, 2003; Caton & Santos, 2009; McGehee, 2002). Looking back now at what has transpired, industry and academics alike are searching for ways to re-invent volunteer tourism to rectify the issues and problems that it has created (Burrai & Hannam, 2018).

Arguably, volunteer tourism has carved a niche by turning need and perceived need into a new tourism product type. However, as discussed above, criticism and international vol-unteering go hand in hand. Crucially, the industry and the research community have had some difficulty answering questions, especially regarding tourists' contributions and where the money goes (Lupoli et al., 2014; Tomazos & Butler, 2009; Tomazos & Cooper 2012). At least at face value, this is a reasonable question for any consumer that makes a hybrid purchase, part buying experiences, and part donating to a good cause. Another issue that persists about the sector is how the volunteers' projects are need-based and not staged for

Agriculture	AIDS	Animal Welfare	Anthropology	Archaeology	Arts	Biological Research	Building & Construction Projects	Business
Childcare & Children	Community Centres	Community Development	Computer Training	Conflict Resolution	Conservation	Cooking	Counselling	Culture
Dental	Disability Issues	Disaster Relief	Drama	Driving	Drug & Alcohol Recovery	Eco-Tourism	Economic Development	Education
English Teaching	Environment	Equestrian	Festivals	Gender Issues	Geology	Grassroots Organization	Health	Health Care
Health Education	Historic Preservation	Hospital	Human Rights	Journalism	Law	Legal Aid	Marine Conservation	Marketing
Media	Medicine	Microfinance	Music	Nursing	Nutrition	Organic Farming	Orphans	Parks Volunteer
Pastoral Work	Public Health	Public Policy	Recreation	Reforestation	Refugee Relief	Renewable Energy	Senior Citizens	Small Business Development
Social Work	Sports	Street Children	Teaching	Tourism	Trail Building	Translation	Tree Planting	Tutor
Veterinary Science	Volunteer Management	Water Projects	Wildlife	Women	Writing	Youth	Youth Development	Youth Ministry

Figure 29.1 Proliferation of projects

tourist consumption (Kontogeorgopoulos, 2017; Mostafanezhad, 2013). Finally, in the spirit of *primum non nocere*, the most lingering question is volunteer tourism's potential to do more harm than good (Brown, 2003). This is a particular risk when different agents, recipients, brokers, local businesses, governments and non-government entities come together in a very ambiguous interplay of interests. In this process, they face different ethical dilemmas, and they make choices in the context of competing institutional logics, which offer opportunities for initiatives that, when pursued, generate specific outcomes (Tomazos, 2020). For example, becoming a volunteer tourist encompasses a combination of fun and mission, and the literature concedes that it is almost impossible to separate volunteer tourism from its tourism/fun element (Easton & Wise, 2015; Steele, Dredge & Scherrer, 2017; Tomazos & Butler, 2010, 2102). Is it acceptable to try to make a difference while also having a good time? What about volunteers who have fundraised to afford the trip; is their sense of duty greater than that of others?

On the same token, if the emphasis is placed on the fun element, how much leniency or strict control would be acceptable on the part of project management? Project managers have to choose which approach to adopt. Opting for a strict and regimented approach could put off fun-loving volunteer tourists. Going for a more laissez-faire attitude could disillusion volunteers who prioritise the mission, and it could pose a risk for the project.

Is it ethical to stage need if it means that a small number of locals can benefit? Can we accept the commoditisation of volunteer tourism's heroic narrative if it leads to desirable outcomes – even if this means that there is an obsession with social media to signal one's virtue?

On a more practical note, should volunteers accept to take part in projects they do not have the expertise to assist in? Such dilemmas are the leitmotif of debates on international volunteering, and the subsequent discussion on the ethical philosophy of volunteering will help us understand them better.

To a large extent, these questions have persisted in the literature due to the methodologies, ontological assumptions and analytical lenses adapted by researchers. The majority of studies in volunteer tourism or voluntourism (Americanism) have employed a Western lens of interpretation being the work of predominantly Western researchers (for example Andereck et al., 2012; Benson & Henderson, 2011; Brown, 2005; Burrai et al., 2015; Frilund, 2018; Guttentag, 2009; McGehee, 2014; McGehee & Santos, 2005; Mcgloin & Georgeou, 2016; Molz, 2016; Mostafanezhad, 2013, 2016; Raymond & Hall, 2008; Reas, 2013; Smith, 2003; Tomazos & Butler, 2012; Wearing, 2001, 2004; Wickens, 2010; Zahra & McIntosh, 2007) and this is only the tip of the iceberg. Granted, this predominantly Western map expands a bit more when taking into account some studies from other regions such as South Africa – Rogerson and Slater (2014) and Van Zyl, Inversini, and Rega (2015); Singapore – Sin (2009, 2010); China – Chen (2016); Malaysia – Ayobami and Ismail (2014), and also from Thailand – Theerapappisit (2009). However, there still exists a considerable gap in our understanding of volunteer tourism in different cultural contexts and other different social-cultural prisms. As a result of this unconscious preference in research, the literature appears to be one-sided, generally emphasising volunteers' voices rather than the communities they are there to serve (Benson, 2015).

Volunteer tourism and its key stakeholders have ridden a wave of changing travel patterns from the traditional beach escape to volunteering and life-immersion. In the process, they have demonstrated the endless potential of tourism phenomena to gain profit, commoditise contested aspects of human experience (Tomazos, 2020), and create controversy that questions the sector's ethos. Is volunteer tourism at worst a harmful market that exploits and demeans good intentions, or is it at best an excellent way to help local people in communities around the world?

Volunteering and ethical philosophy

The capitalist system fosters a reality where conflicting beliefs and practices can co-exist in an unexamined, symbiotic juxtaposition, which merely makes economic sense (Tomazos, 2020). When forecasting the success of volunteer tourism products, the providers would make very clear projections regarding how these products would do in a competitive market. Borrowing from the conceptualisation of homo economicus (Urbina & Ruiz-Villaverde, 2019), we can assume that people are rational utility maximising, purely self-interested agents that are Bayesian probability operators with consistent time preferences (Wilkinson & Klaes, 2017). Based on this, and drawing parallels with the normative theory of egoism and ethical egoism (Werhane, 2000), the most socially responsible thing a company can do is maximise their profits as it will benefit more people through the cyclical flow of income. Ethical egoism assumes that everyone acts in their self-interest and makes it ethically correct to do so when observing the consequences of said actions (Machan, 1979). However, in the context of volunteering, one must not overlook the ethics of duty.

Our duty to others is the crux of Immanuel Kant's ethical philosophy, which encompasses the idea that people should never be considered a means to other people's ends and that everyone is equal (Bowie, 2002). He argued that the intention of the action, as opposed to the consequence, determines its morality (Baron et al., 2018, p. 12). Kant argues that one should utilise free will and rationality to make the most moral choice instead of just choosing what is in one's best interest. Any decision must successfully advance through three Maxims (Categorical Imperative) to determine if it is ethical to take or not (see Baron, 2018; Bowie, 2002). The realistic understanding must temper the deontological approach as it would be very utopic to expect that there will only be winners in any given situation or scenario. We must also consider whom the duty is owed to. From a utilitarian perspective, the duty is owed to the greatest number of people that will benefit from this decision (Ferrell et al., 2013; Posner, 1979).

Arrow (1951) argues that most societies adhere to economic models that assume a utilitarian preference such that the "best configuration of inputs and outputs" and distribution takes hold within society (Bator, 1958, p. 22). The inter-temporal application of utilitarianism is, of course, tricky as it hinges on the idiom of 'The ends justifying the means'. However, the 'ends' are not always measurable at the immediate horizon when decisions are made (see Von Hayek, 1937). Using the outcomes as a strict criterion while adopting a teleological stance will always be challenging. Such an evaluation will still hinge on one's ability to answer with certainty what the outcomes are, or will be, without considering the ambiguity of power structures, and how is it possible to decide what is the greater good, or the greater good for whom (Baron et al, 2018).

In the real world, governments, businesses and individuals are guided by Adam Smith's 'invisible hand' to act chronically rationally within an ethical cocktail of utilitarianism and egoism. Smith was one of the first advocates for the free market, which he explained through the "invisible hand" (Werhane, 2000, p. 186) as the market forces that lead the economy to an equilibrium between supply and demand without the intervention of external actors (Rothchild, 2005; Rothschild, 2001). It pertains that the invisible hand's natural forces lead to an outcome that satisfies society's economic progression and further operates in a way that regulates and constrains businesses' self-interest (Bishop, 1995; Heath, 2004). In this way, it is argued that no two groups of individuals can exploit one another in the long term as it is naturally creating a self-containing system (Werhane, 2000).

Some would argue that egoism can never be used to achieve noble ends (Mele, 2001), while others would reason that enlightened self-interest can be used to 'do well by doing good' (Stieb, 2006). Enlightened self-interest was a concept first discussed by Alexis de Tocqueville (1805–1859) in his work *Democracy in America* (1835). To understand de Tocqueville's notion, one must look at the political and social turmoil that existed in France during his lifetime. His grandfather and aunt had been guillotined, and his parents imprisoned at the time of the French Revolution. This uprising of the masses against the elite made him think that coming together to better everyone's lives was the key to social harmony. He suggested that encouraging the masses to participate in civil associations would take their minds off their struggles(De Tocqueville, 2003). By the same pragmatic token, if the aristocracy appeared to contribute to the welfare and improvement of the lives of the poor, they may minimise the risk of facing the guillotine again. Enlightened Self-interest acknowledges that people are rational and can understand their decisions' full impact and these decisions will not change over time (Stendardi, 1992). Neo-classical economists appeal to the justifications of Enlightened Self-interest and Ethical Egoism to rationalise the use of laissez-faire capitalism, which Smith argued is the most ethical form of trade (Stendardi 1992; Werhane, 2000).

This view, which neoliberal thinking embraced, accepts that collective and individualistic goals can exist and that there can be no conflict of interest (Klein, 2007). One of the most prominent defenders of this view is Ayn Rand (1964) who, to make a point contrasts egoism with extreme altruism. She argues that selfless acts can be innately selfish, building on Nietzsche's sophism that, if you do not look after yourself, others will have to look after you (Sleinis, 1994). When applied to international volunteering, one could accept a rational desire to increase the number of paying volunteers to increase revenue. However, increased numbers and further commoditisation have brought consequences which in the long term could reduce profits or endanger the sector as a whole.

Volunteering as commodity

Understanding commoditisation has two crucial prerequisites. First and foremost, to understand that there are no specific individuals or organisations with the sole remit to commoditise; and second, it takes time, and its effects may or may not be visible at any single given moment in time or any particular space. It is an emanation of human ingenuity and endeavour and linked with the process in which goods, services and practices come into existence (Appadurai, 1994). Some are more marketable than others, and some fall out of favour with consumers/users as critical sumptuary laws may extinguish their marketability (Tomazos, 2020).

In these terms, great ideals are demoted to standard practice. No one remembers or knows how good intentions became a commodity, but it just happened, possibly in an organic way. In many cases, commodities 'appear', and as they become further marketed, a supporting infrastructure rises with them (Appadurai, 1994). By that time it is too late to question ifs and buts, people shrug their shoulders and say, it is just business.

In many ways, through his writings, Marx saw this coming, he foresaw a society on a path of unchecked commoditisation that once it had gathered momentum, would become unstoppable (Marx, 1887). Under the conditions of capitalism, wherein commodities are alienated from their production, Marx highlighted that people view commodities as inherently possessing exchange-value (Dant, 1996; Lloyd, 2008). Therefore, it is as though they have value in and of themselves as material beings when, in reality, their value originates from the human labour that created them (Marx, 1867). For Marx, this stand-in value or commodity fetishism occurs when commodities are infused with powers, characteristics and attributes which they do not, as inanimate objects, possess (Cluley & Dunne, 2012; Lloyd, 2008).

Whilst Marx's contribution to the understanding of symbolic value was groundbreaking, there is widespread agreement that his work did not go far enough (Dant, 1996; Koch & Elmore, 2006; MacCannell, 1976). Specifically, Marx's discussion on commodity fetishism was limited to use-value and exchange-value only (Koch & Elmore, 2006). Accordingly, subsequent literature has attempted to address this shortcoming. Most notably, Baudrillard (1968, 1970, 1972) added an additional value – sign or symbolic value (Kellner, 1989; Koch & Elmore, 2006).

Baudrillard explained that objects exist within a cultural system of signs, developed through increased product differentiation and mass media, particularly, advertising (Baudrillard, 1968, 1970). Under this system, objects are organised into a "hierarchical code of signification," (Baudrillard, 1972, p. 64), wherein they acquire sign value depending upon the extent to which they signify socially desirable qualities such as prestige and status (Kellner, 1989). The more prestigious the object, the greater its sign value (Kellner, 1989). Correspondingly, Baudrillard (1970) argues that consumption centres around manipulating signs, with the objects that people consume serving as a language through which they can communicate and interact with others in society. Thus, the principle here is that a product's physical utility is not the sole factor from which people make their consumption choices, but rather, its symbolic character is also significant. This shift is best encapsulated by Levy (1959, p. 118) who states, "people buy things not only for what they can do but also for what they mean".

On this token, then, a commodity holds great potential to serve commercial ends, and realistically everything has some commodity potential, no matter how little. Still, there may be injunctions or structural issues that skew this 'natural' process and limit innovation and invention capacity. Hence, the challenge then becomes to celebrate those commodities that, on the one hand, promise the highest return, but they also have the least detrimental effect for all stakeholders involved (Tomazos, 2020, p. 18). Should that be the acid test for international volunteering? That may be construed as a rather simplistic attitude that focuses only on whether we can do something; when we should also be asking whether we ought or should be doing something.

Perhaps we need to take a step back and forget about normative ethical theory and look at moral reasoning and decision-making frameworks. Cushman et al. (2013) argue that diverse moral judgment revolves around a dual framework of action-based and outcome-based values. According to this framework, volunteering in tourism can be linked to the intrinsic status of actions (e.g. I volunteer because it is considered good), or to the expected consequences of actions (e.g. Volunteer work will look good on my CV). We must not overlook the importance of reward motivation as people usually aim to maximise subjective expected values, but differ in choosing specific options. In volunteering in tourism, some individuals may choose to complete their shifts, while others choose to be more opportunistic and leave early (Tomazos & Butler, 2012).

Volunteering blurs the lines between the pursuit of self-interest and serving a good cause. Managers and volunteers must balance between egoism and altruism, ethical demands and economic realities, moral and financial costs, and profit motives and ethical imperatives. In a market economy, commoditised volunteering brokers are encouraged to pursue profit and be competitive as this competition will, at least in theory, affect the price and the quality of what they are selling. These brokers can only be successful as viable business ventures if people are willing to pay to participate in these experiences. If prospective customers feel that they are getting what they want, they will be willing to pay for them, and in turn, the brokers will also feel more inclined to make such offering more available (Tomazos, 2020). From the operators' perspective, volunteering as a seemingly simple concept of good intentions and goodwill is misguided when examined under an economics lens. Though seemingly the antithesis of one another, economics and ethics are instrumental in looking at problems in society from a unique perspective.

Without this perspective, volunteers will not extract extra value from their experiences, and suppliers will not have the incentive to deliver such experiences. The absence of prices will make it very challenging for anyone to decide the preferred option. Consumers can interpret increased price as higher quality, allowing them to differentiate in a saturated market (Bai, 2016). While trying to avoid getting political, even planners in the former Soviet Union were following commodity prices in the West to calculate rates for their economic programs. Price then may be explicit or implicit and whether we like it or not the law of supply and demand governs and oversees the provision of goods and services (Rothschild, 2001).

Using the above as a departure point, it becomes apparent that international volunteering encompasses the moral implications of marketing tourist experiences using poverty, deprivation, ecological sensitivity (to name a few) as commodities, which are effectively bought by and sold to well-intentioned individuals. Participation always involves – even before the experience takes place – monetary transactions which leave no choice but to reduce the above phenomena into consumable objects (Tomazos, 2020).

However, the act of a good becoming a commodity is not inherently good or bad, but it hinges on this commodification's outcomes (Radin, 1996). This view has its roots in the pragmatist school of thought and what philosophers may call 'non-ideal justice', or what economists term 'reform' or 'second best' ethics. This ethical stance seeks to improve a present situation, rather than to pursue an idealistic optimum. This non-essentialist approach is innately pragmatic, and accidentalist, and it hinges on social conditions. These social conditions and different outcomes may dictate the formation of value judgments and not a set of pre-existing assumptions. In this light, we should view the exchanges that take place (monetary or other), as an essential part of providing a service to others; no transactions, no income – no income, no support for projects.

Finally, it would be calamitous to discharge international volunteering as damaging or not useful to the needy. In most parts of the world where volunteers operate, there is a strong need to help in various areas and projects. The efforts of volunteers alone will not save the world, and perhaps they are probably taking more out of the experience than what they are putting in. However, we can find solace and hope in knowing that others will follow and build on what they will leave behind. It is this cycle that gives meaning and purpose to international volunteering.

Maybe we should not seek solutions in labels or putting volunteers into brackets that make taxonomic sense. Instead, we should follow Ning and Palmer's (2020) ethics of the heart. Volunteers today find themselves at a very difficult place; they are damned if they do, and damned if they do not. Under a market socialism lens, sacrificial, unconditional volunteering is simultaneously ideologically glorified and socially deviant (Ning & Palmer, 2020). On the one side, there is the moral imperative of altruistic sacrifice propagated from volunteer tradition, and on the other side, there is 'neoliberal' utilitarianism derived from market rationality. Events have proven that the market will always be a step ahead to assign different values or a premium to any form of experience, as long as the discourse meets a marketable niche's needs and desires. This inevitability should not be the defining aspect of international volunteering; instead, we should look at each volunteer and their experience separately. Only then we will truly understand what lies at the heart of volunteering.

There will always be disparities between reality and what we aspire to, which can be frustrating to many. However, the processes of giving and receiving go hand in hand in volunteering, and the ones who give and the ones who receive are infused with a sense of ordinary ethics of responsibility and care that prefigures the precise impulse that drives volunteering (Cloke et al., 2005). The temporal and episodic nature of international volunteering will always offer an appealing setting where the heart's ordinary ethics can thrive in extraordinary spaces (Barnett et al., 2005), heterotopias, where the ethical self and volunteering come together.

References

Allahyari, R. A. (2000). *Visions of charity: Volunteer workers and moral community.* University of California Press.

Andereck, K., McGehee, N. G., Lee, S., & Clemmons, D. (2012). Experience expectations of prospective volunteer tourists. *Journal of Travel Research, 51*(March 2011), 130–141. http://doi.org/10.1177/0047287511400610

Anheier, H. K., & Salamon, L. M. (1999). Volunteering in cross-national perspective: Initial comparisons. *Law and Contemporary Problems, 62*(4), 43–65.

Appadurai, A. (1994). *Commodities and the politics of value. Interpreting Objects and Collections.* London and New York: Routledge, 76–91.

Arrow, K. J. (1951). Alternative approaches to the theory of choice in risk-taking situations. *Econometrica: Journal of the Econometric Society, 19,* 404–437.

Ayobami, O. K., & Ismail, H. N. B. (2014). *The exploration of value domain attribute in Argungu community with an emergent voluntourism economy and its accrued benefits.* International Conference on Urban and Regional Planning. 9–11 May. Universiti Teknologi Malaysia, Johor.

Bai, J. (2016). *Melons as lemons: Asymmetric information, consumer learning and seller reputation.* Job Market Paper, Department of Economics, Massachusetts Institute of Technology.

Barnett, C., Cloke, P., Clarke, N., & Malpass, A., (2005). Consuming ethics: Articulating the subjects and spaces of ethical consumption. *Antipode, 37,* 23–46. http://dx.doi.org/10.1111/j.0066-4812.2005.00472.x

Baron, J., Gürçay, B., & Luce, M. F. (2018). Correlations of trait and state emotions with utilitarian moral judgements. *Cognition and Emotion, 32*(1), 116–129. http://dx.doi.org/10.1080/02699931.2017.1295025

Baron, M. W. (2018). *Kantian ethics almost without apology.* Cornell University Press.

Bator, F. M. (1958). The anatomy of market failure. *The Quarterly Journal of Economics, 72*(3), 351–379. http://dx.doi.org/10.2307/1882231

Baudrillard, J. (1968). *The system of objects.* Translated by J. Benedict, 1996. London: Verso.

Baudrillard, J. (1970). *The consumer society: Myths and structures.* Translated by J. P. Mayer, 1998. London: Sage Publications. http://dx.doi.org/10.4135/9781526401502

Baudrillard, J. (1972). *For a Critique of the Political Economy of the Sign.* Translated by C. Levin, 1981. St. Louis, Missouri: Telos Press.

Benson, A. M. (2015). Why and how should the international volunteer tourism experience be improved?. *Worldwide Hospitality and Tourism Themes, 7*(2), 208–214. http://dx.doi.org/10.1108/WHATT-01-2015-0001

Benson, A. M., & Henderson, S. (2011). A strategic analysis of volunteer tourism organisations. *Service Industries Journal, 31*(3), 405–424. http://doi.org/10.1080/02642060902822091

Bezruchka, S. (2000). Medical tourism as medical harm to the Third World: Why? For whom? *Wilderness & Environmental Medicine, 2*(11), 77–78.Bilasová, V. (2008). *Výzvy pre etiku v súčasnosti* [Challenges of contemporary ethics]. Prešov: FF PU.

Bishop, J. D. (1995). Adam Smith's invisible hand argument. *Journal of Business Ethics, 14*(3), 165–180. http://dx.doi.org/10.1007/BF00881431

Boetzkes, E., & Waluchow, W. J. (Eds.). (2000). *Readings in health care ethics.* Peterborough: Broadview Press.

Bowie, N. (2002). A Kantian approach to business ethics. In R. Frederick (Ed.), *A companion to business ethics* (pp. 61–71). Oxford: Blackwell. http://dx.doi.org/10.1002/9780470998397.ch1

Brown, P. (2003). Mind the gap: Why student year out may do more harm than good. *The Guardian*, 6th September. https://www.theguardian.com/uk/2003/sep/06/highereducation.gapyears. Accessed on 21/01/2021.

Brown, S. (2005). Travelling with a purpose: Understanding the motives and benefits of Volunteer Vacationers. *Current Issues in Tourism, 8*(6), 479–496. http://doi.org/10.1080/13683500508668232

Burrai, E., Font, X., & Cochrane, J. (2015). Destination stakeholders' perceptions of volunteer tourism: An equity theory approach. *International Journal of Tourism Research, 17*(5), 451–459. http://doi.org/10.1002/jtr.2012

Burrai, E., & Hannam, K. (2018). Challenging the responsibility of 'responsible volunteer tourism'. *Journal of Policy Research in Tourism, Leisure and Events, 10*(1), 90–95. http://dx.doi.org/10.1080/19407963.2017.1362809

Caton, K., & Santos, C. A. (2009). Images of the other: Selling study abroad in a postcolonial world. *Journal of Travel Research, 48*(2), 191–204. http://dx.doi.org/10.1177/0047287509332309

Chen, L. J. (2016). Intercultural interactions among different roles: A case study of an international volunteer tourism project in Shaanxi, China. *Current Issues in Tourism, 19*(5), 458–476. http://doi.org/10.1080/13683500.2015.1005581

Clary, E., Snyder, M., & Stukas, A. (1996). Volunteers, motivations: Findings from a national survey. *Nonprofit and Voluntary Sector Quarterly, 25*, 485–505. http://dx.doi.org/10.1177/0899764096254006

Cloke, P., Johnsen, S., & May, J., (2005). Exploring ethos? Discourses of 'charity' in the provision of emergency services for homeless people. *Environment and Planning A 37*, 385–402. http://dx.doi.org/10.1068/a36189

Cluley, R., & Dunne, S., (2012). From commodity fetishism to commodity narcissism. *Marketing Theory, 12*(3), 251–265. http://dx.doi.org/10.1177/1470593112451395

Cushman, F., Sheketoff, R., Wharton, S., & Carey, S. (2013). The development of intent-based moral judgment. *Cognition, 127*(1), 6–21. http://dx.doi.org/10.1016/j.cognition.2012.11.008

Dant, T., (1996). Fetishism and the social value of objects. *Sociological Review, 44*(3), 495–516. http://dx.doi.org/10.1111/j.1467-954X.1996.tb00434.x

Dekker, P., & Halman, L. (2003). *The values of volunteering: cross-cultural perspectives*. New York: Springer. http://dx.doi.org/10.1007/978-1-4615-0145-9

De Tocqueville, A. (2003). *Democracy in america America* (Vol. 10). Washington, DC: Regnery Publishing.

Dupuis, C. C. (2004). Humanitarian missions in the third world: A polite dissent. *Plastic and Reconstructive Surgery*, May 27th. Brussels http://dx.doi.org/10.1097/01.PRS.0000097680.73556.A3

Easton, S., & Wise, N. (2015). Online portrayals of volunteer tourism in Nepal: Exploring the communicated disparities between promotional and user-generated content. *Worldwide Hospitality and Tourism Themes, 7*(2), 141–158. http://dx.doi.org/10.1108/WHATT-12-2014-0051

Eimhjellen, I., Steen-Johnsen, K., Folkestad, B., & Ødegård, G. (2018). *Changing patterns of volunteering and participation*. In I. Eimhjellen, K. Steen-Johnsen, B. Folkestad, & G. Ødegård (Eds.), *Scandinavian civil society and social transformations* (pp. 25–65). Champaign, IL: Springer. http://dx.doi.org/10.1007/978-3-319-77264-6_2

Eliasoph, N. (1998). *Avoiding politics: How Americans produce apathy in everyday life*. Cambridge: Cambridge University Press. http://dx.doi.org/10.1017/CBO9780511583391

Ferrell, O. C., Crittenden, V. L., Ferrell, L., & Crittenden, W. F. (2013). Theoretical development in ethical marketing decision making. *AMS Review, 3*(2), 51–60. http://dx.doi.org/10.1007/s13162-013-0047-8

Fielding, T. (1824). *Select proverbs of all nations: Illustrated with notes and comments to which is added a summary of ancient pastimes holidays and customs with an analysis of the wisdom of the ancients and of the fathers of the church*. London: Longman Hurst Rees Orme, Brown and Green.

Frilund, R. (2018). Teasing the boundaries of 'volunteer tourism': Local NGOs looking for global workforce. *Current Issues in Tourism, 21*(4), 355–368. http://dx.doi.org/10.1080/13683500.2015.1080668

Godfrey, J. (2018). Commodified volunteer tourism and consumer culture: A case study from Cusco, Peru. *European Journal of Tourism Research, 19*, 136–139.

Green, T., Green, H., Scandlyn, J., & Kestler, A. (2009). Perceptions of short-term medical volunteer work: A qualitative study in Guatemala. *Globalisation and Health, 5*(1), 4. http://dx.doi.org/10.1186/1744-8603-5-4

Guttentag, D. A. (2009). The possible negative impacts of volunteer tourism. *International Journal of Tourism Research, 11*(6), 537–551. http://doi.org/10.1002/jtr.727

Han, H., Meng, B., Chua, B. L., Ryu, H. B., & Kim, W. (2019). International volunteer tourism and youth travelers–an emerging tourism trend. *Journal of Travel & Tourism Marketing, 36*(5), 549–562. http://dx.doi.org/10.1080/10548408.2019.1590293

Heath, J. (2004). A market failures approach to business ethics. In J. Heath (Ed.), *The invisible hand and the common good* (pp. 69–89). Berlin, Heidelberg: Springer. http://dx.doi.org/10.1007/978-3-662-10347-0_5

Holmes, K., & Smith, K. A. (2009). *Managing volunteers within tourism.* Oxford: Butterworth-Heinemann.

Hustinx, L. (2001). Individualisation and new styles of youth volunteering: An empirical exploration. *Voluntary Action, 3*(2), 57–76.

Hustinx, L. (2010). I quit, therefore i am?: Volunteer turnover and the politics of self-actualization. *Nonprofit and Voluntary Sector Quarterly, 39*(2), 236–255. http://dx.doi.org/10.1177/0899764008328183

Hustinx, L., Cnaan, R. A., & Handy, F. (2010). Navigating theories of volunteering: A hybrid map for a complex phenomenon. *Journal for the Theory of Social Behaviour, 40*(4), 410–434. http://dx.doi.org/10.1111/j.1468-5914.2010.00439.x

Hustinx, L., & Lammertyn, F. (2003). Collective and reflexive styles of volunteering: A sociological modernization perspective. *Voluntas: International Journal of Voluntary and Nonprofit Organisations, 14*(2), 167–187.

Kellner, D., (1989). *Jean Baudrillard: From Marxism to postmodernism and beyond.* Stanford, CA: Stanford University Press.

Klein, N. (2007). *The shock doctrine: The rise of disaster capitalism.* New York: Penguin.

Koch, A. M., & Elmore, R., (2006). Simulation and symbolic exchange: Jean Baudrillard's augmentation of Marx's theory of value. *Politics & Policy, 34*(3), 556–575. http://dx.doi.org/10.1111/j.1747-1346.2006.00028.x

Kohlberg, L. (1984). *The psychology of moral development.* San Francisco, CA: Harper & Row.

Komenská, K. (2017). Moral motivation in humanitarian action. *Human Affairs, 27*(2), 145–154. http://dx.doi.org/10.1515/humaff-2017-0013

Kontogeorgopoulos, N. (2017). Forays into the backstage: Volunteer tourism and the pursuit of object authenticity. *Journal of Tourism and Cultural Change, 15*(5), 455–475. http://dx.doi.org/10.1080/14766825.2016.1184673

Levy, S. J. (1959). Symbols for sale. *Harvard Business Review, 37* (July-August), 117–124. http://dx.doi.org/10.4135/9781452231372.n18

Lewis, D. (2005). *Globalisation and international service: A development perspective.* London: Institute for Volunteering Research.

Lloyd, G., (2008). *Commodity fetishism and domination: The contributions of Marx, Lukács, Horkheimer, Adorno and Bourdieu.* Unpublished Master's Thesis. Rhodes University.

Lohmann, R. A., & Van Til, J (1992). *The commons: New perspectives on nonprofit organisations and voluntary action.* San Francisco, CA: Jossey-Bass.

Loiseau, B., Sibbald, R., Raman, S. A., Benedict, D., Dimaras, H., & Loh, L. C. (2016). 'Don't make my people beggars': A developing world house of cards. *Community Development Journal, 51*(4), 571–584. http://dx.doi.org/10.1093/cdj/bsv047

Lough, B. J., Tiessen, R., & Lasker, J. N. (2018). Effective practices of international volunteering for health: Perspectives from partner organisations. *Globalisation and Health, 14*(1), 1–11. http://dx.doi.org/10.1186/s12992-018-0329-x

Lupoli, C. A., Morse, W. C., Bailey, C., & Schelhas, J. (2014). Assessing the impacts of international volunteer tourism in host communities: A new approach to organising and prioritising indicators. *Journal of Sustainable Tourism, 22*(6), 898–921. http://dx.doi.org/10.1080/09669582.2013.879310

MacCannell, D. (1976). *The tourist: A new theory of the leisure class.* Oakland: University of California Press.

Machan, T. R. (1979). Recent work in ethical egoism. *American Philosophical Quarterly, 16*(1), 1–15.

Marx, K. (1887). *Capital: A critique of political economy, volume I, book one: The process of production of capital.* Moscow: Kapital English.

Marx, K. (1867). *Capital: A critique of political economy, volume 1.* Translated by B. Fowkes, 1990. London: Penguin Books Limited.

McGehee, N. G. (2002). Alternative tourism and social movements. *Annals of Tourism Research, 29*(1), 124–143. http://doi.org/10.1016/S0160-7383(01)00027-5

McGehee, N. G. (2014). Volunteer tourism: Evolution, issues and futures. *Journal of Sustainable Tourism, 22*(6), 847–854. http://doi.org/10.1080/09669582.2014.907299

McGehee, N. G., & Santos, C. A. (2005). Social change, discourse and volunteer tourism. *Annals of Tourism Research, 32*(3), 760–779. http://doi.org/10.1016/j.annals.2004.12.002

McGloin, C., & Georgeou, N. (2016). 'Looks good on your CV': The sociology of volun- tourism recruitment in higher education. *Journal of Sociology, 52*(2), 403–417. http://doi. org/10.1177/1440783314562416

Mele, D. (2001). Loyalty in business: Subversive doctrine or real need? *Business Ethics Quarterly, 11*(1), 11–26. http://dx.doi.org/10.2307/3857866

Molz, J. (2016). Making a difference together: Discourses of transformation in family voluntourism. *Journal of Sustainable Tourism, 24*(6), 805–823.

Montgomery, L. M. (1993). Short-term medical missions: Enhancing or eroding health?. *Missiology, 21*(3), 333–341. http://dx.doi.org/10.1177/009182969302100305

Mostafanezhad, M. (2013). The geography of compassion in volunteer tourism. *Tourism Geographies, 15*(2), 318–337. http://doi.org/10.1080/14616688.2012.675579

Mostafanezhad, M. (2016). Organic farm volunteer tourism as social movement participation: A Polany- ian political economy analysis of World Wide Opportunities on Organic Farms (WWOOF) in Ha- wai'i. *Journal of Sustainable Tourism, 24*(1), 114–131. http://doi.org/10.1080/09669582.2015.1049609

Mutchnick, I. S., Moyer, C. A., & Stern, D. T. (2003). Expanding the boundaries of medical ed- ucation: Evidence for cross-cultural exchanges. *Academic Medicine, 78*(10), S1–S5. http://dx.doi. org/10.1097/00001888-200310001-00002

Ning, R., & Palmer, D. A. (2020). Ethics of the heart: Moral breakdown and the aporia of Chinese volunteers. *Current Anthropology: A World Journal of the Sciences of Man, 61*(4), 395–417.

Pinto, A. D., & Upshur, R. E. (2009). Global health ethics for students. *Developing World Bioethics, 9*(1), 1–10. http://dx.doi.org/10.1111/j.1471-8847.2007.00209.x

Posner, R. A. (1979). Utilitarianism, economics, and legal theory. *The Journal of Legal Studies, 8*(1), 103–140. http://dx.doi.org/10.1086/467603

Pyott, A. (2008). Short-term visits by eye care professionals: Ensuring greater benefit to the host com- munity. *Community Eye Health, 21*(68), 62.

Qi, H. (2020). Conceptualising volunteering in tourism in China. *Tourism Management Perspectives, 33*, 1–8.

Radin, M. J. (1996). *Contested commodities: The trouble with trade in sex, children, body parts and other things.* Cambridge, MA: Harvard University Press.

Rand, A. (1964). *Government financing in a free society. The Virtue of Selfishness: A New Concept of Egoism.* New York: New American Library.

Raymond, E. M., & Hall, C. M. (2008). The development of cross-cultural (mis)understanding through volunteer tourism. *Journal of Sustainable Tourism, 16*(5), 530. http://doi.org/10.2167/ jost796.0

Reas, P. J. (2013). 'Boy, have we got a vacation for you': Orphanage tourism in Cambodia and the commodification and objectification of the orphaned child. *Thammasat Review, 16*, 121.

Roberts, M. (2006). Duffle bag medicine. *Jama, 295*(13), 1491–1492. http://dx.doi.org/10.1001/ jama.295.13.1491

Rogerson, J. M., & Slater, D. (2014). Urban volunteer tourism: Orphanages in Johannesburg. *Urban Forum, 25*(4), 483–499. http://doi.org/10.1007/s12132-014-9240-6

Rothchild, J. (2005). Ethics, law, and economics: Legal regulation of corporate responsibility. *Journal of the Society of Christian Ethics, 25*(1), 123–146. http://dx.doi.org/10.5840/jsce200525127

Rothschild, E. (2001). *Economic sentiments: Adam Smith, Condorcet, and the enlightenment.* Cambridge, MA: Harvard University Press. http://dx.doi.org/10.2307/j.ctvjnrtf3

Ryška, T. (2014). *Imaginace pomoci, rozvoje a humanitarismu [Imagining assistance, development, and human- itarianism].* In Z. Gallayová, J. Hipš, & K. Urbanová (Eds.), *Globálne vzdelávanie – context a kritika* [Global education – context and critique] (pp. 78–95). Zvolen: Technická univerzita vo Zvolene.

Salazar, N. B. (2015). Becoming cosmopolitan through traveling? Some anthropological reflections. *English Language and Literature, 61*(1), 51–67.

Sherraden, M. S., Lough, B., & McBride, A. M. (2008). Effects of international volunteering and ser- vice: Individual and institutional predictors. *Voluntas: International Journal of Voluntary and Nonprofit Organizations, 19*(4), 395. http://dx.doi.org/10.1007/s11266-008-9072-x

Silk, J. (2000). Caring at a distance:(im) partiality, moral motivation and the ethics of representation-introduction. *Ethics, Place & Environment, 3*(3), 303–309. http://dx.doi.org/10.1080/713665900

Sin, H. L. (2009). Volunteer tourism—"Involve me and I will learn"? *Annals of Tourism Research, 36*(3), 480–501. http://doi.org/10.1016/j.annals.2009.03.001

Sin, H. L. (2010). Who are we responsible to? Locals' tales of volunteer tourism. *Geoforum, 41*(6), 983–992. http://dx.doi.org/10.1016/j.geoforum.2010.08.007

Sleinis, E. E. (1994). *Nietzsche's revaluation of values: A study in strategies* (Vol. 22). Urbana and Chicago: University of Illinois Press.

Smith, K. A. (2003). Literary enthusiasts as visitors and volunteers. *International Journal of Tourism Research, 5*(2), 83–95. http://doi.org/10.1002/jtr.419

Smith, P. (2014). *International volunteer tourism as (de)commodified moral consumption*. In M. Mostafanezhad & K. Hannam (Eds.), *Moral encounters in tourism. Current developments in the geographies of leisure and tourism* (pp. 31–46). Aldgate: Ashgate.

Stebbins, R. A. (2020). *The serious leisure perspective: A synthesis*. Calgary, Canada: Springer Nature.

Steele, J., Dredge, D., & Scherrer, P. (2017). Monitoring and evaluation practices of volunteer tourism organisations. *Journal of Sustainable Tourism, 25*(11), 1674–1690. http://dx.doi.org/10.1080/096695 82.2017.1306067

Stendardi Jr, E. J. (1992). Corporate philanthropy: The redefinition of enlightened self-interest. *The Social Science Journal, 29*(1), 21–30. http://dx.doi.org/10.1016/0362-3319(92)90014-9

Stieb, J. A. (2006). Clearing up the egoist difficulty with loyalty. *Journal of Business Ethics, 63*(1), 75–87. http://dx.doi.org/10.1007/s10551-005-0847-3

Theerapappisit, P. (2009). Pro-poor ethnic tourism in the Mekong: A study of three approaches in Northern Thailand. *Asia Pacific Journal of Tourism Research, 14*(2), 201–221. http://dx.doi. org/10.1080/10941660902847245

Tomazos, K. (2020). *Contested tourism commodities: What's for sale*. Newcastle Upon Tyne: Cambridge Scholars Publishing.

Tomazos, K., & Butler, R. (2009). Volunteer tourism: The new ecotourism? *Anatolia, 20*(1), 196–211.

Tomazos, K., & Butler, R. (2010). The volunteer tourist as "hero." *Current Issues in Tourism, 4*(13), 363–380. http://doi.org/10.1080/13683500903038863

Tomazos, K., & Butler, R. (2012). Volunteer tourists in the field: A question of balance? *Tourism Management, 33*(1), 177–187. http://doi.org/10.1016/j.tourman.2011.02.020

Tomazos, K., & Cooper, W. (2012). Volunteer tourism: At the crossroads of commercialisation and service?. *Current Issues in Tourism, 15*(5), 405–423. http://dx.doi.org/10.1080/13683500.2011.605112

Tomazos, K., & Luke, S. (2015). Mega-sports events volunteering: Journeys with a past, a present and a future. *VOLUNTAS: International Journal of Voluntary and Nonprofit Organisations, 26*(4), 1337–1359. http://dx.doi.org/10.1007/s11266-014-9484-8

Urbina, D. A., & Ruiz-Villaverde, A. (2019). A critical review of homo economicus from five approaches. *American Journal of Economics and Sociology, 78*(1), 63–93.

van Zyl, I., Inversini, A., & Rega, I. (2015). The representation of voluntourism in search engines: The case of South Africa. *Development Southern Africa, 0*(February), 1–17. http://doi.org/10.1080/0 376835X.2015.1010714

Von Hayek, F. A. (1937). Economics and knowledge. *Economica, 4*(13), 33–54.

Wearing, S. (2001). *Volunteer tourism: Experiences that make a difference*. CABI. Retrieved from https:// books.google.com/books?hl=en&lr=&id=6VRrdFoCCDwC&pgis=1

Wearing, S. (2004). Examining best practice in volunteer tourism. In R. Stebbins & M. Graham *Volunteering as leisure, leisure as volunteering: An international assessment* (pp. 209–224). Cambridge: CABI. http://doi.org/10.1079/9780851997506.0209

Werhane, P. H. (2000). Business ethics and the origins of contemporary capitalism: Economics and ethics in the work of Adam Smith and Herbert Spencer. *Journal of Business Ethics, 24*(3), 185–198.

Wickens, E. (2010). Journeys of the self: Volunteer tourists in Nepal. In A. Benson (Ed.), *Volunteer tourism* (pp. 66–76). London: Routledge.

Wilkinson, N., & Klaes, M. (2017). *An introduction to behavioral economics*. London: Macmillan International Higher Education.

Wollebaek, D., & Selle, P. (2002). Does participation in voluntary associations contribute to social capital? The impact of intensity, scope, and type. *Nonprofit and Voluntary Sector Quarterly, 31*(1), 32–61. http://dx.doi.org/10.1177/0899764002311002

Zahra, A., & McIntosh, A. (2007). Volunteer tourism: Evidence of cathartic tourist experiences. *Tourism Recreation Research, 32*(1), 115–119. http://doi.org/10.1080/02508281.2007.11081530

30

DIVERSITY AND INCLUSION IN SPORT VOLUNTEERING

Ryan Storr

Introduction: the role of volunteers in diversity and inclusion efforts in Australian Sport

In this chapter, the nature of volunteering in Australian sport and its pervasive impact on the delivery of successful diversity and inclusion initiatives across various sporting organisations in Australia is discussed. The aim is to provide an overview of the current landscape of volunteering in sport, by highlighting the lived experience of the volunteers. Two specific cases of diversity volunteering will be presented: volunteering with persons with disability, and volunteering with LGBT+ communities.

Sport in countries such as the UK and Australia is organised through a network of community sports clubs, run and managed by dedicated volunteers (Nichols et al., 2019; Storr et al., 2020). Without the army of committed volunteers, sport activities are at risk of never being delivered. The role volunteers play role in delivering inclusive sporting environments for socially and culturally diverse individuals is indispensable. The extent to which sports clubs operate as an effective tool for diversity goals is a contested space, mainly because there are debates around the role of a sports club; should it be used to promote social welfare goals, or to simply provide opportunities for people to play sport? And accounts of voluntary sports clubs delivering diversity are rarely referenced in the sport volunteering scholarship (Nichols, 2005).

Attending to the demands of delivering participation and social justice objectives, for example the inclusion of people from diverse communities such as those living with disabilities and those who are culturally and linguistically diverse, "requires professionalism in club management, in the sense of a formality of organisation, but the ways in which clubs have responded to these pressures are dependent on the attitudes of key volunteers in the club structures" (Nichols, 2005, p. 345). Until recently, little was known about how community sport volunteers respond to the pressures of increased diversity within western societies. Storr et al. (2020) has identified the different motivations which underpin the decisions of club volunteers to engage with different forms of diversity, and argues that the business case is the dominant discourse and key driver for volunteers and clubs to engage with certain types of diversity work. The business case for diversity in this context means that diversity is promoted and adopted on the understanding that it will increase participation, attract revenue and new fans to the sport or club, in turn improving the overall economic and social value of the club.

DOI: 10.4324/9780367815875-36

Diversity amongst community sport volunteers

Recently, there has been a push to increase diversity efforts within community sport settings and make participation representative of the communities that community sports clubs seek to serve. In the majority of sports clubs in western societies, diversity policies and programs are delivered by volunteers. In the Australian context, there is also a drive to make participation in sport representative of the Australian population (Australian Sports Commission, 2015). This has been a policy imperative in Australia, and with a quarter of all Australians born overseas, "sports participation in Australia should be as equally culturally diverse and representative" (Australian Sports Commission, 2015, p. 2).

It is now known that people from diverse backgrounds are less likely to volunteer than their Anglo-Saxon counterparts in western societies (Low et al., 2007; Volunteering Australia, 2011). There are a range of reasons why people from diverse backgrounds choose not to volunteer. For example, culturally and linguistically diverse people and recently arrived migrants have different cultural understandings and practices associated with volunteering, based on family, religion, or kinship (Oppenheimer, 2008). Further, some families, and single parent households with multiple children, may not have the time or resources to volunteer.

There is little data on demographic variations in sport volunteers in Australia in the last decade. Making volunteering accessible for all is a key priority for many government and volunteering organisations, and this is the same for the sport sector. However, policy rhetoric does not always lead to inclusive volunteering practices, and recent available Australian research on diversity in community sport settings indicates that the majority of volunteers are from white/Anglo and middle-class backgrounds, with little representation from minority groups (Jeanes et al., 2019; Spaaij et al., 2018).

Providing services for a range of cultural groups can be challenging for sport and recreation clubs, and developing "specific cultural strategies is often not feasible, particularly for those clubs that are run by volunteers" (Hanlon & Coleman, 2006, p. 93). Spaaij et al. (2018) show that implementing diversity policies can be challenging for volunteers when there is increased resistance to it, and working against institutional norms can often feel daunting and overwhelming. Backlash and resistance to diversity is an emerging topic of scholarship in sport, and recent findings suggest that key leaders of community sports clubs uphold the *status quo* and resist efforts towards greater diversity (Spaaij, Knoppers & Jeanes, 2020). This is why it is important to promote volunteering within diverse communities, for example LGBT+ communities, so they can be empowered to stand up to and respond to resistance when human rights are challenged or policy changes threaten the livelihood of marginalised people.

With regards to disability and volunteering, we know very little about disabled volunteers. From UK national volunteer surveys, Mawson and Parker (2013) identify that a lack of skills and provision discourages minority groups from volunteering more broadly. Additionally, people with a disability volunteer less in sport than those who do not have a disability (Darcy et al., 2011). This finding corroborates with youth sport volunteering scholarship which shows that youth volunteering programs in sport, based on leadership, can be exclusive in nature and tend to attract young people with high levels of capital and experiences, reproducing inequalities in youth (Storr & Spaaij, 2016).

Attempts to make volunteering more inclusive and representative of diverse communities, "has become a key component of volunteering practice, policy and research" (Rochester et al., 2010, p. 190). However, there are very few, targeted programs to promote volunteering amongst diverse communities in sport. However, as case study 2 in this chapter will show, when marginalised groups in society seek to make environments more inclusive, they will become involved in volunteering to initiate social change.

The role of volunteers in delivering diversity policy and programs

The attitudes of volunteers towards topical social issues such as diversity and inclusion are important for three reasons: to help influence policy, support sports organisations and clubs to respond to increased diversity, and attract more volunteers from diverse backgrounds. The delivery of sport provision, and the challenge of increasing diversity within the sport sector and implementing this, is unfairly placed upon volunteers. This is because they are tasked with addressing complex societal challenges, something that professional sports organisations are still grappling with, without being given the proper training, education, and resources (Auld, 2008).

Furthermore, increased focus must be directed towards the capacity of volunteers within sports clubs, and their skills and abilities (Auld, 2008). Significant research within community sport highlights the important role of key individuals in introducing, and fostering diversity within sports clubs, and it is these 'champions of change' or 'community champions' who are the primary driving forces behind diversity efforts (Ahmed, 2007a, 2007b; Cunningham, 2008; Melton & Cunningham, 2014; Spaaij, Magee & Jeanes, 2014). According to Jeanes et al. (2019) volunteers are increasingly being used as policy implementers around diversity within Australia but are more often than not unsupported by individuals and leaders within their sporting club or state sporting organisation.

In the following sections, I outline and present two case studies in documenting the experiences of volunteers who deliver diversity provision, and of sport volunteers from diverse backgrounds. The first case study concerns the experiences of community sport volunteers who manage and coordinate specialist cricket teams for athletes with intellectual disabilities. The second case study draws upon research with a group of lesbian, gay, bisexual, and transgender (LGBT+) volunteers who oversee and run the Australian Football League (AFL) LGBT+ supporter groups.

Case study 1: volunteer experiences of diversity work in community sports clubs

The first case study explores how community sport volunteers, specifically cricket volunteers, engaged with diversity practices. Diversity practices refer to a particular type of work which is undertaken to promote greater diversity within a specific setting. In this case study, the type of diversity work was disability diversity, where volunteers within a community sports club (cricket) facilitated the participation of athletes with an intellectual disability. The focus of this case study is on the volunteers who engaged with diversity work, through managing, coaching, and facilitating two specialist cricket teams for athletes with intellectual disabilities. In this case study sample of 21 volunteers at a community cricket club, only one was culturally diverse, and very few were women, demonstrating the lack of diversity within the volunteers at the club. I will focus on two key parts of this case study in order to (1) understand the motivations of volunteers who choose diversity work, in this case intellectual disability diversity, and (2) to explore the experiences of those volunteers committed to diversity work. This case study is based on an ethnographic study at a community cricket club in Melbourne, Australia (Storr, 2017, 2020), and the club is referred to as Royal Stakesby

Cricket Club (RSCC). Twenty-one individual interviews were conducted at the club, in addition to over 200 hours of participant observations, and an ethnographic qualitative approach was adopted to understand how diversity was enacted on a day to day basis at the club.

Motivations of volunteers committed to diversity work

We know that the motivations to volunteer within sport can be for a range of reasons, for example, wanting to give back to a club or community, as a parent at a sports club in which their child participates, for leisure, and to meet new people and foster new friendships (Nichols et al., 2016, 2019). At RSCC, the main motives to help with the disability cricket teams were to provide opportunities for marginalised groups to play and engage in sport, and the sense of satisfaction from witnessing the enjoyment of players. As one volunteer stated:

> I do get satisfaction out of seeing the enjoyment in the majority of them [the players]. They... sport is a big part of their lives and it's... to wear that uniform and to mingle with people within the same situation as them and, yes, I can honestly say I've never, ever thought I really don't want to go tonight or today. I've just done it because I get... I do get satisfaction out of the enjoyment of it. Seeing them enjoy it and know that they've got somewhere to go and participate. For giving people a chance to compete and be good at something where they normally wouldn't have a chance to have a competitive game of something, and it does give them a goal to come on a Wednesday and rain, hail or snow, the weather doesn't make any difference, they've got that goal to come and it's so competitive, the teams. I switch the teams around and try and put different ones with different ones. It doesn't always work either. They always say, 'I don't want to play with him' or 'I want to play with her'. To see them so competitive and know that they've got something to do every Wednesday night and the cricket tournament coming up is a really big deal. The boys that I drove home on Sunday said, 'We can't wait for the carnival Olive. We can't wait'. It's something for them to look forward to and that just gives me some satisfaction, I think.

Other volunteers were also motivated by that sense of satisfaction, but also due to the fact that without volunteers to help with diversity programs, the program would not run. As one volunteer highlighted, the availability of volunteers is paramount:

> Well, people power is the main thing you need because you need people to drive buses and organise things. Yeah. Well, they've got the equipment and their uniforms, but your hands on people is what you've got to have.

Another volunteer expressed a similar sentiment:

> If you don't volunteer or help with your child who has a disability in the things that they want to be involved in, those things don't run.

Unfortunately, sports teams do not run themselves, and if there are no volunteers to run the teams and competitions, or umpire matches, players from diverse communities do not get the opportunity to play. This is important because a structured opportunity for people with intellectual disabilities to play cricket offers them a chance to connect and make new friends, and peer support. However, preparing volunteers to work with specialist groups is vital, so that they have appropriate training and education to work and engage with people with intellectual disabilities. Such training might include learning the specific needs of people with intellectual disabilities, and behaviour management. Working with some disability groups can be rewarding but also challenging because of behaviour and specific individual needs. These factors impacted on the volunteer experiences of doing diversity work.

Many volunteers at RSCC had not worked with athletes with intellectual disabilities before, beyond their own child, so it was a new experience for some volunteers. As one volunteer parent highlighted, she was somewhat overwhelmed on her first volunteer session:

> I found it confronting the first few weeks, because we've never been involved in something that was only for people with a disability and some of them were very streetwise which we had not encountered before and certainly it was a little bit you know scary that all these people were swearing and things like that. Like all very diverse people and [son] not being involved and they were all in this inside loud noisy [space], and then... there aren't so many there now but a number of people were coming with carers from centres that you know couldn't speak to... to me thinking that they had no idea where they were or what they were doing and they were just being put in there and I thought oh goodness what's going to happen, but my son [participant in the program] just took to it like a fish to water. It didn't twig with him. There was a ball and let's play.

Additionally, some volunteers found it difficult to manage some of the ongoing behavioural challenges of players. Many volunteers had not received training, nor were they supported by their club. One volunteer, who managed and coordinated the teams spoke of this challenge:

> But that's just part for the course. One of them... some of them went up to Robert last week, the girls, and said, 'Olive doesn't give us a go. You give us a go'. Because I had probably about the 14 best players on show for him to choose the team, but the girls are not quite up... the stronger players, but they think I'm against them, but I'm not. It's just that they're not quite up to it. We have got... I have quite a few behavioural problems. I've never had any training because my son doesn't have behavioural problems, I've only learnt as I've gone along. Even we had a screaming match on last Sunday. I just do not like language. In my days, people didn't swear and I've been brought up with the old school and I just won't stand for it and one of the boys was mouthing off the other day, so we had a screaming match about how I wouldn't stand for it. That happens quite regularly, and I often mentor them with broken romances, deaths in the family, relationship problems.

Findings showed that volunteers committed to diversity work and fostering more inclusive sporting environments need to have the appropriate training and education, in addition to support from their organisation or club. If volunteers are not appropriately supported and their efforts are not valued, they risk burning out and terminating their volunteering commitments. A key finding about the volunteers at RSCC was a critical reliance on their capacity to be able to engage with diversity work. As a volunteer informed me during my fieldwork, "Without volunteers, you get nowhere", which is especially true for diversity work within sport. In case study 1, the motivations of volunteers who facilitate diversity work, specifically intellectual disability as a form of diversity, are outlined. In the following case study, the focus changes to the volunteers from diverse backgrounds and their approach to diversity work.

Case study 2: volunteers doing diversity work – the case of AFL supporter groups

The second case study concerns a group of volunteers who are of diverse sexualities and genders. LGBT+ people experience unwelcoming and hostile sporting environments (Storr, 2020; Storr & Symons, 2020), and although attitudes have changed to become more accepting of LGBT+ people in some sections of society, discrimination still exists across all levels of sport. A primary reason many people choose to volunteer is because of a cause that is close to their heart. Volunteering for a cause or passion is often referred to as benevolent volunteering. Benevolent volunteering refers to situations where volunteers provide care or in other ways help other people in need, as 'unpaid work or service' often within the field of social service (Rochester et al., 2010).

Benevolent volunteering is especially true for case study 2, where a group of volunteers came together to establish a fan/supporters group for a major Australian sporting code. Australian Football League (AFL) supporter groups, such as the Purple Bombers (Essendon) and the Rainbow Swans (Sydney Swans), were established in recent years to provide a network and community of AFL supporters for their respective clubs, to be able to engage with AFL and attend games in a safe and affirming environment.

Members and volunteers host social events, meet up before a game, and often sit together throughout a game. These groups were formed in response to continued acts of homophobia, biphobia, and transphobia in AFL spectators. A group of volunteers came together, in partnership with their club, to establish the Pride groups, and today nearly every professional AFL team in Australia has a pride group. The groups together create a unified AFL Pride Collective, tasked with coordinating and managing efforts to promote LGBT+ inclusion in the AFL community.

Pride groups are a way for LGBT+ people to feel safe and supported to go to live sports games. Research tells us that LGBT+ people report that sports games are not safe spaces and homophobia/biphobia/transphobia are still common (Storr et al., 2019). For example, a report by Goldring (2018) found that 63% of LGBT+ people experienced verbal or physical abuse on the grounds of homophobia and biphobia at football games. Some comments below from volunteers involved in the pride groups outline what a pride group is:

> I'd describe it as essentially, a group of people who maybe feel like they're not represented in the typical way in sport and have just come together to create an environment where all kinds of people can just celebrate sport, celebrate their team while being exactly who they are without any fear of repercussions from the rest of the sporting community.
>
> A supporter group is about creating a safe space for anyone who identifies as L.G.B.T.I.Q. It's about allowing people to still enjoy the sport that they enjoy, having folks there that they can speak to for any kind of issues they might have, for example, I remember sitting with somebody who recently came out as gay, going to a game, but they wanted somebody to sit with and feel safe and enjoy going to the games with. When you hear a lot of attitude, activity, language within those seats, which even though I'm quite tough-skinned, it was hard to hear myself, but it's allowing those safe spaces and also creating events for like-minded people that get together and be a bit more social too.

The research project was funded by Cricket Victoria to understand how to support the creation of LGBT+ pride groups in the Big Bash Cricket League in Australia (for more information on this and the associated methods, see Storr et al., 2019). For this project, individual interviews were conducted with volunteers from a variety of LGBT+ supporter groups across Australia. It is the motives and experiences of this select group of volunteers which are discussed in this case study.

The need for pride groups in Sport

Pride groups were established by volunteers because of ongoing discrimination and hostility to LGBT+ people in AFL, causing members to feel uncomfortable and unsafe at matches. On the persistent homophobic comments heard at games one volunteer reported:

> But yeah, obviously growing up in that sort of environment, and it is obviously a fairly ultra-masculine type of environment. But then coming out I think as an adult, I suppose you do hear, and certainly when I first came out and for a lot of years there was still those homophobic comments in the crowd and things like that.

Safety concerns were discussed in several interviews with volunteers, and fear of large crowds and environments where alcohol was common, which added to fears of homophobia and transphobia:

> One of the things that we do get feedback from people is that a lot of people in our committee have a lot of anxiety about very large crowds, that they don't do large groups of people, boisterous type of environments. And knowing that there could be a possibility that somebody may call out something homophobic that, that's just too scary and too daunting for some people. So... and we know it's improving and it certainly has improved dramatically. But it's still got a way to go. There is still issues that do pop up occasionally. As I said, one of our projects that we've done the last two years is, first year we did three games. This year we did four games where we had that group ticketing. So we were able to specifically have a safe space. We then targeted a few core groups in our community. So one of them was gender diverse people, queer youth was another. Where we raised funds, reduced price of tickets and got them to come.

Targeted efforts to facilitate the engagement of minority groups is not uncommon in sport, and in the above example, the volunteer highlighted that by making some adjustments to how sport is delivered (e.g. prices), marginalised sections of society can engage in sport in meaningful ways. The pride groups are essential because LGBT+ people report that action is still needed to eradicate anti-LGBT+ discrimination in sport, as another volunteer highlighted:

> They're needed because it really does bring a conversation that needs to be had to light and that is, even though there are some people who naturally don't feel comfortable with it, we can't ignore the fact that sport is supposed to be something for everyone. It is supposed to be something everyone can have every right to enjoy and be a part of, be a spectator and be a fan and unfortunately there aren't too many sporting communities that hold a bit of reservation in regards to how to treat fans who are a little different and fans who are a bit of let's say, a minority and so it's really important.

Further, for some members of the pride groups, specifically those who are trans or gender diverse, engaging and attending football games came with increased risks, to the individual and their families. As one trans participant commented:

> What's hard for me as a trans-woman is I come from living a life as a heterosexual man. I was privately bisexual, but I was living a heterosexual life and so I was dealing with blue collar folks who just want to go to a game, drink their beer, have a pint and a pie and watch a game. That was me. I was with my mates and we'd just watch a game and whatever and I want to be able to talk my kids and do these things and have my daughter understand sport is fun, even for young girls. I'm also coming to spaces where going up to bars or dating or whatever as a trans-woman, there's nothing for a rainbow family like me, so to take my kids to the oval and meet a few players and just watch a game and create a family atmosphere, that's so important to me.

This volunteer spoke of the positive ways that being part of a pride group helped her create new friendships and feel supported and safe whilst attending games. Trans and gender diverse people face challenging times in sporting environments, so pride groups provide a safe and affirming way to engage with a sport they are passionate about.

Many volunteers spoke of the numerous benefits derived from participating in volunteering with their respective pride groups, citing that they are helping build a more inclusive sporting sector. Volunteering also offered an avenue for LGBT+ people to connect with sport which does not involve playing, or other social settings such as alcohol or the pub. One volunteer reported:

> So yeah I mean it is, it's my passion. And I think I've... that's multiplied by 10 since I've got involved with [pride group]. So certainly always had a passion for it. I think it's just one of those things where... and I think it's the great thing about it is that it brings people together and it doesn't matter what your background is. So we've been very lucky, the work that we've done as well, we've done a lot of work with the official [AFL club] supporters group. And volunteered and got involved with them. But they have been really openly welcoming to all of us. And it is a quite diverse group of people even within that, you'll find a lot of those footy clubs, there is already quite often a lot of people who are socially awkward or backwards that are quite often involved in... and that is their social aspect in life because they don't fit the mould of going to the pub. So stepping into that sort of environment has been really quite welcoming in that aspect.

Finally, in understanding why LGBT+ people volunteer with a particular group or sporting organisation, the comment below outlines the particular connection that minority groups have with their own community, and why they volunteer to help others like themselves, to change society for the better:

> I think just one of the things that I said right from the word go is that I wanted to ensure that our group was going to be one of the most welcoming LGBTIQ supporter groups in [city]. And you know, you hear from a lot of people in the community that quite often a lot of groups are cliquey or that there's issues and there's this and that. I said from word go to our committee that we need to make sure everyone feels welcomed and included and that's something that we've certainly pushed so I'm quite proud of that. Because people do comment back and say how welcomed they have felt. And so

having that sort of impact, I think, and as I say, the positive feedback that you get from people from that sort of comment. The comments and emails that we've received about seeing the flags, we have members in the UK, in the US, who've seen our flags on Fox Sport overseas. And it's about showing that support for our community members and we receive so much feedback from people about how much of a positive impact it has on them watching the game and seeing those flags there. So it's explaining that to people.

This research on LGBT+ volunteers in supporter groups, however, indicates that people volunteer to help make positive changes in the sport sector, and to help other people across LGBT+ communities in Australia. Further, when LGBT+ people volunteer in sport, they have positive sport experiences and increase their social networks.

Conclusion

This chapter has briefly explored the role of volunteers in promoting greater diversity and inclusion within the sport sector in Australia. It also provided a summary of the relevant research on diversity and volunteering within sport, and the experiences and motivations of volunteers: those who facilitate the delivery of diversity work and programs within community sport, those from a specific marginalised group, and also LGBT+ volunteers. Volunteering in sport, for a specific cause, such as to promote inclusion within a sporting code, or to combat homophobia, biphobia, and transphobia, can lead to several benefits for both the organisation and volunteer, mainly social capital, and fostering new social connections.

A key theme discussed in this chapter relates to the importance and reliance of having diverse volunteers within sport, in order to implement policies and practices which aim to promote diversity and inclusion in sport. The first case study demonstrated that expecting a group of volunteers with little training and education around diversity and inclusion, to implement policies and efforts to promote greater diversity would be challenging for them. This supports findings from Jeanes et al. (2019) which highlights the lack of support volunteers are given in promoting greater diversity within community sport, therefore raising questions about the effectiveness of volunteers being used as policy implementors around diversity and inclusion. Investment needs to be increased into volunteer support, education, and training. The second case study highlights that when those from diverse communities are empowered and supported through their clubs, they feel confident in enacting policies and programs encouraging greater diversity within sport, and there are several benefits to the volunteer in particular. However, volunteers must also be better supported by their organisations and clubs, especially relating to LGBT+ people, around resistance and backlash (Spaaij, Knoppers & Jeanes, 2020). Better volunteer management practices and strategies within the sport sector is evident from findings from both case studies.

There is limited data available on the prevalence of volunteering within marginalised groups, such as persons who are LGBT+, with a disability, or from culturally diverse backgrounds. Future research should seek to capture data on volunteering amongst diverse groups, explore the conditions underpinning people's choice to volunteer, and under what circumstances. Volunteering is still a significant part of cultural life in many societies across the globe and is crucial to the sport sector in a range of countries. Only when sports organisations truly focus their resources and energy on promoting and attracting volunteers from diverse social and cultural backgrounds, will sport be more reflective of diverse communities across the globe. Volunteers are central to diversity efforts in the sport sector internationally, and therefore policy and practice needs to reflect this.

References

Ahmed, S. (2007a). "You end up doing the document rather than doing the doing": Diversity, race equality and the politics of documentation'. *Ethnic and Racial Studies*, *30*(4), 590–609. https://doi.org/10.1080/01419870701356015

Ahmed, S. (2007b). The language of diversity. *Ethnic and Racial Studies*, *30*(2), 235–256. https://doi.org/10.1080/01419870601143927

Auld, C. (2008). Voluntary sport clubs: The potential for the development of social capital. In M. Nicholdson & R. Hoye (Eds.) *Sport and social capital* (pp.143–164). Routledge.

Australian Sports Commission. (2015). *Cultural diversity and the role of sport*. Retrieved from: https://secure.ausport.gov.au/clearinghouse/knowledge_base/organised_sport/sport_and_government_policy_objectives/Cultural_Diversity_and_the_Role_of_Sport

Cunningham, G. (2008). Commitment to diversity and its influence on athletic department outcomes. *Journal of Intercollegiate Sport*, *1*(2), 176–201. https://doi.org/10.1123/jis.1.2.176

Darcy, S., Taylor, T., Murphy, A., & Lock, D. (2011). *Getting involved in sport: The participation and on-participation of people with disability in sport and active recreation*, Australian Sports Commission, Canberra.

Goldring, J., (2018). *LGBT+ end of season survey: A pride in football and football v homophobia report*. Pride Sports.

Hanlon, C., & Coleman, D. (2006). Recruitment and retention of culturally diverse people by sport and active recreation clubs. *Managing Leisure*, *11*(2), 77–95. https://doi.org/10.1080/13606710500520130

Jeanes, R., Spaaij, R., Magee, J., Farquharson, K., Gorman, S., & Lusher, D. (2019). Developing participation opportunities for young people with disabilities? Policy enactment and social inclusion in Australian junior sport. *Sport in Society*, *22*(6), 986–1004. https://doi.org/10.1080/17430437.2018.1515202

Low, N., Butt, S., Ellis, P., & Davis Smith, J. (2007). *Helping out: A national survey of volunteering and charitable giving*. Cabinet Office.

Mawson, H., & Parker, A. (2013). The next generation: Young people, sport and volunteering. In A. Parker & D. Vinson (Eds.) *Youth sport, physical activity and play: policy, intervention and participation* (pp. 152–165). Routledge.

Melton, E., & Cunningham, G. (2014). Who are the champions? Using a multilevel model to examine perceptions of employee support for LGBT inclusion in sport organizations. *Journal of Sport Management*, *28*, 189–206. https://doi.org/10.1123/jsm.2012-0086

Nichols, G. (2005). Stalwarts in sport. *World Leisure Journal*, *47*(2), 31–37. https://doi.org/10.1080/04419057.2005.9674393

Nichols, G., Hogg, E., Knight, C., & Storr, R. (2019). Selling volunteering or developing volunteers? Approaches to promoting sports volunteering. *Voluntary Sector Review*, *10*(1), 3–18. https://doi.org/10.1332/204080519X15478200125132

Nichols, G., Knight, C., Mirfin-Boukouris, H., Uri, C., Hogg, E., & Storr, R. (2016). *Motivations of sport volunteers in England: A review for Sport England*. Sport England.

Oppenheimer, M. (2008). *Volunteering: Why we can't survive without it*. UNSW Press.

Rochester C., Paine A. E., Howlett S., & Zimmeck M. (2010). Making volunteering inclusive. In C. Rochester, A. E. Payne & S. Howlett (Eds.) *Volunteering and society in the 21st century* (pp. 195–205). Palgrave Macmillan. https://doi.org/10.1057/9780230279438_14

Spaaij, R., Knoppers, A., & Jeanes, R. (2020). "We want more diversity but...": Resisting diversity in recreational sports clubs. *Sport Management Review*, *23*(3), 363–373. https://doi.org/10.1016/j.smr.2019.05.007

Spaaij, R., Magee, J., Farquharson, K., Gorman, S., Jeanes, R., Lusher, D., & Storr, R. (2018). Diversity work in community sport organizations: Commitment, resistance and institutional change. *International Review for the Sociology of Sport*, *53*(3), 278–295. https://doi.org/10.1177/1012690216654296

Spaaij, R., Magee, J., & Jeanes, R. (2014). *Sport and social exclusion in global society*. Routledge.

Storr, R. (2017). *'Now that they're here, we just have to deal with it': Exploring how volunteers enact intellectual disability within community sports clubs in Melbourne*, Australia. PhD Thesis, Victoria University.

Storr, R. (2020). "The poor cousin of inclusion": Australian Sporting Organisations and LGBT+ diversity and inclusion. *Sport Management Review*. Online First. https://doi.org/10.1016/j.smr.2020.05.001

Storr, R., Jeanes, R., Spaaij, R., & Farquharson, K. (2020). "That's where the dollars are": Understanding why community sports volunteers engage with intellectual disability as a form of diversity. *Managing Sport and Leisure*, 1–14. https://doi.org/10.1080/23750472.2020.1730226

Storr, R., Knijnik, J., Parry, K., Collison, A., & Staples, E. (2019). *Developing LGBT+ inclusive supporter groups in the Big Bash League*. Western Sydney University.

Storr, R., & Spaaij, R. (2016). "I guess it's kind of elitist": The formation and mobilisation of cultural, social and physical capital in youth sport volunteering. *Journal of Youth Studies*, *20*(4), 487–502. https://doi.org/10.1080/13676261.2016.1241867

Storr, R., & Symons, C. (2020). Promoting LGBT+ inclusion in women's and girls' sport: Lessons from Australia. In E. Sherry & K. Rowe (Eds.) *Developing sport for women and girls* (pp. 69–82). Routledge.

Volunteering Australia (2011). *The latest picture of volunteering in Australia*. Retrieved from: http://www.volunteeringaustralia.org/research-and-advocacy/the-latest-picture-of-volunteering-in-australia/

31

INTERCULTURAL LEARNING OR JUST HAVING FUN?

What volunteer tourism providers can learn from educational volunteering programmes to enhance intercultural competencies

Olga Junek and Celine Chang

Introduction

Volunteering abroad programmes for students and young adults come under many guises and with different aims and considerations attached and are offered by numerous providers. The two main types of organisations offering volunteering opportunities abroad fall into two main categories, those of non-governmental organisations or NGOs (henceforth non-commercial) and those of commercial operators. Both of these types of providers cover different market segments, offer programmes varying in type, length of stay and experiences and are largely driven by the motivations of those who take part as well as by the underlying principles of volunteering, and the promotion and cost of these programmes. Additionally, for the non-commercial providers, a regulatory and policy-based framework strongly guides their operations.

The last two decades have seen an expansion of volunteering abroad, with tourism strongly tied to the volunteering component (Wearing & McGehee, 2013). These programmes are taken up in source markets, mainly within Western countries and tend to be driven by notions of alternative tourism, niche tourism, gap year experiences and other developments leading to the growth of volunteering tourism, often referred to as voluntourism. Amongst the large proliferation of research and subsequent literature in this area, there have also been strong criticisms aimed at this form of travel. It is beyond the scope of this chapter to enter into an examination of the significant research contributions over the many diverse aspects of volunteering tourism, including those listed above.

The aim of this chapter is to focus on the intercultural learning design within the two different categories of volunteering abroad providers in Germany, a country with a long history of international volunteering. Specifically, the chapter examines which elements of the volunteering program design contribute to an increased intercultural understanding and competencies.

Intercultural competencies are considered vital in encouraging mutual understanding of people of different cultures and researchers have identified volunteering abroad as a method for developing these competencies. Lough (2011) and others (Bennett, 2009;

DOI: 10.4324/9780367815875-37

Deardorff, 2008; Fantini & Aqeel, 2006; Pusch & Merrill, 2008) posit that intercultural competence can only develop under the right conditions and that the characteristics and nature of the volunteer, the volunteering activity and the design and capacity of the volunteering organisation all play an important role (Perry & Imperial, 2001; Sherraden, Lough & McBride, 2008).

This chapter seeks to investigate how international volunteering programmes promote intercultural learning, using a qualitative study based on interviews conducted with non-commercial and commercial providers. In addition, subject experts and some past volunteers were also interviewed.

Background – the German context

In Europe, the so-called International Voluntary Services were initiated during and after World War 1 (WW1). These programmes were aimed specifically at fostering peace among countries, which were previously at war and encouraged young people in particular, to be part of consolidating and extending peaceful relations and intercultural understanding (Claessens & Danckwortt, 1957; Danckwortt, 1996). In addition to the international dimension, an educational perspective was added. During these intercultural encounters in the context of volunteering, participants were to learn about other cultures and to develop a thorough understanding through experiencing differences and commonalities (Claessens & Danckwortt, 1957). In Germany after World War 2 (WW2), many new organisations were founded as well as an umbrella organisation. Similar agencies and organisations developed in the UK such as the Voluntary Service Overseas in 1958, and the Peace Corps in the USA in 1961 (Peace Corps Connect, 2020; Voluntary Service Overseas, 2020). In Germany, these international voluntary services were also called 'workcamps' and have had their firm place within the volunteering arena ever since. In Germany, there are 15 publicly funded workcamp organisations, which are involved in about 1,000 workcamps in 80 countries, and take care of 5,000 volunteers each year (Trägerkonferenz, 2020).

Typical workcamps are short-term in the sense that they are usually of two to four weeks duration. Participants pay a participation fee to the provider and cover the travel expenses and spending money themselves and tend to come from industrialised countries. Participants are rarely from developing countries due to financial reasons, unless the voluntary service takes place in their home countries. Other than that, their participation is only possible when workcamp organisations from industrialised countries or other governmental programmes fund their expenses (cf. Chang, 2006). Volunteering projects are usually offered in four areas: construction and renovation, ecological, social, historical and cultural projects. The voluntary work is done for a local project owner who collaborates with the sending institution. Work takes up to five to six hours per day and the rest of the time is free and often used for sightseeing and other outings. The group usually stays together in basic accommodation. An important educational principle of these programmes is the self-organisation, e.g. for self-catering on site or individual travel arrangements. However, workcamps are accompanied by two group leaders (so-called 'teamers'). They do not lead the group in a classical leadership role, but are first contacts for both participants and project owners and responsible for organisational procedures (Chang, 2006).

In addition to workcamps, there are many other options to take part in international voluntary services and within the last decades, they have become more common with many commercial providers entering the market. For the purpose of this research, it is important to distinguish between long-term and short-term options as well as publicly and privately funded programmes and offerings. Subsidised programmes are usually regulated regarding the minimum and maximum duration by national ministries or the European Union. These programmes have goals driven by national and European (development) policies. Usually, non-commercial sending providers operationally implement these programmes for which they receive funding.

Apart from the publicly funded and regulated workcamps, the duration of other regulated volunteering programmes tends to be more long-term with volunteers staying for an average 9–12 months (Seidel & Stammsen, 2018). One key programme in Germany is *weltwärts*, which aims at fostering global learning of young adults through intercultural encounters within the context of volunteering abroad. Launched in 2008, more than 34,000 volunteers from Germany had gone abroad ten years later (Weltwärts, 2020). This programme fits into the category of volunteering for development (V4D), which involves organised contributions to communities outside one's own country for a specific period of time (Haas, 2012; Sherraden et al., 2006). In 2019, around 180 sending institutions (NGOs) from different backgrounds – religion, development, youth exchange and the environment – were registered within this programme and were subsidised up to 75% by the Federal Government (Georgeou & Haas, 2019). This means that almost all costs for volunteers are provided for, including travel expenses, accommodation, insurance and even spending money (Weltwärts, 2020).

Besides these regulated volunteering programmes, there are flexible programmes offered predominantly by commercial providers. These providers are unregulated and operate within a commercial, market-driven economy, despite the promotional rhetoric of "mutual, reciprocity and global civil society and community" (Georgeou & Haas, 2019, p. 1415). The two main characteristics in the more flexible programmes are that volunteers can decide about the timeframe of the volunteering work and have to cover the costs themselves (Seidel & Stammsen, 2018). Some providers also define a minimum time-period for the volunteering assignment. Since longer stays are connected with higher costs, volunteers tend to stay shorter periods, from several weeks to up to three months. In a study by Seidel and Stammsen (2018), the average was 7.3 weeks. There has been an increasing demand for flexible and short-term programmes within the last years with a growing number of commercial providers entering the market. The number of volunteers choosing a flexible programme outnumbers the long-term volunteers in the regulated programmes by far. Similar to other trends in international volunteering, an estimated 15,000–25,000 volunteers from Germany take part in flexible volunteering programmes abroad through commercial providers per year (Monshausen et al., 2018).

Voluntourism or volunteering abroad?

It is important to distinguish between the terminology used by non-commercial and commercial providers in how their programmes are named, designed and promoted. The variety of volunteering organisations (Everingham & Motta, 2020) makes it difficult and also inappropriate to assume that broad similarities result in similar aims and design of the programmes. However, the distinctions between providers and their programmes, and certainly in the German context, are central to the overall aims, programme design and promotion of the programmes that are explored in this research.

Generally, volunteering within the context of funded, regulated programmes have traditionally not been associated with tourism or considered under a tourism perspective. Due to the objectives of the programmes, the most prevalent focus by non-profit organisations and researchers has been on international (youth) exchange and the enhancement of global and intercultural competency building. Research on exchange programmes has usually focused on evaluating the effects of international exchange programmes on participants (Thimmel & Schäfer, 2019), of which volunteering programmes are one category (cf. Thomas, Chang & Abt, 2007).

On the other hand, with the increasing number of providers from the tourism sector, even from large tour operators such as TUI, voluntourism has been predominantly associated with flexible programmes that focus on the volunteers' demands and needs as customers. It is seen as a vacation with a high level of adventure and intensive experience including the feeling of "to do good" (Monshausen et al., 2018, p. 6). The advantage of these tour operators from the customer perspective is their ability to organise the whole trip, with volunteering being one component next to others, such as a safari or hiking. However, volunteer tourism is also referred to as a form of alternative tourism (Germann Molz, 2016; Wearing & McGehee, 2013), and a type of tourism that is more authentic and reflexive (McIntosh & Zahra, 2007), capable of raising tourists' awareness of social injustice (McGehee & Santos, 2005), creating a strong global civil society (Sherraden et al., 2006) and resulting in some kind of transformative experience (Magrizos, Kostopoulos & Powers, 2020).

As a result of the diverging views on volunteer tourism, two streams of literature have developed regarding volunteer tourism; one stream that regards it predominantly as beneficial on a number of different levels (Magrizos et al., 2020; McGehee, 2014; Sin, 2009). In direct contrast, the other stream reflects the many criticisms of these programmes over the last decade (Guttentag, 2009; Ong et al., 2017; Sin, 2010; Wearing & McGehee, 2013) that purport rationalising poverty, the demonstration effect, unequal social relations, exploitation of the host communities and neo-colonialism elements (Guttentag, 2009; Lyons et al., 2012; Palacios, 2010; Sin, 2010; Vrasti & Montsion, 2014).

Research on volunteer tourism does not often distinguish between programme providers. It usually acknowledges volunteering in the context of travelling or as a holiday component where a balance between contributing to local projects and having a good time is the main pull factor (see Wearing, 2001, and others). One of the major criticisms of commercial voluntourism has been the weak linkages and few collaborative approaches between providers and local partner organisations (Guttentag, 2009). Indeed, Guttentag (2009) asks the question as to whose needs should come first, the volunteer's or the community's and suggests that commercial providers may not always fulfill the aims of the local projects alongside their commercial priorities. In the case of the non-commercial providers and the regulatory nature of these, the conditions ensure that there is a local partner organisation, and the relationship is a collaborative one with a focus on reciprocity with the local organisation or project (Georgeou & Haas, 2019).

Further research is needed to ascertain the major differences between commercial and non-commercial providers, not just in their overall aims, operations and structures, but also in the design of their programmes and how these can add to mutual benefits of participants, local organisations and host communities. The 'holiday and travel' part of the programme in the case of commercial providers needs to be evaluated to determine the role it plays and how this contributes or diminishes the overall voluntourism experience.

In terms of intercultural learning and the development of intercultural competence within volunteer tourism it has been suggested that positive effects are probably over-estimated and that on the contrary, negative stereotypes and intercultural misunderstandings are developed (Guttentag, 2009; Raymond & Hall, 2008). Here, the role of the sending organisations, the provider, comes into place. Raymond and Hall (2008) argue, for example, that the development of cross-cultural understanding should be a goal of the sending organisations rather than an expected outcome of sending volunteers abroad. Providers should actively facilitate this goal before, during and after the voluntary service. In the slightly different context of studying abroad, but one that has high relevance, Trede, Bowles and Bridges (2013) argue that a semi-formal type of assessment on a relevant topic, such the economy or tourism or culture should be part of the programme and highlight the importance of thoughtfulness and preparation. Furthermore, reflection as suggested by Lough (2011) needs to be incorporated into the programme, through the guidance of a leader or mentor to optimise the experiential learning taking place.

While research evidence regarding the development of intercultural competence within volunteer tourism literature is mixed, there is strong evidence from empirical studies that evaluated the effects of international youth exchange programmes, where international voluntary services are one programme type (Thomas et al., 2007). In a quasi-experimental study on international workcamps by Chang (2006) that used a pre-post design and psychometric scales, significant effects on abilities related to intercultural competence such as openness, flexibility and self-efficacy were shown. In addition, there were significant effects on the participants' self-evaluation of their intercultural competence development due to the workcamp experience. Most effects remained stable as a follow-up assessment three months after finishing the voluntary service revealed. In terms of motives for participating, the study also showed that while voluntary work ranked behind getting to know new people from different cultures and to improve foreign language skills, the voluntary work itself was evaluated as an important venue for intercultural learning. To have fun at the voluntary work was a significant predictor for developing intercultural competence as several regression models on the effects revealed.

Thus, in research on the effects of volunteering abroad in programmes by non-commercial providers, the development of intercultural competence has been evidenced. These programmes also follow defined educational goals. This brings us back to the purpose of this chapter. Since non-commercial providers have a long history in optimising their programmes to meet their educational goals with the development of intercultural competence as one important goal, commercial providers of volunteer tourism, that have not taken this goal into account so far, could learn from their expertise.

Intercultural competence

Beyond providing intercultural encounters we would argue that all volunteer tourism organisations have a role and responsibility in designing programmes to foster and develop international understanding and competence in their participants or customers. Intercultural understanding and competencies are considered vital in encouraging mutual understanding of different cultures in the context of volunteer tourism. However, Lough (2011) and others (Bennett, 2009; Deardorff, 2008; Fantini & Aqeel, 2006; Pusch & Merrill, 2008) posit that the development of intercultural competence can only grow under the right conditions and that the characteristics and nature of the volunteer, the volunteering activity and the design and capacity of the volunteering organisation all play an important role (Perry & Imperial, 2001; Sherraden et al., 2008).

Intercultural competence has been defined in a multitude of ways depending on context and area of study (Bennett, 2009; Deardorff, 2008; Lough, 2011; McAllister et al., 2006; McRae & Ramji, 1996; Trede et al., 2013). Four main dimensions are considered as the basic tenets of intercultural competence, those of knowledge, attitude, skills and behavior (Bennett, 2009; Lustig & Koester, 2006; Perry & Southwell, 2011) while others, for example, Deardorff (2006) see it as a process. Cultural tolerance, flexibility, language proficiencies, intercultural sensitivity, respect, empathy for others (Heyward, 2002; Hiller & Woźniak, 2009) and other behavioral, attitudinal, cognitive and affective nuances have also been included in research of the concept of intercultural competence. For the purpose of this chapter the authors see intercultural competence as "the ability to effectively and appropriately interact in an intercultural situation or context" (Perry & Southwell, 2011, p. 453) as well as *the* "socio-cultural context and dispositions that inform abilities to engage with intercultural and global situations" (Chappell, Gonczi & Hager (2000) in Trede et al., 2013, p. 444). As such, intercultural competence should include intercultural communication skills and the incorporation of the knowledge of culture and the host community into those skills (Arasaratnam, 2009; Gudykunst et al., 2005) as well as intercultural sensitivity (Hammer, Bennett & Wiseman, 2003) and understanding (Deardorff, 2006; Hill, 2006).

As an important part of global citizenship, intercultural competence can also play a major role in creating good global citizens. Global citizenship is conceived as a "conceptual value framework underpinned by social responsibility, global equality and human rights" and thus "aligns well with notions of intercultural competence" (Trede et al., 2013, p. 443) and inclusion of the concepts of intercultural competence, intercultural understandings as well as social responsibility and global engagement has also been strongly advocated (Butcher & Smith, 2015; McGehee, 2012; Morais & Ogden, 2010; Trede et al., 2013).

There is relatively little research on volunteering abroad participants and what elements of their experience may (or may not) have contributed to intercultural understanding and intercultural competence (Everingham & Motta, 2020; Lough, 2011). Additionally, much of the research thus far, except Georgeou and Haas (2019), does not differentiate between the participants of non-commercial and commercial providers. For these reasons, we would suggest that, as a first step, a lens needs to be focused on the design of volunteering abroad programmes of both types of providers.

Research objectives

To understand fully how intercultural competence is incorporated into the design of volunteering programmes and to establish the potential benefits of the design and operational aspects of the programme, the following research objectives were developed:

- What programme elements and activities specifically enhance the intercultural competence of the participants?
- How can the offerings of providers of voluntourism and of non-commercial providers of international voluntary work be characterised (goals, schedule, costs)?
- What do non-commercial providers do differently than commercial providers with regard to fostering intercultural competence development?
- What learnings can be drawn for both types of providers?

Methodology

Due to the lack of research with this particular focus, an exploratory research design was chosen using semi-structured interviews (cf. Bortz & Döring, 2016; Jennings 2010; Picken, 2018). It included a multi-perspective approach by integrating representatives from both commercial and non-commercial providers as well as a few subject matter experts and former volunteers into the sample. Initially, a list of commercial and non-commercial providers of international volunteering services was created based on desktop research of providers' websites as well as information portals for target audiences. Subject matter experts were selected based on publications, personal network and recommendations through other experts. The subject matter experts have a working history in policymaking organisations, umbrella organisations in tourism and international youth exchange organisations as well as in academia, and have a broad and independent view on the subject matter. Former international volunteers were included as an ad-hoc sample (cf. Bortz & Döring, 2016). Besides one or more international volunteering experiences, criteria for being included in the study were high levels of self-reflection and reflection of the volunteering experience. These findings were assessed by the interviewers in a short conversation, pre-interview, with the former volunteers.

Potential interview partners were initially contacted via email but due to the Covid-19 pandemic situation and the lock-down in Germany, the response rate for commercial providers was low. When followed up, most said that the current situation forces them to focus on other pressing issues. The non-commercial providers were much more willing to support the study, even though their programmes were affected by Covid-19 as well. However, since they mainly receive public funds, they had no real economic concerns. In total, 21 interviews were conducted out of which 10 were with non-commercial providers, 2 with commercial providers, 4 subject matter experts and 5 former participants. In order to back up the information on commercial providers, a complementary analysis of a random sample of 22 providers' websites was conducted. The focus of the analysis was to find out more about their offerings, marketing, local partners for volunteering projects and any information that indicated the purpose to enhance intercultural learning and competence development, such as motivation letters or preparatory seminars.

Due to the Covid-19 pandemic situation, all interviews were held via Zoom. The interview duration was 45 minutes on average. The interviews were recorded, transcribed and analysed by means of a qualitative content analysis (Mayring, 2014) using the MAXQDA, a software package for qualitative and mixed-method research (Kuckartz & Rädiker, 2019).

Results

Provider market and provider characteristics

Generally, the respondents agreed that the market for volunteering abroad has been increasing in the last years, especially through commercial providers like tour operators. They have noticed a trend towards individual programmes as opposed to group-based programmes. Therefore, participants for workcamps have been declining. As for programme duration, the interviewees had slightly differing views and see a trend towards flexible programmes, both short-term and long-term. The Covid-19 pandemic has had a great impact on volunteering abroad and many programmes could not take place in 2020. The long-term effects of the pandemic on international volunteering needs are not foreseeable at the time of this research. Some providers see the need to reposition themselves based on the new circumstances. They predict both higher expectations regarding programme quality as well as an increase in short-term programmes since they are more predictable in these times.

The findings show that in the non-commercial area, there are numerous organisations, some of which have a longstanding history with a focus on volunteering. Commercial providers are often tour operators that either specialise in volunteering or offer packages including volunteering. The characteristics of both types of providers are summarised in Table 31.1.

Table 31.1 Characteristics of commercial and non-commercial international volunteering providers

	Non-commercial providers	Commercial providers
Fees	Covering of costs Funded by government programs, donations and sponsorship Participants pay small fee and their travel costs	Profit-oriented Fees range between 700 and 4,500 euros (not including airfares) Small portion of the fees goes to funding local projects
Type of projects	Projects that facilitate personal and social learning Projects selected on needs of local organisations (not attractiveness) Mainly work camps, group based and individual	Providing programs that appeal to customers. Often dependant on type of project and destination that has current appeal Social (working with children or teens), wildlife, construction
Duration	Short (2–4 weeks) and long-term (> 6 months –1 year)	Mainly short-term, long-term offerings available but chosen infrequently
Participant characteristics	Young adults, mainly females; high school and/or university graduates	Mostly female, 16–26 years of age, recently completed secondary school
Participant motivations	To improve languages skills and intercultural competence To bridge gap time between high school and university To do something useful	Focus on vacation, adventure and pleasure
Planning times for participants	Long-term planning required	Short-term planning
Participant requirements	Long selection process Motivation letter before interview	No selection criteria
Preparation/ training	Preparatory seminars (1–7 days), training components such as role-play are included	No preparation seminar/training Often language courses are offered before starting project work
In-field expectations	Long-term programs include one or more seminars; learning tools such as reflection diaries	
In-field support	Contacts from partner organisations and sending institutions, teamer, sometimes additional external mentors Support persons have been trained in enhancing intercultural learning	Contacts from partner organisations and sending institutions
Promotion/ marketing	Intercultural competence and learning Low marketing funds	Focuses on special travel experience with a purpose To get to know people from other cultures Service oriented High marketing budget Easier to find through search engines
Follow-up; debriefing	Debriefing seminars, individual reports	Rarely offered and not obligatory

(Continued)

Table 31.1 (Continued)

	Non-commercial providers	Commercial providers
Travel arrangements	Individually arranged	Can be booked by provider
Inclusions	Accommodation, food, sometimes outings	Outings and some travel components often included in total cost
Other characteristics		Participants are sometimes reluctant to work Often want to meet other Germans more than locals

Travel or volunteering?

One of the major differences between the two types of providers are the goals of each. Programmes by the non-commercial organisations usually have an educational goal that promotes reflective learning and is seen to lead to better intercultural understanding and resulting intercultural competence.

> (...) This whole package [preparation, on-site seminar and reflections, evaluation meeting] contributes to the development of intercultural competencies. That you learn to be empathetic, to stand back, to control oneself and not to automatically rate everything that you see in a different culture and also to critically evaluate one's own culture.
>
> *(E02, 22)*

The commercial providers do use a lot of words in their promotional materials that can be interpreted as semi-education, for example 'mindful volunteering', 'finding yourself', 'social engagement' but at the same time they also promote the experiences as 'fleeing the everyday', 'unforgettable', 'travel for world explorers' and so on.

Our research has shown that non-commercial providers with a background in international youth exchange programmes in the context of volunteering services do not identify with the term 'voluntourism'. Many criticise that the focus of voluntourism is on customer demand only and that it does not consider how local people are affected by the voluntary services. Criticism of voluntourism from the non-commercial providers extends to low benefit for those in need, too profit-oriented and low development of the participants' intercultural competence.

Intercultural programme design

The underlying philosophy and vision of the non-commercial providers are focused heavily on intercultural competence and learning. Due to government financial support and underlying principles of global peace and understanding this is to be expected, and intercultural programme design plays a major role. This is evidenced in the selection process, preparation and training and post-return reporting and debriefing. In addition, the non-commercial providers ensure there is a good fit between the participants and the selected project. They provide active support by project leaders and/or contact persons of the partner organisation in-field. Overall, it is notable, that the programme design follows educational principles that promote reflection and thus experiential learning that goes beyond stereotyping (Lough, 2011).

On the other hand, most commercial providers have little or no selection criteria, minimal training or preparation except written material, or sometimes an optional preparation seminar and/or language courses, no debriefing and rather passive support in-field. Once in the field, if problems arise, participants might talk to the local contacts; the host family is also suggested as a mediator if problems arise. It is uncertain (yet unlikely) if contacts in-field have been trained in guiding learning processes, reflections or mediation.

However, some of the non-commercial providers also mentioned that the reality of the international programmes is at times somewhat different to their guiding principles. This included no realistic preparation for possible conflict situations, change or dropping out of participants during stay and lack of quantifiable project evaluations. Nevertheless, if commercial providers want to improve their offerings in terms of the enhancement of intercultural competencies, it is exactly the educational programme that the non-commercial providers have incorporated into the volunteering service that are lacking. Thus, they would need to define an educational strategy and offer instruments that enhance intercultural learning, such as obligatory preparation, debriefing and on-site reflection opportunities as the following quote of one expert reflects:

> (…) but specific components for preparation or on-site learning, such as role-play or digital learning offerings, opportunities for reflection, making available of learning material (…). To offer these more intensely, this is what commercial providers could do.
>
> *(E03, 29–30)*

Apart from the enhancement of intercultural competence, a number of interview partners stressed that it is not unidirectional learning from non-commercial providers. In fact, they pointed out some valuable practices they could learn from the commercial providers in terms of marketing, customer orientation and service quality. Some see a synergy potential if commercial and non-commercial providers were to collaborate more in order to stay successful in a changing and challenging market. For instance, the combination with other products (e.g. language classes, adventure tourism) is seen as an asset to make volunteering abroad more attractive to participants. Hence, the easy-to-draw conclusion that programmes by non-commercial providers are 'all good' (cf. Guttentag, 2009), is seen as over-simplistic. On the contrary, some stress that there are commercial providers that have very good educational programmes and that all providers have the opportunity to make use of the educational potential of volunteering abroad.

> I am happy that they [commercial providers] are there, because they create a link between tourism and an educational event. (…) This is not different in youth work where we have a link between leisure and education (…). And there are smart examples of commercial providers that offer a great preparation and debriefing, and appreciative interaction, (…) etc. where non-commercial providers can also learn from commercial providers with regards to specific organisational questions.
>
> *(E03, 30)*

Discussion

We started with the provocative title, as to what volunteer tourism providers can learn from educational volunteering programmes to enhance intercultural competencies of their participants and customers. Results suggest that maybe the question should be narrowed to those commercial providers that are interested in doing so. While doing the research, it became clear that this does not seem to be their focus or indeed, priority, apart from a few exceptions.

Therefore, two questions arise that need to be further investigated through empirical research. One refers to the main criteria for target audiences on which to choose a provider. The range might span from visibility on the internet, costs, destination marketing and projects offered. The assumption based on what the experts said, is that many commercial providers invest more in marketing and are thus easier to be found online. In addition, many potential participants are not aware of all the different options offered in the range of providers, commercial and non-commercial. This is why umbrella platforms and individual guidance such as that offered by Eurodesk (see https://eurodesk.eu/) are helpful for interested participants, including their parents, as one expert pointed out. Otherwise, with their professional marketing, commercial providers have a clear advantage to win the competition based on online searches. An important question to ask is if commercial and non-commercial providers generally attract different participants in terms of individual goals, values and interests related to the voluntary services. Based on the results, it seems that this is likely to be the case. Even though participants of both provider categories are similar in age, gender and educational background, the hypothesis is that participants of commercial providers actually do see volunteering abroad as a quasi-vacation, and as part of a more adventurous, but also more meaningful type of travel. Therefore, the motives for choosing which programme and provider should be further investigated as well as the relationship between motives and the level of intercultural competence built in and offered in the context of the experience. A significant difference of participants' motives would indicate that non-commercial providers and commercial providers do not share the same market, even though there might be some overlap. If intercultural learning, intercultural competence and the notion of reciprocity are important motivational reasons for volunteering, then the non-commercial providers have a great deal to offer to reach those aims.

The focus of this chapter has been on the fostering of intercultural competence through volunteering abroad and how programme design of providers can contribute to the learning process. It is safe to assume that no provider, non-commercial and commercial, would really dispute the importance of intercultural competence resulting from the volunteering abroad experience.

> In the end nobody will say 'I am against it', but the big question is, what instruments do you offer that it really happens.
>
> *(E03, 26)*

However, commercial providers are forced to ask themselves about the return on investing in instruments that enhance intercultural competence of customers. With the growing number of commercial providers in the market, it might be argued, that could be a unique selling point among commercial providers. In addition, if customers see the benefit of having developed their intercultural competence further it might result in higher levels of customer satisfaction, customer loyalty and the perception of a high-quality product. This might lead to returning customers, a good reputation and thus a positive effect on acquiring new customers.

Having educational and intercultural aims and outcomes guiding the programme design is the important first step towards achieving the goal of intercultural competence and these were certainly present amongst the non-commercial providers. But beyond the aims of the programmes, there are other elements as Lough (2011) points out in his study on volunteers from two different non-commercial providers. In the study, Lough (2011) measured the responses of returned volunteers on the *duration, relationships, immersion, guided reflection* and *contact reciprocity,* all of which he saw as important aspects of their experience and their intercultural learning (Lough, 2011, p. 5). Our respondents highlighted these elements and we see the need to incorporate them in the design of volunteering abroad programmes, if intercultural competence, beyond the superficial, is a desired learning outcome.

In terms of duration and immersion, the longer volunteers participate in a programme, the more likely they are to build relationships and be immersed in the programme together with locals. This takes place in the home stay environment, the work place and in social activities outside of work. Immersion can be achieved through home stay accommodation and the work context situation, thereby offering a chance to live and interact with locals. The non-commercial providers were aware of the need to provide structured opportunities and activities for interaction between the local community and the volunteers.

Guided reflection, both as individuals and in groups, was considered important for the learning outcomes (Lough, 2011) but the difficulty of embedding this in the programme also needs to be acknowledged. Providing social activities, individual time to reflect and encouraging the importance of reflection opportunities can all be regarded as guided reflection.

> (…) I think it is important to offer participants this protected space where they can practice. Where it is talked about what went wrong, why things didn't work and what this has to do with me and my cultural imprint. To create awareness.
>
> *(NP05, 121)*

From the participants' perspective this resulted in several realisations:

> I have become more open and yes, I think differently and have less prejudice in my head.
>
> *(T03, 52)*

> It has simply been a good experience to work even though you don't earn money for it. Simply to do which you do from you heart and this is why I would say, that it has influenced me.
>
> *(T03, 60)*

Within intercultural competence, the three domains of intercultural ability (Fantini & Aqeel, 2006, p. 27) should be at the forefront of the aims and learning outcomes of volunteering abroad programmes – *relationship building, communication skills, and co-operative and collaborative behavior.* To achieve competency in these domains, directed and operationalised activities should be incorporated into the programme structure.

Contributions

Literature on voluntourism does not differentiate enough between commercial and non-commercial providers and programme designs that enhance intercultural competence. Results indicate that this is important when evaluating goals, programme design and effects, such as intercultural competence, and as such they provide the firsts step in furthering research on volunteering abroad providers. This exploratory study showed that from the provider and expert perspective, programme design and educational guidance positively influences the depth and level of intercultural competence development among participants. Therefore, in line with Raymond and Hall (2008), the development of intercultural competence should be a goal of providers rather than an expected outcome.

Limitations and further research

As a first exploratory study on this particular subject matter, it has some limitations. First, results mainly reflect the non-profit provider perspective and therefore results might be biased. Consequently, more commercial providers should be included in a follow-up study investigating their specific situation regarding the enhancement of intercultural competence among participants. As outlined before, further research needs to investigate the philosophy of programme design as well as participants' motives in comparison to those of non-commercial providers that have the goal to enhance intercultural competence through their programmes.

In addition, research on the effects of international volunteering has been largely qualitative in nature. In order to be able to safely generalise across the population of participants, a quasi-experimental pre-post design with control groups is needed. This kind of research is difficult to find so far, neither in the area of voluntourism nor in the area of international exchange programmes (cf. Chang, 2006, on workcamps).

Even though the perspectives of various stakeholder groups were included, one important one was missing. The perspective of the local project owners or managers respectively. When looking at the voluntourism literature, this perspective has not been empirically investigated sufficiently. This perspective needs to be included in further research in this topic area since it would highlight programme design needs of these important stakeholders to enhance intercultural competence, to embark on the concept of reciprocity (Lough, 2011) and to avoid the potential negative effects on people and communities involved in the local volunteering projects.

Conclusion

International volunteering provides a special space for intercultural learning in comparison with other forms of tourism, since participants need to interact more and at a different levels with locals and thus become more involved in the culture of the destination and its people. In addition, many volunteers work alongside volunteers from across the world, which adds to the intercultural learning experience. However, in order to benefit the most from volunteering abroad, it can be argued that programmes need to include specific aims and learning outcomes to enhance this intercultural learning and result in the enhancement of intercultural competence. Thus, most commercial providers need to decide if they want to improve their offerings in that area. For commercial providers, this is a business decision that might be influenced by several factors such as market developments and return on investment.

With the enduring Covid-19 pandemic and its effects on travelling abroad, both commercial and non-commercial providers are forced to re-evaluate their offerings since they need to deal with travelling restrictions, health and security regulations as well as potential changes of customer motives and demands. How the market for international volunteering will change cannot be predicted yet. However, one positive effect of the pandemic might be an increase in collaboration between commercial and non-commercial providers in order to remain successfully in the market.

References

Arasaratnam, L. A. (2009). *The development of a new instrument of intercultural communication competence.* http://www.immi.se/intercultural/nr20/arasaratnam.htm

Bennett, M. J. (2009). Defining, measuring, and facilitating intercultural learning: a conceptual introduction to the Intercultural Education double supplement. *Intercultural Education, 20*(4), 1–13. https://doi.org/10.1080/14675980903370763

Bortz, J. & Döring, N. (2016). *Forschungsmethoden und evaluation in den sozial- und humanwissenschaften* [Research methods and evaluation in the social and human sciences] (5th ed.). Heidelberg: Springer.

Butcher, J. & Smith, P. (2015). *Volunteer tourism: The lifestyle politics of international development.* London: Routledge.

Chang, C. (2006). *Veränderungen von Selbstschemata im Kontext der Teilnahme an internationalen Workcamps* [Changes of self-schemes in the context of particaption in international workcamps]. Aachen: Shaker.

Chappell, C., Gonczi, A. & Hager, P. (2000). Competency-based Education. In F. Griff (Ed.), *Understanding adult education and training* (2nd ed., pp. 191–205). Crows Nest: Allen & Unwin.

Claessens, D. & Danckwortt, D. (1957). *Jugend in Gemeinschaftsdiensten: Eine soziologisch-psychologische Untersuchung über die Arbeit in den internationalen Jugendgemeinschaftsdiensten* [Youth in community services: A sociological-psychological study of work in international youth community services]. München: Juventa.

Danckwortt, D. (1996). Forschungs- und Praxisfelder interkulturellen Personenaustauschs [Fields of research and practice of intercultural exchange of people]. In A. Thomas (Ed.), *Psychologie interkulturellen Handelns* (pp. 269–281). Göttingen: Hogrefe.

Deardorff, D. K. (2006). Identification and assessment of intercultural competence as a student outcome of internationalization. *Journal of Studies in International Education, 10*(3), 241–266. https://doi.org/10.1177/1028315306287002

Deardorff, D. K. (2008). Intercultural competence: A definition, model, and implications for education abroad. In V. Savicki (Ed.), *Developing intercultural competence and transformation: Theory, research, and application in international education* (pp. 32–52). Sterling, VA: Stylus.

Everingham, P. & Motta, S. C. (2020). Decolonising the 'autonomy of affect' in volunteer tourism encounters. *Tourism Geographies*, 1–21. https://doi.org/10.1080/14616688.2020.1713879

Fantini, A. E. & Aqeel, T. (2006). Exploring and assessing intercultural competence. *World Learning Publications*, Paper 1. http://digitalcollections.sit.edu/worldlearning_publications/1

Georgeou, N. & Haas, B. (2019). Power, exchange and solidarity: Case studies in youth volunteering for development. *VOLUNTAS: International Journal of Voluntary and Nonprofit Organizations, 30*(6), 1406–1419. https://doi.org/10.1007/s11266-019-00103-w

Germann Molz, J. (2016). Making a difference together: Discourses of transformation in family voluntourism. *Journal of Sustainable Tourism, 24*(6), 805–823. https://doi.org/10.1080/09669582.2015.1088862

Gudykunst, W. B., Lee, C.M, Nishida T. & Ogawa, N. (2005). Theorizing about intercultural communication. In W. B. Gudykunst (Ed.), *Theorizing about intercultural communication* (pp. 3–32). Thousand Oaks, CA: Sage.

Guttentag, D. A. (2009). The possible negative impacts of volunteer tourism. *International Journal of Tourism Research, 11*(6), 537–551. https://doi.org/10.1002/jtr.727

Haas, B. (2012). *Ambivalence of reciprocity. Reciprocity forms of the weltwärts-volunteer service in the mirror of postcolonial theory, interdisciplinary studies on voluntary services* (Vol. 2). Cologne: Kölner Wissenschaftsverlag.

Hammer, M. R., Bennett, M. J. & Wiseman, R. (2003). Measuring intercultural sensitivity: The intercultural development inventory. *International Journal of Intercultural Relations, 27*(4), 421–443. https://doi.org/10.1016/s0147-1767(03)00032-4

Heyward, M. (2002). From international to intercultural: Redefining the international school for a globalized world. *Journal of Research in International Education, 1*(1), 9–32. https://doi.org/10.1177/1475240902001001266

Hill, I. (2006). Student types, school types and their combined influence on the development of intercultural understanding. *Journal of Research in International Education, 5*(1), 5–33. https://doi.org/10.1177/1475240906061857

Hiller, G. G. & Woźniak, M. (2009). *Developing an intercultural competence programme at an international cross-border university. Intercultural Education, 20*(4), 113–124. https://doi.org/10.1080/14675980903371019

Jennings, G. (2010). *Tourism research* (2nd ed.). Australia: John Wiley & Sons.

Kuckartz, U. & Rädiker, S. (2019). *Analyzing qualitative data with MAXQDA: Text, audio, and video.* Wiesbaden: Springer VS.

Lustig, M. W. & Koester, J. (2006). *Intercultural competence: Interpersonal communication across cultures* (5th ed.). Boston, MA: Pearson.

Lough, B. J. (2011). International volunteers' perceptions of intercultural competence. *International Journal of Intercultural Relations, 35*(4), 452–464. https://doi.org/10.1016/j.ijintrel.2010.06.002

Lyons, K., Hanley, J., Wearing, S. & Neil, J. (2012). Gap year volunteer tourism: Myths of global citizenship? *Annals of Tourism Research, 39*(1), 361–378. https://doi.org/10.1016/j.annals.2011.04.016

Magrizos, S., Kostopoulos, I. & Powers, L. (2020). Volunteer tourism as a transformative experience: A mixed methods empirical study. *Journal of Travel Research*, April 2020. https://doi.org/10.1177/0047287520913630

Mayring, P. (2014). *Qualitative content analysis: Theoretical foundation, basic procedures and software solution.* Klagenfurt. URN: http://nbn-resolving.de/urn:nbn:de:0168-ssoar-395173

McAllister, L., Whiteford, G., Hill, B., Thomas, N. & Fitzgerald, M. (2006). Reflection in intercultural learning: Examining the international experience through a critical incident approach. *Reflective Practice, 7*(3), 367–381. https://doi.org/10.1080/14623940600837624

McGehee, N. G. (2012). Oppression, emancipation, and volunteer tourism. *Annals of Tourism Research, 39*(1), 84–107. https://doi.org/10.1016/j.annals.2011.05.001

McGehee, N. G. (2014). Volunteer tourism: Evolution, issues and futures. *Journal of Sustainable Tourism, 22*(6), 847–854. https://doi.org/10.1080/09669582.2014.907299

McGehee, N. G. & Santos, C. A. (2005). Social change, discourse and volunteer tourism. *Annals of Tourism Research, 32*(3), 760–779. https://doi.org/10.1016/j.annals.2004.12.002

McIntosh, A. J. & Zahra, A. (2007). A cultural encounter through volunteer tourism: Towards the ideals of sustainable tourism? *Journal of Sustainable Tourism, 15*(5), 541–556. https://doi.org/10.2167/jost701.0

McRae, N. & Ramji, K. (1996). Enhancing cultural intelligence through cooperative and work-integrated education. In R. K. Coll & K. E. Zegwaaard (Eds.), *International handbook for cooperative and work-integrated education* (2nd ed., pp. 269–281). Lowell, MA: WACE World Association for Cooperative Education.

Monshausen, A., Plüss, C., Jäger, L., Köhrer, E., Kosche, M., Lukow, M. Maurer, M. Hertwig, F. (2018). *Vom Freiwilligendienst zum Voluntourismus: Herausforderungen für die verantwortungsvolle Gestaltung eines wachsenden Reisetrends* [From volunteering programmes to voluntourism: Challenges for a responsible design of a growing travel trend]. https://www.tourismwatch.de/system/files/document/Profil18_Voluntourismus.pdf

Morais, D. B. & Ogden, A. C. (2010). Initial development and validation of the global citizenship scale. *Journal of Studies in International Education, 15*(5), 445–466. https://doi.org/10.1177/1028315310375308

Ong, F., King, B., Lockstone-Binney, L. & Junek, O. (2017). Going global, acting local: Volunteer tourists as prospective community builders. *Tourism Recreation Research, 43*(2), 135–146. https://doi.org/10.1080/02508281.2017.1391449

Palacios, C. M. (2010). Volunteer tourism, development and education in a postcolonial world: Conceiving global connections beyond aid. *Journal of Sustainable Tourism, 18*(7), 861–878.

Peace Corps Connect (2020). https://www.peacecorpsconnect.org/ Accessed December 10, 2020.

Perry, J. L. & Imperial, M. T. (2001). A decade of service-related research: A map of the field. *Nonprofit and Voluntary Sector Quarterly, 30*(3), 462–479. https://doi.org/10.1177/0899764001303004

Perry, L. B. & Southwell, L. (2011). Developing intercultural understanding and skills: Models and approaches. *Intercultural Education, 22*(6), 453–466. https://doi.org/10.1080/14675986.2011.644948

Picken, F. (2018). The interview in tourism research. In W. Hillman & K. Radel (Eds.), *Qualitative methods in tourism research* (pp. 200–222). Clevedon Hall: Channelview Publications.

Pusch, M. D. & Merrill, M. (2008). Reflection, reciprocity, responsibility, and committed relativism. In V. Savicki (Ed.), *Developing intercultural competence and transformation: Theory, research, and application in international education* (pp. 53–73). Sterling, VA: Stylus.

Raymond, E. M. & Hall, C. M. (2008). The development of cross-cultural (mis)understanding through volunteer tourism. *Journal of Sustainable Tourism, 16*(5), 530–543. https://doi.org/10.2167/jost796.0

Seidel, F. & Stammsen, P. (2018). Die Dauer von flexibler Freiwilligenarbeit im Ausland [The duration of flexible volunteering work abroad]. *Voluntaris, 6*(2), 270–288. https://doi.org/10.5771/2196-3886-2018-2-270

Sherraden, M. S., Lough, B. J. & McBride, A. M. (2008). Effects of international volunteering and service: Individual and institutional predictors. *VOLUNTAS: International Journal of Voluntary and Nonprofit Organizations, 19*(4), 395–421. https://doi.org/10.1007/s11266-008-9072-x

Sherraden, M. S., Stringham, J., Sow, S. C. & McBride, A. M. (2006). The forms and structure of international voluntary service. *VOLUNTAS: International Journal of Voluntary and Nonprofit Organizations, 17*(2), 156–173. https://doi.org/10.1007/s11266-006-9011-7

Sin, H. L. (2009). Volunteer tourism – "Involve me and I will learn"? *Annals of Tourism Research, 36*(3), 480–501. https://doi.org/10.1016/j.annals.2009.03.001

Sin, H. L. (2010). Who are we responsible to? Locals' tales of volunteer tourism. *Geoforum, 41*(6), 983–992. https://doi.org/10.1016/j.geoforum.2010.08.007

Thimmel, A. & Schäfer, S. (2019). Wirkungsforschung in der internationalen Jugendarbeit. In M. Begemann, C. Bleck & R. Liebig (Eds.), *Wirkungsforschung zur Kinder- und Jugendhilfe: Grundlegende Perspektiven und arbeitsfeldspezifische Entwicklungen* [Research on effectiveness of children and youth aid: General perspectives and work field specific developments] (pp. 234–252). Weinheim: Beltz Juventa.

Thomas, A., Chang, C. & Abt, H. (2007). *Erlebnisse, die verändern: Langzeitwirkungen der Teilnahme an internationalen Jugendbegegnungen* [Experiences, that make a change: Long term effects of the participation in international youth encounters]. Göttingen: Vandenhoeck & Ruprecht.

Trägerkonferenz. (2020, September 7). *Workcamps.* https://www.workcamps.org/

Trede, F., Bowles, W. & Bridges, D. (2013). Developing intercultural competence and global citizenship through international experiences: academics' perceptions. *Intercultural Education, 24*(5), 442–455. https://doi.org/10.1080/14675986.2013.825578

Voluntary Service Overseas (VSO). (2020). https://www.vsointernational.org/about/our-history. Accessed December 10th, 2020.

Vrasti, W. & Montsion, J. M. (2014). No good deed goes unrewarded: The values/virtues of transnational volunteerism in neoliberal capital. *Global Society, 28*(3), 336–355. https://doi.org/10.1080/13600826.2014.900738

Wearing, S. (2001). *Volunteer tourism. Experiences that make a difference.* Wallingford: CABI publishing.

Wearing, S. & McGehee, N. G. (2013). Volunteer tourism: a review. *Tourism Management, 38*, 120–130. https://doi.org/10.1016/j.tourman.2013.03.002

Weltwärts. (2020, September 7). *weltwärts – eine Erfolgsgeschichte. Wir blicken zurück. [weltwärts – a success story. A retrospective.]* https://www.weltwaerts.de/de/rueckblick-ueber-weltwaerts.html

32

SERVICE LEARNING AND VOLUNTEERING

A case study of service learning in Chinese business events volunteering

Guoyang Chen and Hongxia Qi

Introduction

Service learning, which is rooted in experiential learning, combines learning objectives with service obligations (Wilson et al., 2020). It has been welcomed worldwide as an important educational method for many years. Service learning can promote students' critical thinking, problem-solving skills, interpersonal skills, communication skills, teamwork spirit and sense of civic responsibility (Mak et al., 2017). Moreover, service learning moves beyond simply offering service and help to a recipient, but it requires reciprocity between community and students (Riner, 2011). Research on service learning has been rapidly developed and scholars are seeking different mechanisms to better facilitate service learning experience to accommodate contemporary students. Similar to service learning, volunteering has a long history and tradition to promote civic engagement among young people (Nickels, 2017). Volunteering and service learning overlap, as a volunteer placement can be used as a format for service learning but volunteering is enormously diverse and not all service learning involves volunteering. Some roles in volunteering also require similar basic components of effective service learning (Nickels, 2017). Therefore, with careful administrative consideration and close collaboration between educational institutions, community organisations and students, the service learning experience can be successfully facilitated through volunteering.

This chapter explores the opportunity for facilitating service learning experiences in volunteering activities. The chapter initially considers the literature on service learning and volunteering. Then, the case study of service learning in Chinese business events volunteering will be presented to explain the service learning experience through volunteering. Lastly, the conclusion will provide implications and recommendations for future research.

Literature review

The connections between service learning and volunteering are subtle. Scholars state that "volunteer experience crossed over with elements of service learning" (Nickels, 2017, p. 40) or "servicing learning is more than just volunteering" (Lavery & Richards, 2006, p. 17). In this section, first, the literature review will focus on service learning and its development. Then, service learning in volunteering will be explained.

DOI: 10.4324/9780367815875-38

The definitions of service learning are varied. Most researchers (Guo et al., 2016; Lindsay, 2013) define service learning as a teaching method, which integrates academic knowledge and community service. Besides these two critical elements, other researchers (Ma, 2018; Parker et al., 2009) point out the importance of reflection in defining service learning. Service learning is also widely explained as a form of experiential learning, which combines community service and academic knowledge (Lavery & Richards, 2006; Moorman & Arellano-Unruh, 2002). Ma et al. (2018) explain that service learning includes training, reflection, assessments, observation of a community, academic learning and applications of theory in service.

In the early 20th century, American higher education began to advocate service learning (Ma, 2018). Since the 1980s, service learning programs have been rapidly introduced in university campuses as a new form of learning for the students through participating community service (Wilson et al., 2020). Nowadays, service learning is becoming one of the most popular learning methods in many countries. Service learning is treated as a major channel to bring academic learning into the real world (Ngai, 2009) and the studies on service learning have been increasingly developed globally (Gelmez-Burakgazi, 2018; Ma et al., 2018; Parker et al., 2009).

The positive outcomes from participating in service learning have been demonstrated as fostering civic responsibility, acceptance of diversity, leadership skills, and becoming dedicated and engaged citizens (Cox et al., 2014). In the past two decades, research on service learning has more focused on the mechanism of effective service learning, such as program characteristics and service type (Ngai, 2009). Lavery and Richards (2006) summarised the basic elements to effective service learning: efficient preparation; performing the service and analysing the experiences through a process of reflection or debriefing; and reciprocity between those serving and the person or group being served. The service work, such as welfare, empowerment and advocacy (Lavery & Richards, 2006), is deeply connected with communities. Gelmez-Burakgazi (2018) summarised a few issues tightly associated with community service: multiculturalism, civic engagement, social justice, citizenship and personal fulfilment. Many disciplines have incorporated service learning in their courses, such as nursing, education, business and engineering (Parker et al., 2009).

International service learning has also become popular among students. International service learning can be simply defined as combing "academic construction and community-based service in an international context" (Crabtree, 2008, p. 18). International service learning links international travel, education and community service together to promote global awareness, intercultural understanding, civic mindedness and leadership skills (Crabtree, 2008). Travel is an important component compared to other service learning. Volunteer tourism, which promotes sustainable and responsible travel experiences (Wearing et al., 2017), overlaps with international service learning. Learning is one of the strongest motivations for volunteer tourists (Boluk et al., 2017). Research showed that Millennials were more highly motivated to travel than any other age group (PR Newswire, 2014). Therefore, Millennials are a cohort most likely to engage in volunteering as a form of service learning.

Service learning stresses to bring all stakeholders together. Students, communities and educational institutions are the key actors in service learning programs (Bringle & Hatcher, 1995; Gazley et al., 2012). Gelmez-Burakgazi (2018) asserts that, in service learning, students are the service providers as well as receivers, and schools and community organisations become co-educators. For the educational institutions, it is important to assess students' performance and reflection in service learning programs, so lecturers can understand students' progress, and then further improve the programs (Ma et al., 2018). For the community organisations, they should strengthen volunteer management efficiency to student engagement (Gazley et al., 2012). Overall, service learning, which is embraced by all stakeholders, has been developed and involved in many forms over the years. It contributes to foster civic responsibility and acceptance of social diversity (Cox et al., 2014; Parker et al., 2009; Xiang & Luk, 2012).

Volunteering is another popular approach to civic engagement (Nickels, 2017). The notion of volunteerism emphasises a desire to take actions, which are voluntary without expectation of payment for the common good (Schroeder et al., 2014). Volunteering creates a wide range of benefits. It provides community service and can generate social capital, as well as making an important contribution to the global economy (Wu, 2011). Volunteers are valuable for all kinds of public and private and not for profit organisations to continue to successfully develop the programs (Silverberg et al., 1999).

Even though there are some similarities between the ideologies of service learning and volunteering, many researchers have recognised the differences. Lindsay (2013) indicates that volunteering is not necessarily integrated with learning objectives. Nickels (2017) states that reflection is rarely requested in completing volunteering tasks. However, volunteering has a vast spectrum and some volunteering activities may require participants to prepare or reflect more than others (Nickels, 2017). Therefore, volunteering can generate service learning experiences through careful consideration and facilitation (Cloyd, 2017; Gelmez-Burakgazi, 2018). In addition, service learning which involves volunteering can positively impact participants' attitude towards volunteerism (Wilson et al., 2020).

Globally, research has shown that the numbers of volunteers have declined in recent years. Wilson et al. (2020) pointed out that young volunteers (ages 16–24) in the United States has seen a downward shift in numbers since 2011. Similarly, Sparks (2013) noted a decrease in volunteering for older high school students. Some researchers looked for new directions to increase the volunteering rate through combining service learning experiences. Cox et al. (2014) suggested that international service learning programs might encourage more young people to volunteer because the travel component is desired among Millennials. In Brewis' (2010) report, she showed that the volunteering activities within UK universities have moved from student-organised community action to in-built service learning-type programs. Moreover, Chinese higher education considers service learning as a valid means to improve participation in volunteerism (Ma et al., 2018).

In the booming global event industry, a big number of volunteers are involved in and perform a wide range of roles such as on-site guidance, food and beverage, and security check, playing a key role in helping the success of events. As the event phenomena gained momentum in recent years, there was an increase in event volunteering research, mainly focusing on sports event volunteering (Smith et al., 2014). A variety of benefits and impacts of event volunteering have been explored, which develop volunteers' skills and facilitate service learning (e.g., Venske, 2019). Research on how event volunteering, particularly business events volunteering, impacts service learning is still in its infancy in the literature, which needs to be further examined in light of this fast developing phenomenon. The next section will introduce a novel case study on service learning in Chinese business events volunteering.

Case study: service learning in Chinese business events volunteering

The case study in this chapter is drawn from one of the authors' PhD projects on *Student Volunteering at Business Events in China* (Qi, 2018). The project systematically explores the phenomenon of student volunteering in the context of Chinese business events through a grounded theory approach. The investigator's rich experience as a student volunteer equips her with valuable insights of the investigated phenomenon, which act as the starting point of the project. The data consist of two main sources: auto-ethnographic data (i.e., the investigator's own volunteer experiences and insights) and in-depth interview data. For the interviews, three groups of interviewees are involved: student volunteers, higher educational institution officers and business event organisers. In total, there are 39 interview participants. The two types of data are merged and thematically analysed by coding.

The project demonstrates that there are diverse motivations and conceptualisations of the volunteering phenomenon, but it is evident that volunteering at business events is an effective service learning experience. To gain a comprehensive understanding of the different stakeholders' perspectives, key findings from the project are summarised in this chapter.

Background of business events volunteering

The booming of business event industry

Business event is one of the fastest growing segments of the global event industry and China is no exception. It has become an emerging trend for a destination to promote itself as an international business event destination due to the great economic effects as well as cultural prosperity and diversity that business events can bring. According to the Statistical Analysis Report on China's Exhibition Industry Development from China Convention/Exhibition/Event Society (2019), more than 11,000 exhibitions were held in China in 2019. For large-scale business events like Canton Fair, hundreds of on-site volunteers are needed. Even for local events like Qingdao Furniture Exhibition, dozens of volunteers are needed. Moreover, most events are held regularly. This fast growth of the business event industry has led to an increasing need for on-site staff, including volunteers, which has brought the challenge of finding enough staff among event organisers.

Students as the main force of volunteers

In China, youth, particularly university students, are the main force of volunteers. Taking the 2008 Beijing Olympic Games as an example, the number of applicants from Beijing was 256,000 of which 181,500 (71%) were students (Zhang, 2009). The project identifies that this is also the same for business events with the majority of volunteers being university students. Volunteering is one of the most important forms for students' social practice activities, which are designed to encourage students to connect with the local community and enhance learning through practice.

There are many roles that a volunteer may perform during a business event, including customer service at the registration desk, protocol and languages, and operational support for attendees. In most cases, volunteers represent the event organiser providing service for event attendees.

Collaboration model between event organisers and educational institutions

For the business events volunteering, it is a common practice for the event organisers to establish a long-term collaboration with local educational institutions. Most business events are held regularly and the young generation prefers one-off and short-term volunteering activities. The collaboration model is helpful in ensuring that event organisers can recruit enough volunteers and it is also a strategy to cope with the declining trend of volunteer participation. The model brings reciprocal benefits to different stakeholders. For student volunteers, they have the chance to learn and practice through volunteering at events. For event organisers, they can find enough volunteers for their events. For higher educational institutions, the model provides a good platform to enhance students' learning and provide professional training.

Service learning in business events volunteering: understandings from three perspectives

Student volunteers: service learning through volunteering

A diverse range of instrumental and individual motivations were identified in this case study. Data analysis revealed that the desire to help the event and ensure its success, and the willingness to help the community and the country was common among students. To learn was identified as a key component of the motives of student volunteers at business events in China. Many interviewees saw volunteering at business events as instrumental for learning related to their study, such as to gain knowledge of new trends in the industry, to learn by doing, to apply what they have learned from books in service, to gain skills to prepare for the future employment and to learn about the event industry. This case study also demonstrates that volunteering at business events is believed to be an effective way to connect with communities, as a complement to the classroom-oriented study model. The co-existence of the willingness to help and the motivation for learning demonstrates that volunteering at business events is essentially a type of community service learning.

Moreover, many of the student volunteer interviewees expressed that they reflected during and after the volunteer activity. They summarised what they learned from the service. Through this, the students express the effects of the experience on improving themselves from different aspects. Business event volunteer behaviour is an enlightening process that enables students to reflect on how an experience relates to their knowledge, how they see themselves and how to prepare for future employment. Taking career-related motivation as an example, volunteers are motivated by the networking opportunities in volunteering at business events. The short-term volunteer experiences enable students to reflect on issues such as future careers in the business event industry and their suitability, interest and skills, which are believed to be valuable for their future employment. These three aspects are in accordance with the characteristics of learning, reciprocity and reflection of service learning.

Educational institutions: volunteering as a type of service learning

From the educational institutions' perspective, business events volunteering is launched as a type of service learning with the goal of enhancing students' learning of event knowledge through providing service to event organisers and visitors. The use of service learning as a teaching method is believed to bring students multifaceted benefits. The case study demonstrates that in many higher educational institutions, students studying event management are deeply linking theory with practice. As such, they are required to volunteer at a certain number of events in order to gain their degree.

The higher educational institution officers who participated in this study emphasised the original intention of providing students with the opportunities of learning when they talk about the reasons for setting up the volunteer programs with the event industry. They proposed that volunteering at business events is an effective way for pursuing service learning and deliberately aim to blend the study undertaken by students within the classroom with the experience of practices in the workplace. This emphasises the growing importance of the concept of learning from practising, which is becoming more and more popular among higher educational institutions in China. According to the higher educational institution officers in this project, another reason contributing to volunteering being launched as a type of service learning is that students have limited opportunities to access social practice in China.

With the pursuit of service learning as a modern pedagogical strategy, the educational institutions believe that students can seek out first-hand experiences through volunteering at business events, which would provide a practical foundation to their studies and future employment. This can help explain why colleges incorporate this model in their teaching schedule and why students emphasise the significance of 'experience' for their college life when talking about motivations. It has become a trend among higher educational institutions to provide students the opportunities to volunteer at business events as a way to combine academic knowledge and community service, and gain professional training (Qi, 2020).

Event organisers: reciprocal process of volunteering at business events

For the business event organisers, the large number of volunteers is a valuable workforce. University students or youth are the main force of volunteers at business events. The event organisers highlight that student volunteering is a good strategy to respond to the decline of volunteering, enabling them to find enough volunteers for their events. Moreover, students are equipped with good knowledge and skills, so they can provide professional services to the event, which is valued by business event organisers. In this project, the interviewed event organisers widely propose that volunteering at business events provides students a good platform to learn and to practice, transforming event organisers into co-educators for students' community learning, while addressing the labour issue, which is a reciprocal process.

Overall, learning through the servicing of business events is one of the main motivations for student volunteers, while volunteering is adopted as a pedagogical strategy that highlights service learning as a means to seek out first-hand experiences. This indicates the blurred boundaries between business events volunteering and service learning. Service learning has a wider scope, which is "a process where the learner needs to reflect upon the experience and derives new learning" (Osland et al., 1971, p. 67), and it is part of a broader set of educational tools termed experiential learning. There are a variety of methods in service learning such as class discussion and academic material guidance. Business events volunteering is one part of service learning. The goal of volunteer activities at business events is to learn and practice, and is relatively smaller in scope than service learning. However, service learning is shown to be an effective means to improve volunteerism in this study.

Conclusions

As one of the service learning types, business events volunteering is introduced in this chapter. It is found that volunteering at business events is an effective and emerging service learning experience. Students gain the opportunity to learn, practice and reflect from volunteering at business events. The identified impacts for students in this project confirm previous studies that explored the value of service learning (e.g., Ngai, 2009). For higher educational institutions, business events volunteering is launched as a pedagogical strategy and a type of service learning with the goal of equipping students with first-hand experiences. This shares similarities with the existing literature on service learning (e.g., Ma et al., 2018), but expands the current scholarly attention from nursing and social work to business. From the event organisers' perspective, student volunteering at business events is believed to be more like a service learning experience due to the consideration of students lacking work experience. Nevertheless, the involvement of a large number of students helps address the issue of labour shortage in the business events industry.

Research on service learning has grown steadily over the past several decades, demonstrating new and emerging service learning types. For example, international service learning, linking the travel component with education and community service, has gained popularity among the younger generation (PR Newswire, 2014). The concept of service learning originated and spread in the medical, nursing and social work fields and is becoming more popular in many other sectors including business. This chapter is one of the pioneering attempts to explore service learning in business, more specifically in the business events area. Volunteering at business events is launched as a type of service learning with the goal of enhancing learning through service and connecting with communities. The co-existence of the motivations of helping and learning demonstrates that volunteering at business events is a type of community service learning. The growing number of business events in the global context brings students a platform to learn through practice, service and reflection. The real-world environment produces several benefits for students, particularly those studying event management. Volunteering at business events is a relatively new and booming service learning type, attracting the involvement of a large number of students. This chapter is a timely contribution to the literature and will hopefully act as a stepping stone to further investigation in this field.

This chapter also highlights important implications for related stakeholders. Volunteering at business events is an effective way of delivering service learning, whereby students can not only learn and develop skills, but also connect with the community. Due to the explorative nature of research in this field, service learning programs need to be further developed to maximise the benefits to students, including the cooperation model with event organisers and student performance assessment. Lastly, business event organisers, as community organisations and co-educators, should not just see student volunteering as a way to address the labour shortage issue, but also play a role in educating the next generation.

References

Boluk, K., Kline, C., & Stroobach, A. (2017). Exploring the expectations and satisfaction derived from volunteer tourism experiences. *Tourism and Hospitality Research, 17*(3), 272–285. https://doi.org/10.1177/1467358415600212

Brewis, G. (2010). From service to action? Students, volunteering and community action in mid twentieth-century Britain. *British Journal of Educational Studies, 58*(4), 439–449. https://doi.org/10.1080/00071005.2010.527668

Bringle, R. G., & Hatcher, J. A. (1995). A service-learning curriculum for faculty. *Michigan Journal of Community Service Learning Fall, 2*, 112–122. https://scholarworks.iupui.edu/bitstream/handle/1805/4591/bringle-1995-service-learning.pdf?sequence=1&isAllowed=y

China Convention/Exhibition/Event Society. (2019). *Statistical analysis report on China's exhibition industry development.* https://www.cces2006.org/index.php/home/index/detail/id/13890

Cloyd, M. (2017). When volunteering is mandatory: A call for research about service learning. *Multicultural Education, 24*(3–4), 36–40.

Cox, T., Murray, L. I., & Plante, J. D. (2014). Undergraduate student diversity paradigm expansion : The role of international service learning. *International Forum of Teaching and Studies, 10*(1), 3–13.

Crabtree, R. (2008). Theoretical foundations for international service-learning. *Michigan Journal of Community Service Learning, 15*(1), 18–36. papers://daf6d064-3453-45f6-a1b3-8d1f363fea23/Paper/p197

Gazley, B., Littlepage, L., & Bennett, T. A. (2012). What about the host agency? Nonprofit perspectives on community-based student learning and volunteering. *Nonprofit and Voluntary Sector Quarterly, 41*(6), 1029–1050. https://doi.org/10.1177/0899764012438698

Gelmez-Burakgazi, S. (2018). Volunteering: Evaluation of community service learning. *Turkish Online Journal of Qualitative Inquiry, 9*(4), 342–372. https://doi.org/10.17569/tojqi.410893

Guo, F., Yao, M., Zong, X., & Yan, W. (2016). The developmental characteristics of engagement in service-learning for Chinese college students. *Journal of College Student Development, 57*(4), 447–459. https://doi.org/10.1353/csd.2016.0042

Lavery, S., & Richards, J. (2006). Service-learning: More than just volunteering. *Principal Matters, 66*(autumn), 17–18.

Lindsay, P. (2013). Working adult undergraduate students' interest and motivation in service learning and volunteering. *The Journal of Continuing Higher Education, 61*(2), 68–73.

Ma, H. C. (2018). The concept and development of service-learning. In H. C. Ma, C. A. Chan, C. A. Liu, & M. F. Mak (Eds.), *Service-Learning as a New Paradigm in Higher Education of China Book* (pp. 17–43). Michigan State University Press.

Ma, H. C., Mak, M. F., & Liu, C. A. (2018). Service-learning and the aims of Chinese higher education. In H. C. Ma, C. A. Chan, C. A. Liu, & M. F. Mak (Eds.), *Service-Learning as a New Paradigm in Higher Education of China* (pp. 17–43). Michigan State University Press.

Mak, B., Lau, C., & Wong, A. (2017). Effects of experiential learning on students: An ecotourism service-learning course. *Journal of Teaching in Travel & Tourism, 17*(2), 85–100. https://doi.org/10.1080/15313220.2017.1285265

Moorman, M. K., & Arellano-Unruh, N. (2002). Community service-learning projects for undergraduate recreation majors. *Journal of Physical Education, Recreation & Dance, 73*(2), 42–45. https://doi.org/10.1080/07303084.2002.10607753

Ngai, S. S. Y. (2009). The effects of program characteristics and psychological engagement on service-learning outcomes: A study of university students in Hong Kong. *Adolescence, 44*(174), 374–389.

Nickels, H. (2017). Service-learning, volunteering and inclusion from a pre-service teacher's perspective. In S. Lavery, D. Chambers, & G. Cain (Eds.), *International Perspectives on Inclusive Education* (Vol. 12, pp. 39–51). Emerald Publishing Limited. https://doi.org/10.1108/S1479-363620170000012003

Osland, J., Kolb, D., Rubin, I. M., & Turner, M. E. (1971). *Organizational Behavior: An Experiential Approach*. Prentice Hall.

Parker, E. A., Myers, N., Higgins, H. C., Oddsson, T., Price, M., & Gould, T. (2009). More than experiential learning or volunteering: A case study of community service learning within the Australian context. *Higher Education Research and Development, 28*(6), 585–596. https://doi.org/10.1080/07294360903161147

PR Newswire. (2014). *Hotwire Predicts 2015 Will Be Year of Millennial Traveler*. https://www.prnewswire.com/news-releases/hotwire-predicts-2015-will-be-year-of-millennial-traveler-300014321.html

Qi, H. (2018). *Student Volunteering at Business Events in China: Motivations and Conceptualizaton*. Victoria University of Wellington.

Qi, H. (2020). Conceptualizing volunteering in tourism in China. *Tourism Management Perspectives, 33*(November 2019), 100618. https://doi.org/10.1016/j.tmp.2019.100618

Riner, M. E. (2011). Globally engaged nursing education: An academic program framework. *Nursing Outlook, 59*(6), 308–317. https://doi.org/10.1016/j.outlook.2011.04.005

Schroeder, A., Graziano, W. G., Stukas, A. A., Snyder, M., & Clary, E. G. (2014). Volunteerism and community involvement: Antecedents, experiences, and consequences for the person and the situation. In D. A. Schroeder & W. Graziano (Eds.), *The Oxford Handbook of Prosocial Behavior* (Issue March 2014). Oxford University Press. https://doi.org/10.1093/oxfordhb/9780195399813.013.012

Silverberg, K., Ellis, G., Backman, K., & Backman, S. (1999). An identification and explication of a typology of public parks and recreation volunteers. *World Leisure & Recreation, 41*(2), 30–34. https://doi.org/10.1080/10261133.1999.9674148

Smith, K., Lockstone-Binney, L., Holmes, K., & Baum, T. (2014). *Event Volunteering: International Perspectives on the Event Volunteer*. Routledge.

Sparks, S. (2013). Community service requirements seen to reduce volunteering. *Education Week, 33*(1), 6.

Venske, E. (2019). Event volunteering as an educational resource in business tourism. *Tourism, 67*(3), 268–280.

Wearing, S., Young, T., & Everingham, P. (2017). Evaluating volunteer tourism: has it made a difference? *Tourism Recreation Research*, *42*(4), 512–521. https://doi.org/10.1080/02508281.2017.1345470

Wilson, R., Látková, P., Yoshino, A., & Sheffield, E. (2020). Changes in volunteerism perception:
Results from an international service learning case study. *SCHOLE: A Journal of Leisure Studies and
Recreation Education*, 1–11. https://doi.org/10.1080/1937156x.2020.1718038

Wu, H. (2011). *Social Impact of Volunteerism*. Points of Light Foundation. https://www.yumpu.com/en/
document/read/51218070/social-impact-of-volunteerism-points-of-light-foundation

Xiang, R., & Luk, T. C. (2012). Service learning as a social work pedagogy of China. *China Journal of
Social Work*, *5*(3), 223–236. https://doi.org/10.1080/17525098.2012.721179

Zhang, P. (2009). Research on the issues of volunteer service legislation. *Legal and Economy*, *10*(2), 32–34.

33

VOLUNTEERING AND OBLIGATION

Positive and negative

Robert A. Stebbins

Volunteering as leisure activity

Whether it is leisure studies specialists looking at volunteering or voluntary action specialists looking at leisure, the result has been much the same: neither field has been inclined to view its own subject matter through the eyes of the other. Still, significant exceptions exist, some of which will be reviewed here to show how the theoretical link between leisure and volunteering has evolved in recent decades.

Some of the earliest theoretical stirrings in this area came from Philip Bosserman and Richard Gagan (1972), who argued that, at the level of the individual, all leisure activity is voluntary action. More precise statements were made subsequently and somewhat later by Max Kaplan (1975) and John Neulinger (1981), two leisure studies specialists who observed in passing how leisure can serve either oneself or other people, if not both. It is presumed that they had volunteerism in mind, even though some amateur and hobbyist activities also have this dual function (e.g. community music, theater, sports like curling and ice and powerboat racing). From the side of voluntary action research, Kenneth Boulding (1973) theorized that voluntary service borders on leisure, frequently even overlapping it. Alex Dickson (1974) observed that leisure is seen in commonsense as part of voluntary action and does in fact "carry this spare-time connotation" (p. 13).

Karla Henderson (1981, 1984) examined the leisure component of volunteering both empirically and theoretically. She noted that in the 1980s social scientists ordinarily regarded volunteering in the same way as they regarded paid work, as having an external, or extrinsic, orientation – the volunteer has a job to complete for the benefit of the community. This contrasts with the (volitional) view they hold of leisure as oriented by internal, or intrinsic, interests – the participant enjoys the activity for itself and for the self-expression, self-enrichment, and self-fulfillment it can engender. Henderson found that her sample of 4-H workers in the United States defined their volunteering as leisure. For them, volunteering was part of their leisure world.

A few years later, Stanley Parker (1987) reported findings from research on a group of peace workers. He discovered that, whereas they worked as volunteers for the cause of peace, they considered this activity part of their leisure. Parker also completed a second study around this time centered on the serious leisure activities of two samples of volunteers,

DOI: 10.4324/9780367815875-39

one drawn in Britain, and the other drawn in Australia (reported in Parker, 1992). Here, he found that one person in five engaged in some form of activity classifiable as volunteering. Almost invariably, the people sampled described their volunteering as leisure, as a primarily rewarding activity and secondarily a helping activity. Their leisure was nonetheless most substantial; in reality, it was serious leisure. Robert Stebbins' (1998) study of francophone career volunteers in Calgary and Edmonton in Canada revealed an even distribution among those who saw this kind of activity as leisure, work, or as a separate activity distinct from these two (reported in Stebbins, 2000).

While Parker was studying peace workers, Susan Chambré (1987) was examining elderly volunteers. She reached similar conclusions: her respondents also defined their volunteering as leisure activity. As with Henderson, she wrestled with the extrinsic-intrinsic and the altruistic-self-interested dimensions, both of which pervade leisure volunteering. Volunteering is a work-like activity wherein a person accomplishes a task without remuneration. At the same time, the activity, which is freely chosen, provides many a satisfying experience. Chambré (1987) found, however, that the motives given by the elderly for taking up a volunteer role differed from those given for continuing it. Although their sense of altruism often led them to volunteer in the first place, they were highly motivated by the intrinsic satisfaction they found there to continue in this role.

Working from Chambré's conclusion that volunteering is leisure, Lucy Fischer and Kay Schaffer (1993) set out to explore the patterns of cost and reward the elderly experience when they participate in this kind of activity. Following a comprehensive review of the current research and case study literature, the authors concluded that certain costs (e.g. time, hazards, inconveniences) are typically offset by numerous special rewards. These rewards included the following: feeling competent to do the volunteer work, sensing ideological congruence with the organization, and being satisfied with the job done (i.e., work is interesting, professional growth is possible, personal skills are used). Self-actualization, self-enrichment, and opportunities for social interaction were also found to be highly appealing (Fischer & Schaffer, 1993). Moreover, it appears that the elderly are not alone in their feelings that volunteering is a highly rewarding form of leisure. Alexander Thompson and Barbara Bono (1993) found similar sentiments in their sample of volunteer firefighters whose activities fostered self-actualization, group accomplishment, and a special self-image.

Thomas Rotolo and John Wilson (2007) touch more obliquely on the question of volunteering when they observe that sex segregation in the workplace – the tendency for men and women to work in different occupations and jobs – remains widespread. Domestic chores are also sex-typed, but the extent to which sex segregation is found in other forms of non-waged work, such as volunteering, is unknown. The authors used maximum likelihood probit models with selection to estimate the incidence of sex segregation among volunteers in a nationally representative sample of adult Americans ($n = 91,807$). To explain this finding, they note one line of argument which states that any gender differentiation found in other work environments spills over into volunteer work.

A competing argument, which is based on the Serious Leisure Perspective (SLP) (see Stebbins 2007/2015 and www.seriousleisure.net), contends that, in effect, this spillover theory overlooks an important characteristic of volunteer work: compared with work performed for pay or domestic chores, volunteering is an agreeable obligation. Volunteering is what we do in our non-work where, presumably, we have free choice. According to this argument, neither men nor women need conform to the pattern of sex segregation found in other work spheres. Thus, women can either ignore the constraints placed on them at work and at home or look for ways to overturn them. Indeed, Rotolo and Wilson (2007) write that volunteerism can be an alternative career for women, a source of empowerment and freedom. Nevertheless, their study suggests that sports and recreational activities *are* highly gendered. That we are not compelled by need or social obligation to engage in or watch these activities seems not to vitiate the force of gender ideologies on our thoughts about the kinds of activities held to be appropriate for men and women.

Volunteering as obligation

Obligation outside that experienced while pursuing a livelihood is terribly understudied; much of it has to do with the family or domestic life, if not both, while obligatory communal involvements are also possible. The latter are sometimes seriously misunderstood as in coerced volunteering. To speak of obligation, is to speak not about how people are prevented from entering certain leisure activities, the object of much of research on leisure constraints, but about how people fail to define a given activity as leisure or redefine it as other than leisure, that is, as an unpleasant obligation. Obligation is both a state of mind, an attitude (a person feels obligated), and a form of behavior (they must carry out a particular course of action and engage in a particular activity). But even while obligation is substantially mental and behavioral, it is also embedded in the social and cultural world of the obligated actor. Consequently, we may even speak of a culture of obligation that takes shape around many work, leisure, and non-work activities (discussed later).

Obligation fits in this discussion in at least two ways: leisure may include certain agreeable obligations and the third domain of life, non-work obligation which consists of disagreeable requirements capable of undermining life's positiveness. Agreeable obligation is very much a part of some leisure, evident when such obligation accompanies positive commitment to an activity that evokes pleasant memories and expectations. These two are essential features of leisure according to Kaplan (1960). Still, it might be argued that agreeable obligation in leisure is not really felt as obligation, since the participant wants to do the activity anyway. Still, my research in serious leisure suggests a more complicated picture. My respondents knew that they were supposed to be at a certain place or do a certain thing and knew that they had to make this a priority in their day-to-day lives. They not only wanted to do this, but they were also required to do it; other activities and demands could wait. At times, the participants' intimates objected to the way he or she prioritised everyday commitments, and this led to friction, creating costs for the participants that somewhat diluted the rewards of the leisure in question. Agreeable obligation is also found in devotee work and the other two forms of leisure (casual and project-based leisure), though possibly less so in the casual form.

On the other hand, disagreeable obligation has no place in leisure, because, among other reasons, it fails to leave the participant with a pleasant memory or expectation of the activity. Rather it is the substance of the third domain: non-work obligation. This domain is the classificatory home of all we must do that we would rather avoid that is not related to work (including moonlighting). So far, I have been able to identify three types (Stebbins, 2009, pp. 24–26).

Unpaid labor: activities people do themselves even though services exist which they could hire to carry them out. These activities include mowing the lawn, housework, shoveling the sidewalk, preparing the annual income tax return, do-it-yourself, and a myriad of obligations to friends and family (e.g. caring for a sick relative, helping a friend move to another home, arranging a funeral).

Unpleasant tasks: required activities for which no commercial services exist or, if they exist, most people would avoid using them. Such activities are exemplified in checking in and clearing security at airports, attending a meeting on a community problem, walking the dog each day, driving in city traffic (in this discussion, beyond that related to work), and errands, including routine grocery shopping. There are also obligations to family and friends in this type, among them, driving a child to soccer practice and mediating familial quarrels. Many of the 'chores' of childhood fall in this category. Finally, activities sometimes mislabelled as volunteering are, in fact, disagreeable obligations from which the individual senses no escape. For example, some parents feel this way about coaching their children's sports teams or about helping with a road trip for the youth orchestra in which their children play.

Self-care: disagreeable activities designed to maintain or improve in some way the physical or psychological state of the individual. They include getting a haircut, putting on cosmetics, doing health-promoting exercises, going to the dentist, and undergoing a physical examination. Personal and family counselling also fall within this type, as do the activities that accompany getting a divorce.

Some activities in these types are routine obligations, whereas others are only occasional. Moreover, for those who find some significant measure of enjoyment in, say, grocery shopping, walking the dog, do-it-yourself, or taking physical exercise, these obligations are defined as agreeable; they are effectively leisure. Thus, what is disagreeable in the domain of non-work obligation rests on personal interpretation of the actual or anticipated experience of an activity. So, most people dislike or expect to dislike their annual physical examination, though not the hypochondriac.

Non-work obligation, even if it tends to occupy less time than the other two domains, is not inconsequential. I believe the foregoing types support this observation. Moreover, some of them may be gendered (e.g. housework), and accordingly, occasional sources of friction and attenuated positiveness of lifestyle for all concerned. Another leading concern for positive sociology laid down by non-work obligation is that it reduces further (after work is done) the amount of free time for leisure and, for some people, devotee work. Such obligation may threaten devotee work because it may reduce the time occupational devotees who, enamored as they are of their core work activities, would like to put in at work as overtime.

Culture of obligation

It was stated earlier that obligation is substantially mental and behavioural. Nonetheless, it is embedded in the social and cultural world of the obligated actor. Consequently, we may also speak of a culture of obligation that takes shape around many work, leisure, and non-work activities (Stebbins, 2009). What does this culture look like?

The essence of the culture of obligation is the shared sentiment of feeling obliged to engage in a particular activity. Let us look, first, at the disagreeable face of obligation. For example, the mother who laments to a friend that she is getting tired of taking her young son to hockey practice at 6:00 in the morning three times a week is highly likely to find a sympathetic ear among other parents saddled with the same responsibility. Or the man who complains to his neighbor about having, once again, to mow the lawn voices his lament anticipating shared sentiment with the listener. Since we all have to carry out at various points in life some disagreeable obligations, we can often empathize with others forced to do the same.

The areas of life in which disagreeable obligation tends to concentrate constitute another facet of this culture. The three types set out above also serve as labels for these areas: unpaid labor, unpleasant tasks, and self-care. Additionally, taking now an institutional approach, much of this obligation falls under the heading of family or domestic life, sometimes both, but with disagreeable communal involvements also being possible. Illustrative of the latter is the feeling that many householders might well have who, in facing possible decline in property values, know they should attend a public meeting about, say, an expressway or halfway house for ex-offenders being proposed for their neighborhood. Note here, as well, the power of certain social conditions to frame such obligations, including vested community interests of the 'not-in-my-backyard' variety and the professional authority of city planners.

And, while on the institutional plane, note that disagreeable obligation may also be experienced at work as well as in some leisure. Among the aspects of work that people dislike are certain activities they are required to engage in while there. Some of these may be fatiguing such as lifting heavy objects and standing for long periods of time. Others, though not fatiguing, may be boring or otherwise unpleasant, including diagnosing and treating the common cold in medicine (boring), grading examinations in teaching (boring), and attending to injured young children in emergency medical service (emotionally upsetting).

As for the agreeable side of the culture of obligation, consider the following examples. In each, the obligated participants also want very much to engage in the activity. Thus, imagine the amateur poet who has accepted an invitation to present some of her works at a local coffee house. Both the poet and the person who extended the invitation are aware of her obligation to perform once the invitation is accepted. It is likewise for a member of an amateur basketball team whose teammates depend on him to play the next match. The sense of obligation to do this is shared by all concerned. Finally, many volunteers and those whom they serve know well the obligation of the former to be present at the appointed time and place to volunteer as promised.

Staying on the institutional level, note that the culture of obligation is found throughout leisure, whether serious, casual, or project-based. That is, in all three forms people may feel obliged to do something that they also want to do. Yet the institutional location of agreeable obligation is even more complex than this. People can feel pleasantly obliged to engage in leisure activities within the family (e.g. to have a picnic, play a board game with the children, or go out to eat with one's spouse). Nonetheless, there are also many pleasant obligatory activities to be enacted in devotee work, seen in performing as a guest concert pianist with a renowned symphony orchestra, providing expert advice as a counselor in a challenging marital dispute, and repairing string instruments as a self-employed luthier.

It is evident that obligation, agreeable or not, is also relational, or social. We are not only obliged to undertake certain activities – we are also obliged to the individuals who have an interest in them. All the foregoing examples, with the possible exception of mowing the lawn, presuppose the presence of one or more other people who depend on the obligated person to honor their commitment. There is thus a personal tie, a relationship of some duration, between what Cuskelly and Harrington (1997) call 'obligees' (e.g. feel they must help a friend or a nonprofit group) and 'role dependee' (e.g. young members of a family participating in an activity, for which, to ensure its survival, a parent must volunteer). Again, returning to the conditional level of analysis, we must also, for a complete explanation, inquire into the structural and cultural arrangements underlying this obligation for the role dependee. Is it ultimately caused by a failure of municipal support for the activity, a sudden surge in its popularity, a shortage of qualified personnel to provide it, or a combination of these factors and others?

Personal implications of obligatory volunteering

Obligatory volunteering, inherently agreeable as it is, is commonly motivated by a sense of responsibility for executing the volunteer activity. Thus, participants know it is up to them to clear the snow in front of their place of worship before religious services, write up the minutes of the meeting of the board of directors (as secretary), and publicize the next concert of the community orchestra (as person responsible for this function). Such volunteering brings with it a feeling of satisfaction (possibly pride) at being responsible, of successfully or admirably discharging a duty.

All volunteering is voluntary action, whereas some of the latter, though also volunteering, is more accurately defined as 'civic engagement'. It is a "duty or obligation felt by citizens to participate through some sort of civic engagement or civil labor in the civil society in which they live" (Smith, Stebbins & Dover, 2006, p. 42). There are requirements in community life that pressure (i.e., obligate) its citizens to 'voluntarily' act in certain ways. These requirements include political participation (e.g. voting, protesting, volunteering for a political party), carrying out civic duties like refraining from littering, cleaning up when one's dog fouls the landscape, and not smoking in smoke-free areas.

At the organizational level, felt obligation blends with commitment to the group such that volunteers are also inspired by a significant attachment to it and its goals. Bateman, Gray, and Butler (2006) studied this variety of commitment in community volunteering. They found it varied with the nature of online volunteer activity required by their organization. The strength of organizational commitment is also a powerful force in those groups that energize social movements and those that drive political participation.

Additionally, some community requirements consist of refraining from acting in ways objected to by a majority of its members. Leisure and the study of it are generally positive, but certain kinds of leisure are unwelcomed by particular segments of society or in different parts of the community. That is, leisure, positive as it is for its participants, is sometimes defined negatively by non-participants who observe it, who for the most part see, hear, or smell aspects of a leisure activity that offends them. Moreover, the leisure experience encountered under conditions of an obvious negative public reception is undoubtedly different from that experience when the activity is widely accepted. Elsewhere, Stebbins (2017) has mentioned female street prostitution (leisure for the 'john'), raucous behavior by patrons leaving bars at closing time, and noisy late-night parties in neighborhood backyards and urban apartment buildings.

Ambivalence about obligations

To be sure, not all citizens respect these community requirements; they may be uncertain about them. Furthermore, there are those who generally do respect them, but still fail for some reason to act responsibly in the moment. They may regret ignoring these requirements, perhaps even feeling a touch of guilt. This is where voluntary obligation may become disagreeable, though possibly only briefly.

Yet, for some people, relief (momentary well-being) may be the dominant response to having met an unpleasant obligation. An individual might say that, at last, they have successfully finished constructing the playroom in the basement, shoveling the sidewalk after a major snowstorm, or filling in a complicated tax return. The obligation is unpleasant, but capable of generating a sense of release, liberation, even accomplishment once the activity is finished.

Another sphere of obligatory volunteering is that of service learning. It is defined as a "school or university-based program in which students receive course credit for volunteer work usually doing community service in a nonprofit agency or volunteer program in their community" (Smith et al., 2006, p. 209). Service learning shows that volunteering is not always a purely free, unconstrained activity. There are many similar examples where it involves some element of obligation or even coercion (for a quantitative examination of this matter, see Gallant, Smale & Arai, 2017). Still, it can be argued that this is really 'marginal' volunteering, where coercion to act is a salient condition (Stebbins, 2001).

There is also the issue of the gap in knowledge about whether volunteers' sense of obligation to their roles and host organizations can change over time. Indeed, it may be that, as the years pass, an initially agreeable volunteering activity becomes onerous. In short, it is at present difficult to create a rich portrait of career volunteering as we have for other serious leisure activities (see Stebbins, 2014), at least until we have conducted much more research on the matter.

Scientifically speaking, obligatory volunteering is a difficult process to study. It is subject to personal interpretation, buffeted by occasional selfishness, judged by universalistic community standards, among undoubtedly other factors. What is more, the force of obligation as a responsibility may wax and wane in situ; that is, one may feel uncomfortably obliged doing the volunteer activity at one point, and excited and interested in doing it at another. These feelings are real to participants, and they help determine whether they will count such volunteering as serious leisure and return to experience more of it.

Conclusions

Obligation, I have argued here, is at once an individual thought and activity of being responsible and a central concept in the culture of obligation. It pervades volunteering, in that volunteers promise and offer one or more services to their targets of help. In brief, they are therefore obligated to do as best they can what they say they will do.

In its essence, volunteering is leisure, notwithstanding its occasional disagreeable aspects. This is in fact a feature of all serious leisure, including that found in volunteering being referred to in this chapter and elsewhere as career volunteering (Stebbins, 2007/2015). A main way that the serious pursuits are set off from other kinds of work and leisure is by the extraordinary rewards they offer. These rewards act as powerful motives for getting and staying involved in one or more of those pursuits. Still, all serious pursuits are further distinguished by the fact that participants sometimes encounter costs while engaging in such activities. Among these costs are the disagreeable obligations occasionally encountered while volunteering. In practice, this becomes an individual process of balancing the costs and rewards, wherein the first are defined by that person as insignificant compared to the second. The latter are powerful, experienced in, for example, self-fulfillment, self-expression, and deep involvement in a special social world of participants, relationships, groups, clients, and service providers (further discussed in Stebbins, 2018). The profile of rewards and costs places the serious pursuits at odds with the popular images of work as drudgery and leisure as an unalloyed good time (Stebbins, 2014). It explains why the interviewees in my various exploratory studies kept insisting that their leisure was out of the ordinary, quite unlike that of most other people.

Were it even possible, would it be good to try to eliminate obligation from the leisure lifestyle of career volunteers? My position on this question is that such an effort would be shortsighted. Obligation stems from responsibility, which has its own rewards. It anchors its holders in some kind of group or organizational structure, as for instance, being a treasurer, committee chair, tour guide, or docent at a zoo. These volunteers have acquired through such leisure a recognizable and respectable place in the community. Moreover, the obligation to volunteer helps justify the activity that it inspires, a critical orientation when participants are often faced with demands on their time from employer, spouse, close friends, or relatives.

Regarding structure, serial obligations add temporal structure to everyday life. For instance, volunteer coaches in a sport know they must be present at scheduled practices and matches. Hospital volunteers agree to offer their services during specified periods on a weekly basis. Less precise but nonetheless capable of establishing temporal demands are the activities of various outdoor volunteers. These people who, serving (usually) nonprofit organizations, shovel sidewalks, water and weed gardens, maintain hiking trails and the like, work when the weather sporadically permits. Theirs is an on-call kind of time structure.

Fourth, having an obligation may serve as an antidote to procrastination. The psychology of procrastination takes a largely disapproving view of the subject, at least that is how it is summed up in *Psychology Today* (2019). It is said to be personally harmful for a person to procrastinate, to delay meeting an obligation to self or someone else. Discussions of the practice in psychology and management share this focus on the negative antecedents of procrastinatory behavior. Nevertheless, when the obligation is positive, as it commonly is in career volunteering, procrastination seems seldom to occur. Rather, the activity's powerful appeal paints its obligatory nature in attractive colors.

Sir Humphrey Davy observed that "life is made up, not of great sacrifices or duties, but of little things, in which smiles and kindness, and small obligations given habitually, are what preserve the heart and secure comfort". Though he made his living as a renowned chemist in late 18th and early 19th century England, he also saw the importance of the little things in life, including the rewarding everyday obligations we find there. Volunteering boosts the significance of this local manifestation of altruism, in that a part of the wider community now benefits from it as well.

References

Bateman, P., Gray, P., & Butler, B. (2006). Community commitment: How affect, obligation, and necessity drive online behaviors. *ICIS 2006 Proceedings, 63*, http://aisel.aisnet.org/icis2006/63.

Bosserman, P., & Gagan, R. (1972). Leisure behavior and voluntary action. In D.H. Smith, R.D. Reddy, & B.R. Baldwin (Eds.), *Voluntary action research* (pp. 109–126). D.C. Heath.

Boulding, K. (1973). *The economy of love and fear.* Wadsworth.

Chambré, S.M. (1987). *Good deeds in old age: Volunteering by the new leisure class.* Lexington Books.

Cuskelly, G., & Harrington, M. (1997). Volunteers and leisure: Evidence of marginal and career volunteerism in sport. *World Leisure & Recreation, 39*(3), 11–18. https://doi.org/10.1080/10261133.1997.9674073

Dickson, A. (1974). Preface. In D.H. Smith (Ed.), *Voluntary action research: 1974* (pp. xii–xx). D.C. Heath.

Fischer, L.R., & Schaffer, K.B. (1993). *Older volunteers: A guide to research and practice.* Sage.

Gallant, K., Smale, B., & Arai, S. (2017). Measurement of feelings of obligation to volunteer: The obligation to volunteer as commitment (OVC) and obligation to volunteer as duty (OVD) scales. *Leisure Studies, 36*(4), 588–601. https://doi.org/10.1080/02614367.2016.1182204

Henderson, K.A. (1981). Motivations and perceptions of volunteerism as a leisure activity. *Journal of Leisure Research, 13*, 208–218. https://doi.org/10.1080/00222216.1981.11969484

Henderson, K.A. (1984). Volunteerism as leisure. *Journal of Voluntary Action Research, 13*, 55–63. https://doi.org/10.1177/089976408401300106

Kaplan, M. (1960). *Leisure in America: A social inquiry.* Wiley.

Kaplan, M. (1975). *Leisure: Theory and policy.* Wiley.

Neulinger, J. (1981). *To leisure: An introduction.* Allyn and Bacon.

Parker, S.R. (1987). Working for peace as serious leisure. *Leisure Information Quarterly, 13* (4), 9–10.

Parker, S.R. (1992). Volunteering as serious leisure. *Journal of Applied Recreation Research, 17,* 1–11.

Psychology Today (2019). Procrastination. https://www.psychologytoday.com/ca/basics/procrastination

Rotolo, T., & Wilson, J. (2007). Sex segregation in volunteer work. *The Sociological Quarterly, 48*(3), 559–585. https://doi.org/10.1111/j.1533-8525.2007.00089.x

Smith, D.H., Stebbins, R.A., & M. Dover (2006). *A dictionary of nonprofit terms and concepts.* Indiana University Press.

Stebbins, R.A. (1998). The urban francophone volunteer: Searching for personal meaning and community growth in a linguistic minority. *New Scholars-New Visions in Canadian Studies Quarterly Monographs Series, 3*(2). University of Washington, Canadian Studies Centre.

Stebbins, R.A. (2000). Antinomies in volunteering: Choice/obligation, leisure/work. *Société et Loisir/Society and Leisure, 23,* 313–326. https://doi.org/10.1080/07053436.2000.10707533

Stebbins, R.A. (2001). Volunteering - marginal or mainstream: Preserving the leisure experience. In M. Graham & M. Foley (Eds.), *Leisure volunteering: Marginal or inclusive?* (pp. 1–10). Leisure Studies Association, University of Brighton.

Stebbins, R.A. (2007/2015). *Serious leisure: A perspective for our time.* Transaction. Routledge (published in paperback in 2015 with new Preface).

Stebbins, R.A. (2009). *Personal decisions in the public square: Beyond problem solving into a positive sociology.* New Brunswick, NJ, Transaction. New York, Routledge.

Stebbins, R.A. (2014). *Careers in serious leisure: From dabbler to devotee in search of fulfillment.* Palgrave Macmillan.

Stebbins, R.A. (2017). *Leisure's legacy: Leisure studies in a global era.* Palgrave Macmillan.

Stebbins, R.A. (2018). *Social worlds and the leisure experience.* Bingley, UK, Emerald Group.

Thompson, A.M., III, & Bono, B.A. (1993). Work without wages: The motivation of volunteer firefighters. *American Journal of Economics and Sociology, 52,* 323–343. https://doi.org/10.1111/j.1536-7150.1993.tb02553.x

34

GLOCAL CITIZENSHIP

Lofty ideals in regional space

Faith Ong

Introduction

International volunteer tourism has received much attention in popular media and academic research, with the latter going through advocacy, cautionary, adaptancy and scientific platform phases in the two decades since its first definition was proposed (Wearing & McGehee, 2013). Programmes espouse the development of participants into global citizens, appealing to a loftier goal of becoming citizens who perform moral good across the world for the benefit of others (Brown, 2005; Brown & Morrison, 2003; Coghlan, 2006; Coghlan & Fennell, 2009; Stoddart & Rogerson, 2004). This chapter examines global citizenship in context, and posits that in between the international and local forms of volunteering lies domestic travel volunteering, which has a potential to satisfy travel impetus as well as global citizenship ideals. This chapter will proceed first by exploring global citizenship, its enactment through international volunteer tourism and the current state of domestic travel volunteering research. Through understanding global citizenship dimensions and the outcomes of volunteer tourism, the chapter will conclude with a future research agenda for exploring the advocacy potentials of domestic travel volunteering in encouraging glocal citizenship.

Global citizenship

Global citizenship has been popularised as a concept of citizenship and belonging that de-emphasises political citizenship as characterised by national identities (Butcher, 2017). While citizenship typically brings to mind associations with sovereignty, identity and rights, the rhetoric of global citizenship acknowledges, but delineates itself from, nation-based political entities such as sovereign governments and unions (Standish, 2012). Eschewing the polarity wrought by equating notions of citizenship with identity and rights, global citizenship calls on a universality and morality that transcends these largely geographically bound concepts (Oxley & Morris, 2013). Generally applied in the field of education, but fast expanding in scope and applicability, global citizenship presents itself as free of political judgment, but concerned with awareness, responsibility and caring (Butcher, 2017).

In positioning itself as distinct from citizenship that is concerned with nationhood, global citizenship has been discussed in many forms. While some researchers have explored the

434

DOI: 10.4324/9780367815875-40

concept in terms of dichotomy – defining the positive and negative polarising conceptions of global citizenship (Shultz, 2007; Tully, 2008) – others focus on the desired attributes of global citizens (Gerzon, 2010; Veugelers, 2011). The latter, in particular, provide normative visions of global citizenship, but are weakly linked to its fundamental concepts such as human rights, actions and social dynamics (Oxley & Morris, 2013). The move away from assigning attributes to global citizens has produced typologies based on ideological underpinnings instead, focusing on core concerns and intentions (Schattle, 2007, 2008).

Broadening the conceptualisation of global citizenship, Oxley and Morris (2013) offer a typology based on cosmopolitanism and advocacy that will be referred to in this chapter. This typology, consisting of eight forms, was conceptualised to encompass the diversity of forms that comprise global citizenship. These forms are summarised in Table 34.1 below.

While the cosmopolitan types of global citizenship are universalist in nature, they are typically seen to be set within institutions and practices that are West-centric (Tully, 2008), and thus considered to reinforce hegemonic conceptions of same-ness. The advocacy types of global citizenship, on the other hand, focus on relativist ideologies led by creation of change through advocacy.

Table 34.1 Typology of global citizenship

Type	Conception	Focus
Cosmopolitan	Political global citizenship	A focus on the relationships of the individual to the state and other polities, particularly in the form of cosmopolitan democracy.
Cosmopolitan	Moral global citizenship	A focus on the ethical positioning of individuals and groups to each other, most often featuring ideas of human rights.
Cosmopolitan	Economic global citizenship	A focus on the interplay between power, forms of capital, labour, resources and the human condition, often presented as international development.
Cosmopolitan	Cultural global citizenship	A focus on the symbols that unite and divide members of societies, with particular emphasis on globalisation of arts, media, languages, sciences and technologies.
Advocacy	Social global citizenship	A focus on the interconnections between individuals and groups and their advocacy of the 'people's' voice, often referred to as global civil society.
Advocacy	Critical global citizenship	A focus on the challenges arising from inequalities and oppression, using critique of social norms to advocate action to improve the lives of dispossessed/subaltern populations, particularly through a post-colonial agenda.
Advocacy	Environmental global citizenship	A focus on advocating changes in the actions of humans in relation to the natural environment, generally called the sustainable development agenda.
Advocacy	Spiritual global citizenship	A focus on the non-scientific and immeasurable aspects of human relations, advocating commitment to axioms relating to caring, loving, spiritual and emotional connections.

Adapted from Oxley and Morris (2013, p. 306).

As a set of action-oriented global citizenship categories, the advocacy types will form a lens through which volunteer tourism will be examined. These dimensions of global citizenship, in the face of a citizen set adrift from geopolitical definitions, are pertinent to the focus of volunteer tourism as tools of global citizenship development. They are action and activity-focused, which is the often-touted focus of volunteer tourism programmes as well (Broad & Jenkins, 2007; McGehee, 2002). In pursuit of a world where growth of global citizenship is meant to benefit the global population at large, volunteer tourism will be examined for its ability to contribute to global citizenship and grow a global citizenry.

Global citizenship through volunteer tourism

The act of travel, since the days of the Grand Tour, has been lauded as a way to see and understand the world at large (Chard, 1997; Wearing, 2001). As travel has become more accessible, those who can afford the time and expenses to travel have had the opportunity to expand their experience of the world beyond their immediate geographical and social confines. This burgeoning of travel has also served to shine the spotlight on the consumption of natural and socio-cultural resources in the context of travel, and called to question the sustainability of such practices (Buckley, Gretzel, Scott, Weaver & Becken, 2015). It is within the background of this criticality in regard to overconsumption and the extractive nature of the tourism industry that the conversation has flipped to ask what travel can contribute around the world instead of focusing on what travellers can consume from destinations (Scheyvens & Hughes, 2019). As a part of the global citizenry that has come to the forefront of consciousness in recent times, tourists are increasingly attracted to forms of travel which promise to entertain while minimising negative impact on the destination (Ateljevic, 2020). It is on the back of this mindset that the phenomenon of volunteer tourism continues to prosper, having developed from preceding international volunteering programmes (VolunTourism.org, 2012).

Over the years, international volunteer tourism has attracted much attention in regard to its intended ways of giving back and the practicalities of doing so (Eckardt, Font & Kimbu, 2020). It is also seen to be contributing to the host community while operating as a feel-good mission for the tourist (Han, Lee & Hyun, 2020). Arising from this idealistic notion is a myriad of expectations which volunteer tourists hold on to in evaluating their experiences. By holding on to such expectations, volunteer tourists may be inspired or inhibited by their trip experiences to participate in further activities that contribute to the betterment of their environment or global citizenry (Ong, King, Lockstone-Binney & Junek, 2018).

From a global perspective, volunteer tourism has also been criticised for reinforcing the Global North/South divide that exacerbates economic and social inequalities between economic hemispheres (Zeddies & Millei, 2015). Research has oftentimes ventured to label volunteer tourism as a form of neocolonialism that can inadvertently dictate who should be helped and how (Epprecht & Tiessen, 2012; Lyons, Hanley, Wearing & Neil, 2012; Palacios, 2010). The involvement – and subsequent exploitation – of local children in the name of good intentions vis-à-vis volunteer tourism and its framing of help for the helpless has also created a lightning rod for volunteer tourism's critiques (Cheer, Mathews, van Doore & Flanagan, 2019; Zeddies & Millei, 2015).

In relation to global citizenship, much has been explored in relation to international volunteer tourists and their development as part of the global citizenry through the act of volunteering via travel. International volunteer tourism is often framed as working *for* the marginalised rather than *with* them in the name of global citizenship, reinforcing the Global North/South divisive narrative of 'helping' (Jakubiak & Iordache-Bryant, 2017). In response to this, there has also been a move towards conceptualising international volunteer tourism along the lines of mutuality and decommodification (Everingham, 2016; Wearing, Young & Everingham, 2017). This reframing is a critical first step towards reducing inequalities in power relations and forming relationships in international volunteer tourism projects that start on a more equal foot.

In regard to questioning the broader impacts of volunteer tourism beyond the trip's temporal confines, both Lee and Yen (2015) and Ong et al. (2018) found that returnees of international volunteer tourism often intended to participate in further international volunteer tourism programmes. However, looking beyond just international volunteer tourism, Ong (2016) found that these experiences did not lead to greater volunteer participation in other forms when volunteer tourists returned home. Conversely, more returnees reported that they did not intend to participate in their own local communities through volunteering post-trip than pre-trip. While the Ong et al. (2018) research did not explore the reasons behind this increasing unwillingness to volunteer in their own communities, it is sufficient impetus to wonder if other forms of travel volunteering might be more suited to encouraging continued global citizenship behaviour in the longer term than international volunteer tourism. After all, the dimensions of global citizenship could reasonably be enacted within home communities as they would in other destinations; in fact, one might argue that the building of a global citizenry would ideally encompass contributions to both local and other communities in this act of globalism.

While international travel has never been more accessible, the large-scale international travel restrictions enacted in response to the COVID-19 global pandemic have brought to the fore realities of international travel as a function allowed by geopolitical powers. This curtailment of travel can severely impact the practice of global citizenship through international travel as has been typically espoused. Instead, calling on the dimensions of global citizenship and considering other forms of enactment this global citizenship can take, this chapter explores alternatives for the global citizenry to transform their ideals into action. In particular, a form of travel volunteering within geographical borders called domestic travel volunteering is explored as a means of satisfying the urge to travel while enacting values that align with global citizenship.

Domestic travel volunteering

While volunteer tourism typically evokes images of traveling overseas to exotic locations to carry out volunteer work, domestic travel volunteering has been increasingly recognised as a form of volunteering and travel. This phenomenon is particularly applicable to countries, which have a large landmass, such as Australia. Domestic travel volunteering has largely been examined from a volunteering-first perspective, with an array of activities explored and suggested for inclusion. Some examples include volunteering for major events, such as the hosting of Olympic Games or the Cricket World Cup in cities around the world (Holmes, Smith, Lockstone-Binney & Baum, 2010; Nichols & Ralston, 2014; Smith, Wolf & Lockstone-Binney, 2014). These large-scale events have necessitated large workforces, of which volunteers from around host countries have been integral despite having to travel into the host cities to fulfil these roles. Another commonly regarded form of domestic travel volunteering is organic farm volunteering such as in the case of World Wide Opportunities on Organic Farms (WWOOF), which provide food and accommodation in exchange for farm labour (McIntosh & Bonnemann, 2006; Miller & Mair, 2015). Within Australia, there are programmes linked with regional and Indigenous communities that match skilled volunteers with the host-identified needs of a regional community, encouraging volunteering and skilled participation with these communities (Community First Development, n.d.; Outback Links, 2020). Active conservation has also driven a sub-segment of 'hard' ecotourists to undertake domestic travel to focus on research and conservation related to mammals, reptiles, fish, birds, plants and insects (Cousins, 2007). Such conservation-led domestic travel has often been supported by conservation trusts (national and international), in addition to being enfolded within other commercial tour operations (Cousins, 2007).

Another area, which has received some focus is the grey nomad segment, those above the age of 50 who adopt an extended period of independent travel within their own country and are not part of any commercial tourism event (Leonard & Onyx, 2007). In the course of their travel, such grey nomads may choose to give back to communities they have interacted with along their self-drive journeys (Leonard & Onyx, 2009) or contribute to the continued preservation of landscapes they have enjoyed in their domestic travels (Weaver, 2015). This older demographic also prefer to undertake community-enhancing projects such as assisting historical preservation, sharing their personal histories with younger children and helping Aboriginal community projects (Leonard & Onyx, 2009). The largely grey nomad segment that makes up campground hosts in national park camping grounds in Australia has also received some attention as a viable alternative programme that leverages the increasing grey nomad camping population (Weiler & Caldicott, 2020). Though not remunerated, all the activities described above require relocation and for the volunteer to cover the associated travel expenses. This emphasis on travel as an integral part of volunteer tourism is crucial to its examination, as it is not immune to the issues affecting other forms of tourism. Such issues include the tourist's perception of the host community and the host community's receptivity to the traveller's contributions. Grey nomad domestic travel volunteering has also been explored as a way of attracting retirees to join regional communities in supporting the preservation and survival of these waning communities (Bates, 2007).

Beyond the Australian context, others have examined the socio-political and moral imperatives driving domestic travel volunteering. In particular, Chaisinthop (2017) provided an in-depth exploration into domestic travel volunteering in Thailand, which is dominated by participants from the middle-class, urban populace. While the activities provided participants with the opportunity to enact cherished social values, Chaisinthop (2017) also found that many of these organised domestic travel volunteering programmes tended to reproduce existing power relations that serve to preserve rather than challenge political status quo. This echoes the criticisms of the global North/South divide in volunteer tourism, where the well-intentioned practices of volunteer tourism can inadvertently reinforce hegemonic social and political power structures (Bandyopadhyay & Patil, 2017). In their study of Ride for Love, a student-led programme providing education support for disaster-hit and remote regions, Wen, Lin and Peng (2018) interviewed students who rode their bicycles to these regions. Their findings indicated that the programme's impacts were left on both youth volunteers – who learnt invaluable interpersonal skills – as well as hosts – who were encouraged by these volunteers to invest in their children's education.

In the face of volunteer tourism's increasing critique in the context of growing global citizenship, the domestic travel volunteering space then presents fertile ground for growing the practice and development of the global citizenry. Chief amongst these are the areas which are suggested in the future research section which follows.

Future research

The path to global citizenship can be conceived as smaller stepping stones enacted within one's own geographic neighbourhood, rather than conceived solely as a panacea to entire global issues. Global citizenship is not merely a concern with the 'other' that exists outside our geographical borders; they exist around us, and interstate as well. Thus, with a view to understanding the role domestic travel volunteering can contribute to global citizenship – referred to here as glocal citizenship – particularly in the enactment of advocacy that recognises that global inequalities and injustices can happen in one's own backyard, the following research agenda is proposed to this end.

Understanding glocal citizenship in domestic travel volunteering.

Answering the paucity of literature around domestic travel volunteering, it is imperative to first set the scene as to what qualifies local home volunteering in relation to domestic travel volunteering. Delineation could be conceived as particular distances from home (or regions that are considered home) or in relation to the crossing of state lines, particularly of countries with larger land areas such as Australia, China and Russia. Beyond volunteer activities, what are the considerations beyond activity-compatibility and location convenience that drive domestic volunteer tourists to undertake this form of travel volunteering? Just as there are different spectra of volunteering (from serious leisure to casual (Stebbins, 2004)) and volunteer tourism (Tomazos & Butler, 2012), one could conceive that the skills required and distances undertaken would form part of the characteristics that help us understand domestic travel volunteering in general. However, the extent that these factors play into the conceptualisation of domestic travel tourism has yet to be explored.

Social global citizenship

In exploring the potential of domestic travel volunteering as a vehicle of social global citizenship, where the focus is on interconnections between people and their advocacy of the people's voice to build global civil society, the following questions are proposed to develop understanding in the area. What structures of domestic travel volunteering facilitate social instead of transactional interactions between domestic travel volunteers and the communities into which they are invited? Without positioning communities that accept help as vulnerable, helpless or in any way less-than, what are the ways in which domestic travel volunteers can fulfil their altruistic desires while forming mutual connections with local communities?

Critical global citizenship

Since the world population became an urban majority in 2007, there have been estimates that nearly two-thirds of the world population will reside in urban areas by 2050 (United Nations, 2018). This tipping of population majorities toward the urban has resulted in a disenfranchisement of regional and rural communities, which feel left out of decisions led by the urban majority. A redistribution of population via domestic travel volunteering would not be feasible due to the large numbers that would be needed to correct the imbalance in this complex matter. However, fostering global citizenship through domestic travel volunteering could refocus the challenges arising from these inequalities, particularly in one's own backyard. Therefore, could domestic travel volunteering encourage the critical global citizenship characterised by challenges to inequalities and its resultant economic and social oppression? What are the potentials in this form of travel volunteering that could exhort tourists to understand that global citizenship concepts are just as applicable in their own countries as they are across borders?

Environmental global citizenship

As the COVID-19 pandemic has clearly exemplified, international and even interstate borders can be tightly controlled, especially in the Australian context. Is encouragement of domestic travel volunteering a viable means of bolstering local volunteer forces in times of need, particularly in cases of disaster and recovery? While Wen et al. (2018) have examined this in the context of Chinese university students, the human response to environment disasters in the context of domestic travel volunteering is not widely explored. Furthermore, even as environmental restoration forms a part of the conceptualisation of volunteer tourism offered by Wearing (2001) nearly two decades ago, the potential of domestic travel volunteering as a means of environmental restoration without the high carbon emissions of international travel warrants more attention.

Spiritual global citizenship

Intimacy, affect and emotional experiences have been widely explored in international volunteer tourism (see Conran, 2011; Crossley, 2012; Everingham, 2016; Everingham & Motta, 2020). There is a comparative lack in the focus on human relations related to caring, loving, spiritual and emotional connections in domestic travel volunteering. In exploring the social impacts of domestic travel volunteering, it is pertinent to shine the spotlight on the forms and depths of social bonds that are created through this form of travel/volunteering. Such knowledge could have an impact on how the interconnectedness of populations is affected by the encouragement of domestic travel volunteering, and inform the development of such programmes to encourage solidarity initiatives in times of need.

Conclusion

Given the continued efforts to transform travel from its extractive form into versions that are contributively transformational for host communities and regenerative in intent (Cave & Dredge, 2020), the nexus of home and host in domestic travel volunteering represents opportunity to study glocal citizenship. Growing income equality between and within countries has given rise to encouragement of greater empathy and understanding amongst communities as a means towards a future that is less fractured by difference (Ateljevic, 2020). With international volunteer tourism producing mixed results in relation to its ability to encourage global citizenship amongst participants, the rise and potential of domestic travel volunteering present a viable alternative.

By encouraging the intermingling of populations within larger nations, this form of travel volunteering possesses the means to encourage relationality and empathy within populations, instead of defaulting to a polarising conceptualisation of 'us' versus 'them'. Even as domestic travel volunteering provides avenues toward interaction, this form of travel volunteering could contribute positively to the practice of global citizenship principles in the most accessible and familiar contexts. While domestic travel volunteering may pale in comparison to the diversity of options offered by its international counterpart, it nevertheless opens a plethora of opportunities to foster commonality and boost intra-regional solidarity. These are the same ideals espoused in global citizenship, and it is time that one's backyard – in the form of domestic travel – is recognised as a valued segment of the global population that is equally deserving of awareness, responsibility and caring.

References

Ateljevic, I. (2020). Transforming the (tourism) world for good and (re)generating the potential 'new normal'. *Tourism Geographies, 22*(3), 467–475. doi:10.1080/14616688.2020.1759134

Bandyopadhyay, R., & Patil, V. (2017). 'The white woman's burden' – the racialized, gendered politics of volunteer tourism. *Tourism Geographies, 19*(4), 644–657. doi:10.1080/14616688.2017.1298150

Bates, K. (2007). Volunteering on the move: Grey nomads and volunteering. *Australian Journal on Volunteering, 11*(2), 68–69.

Broad, S., & Jenkins, J. M. (2007). Gibbons in their midst? Conservation volunteers' motivations at the Gibbon Rehabilitation Project, Phuket, Thailand. In K. Lyons & S. Wearing (Eds.), *Journeys of discovery in volunteer tourism: International case study perspectives* (pp. 72–85). Wallingford, UK: CABI.

Brown, S. (2005). Travelling with a purpose: Understanding the motives and benefits of volunteer vacationers. *Current Issues in Tourism, 8*(6), 479–496. doi:10.1080/13683500508668232

Brown, S., & Morrison, A. (2003). Expanding volunteer vacation participation: An exploratory study on the mini-mission concept. *Tourism Recreation Research, 28*(3), 73–82. https://doi.org/10.1080/0 2508281.2003.11081419

Buckley, R., Gretzel, U., Scott, D., Weaver, D., & Becken, S. (2015). Tourism megatrends. *Tourism Recreation Research, 40*(1), 59–70. doi:10.1080/02508281.2015.1005942

Butcher, J. (2017). Citizenship, global citizenship and volunteer tourism: A critical analysis. *Tourism Recreation Research, 42*(2), 129–138. doi:10.1080/02508281.2017.1295172

Cave, J., & Dredge, D. (2020). Regenerative tourism needs diverse economic practices. *Tourism Geographies, 22*(3), 503–513. doi:10.1080/14616688.2020.1768434

Chaisinthop, N. (2017). Domestic volunteer tourism in Thailand. *South East Asia Research, 25*(3), 234–250. doi:10.1177/0967828X17718880

Chard, C. (1997). Grand and ghostly tours: The topography of memory. *Eighteenth-Century Studies, 31*(1), 101–108. doi:10.2307/30053648

Cheer, J., Mathews, L., van Doore, K. E., & Flanagan, K. (2019). *Modern day slavery and orphanage tourism*. Oxfordshire, UK: CABI.

Coghlan, A. (2006). Volunteer tourism as an emerging trend or an expansion of ecotourism? A look at potential clients' perceptions of volunteer tourism organisations. *International Journal of Nonprofit and Voluntary Sector Marketing, 11*(3), 225–237. doi:10.1002/nvsm.35

Coghlan, A., & Fennell, D. (2009). Myth or substance: An examination of altruism as the basis of volunteer tourism. *Annals of Leisure Research, 12*(3–4), 377–402. doi:10.1080/11745398.2009.9686830

Community First Development. (n.d.). *Volunteers - Community first development*. Retrieved from https://www.communityfirstdevelopment.org.au/volunteers

Conran, M. (2011). They really love me!: Intimacy in Volunteer Tourism. *Annals of Tourism Research, 38*(4), 1454–1473. doi:10.1016/j.annals.2011.03.014

Cousins, J. A. (2007). The role of UK-based conservation tourism operators. *Tourism Management, 28*(2007), 1020–1030.

Crossley, É. (2012). Affect and moral transformations in young volunteer tourists. In D. Picard & M. Robinson (Eds.), *Emotion in motion: Tourism, affect and transformation* (pp. 85–97). Surrey, UK: Ashgate Publishing Ltd.

Eckardt, C., Font, X., & Kimbu, A. (2020). Realistic evaluation as a volunteer tourism supply chain methodology. *Journal of Sustainable Tourism, 28*(5), 647–662. doi:10.1080/09669582.2019.1696350

Epprecht, M., & Tiessen, R. (2012). Introduction: Global citizenship education for learning/volunteering abroad. *Journal of Global Citizenship & Equity Education, 2*(1).

Everingham, P. (2016). Hopeful possibilities in spaces of 'the-not-yet-become': Relational encounters in volunteer tourism. *Tourism Geographies, 18*(5), 520–538. doi:10.1080/14616688.2016.1220974

Everingham, P., & Motta, S. C. (2020). Decolonising the 'autonomy of affect' in volunteer tourism encounters. *Tourism Geographies, 1–21.* doi:10.1080/14616688.2020.1713879

Gerzon, M. (2010). *American citizen, global citizen.* Boulder, CO: Spirit Scope Publishing.

Han, H., Lee, S., & Hyun, S. S. (2020). Tourism and altruistic intention: Volunteer tourism development and self-interested value. *Sustainability, 12*(5). doi:10.3390/su12052152

Holmes, K., Smith, K. A., Lockstone-Binney, L., & Baum, T. (2010). Developing the dimensions of tourism volunteering. *Leisure Sciences, 32*(3), 255–269. doi:10.1080/01490401003712689

Jakubiak, C., & Iordache-Bryant, I. (2017). Volunteer tourism in Romania as/for global citizenship. *Tourism Recreation Research, 42*(2), 212–222. doi:10.1080/02508281.2017.1299344

Lee, S., & Yen, C.-L. (2015). Volunteer tourists' motivation change and intended participation. *Asia Pacific Journal of Tourism Research, 20*(4), 359–377. doi:10.1080/10941665.2014.898672

Leonard, R., & Onyx, J. (2007). Constructing short-term episodic volunteering experiences match Grey Nomads and the needs of small country towns. *Third Sector Review, 13*(1), 121–139.

Leonard, R., & Onyx, J. (2009). Volunteer tourism: The interests and motivations of grey nomads. *Annals of Leisure Research, 12*(3–4), 315–332. doi:10.1080/11745398.2009.9686827

Lyons, K., Hanley, J., Wearing, S., & Neil, J. (2012). Gap year volunteer tourism: Myths of Global Citizenship? *Annals of Tourism Research, 39*(1), 361–378. doi:10.1016/j.annals.2011.04.016

McGehee, N. G. (2002). Alternative tourism and social movements. *Annals of Tourism Research, 29*(1), 124–143. doi:10.1016/s0160-7383(01)00027-5

McIntosh, A. J., & Bonnemann, S. M. (2006). Willing Workers on Organic Farms (WWOOF): The alternative farm stay experience? *Journal of Sustainable Tourism, 14*(1), 82–99. doi:10.1080/09669580608668593

Miller, M. C., & Mair, H. (2015). Organic farm volunteering as a decommodified tourist experience. *Tourist Studies, 15*(2), 191–204.

Nichols, G., & Ralston, R. (2014). The 2012 Ambassadors: second-class Olympic volunteers, or the best potential for developing a volunteer legacy from the Games? In K. A. Smith, L. Lockstone-Binney, K. Holmes, & T. Baum (Eds.), *Event volunteering: International perspectives on the event volunteering experience* (pp. 154–164). New York: Routledge.

Ong, F. (2016). *Towards global citizens: Harnessing the expectations of volunteer tourists.* (Doctor of Philosophy Monograph), VIctoria University, Melbourne, Australia.

Ong, F., King, B., Lockstone-Binney, L., & Junek, O. (2018). Going global, acting local: Volunteer tourists as prospective community builders. *Tourism Recreation Research, 43*(2), 135–146. doi:10.1080/02508281.2017.1391449

Outback Links. (2020). *Outback links - Frontier services.* Retrieved from https://frontierservices.org/how-we-help/outback-links/

Oxley, L., & Morris, P. (2013). Global citizenship: A typology for distinguishing its multiple conceptions. *British Journal of Educational Studies, 61*(3), 301–325. doi:10.1080/00071005.2013.798393

Palacios, C. M. (2010). Volunteer tourism, development and education in a postcolonial world: Conceiving global connections beyond aid. *Journal of Sustainable Tourism, 18*(7), 861–878.

Schattle, H. (2007). *The practices of global citizenship.* Lanham, MD: Rowman & Littlefield Publishers.

Schattle, H. (2008). Education for global citizenship: Illustrations of ideological pluralism and adaptation. *Journal of Political Ideologies, 13*(1), 73–94. doi:10.1080/13569310701822263

Scheyvens, R., & Hughes, E. (2019). Can tourism help to "end poverty in all its forms everywhere"? The challenge of tourism addressing SDG1. *Journal of Sustainable Tourism, 27*(7), 1061–1079. doi:10.1080/09669582.2018.1551404

Shultz, L. (2007). Educating for global citizenship: Conflicting agendas and understandings. *Alberta Journal of Educational Research, 53*(3), 248–258.

Smith, K. A., Wolf, N., & Lockstone-Binney, L. (2014). Volunteer experiences in the build-up to the Rugby World Cup 2011. In K. A. Smith, L. Lockstone-Binney, K. Holmes, & T. Baum (Eds.), *Event volunteering: International perspectives on the event volunteering experience* (pp. 111–125). New York: Routledge.

Standish, A. (2012). *The false promise of global learning: Why education needs boundaries.* London: Continuum International Publishing Group.

Stebbins, R. A. (2004). Serious leisure, volunteerism and quality of life. In J. T. Haworth & A. J. Veal (Eds.), *Work and leisure* (pp. 200–212). New York: Routledge.

Stoddart, H., & Rogerson, C. M. (2004). Volunteer tourism: The case of habitat for humanity South Africa. *GeoJournal, 60*(3), 311–318. doi:10.1023/B:GEJO.0000034737.81266.a1

Tomazos, K., & Butler, R. (2012). Volunteer tourists in the field: A question of balance? *Tourism Management, 33*(1), 177–187. doi:10.1016/j.tourman.2011.02.020

Tully, J. (2008). Two meanings of global citizenship: modern and diverse. In M. A. Peters, A. Britton, & H. Blee (Eds.), *Global citizenship education: Philosophy, theory and pedagogy* (pp. 15–40). Rotterdam: Sense.

United Nations. (2018, 16 May 2018). *68% of the world population projected to live in urban areas by 2050, says UN*. Retrieved from https://www.un.org/development/desa/en/news/population/2018-revision-of-world-urbanization-prospects.html#:~:text=News-, 68%25%20of%20the%20world%20population%20projected%20to%20live%20in, areas%20by%202050%2C%20says%20UN&text=Today%2C%2055%25%20of%20the%20world's, increase%20to%2068%25%20by%202050.

Veugelers, W. (2011). The moral and the political in global citizenship: Appreciating differences in education. *Globalisation, Societies and Education, 9*(3–4), 473–485. doi:10.1080/14767724.2011.605329

VolunTourism.org. (2012). *History of voluntourism*. Retrieved from http://www.voluntourism.org/inside-history.html

Wearing, S. (2001). *Volunteer tourism: Experiences that make a difference*. Wallingford: CAB International.

Wearing, S., & McGehee, N. G. (2013). Volunteer tourism: A review. *Tourism Management, 38*(0), 120–130. doi:http://dx.doi.org/10.1016/j.tourman.2013.03.002

Wearing, S., Young, T., & Everingham, P. (2017). Evaluating volunteer tourism: Has it made a difference? *Tourism Recreation Research, 42*(4), 512–521. doi:10.1080/02508281.2017.1345470

Weaver, D. (2015). Volunteer tourism and beyond: Motivations and barriers to participation in protected area enhancement. *Journal of Sustainable Tourism*, 1–23. doi:10.1080/09669582.2014.992901

Weiler, B., & Caldicott, R. (2020). Unpacking the factors that contribute to successful engagement of stakeholders in a volunteer Camphost programme. *Tourism Recreation Research, 45*(2), 247–264. doi:https://doi.org/10.1080/02508281.2019.1640445

Wen, J. J., Lin, Q.-q., & Peng, B.-q. (2018). The interpersonal interaction and socialisation of volunteers: Case study of ride for love. In C. Khoo-Lattimore & E. C. L. Yang (Eds.), *Asian youth travellers: Insights and implications* (pp. 175–196). Singapore: Springer Singapore.

Zeddies, M., & Millei, Z. (2015). "It takes a global village": Troubling discourses of global citizenship in United Planet's voluntourism. *Global Studies of Childhood, 5*(1), 100–111. doi:10.1177/2043610615573383

PART 7

New directions in volunteering research

35

PROFILING RESEARCH ON VOLUNTEERING IN EVENTS, SPORT AND TOURISM

Andrzej Lis and Mateusz Tomanek

Introduction

Volunteering is defined as

> any activity in which time is given freely to benefit another person, group or cause. Volunteering is part of a cluster of helping behaviours, entailing more commitment than spontaneous assistance but narrower in scope than the care provided to family and friends.
>
> *(Wilson, 2000, p. 215)*

As manifested in the high-frequency keywords attached to publications dealing with the topics of volunteering and volunteerism, indexed in the Scopus database, volunteers support a variety of sectors and areas including among others: education, social welfare, health care, religious organisations and developing countries. Regardless of the area where volunteering is practiced, the phenomenon has been gaining popularity as an object of scientific inquiry, and in consequence the number of research publications has been constantly growing. The same tendency is observed in regard to volunteering in events, sport and tourism (cf. Figure 35.1).

Volunteering in events is the first focal point of this Handbook. Event volunteering is well suited to the needs of those who want to engage in voluntary activities on a short term or occasional basis. This kind of involvement, called 'episodic' volunteering, is typical of sport, cultural and/or business events (Smith, Baum et al., 2014, p. 3). The scientific output dealing with volunteer management in events is explored by Kim and Cuskelly (2017). Their systematic quantitative literature review includes some components of research profiling focusing on the geographical and time distribution of research, and the profile of journals publishing the findings. Moreover, they analyse the variety of methodological approaches and theoretical foundations of research in the field as well as key concepts, constructs and research questions. The authors observed that the majority of analysed publications were characterised by unclear theoretical frameworks and the studies used questionnaire surveys as the primary collection technique to gather data from volunteers. Kim and Cuskelly (2017) also note that the research on volunteering in events requires more engagement of scholars representing

DOI: 10.4324/9780367815875-42

various countries and research perspectives. The collection combining the studies presenting *International perspectives on the event volunteering experience*, edited by Smith, Lockstone-Binney et al. (2014), may be considered as an example of such a comprehensive approach.

Volunteering in sport is the second area of interest. As observed by Doherty (2006, p. 105) "[s]port volunteering is critical to the sport industry itself, and to the voluntary sector as a whole". Thus, it is considered to be an interesting area for research exploration. The potential of scientific inquiry focused on sport volunteering is highlighted, among others, by the special issue of *Sport Management Review*, introduced by Doherty (2006). The amassing production in the field is discussed by Wicker (2017, p. 325) in an article that "reflects on existing research examining volunteerism and volunteer management in sport from individual, institutional, multi-level, and policy perspectives".

Tourism volunteering constitutes the third central focus of our study. As noticed by Holmes et al. (2010, p. 255),

> [t]ourism volunteering encompasses individuals volunteering in their own community (i.e., host volunteering) and tourists volunteering at a destination (i.e., volunteer tourism). Volunteers in tourism on the whole are engaged in the process of assisting the leisure experiences of others while simultaneously undertaking a recreational activity either in their home community or in a destination further afield.

Host volunteering "involves residents as volunteers within their own community, and takes place in visitor attractions, at events, and in destination service organisations such as visitors centres" (Smith & Holmes, 2012, pp. 562–563). As defined by Wearing (2001), volunteer tourism

> applies to those tourists who, for various reasons, volunteer in an organised way to undertake holidays that may involve aiding or alleviating the material poverty of some groups in society, the restoration of certain environments, or research into aspects of society or environment.

A review of the state of research on volunteer tourism was conducted by Wearing and McGehee (2013), who analysed available literature from the perspectives of stakeholders, i.e., volunteer tourists and their motivations, organisations involved in facilitating of this kind of tourism, and host communities. Moreover, attention was paid to the emerging area of studies on the impact of volunteer tourism on changing behaviours after returning home. Another important contribution was made by McGehee (2014), who "reviews the 30-year evolution of volunteer tourism as phenomenon, industry and research area" (p. 847). In addition to classical aspects of volunteer tourism research dealing with: commodification of the industry, tourists' motivations and a lack of commonly accepted theoretical foundations, McGehee (2014) highlighted emerging topics such as: the employment of new technologies for volunteer tourism purposes, certifying the quality of volunteer tourism and its religious and spiritual aspects.

In last two decades, the number of research publications on volunteering in events, sport and tourism has increased significantly. Nevertheless, the amassing research output across these foci has been neither mapped bibliometrically, nor profiled, so far. Searching in Scopus and Web of Science databases, as of 8 February 2021, we found limited publications mapping the research field with the use of bibliometric methods, and a research profiling methodology in particular. The exception is the aforementioned review of event volunteer management by Kim and Cuskelly (2017), which includes some elements of research profiling. Thus, we consider it to be of paramount importance to contribute to theory development with a bibliometric study profiling research production in the field. The aim of the study was to profile the research output on volunteering in events, sport and tourism. The research process was guided by the three following questions: (1) How has research on volunteering in events, sport and tourism evolved over time? (2) Who are the main contributors (countries, research institutions, authors, source titles) to research progress? (3) What are the core references in the field?

Methods of study

The study employed the method of research profiling (Porter et al., 2002), categorised among bibliometric descriptive studies, and the method of direct citation analysis, representing science mapping methodologies (Zupic & Čater, 2015). Research profiling is considered to be an effective supplement of traditional literature reviews aimed at mapping research production in a field of academic study (Porter et al., 2002). Full-scale research profiling consists of three components, i.e., general publication profiling, subject area profiling and topic profiling (cf. Martinez et al., 2012; Sudolska, Lis & Błaś, 2019; Sudolska, Lis & Chodorek, 2019). Nevertheless, the scope of our study was limited to the component of general publication profiling, while subject area profiling and topic profiling were excluded. The general publication profiling was oriented to profiling the most productive contributors to research output in the field, i.e., countries, research institutions, authors and source titles. In all the components of research profiling, the full counting method was used to calculate research contributions, i.e., the total count of a multi-authored publication (and citations it received) was attributed to all the authors. In regard to scholars' affiliations, in the component of author profiling, we linked scholars with institutions listed as their official affiliations in Scopus, while in the component of research institution profiling, contributions were shared between the institutions a given author has been affiliated with in the period under the study (2000–2021), e.g., Stephen Wearing's output was divided between the University of Technology Sydney, where he has been until recently and the University of Newcastle, where he serves now. Direct citation analysis (Smith, 1981), supported with VOSviewer software (van Eck & Waltman, 2010), was employed to identify core references, i.e., those of the highest number of citations. We supplemented the analysis of the number of citations with the attribute of the normalised number of citations in order to mitigate against the method being biased towards older publications (van Eck & Waltman, 2020, p. 37). Both the methods of research profiling and direct citation analysis contributed to the resulting assessment of productivity growth in the field.

We used the Scopus database as a source of bibliometric data for analysis. The research sampling process, conducted on 8 February 2021, consisted of three steps. First, we searched for the conjunction of phrases 'volunteer*' and ('event' or 'sport' or 'tourism') in the titles of the Scopus indexed publications. We employed the stemming technique, i.e., putting the truncation symbol at the end of the word 'volunteer', in order to broaden our search and include words with various endings. We retrieved 686 documents. Second, having checked the relevance of publications, we restricted the sample to 584 publications indexed in the following subject areas (defined automatically by Scopus): Business, Management and Accounting, Social Sciences, Environmental Science, Economics, Econometrics and Finance, Psychology and Decision Sciences. Thirdly, we confined the sample and excluded publications issued prior to 2000. In total, the research sample comprised 575 items. The majority of them were journal articles (447), followed by: book chapters (76), conference papers (12), editorials (10), reviews (10), books (9), notes (5), letters (4) and errata (2). Moreover, in order to identify core references in the thematic areas (sub-fields), we retrieved sub-samples including the publications related to volunteering in events ($N = 169$), volunteering in sport ($N = 186$) and tourism volunteering ($N = 284$). The sub-samples followed the same exclusion criteria as the main sample. The sub-samples were established on a non-exclusive basis, i.e., articles were coded in more than one sub-sample if they contained relevant keywords (there were 63 items coded in two sub-samples, and 1 item coded in all three sub-samples). Moreover, for the purposes of the core references analysis, following the rule of snowball sampling, we added the works of Simpson (2004) and Farrell et al. (1998), which were excluded in the research sampling process for the needs of general publication profiling.

Research productivity

We measured productivity in volunteering research in events, sport and tourism with the attributes of the yearly number of publications and the number of received citations. The findings from the analysis are displayed in Figure 35.1. Among 575 publications, comprising the research sample, 569 items were published between 2000 and 2020, which translates into an average annual production equal to 27.09 documents. The publications in total received 10,220 citations (10,036 citations excluding 2021), which makes an average of 17.63 citations per one publication and 477.90 citations per year.

Research productivity in the field, defined by the number of publications and the number of citations, may be considered as a manifestation of the stage of the research field lifecycle (Czakon, 2011). In the period of 2000–2020, three stages may be observed in the progression of research on volunteering in events, sport and tourism. First, from 2000 to 2007, several publications were noticed every year, reaching the maximum output level of ten items. The yearly number of received citations increased from none in 2000 to 52 in 2007. We label

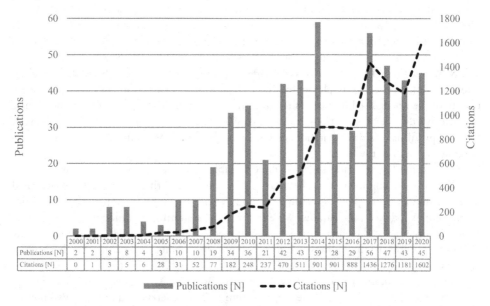

	2000	2001	2002	2003	2004	2005	2006	2007	2008	2009	2010	2011	2012	2013	2014	2015	2016	2017	2018	2019	2020
Publications [N]	2	2	8	8	4	3	10	10	19	34	36	21	42	43	59	28	29	56	47	43	45
Citations [N]	0	1	3	5	6	28	31	52	77	182	248	237	470	511	901	901	888	1436	1276	1181	1602

▬▬ Publications [N]   ● ● ● ● Citations [N]

Figure 35.1   Productivity in research on volunteering in events, sport and tourism

Source: Own study based on data retrieved from Scopus (8 February 2021).

this time as the start-up period of the research field. Second, between 2008 and 2014, yearly production increased from 19 to 59 publications, with the exception of 2011, when the number of publications dropped to 21. The number of citations followed the growth trend and moved up from 77 in 2008 to 901 in 2014. This period may be tagged as the growth stage. Thirdly, a decrease in research output was observed in 2015–2016 (to around 30 publications per year), followed by an increase in 2017 (to 56 items), and the stabilisation trend in 2018–2020 (at the level of 45 publications). The decrease in the number of published papers in 2015–2016 resulted in growth inhibition of the number of citations (at the level of around 900). Then, since 2017, the situation has improved. In 2020, more than 1,600 citations were reported. Thus, the period of 2015–2016 deserves the label of the shakeout stage.

Top contributors

In order to profile research on volunteering in events, sport and tourism, we identified the leading contributors to the field including the categories of the most productive countries, research institutions, source titles and authors (cf. Table 35.1.). We used the following measures of productivity and citation impact: the total number of publications (TP), the total number of received citations (TC), the citation count per one publication (C/P) and the h-index (Hirsch index).

Country profiling

Research production on volunteering in events, sport and tourism was distributed over 56 countries. Among them, there were 13 contributors with 10 and more publications. The leaders with the output exceeding 100 publications were: Australia, the United Kingdom and the United States. They were followed by Canada and New Zealand with the total count of around 40–50 publications. The scholars in the aforementioned nations were highly cited. Australia, the United Kingdom, and the United States received more than 2,000 citations each. Publications affiliated with institutions in Canada and New Zealand reached the level of around 1,000 citations per country. For all of the aforementioned nations except the United Kingdom, the index of the average number of citations per publication was higher than 20. The h-indexes range from 14 (New Zealand) to 30 (Australia).

Among remaining top contributors, there were three European continental nations (Germany, Spain and Norway) and two Asian nations (South Korea and China). Moreover, taking into account the number of citations, the contributions of Singapore (399 citations) and Peru (314) are worth mentioning. The analysis of the most productive countries in the field indicates the leading role of developed economies, and Anglo-Saxon countries in particular. Among the top 10 contributors, there was only one emerging economy, i.e., China, the production of which was characterised by much lower values of citation impact indices. Similar tendencies were noticed in the sub-samples dealing with volunteering in events, volunteering in sport and tourism volunteering. Anglo-Saxon countries were the top contributors in all three areas. In event volunteering, Australia, the United States, the United Kingdom, Canada and New Zealand were followed by South Korea, Spain, Norway, China and Germany. In sport volunteering, the United Kingdom was the leader, succeeded by Australia, the United States, Canada, Germany, South Korea, Norway, China, Belgium and the Russian Federation. What is surprising is that New Zealand was left out of the top ten contributors. In tourism volunteering, in addition to the top five aforementioned

Table 35.1 Most productive contributors to research on volunteering in events, sport, and tourism

Items	TP	TC	C/P	h
Country profiling				
Australia	136	2860	21.0	30
United Kingdom	135	2022	15.0	25
United States	117	2554	21.8	27
Canada	50	1155	23.1	18
New Zealand	43	988	23.0	14
South Korea	23	186	8.1	8
Germany	20	261	13.1	9
China	17	71	4.2	5
Spain	15	151	10.1	5
Norway	12	198	16.5	7
Research institution profiling				
Griffith University	30	634	21.1	15
University of Technology, Sydney	19	535	28.2	12
University of Brighton	18	186	10.3	8
Victoria University	17	204	12.0	8
Victoria University of Wellington	16	149	9.3	7
University of Newcastle, Australia	13	513	39.5	11
University of Western Ontario	13	341	26.2	9
Deutsche Sporthochschule Köln	12	194	16.2	6
University of Hawai'i at Mānoa	12	312	26.0	7
University of Waterloo	12	336	28.0	8
University of Strathclyde	12	215	17.9	7
Curtin University	12	111	9.3	6

Items	TP	TC	C/P	h
Source title profiling				
Journal of Sustainable Tourism	29	1259	43.4	16
Tourism Recreation Research	26	666	25.6	11
Event Management	24	366	15.3	9
Sport Management Review	20	465	23.3	12
Annals of Tourism Research	19	1166	61.4	13
Current Issues in Tourism	13	141	10.8	6
European Sport Management Quarterly	12	209	17.4	8
Annals of Leisure Research	11	153	13.9	8
Managing Leisure	11	283	25.7	10
Volunteer Tourism Theoretical Frameworks and Practical Applications	11	89	8.1	5
Author profiling				
Benson, A. M.	16	137	8.6	6
Wearing, S.	16	665	41.5	11
Cuskelly, G.	14	226	16.1	10
Nichols, G.	14	151	10.8	6
Mostafanezhad, M.	13	302	23.2	8
Holmes, K.	12	113	9.4	6
Smith, K. A.	12	112	9.3	6
Lockstone-Binney, L.	11	106	9.6	6
Bang, H.	9	203	22.6	7
Baum, T.	9	118	13.1	5
Coghlan, A.	9	350	38.9	8
Doherty, A.	9	235	26.1	6

Source: Own study based on data retrieved from Scopus (8 February 2021).

Anglo-Saxon nations, some Asian and African countries (South Africa, South Korea, China, Malaysia and Thailand) were reported among the most productive nations.

Research institution profiling

The dominant position in research on volunteering in events, sport and tourism occupied by Anglo-Saxon nations was confirmed by institutional profiling. Eleven among the top 12 institutions, which contributed with at least 12 publications, were located in Anglo-Saxon countries (Australia – 5, Canada and the United Kingdom – 2 universities in each country, New Zealand and the United States – 1). German Deutsche Sporthochschule Köln was the only institution from a non-native English-speaking country among the top contributors. Griffith University (Australia) was the unquestioned most productive institution in the field. The followers are: the University of Technology Sydney and Victoria University, the University of Brighton and New Zealand's Victoria University of Wellington. Taking into account the attribute of the number of citations per publication, among the top contributors, the following institutions are worth highlighting: the University of Newcastle Australia, the University of Technology Sydney, the University of Waterloo, the University of Western Ontario and the University of Hawai'i at Mānoa. While analysing the contribution to thematic sub-fields, some differences were noticed. Griffith University and Victoria University of Wellington are the top contributors to research on volunteering in events. The issues of volunteering in sport are mostly studied at Griffith University, the University of Western Ontario and Deutsche Sporthochschule Köln. Moreover, the contributions of British Liverpool John Moores University and Sheffield University are worth noting. In tourism volunteering, the University of Technology Sydney, the University of Brighton and the University of Newcastle are the leaders. Interesting shifts are noticed while analysing the dynamics of contributions by research institutions. On the one hand, the position of some of them in the field seemed to weaken. For instance, Victoria University, which was very active in 2009–2014, currently shows lower productivity in the field. On the other hand, new important players emerged. Among the leading contributors to the field in 2016–2021, besides Griffith University, Liverpool John Moores University and Sejong University were recognized.

Source title profiling

The *Journal of Sustainable Tourism* (with 29 publications) was found to be the most frequently chosen source title to publish findings from research on volunteering in events, sport and tourism. The followers are: *Tourism Recreation Research* (26 papers), *Event Management* (24) and *Sport Management Review* (20). In regard to the number of received citations and subsequently the h-index, *Journal of Sustainable Tourism* (1,259) and *Annals of Tourism Research* (1,166) stand out from the crowd. Moreover, taking into account the number of received citations (200 and more), the following source titles not listed in Table 35.1. are worth mentioning: *Tourism Management* (322 citations), *International Journal of Tourism Research* (310), *Journeys of Discovery in Volunteer Tourism* (302) and the *Journal of Sport Management* (210). The primary choices for publishing papers in thematic sub-fields were: *Event Management* for volunteering in events as well as *Sport Management Review* and *European Sport Management Quarterly* for volunteering in sport, and the *Journal of Sustainable Tourism* and *Tourism Recreation Research* for tourism volunteering.

Author profiling

Angela Benson (the University of Brighton) and Stephen Wearing (the University of Newcastle), each of them with 16 publications, are the most prolific authors researching on volunteering in events, sport and tourism. They are followed by: Graham Cuskelly (Griffith University), Geoff Nichols (the University of Sheffield) and Mary Mostafanezhad (the University of Hawai'i at Mānoa). Taking into account the number of received citations (more than 350), the following scholars are also notable: Nancy Gard McGehee from Virginia Polytechnic Institute and State University (736 citations), Ann Zahra affiliated with the University of Waikato (373), Harngluh Sin from the National University of Singapore (358) and Alexandra Coghlan from Griffith University (350). The leading contributors to thematic sub-fields are: in volunteering in events – Karen Smith (Victoria University of Wellington), in volunteering in sport – Geoff Nichols, Graham Cuskelly and Alison Doherty (the University of Western Ontario, Canada), in tourism volunteering – Stephen Wearing, Mary Mostafanezhad and Angela Benson.

Core references

Direct citation analysis of publications comprising the research sample indicates two distinctively separate branches in the research field, with the focus on tourism volunteering and volunteering in sport. There are only three documents combining together the aforementioned thematic areas. The publications dealing with event volunteering make a kind of a 'bridge' linking these two sub-fields. Nevertheless, they are much more integrated with the theme of volunteering in sport (phrases 'event' and 'sport' are mentioned together in the titles of 58 documents) rather than tourism volunteering (7 documents). There was only one publication found comprising the three expressions together in its title (Jarvis & Blank, 2011), which analyses tourism related motivations among sport event volunteers. Simultaneously, direct citation analysis points out significant variety in the number of citations among the sub-fields, i.e., research on tourism volunteering is much more cited than publications on volunteering in events or sport. Therefore, we decided to identify and explore the core references in each of the three sub-fields.

In the tourism volunteering sub-field and across the whole research field, the highest number of citations was received by: Simpson (2004) (344 citations), McGehee and Santos (2005) (244), Sin (2009) (219), and Guttentag (2009) (212). The followers are: Raymond and Hall (2008) (197 citations), Wearing and McGehee (2013) (178), Palacios (2010) (178), and Lyons et al. (2012) (170). Taking into account the attribute of the normalised number of citations, in order to mitigate the bias of direct citations analysis towards older documents, the following publications are worth noting: Meng et al. (2020) (the normalised number of citations equal to 7.03), Lyons et al. (2012) (6.67), Han et al. (2019) (6.02), Coghlan and Weiler (2018) (5.84), Wearing and McGehee (2013) (5.61), and Palacios (2010) (5.50).

Among the aforementioned core references, Simpson (2004) focuses on 'gap year' tourism, i.e., leaving daily duties (work, studies) for a longer period of time and travelling in order to discover skills, gain experience and contribute to development. This study analyses "the ways development and the 'third world' are presented and sold to gap year participants" and "how these representations then shape the way participants experience the 'other' that they encounter through their gap year" (Simpson, 2004, p. 682). McGehee and Santos (2005) analyse the cases of three US volunteer tourism organisations to discuss implications for volunteer tourism. Their study indicates that "participation in volunteer tourism had a positive effect on both intended post-trip social movement activities and support for activism" (McGehee & Santos, 2005, p. 760). Whilst Sin (2009) was mainly interested in motivations of volunteer tourists and their satisfaction in meeting these expectations, Guttentag (2009, p. 537) focused his research on potential negative consequences of volunteer tourism, listing among them: "a neglect of locals' desires, a hindering of work progress and completion of unsatisfactory work, a disruption of local economies, a reinforcement of conceptualisations of the 'other' and rationalisations of poverty, and an instigation of cultural changes". Similarly, Raymond and Hall (2008) pointed out excessive optimism regarding volunteer tourism in the extant literature, while noting that insufficiently managed volunteer tourism programmes may result in cross-cultural misunderstandings and the strengthening of cultural stereotypes.

Wearing and McGehee (2013) provide a review of research on volunteer tourism, including the motivations of participants, acquired experiences, the roles of coordinating organisations and the attitudes of local societies. They stress that

> [f]or volunteer tourism to succeed it has to be sustainable for both the social and natural environments of the area visited, while also not becoming another form of tourism based mainly on the commodification of at least partly altruistic intent.
>
> *(Wearing & McGehee, 2003, p. 127)*

The aforementioned balance is important as there is a risk that volunteer tourism may become a form of charity tourism (Butcher, 2011). Palacios (2010) notices that the benefits from short term internships for students may be similar to those of international volunteering and service initiatives, including increases in engagement and development of career and cross-cultural competencies. Embedded in the context of Australian gap year programmes, the study of Lyons et al. (2012, p. 363) analysed "the valorisation of cross-cultural understanding and mutual respect through volunteer tourism". Meng et al. (2020) studied the theoretical framework of volunteer tourists' motivations to continue engagement in volunteer tourism programs, giving attention to their quality, levels of trust in the organisations conducting programmes and needs awareness. Coghlan and Weiler (2018) analyse the process of transformational changes in volunteer tourism. Han et al. (2019) explore relationships between motivations for volunteer tourism and satisfaction, trust and the behavioural intentions of participants. They notice that, in contrast to mass tourism, volunteer tourism contributes both to the personal fulfilment of participants and development of local societies. Although our study encompassed both host volunteering and volunteer tourism, we realised that research in host volunteering was very limited (e.g., see Paraskevaidis & Andriotis, 2017; Qi, 2021), while volunteer tourism occupied a dominant position in the research field.

In the sub-field focused on volunteering in sport, the most cited references are: Farrell et al. (1998) (206 citations), Doherty (2009) (105), Kay and Bradbury (2009) (75), Harvey et al. (2007) (74), and Doherty and Carron (2003) (74). Farrell et al. (1998) tested the Special Event Volunteer Motivation Scale (SEVMS) and measured the satisfaction of volunteers engaged in the Canadian Women's Curling Championship in 1996. Analysing the experiences of more than 1,000 volunteers contributing to the 2001 Canada Summer Games, Doherty (2009) differentiates between volunteers engaged in cyclical sport events (e.g. league competitions) and one time (or episodic) events as well as between those who are involved in the event preparation process (usually lasting for a few months) and those who support the direct conduct of the event. In reference to the sport policy of the United Kingdom, Kay and Bradbury (2009) highlight the capability of sport volunteering to develop social capital and relationships for youth. Similarly, the study by Harvey et al. (2007) focuses on the relationship between sport volunteering and social capital. In this case, a pilot Canadian study showed a strong relationship between these two variables. Doherty and Carron (2003) focused their attention on volunteers working for sport non-profit organisations. Their findings indicated cohesion of tasks to be stronger than social cohesion in relation to the satisfaction of volunteers, their engagement and willingness to continue volunteering. In addition to the aforementioned core references, taking into account the attribute of the normalised number of citations, the already discussed study by Wicker (2017) is notable among the most influential works on volunteering in sport.

In the sub-field of event volunteering, the already mentioned study by Doherty (2009) is the most cited publication with 105 citations. Other core references are the works of: Costa et al. (2006) (104 citations), Giannoulakis et al. (2008) (65), Coyne and Coyne (2001) (65), and Monga (2006) (64). Creating a 'bridge' among participants, organisers and fans/audience, volunteers play a role of paramount importance for numerous sport events (Doherty, 2009). Therefore, providing adequate training of volunteers and building a positive atmosphere and the feeling of commitment among them are prerequisites of effective event management. Although, volunteers' willingness to take part in subsequent events was considered to be the most visible manifestation of their satisfaction, Costa et al. (2006) measured volunteers' contentment, organisational engagement, sense of community and satisfaction with volunteer training. They found that a sense of community positively influences volunteers' engagement in organising an event, which in turn increases satisfaction. Volunteer motivation is the theme of the study by Giannoulakis et al. (2008), who surveyed the volunteers participating in the Olympic Games 2004 in Athens, Greece. The authors used the Olympic Volunteer Motivation Scale (OVMS) to identify volunteer motivations to engage with the event. As measuring volunteers' satisfaction and motivation is an issue of paramount importance for event management, it is worth mentioning the study by Monga (2006), who developed and tested "a measurement scale for motivation to volunteer for special events" (p. 47). Coyne and Coyne (2001) analysed the issue of recruiting and retaining volunteers for golf tournaments. They found that 'love of golf' among volunteers was an indispensable condition to attract them to contribute to organising mass golf events. Besides the aforementioned most cited publications on volunteering in events, while taking into account the normalised number of citations (5.33), it is worth noting Cho et al.'s (2020) study of volunteers' intentions to continue engagement in sport events.

Conclusion

Summing up, in response to the first study question, taking into account the annual numbers of publications and received citations, we have identified three periods in the development of research on volunteering in events, sport and tourism: (1) start-up (2000–2007), (2) growth (2008–2014) and (3) shakeout (2015–2020). In response to the second study question, we have recognised the Anglo-Saxon nations (Australia, the United States, the United Kingdom, Canada and New Zealand) as the main contributors to research production in the field. We hypothesise that it may be a consequence of high volunteering rates in these societies. For instance, all the aforementioned countries are listed among the most generous nations in the CAF World Giving Index: the United States (rank 1), New Zealand (3), Australia (4), Canada (6), the United Kingdom (7) (CAF World Giving Index, 2019). Similarly, they are within the top ten societies volunteering their time: the United States (rank 1), New Zealand (2), Canada (4), Australia (5), the United Kingdom (10) (NationMaster, n.d.).

Australia's Griffith University was found to be the most productive research institution, while the University of Newcastle was the leader in regard to the number of citations per publication. The most prolific authors in the field were Angela Benson (University of Brighton) and Stephen Wearing (University of Newcastle). The researchers, whose works have received the most academic attention manifested by the number of citations were: Nancy Gard McGehee and Stephen Wearing. The *Journal of Sustainable Tourism* was recognised as the most productive and prestigious source title in the field. In response to the third study question, we noticed that the majority of the most cited references in the field are focused on the sub-field of tourism volunteering, and volunteer tourism mostly. The studies on tourism volunteering and volunteering in sport constitute separate branches in the research field. Publications dealing with event volunteering make a kind of a 'bridge' linking these two sub-fields.

In discussing the findings, the limitations of the study process should be taken into account. First, the research sampling process was narrowed to Scopus only, which provides the risk of omitting valuable publications not indexed in this database. Moreover, Scopus shows favouritism towards papers written in English. Second, employing strict research sampling criteria, based on keyword searches in bibliometric databases, may result in the risk of omitting some important publications, as noted above in regard to works of Simpson (2004) and Farrell et al. (1998). Thirdly, the inherent weaknesses of direct citation analysis, such as a bias toward older publications, should be noted. We attempted to mitigate this limitation by employing the normalised number of citations in the analysis process. Nevertheless, this attribute is likely changing over time and it depends very much on other publications in the sample. As the sub-samples used for identifying core references were relatively small, there is a risk of lower accuracy of this measure. Fourthly, the employed methodology provided a holistic picture of the research field, but had limitations in portraying the dynamics of contributions to the field over the last two decades e.g., differentiating between research institutions and authors productive in the past and those active recently or observing movements of scholars between institutions. Fifthly, the research field taken for analysis shows some heterogeneity and analysing the issue of volunteering in the contexts of events, sport and tourism all together may lead to some generalisations, thereby neglecting distinctive features of the thematic areas in the research field.

As already mentioned, bibliometric studies of research on volunteering in events, sport and tourism have been very limited, so far. Thus, in our opinion, the identified research gap offers interesting opportunities for further research with the use of science mapping methods, including: direct citation analysis, co-citation analysis, bibliographic coupling, co-author analysis and co-word analysis (Zupic & Čater, 2015). First, we recommend to explore the conceptual structure of the field in order to identify leading and emerging research themes as well as dynamics in this aspect. Second, mapping the intellectual structure of literature may contribute to exploring and better understanding relationships among the publications in the research field. Thirdly, mapping the social structure may be useful to discover collaborative links among scholars, research institutions and countries, and their impact on the quantity and quality of research production.

References

Butcher, J. (2011). Volunteer tourism may not be as good as it seems. *Tourism Recreation Research, 36*(1), 75–76. https://doi.org/10.1080/02508281.2011.11081662

CAF World Giving Index. (2019). https://www.cafonline.org/docs/default-source/about-us-publications/caf_wgi_10th_edition_report_2712a_web_101019.pdf

Cho, H., Li, C., & Wu, Y. (2020). Understanding sport event volunteers' continuance intention: An environmental psychology approach. *Sport Management Review, 23*(4), 615–625. https://doi.org/10.1016/j.smr.2019.08.006

Coghlan, A., & Weiler, B. (2018). Examining transformative processes in volunteer tourism. *Current Issues in Tourism*, *21*(5), 567–582. https://doi.org/10.1080/13683500.2015.1102209

Costa, C. A., Chalip, L., Green, B. C., & Simes, C. (2006). Reconsidering the role of training in event volunteers' satisfaction. *Sport Management Review*, *9*(2), 165–182. https://doi.org/10.1016/S1441-3523(06)70024-9

Coyne, B. S., & Coyne, E. J. (2001). Getting, keeping and caring for unpaid volunteers for professional golf tournament events. *Human Resource Development International*, *4*(2), 199–216. https://doi.org/10.1080/13678860121999

Czakon, W. (2011). Metodyka systematycznego przeglądu literatury. *Przegląd Organizacji*, *3*, 57–61. https://doi.org/doi:10.33141/po.2011.03.13.

Doherty, A. J. (2006). Sport volunteerism: An introduction to the special issue. *Sport Management Review*, *9*(2), 105–109. https://doi.org/10.1016/S1441-3523(06)70021-3

Doherty, A. J. (2009). The volunteer legacy of a major sport event. *Journal of Policy Research in Tourism, Leisure and Events*, *1*(3), 185–207. https://doi.org/10.1080/19407960903204356

Doherty, A. J., & Carron, A. V. (2003). Cohesion in volunteer sport executive committees. *Journal of Sport Management*, *17*(2), 116–141. https://doi.org/10.1123/jsm.17.2.116

Farrell, J. M., Johnston, M. E., & Twynam, G. D. (1998). Volunteer motivation, satisfaction, and management at an elite sporting competition. *Journal of Sport Management*, *12*(4), 288–300. https://doi.org/10.1123/jsm.12.4.288

Giannoulakis, C., Wang, C. H., & Gray, D. (2008). Measuring volunteer motivation in mega-sporting events. *Event Management*, *11*(4), 191–200. https://doi.org/10.3727/152599508785899884

Guttentag, D. A. (2009). The possible negative impacts of volunteer tourism. *International Journal of Tourism Research*, *11*(6), 537–551. https://doi.org/10.1002/jtr.727

Han, H., Meng, B., Chua, B. L., Ryu, H. B., & Kim, W. (2019). International volunteer tourism and youth travelers: An emerging tourism trend. *Journal of Travel and Tourism Marketing*, *36*(5), 549–562. https://doi.org/10.1080/10548408.2019.1590293

Harvey, J., Lévesque, M., & Donnelly, P. (2007). Sport volunteerism and social capital. *Sociology of Sport Journal*, *24*(2), 206–223. https://doi.org/10.1123/ssj.24.2.206

Holmes, K., Smith, K. A., Lockstone-Binney, L., & Baum, T. (2010). Developing the dimensions of tourism volunteering. *Leisure Sciences*, *32*(3), 255–269. https://doi.org/10.1080/01490401003712689

Jarvis, N., & Blank, C. (2011). The importance of tourism motivations among sport event volunteers at the 2007 World Artistic Gymnastics Championships, Stuttgart, Germany. *Journal of Sport and Tourism*, *16*(2), 129–147. https://doi.org/10.1080/14775085.2011.568089

Kay, T., & Bradbury, S. (2009). Youth sport volunteering: Developing social capital? *Sport, Education and Society*, *14*(1), 121–140. https://doi.org/10.1080/13573320802615288

Kim, E., & Cuskelly, G. (2017). A systematic quantitative review of volunteer management in events. *Event Management*, *21*(1), 83–100. https://doi.org/10.3727/152599517X14809630271195

Lyons, K., Hanley, J., Wearing, S., & Neil, J. (2012). Gap year volunteer tourism. Myths of global citizenship? *Annals of Tourism Research*, *39*(1), 361–378. https://doi.org/10.1016/j.annals.2011.04.016

Martinez, H., Jaime, A., & Camacho, J. (2012). Relative absorptive capacity: A research profiling. *Scientometrics*, *92*(3), 657–674. https://doi.org/10.1007/s11192-012-0652-6

McGehee, N. G. (2014). Volunteer tourism: Evolution, issues and futures. *Journal of Sustainable Tourism*, *22*(6), 847–854. https://doi.org/10.1080/09669582.2014.907299

McGehee, N. G., & Santos, C. A. (2005). Social change, discourse and volunteer tourism. *Annals of Tourism Research*, *32*(3), 760–779. https://doi.org/10.1016/j.annals.2004.12.002

Meng, B., Ryu, H. B., Chua, B. L., & Han, H. (2020). Predictors of intention for continuing volunteer tourism activities among young tourists. *Asia Pacific Journal of Tourism Research*, *25*(3), 261–273. https://doi.org/10.1080/10941665.2019.1692046

Monga, M. (2006). Measuring motivation to volunteer for special events. *Event Management*, *10*(1), 47–61. https://doi.org/10.3727/152599506779364633

NationMaster. (n.d.). *Volunteered your time*. https://www.nationmaster.com/country-info/stats/Lifestyle/Society/Volunteering-and-social-support/Volunteering/Volunteered-your-time

Palacios, C. M. (2010). Volunteer tourism, development and education in a postcolonial world: Conceiving global connections beyond aid. *Journal of Sustainable Tourism*, *18*(7), 861–878. https://doi.org/10.1080/09669581003782739

Paraskevaidis, P., & Andriotis, K. (2017). Altruism in tourism: Social exchange theory vs altruistic surplus phenomenon in host volunteering. *Annals of Tourism Research*, *62*, 26–37. https://doi.org/10.1016/j.annals.2016.11.002

Porter, A. L., Kongthon, A., & Lu, J.-C. C. (2002). Research profiling: Improving the literature review. *Scientometrics*, *53*(3), 351–370. https://doi.org/10.1023/A:1014873029258

Qi, H. (2021). Host volunteering in tourism as a voluntary exchange. *Current Issues in Tourism*, *24*(6), 857–870. https://doi.org/10.1080/13683500.2020.1758042

Raymond, E. M., & Hall, C. M. (2008). The development of cross-cultural (mis)understanding through volunteer tourism. *Journal of Sustainable Tourism*, *16*(5), 530–543. https://doi.org/10.2167/jost796.0

Simpson, K. (2004). "Doing development": The gap year, volunteer-tourists and a popular practice of development. *Journal of International Development*, *16*(5), 681–692. https://doi.org/10.1002/jid.1120

Sin, H. L. (2009). Volunteer tourism - "Involve me and I will learn?" *Annals of Tourism Research*, *36*(3), 480–501. https://doi.org/10.1016/j.annals.2009.03.001

Smith, K. A., Baum, T., Holmes, K., & Lockstone-Binney, L. (2014). Introduction to event volunteering. In K. A. Smith, L. Lockstone-Binney, K. Holmes, & T. Baum (Eds.), *Event volunteering: International perspectives on the event volunteering experience* (pp. 1–16). Routledge. https://doi.org/10.4324/9780203385906

Smith, K. A., & Holmes, K. (2012). Visitor centre staffing: Involving volunteers. *Tourism Management*, *33*(3), 562–568. https://doi.org/10.1016/j.tourman.2011.06.010

Smith, K. A., Lockstone-Binney, L., Holmes, K., & Baum, T. (Eds.). (2014). *Event volunteering: International perspectives on the event volunteering experience*. Routledge.

Smith, L. C. (1981). Citation analysis. *Library Trends*, *30*(1), 83–106.

Sudolska, A., Lis, A., & Błaś, R. (2019). Cloud computing research profiling: Mapping scholarly community and identifying thematic boundaries of the field. *Social Sciences*, *8*(4), art. 112. https://doi.org/10.3390/socsci8040112

Sudolska, A., Lis, A., & Chodorek, M. (2019). Research profiling for responsible and sustainable innovations. *Sustainability*, *11*(23), art. 6553. https://doi.org/10.3390/su11236553

van Eck, N. J., & Waltman, L. (2010). Software survey: VOSviewer, a computer program for bibliometric mapping. *Scientometrics*, *84*(2), 523–538. https://doi.org/10.1007/s11192-009-0146-3

van Eck, N. J., & Waltman, L. (2020). *VOSviewer Manual*. https://www.vosviewer.com/documentation/Manual_VOSviewer_1.6.15.pdf

Wearing, S. (2001). *Volunteer tourism: Experiences that make a difference*. CABI Publishing.

Wearing, S., & McGehee, N. G. (2013). Volunteer tourism: A review. *Tourism Management*, *38*, 120–130. https://doi.org/10.1016/j.tourman.2013.03.002

Wicker, P. (2017). Volunteerism and volunteer management in sport. *Sport Management Review*, *20*(4), 325–337. https://doi.org/10.1016/j.smr.2017.01.001

Wilson, J. (2000). Volunteering. *Annual Review of Sociology*, *26*, 215–240. https://doi.org/10.1146/annurev.soc.26.1.215

Zupic, I., & Čater, T. (2015). Bibliometric methods in management and organization. *Organizational Research Methods*, *18*(3), 429–472. https://doi.org/10.1177/1094428114562629

36

TRENDS IN VOLUNTEERING

Colin Rochester

Introduction

Writing a chapter on 'Trends in Volunteering' is challenging at any time but the task is made all the more demanding by the current uncertainty about the progress of the COVID-19 pandemic. This chapter has been written in August 2020 when the pandemic has not run its course and the full impact of the virus and the measures taken to control it – let alone their implications in the longer-term – cannot yet be known. It is, however, already clear that volunteering has been significantly affected by COVID-19 and both the ways in which people are involved in voluntary action and the nature of the volunteer experience will to some extent be shaped by the experience of the current crisis. In the circumstances the chapter will first review the trends in volunteering discernible before the onset of the pandemic, then discuss its impact on voluntary action and its implications, and conclude by outlining the possible ways in which we might expect to see the trends in volunteering continue.

This still leaves the author with the original challenge for the chapter – how to do justice to the full range of activities covered by the term volunteering and the variety of organisational contexts in which they take place. Much of the literature – practitioner and academic alike – concentrates its attention on just one form of voluntary action which has been characterised as 'the non-profit paradigm' (Lyons et al., 1998) or the 'default setting' for volunteering (Rochester, 2013). This assumes that volunteers are involved in making a contribution to the broad field of social welfare, are involved in the work of large formally structured organisations, and are 'managed' by members of the staff of those bodies. It ignores or excludes self-governing voluntary action by people involved in self-help, mutual aid and campaigning activities – 'the civil society paradigm' (Lyons et al., 1998) and volunteering as serious leisure (Stebbins, 1996) where volunteers engage in the fields of arts and culture and sports and recreation. The 'dominant paradigm' also fails to go beyond the formal, professionally staffed agency of the non-profit paradigm to include smaller, less structured and volunteer-led associations. In addition, the common division between formal volunteering – undertaken within organisations, and informal volunteering – undertaken between individuals – is increasingly recognised as blurred as the definition of what constitutes an organisation comes under scrutiny (see Billis, 2020, for a detailed examination of this form of hybridity).

DOI: 10.4324/9780367815875-43

This rather lengthy introductory section is justified by the need to ensure that we try to avoid the common fault of treating volunteering as a homogenous phenomenon and the risk of assuming that trends we may discern in some areas of volunteering will also apply to other – very different – forms of activity.

Overall trends: what the surveys tell us – and what they do not

A considerable amount of time, energy and funding has been invested in attempts to measure the extent and scale of volunteering both nationally and internationally. These have not led to much reliable data for measuring overall trends owing to inconsistent approaches to the methodology used and differences in ways of defining volunteering (Rochester et al., 2010). One possible exception to the failure to chart overall trends has been advanced by Lindsey and Mohan (2018) who argue that the 'headline rates' of volunteering activity in England have not changed significantly over the years. They report (Lindsey & Mohan, 2018, p. 61) that Beveridge's social researchers in the 1940s estimated that "up to one-third of adults were giving unpaid voluntary help at least once a month" which was strikingly similar to present day rates of engagement in regular formal volunteering. Despite the striking changes in the economic and social environment of Britain since 1979 and frequent government initiatives aimed at promoting volunteering (reviewed by Zimmeck, 2010), changes in the levels of voluntary action during this period are regarded by Lindsey and Mohan as insignificant.

The unlikelihood of major changes in the headline rates of volunteer participation may also be matched by the continuing existence of a 'civic core' of the 'old stalwarts' among the volunteering population. Following Reed and Selby's (2001) pioneering study in Canada, a study by Mohan and Bulloch (2012) has located a similar core of civic-minded people in England who constitute 30% of the population but contribute between 80% and 90% of the total hours given to pro-social activities.

Overall, then, the evidence from the rich survey data collected in the past 40 or so years in England suggest that the overall numbers participating in voluntary action have remained stable and that the great majority of the activities in which volunteers are involved are undertaken by a very active minority of them. On the other hand, volunteering has not stood still; there are important changes in the environment in which volunteering takes place and in the way volunteers are engaging in voluntary activity; these trends will be discussed in the next two sections of the chapter.

The changing environment for volunteering

Changing institutions and the weakening of social ties

The later years of the last century and the first two decades of the current one have witnessed a number of important changes in the way our social institutions have changed. While different societies may have experienced these changes in different ways, they all will have felt some impact from them. This is true of the basic building blocks of the family or household, of involvement in political systems, and on the changing role of the 'intermediate' institutions that serve to bridge the gap between these two poles.

In the case of the family, the 'traditional' examples of the 'nuclear family' composed of a – usually married – heterosexual couple and their children or the 'extended family' involving a number of members across two or three generations are less prevalent and have given way to what Evans and Saxton (2005) have termed the 'any way up' family: "Half a century ago a child", they write, "was typically a part of a broad family unit made up of grandparents and parents as well as a number of uncles, aunts, cousins and siblings". Over time, families have become 'taller' – children are less likely to know their grandparents – and 'narrower' – as they know fewer aunts, uncles and cousins. The growing tendency for divorce and separation between couples has led to increasing numbers of single-parent families: "[T]he widespread fracturing and restructuring of the family unit has resulted in some very complex and disjointed family arrangements" (2005, p. 16).

In most countries there has been a marked decline in the involvement of citizens in the conventional political system at a national and local level. Fewer people vote in general elections, and the membership of mainstream political parties – and active involvement in their activities – have fallen sharply. By contrast, there has been an increase of participation in single-issue politics and new kinds of campaigning activities for new kinds of causes (for the UK, see the Power Inquiry, 2006; Carnegie UK Trust, 2007).

And at the 'intermediate' level there has been a major shift in the nature of 'community': "Even though more people than ever are physically packed together in cities, they are becoming more rather less isolated socially" as the result of increased mobility (Zimmeck, 2001, p. 7). In many countries there has been a major shift towards secularisation and a loss of shared activity in religious adherence (Olson & Beckworth, 2011; Torry, 2014). And in the UK, there has been a similar decline in attendance at another – very different, British institution – the local public house.

Growth of consumerism and the impact of marketisation

The decline of traditional family, neighbourhood and community ties has been widely associated with a rising tide of individualism and increasing opportunities to exercise consumer choice. There is some evidence, however, that this has reached its apogee and that people are beginning to place more emphasis on seeking the kinds of well-being that cannot be achieved through consumption and are looking for better public spaces and better social connections with their communities (Carnegie UK Trust, 2007).

The extent to which these 'social' aspirations will be achieved is restricted by the extent to which our society has become 'marketised'. As Michael Sandel explains (2012, pp. 10–11): "A market society is a way of life in which market values seep into every aspect of human endeavor. It's a place where social relations are made over in the image of the market" and where market values have crowded out non-market norms in a whole series of arenas where public goods – 'the good things' in life – are corrupted or debased by being turned into commodities. While some commentators take the view that Sandel overstates his case, there can be little doubt that, in an increasingly 'marketised' society, there is a real threat to the values of volunteering.

Inequality and poverty

As in other highly developed countries, Britain has become wealthier since the 1970s and has managed to continue to grow richer despite the financial crisis of 2008 but this growing wealth has not been equally shared, and the gap between the richest and the poorest has widened and is continuing to widen (Equality Trust, 2017). According to the Joseph Rowntree Foundation, "14 million people live in poverty in the UK – over one in five of the population" (2017, p. 4.).

There are two specific places where the impact of rising poverty will be felt on volunteering. In the first place there are growing numbers of people whose position in the labour market has become more insecure. The use of 'zero hours' contracts, short-term employment contracts and the increasing use of the 'gig' economy have all contributed to large numbers of people whose hours of work and terms of employment make it difficult for them to commit to volunteering on any kind of regular basis (Wilson, 2017).

This has been exacerbated by the growing volatility of the housing market where the long-term security and stability provided by the provision of municipal and other social housing has become rarer and the growing gap in the need for housing has been filled by private landlords who increasingly deal in short-term tenancies. Growing numbers of households who may move house frequently and at short notice are unlikely to strike deep roots in the communities through which they may pass. As the population becomes increasingly transient, the opportunities for involvement in community life and voluntary action become more limited (DGCMS, 2020; Paris et al., 2014).

An ageing population

In common with other industrialised countries, Britain has experienced and is expected to continue to experience a very significant increase in the proportion of older people in its population. This has been due to a combination of an increasing number of older people and a decreasing number of younger ones. Between 1981 and 2003, for example, the number of people aged 65 and over rose by 28% while the number of people under 16 fell by 18% (Hughes, 2009). The Carnegie Trust (2007) has calculated that there will be more over 60s than under 25s by 2025.

The growing number of older people can be seen as an important plus for the size of the volunteer population: people who are living longer and remain in good health provide what is potentially, at least, a growing body of volunteers. On the other hand, the demand for volunteer help is likely to increase: the need for care and support for older people as they become frailer and more vulnerable will be a major concern as the population of older people increases.

A further area of concern is the impact on the cohort of potential volunteers of the growing numbers of carers required to meet the needs of older members of their own families. This will reduce the pool of volunteers available to meet the needs of older people outside the family circle.

Growing social isolation

A second important consequence of recent changes in the demography of the UK and other developed countries has been a major increase in the number of single-person households. This is an important contributory factor in the growth of problems of social isolation that volunteering has been seen as an important means of addressing (Ockenden, 2007), especially in the cases of older people (Low et al., 2007) and people experiencing mental health issues (Murray et al., 2008).

But the relationship between social isolation and volunteering is complex. On the one hand it is clear that volunteering can play an important role in addressing and overcoming isolation (Volunteer Now, 2017). On the other hand, there is no shortage of evidence that people who are isolated are unlikely to look for opportunities for volunteering or to take up those that are offered to them. Many of them lack the confidence and a shared culture of participation that encourage people into volunteering activities (Lim & Laurence, 2015).

The impact of the digital revolution

Perhaps the most significant set of changes in the current and future environment for volunteering involves the revolutionary impact of developments in internet technology and communications. The speed and scope of these developments are not easy to grasp – especially for the older generation which grew up before the arrival of the internet and does not have the facility of the later generation of 'digital natives' who are at home in this brave new world. For most of the older generation – and practically all of their juniors – the internet and its applications are part of their everyday life. As well as the ability to access and process data, digital technology has increasingly become the means of producing and publishing material, on the one hand, and a way of establishing and maintaining social contacts with large numbers of people, on the other (Rochester et al., 2010).

The younger generations

Arguably, the younger generations of 'Generation X' and 'Generation Y' not only have a significantly different experience of the electronic environment and use the new technology in new ways, but have also shaped their environment into a whole new set of social contacts and new ways of using them.

The members of Generation X were born between 1966 and 1976 and have been referred to as the first generation of 'latchkey' kids, exposed to lots of daycare and divorce. Known to have the lowest voting participation rate of any generation, they were described by *Newsweek* as the generation that "dropped out without ever turning on the news or tuning in to the social issues around them" (Schroer, 2017). Gen X is often characterised by high levels of scepticism and 'what's in it for me' attitudes. They have formed families with a higher level of caution and pragmatism than their parents demonstrated.

Their successors – Generation Y or the 'Millennials' – were born 1977–1994 and have been described as "incredibly sophisticated, technology wise, immune to most traditional marketing and sales pitches … as they not only grew up with it all, they've seen it all and been exposed to it all since early childhood" (Schroer, 2017, unpaginated). Generation Y are "less brand loyal and the speed of the Internet has led the cohort to be similarly flexible and changing in its fashion, style consciousness and where and how it is communicated with" (ibid). Members of this generation are unlikely to commit to longer term volunteering roles and can be expected to volunteer for short-lived experiences and changing commitments in line with the changing influences encountered on-line (op cir)

A new public administration regime?

Pestoff (2020) has suggested that a new communitarian public administration regime has begun to emerge in place of earlier regimes based on the concept of citizens as passive recipients of public services (the traditional) and on the notion that citizens should be seen as consumers (the new public management regime). Following the example of the UK Coalition Government's idea of the 'Big Society' in 2010 but also seen in Japan, Thailand and parts of Europe, this approach seeks to change the status of citizens by turning them into active co-producers of services. For Britain, this has meant major reductions in financial support for public services previously seen as an essential part of state provision and the expectation that the gaps thus created would be filled by voluntary action.

This major change has led to attempts to recruit increasing numbers of volunteers in public libraries, health and social care services, schools and in the police service where they are expected to make a significant contribution not only to balancing the books but also to enhancing the quality of service (Rochester et al., 2020).

Trends in volunteering attitudes and behaviour

The growth of managerialism

The combination of an approach to management drawn from the experience of private and public sector organisations and the impact of a number of external pressures has led to what Ellis Paine and her colleagues (2010, p. 99) have called "A dominant model of volunteer management ... with a common set of prescribed codes and good practices". This has increasingly displaced an earlier more 'home-grown' and less bureaucratic alternative approach to organising the work of volunteers (Zimmeck, 2001). Driven in part by the demands of funders and regulators and the needs to meet service levels and comply with contracts, this approach has also been adopted by the growing numbers of volunteer managers as a means of identifying their professional status. There is little doubt that the volunteer experience has been improved by the development of better ways through which their activities have been organised and supported; the finding from a 1997 survey that 71% of those contacted felt that their volunteering could be better organised (Davis Smith, 1998) is highly unlikely to be repeated. On the other hand, volunteers are unhappy with the overly formal and highly bureaucratised ways in which they are managed; some have stopped volunteering as a result and other potential volunteers have been discouraged from getting involved because of what they saw as excessive bureaucracy. And, perhaps most importantly, over formal approaches put at risk the sociability and team spirit that have been prized by many volunteers (Ellis Paine et al., 2010). As Gaskin (2003) has suggested what volunteers need is a 'choice blend', combining well organised volunteer roles and support with an informal and flexible approach to delivering them.

Volunteer roles and responsibilities

There is some evidence about the changes that have happened to the ways in which volunteers are involved in terms of the roles they undertake and the responsibilities they accept. Rochester et al. (2020) suggest that, as voluntary sector organisations increasingly take on some of the distinctive characteristics of the public and private sectors, many volunteers no longer play a part in shaping the mission and strategic purpose of the organisation and no longer exercise a considerable degree of autonomy over the ways in which they carry out their roles. Instead, they tend to be restricted to performing very specific functions designed by and subject to the supervision of paid managers. In the case of the growing numbers of volunteers involved in the public sector, the same authors have identified three models of volunteer involvement. In the first place, volunteers play an auxiliary role providing cheap labour or carrying out specific tasks not seen as essential functions for the paid staff. Second, volunteers can be seen as substitutes for paid staff and are treated in very much the same way as those they have replaced. And, in the third model, volunteers are seen to bring something distinctive to the organisation with which they are involved which adds a new dimension to the work of its paid staff.

A 'new model' of volunteering

The more limited, instrumental and 'managed' form of volunteer involvement outlined above fits very well into the new model of volunteering identified by Hustinx (2001) as an alternative to the 'classic' approach to volunteering. This is similar to the distinction made by Evans and Saxton (2005) between the decreasing number of 'time-driven' volunteers and the growing number of those who are 'cause-driven'. Rather than treating volunteering as a means of pursuing a cause, people are increasingly seeking specific experiences and rewards. This newer attitude to volunteering has been described by some Dutch organisations as a 'revolving door' approach (Dekker & Halman, 2003).

Similar changes in engagement in sports volunteering have been detected by Gratton and colleagues, who "concluded that a European trend towards more informal participation in health and fitness-related sports and a decline in more traditional team sports was replicated in England" (2011 quoted by Nichols, 2017, p. 16). This was seen as part of a

> change from a modernist society in which leisure is explained by structural factors such as occupation, ethnicity, sex and family roles to a post-modern one in which class and gender are replaced by more fluid identity politics and experiences are more individual than collective.
>
> *(Nichols, op cit.)*

Episodic volunteering

In concrete terms, this new model takes the form of 'episodic' volunteering which is widely reported to be a growing phenomenon (Hyde et al., 2014; Dunn et al., 2016). Older-style volunteers were typically involved in high levels of time and commitment to a cause and an organisation and might adapt their volunteering to the changing long-term needs of an organisation. Episodic volunteering was just one of the ways in which people used their time and was clearly limited in its scope and the amount of time involved and was expected to be intrinsically rewarding. The growth in episodic volunteering has been a positive trend for events. However, it is less beneficial for organisations that require ongoing volunteer roles, such as sports clubs seeking committee members.

The ways in which people take part in episodic volunteering vary quite significantly. Some commit themselves to a time and a task on one specific occasion (for example, at major sporting or cultural events); others may be involved in a series of events over a period of time; and a third group combined their episodic volunteering with long-term involvement within the same or another organisation (Macduff, 2005; Handy et al., 2006).

The ultimate form of episodic volunteering has been the recent development of micro-volunteering (NCVO, 2013) which, as Charlotte Jones suggests in the *Guardian*, takes a simple idea – that people are more likely to volunteer their time in short and convenient, bite-sized chunks – and turns it into a new approach to community action. (13th April, 2017). In 2016, 80% of micro-volunteering was carried out on line – usually on smart phones – mainly by young people and it has been most popular in the UK where more than half of all micro-volunteering actions took place in 2015.

Volunteering in a digital society

It is only very recently that we have begun to see just how radically the digital society has the capacity to change the way we go about volunteering. It has become fairly routine for the ways in which volunteering is organised to adapt to the new technology. It has become an important tool for communicating news about opportunities for volunteering to large numbers of people and without delay. It provides a means for potential volunteers to identify the cause with which they identify and the roles that they find most appropriate. And, perhaps most importantly, it has enabled people who find it difficult to leave their homes to find ways of involving themselves in voluntary action without going outside.

But these are largely about adapting existing activities for remote use. More recently social media has enabled people to engage in collective activities: groups have been able to meet and organise collective activities by using their social media connections and have drawn on their collective resources to negotiate with local government agencies and other bodies.

Change in the kinds of activity volunteers are involved in

Lindsey and Mohan's (2018) review of the data sources for the period 1979 to 2017 essentially reflects long-term continuity in the kinds of formal volunteering recorded in England; they refer to "broad stability in the activities being carried out by volunteers" (p. 217). And they go on to say that "when it comes to the groups and organisations assisted by volunteers, there is consistency in the rankings: sport, hobbies and recreation, religious groups, children's education and youth activities have remained at the top of the list" (p. 218). But there have been some changes: the proportion of those volunteering in the health, education and disability fields and those working with older people has fallen while those engaged in environmental groups has grown (Lindsey & Mohan, 2018, p. 91). One possible explanation for these changes is that volunteering is increasingly seen as an activity to be enjoyed for its own sake and not solely or primarily as a service to other people. Recreational activities remain very popular and the rising interest in the environment not only reflects popular concern about issues like climate change but also highlights the ways in which volunteering in tourism can be intrinsically rewarding.

Formal and informal volunteering

Another recent development in the ways in which researchers have studied volunteers has been the increased blurring of the clear distinction between formal and informal volunteering. Ellis Paine and her colleagues have suggested that it would be more helpful to introduce an intermediate category. Alongside 'organised' or formal volunteering and 'individual' or informal volunteering, they would add 'collective' volunteering undertaken in groups which are not formally constituted but come together to address a common need or interest (2014, pp. 18–19). Billis (2020) has explored the overlapping territory between the world of organisations and the personal world made up not only of family and friends but also groupings "that may be defined as the personal world arrangements for doing things" (p. 523). Two examples of the growth of this form of collective voluntary action are the prevalence of book clubs (Hartley, 2002; Billis, 2020) and food banks (Tyler, 2020). Many recreational activities are arranged along these lines: friends or workmates agree to play sport or games on a more or less regular basis while informal groups of people come together to join in a bike ride or an excursion to an interesting destination. These kinds of group activity require a basic level of coordination but do not demand the creation of a permanent or formal organisation.

The potential importance of these insights has been enhanced by some of the recent trends already noted above. Looser-knit forms of collective volunteering enable the involvement of the 'new model' of volunteering, are suitable for some forms of episodic volunteering, provide the framework for some virtual forms and may well offer ways through which Generations X and Y can develop opportunities for voluntary action.

Volunteering and COVID-19

The COVID-19 pandemic and the measures taken by government to slow the spread of infection have had a far-reaching impact both on the need for voluntary action and on the problems involved in participating in it. The dislocation of normal social life caused by the lockdown and restrictions on contact with other people brought the normal activities of many volunteers to an abrupt end. It has been suggested (by Grotz et al., 2020, pp. 14–15.) that many of the most regular volunteers had been put at risk of negative health outcomes "because they were self isolating as they were at additional risk or because their usual volunteering activities in charity shops, museums and stately homes – and of course hospitals – were suspended".

The impact of the lockdown on the wider community was also both significant and widespread: people faced not only practical difficulties such as shopping for food and other necessities and collecting medicines but the problems of social isolation and loneliness that might impinge of their mental health and well-being. Many people on low incomes and in insecure employment also found themselves in need of food and other essential items. Addressing these problems put acute pressure on statutory services and voluntary sector organisations and created the need for a large-scale response from volunteers.

This response took two forms. The first of these was an attempt by government to harness voluntary action in support of the health service and those at risk of the pandemic. This was a 'top-down' initiative aimed at recruiting volunteers to assist the work of the National Health Service by addressing four needs. These were: to collect and deliver shopping, medication or other essential supplies to vulnerable people; to provide transport for patients on discharge; to transport equipment, supplies or medication between National Health Service services and sites; and to provide telephone support to individuals at risk of loneliness. The programme was run on a national level and was designed to connect volunteers to those in need of their service by means of a specially designed 'app'.

The appeal was originally intended to recruit 250,000 volunteers but the response was so enthusiastic that the target was rapidly revised upwards and in the end the programme accepted 750,000 responses – the largest peacetime mobilisation of volunteers (Delany, 2020).

Unfortunately the scheme was ill-considered and poorly executed. The Association of Directors of Adult Social Services felt it was 'shameful' that local councils had not been involved in designing the programme and it had "diverted 750,000 volunteers away from supporting local communities and left them with nothing to do for the first three weeks of the epidemic" (Hill, 2020, unpaginated). Of the 750,000 who came forward, only 360,000 were approved and accepted onto the scheme and, of those, only 220,000 had been offered tasks by early July 2020. As a result, many who volunteered for the programme were given nothing to do despite waiting for as long as 90 hours on duty (Gregory, 2020: unpaginated).

The second form of response to the crisis in the shape of voluntary action was spontaneous activity by large numbers of individuals and groups. This included not only help from neighbours and friends but also the contribution of a variety of local groups, many of which seem to have appeared in response to the pandemic alongside existing organisations that had engaged with the impact of COVID-19. Almost 4,000 of these groups have been included in a central website for COVID-19 mutual aid groups across England and Wales (https://covidmutualaid.com) but this number is unlikely to include many groups that have come together on a very local level such as a group of residents in a block of flats or a local street.

This "rapid and large-scale mobilisation of community action" is involved in "fulfilling practical tasks such as grocery shopping and collecting medication, but also providing invaluable emotional support and advice to members of the community, many of whom are struggling with physical and mental health issues as well as economic disadvantage" (O'Dwyer, 2020, p. 2). And, alongside these activities, a completely new form of volunteering has sprung up in response to a nationwide shortage of 'scrubs' and other protective clothing and equipment for health and care workers. Described as "a network of voluntary community groups who love to sew, and are making scrubs to order for NHS staff who are struggling to get them during this crisis" (Scrub Hub, 2021), the scrubs movement is an innovative and flexible response to a very specific response to the pandemic.

The longer term impact of voluntary action on the different responses to the crisis is difficult to predict. Volunteer managers have three ongoing concerns about what will happen when the crisis is lifted: they are concerned about liability for those involved; sustainable safeguarding for vulnerable adults; and the anxiety to be expected on the part of those returning to volunteering (Grotz et al., 2020). The willingness of volunteers to return to their activities might also be affected by the abrupt ending of their involvement and a lack of enthusiasm to re-engage. The impact of the more or less spontaneous response to COVID-19 is more difficult to assess. Will the upsurge in mutual aid groups and the setting up of the scrubs movement lead to a new involvement in voluntary action or will these phenomena come to an end with the finish of the crisis? And will the use of social media prevalent in the new groups set a pattern for the ways in which volunteering will become increasingly the norm after COVID-19?

Some tentative conclusions

This chapter set out to identify trends in the many ways in which volunteering will develop in the future. It has suggested ways in which voluntary action might be affected by wider changes in the social environment; discussed how attitudes towards volunteering and the ways in which volunteers behave have changed; and made a tentative assessment of the ways in which the response of voluntary action to the pandemic might help to shape its future development.

We can identify a number of trends that are specific to different strands of volunteer activity, which can be placed on a spectrum from the most to the least formally organised context in which it takes place.

1   The most formally organised kind of volunteering has become increasingly organised and structured by the kind of modern managerial methods applied to human resource management. This development has enabled volunteer involving organisations to make maximum use of their volunteer workforce but has received mixed reactions from the volunteers themselves. It is a trend that will be reinforced by the increasing expectation that volunteers can fill the gaps in public service provision created by the emergent communitarian regime. This regime can also be adopted for the organisation and management of the large numbers of volunteers involved in major sporting events like the Olympic Games when each volunteer role needs to be carefully designed and implemented by the organisers. This managerial approach, however, excludes volunteers

from the roles some used to play in shaping the mission and strategic purposes of the organisation with which they are involved. It would thus be less suitable for community led events where volunteers are needed to play more strategic roles.

2   The newer models of volunteering associated (by Hustinx, Evans and Saxton and Nicholls among others) with a post-modern society can be seen as compatible with this very formal or 'managerial' approach. Volunteers tend to move from one organisation to another in search of the specific kinds of experiences that meet their personal expectations. A tightly organised and structured managerial organisation can offer volunteers clear and defined roles with which to meet their aspirations.

3   The increasingly widespread adoption of digital media may contribute to the managerial approach to volunteering: it is easier to find opportunities to get involved; it enables people to volunteer without leaving their homes; and helps them to select the cause or organisation they can support. On the other hand, social media provides alternative ways of involvement in voluntary action: people have been able to meet and organise their collective activities using Facebook and other applications. In particular the younger people who are 'digital natives' find this kind of involvement more natural than face-to-face meetings.

4   The rise of social media has made a major impact on the less formally organised forms of voluntary action often rather dismissively described as 'below the radar' organisations (Phillimore et al., 2010). The uncounted numbers of associations, more or less organised groups and informal groupings appear to have been increasing even without the spread of information technology – one estimate (Hartley, 2002, p. vii) put the number of book reading groups as high as 50,000 in the UK and 5,000,000 in the USA. But there can be little doubt that technology has given new emphasis to the growth in these kinds of collective voluntary activity including mutual aid groups, local campaigns, those involved in leisure activities, and others organised around the need to address social isolation and to foster sociability. It is difficult to assess the extent to which the growing numbers of less formal groupings are supplanting more 'traditional' kinds of volunteering but one trend that has been noted is a decline in the participation in some formally constituted sports clubs and an increase in less organised activities such as parkrun.

5   Some of these trends, at least, have been accentuated by the impact of COVID-19. While it is difficult to predict the longer-term consequences of this experience, some strengthening of the trends seems likely. Concern for the health and safety of volunteers and those with whom they interact will increase the tendency towards more managerial approaches to volunteering but may well make the involvement less attractive. The increased use of social media during the pandemic will facilitate more flexible forms of volunteering and add to the increased adoption of 'new' models. The upsurge in locally based and informal voluntary action may help to offset the weakening of social ties and growing isolation that have characterised recent developments.

This chapter has explored some of the ways in which various kinds of voluntary action have developed and how they may continue to change the ways in which people engage in volunteering. It has offered some tentative conclusions about the impact and longer-term implications of COVID-19 and the restrictions this has placed on social life. And, beyond that, it has aimed to illustrate how, while the overall rates of voluntary activity have remained stable, the different ways in which volunteers are involved have developed in an environment in which new challenges and opportunities take their place alongside continuing needs.

References

Billis, D. (2020). Hybrid organisations in the overlapping territory with the personal world in D. Billis and C. Rochester (eds.), *Handbook on hybrid organisations*. Edward Elgar, Cheltenham. DOI 01.4337/9781785366116

Carnegie UK Trust. (2007.) *The shape of civil society to come*. Carnegie UK Trust, London.

Davis Smith, J. (1998). *The 1997 survey of volunteering*. National Centre for Volunteering, London.

Dekker, P., & Halman L. (2003). *The values of volunteering: Cross-cultural perspectives*. Kluwer Academic/Plenum, New York.

Delany, S. (2020). *NHS Responders: The largest peacetime mobilisation of volunteers*. http//blogs.ncvo.org.uk/2020/04/06.

Department for Digital, Culture, Media and Sport (DGCMS) (2020). *Community life study 2019–2020*. Retrieved from https://www.gov.uk/government/statistics/community-life-survey-201920

Dunn, J., Chambers, S., & Hyde, M. (2016). Systematic review of motives for episodic volunteering. *Voluntas, 27*, 425–464. https://doi.org/10.1007/s11266-015-9548-4

Ellis Paine, A., Hill, M., & Rochester C. (2014). 'A rose by any other name': Revisiting the question 'what exactly is volunteering'. Working Paper 1: Institute for Volunteering Research, London.

Ellis Paine, A., Ockenden, N., & Stuart, J. (2010). Volunteers in hybrid organizations: A marginalized majority? In D. Billis (ed.), *Hybrid organizations and the third sector* (pp. 206–220). Basingstoke: Palgrave Macmillan.

Equality Trust. (2017). *The scale of economic inequality in the UK*. Retrieved from: https://www.equalitytrust.org.uk/scale-economic-inequality-uk

Evans, E., & Saxton, J. (2005). *The 21st century volunteer: A report on the changing face of volunteering in the 21st century*. nfpSynergy, London.

Gaskin, K. (2003). *A choice blend: What volunteers want from organisation and management*. Institute for volunteering Research, London.

Gregory, A. (2020). 140,000 NHS volunteers left idle. *Sunday Times*, 5th July.

Grotz, J., Dyson, S., & Birt, L. (2020). Health and wellbeing effects of cessation of volunteering on older adults. *Quality in Ageing and Older Adults, 20*(3). DOI 10/1108 OADA-07-2020-0032

Handy, F., Brodeur, M., & Cnaan, R. (2006) Summer on the island: Episodic volunteering. *Voluntary Action, 7*(3), 31–46.

Hartley, J. (2002). *Reading groups*. Oxford University Press, Oxford.

Hill, J. (2020). *Exclusive: Social service directors attack Whitehall COVID response*. Retrieved from https://www.lgcplus.com/politics/coronavirus/exclusive-social-services-directors-attack-whitehall-covid-19-response-15-04-2020/

Hughes, M. (2009). *Social trends 35*. Palgrave Macmillan, Basingstoke.

Hustinx, L. (2001). Individualisation and new styles of youth volunteering: An empirical investigation. *Voluntary Action, 3*(2), 47–55.

Hyde, M., Dunn J., Bax, C., & Chambers, S. (2014). Episodic volunteering and retention: An integrated theoretical approach. *Nonprofit and Voluntary Sector Quarterly, 45*(1), 45–63. https://doi.org/10.1177/0899764014558934

Jones, C. (2017.) *Microvolunteering: What is it and why should you do it?* Retrieved from https://www.theguardian.com/voluntary-sector-network/2017/apr/13/ on 10th November 2019.

Joseph Rowntree Foundation. (2017). *UK Poverty 2017*. Retrieved from: https://www.jrf.org.uk/report/uk-poverty-2017

Lim, C., & Laurence, J. (2015). Doing good when times are bad: Volunteering behaviour and economic hard times. *British Journal of Sociology, 66*(2), 319–344. https://doi.org/10.1111/1468-4446.12122

Lindsey, R., & Mohan, J. (2018). *Continuity and change in voluntary action*. The Policy Press, Bristol.

Low, N., Butt, S., Ellis Paine, A., & Davis Smith, J. (2007). *Helping out: A national survey of volunteering and charitable giving*. Cabinet Office, Office of the Third Sector, London.

Lyons, M., Wijkstrom, P., & Cary G. (1998). Comparative studies of volunteering: What is being studied? *Voluntary Action, 1*(1), 45–54.

Macduff, N. (2005). Societal changes and the rise of the episodic volunteer in J. Brudney (ed.) *Emerging areas of volunteering*. ARNOVA Occasional Paper 1 (2), ARNOVA, Indianapolis.

Mohan J., & Bulloch S. (2012). The idea of a 'civic core': What are the overlaps between charitable giving, volunteering, and civic participation in England and Wales? *Third Sector Research Centre, Working Paper 73*. TSRC, Birmingham.

Murray, J., Bellinger, S., & Easter, A. (2008). *Evaluation of capital volunteering, Fourth interim report.* Institute of Psychiatry, London

NCVO. (2013). *Micro volunteering on the rise.* Retrieved from https://www.ncvo.org.uk/about-us/media-centre/press-releases/484-micro-volunteering-on-the-rise-new-research

Nichols, G. (2017). Volunteering in community sports associations: A literature review. *Voluntaristics Review, 2*(1), 1–75. https://doi.org/10.1163/24054933-12340015

Ockenden, N. (2007). *Volunteering works: Volunteering and social policy.* Commission on the Future of Volunteering, London.

O'Dwyer, E. (2020). *COVID-19 mutual aid groups have the potential to increase intergroup solidarity – but can they actually do so?* Retrieved from https://blogs.lse.ac.uk/politicsandpolicy/covid19-mutual-aid-solidarity/ 11.08.2020

Olson, P., & Beckworth, D. (2011). Religious change and stability: Seasonality in church attendance from the 1940s to the 2000s. *Journal for the Scientific Study of Religion, 50*(2), 388–396. https://doi.org/10.1111/j.1468-5906.2011.01574

Paris, C., Palmer, J., & Williams, P. (2014). *Demographic change and housing need in Northern Ireland.* Northern Ireland Housing Executive, Belfast.

Pestoff, V. (2020). Public administration regimes and co-production in hybrid organisations in D. Billis and C. Rochester (eds.), *Handbook on hybrid organisations.* Edward Elgar, Cheltenham. DOI 01.4337/9781785366116

Phillimore, J., McCabe A., Soteri Proctor A., & Taylor, R. (2010). *Understanding the distinctiveness of small-scale third sector activity.* Third Sector Research Centre Working Paper 33.

The Power Inquiry. (2006). *Power to the people: The report of an independent enquiry into Britain's democracy.* York Publishing Services, York.

Reed P., & Selby K. (2001). The civic core in Canada: Disproportionality in charitable giving, volunteering and civic participation. *Nonprofit and Voluntary Sector Quarterly, 30*(4), 761–780. https://doi.org/10.1177/0899764001304008

Rochester, C. (2013). *Rediscovering voluntary action; the beat of a different drum.* Palgrave Macmillan, Basingstoke.

Rochester, C., Ellis Paine, A., & Hill, M. (2020). Volunteers and hybrid organisations in D. Billis and C. Rochester (eds.), *Handbook on hybrid organisations.* Edward Elgar, Cheltenham. DOI 01.4337/9781785366116

Rochester, C., Ellis-Paine, A., Howlett S., & Zimmeck M. (2010). *Volunteering in the 21st century.* Palgrave Macmillan, Basingstoke

Sandel, M. (2012). *What money can't buy: The moral limits of markets.* Harmondsworth, Allen Lane.

Schroer, W. J. (2017). *Generations X, Y, Z and others.* Retrieved from http://socialmarketing.org/archives/generations-xy-z-and-the-others/

Scrub Hub. (2021). *Scrub Hub.* Retrieved from https://scrubhub.org.uk

Stebbins, R. (1996). Volunteering: A serious leisure perspective. *Nonprofit and Voluntary Sector Quarterly, 2*(2), 211–224. https://doi.org/10.1177/0899764096252005

Torry, M. (2014). *Managing religion: The management of Christian religious and faith-based organisation.* Palgrave Macmillan, Basingstoke.

Tyler, G. (2020). *Food banks in the UK.* House of Commons Library Briefing Paper Number 8585 15 July 2020.

Volunteer Now. (2017.) *Volunteering and combating social isolation and loneliness: A report of a survey into the link between volunteering and combating social isolation in older people.* Volunteer Now, Belfast.

Wilson, B. (2017). *What is the 'gig' economy?* Retrieved from http://www.bbc.co.uk/news/business-38930048

Zimmeck, M. (2001). *The right stuff: New ways of thinking about managing volunteers.* Institute for Volunteering Research. London.

Zimmeck, M. (2010). Government and volunteering: Towards a history of policy and practice in C. Rochester, A. Ellis-Paine, S. Howlett & M. Zimmeck (eds.), *Volunteering in the 21st century.* Palgrave Macmillan, Basingstoke.

37

INFORMAL VOLUNTEERING

Lili Wang

Introduction

Volunteering is a pro-social behaviour that provides "help to others, a group, an organization, a cause, or the community at large, without expectation of material reward" (Musick & Wilson, 2008, p. 3). It is done in leisure time, involving the allocation of free time to non-obligatory and uncoerced activities (Downward, Hallmann & Rasciute, 2020), and considered *serious leisure* by some scholars (i.e., Stebbins, 1996).

A broad definition of volunteering includes both formal and informal volunteering. Formal volunteering (FV) has been a topic of interest for decades, yet scholarly interest in informal volunteering (INV) is fairly nascent. While it remains an understudied topic compared to FV, the literature on INV has grown significantly in recent years. This chapter provides a review of the extant literature on INV, focusing on the definition and measurement of INV, the scope and variation of INV by countries, factors that shape INV, the relationship between FV and INV, and the benefits of INV, proposes future research on INV, and concludes with the implication of INV research on policies and practices.

Definition and measurement of informal volunteering

Although volunteering is a seemingly easy concept, defining what it exactly means and what activities are included is not an easy task (Carson, 1999). Scholars continue to debate how to accurately describe and measure volunteering. Should activities benefiting the volunteer's family or friends be considered volunteering? Should volunteering include compulsory participation, such as ex-offenders performing court-ordered community services? Should participating in volunteer programs that pay stipends or scholarships, such as the Peace Corps and AmeriCorps programs in the US, be considered volunteering? Is helping a sick neighbour with yardwork a volunteering activity and how is it different from performing these tasks for someone through one's church? Is self-organized mutual help in immigrant communities volunteering if these help activities are not organized by any institutions (Carson, 1999; Salamon, Sokolowski & Haddock, 2011)? Given all these questions on volunteering, it is "unlikely that a single definition can cover the different manifestations of volunteering across cultures and capture and neatly explain all

DOI: 10.4324/9780367815875-44

of the conceptual difficulties" (Carson, 1999, p. 69), which explains the variety of definitions and measurements of volunteering we see in the literature.

Western studies of volunteering used to focus predominantly on FV, particularly in the field of leisure volunteering as it is mostly done in a formal setting. However, more scholars and institutions (i.e., the United Nations General Assembly) have started to adopt a broader definition of volunteering, including both FV and INV (Gavelin & Svedberg, 2011). Formal volunteering refers to any volunteering activities that are undertaken through a group, club, formal organization or government program, such as museums, visitor information centres, parks, sporting, and other types of events, while informal volunteering is engaging in some unpaid helping activity not coordinated by a formal organization (Einolf et al., 2016; Wang, Mook & Handy, 2017). While there is no uniform definition of INV, scholars generally agree that INV takes place outside of the organizational context or formal settings (Lee & Brudney, 2012). It may include a number of unpaid, informal neighbourly support activities (e.g. doing yardwork, providing child care, coaching sports to kids in the neighbourhood, taking care of pets, cooking meals, doing household repairs, helping someone move, helping with shopping and errands, and offering rides to appointments), and other unpaid activities helping a stranger, such as a homeless or hungry person, which are not usually thought of as volunteering (Cnaan et al., 1996; Einolf et al., 2016). Although simply helping out or informally volunteering is not viewed as serious leisure, it still involves the allocation of leisure time to nonobligatory and uncoerced activities that are intentionally productive and altruistic (Downward et al., 2020; Stebbins, 1996, 2013).

As INV encompasses a myriad of helping activities, scholars have developed typology or classification of INV to further our understanding of the helping behaviour. For example, using factor analysis, Finkelstein and Brannick (2007) group INV into people-oriented and task-oriented INV. The former includes helping a homeless or hungry person, child or teenager, disabled person, or immigrant, helping one's neighbourhood or community, bringing people of one's ethnic background together, advancing the rights of minorities, babysitting without pay, and helping someone move. The latter includes helping take care of animals, housework, yard or maintenance work, shopping or driving to appointments, helping with the operation of a business, making food, and helping with renovations. Some scholars divide INV into two categories, helping people known personally, which is a planned and repeated helping behaviour, and helping strangers, which is almost always spontaneous (Amato, 1990). Most INV is directed at people one knows, and helping strangers is less common. INV for friends, neighbours, and other familiar individuals is more likely to occur in social groups or communities that have strong norms of reciprocity and mutual assistance as members of these groups may believe helping friends, acquaintances, and other community members is the neighbourly thing to do when there is a need. They may risk losing status and friendships or even be ostracized from the group if they refuse to help others when they are needed (Einolf et al., 2016).

Volunteering in the sports, tourism, and events area is mostly formal volunteering done through an organization or in an organized way, and therefore there is no systematic study of informal volunteering in these areas. However, there are some traditionally informal volunteering activities, such as helping travellers via couch surfing and hitchhiking or riding sharing, which have recently become more formalized through organizations or online platforms. For example, CouchSurfing.com is an online platform where members locate accommodations while traveling by staying in the homes of other members (Rosen, Lafontaine & Hendrickson, 2011). Additionally, some participants' self-organized volunteering activities started as informal volunteering but later become organized. For example, organizing a casual run in the park is now Parkrun.

The informal and spontaneous nature of INV also presents certain challenges to accurate measurement of this type of helping behaviour. For example, local residents may not recall offering a lift to tourists or may not consider it informal volunteering.

Many surveys collect information on FV, but only a few ask questions on INV or both types of volunteering. For example, the Charity Aid Foundation (CAF) World Giving Index (WGI) survey asks whether the respondent has helped a stranger or someone he/she did not know who needed help, volunteered time to an organization, and donated money to a charity in the past month. It measures INV as helping a stranger, which leads to great underestimation as most INV is done for friends, neighbours, and other acquaintances. The survey is conducted annually since 2010 and 128 countries have participated in at least eight surveys in the last ten years (Charity Aid Foundation, 2019). The 2001 International Social Survey Program (ISSP) is another cross-national survey examining INV in 27 countries. It asks respondents "During the past 12 months, how often have you done any of the following things for people you know personally, such as relatives, friends, neighbours or other acquaintances?": (1) "Helped someone outside of your household with housework or shopping"; (2) "Lent quite a bit of money to another person"; (3) "Spent time talking with someone who was a bit down or depressed"; (4) "Helped somebody to find a job". The INV in this survey only measures informal helping of people known personally, not strangers.

The 2001 Independent Sector (IS) Giving and Volunteering in the United States (G&V) survey collects information on FV and INV (Toppe, Kirsch & Michel, 2002). To assess INV, the survey asks, "In the past month, did you volunteer some of your time to help relatives who didn't live with you, including children and parents, neighbours, friends, or strangers? Please do not include help given to people living in your household." This question measures informal help to both people one knows and strangers, providing a more accurate measure of INV. The 2008 General Social Survey (GSS) of Canada asks questions on the number of hours a respondent spent last week on informal care (e.g., providing unpaid care or assistance to one or more seniors living outside of his/her household) and informal help (e.g., doing unpaid housework, yardwork, or home maintenance for persons living outside of his/her household). The various ways that these surveys ask questions about INV suggest that it is critical for scholars who study INV to be aware of the different measurements across studies and be extra careful in making comparisons and conclusions based on the data of INV of different groups or countries.

The accurate measurement of INV can also be challenged by recall bias. People often fail to recall INV when responding to surveys due to its commonplace and episodic nature, resulting in underestimation of its prevalence. Time-use diaries can help alleviate recall bias (Einolf et al., 2016). Havens and Schervish (2001) find that people reported almost three times as much informal volunteering hours in time diaries as they did in the IS G&V survey, suggesting that time diary is a better methodology at estimating INV than survey or interview questions.

The scope of informal volunteering in various countries

Informal volunteering is the most common help behaviour predates the existence of formal voluntary associations. Compared with FV and state assistance, INV "has historically been the most important way that people received assistance when they needed it" (Einolf et al., 2016, pp. 224–225). Today, INV is still more common than FV in most countries. A study using Johns Hopkins Project data indicates that approximately 971 million people volunteer in a typical year across the globe, with 36% being formal volunteers and 64% being informal volunteers (Salamon et al., 2011).

As INV is not coordinated by a formal organization, its prevalence is not dependent on the development of formal voluntary associations in a country. Hence, the rates of INV can be similar between industrialized countries, where formal associations are more developed, and non-industrialized ones. For instance, the WGI survey finds that INV, or helping a stranger, is not significantly correlated with gross domestic product (GDP) (CAF, 2019). Over the last decade, an average of nearly half (48.3%) of the world's adults have helped a stranger, and the top-ranked 11 countries in INV include Liberia (77%), Sierra Leone (74%), US (72%), Kenya (68%), Zambia (67%), Uganda (66%), Nigeria (66%), Iraq (65%), Canada (64%), Malawi (64%), and New Zealand (64%). Seven of the top countries where people are most likely to help a stranger are located in Africa and only three of the top-ranked countries are developed countries. The high rates of informal help in African countries is likely a result of Ubuntu, a philosophy that guides the way people live across almost all of Africa. It can be described as "the capacity in an African culture to express compassion, reciprocity, dignity, humanity and mutuality in the interests of building and maintaining communities with justice and mutual caring" (CAF, 2019, p. 15).

In addition to cross-country comparative studies, several country-specific studies have examined the scope of INV. For example, the 2001 IS G&V survey of US finds that 61% of respondents volunteered informally in the past month and those volunteers spent an average of 26 hours in the month on these activities (Toppe et al., 2002). A 2016 national study of volunteerism in Australia indicates that 46% of respondents participated in INV in the last 12 month (PwC, 2016). The *United Kingdom Civil Society Almanac 2020* reports that 52% of people volunteered informally at least once in 2018–2019, and 26% of people took part in INV regularly (NCVO, 2020). The first national volunteer survey in Mexico, the 2008 National Survey on Solidarity and Volunteer, finds that 66% of the adult Mexicans (41.4 million) volunteered and 32% of the volunteers participated in an individual manner, 24% participated in informal groups (i.e., with neighbours and friends), and 44% volunteered in a formal institution. Scholars believed that a majority of voluntary activity in Mexico is informal as legal and fiscal circumstances do not foster the creation of formal civil society organizations in the country and there is an underlying mistrust of individuals towards Mexican institutions as well as a lack of culture of formal group participation (Butcher, 2010).

The scope of INV in various countries suggests that it is more prevalent than FV and it does not depend on the economic development or the development of formal associations in a country.

Factors that shape informal volunteering

The literature shows that INV are associated with individuals' demographic and socio-economic characteristics (i.e., age, gender, race/ethnicity, immigration status, education, income), available time, the influences of family and culture (i.e., family structure, religiosity), health status, psychologic motivations, social capital, and local connections. Additionally, contextual factors, such as community features and a country's historical background, influence INV.

Regarding demographic characteristics, studies show that older Americans are more likely to engage in INV (Finkelstein & Brannick, 2007; Lee & Brudney, 2012). The 2003 AARP survey of Americans aged 45 and older shows that 51% of respondents volunteered for organizations and an additional 36% of respondents performed INV activities that benefit specific individuals or the community as a whole (Finkelstein & Brannick, 2007). This is likely due to the greater need for help among the peer social networks of older people or the need of childcare. However, the association between age and INV is inconsistent in other countries. For example, the 2008–2009 Citizenship Survey in the United Kingdom (UK) shows that people aged 16 to 25 were regular informal volunteers (38%) compared with those aged 26 to 64 (33–34%) (Drever, 2010), while the ONS UK Time Use Survey 2000 indicates that age is positively associated with INV (Egerton & Mullan, 2008).

Women are consistently more likely to engage in INV than men in countries such as the UK, Switzerland, Germany, Australia, and US (Bittman & Fisher, 2006; Egerton & Mullan, 2008; Gundelach, Frietag & Stadelmann-Steffen, 2010; Hank & Stuck, 2008; Helms & McKenzie, 2014; Hook, 2004; Lee & Brudney, 2012). Wang and co-authors (2017) find that women are more likely to provide unpaid care for children and assist seniors outside of household than men, but less likely to provide informal help with house/yardwork, in Canada. Using data from the 2004 Survey of Health, Ageing and Retirement in Europe, Hank and Stuck (2008) indicate that women aged 50 and above in 11 European countries are more likely to care for a sick or disabled adult or provide help to family, friends, or neighbours than men.

Scholars argue that racial/ethnic minorities and immigrants have a richer tradition of mutual help and close kinship, and thus are more likely to engage in INV (Carson, 1999; Wilson & Musick, 1997), but the empirical results are mixed. Lee and Brudney (2012) find that for African American or Hispanic/Latino in the US, INV is a more dominant type of volunteering than FV; yet they are as likely as other racial/ethnic groups to volunteer informally. However, another study shows that 41% of African-Americans 45 and older volunteered informally, compared with 36% of whites (Rozario, 2006). In Canada, immigrants are found to be less likely to provide informal help with house/yardwork than native-born Canadians (Wang et al., 2017). Similarly, Gundelach et al. (2010) show that foreigners involve less in informal voluntary activities than Swiss nationals.

Education is a human capital that increases FV. Its relationship with INV is inconsistent in the literature. Educational attainment is not significantly associated with INV in Switzerland (Gundelach et al., 2010). Lee and Brudney (2012) and Wang et al. (2017) report similar findings in the US and Canada, respectively. However, Plagnol and Huppert (2010) find that better educated people are more engaged in INV in 23 European countries. Higher education level is also found to be related to INV among elderly Dutch (Cramm & Nieboer, 2015). In terms of income, some studies show that income does not affect INV (Wang et al., 2017), while others find that household income is positively associated with the likelihood of INV (Lee & Brudney, 2012), yet another study of INV in southern Africa (Wilkinson-Maposa & Fowler 2009) shows that INV is the most common type among poor people in that region.

Time spent in paid work, study, leisure activities, and family care all influence the time available for voluntary work. Egerton and Mullan (2008) find that time spent on other activities reduces INV in the UK. Time spent on paid work, house work, domestic care, and educational activities also lowers the propensity of INV according to the 2009 American Time Use Survey, but time with family members and friends both increase INV (Taniguchi, 2011). Additionally, retired people are found to be more likely to help with house/yardwork for friends and neighbours than full-time employees in Canada (Wang et al., 2017). Similarly, non-working and part-time workers engage more frequently in INV than full-time workers in Switzerland (Gundelach et al., 2010).

Family structure, particularly the number and the age of children, influences the amount of house work, and thus may affect the amount of time people can spend on INV. On the other hand, having children will shape people's social network, making them more aware of the need of care in the community, and hence increase their chances of helping others.

Hook (2004) finds that the number of children less than five years old increases the probability of providing informal support in Australia, and having a child at home increases INV in Switzerland (Gundelach et al., 2010). However, Taniguchi (2011) indicates that having children aged 6 or younger, and between 6 and 12 both lower the propensity of INV in the US. The 2006 European Social Survey also shows that having a child at home lowers the chance of INV (Plagnol & Huppert, 2010). Additionally, Wang et al. (2017) find that having more children living in the household increases the propensity of helping others in taking care of their children or assisting seniors, but lowers the chance of helping others with house/yardwork.

Family and culture influences on INV are also manifested in parents' influence on children and religiosity. Parents are role models for their children and religions encourage people to be more empathetic. Studies suggest that children whose parents had volunteered and who were active in religious organizations were more inclined to engage in INV as adults (Jones, 2000; Perks & Haan, 2011). Plagnol and Huppert (2010) reveal that religious people are more engaged in INV in 23 European countries of their study. Interestingly, the study also finds that those who held the cultural values of benevolence (the desire to enhance the welfare of people who are close to the individual), universalism (the desire to protect the welfare of all of society and nature), hedonism (seek pleasure for themselves), and achievement (aim for personal success) all engage more in INV, while only those who value power (aim of gaining social status and control over other people) are less engaged in INV.

Voluntary engagement relies on individuals' physical and mental health. Healthy individuals are more engaged in INV in Europe (Plagnol & Huppert, 2010). Among Dutch independently living older adults aged 70 and above, social function is positively associated with INV in the baseline year of 2011, and older adults with lower levels of physical function are less likely to engage in INV two years later (Cramm & Nieboer, 2015). Studies have also examined the association between psychologic motivations and INV. Finkelstein and Brannick (2007) show that six motivations of the 'Volunteer Functions Inventory' (Clary et al., 1998), role identity, and prosocial personality predict informal volunteering in a similar way they predicted FV.

Concerning social capital, studies indicate that membership in religious and secular organizations is positively related to INV in the US and Canada (Lee & Brudney, 2012; Wang et al., 2017). Similarly, Plagnol and Huppert (2010) show that individuals who are more socially integrated (i.e., meet people, take part in social activities, attend religious services) engage more in INV in Europe. Cramm and Nieboer (2015) find that Dutch older adults' social capital, measured by a combined score of group membership, support from groups and support from individuals, trust, social harmony, sense of belonging and sense of fairness, is positively and consistently associated with their INV at baseline as well as two years later.

Social connections tend to grow as individuals live longer in a community, and thus INV is likely to increase with the length of local residence. Wang et al. (2017) show that the length of time a person has lived in current city or local community is positively associated with informal care and informal house/yardwork in Canada. Gundelach et al. (2010) also find that duration of residence is positively associated with INV in Switzerland.

In addition to individuals' characteristics, studies have also examined contextual factors that shape INV. For example, the 2000 General Household Survey shows that INV is more common than FV in UK's Northern regions which are poor and losing population (Williams, 2003). The degree of urbanization has a negative impact on INV in Switzerland (Gundelach et al., 2010). Additionally, a region's cultural and institutional background shapes the INV of its residents. The German-speaking regions which are liberal have a significantly higher level of INV than the French-speaking and Italian-speaking regions which are conservative (Gundelach et al., 2010).

In sum, individuals' socio-demographics, available time, family and culture influences, health, motivations, social capital, and local connections, as well as the socioeconomic, cultural, and institutional context of a community or a country shape INV.

Formal volunteering and informal volunteering

FV and INV are two distinct types of voluntary behaviour. The question is whether they compete with one another or they complement each other. Scholars who hold the 'competition hypothesis' would argue that individuals involved in FV would be less likely to provide informal help to others as they have finite amount of time, and therefore FV and INV would have a negative correlation (Plagnol & Huppert, 2010). In contrast, those who support the 'complement hypothesis' would argue that individuals involved in FV are more likely to engage in INV, or vice versa, as they tend to be altruistic, care about others, or have a high motivation to help others, and therefore we would observe a positive correlation between FV and INV (Hank & Stuck, 2008; Lee & Brudney, 2012; Taniguchi, 2011).

The relationship between FV and INV may vary by socio-demographic groups and the social, cultural, and political context of countries. Several scholars have examined FV and INV among older adults in different countries, which provide empirical support of either the 'competition hypothesis' or 'complement hypothesis'. In a study exploring barriers to participating in FV among older non-volunteers in Western Australia, Pettigrew et al. (2017) find that individuals who provide informal help to family and friends felt too committed to also engage in FV, supporting the 'competition hypothesis'. The competition between the two types of volunteering are evident in three factors: temporal factors (the time taken to perform INV duties), logistical factors (the need to be flexible to accommodate short-notice requests for assistance from family and friends), and psychological factors (the cognitive dissonance associated with cancelling the FV commitments which clash with the INV commitments that were of higher priority). However, based on the German Survey on Volunteering 2014, Simonson (2017) finds that the rates of FV and INV among people aged 65 years and older are similar (34% vs. 31.8%) with a positive correlation. The study also shows that less educated individuals have lower participation rates in both forms of volunteering, suggesting restrictions for individuals with fewer resources to participate in volunteering. In another study of older migrants living in Germany using the same survey data, Vogel (2017) finds that volunteering opportunities are unequally distributed and migrants are less likely to volunteer in formal organizations than citizens born in Germany. However, migrants aged 50 and above are found to be as likely to volunteer informally as older non-migrants. Additionally, older migrants who volunteer formally are also more likely to volunteer informally, suggesting that INV provides immigrants an additional rather than an alternative route into social participation.

Studies also show that FV and INV vary by gender. Using a Time Use Survey in Germany, Helms and McKenzie (2014) find strong evidence that women are more likely to volunteer formally if they also volunteer informally, which suggests that the decisions of these two types of volunteering are complementary. However, for men the decisions of FV and INV are not significantly related. Moreover, people of different social status may engage in FV and INV differently. Perpék (2012) compared FV and INV in Hungary and found that the groups of formal and informal volunteers significantly differ from each other. FV is preferred by higher social status holders, and moved by 'modern' motivations.

The relationship between FV and INV may also be shaped by countries' social, cultural, and political contexts. For example, social welfare countries, where government provides various social services, may have little need of informal helping, and thus *crowd out* informal volunteering (Gundelach et al., 2010).

Benefits of informal volunteering

As a productive activity that individuals engage in during leisure time, INV not only generates economic values to the society, but also contributes to the overall well-being of the volunteers.

Concerning the economic values, Egerton and Mullan (2008) estimate that INV contributes £15 billion per annum to the UK economy, which is much higher than that of FV (£5.6 billion). Additionally, women contribute more to the economy through INV than men. In Australia, the estimated value of the time donated to welfare services by volunteers reached $27.4 billion, about twice the amount spent by all government and non-government sources, and informal help to family, friends, and neighbours accounted for over two-thirds of the estimated value of services (Bittman & Fisher, 2006).

Scholars suggest that helping others, either through FV or providing informal help to social network members, can enhance the self-esteem of helpers, make them believe that they can have greater control over their own lives, and help them shift their focus away from the problems they may be grappling with, and thus lead to better physical and mental health (Krause, 2009). While INV should arguably provide many of the same health benefits as FV, the empirical findings remain inconclusive. Some studies indicate a positive association between INV and volunteers' well-being. For example, using a panel data of older religious congregation members in the US, Krause (2009) shows that those who provide informal help to their coreligionists tend to have better self-rated health over time. Plagnol and Huppert (2010) also find that INV is positively associated with level of happiness, a sense of accomplishment, a sense of doing something worthwhile, and a multi-item measure of positive effect in all 23 European countries in their study.

Other studies show that INV can help widows cope with their loss and recover from depression (Brown et al., 2008; Li, 2007). However, a study of FV and INV and health across Mediterranean European Countries shows that INV is negatively associated with self-perceived health in Italy (Fiorillo & Nappo, 2015). Furthermore, Li and Ferraro (2005) found that FV reduces depressive symptoms among older adults in the US, but INV does not help. These inconsistent findings suggest that the relationship between INV and health may be mediated by some other factors (Einolf et al., 2016). For example, a study of older Americans finds that INV only increases positive impact and decreases negative impact among Black men and White women (McIntosh & Danigelis, 1995).

The literature suggests that the benefits of INV go beyond the economic values it generates and the health benefits it brings to volunteers. INV can strengthen social connections among community residents, help build community culture and spirit, make people care for their environment and the people around them, and enhance the capacity of community members to resolve some problems themselves (Bittman & Fisher, 2006; Williams, 2003).

Future research

Given that INV remains a relatively new and understudied research topic, future studies can focus on the following areas to advance our knowledge of this pro-social behaviour across the globe.

First, surveys on INV need to include informal help provided to friends, neighbours, or other acquaintances as well as to strangers. Existing surveys vary significantly on the questions regarding INV. Some focus on help provided to strangers, while others focus on help directed at people one knows. Future surveys should include both categories of informal help to have a better measurement of INV, for example, informal help provided to tourists and sports coaching for kids in the neighbourhood. Additionally, developing some common survey questions on INV would allow cross-national comparative study and a meaningful comparison of the scope of INV across studies.

Second, existing studies of INV primarily come from western developed countries, such as the US, UK, Canada, Australia, and European countries. Scholars need to focus more on INV in other nations, such as countries in Asia, Africa, and South America, examining the factors that shape informal volunteering in these countries with different social, cultural, and political context. For example, the culture of hospitality towards guests in some countries may lead to informal help provided to tourists.

Third, many existing studies on the potential benefits of INV uses cross-sectional rather than longitudinal data, which cannot establish the direction of causality. In addition, most existing studies on the benefits of INV focus on its benefits to individuals. Future efforts can be made to conduct more longitudinal studies of INV and examine its benefits to the broader communities, such as community cohesion and community safety.

Conclusion

With the growing devolution of government responsibilities and increasing demand for social services in the past few decades, countries around the world have been relying more on volunteers to meet human needs. INV is an important way people directly help others. It is more common than FV and its prevalence is not constrained by the economic development or the development of formal associations of a country.

Previous research shows that older adults, women, people with time (e.g., retired or part-time employees), religious, healthy, having strong social capital, and local connections are more likely to engage in INV, and most studies indicate that people who engage in INV are also more likely to volunteer formally, meaning that the two leisure activities complement each other. The findings suggest that targeting informal volunteers could be a cost-effective strategy for public and nonprofit programs to recruit formal volunteers.

The economic contribution of INV and its impact on volunteers and communities imply that encouraging informal volunteering could be an effective community building tool. Government agencies or nonprofit organizations can facilitate INV by providing a platform that shares information on help needed in the community and establishing a mechanism to reward INV. Examples of current policies implemented include Local Exchange and Trading Schemes, time banks, and 'employee mutuals' in the UK (Williams, 2004). These policies will likely promote a participatory culture and encourage a productive use of leisure time.

While informal volunteering has not been systematically studied in the sports, events, and tourism areas, scholars can examine self-organized voluntary activities, such as sports coaching, book clubs, or other mutual aid groups in communities, and local residents' spontaneous helping behaviour towards tourists. The extant literature may help advance the future research of informal volunteering in sports, events, and tourism.

References

Amato, P. R. (1990). Personality and social network involvement as predictors of helping behavior in everyday life. *Social Psychology Quarterly, 53*, 31–43. https://doi.org/10.2307/2786867

Bittman, M., & Fisher, K. (2006). *Exploring the economic and social value of present patterns of volunteering in Australia*. Social Policy Research Paper No. 28. Department of Families, Community Services and Indigenous Affairs, Canberra, Australia.

Brown, S. L., Brown, R. M., House, J. S., & Smith, D. M. (2008). Coping with spousal loss: Potential buffering effects of self-reported helping behavior. *Personality and Social Psychology Bulletin, 34*, 849–886. http://doi.org/10.1177/0146167208314972

Butcher, J. (2010). Mexican solidarity: Findings from a national study. *Voluntas, 21*, 137–161. http://doi.org/10.1007/s11266-010-9127-7

Carson, E. D. (1999). On defining and measuring volunteering in the United States and abroad. *Law and Contemporary Problems, 62*(4), 67–71. http://doi.org/10.2307/1192267

Charity Aid Foundation. (2019). *CAF World Giving Index: Ten years of giving Trends*. Retrieved from https://www.cafonline.org/docs/default-source/about-us-publications/caf_wgi_10th_edition_report_2712a_web_101019.pdf

Clary, E. G., Snyder, M., Ridge, R., Copeland, J., Haugen, J., & Miene, P. (1998). Understanding and assessing the motivations of volunteers: A functional approach. *Journal of Personality and Social Psychology, 74*, 1516–1530. http://doi.org/10.1037//0022-3514.74.6.1516

Cnaan, R., Handy, F., & Wadsworth, M. (1996). Defining who is a volunteer: Conceptual and empirical considerations. *Nonprofit and Voluntary Sector Quarterly, 25*(3), 364–383. http://doi.org/10.1177/0899764096253006

Cramm, J. M., & Nieboer, A. P. (2015). Background characteristics, resources and volunteering among older adults (aged≥ 70 years) in the community: A longitudinal study. *Geriatrics & Gerontology International, 15*(8), 1087–1095. https://doi.org/10.1111/ggi.12404

Downward, P., Hallmann, K., & Rasciute, S. (2020). Volunteering and leisure activity in the United Kingdom: A longitudinal analysis of males and females. https://doi.org/10.1177/0899764020901815

Drever, E. (2010). *2008–09 citizenship survey: Volunteering and charitable giving topic report*. United Kingdom Department for Communities and Local Government. Retrieved from https://www.bl.uk/collection-items/200809-citizenship-survey-volunteering-and-charitable-giving-topic-report#

Egerton, M., & Mullan, K. (2008). Being a pretty good citizen: An analysis and monetary valuation of formal and informal voluntary work by gender and educational attainment. *British Journal of Sociology, 59*, 145–164. https://doi.org/10.1111/j.1468-4446.2007.00186.x

Einolf, C. J., Prouteau, L., Nezhina, T., Ibrayeva, A. R. (2016). Informal, unorganized volunteering. In D. H. Smith, R. A. Stebbins & J. Grotz (eds.). *The Palgrave handbook of volunteering, civic participation, and nonprofit associations* (pp. 223–241). Palgrave Macmillan: London, United Kingdom.

Finkelstein, M. A., & Brannick, M. T. (2007). Applying theories of institutional helping to informal volunteering: Motives, role identity, and prosocial personality. *Social Behavior and Personality, 35*, 101–114. https://doi.org/10.2224/sbp.2007.35.1.101

Fiorillo, D., & Nappo, N. (2015). Formal and informal volunteering and health in Mediterranean Europe. *Athens Journal of Mediterranean Studies, 1*(4), 297–310. http://doi.org/10.30958/ajms.1-4-1

Gavelin, K., & Svedberg, L. (2011). *Estimating the scope and magnitude of volunteerism worldwide*. Bonn: United Nations Volunteers, External Paper BP1, State of the World's Volunteerism Report Project.

Gundelach, B., Frietag, M., & Stadelmann-Steffen, I. (2010). Making or breaking informal volunteering: Welfare statism and social capital in a sub-national comparative perspective. *European Societies, 12*, 627–652. https://doi.org/10.1080/14616696.2010.497224

Hank, K., & Stuck, S. (2008). Volunteer work, informal help, and care among the 50+ in Europe: Further evidence for 'linked' productive activities at older ages. *Social Science Research, 37*, 1280–1291. http://doi.org/10.1016/j.ssresearch.2008.03.001

Havens, J. J., & Schervish, P. G. (2001). The methods and metrics of the Boston area diary study. *Nonprofit and Voluntary Sector Quarterly, 30*, 527–550. https://doi.org/10.1177/0899764001303010

Helms, S., & McKenzie, T. (2014). Gender differences in formal and informal volunteering in Germany. *Voluntas, 25*, 887–904. https://doi.org/10.1007/s11266-013-9378-1

Hook, J. L. (2004). Reconsidering the division of household labor: Incorporating volunteer work and informal support. *Journal of Marriage and Family, 66*(1), 101–117. https://doi.org/10.1111/1467-6478.00050-i1

Jones, F. (2000). Community involvement: The influence of early experience. *Canadian Social Trends, 57*, 15–19.

Krause, N. (2009). Church-based volunteering, providing informal support at church, and self-rated health in late life. *Journal of Aging and Health, 21*, 63–84. https://doi.org/10.1177/0898264308328638

Lee, Y., & Brudney, J. (2012). Participation in formal and informal volunteering: Implications for volunteer recruitment. *Nonprofit Management and Leadership, 23*(2), 159–180. http://doi.org/10.1002/nml.21060

Li, Y. (2007). Recovering from spousal bereavement in later life: Does volunteer participation play a role? *Journal of Gerontology: Series B: Psychological Sciences and Social Sciences, 62*, S257–S266. https://doi.org/10.1093/geronb/62.4.S257

Li, Y., & Ferraro, O. F. (2005). Volunteering and depression in later life: Social benefit or selection processes? *Journal of Health and Social Behavior, 46*, 68–84. http://doi.org/10.1177/002214650504600106

McIntosh, B. R., & Danigelis, N. L. (1995). Race, gender, and the relevance of productive activity for elders' affect. *Journal of Gerontology: Social Sciences, 50B*(4), 5229–5239. https://doi.org/10.1093/geronb/50B.4.S229

Musick, M. A., & Wilson, J. (2008). *Volunteers: A social profile*. Indianapolis: Indiana University Press.

National Council of Voluntary Organizations (NCVO). (2020). *UK civil society almanac 2020*. Retrieved from https://data.ncvo.org.uk/volunteering/

Perks, T., & Haan, M. (2011). Youth religious involvement and adult community participation: Do levels of youth religious involvement matter? *Nonprofit and Voluntary Sector Quarterly, 40*, 107–129. https://doi.org/10.1177/0899764009357794

Perpék, É. (2012). Formal and informal volunteering in Hungary. Similarities and differences. *Corvinus Journal of Sociology and Social Policy, 3*(1), 59–80.

Pettigrew, S., Jongenelis, M., Newton, R., Warburton, J., & Jackson, B. (2017). Aspects of the competition between informal and formal volunteering among older people. *Innovation in Aging, 1*(Suppl 1), 1396. https://doi.org/10.1093/geroni/igx004.5138

Plagnol, A. C., & Huppert, F. A. (2010). Happy to help? Exploring the factors associated with variations in rates of volunteering across Europe. *Social Indicators Research, 97*(2), 157–176. https://doi.org/10.1007/s11205-009-9494-x

PricewaterhouseCoopers Australia (PwC). (2016). *State of volunteering in Australia*. Retrieved from https://www.volunteeringaustralia.org/wp-content/uploads/State-of-Volunteering-in-Australia-full-report.pdf

Rosen, D., Lafontaine, P. R., & Hendrickson, B. (2011). CouchSurfing: Belonging and trust in a globally cooperative online social network. *New Media & Society, 13*(6), 981–998. https://doi.org/10.1177/1461444810390341

Rozario, P. A. (2006). Volunteering among current cohorts of older adults and baby boomers. *Generations, 30*(4), 31–36.

Salamon, L. M., Sokolowski, S. W., & Haddock, M. A. (2011). Measuring the economic value of volunteer work globally: Concepts, estimates, and a roadmap to the future. *Annals of Public and Cooperative Economics, 82*(3), 217–252. https://doi.org/10.1111/j.1467-8292.2011.00437.x

Simonson J. (2017). Formal and informal volunteering among older people in Germany– Complement or competition? *Innovation in Aging, 1*(Suppl 1), 1396. https://doi.org/10.1093/geroni/igx004.5139

Stebbins, R. A. (1996). Volunteering: A serious leisure perspective. *Nonprofit and Voluntary Action Quarterly, 25*, 211–224. https://doi.org/10.1177/0899764096252005

Stebbins, R. A. (2013). Unpaid work of love: Defining the work-leisure axis of volunteering. *Leisure Studies, 32*(3), 339–345. https://doi.org/10.1080/02614367.2012.667822

Taniguchi, H. (2011). The determinants of formal and informal volunteering: Evidence from the American Time Use Survey. *Voluntas, 23*(4), 920–939. https://doi.org/10.1007/s11266-013-9378-1

Toppe, C. M., Kirsch, A. D., & Michel, J. (2002). *Giving and volunteering in the United States*. Independent Sector.

Vogel C. (2017). Informal volunteering among older migrants – An alternative route into social participation? *Innovation in Aging, 1* (Suppl 1), 1396. https://doi.org/10.1093/geroni/igx004.5141

Wang, L., Mook, L., & Handy, F. (2017). An empirical examination of formal and informal volunteering in Canada. *Voluntas, 28*, 139–161. https://doi.org/10.1007/s11266-016-9725-0

Wilkinson-Maposa, S., & Fowler, A. (2009). *The poor philanthropist. II: New approaches to sustainable development*. University of Cape Town. Cape Town, South Africa.

Williams, C. C. (2003). Developing community involvement: Contrasting local and regional participatory cultures in Britain and their implications for policy, *Regional Studies, 37*(5), 531–541. https://doi.org/10.1080/0034340032000089086

Williams, C. C. (2004). Informal volunteering: Some lessons from the United Kingdom. *Journal of Policy Analysis and Management, 23*(3), 613–661. https://doi.org/10.1002/pam.20030

Wilson, J., & Musick, M. A. (1997). Who cares? Toward an integrated theory of volunteer work. *American Sociological Review, 62*(5), 694–713. https://doi.org/10.2307/2657355

38

METHODS FOR RESEARCHING VOLUNTEERS

Richard Shipway and Leonie Lockstone-Binney

Introduction

As demonstrated by the contributions to this Handbook, there is a burgeoning interest in understanding event, sport and tourism (EST) volunteering. Although referenced specifically in relation to sports volunteering research, we echo and extend to tourism and events, Hoye et al.'s (2019) call for researchers to adopt a broader range of methodologies to examine volunteering in these fields. Bringing together these contrasting perspectives, this chapter first discusses the dominance of quantitative investigations and their application to date. This discussion lays the groundwork for appeals for increased qualitative and mixed-methods studies to demonstrate the breadth of methods that can be applied to the study of EST volunteering.

Following, a more instructional approach is taken to outline how quantitative and qualitative methods can be utilised to support volunteering research in our fields. Issues of questionnaire design, administration and sampling are quantitative considerations that are discussed. Further discussed are contextualised examples of guidelines and tools for conducting qualitative approaches including participant observation and interviews. The chapter briefly concludes with a discussion of opportunities for methodological expansion in respect of EST volunteering.

The use of quantitative approaches to support EST volunteering research

Quantitative studies have dominated the field of EST volunteering research to date (Lockstone-Binney et al., 2010, 2014; Smith, Lockstone-Binney & Holmes, 2019). Jennings (2010, p. 21) aligns the quantitative approach to positivism/post positivism and notes that it "takes the tourism experience, event or phenomenon and abstracts it to the level of numerical representation". Finn, Elliott-White and Walton (2000, p. 8) highlight that the "quantitative researcher can reach large numbers of people by oversimplifying reality, whereas the qualitative researcher deals with the complexity of reality but with more limited numbers". The potential of applying quantitative methods to study EST volunteering lies in their ability to describe the characteristics of sample populations (through descriptive research) and

DOI: 10.4324/9780367815875-45

examine the predictors and outcomes of volunteering experiences (through explanatory or causal research) (Jennings, 2010).

Applied to the events and festivals context more broadly, Shipway, Jago and Deery (2020, p. 307) note that quantitative methods have been primarily employed "to assess, if not understand, the motives, attitudes, satisfaction, behaviour (including expenditure), and future intentions of event and festival attendees". Applied to EST volunteering, similar topic areas have been brought to light using quantitative methods.

In relation to tourism volunteering, for example, encompassing both host/local resident volunteering and volunteer tourism, studies of volunteer profiles (Han et al., 2019); motivations, expectations, experiences and satisfaction (Andereck et al., 2012; Chen, Liu & Legget, 2019; Han et al., 2019); and trends and management issues in volunteering settings (Kwiatkowski et al., 2020), are popular topics of study. Interactions with host communities and aspects of self and cultural identity have been additional topics studied in relation to volunteer tourism using quantitative methods (Bailey & Russell, 2010; Ong et al., 2018).

There are commonalities in the above sample body of work that apply to how volunteering is quantitatively examined in other leisure settings including sports and events. Using the further example, in respect of event volunteering, the following topics have been quantitatively examined: volunteer profiles, motivations and expectations (Ahn, 2018; Farrell, Johnston & Twynam, 1998; Jiang, Potwarka & Xiao, 2017; Strigas & Jackson, 2003; Vetitnev, Bobina & Terwiel, 2018); experiences and satisfaction (Farrell et al., 1998; Giannoulakis, Wang & Felver., 2015; Hallmann, Downward & Dickson, 2018) and aspects of commitment (Aisbett & Hoye, 2015; Green & Chalip, 2004; Mykletun & Himanen, 2016).

Having outlined various topic areas that quantitative studies of EST volunteering have illuminated, we now turn to discuss the practical application of quantitative research methods within a volunteering context.

Quantitative research methods

When discussing quantitative research, it is important to understand (i) why this approach has been so widely adopted in volunteering contexts, (ii) what comprises quantitative research and (iii) when should it be used as the preferred approach. In the volunteering context, a quantitative approach will generally be adopted in order to assess, if not understand, the motives, attitudes, satisfaction, behaviour and future intentions of volunteers. Data are generally obtained via a survey of a sample of the appropriate population or in some cases a census using a carefully designed questionnaire, and although the questionnaire is the key 'tool of trade' for quantitative researchers (Shipway et al., 2020), the design and administration process adopted in its application need to very carefully considered as inadequate processes put into question the results obtained.

Questionnaire design

The design of the questionnaire is fundamental to the success of quantitative research; if the questionnaire does not ask relevant questions in relation to the overall objective of the study or if the questions are not clear to respondents, then the data obtained will be flawed. As a starting point in the design of the questionnaire, it must be clear what data are needed in order to address the overall objectives of the study (Shipway et al., 2020). In questionnaire design, there is often a temptation to add questions that would be 'nice to know' but are perhaps not fundamental to the study of EST volunteering. This will often lead to questionnaires that are too long, thereby impinging on respondents' time and generally resulting in lower response rates (Dillman et al., 2009). As many questionnaires used to collect data in EST domains linked to volunteering will require that the data be collected at a specific time point (i.e., during or after an event), it is crucial that the questionnaire is not too long, as completing this task takes the respondent away from enjoying their respective volunteering experience.

Choosing appropriate scales for respondents to answer the various questions is an important decision that is often overlooked in questionnaire design. To decide on appropriate answers, options or scales for the various parts of the questionnaire requires a clear understanding of the overall research objective and the data analytical techniques that will best address this objective (Shipway et al., 2020). Often, discrete answer options are provided on questionnaires when it would be more appropriate to provide continuous Likert scales so that a more comprehensive range of statistical techniques can be employed to analyse the data. Dichotomous 'yes – no' answer options are often far too blunt for respondents to provide their true opinions/attitudes and thus valuable information is lost. In collecting data from volunteers about their satisfaction with volunteering, it is much better to ask 'how satisfied they were with their volunteering experience' using a five, seven or ten point scale than it is to simply ask 'were they satisfied or not' with a categorical 'yes or no' answer option. Clearly, this does not apply to all areas such as demographic questions for which most questions will require discrete answer selections.

For ease of data entry and analysis, it is often easier to ensure that the questionnaire is largely comprised of closed questions, that is, questions for which there are specific answer options. Despite this, there are significant benefits in also providing respondents with an opportunity to explain their responses in an open format. The data thus obtained helps one understand the reasons for a particular viewpoint. For example, asking a volunteer about their overall level of satisfaction identifies how satisfied s/he was with their volunteering experience, but not why this was the case. There is value in having a supplementary question that asks the respondent the main reasons for this level of satisfaction. The open answers obtained can be invaluable for helping volunteer managers modify aspects of subsequent volunteering roles and duties to further enhance overall satisfaction. A pilot study is advisable to test a questionnaire for use in data collection within a volunteering context, and as such, it is essential that representatives of the target audience be identified and engaged.

Questionnaire administration

There are a variety of methods that can be used to administer a questionnaire and each of these has various advantages and disadvantages to be considered. This section identifies key methods and presents some of the items to consider when selecting the most appropriate method, particularly in relation to EST volunteering research. In recent years, response rates in most studies have fallen substantially (Dillman et al., 2009) as we are inundated with an ever-increasing number of surveys and become jaded. It is critical, therefore, to consider the cost per completed questionnaire, and not just the cost of administering the questionnaire when deciding which method is most suitable for a particular study.

The most common method that has been used in EST research is the distribution of self-complete questionnaires. Participants are generally asked to either complete them at that time and return the completed questionnaires to an identified collection point or to complete the questionnaire once they return home and to mail it back using an enclosed stamped self-addressed envelope. Whilst this approach is relatively low in terms of cost as it simply requires staff to distribute a questionnaire, it has the problem of often only achieving very low response rates. In the context of EST, a low response rate is problematic as once the holiday, event or sporting activity has taken place, it is impossible to administer the questionnaire again or to continue the distribution of questionnaires, which are options for many other areas of study (Shipway et al., 2020).

Another popular means of administering questionnaires, although involving a higher cost than the aforementioned approach, is the use of intercept interviewers to collect data in situ. In a volunteering setting, this means that a number of interviewers are required to intercept volunteers and ask them questions and note their responses. A key advantage of this approach is the response rate can be monitored and achieved in real time and additional interviewers can be arranged if the response rate is not as high as intended. Using this approach, the interviewer can also assist respondents if they do not understand some of the questions. There are some disadvantages with this approach. First, the fact that respondents must give up their time to answer the questionnaire can detract from their overall 'volunteer' experience. Also, some questions may require respondents to have participated in the full volunteering experience prior to them being able to answer with any reliability. For example, a volunteer may have just started volunteering and will not be able to comment in a meaningful way about their level of volunteering satisfaction as they will not have truly experienced the roles, tasks and duties involved and many aspects of volunteering may not yet have occurred.

A variation on the intercept interview approach outlined above is for intercept interviewers to collect telephone numbers or email addresses from volunteers at the time and advise them that they will be contacted at a later date. The questionnaire can then be administered to volunteers who agree to this request either via telephone or email. The advantages of this approach are that it is less intrusive, and questions can be answered more accurately afterwards.

A more recent method of questionnaire administration, gaining popularity is the use of online research panels from which a sample of volunteers can be selected to complete an online questionnaire. This approach has relevance to studies where one may be seeking to obtain information relating to volunteer attitudes, motives, satisfaction and behaviour in general. An advantage of this approach is that online research panels are now so large that it is possible to select respondents who conform to quite tightly defined demographic and behavioural characteristics. Whilst they can be expensive to use, the cost per completed questionnaire is often relatively low compared to other techniques and the data can be collected quickly.

Sampling

It is possible to collect data from all members of a particular population rather than simply from a sample of the population and this is termed a census. Clearly, it is generally only viable to consider a census when the relevant population is relatively small, identifiable and easily accessible. In the volunteering context, a census approach could be a viable option to collect data from the volunteers at a specific sport or cultural event. Here the total number of volunteers is often relatively small and the group is generally easily accessible through the volunteer manager(s) or event organiser.

Given that it is not normally economically or logistically feasible to adopt a census approach for most studies, data must be collected from a sample of the relevant volunteer population. In quantitative research, the usual intention is to draw conclusions about the attitudes, motives or behaviours about the total relevant volunteering population based on the findings drawn from a sample of that population (Shipway et al., 2020). It is therefore vital that the sample be as random as possible and large enough in size so that the variations in the total volunteer population are reflected in the sample. Although it is very difficult to obtain a sample that is truly random, there are techniques that can be used to enhance the randomness of the sample. In surveying volunteers, this might require the interviewer to approach every 'nth' volunteer.

One of the main sampling errors that could potentially occur in a volunteer setting relates to the days on which surveying is done. There are quite a number of EST activities staged over four to seven days, only two of which are weekend days. However, because the weekend days tend to have the largest crowds, surveying of volunteers often occurs over the weekend. As such, when the results of the survey are scaled up to the total population of volunteers, there is a likelihood that findings will be skewed. Hence, it is important that volunteer sampling takes place on each day to ensure proportional returns.

For some volunteer studies, there may be the need to understand the attitudes or behaviour of specific roles and positions within the total relevant volunteer population and a random sample may not capture sufficient numbers of particular groups to enable this analysis to occur. As such, there may be a need for a stratified sample where specific numbers of volunteers are required to reflect different volunteering roles and responsibilities. For example, it might be possible to set targets for the number of volunteer respondents obtained from outside the local area, city or region so that an understanding of this group can be obtained.

The use of a survey technique leads to data collection through intercept interviews, phone interviews, mailout self-complete questionnaires or online questionnaire completion (Shipway et al., 2020), the choice, design and administration of which must be carefully considered.

The use of qualitative approaches to support volunteering research

While qualitative methods are less widely used to study EST volunteering, these are increasing in prevalence. Across the EST domains, qualitative approaches have been more commonly used in studying the lived experiences of volunteer tourists, including aspects of personal transformation and learning (Coghlan & Weiler, 2018; Müller, Scheffer & Closs, 2020; Pan, 2017) and volunteering motivations (Chen & Chen, 2011; Grimm & Needham, 2012; Proyrungroj, 2017).

In relation to events/sporting events, recent qualitative examples include studies using interviews (Jæger & Olsen, 2017; Nichols, Ralston & Holmes, 2017; Schnitzer, Kristiansen & Hanstad, 2018) and also focus groups (Aisbett & Hoye, 2014; Ragsdell & Jepson, 2014). Wilks (2016) drew on the reflective diaries kept by volunteers at the London 2012 Olympic and Paralympic Games to consider the lived experiences of those participating, and Clayton (2016) used diaries and interviews of volunteers involved in UK music festivals to understand volunteers' knowledge management activities. Tomazos and Luke (2015) adopted narrative inquiry, and autographical studies are emerging (Qi, Smith & Yeoman, 2018; Sadd, 2018; Wise, 2017).

This section of the chapter will explore some of the research tools associated with qualitative research in volunteering. At the centre of any quantitative-qualitative discussion is the philosophical debate that qualitative researchers generally operate under different epistemological assumptions from quantitative researchers (Shipway et al., 2020). However, volunteering related research, especially in the domains of EST, is far richer for the wide variety of views and methods that the debate generates.

Volunteer researchers are confronted with a host of approaches when starting their research, the choice of which is a reflection of the subjectivity, culture and preferences of the researcher as well as the topic under study (Brewer, 2000). The three most common qualitative research methods are participant observation, in-depth interviews and focus groups. Each method is particularly suited for obtaining a specific type of data. Participant observation is appropriate for collecting data on naturally occurring behaviours in their usual contexts; in-depth interviews are appropriate for collecting data on individuals' life histories, experiences and perspectives, especially when sensitive issues and topics are being explored; and focus groups are appropriate in extracting data on the cultural norms of a group and to generate broad overviews of issues of concern to the cultural groups represented (Shipway et al., 2020).

This section will explore the two primary qualitative methods of enquiry, namely, participant observation including an exploration of ethnography; and the interview method, which if used properly can enhance the understanding of various aspects of volunteering. Examples and scenarios are included from a sport event volunteering context, along with an explanation of some appropriate research techniques and approaches to be adopted.

Participant observation

Participant observation is the act of looking at the setting and people in detail and over time, systematically studying what goes on and noting and reporting it. Volunteering researchers as participant observers will look at people in their natural settings. Participant observation is an inductive approach that has origins in anthropology and sociology and from the early periods of fieldwork, when researchers became part of the culture they studied, and examined the actions and interactions of people 'in the field'. In relation to volunteering generally, the experiences and social, cultural and personal meanings attached by volunteers represents an area that is still fruitful for further in-depth exploration (Mackellar, 2013).

Prolonged engagement and involvement is one significant characteristic of participant observation, which is needed to learn about the volunteering setting and people being studied. Whilst observation is considered less disruptive (Mackellar, 2013) and more unobtrusive than interviews, participant observation does not just involve watching, but also listening and talking to the people being studied. Participant observation can be conducted in open and closed volunteering settings. The participant-observer enters the setting without intending to limit the observations to particular people or situations and adopts an unstructured approach. Certain ideas might emerge in the early stages, but usually observation would progress from being unstructured to the more detailed and focused until specific actions become the main interest of the researcher. Researchers can then observe social processes as they happen and develop, and situations can be analysed.

Holloway (2008) notes that observers can examine events and ongoing actions, however, they cannot explore past events and the thoughts of participants, which is only possible in interviews. When participant observation is successful, it will uncover interesting patterns and developments that are grounded in the real world of the volunteering participants' daily lives. It was Holloway (2008) who highlighted that the task of both exploration and discovery is, after all, the aim of qualitative research. The observation of a variety of contexts within a volunteering setting is important. Spradley (1980) states that all participant observation takes place in social situations, and provides a framework in order to guide researchers, which are applicable to volunteering. In Figure 38.1, Spradley's framework for participant

---

The Virgin Money London Marathon

Space: The Event location, e.g., *the streets of London.*

Actor: The person in the Event setting, e.g., *the runners, the security personnel, the police officers, the spectators, the co-volunteers.*

Activity: The behaviour and actions of those in attendance.

Object: The items located in the setting, e.g., *drink stations, mile markers, medical support.*

Act: The single action, e.g., *policing the event, marshalling runners and spectators, music.*

Events: What is happening (in the period post, during and pre)? e.g., *the context and importance of charity focused mass participation sports events in the UK, or proposed event impacts and legacies.*

Time: Time frame and sequencing, e.g., *media build-up (traditional press and online), planning and organisation activities leading up to the main days of the Marathon, post-event activities such as clean-up operations.*

Goal: What volunteers are aiming to achieve, e.g., *(depending on actor role) raising awareness, minimising disruption, fun and enjoyment, profiling London and the UK as tourist destinations.*

Feeling: The emotions of volunteers, spectators and runners, e.g., *accessible through observation on the days; the press in the build-up to the event; and the atmosphere on the Marathon course.*

Figure 38.1 Volunteering at the Virgin Money London Marathon
Adapted from Spradley (1980, p. 78)

observation is applied to a volunteering context. Using the annual Virgin Money London Marathon as a point of illustration allows the reader to grasp the applicability of the technique for volunteering research.

Through using an inductive approach, the focus of observation will inevitably change in response to the data generated as the research proceeds. The qualitative researcher has to be flexible and responsive to the conditions of the research setting; in this case, the Virgin Money London Marathon.

Spradley (1980) suggests that observers take three main steps: they use *descriptive, focused* and finally, *selective* observation. Descriptive observation incorporates general ideas that the observer has in mind, and everything taking place in the situation becomes a source of data and should be recorded, including smells, colours or appearances of people in the chosen setting. Description involves all five senses (Holloway & Wheeler, 2010). As time progresses, certain important aspects or areas of the setting should become more obvious, and the researcher will be able to focus on these. Finally, the observation will then become highly selective. To aid data collection, we suggest that volunteering researchers can utilise the observation guidelines provided by Le Compte, Preissle and Tesch (1993). These guidelines, detailed in Figure 38.2, will be useful when starting volunteer related field research.

To illustrate the usefulness of the data collection techniques outlined above, there now follows a more specific exploration of ethnography as a qualitative method of enquiry, highlighting its applicability and relevance within the domain of volunteering studies.

---

1. The **'who'** questions

Who and how many people were present in the volunteering event setting or taking part in activities and events? What were their characteristics and roles for volunteers within the environment?

2. The **'what'** questions

What is happening in the volunteering setting, what are the actions and rules of behaviour of those present? What are the variations in the behaviour observed?

3. The **'where'** questions

Where do interactions between volunteers and / or attendees take place? Where are they located in the physical space of the volunteering setting?

4. The **'when'** questions

When do conversations and interactions take place? What is the timing of the activities or actions; and do discussions and interactions take place at different times?

5. The **'why'** questions

Why do volunteers and / or attendees in the setting act the way they do? Why are there variations in behaviour amongst volunteers?

Figure 38.2   Observational guidelines for volunteering

Ethnography in volunteering

Ethnography is a qualitative research approach where, through participant observation, the researcher is immersed in the day-to-day lives of the people, or conducts one-on-one interviews with members of a group (Shipway et al., 2020). Ethnography is defined as the description and interpretation of a culture or social group; its aim is to understand social reality by focusing on ordinary, everyday behaviour and to provide an in-depth study of a culture (Holloway, Brown & Shipway, 2010). The utility of ethnography as a qualitative research approach in the field of volunteering is clear: it permits both observations and interviews with key informants, a full picture of the volunteering experience can be captured by the researcher, who by assuming the role of participant, gains privileged access to the subculture.

In an event setting, the work of Stadler, Reid and Fullagar (2013) is a notable example of the use and application of ethnography as an interpretative methodology for researching knowledge practices and some of the constraints of ethnographic research. Their ethnographic approach incorporated two methods of data collection, namely, participant observation and in-depth interviews. Booth (2016) also very effectively utilised ethnography to examine the producers of Indian cultural events in both global and localised contexts. In her work, she reinforced that ethnography as a research method rested on the dual techniques of participant observation and interviewing. Booth also argued how in an event setting it is important to understand how the researcher can affect the outcome of the findings.

The value of ethnography is in describing and understanding cultures, which could be replicated within any volunteering setting; ethnography alone permits the study of the culture created by participants. Applying ethnographic methods – especially observation – will help volunteering researchers to contextualise behaviours, beliefs and feelings, and identify the cultural influences on the individuals and groups they study (Shipway et al., 2020). In addition to participant observation, interviews are possibly the best way to access volunteer experiences, allowing volunteers to express themselves in their own words and at their own pace (Brewer, 2000).

The interview

Jones (2015) suggested that the simplest way to obtain information from someone is to simply ask them! This is the underlying principle of the research interview and in its most basic form, the interviewer is trying to gain the perspectives, feelings and perceptions from the participant(s) and/or their description of the phenomenon being studied (Holloway, 2008). The depth and richness of qualitative data are functions of the ability to sensitively explore topics of importance with informants (Mason, 2002). Qualitative interviews will vary in their degree of structure, ranging from the unstructured to the structured interview. Qualitative researchers in the volunteering domain would normally employ the unstructured or semi-structured interview. The one-to-one interview is the most common method by which qualitative data is collected in volunteering-related research, which collects highly structured data. The researcher is a key element of the interview process (Shipway et al., 2020), and their skills, attributes and interviewing technique are all integral to obtaining 'rich' qualitative data.

There are both advantages and disadvantages of the interview method. Participants will be able to talk about their own volunteering experiences and in their own words, elaborate on areas of interest and importance, and they provide an opportunity for unexpected data to emerge, which might not have been readily apparent. Importantly, the volunteer researcher must be careful to avoid interviewer bias and avoid influencing the study either positively or negatively, depending on various external factors.

Unstructured interviews draw on the social interaction between the informant and the interviewer to gather information. Informants can let their thoughts wander, and although structuring and ordering of the questions are not utilised, there is an element of controlled communication relating to the interests of the interviewer (Edwards & Skinner, 2009). As such, it is important in the unstructured interview to ask questions that are open-ended, to get interviewees talking about a broad topic area, whilst remembering that the informant guides the content (Spradley, 1979). Unstructured interviews are useful when little is known about the area of study or perhaps during a preliminary volunteering study to test what the responses might be to a particular issue within the chosen volunteering context. Even unstructured interviews are usually supported by an *aide memoire*, an agenda or a list of topics that will be covered, as illustrated in Figure 38.3.

"Tell me about your experience volunteering at the Hay Literary Festival (Wales)".

Aide memoire

- Explore feelings when entering the Festival site or starting your voluntary role.

- Interaction between the crowd and volunteers throughout the duration of the Hay Literary Festival.

- Thoughts on the job roles and responsibilities undertaken at the Festival.

Figure 38.3 Unstructured interview questions and *aide memoires* for volunteering research

This form of unstructured interviewing allows flexibility and lets the researcher follow the interests and thoughts of the informant and whilst they generate the richest data, they also have the highest level of material of no particular use, or what Holloway (2008) calls the *dross rate*. There is also a danger with this type of interview that much of the data will lack focus. Another disadvantage of unstructured interviews is that the researcher working in a volunteering environment is vulnerable to interpretations and subjective insights of informants.

A semi-structured interview has a more specific research agenda and is more focused, however, the informants still describe the situation in their own time and words. It is possible for the researcher to ensure through the tighter structure of semi-structured interviews that they collect important information, while still allowing the informant to express their own thoughts and feelings. A semi-structured interview will allow for more guidance and direction from the researcher. It is suggested that volunteering researchers develop an appropriate interview guide. The researcher can then develop questions and decide which issues to pursue.

When compiling a list of questions for semi-structured interviews, it is important to reflect that the researcher will not wish to lead the participant, but on the other hand, it is necessary to prepare enough questions in case conversation is limited (Shipway et al., 2020). The order of the questions will depend on the answers of each individual, and will therefore not be the same for each participant. The interview is likely to become more centred through progressive focusing, and it is important not to control the answers, but be guided by the informants' ideas and thoughts (Holloway & Wheeler, 2010). We would suggest questions of short to medium length with the use of prompts, similar to those provided in Figure 38.4. These are hypothetical examples from the Red Bull Rampage invitation-only freeride mountain bike competition in Utah, USA.

When asking questions, interviewers can use a variety of techniques. Patton (1990) highlights certain types of questions, for example, *experience, feeling* and *knowledge* questions, examples of which are provided in Figure 38.5.

Spradley (1979) also recommends the use of grand-tour or experience questions in the opening interview, followed by focused mini-tour or example questions, depending on the interviewee's response. They often begin with a broad question within the topic area, such as 'Tell me about volunteering at the 2016 Paralympic Games in Rio, Brazil' or 'What were

---

Red Bull Rampage Mountain Bike Event, Zion National Park, Utah.

Tell me about the time when you volunteered at the Red Bull Rampage invitation event in Utah.

- How did you feel prior to the Rampage?

- Tell me about the actual freeride mountain bike competition, and the route taken by the competitors?

- How did you feel when volunteering throughout the competition?

- What happened after the competition ended?

- How did your friends and family react to your volunteering at the Red Bull Rampage?

And so on.

Figure 38.4 Interview questions and prompts

Experience questions

- Could you tell me about your experience volunteering at the 2023 World Expo in Buenos Aires, Argentina?

- Tell me about your experience of volunteering at the Lesbisch Schwules Stadfest Parade in Berlin, Germany.

Feeling questions

- How did you feel when you were allocated your volunteering tasks at the Belfast International Arts Festival in Ireland?

- As a volunteer, what did you feel when the first act came on stage at the Glastonbury Music Festival in Somerset, UK?

Knowledge questions

- What support services were available for Republican volunteers at the annual Conservative Political Action Alliance Conference (CPAC)?

- How did you cope with spending fourteen days volunteering at the 2022 FIFA World Cup Tournament in Doha, Qatar?

Figure 38.5 Volunteering experience, feeling and knowledge questions

your volunteering experiences at the 2018 Winter Olympic Games in PyeongChang, South Korea'? Grand-tour questions are broader, while mini-tour questions are more specific. A hypothetical example of a grand-tour question could be 'Can you describe a typical day organising staff at the Hong Kong Arts Festival' to an event volunteer manager, or 'How do you see your voluntary role at the Hong Kong Arts Festival' to an event volunteer. In contrast, a mini-tour question could be 'What were your expectations when volunteering at the Sundance Film Festival in the USA' to a festival volunteer, or 'Can you describe what happens when you have a problem with one of the volunteers', to an event volunteer manager of the Cherry Blossom Festival in Japan.

Ragsdell and Jepson (2014) also effectively used semi-structured interviews with volunteers in key festival roles and conducted focus groups with a range of other volunteers. Exploring the role of corporates at sports mega events, Lockstone-Binney et al. (2018) used in depth interviews to examine volunteering legacies at the Sydney 2000 and London 2012 Olympic Games. Their study for the International Olympic Committee (IOC) incorporated 25 semi-structured interviews with senior key stakeholders involved in legacy planning and governance across the Olympic planning cycle.

In summary, the qualitative research interview in a volunteering setting will depend largely on the participants whose ideas, thoughts and feelings the researcher will try to explore, thereby obtaining the insiders' perspective. Due to its flexibility, researchers have freedom to prompt for more information, and participants are able to explore their own thoughts and exert more control over the interview as their ideas have priority. However, the collection and analysis of interview data is time consuming. Despite the need to embrace new paradigms in volunteering studies, there is still a need to further understand the underlying experiences, feelings and emotions related to volunteer behaviour and activity. This section of the chapter suggests that the strength of qualitative research for volunteer related studies, be it participant observation, interviews or any other form of qualitative method of enquiry, is the ability to lift the veil on certain aspects of volunteering, and to make visible unknown cultural phenomena (Edwards & Skinner, 2009; Jones, Brown & Holloway, 2012).

Conclusion

We support calls (Shipway et al., 2020; Smith et al., 2019) for moves away from the dominance of quantitative studies on EST volunteering. We would argue that most quantitative volunteer research conducted in leisure settings focuses on a single organisation or event (exceptions include Cuskelly et al., 2004; Dickson, Benson & Terwiel, 2014; Handy, Brodeur & Cnaan, 2006; Mykletun & Himanen, 2016; Schnitzer et al., 2018), limiting comparisons across multiple contexts and over time. Longitudinal research is particularly needed to evaluate the longer-term benefits of EST volunteering participation in respect of evidencing much lauded mega event legacy outcomes and individual outcomes for the volunteer, for example, as a result of participating in a volunteer tourism program (Ong et al., 2018).

Hoye et al. (2019, p. 175), in their compendium on sport volunteering lamented that related research had to move beyond "descriptive studies of volunteer motives or satisfaction" and "bespoke measurement scales developed by researchers". Smith et al. (2019) raised similar concerns in their review of event volunteering research over the period of 2014–2018. Wicker and Hallmann's (2013, p. 127) review of individual, group and institutional factors affecting the decision to engage in sport volunteering found that the dominance of quantitative studies were also mostly limited to descriptive statistics, "thus, the portfolio of statistical tests has not yet been fully exploited". The challenge for quantitative EST volunteering researchers is to expand the arsenal of statistical techniques applied to study the phenomena. The further challenge is to expand beyond replication studies applied to different EST contexts, which lack theoretical extensions.

There is ample scope for researchers to adopt a broader range of methodologies to examine EST volunteering. Wider adoption of qualitative and mixed-methods studies will supplement the breadth of methods that can be applied to the study of EST volunteering including focus groups and autoethnography and other methods not discussed here (e.g. participant diaries). In addition, there is particular value in conducting cross-case comparative studies, whether qualitative, quantitative or mixed methods, to uncover the generalisability of the volunteer experience across these leisure contexts.

References

Aisbett, L., & Hoye, R. (2014). The nature of perceived organizational support for sport event volunteers. *Event Management, 18*(3), 337–356. https://doi.org/10.3727/152599514X13989500765880

Aisbett, L., & Hoye, R. (2015). Human resource management practices to support sport event volunteers. *Asia Pacific Journal of Human Resources, 53*(3), 351–369. https://doi.org/10.1111/1744-7941.12062

Ahn, Y.-J. (2018). Recruitment of volunteers connected with sports mega-events: A case study of the PyeongChang 2018 Olympic and Paralympic Winter Games. *Journal of Destination Marketing and Management, 8*, 194–203. https://doi.org/10.1016/j.jdmm.2017.04.002

Andereck, K., McGehee, N. G., Lee, S., & Clemmons, D. (2012). Experience expectations of prospective volunteer tourists. *Journal of Travel Research, 51*(2), 130–141. https://doi.org/10.1177/0047287511400610

Bailey, A. W., & Russell, K. C. (2010). Predictors of interpersonal growth in volunteer tourism: A latent curve approach. *Leisure Sciences, 32*(4), 352–368. https://doi.org/10.1080/01490400.2010.488598

Booth, A. (2016). Ethnography in the diaspora: Indian cultural production and transnational networks. In T. Pernecky (Ed.), *Approaches and Methods in Event Studies* (pp.147–162). Routledge.

Brewer, J. (2000). *Ethnography*. Open University Press.

Chen, L.-J., & Chen, J. S. (2011). The motivations and expectations of international volunteer tourists: A case study of 'Chinese village traditions'. *Tourism Management, 32*(2), 435–442. https://doi.org/10.1016/j.tourman.2010.01.009

Chen, X., Liu, C., & Legget, J. (2019). Motivations of museum volunteers in New Zealand's cultural tourism industry. *Anatolia, 30*(1), 127–139. https://doi.org/10.1080/13032917.2018.1542521

Clayton, D. (2016). Volunteers' knowledge activities at UK music festivals: A hermeneutic-phenomenological exploration of individuals' experiences. *Journal of Knowledge Management, 20*(1), 162–180. https://doi.org/10.1108/JKM-05-2015-0182

Coghlan, A., & Weiler, B. (2018). Examining transformative processes in volunteer tourism. *Current Issues in Tourism,* 21(5), 567–582. https://doi.org/10.1080/13683500.2015.1102209

Cuskelly, G., Auld, C., Harrington, M., & Coleman, D. (2004). Predicting the behavioural dependability of sport event volunteers. *Event Management, 9,* 73–89. https://doi.org/10.3727/1525995042781011

Dickson, T. J., Benson, A. M., & Terwiel, F. A. (2014). Mega-event volunteers, similar or different? Vancouver 2010 vs London 2012. *International Journal of Event and Festival Management, 5*(2), 164–179. https://doi.org/10.1108/IJEFM-07-2013-0019

Dillman, D., Phelps, G., Tortora, R., Swift, K., Kohrell, J., Berck, J., & Messer, B. (2009). Response rate and measurement differences in mixed-mode surveys using mail, telephone, interactive voice response (IVR) and the Internet. *Social Science Research, 38*(1): 1–18. https://doi.org/10.1016/j.ssresearch.2008.03.007

Edwards, A., & Skinner, J. (2009). *Qualitative Research in Sport Management.* Elsevier Butterworth-Heinemann.

Farrell, J. M., Johnston, M. E., & Twynam, D. G. (1998). Volunteer motivation, satisfaction and management and an elite sporting competition. *Journal of Sport Management, 12,* 288–300. https://doi.org/10.1123/jsm.12.4.288

Finn, M., Elliott-White, M., & Walton, M. (2000). *Tourism and Leisure Research Methods: Data Collection, Analysis and Interpretation.* Pearson.

Giannoulakis, C., Wang, C.-H., & Felver, N. (2015). A modeling approach to sport volunteer satisfaction. *International Journal of Event and Festival Management, 6*(3), 182–199. https://doi.org/10.1108/IJEFM-04-2014-0010

Green, B. C., & Chalip, L. (2004). Paths to volunteer commitment: Lessons from the Sydney Olympic Games. In R. Stebbins & M. Graham (Eds.), *Volunteering as Leisure/Leisure as Volunteering: An International Assessment* (pp. 49–67). CABI International.

Grimm, K. E., & Needham, M. D. (2012). Moving beyond the "i" in motivation: Attributes and perceptions of conversation volunteer tourists. *Journal of Travel Research, 51*(4), 488–501. https://doi.org/10.1177/0047287511418367

Hallmann, K., Downward, P., & Dickson, G. (2018). Factors influencing time allocation of sport event volunteers. *International Journal of Event and Festival Management, 9*(3), 316–331. https://doi.org/10.1108/IJEFM-01-2018-0004

Han, H., Meng, B., Chua, B.-L., Ryu, H. B., & Kim, W. (2019). International volunteer tourism and youth travellers: An emerging tourism trend. *Journal of Travel and Tourism Marketing, 36*(5), 549–562. https://doi.org/10.1080/10548408.2019.1590293

Handy, F., Brodeur, N., & Cnaan, R. A. (2006). Summer on the island: Episodic volunteering. *Voluntary Action, 7*(3), 31–46.

Holloway, I. (2008). *A-Z of Qualitative Research in Healthcare and Nursing.* Blackwell.

Holloway, I., Brown, L., & Shipway, R. (2010). Meaning not measurement: Using ethnography to bring a deeper understanding to the participant experience of festivals and events. *International Journal of Event and Festival Management, 1*(1), 74–85. https://doi.org/10.1108/17852951011029315

Holloway, I., & Wheeler, S. (2010). *Qualitative Research in Nursing and Healthcare* (3rd ed.). Wiley-Blackwell.

Hoye, R., Cuskelly, G., Auld, C., Kappelides, P., & Misener, K. (2019). *Sport Volunteering.* Routledge.

Jæger, K., & Olsen, K. (2017). On commodification: Volunteer experiences in festivals. *Journal of Tourism and Cultural Change, 15*(5), 407–421. https://doi.org/10.1080/14766825.2016.1168827

Jennings, G. (2010). *Tourism Research* (2nd ed.). John Wiley & Sons.

Jiang, K., Potwarka, L. R., & Xiao, H. (2017). Predicting intention to volunteer for mega-sport events in China: The case of Universiade event volunteers. *Event Management, 21,* 713–728. https://doi.org/10.3727/152599517X15073047237232

Jones, I. (2015). *Research Methods for Sport Studies.* Routledge.

Jones, I., Brown, L., & Holloway, I., (2012). *Qualitative Research in Sport and Physical Activity*. Sage.

Kwiatkowski, G., Hjalager, A.-M., Liburd, J., & Simonsen, P. S. (2020). Volunteering and collaborative governance innovation in the Wadden Sea National Park. *Current Issues in Tourism, 23*(8), 971–989. https://doi.org/10.1080/13683500.2019.1571022

Le Compte, M. D., Preissle, J., & Tesch, R. (1993). *Ethnography and Qualitative Design in Educational Research* (2nd ed.). Academic Press.

Lockstone-Binney, L., Holmes, K., Baum, T., & Smith, K. (2014). Event Volunteering Evaluation (EVE): Challenging the methodological limits of event volunteering research. In K. Smith, L. Lockstone-Binney, K. Holmes & T. Baum (Eds.), *Event Volunteering: International Perspectives on the Volunteering Experience* (pp. 167–181). Routledge Advances in Event Research Series. Routledge.

Lockstone-Binney, L., Holmes, K., Smith, K., & Baum, T. (2010). Volunteers and volunteering in leisure: Social science perspectives. *Leisure Studies, 29*(4), 435–455. https://doi.org/10.1080/02614 367.2010.527357

Lockstone-Binney, L., Holmes, K., Smith, K., & Shipway, R. (2018). The role of corporates in creating sustainable Olympic legacies. *Journal of Sustainable Tourism, 26*(11), 1827–1844. https://doi.org/ 10.1080/09669582.2018.1513007

Mackellar, J. (2013). Participant observation at events: Theory, practice and potential. *International Journal of Event and Festival Management, 4*(1), 56–65. https://doi.org/10.1108/17582951311307511

Mason, J. (2002). *Qualitative Researching* (2nd ed.). Sage.

Müller, C. V., Scheffer, A. B. B., & Closs, L. Q. (2020). Volunteer tourism, transformative learning and its impacts on careers: The case of Brazilian volunteers. *International Journal of Tourism Research, 22*(6), 726–738. https://doi-org./10.1002/jtr.2368

Mykletun, R. J., & Himanen, K. (2016). Volunteers at biking race events: Antecedents of commitment and intention to remain volunteering at future events. *Sport, Business and Management: An International Journal, 6*(3), 246–273. https://doi.org/10.1108/SBM-12-2014-0051

Nichols, G., Ralston, R., & Holmes, K. (2017). The 2012 Olympic ambassadors and sustainable tourism legacy. *Journal of Sustainable Tourism, 25*(11), 1513–1528. https://doi.org/10.1080/09669582.20 17.1291648

Ong, F., King, B., Lockstone-Binney, L., & Junek, O. (2018). Global global, acting local: Are volunteer tourists prospective community builders? *Tourism Recreation Review, 43*(2), 135–146. https:// doi.org/10.1080/02508281.2017.1391449

Pan, T.-J. (2017). Personal transformation through volunteer tourism: The evidence of Asian students. *Journal of Hospitality & Tourism Research, 41*(5), 609–634. https://doi-org.libraryproxy.griffith.edu. au/10.1177/1096348014538048

Patton, M. (1990). *Qualitative Evaluation and Research Methods* (2nd ed.). Sage.

Proyrungroj, R. (2017). Orphan volunteer tourism in Thailand: Volunteer tourists' motivations and on-site experiences. *Journal of Hospitality & Tourism Research, 41*(5), 560–584. https://doi. org/10.1177/1096348014525639

Qi, H., Smith, K. A., & Yeoman, I. (2018). Cross-cultural event volunteering: Challenge and intelligence. *Tourism Management, 69*, 596–604. https://doi.org/10.1016/j.tourman.2018.03.019

Ragsdell, G., & Jepson, A. (2014). Knowledge sharing: Insights from Campaign for Real Ale (CAMRA) Festival volunteers. *International Journal of Event and Festival Management, 5*(3), 279–296. https://doi.org/10.1108/IJEFM-11-2013-0028

Sadd, D. (2018). Proud to be British: An autoethnographic study of working as a Games Maker at London 2012. *Event Management, 22*, 317–332. https://doi.org/10.3727/152599518X15239930463136

Schnitzer, M., Kristiansen, E., & Hanstad, D. V. (2018). Comparing the expectations, experiences and legacies of volunteers at the FIS Nordic World Ski Championships in Oslo in 2011 and Val di Fiemme 2013. *Current Issues in Sport Science, 3*, 1–8. https://doi.org/10.15203/CISS_2018.002

Shipway, R., Jago, L., & Deery, M., (2020). Quantitative and qualitative research tools in events. In S. J. Page & J. Connell (Eds.), *Routledge Handbook of Events* (2nd ed., pp. 306–327). Routledge.

Smith, K. A., Lockstone-Binney, L., & Holmes, K. (2019). Revisiting and advancing the research agenda for event volunteering. In J. Armbrecht, E. Lundberg & T. G. Andersson (Eds.), *A Research Agenda for Event Management* (pp. 126–153). Edward Elgar Publishing.

Spradley, J. P. (1979). *The Ethnographic Interview*. Holt, Rinehart and Winston.

Spradley, J. P. (1980). *Participant Observation*. Holt, Rinehart and Winston.

Stadler, R. Reid, S., & Fullagar, S. (2013). An ethnographic exploration of knowledge practices within the Queensland Music Festival. *International Journal of Event and Festival Management, 4*(2), 90–106. https://doi.org/10.1108/17582951311325872

Strigas, A. D., & Newton Jackson Jr, E. (2003). Motivating volunteers to serve and succeed: Design and results of a pilot study that explores demographics and motivational factors in sport volunteerism. *International Sports Journal, 7*(11), 111–123.

Tomazos, K., & Luke, S. (2015). Mega-sports events volunteering: Journeys with a past, a present and a future. *Voluntas: International Journal of Voluntary and Nonprofit Organizations, 26*(4), 1337–1359. https://doi.org/10.1007/s11266-014-9484-8

Vetitnev, A., Bobina, M., & Terwiel, F. A. (2018). The influence of host volunteer motivation on satisfaction and attitudes toward Sochi 2014 Olympic Games. *Event Management, 22*, 333–352. https://doi.org/10.3727/152599518X15239930463145

Wicker, P., & Hallmann, K. (2013). A multi-level framework for investigating the engagement of sport volunteers. *European Sport Management Quarterly, 13*(1), 110–139. http://dx.doi.org/10.1080/16184742.2012.744768

Wilks, L. (2016). The lived experience of London 2012 Olympic and Paralympic Games volunteers: A serious leisure perspective. *Leisure Studies, 35*(5), 652–667. https://doi.org/10.1080/02614367.2014.993334

Wise, N. (2017). Living abroad and volunteering at the 2014 Commonwealth Games in Glasgow. In A. M. Benson & N. Wise (Eds), *International Sports Volunteering* (pp. 60–76). Routledge.

39

THE FUTURE OF VOLUNTEERING AND WORK

Tom Baum, Leonie Lockstone-Binney, Karen A. Smith,
Richard Shipway and Kirsten Holmes

Introduction

This concluding chapter seeks to situate the future of volunteering relative to wider debates and general socio-economic, demographic and technological trends affecting the world of work. Cognisant that this chapter is written very much in the COVID era, an initial debate about whether COVID-19 represents a seismic change or a blip on the graph for event, sport and tourism (EST) volunteering, and volunteering in general, is discussed. With its prominent focus in the EST volunteering literature (see Lis and Tomanek's chapter of this Handbook), and its inherent travel requirement, the future of volunteer tourism is also discussed.

This chapter references other chapters from the Handbook, linking key debates and topics where possible. It draws on generic and sector specific themes to support discussion about where volunteering lies in relation to paid work and unpaid work and briefly touches on its boundaries with leisure.

The chapter concludes that the EST sectors will continue post-COVID as essential to the physical and mental well-being of communities. The role of volunteers with respect to this significant transition is discussed and an associated research agenda is highlighted.

Volunteering, work and employment in the 21st century

Volunteering has been conceptualised in three forms: as unpaid work, activism and serious leisure (Rochester et al., 2010). Beginning with volunteering as unpaid work, we examine developments in the world of work and implications for volunteering. Drivers of debate about the future of work centre on the Fourth Industrial Revolution (Rotatori et al., 2021), with its focus on technological developments in robotics, artificial intelligence and genetics and the implications such developments might have for the labour market. However, alongside this technological revolution, there are broader socio-economic, geopolitical and demographic drivers of change that might have even more significant and longer lasting influences on the world of work.

Changes in population structures in both the Global North (ageing populations and sustained in-bound talent migration) and the Global South (continued growth in child and youth populations and outward talent leakage) require polar opposite responses in terms of

DOI: 10.4324/9780367815875-46

job creation and automation. The consequences of sustained investment in education and skills development, while facilitating many of the technology-driven changes to work and society, also creates expectations of participation in new opportunities which, in reality, may not be deliverable to all those who are qualified.

To emphasise that we live in uncertain times where many forms of work and employment have been, and continue to face major change, is to highlight the obvious. The nature of work has always been in flux as societies have evolved over the centuries, driven by a combination of, inter alia, economic, social, cultural and technological change. In recent years, much of the discussion about the future of work has focused on the increasing role that automation, robotisation and artificial intelligence have in the execution of routine and increasingly complex work functions. Some commentators such as Susskind (2020) go so far as to envisage a world where there will not be sufficient paid work for everyone to do as a result of technological change. In this dystopian scenario, the future is one of mass technological unemployment, precarious work, workers with little or no bargaining power and growing skills gaps as the population in the Global North ages (OECD, 2019). The Organisation for Economic Co-operation and Development (OECD) take, however, is to focus on the positive potential of technology to create new jobs on a globalised scale, to improve the quality of existing jobs and to bring previously underrepresented groups into the labour market. The reality is that the future probably holds a scenario somewhere between these extremes and the social and political challenge will be to manage the process of change in the best interests of all stakeholder groups across the globe. For volunteering, technology offers new ways in which people can both volunteer (online) (Haski-Leventhal et al., 2020) and also organise volunteering through social media.

Susskind's take on volunteering, in this context, is to depict the encouragement of such action by governments as a subset of wider leisure policies to ensure that the adult population has challenging and engaging things to do in the potential absence of work. Other writers question the value of work that is on offer to many people in developed economies. Graeber (2018), for example, questions the social value of many contemporary 'bullshit jobs', in many respects echoing George Orwell's (1933) questioning of the social purpose of the work of the plongeur in Parisian restaurants.

Given the close association between voluntary work and government and its agencies, the rise of New Public Management (NPM) since the 1980s has already had significant impacts on the work expectations that third sector volunteer organisations, as well as publicly accountable major/ mega events, have of their volunteer workforces (Bartram et al., 2017; O'Rourke, 2020). NPM can be described as ways of reorganising public sector bodies to bring their management approaches closer to business methods. NPM includes the emergence of markets and quasi-markets within public services, the empowerment of accountable management along with active performance measurement and management. This cultural change places volunteer engagement in the delivery of services on a very different footing to that which might have attracted 'traditional' volunteers, seeking to contribute to areas of meaning to them at a personal level in a social, cultural or sporting sense. Our consideration of the future of volunteering, therefore, needs to be seen in the context of these macro-trends in relation to work and employment.

Volunteering as unpaid work

Unpaid work, including volunteering, compared to paid forms, has received considerably less attention from researchers (Grant-Smith & McDonald, 2017). Volunteering is a productive activity, yet it is rarely studied as a form of non-paid labour (Taylor, 2004) or as a serious leisure pursuit (Elkington & Stebbins, 2014). It is also rarely considered or included when discussing the changing nature of paid work.

Entrenched perceptions of volunteering as a lightweight leisure pursuit or feel-good activity of little real economic value persist despite increasing evidence to the contrary (Productivity Commission, 2010; UNV, 2018). Also, research evidence suggests that people view activities that cost the volunteer a lot of effort and give little in the way of personal benefits as being more akin to pure volunteering than easy activities that give ample bene-fits (Handy et al., 2000). The net-cost perception threatens to trivialise EST volunteering, where much of the activity could be considered as a form of leisure or fun when contrasted with social services style volunteering. This view further embeds the traditional paradigm of work as only concerning paid work.

As noted in Rochester's chapter (this volume), in recent decades, too, like paid work, volunteering has changed and diversified to encompass a range of flexible and temporal forms, such as episodic volunteering (Hyde et al., 2016), online volunteering and micro-volunteering, all enhanced by social media, new technologies and mobile lifestyles (Bimber et al., 2012). Volunteering has expanded beyond the not-for-profit sector to include third parties such as corporates, government and educational institutions (Haski-Leventhal et al., 2010). At the same time, this diversification has witnessed a shift from the traditional model of volunteering as a face-to-face service activity, undertaken in a designated location and at a designated time, through an organisation or group (Haski-Leventhal et al., 2018). Wang (this volume) considers informal volunteering, which contributes enormously in many sectors but for which we have a limited understanding in the EST sectors.

Concurrently, a decline in volunteer participation rates has been noted in several coun-tries (for example, ABS, 2020; Bureau of Labor Statistics, 2016; Grimm & Dietz, 2018). Combined with this, the roles and expectations of volunteers by governments has shifted, particularly in developed economies, where essential health and community services are increasingly delivered by volunteers through the contracting out of services (Casto, 2016; Oppenheimer et al., 2014), in response to the withdrawal of direct government involve-ment in core service delivery (Lockstone-Binney et al., 2016; Pick et al., 2011). The rise of neo-liberalism and economic rationalism, the winding back of the welfare state and ideas of smaller governments have contributed to the explosion of public/private partnerships between the voluntary sector and the state (Davis Smith, 2003). Competition for volunteers, therefore, is fierce, with volunteer-involving organisations needing to adapt as individuals become more discretionary about where they volunteer, for how long and in what types of roles (Winterton et al., 2013).

Tomazos (in this volume) interprets EST volunteering in a very catholic and inclusive way, recognising that this does not necessarily match standard definitions of volunteering in these sectors or of volunteer tourism (or voluntourism). He rightly makes no apologies for this as this approach embraces emerging areas of work, notably with regard to the sharing economy, that do not generally feature under this classification. However, this does point to an increased blurring of the boundaries between paid employment, unpaid work and volun-tary work. Paid employment should be, perhaps, the simplest of these three to comprehend although the emergence of the sharing economy, in particular its manifestations in tourism, sports and events in the accommodation and transport sectors raise questions about the con-tractual status of such work.

The question of whether volunteering is always a free and unconstrained activity aligned to core volunteering definitions (Cnaan et al., 1996; Handy et al., 2000) is questionable for some forms of volunteering. For example, the requirement for youth to engage in voluntary community service as part of an educational credit is a case where volunteerism involves some element of obligation and control, similar to paid work. Chen and Qi (this volume) examines service learning for students at business events, where students may be required to volunteer in order to gain the experience needed to secure paid employment. The interpretation placed on the concept of voluntary work and volunteerism, and particularly on the extent of obligation or coercion, varies greatly across social, cultural and national contexts (Handy et al., 2000; Merrill, 2006). With some exceptions (Tuan, 2005; Qi, 2020), the preponderance of reference to these concepts in the literature, however, appears to be located within a westernised, developed world context (Russell, 2016).

Volunteering can be stressful (Holmes & Lockstone-Binney, 2014), particularly when the commitment becomes onerous and work-like in nature. Thus, volunteering out of disagreeable obligation (Stebbins, 2000) may be seen as a misuse of the term 'volunteer' as the activity is not truly voluntary. Stebbins argues that this is especially true in the case of people who are volunteering for work experience and internships, and this type of activity has been particularly difficult to reconcile with volunteering definitions (Parker, 1997). Likewise, it is arguable that those taking unpaid or underpaid first jobs in sectors such as the creative industries are, de facto, volunteering part or all of their time (Alacovska, 2018; Shade & Jacobson, 2015). The effect of these contexts is to further blur the boundaries between voluntary and involuntary volunteering, acknowledging that individuals whilst volunteering in these more coerced forms may still benefit by gaining relevant work experience, together with additional personal, social and skills development (Haski-Leventhal et al., 2018).

Voluntary work – a Global North luxury? The context of volunteer tourism

Hawksley and Georgeou (2019) argue that the neo-liberal turn inherent in much of the discourse on volunteering in Western societies negates the involvement of volunteers to the role of cheap labour in response to the withdrawal of government in the provision of core essential services. As such, volunteering is viewed less as a form of meaningful community empowerment. Howard and Burns (2015) share this view and further argue for a post-colonial approach to be taken to international volunteering, which would overcome the privileging of Northern perspectives of volunteering as a form of work.

It is a common but somewhat myopic and neo-colonial perspective on volunteering to see this as predominantly a North-South or North-North phenomenon, whereby the Global South is seen as the place that hosts volunteers from the Global North (Baillie Smith et al., 2018; Butcher & Einolf, 2016). Baillie Smith et al. (2018) highlight that alternative flows are well-established through the major role that South-South voluntary action plays in supporting regional development. They also make the strong case that non-Western volunteers are better prepared in cultural, linguistic and technical terms, to undertake the development work that is required. Further, engagement that mirrors volunteering in other contexts but is seen as part of wider responsibility to community is commonplace within many Global South contexts, especially in indigenous and other more traditional societies (Kerr et al., 2001; Warburton & Winterton, 2010).

The future of more expansive and inclusive conceptualisations of volunteering may lie in recognition of its global importance for realising the universal development agenda set out in the United Nations Sustainable Development Goals (SDGs). The *Transforming our world: The 2030 agenda for sustainable development* (Agenda 2030) notes "volunteer groups" are one of the key stakeholder groups that governments must work with on SDG implementation, together with regional authorities, international institutions, academia and philanthropic organisations, amongst others (UNGA, 2015, p. 11). Volunteering has further been acknowledged as a means to

> expand and mobilize constituencies, and to engage people in national planning and implementation for sustainable development goals. And volunteer groups can help to localize the new agenda by providing new spaces of interaction between governments and people for concrete and scalable solutions.
>
> *(UNGA, 2014, p. 36)*

We acknowledge that COVID-19 has recently reversed progress towards achieving the SDGs (UN, 2020) but there remains a significant role for volunteers to play in realising this agenda.

COVID-19: seismic change or a blip on the graph?

This chapter has already raised a wide range of challenges impacting on EST volunteering. Yet at the time of writing, we must add COVID-19 to this list. Rochester, in this volume, grapples with the almost impossible task of assessing underlying trends in voluntary engagement while at the same time recognising the impact of context in the shape of a global pandemic. This has clearly accentuated trend changes while also, arguably, shifting the focus of volunteering or, indeed, offering a phase of pause to some forms. Rochester highlights the heterogeneity of volunteering and the challenges of generalising about phenomena that show such distinct diversity in terms of scale, context, agency and formalisation.

The pandemic has substantially put EST volunteering on hold in many countries as opportunities at all levels have disappeared. International tourism all but stalled from early 2020 (UNWTO, 2020), with only limited prospects for a global recovery in 2021, while domestic travel has not compensated for this loss in any significant measure. As a consequence, voluntary roles, whether in cultural institutions, as destination ambassadors or as voluntourists, have correspondingly disappeared. In the areas of sports and events, there was widespread cancellation or postponement of mega and major fixtures and, when they did take place, generally this occurred without spectators or with significantly reduced numbers. The Tokyo Olympics, for example, were postponed to 2021 (Tokyo 2020, 2020) and with that opportunities for thousands of Japanese and international volunteers to participate. At a local level, many countries saw the curtailment of junior and adult amateur sports and, with it, the volunteering contribution of coaches, referees and parents, among others. Other major and mega events suffered the same fate in 2020, such as the Dubai Expo and the Edinburgh Festivals, as well as a myriad of community events and festivals, all of which also were planned to utilise volunteers to a significant degree. How and in what form volunteering returns after the global pandemic remains to be seen.

Kostas Tomazos, in his chapter in this volume, provides critical perspectives on volunteer tourism with, perhaps, rather more balance than some critics of the growth of this industry sector, who advocate a ban on most commercial practices in this regard (Guttentag, 2009). Prior to March 2020, volunteer tourism was a growing form of alternative travel with non-governmental organisations (NGOs) and, increasingly, commercial interests as the primary institutions placing volunteers abroad (Barbieri et al., 2012; Keese, 2011).

The COVID-19 pandemic has put a temporary hold on international travel and perhaps this is an opportunity to pause that can also enable some level of reflection on the ethical and practical concerns that Tomazos raises in relation to volunteer tourism. Huish (2021), indeed, is rather less circumspect in his argument, taking the definitive line that the combination of increased youth awareness of the environmental consequences of long-haul travel with the shock of COVID-19 will significantly reduce, if not eliminate, both international study and international volunteering. Others are suggesting that countries in the Global South need to seek alternative childcare models for orphaned children within communities rather than looking to external support through volunteering (Ladaphongphatthana, 2021). However, there is some emerging evidence that the loss of income and support derived from volunteer tourism programmes in countries such as Cambodia is having a direct and negative impact on key service providers such as orphanages (Khadka & Sem, 2020).

In addition, the travel disruption and closed borders have refocused tourism on local and domestic markets. A long term limitation of international volunteer tourism has been the inability of domestic organisations to partner with volunteer tourism providers to harness the volunteer energy of returning tourists (Coghlan, 2015). Ong's chapter (this volume) considers how to turn global volunteer tourism into glocal support.

Resilience and reinvention for EST volunteering

The COVID-19 global pandemic has highlighted two key areas where volunteering can facilitate critical societal roles in future years, most notably within the broad leisure industry encompassing sectors ranging from sport and tourism to events, hospitality and entertainment. These are (i) the importance of volunteering in times of crisis and how volunteering can foster and address community needs whilst contributing towards societal *well-being*, and (ii) the central role of volunteering in both supporting and enhancing social/community *resilience*. However, the pandemic has also exposed vulnerabilities within the volunteer ecosystem in some countries, albeit possibly as a temporary phenomenon as older volunteers withdrew their services because of their health vulnerabilities to the effects of the virus (Roche, 2020). This, however, locates the decline as part of a general trend in some countries (e.g. the UK) towards a younger volunteer profile, exacerbated, perhaps, by the crisis and highlighting the perceived value of volunteering as a means of enhancing employability to access a career ladder (Paine et al., 2013).

The pandemic further illustrated how volunteering can provide an effective mechanism for addressing broad community needs, and how volunteering can also contribute towards health and well-being for both volunteers and the leisure sector more generally. During times of crises, volunteers play an important social role in both supporting community recovery, and also sharing a sense of belonging and identity amongst volunteer group members who are often operating in affected communities (Miles & Shipway, 2020). This was increasingly evident during 2020–2021 by boosting community morale and mobilising resources within affected communities. For example, in the UK, the mass vaccination programme, that started in December 2020, highlighted the contribution of the voluntary sector to assist with supporting government policy and mass vaccination implementation. Similarly, Miao, Schwarz and Schwarz (2021) report how, in China, large numbers of volunteers were mobilised through the country's leading digital volunteering platform to augment public health services in the early stages of the pandemic. Interestingly, those recruited were experienced volunteers who were, in practice, co-producers of local community responses to the crisis.

Organisations, for example in the travel sector, took the lead in encouraging employees who normally work in customer-facing roles, to volunteer to support local healthcare and community services as airline routes were rapidly shut down in 2020 (CNA, 2020;

Jones, 2020). At the same time, the global crisis has also exposed some of the challenges that formal bureaucracies have in responding to and accommodating large-scale volunteer responses. As an example, this was highlighted during the early stages of the pandemic in the UK when the National Health Service (NHS) was initially unable to deploy the large numbers who offered their services on a voluntary basis (Marsh & Sabbagh, 2020).

Ironically, a volunteering paradox exists in sport, events and tourism management. On the one hand, volunteers clearly play a vital component part in the 'bounce-back-ability' of the broader leisure sector. However, during times of crises the primary aim of many EST organisations and clubs will initially be one of basic survival through the crises. These organisations must primarily ensure they remain as viable functioning operations that are actually able to effectively embrace and support volunteers, and thus be in a position to 'bounce back better' (Shipway & Miles, 2020).

EST environments, be they clubs or organisations, serve a vital role as leisure-based settings whereby volunteers can help rebuild a sense of well-being in the post-crises era. There is further scope for research that explores how these symbolic interactions help shape social behaviour, and how volunteers within the leisure-related sectors can respond to crises that might lead to broader well-being outcomes for both individual volunteers and also for the communities in which they volunteer. Moving the research agenda forward, there is a paucity of studies about how EST volunteers and voluntary organisations, during times of crises, can help shape volunteering, and the subsequent implications for both individual and community well-being.

When considering the broader volunteer landscape, there is also potential for future research which takes a more macro approach and explores linkages between EST volunteering and the nuances and roles of social/community resilience. The global volunteer responses to the COVID-19 pandemic illustrated the increasingly important role of social/community based, bottom-up approaches within the voluntary sector to dealing with global crises and in doing so, to foster greater resilience.

For the purpose of this chapter, volunteer resilience is the ability of volunteer communities to *absorb* and *recover* from these shocks, whilst positively *adapting* and *transforming* their volunteering structures and means for delivering volunteering activity in the face of uncertain impacts of stresses. It is also the ability of those volunteer communities to *manage change* by maintaining and transforming the provision of volunteering in the face of shocks and stresses (Shipway & Miles, 2020). At the heart of notions of community resilience for volunteering is the assumption that communities may become active in seeking to maintain the integrity, identity, livelihoods and resources of their respective communities when under challenge or threat (Shipway et al., 2021). In the EST contexts, a more resilient volunteer community will be one that is both socially cohesive and connected.

Substantial research has found a positive link between volunteering and the volunteer's well-being, while being a member of a volunteer group can increase the group's social capital (Mellor et al., 2009). However, future studies are required which explore when and how being a volunteer, or having membership of an EST volunteering group, might affect personal and collective well-being. A core argument here is that being part of a volunteering community can contribute to the well-being of both the volunteer and the communities in which they are active, and help support recovery from times of crises.

Effective response to, and recovery from, a crisis will require a substantial amount of social support, which may come in either tangible, emotional or informational forms (Inoue & Havard, 2015). Volunteers fulfil these vital roles, either through the provision of services, affective assistance and comfort, or sharing information and advice. In summary, the global pandemic has shown that increasing not only the amount, but also the perceived availability of social support by volunteers was crucial for (i) promoting well-being, (ii) highlighting the underlying power of volunteering and (iii) fostering a sense of purpose and meaning in life.

Conclusion

In concluding this chapter and, indeed, this volume, we have sought to place volunteering in EST in the wider context of trends and developments in society, touching on aspects of social and demographic change, social policy and practice and the nature of work that we may see emerge in the future. Such discussion, of course, must always be fraught with dangers and footnoted with multiple caveats because of the diverse contexts within which EST volunteering is located, globally and because any speculative future view can never be more than, well, speculative! The inherent challenges of informed future-gazing have been thrown into sharp relief by the global pandemic and we have tried to reflect some of the impact of COVID-19 on volunteering in general and tourism, sports and events in particular in this chapter.

What appears inevitable is that, for the foreseeable future, volunteering roles will change from the past normal as a consequence of health-related social distancing, potentially discriminatory limitations to travel and the erosion of social confidence among key volunteer groups, notably older participants. There may well be less front-facing volunteer roles, as is likely during the Tokyo Olympics and the roles of volunteers may also further change (Lockstone-Binney et al., 2015), with a greater focus on specialist rather than general support roles. Models of 'virtual volunteering' as part of EST volunteering may gain greater prominence, whereby voluntary participation moves to remote roles away from sites and venues. Beyond COVID, changes to work itself, driven by technology, may also reduce demand for on-the-ground-volunteering.

This all said, there is little doubt that the tourism, sports and events sectors as a whole would lose out hugely were the diverse contributions of volunteers to be lost for health, technological or wider societal reasons at a time when demographic change, especially in the Global North, will place increased pressure on communities and families to care for their own with limited state support and, therefore, increase demand for other forms of genuine or enforced 'volunteering' or unpaid social care. Tourism, sports and events are essential to the physical and mental well-being of all communities and much important activity in this regard will wither away without vital volunteer contributions.

References

Alacovska, A. (2018). Informal creative labour practices: A relational work perspective. *Human Relations, 71*(12), 1563–1589. https://doi.org/10.1177/0018726718754991

Australian Bureau of Statistics (ABS). (2020). *General social survey: Summary results, Australia methodology, 2019.* Canberra: ABS.

Baillie Smith, M., Laurie, N., & Griffiths, M. (2018). South-South volunteering and development. *The Geographical Journal, 184*(2), 158–168. https://doi.org/10.1111/geoj.12243

Barbieri, C., Almeida Santos, C., & Katsube, Y. (2012). Volunteer tourism: On-the-ground observations from Rwanda. *Tourism Management, 33*, 509–516. http://DOI.org/10.1016/j.tourman.2011.05.009

Bartram, T., Cavanagh, J., & Hoye, R. (2017). The growing importance of human resource management in the NGO, volunteer and not-for-profit sectors. *International Journal of Human Resource Management, 28*(14), 1901–1911. https://doi.org/10.1080/09585192.2017.1315043

Bimber, B., Flanagin, A., & Stohl, C. (2012). *Collective action in organizations: Interaction and engagement in an era of technological change.* New York: Cambridge University Press. https://doi.org/10.1017/CBO9780511978777

Bureau of Labor Statistics. (2016). *Volunteering in the United States – 2015.* Washington, DC: US Department of Labor.

Butcher, J., & Einolf, C. (2016). *Perspectives on volunteering. Nonprofit and civil society studies.* New York: Springer.

Casto, H. (2016). Just one more thing I have to do: School-community partnership. *School Community Journal, 26,* 139–162.

Channel News Asia (CNA) (2020). COVID-19: Singapore Airlines to provide 300 'care ambassadors' to fill manpower gap at hospitals, 3rd April, accessed at https://www.channelnewsasia.com/news/singapore/covid-19-singapore-airlines-care-ambassadors-hospital-manpower-12608118 on 26th February 2021.

Cnaan, R., Handy, F., & Wadsworth, M. (1996). Defining who is a volunteer: Conceptual and empirical considerations. *Nonprofit and Voluntary Sector Quarterly, 25*(3), 364–383. https://doi.org/10.1177/0899764096253006

Coghlan, A. (2015). Prosocial behaviour in volunteer social. *Annals of Tourism Research, 55,* 46–60. https://doi.org/10.1016/j.annals.2015.08.002

Davis Smith, J. (2003). Government and volunteering. *Voluntary Action, 5,* 23–23.

Elkington, S., & Stebbins, R. A. (2014). *The serious leisure perspective: An introduction.* London: Routledge.

Graeber, D. (2018) *Bullshit jobs. A theory.* London: Allen Lane.

Grant-Smith, D., & McDonald, P. (2017). Ubiquitous yet ambiguous: An integrative review of unpaid work. *International Journal of Management Reviews, 20,* 559–578. https://doi.org/10.1111/ijmr.12153

Grimm, R. T. Jr., & Dietz, N. (2018). *Where are America's volunteers? A look at America's widespread decline in volunteering in cities and states.* College Park, MD: Do Good Institute, University of Maryland.

Guttentag, D. (2009). The possible negative impacts of volunteer tourism. *International Journal of Tourism Research, 11,* 537–551. https://doi.org/10.1002/jtr.727

Handy, F., Cnaan, R. A., Brudney, J., Ascoli, U., Meijs, L. C. P. M., & Ranade, S. (2000). Public perception of "who is a volunteer": An examination of the net-cost approach from a cross-cultural perspective. *Voluntas, 11,* 45–65.

Haski-Leventhal, D., Alony, I., Lockstone-Binney, L. Holmes, K., Meijs, L., & Oppenheimer, M. (2020). Online volunteering at DigiVol: An innovative crowd-sourcing approach for heritage tourism artefacts preservation. *Journal of Heritage Tourism, 15*(1), 14–26. https://doi.org/10.1080/1743873X.2018.1557665

Haski-Leventhal, D., Meijs, L. C., & Hustinx, L. (2010). The third-party model: Enhancing volunteering through governments, corporations and educational institutes. *Journal of Social Policy, 39,* 139–158. https:// doi.org/10.1017/S0047279409990377

Haski-Leventhal, D., Meijs, L. C. P. M., Lockstone-Binney, L., Holmes, K., & Oppenheimer, M. (2018). Measuring volunteerability and the capacity to volunteer among non-volunteers: Implications for social policy. *Social Policy and Administration, 52*(5), 1139–1167. https://doi.org/10.1111/spol.12342

Hawksley, C., & Georgeou, N. (2019). Gramsci 'makes a difference': Volunteering, neoliberal 'common sense', and the sustainable development goals. *Third Sector Review, 25*(2), 27–56.

Holmes, K., & Lockstone-Binney, L. (2014). An exploratory study of volunteer stress management: The organizational story. *Third Sector Review, 20,* 1–7.

Howard, J., & Burns, D. (2015). Volunteering for development within the new ecosystem of international development. *IDS Bulletin, 46*(5), 5–16. https://doi.org/10.1111/1759-5436.12171

Huish, R. (2021). Global citizenship amid COVID-19: Why climate change and a pandemic spell the end of international experiential learning. *Canadian Journal of Development Studies.* https://doi.org/10.1080/02255189.2020.1862071

Hyde, M. K., Dunn, J., Bax, C., & Chambers, S. K. (2016). Episodic volunteering and retention: An integrated theoretical approach. *Nonprofit and Voluntary Sector Quarterly, 45*(1), 45–63. https://doi.org/10.1177/0899764014558934

Inoue, Y., & Havard, C. T. (2015). Sport and disaster relief: A content analysis. *Disaster Prevention and Management: An International Journal, 24*(3), 355–368. https://doi.org/10.1108/DPM-12-2014-0276

Jones, L. (2020) Airline staff volunteer to support healthcare workers, 6th April, accessed at https://samchui.com/2020/04/06/grounded-airline-crews-now-healthcare-heroes/#.YDiZfmj7SUk on 26th February 2020.

Keese, J. (2011). The geography of volunteer tourism: Place matters. *Tourism Geographies, 13*(2), 257–279. https://doi.org/10.1080/14616688.2011.567293

Kerr, L., Savelsberg, H., Sparrow, S., & Tedmanson, D. (2001). *Experiences and perceptions of volunteering in Indigenous and non-English speaking background communities.* Adelaide: University of South Australia.

Khadka, S., & Sem, B. (2020). Caring for children left behind in residential care during COVID-19. UNICEF, accessed at https://www.unicef.org/cambodia/stories/caring-children-left-behind-residential-care-during-covid-19 on 23rd March 2021.

Ladaphongphatthana, K. (2021). Holistic orphan care: A call for change in caring for orphans and vulnerable children. *Transformations, 38*(1), 78–92. https://doi.org/10.1177/0265378820983355

Lockstone-Binney, L., Smith, K., Holmes, K., & Baum, T. (2015). Exploring future forms of event volunteering. In I. Yeoman, M. Robertson, U. McMahon-Beattie, E. Backer & K. Smith (Eds.), *The future of events & festivals* (pp. 175–186). Routledge Advances in Events Book Series. Abingdon: Routledge.

Lockstone-Binney, L., Whitelaw, P. A., & Binney, W. (2016). Crown land management from a volunteer perspective: The Victorian example. *Australasian Journal of Environmental Management, 23*, 130–140. https://doi.org/10.1080/14486563.2015.1094751

Marsh, S., & Sabbagh, D. (2020) NHS says coronavirus volunteer scheme taking time to get up to speed, *The Guardian*, 10th April, accessed at https://www.theguardian.com/society/2020/apr/10/nhs-coronavirus-volunteer-ionger-than-expected on 26th February 2021.

Mellor, D., Hayashi, Y., Stokes, M., Firth, L., Lake, L., Staples, M., Chambers, S., & Cummins, R. (2009). Volunteering and its relationship with personal and neighbourhood wellbeing. *Nonprofit and Voluntary Sector Quarterly, 38*(1), 144–159. https://doi.org/10.1177/0899764008317971

Merrill, M. V. (2006). Global trends and the challenges for volunteering. *The International Journal of Volunteer Administration, XXIV*(1), 9–14.

Miao, Q., Schwarz, S., & Schwarz, G. (2021). Responding to COVID-19: Community volunteerism and coproduction in China. *World Development, 137*. https://doi.org/10.1016/j.worlddev.2020.105128

Miles, L., & Shipway, R. (2020). Exploring the COVID-19 pandemic as a catalyst for stimulating future research agendas for managing crises and disasters at international sport events. *Event Management, 24*(4), 537–552. https://doi.org/10.3727/152599519X15506259856688

OECD. (2019). *Future of work.* Paris: OECD.

Oppenheimer, M., Warburton, J., & Carey, J. (2014). The next "new" idea: The challenges of organisational change, decline and renewal in Australian Meals on Wheels'. *Voluntas, 29*, 1550–1569.

O'Rourke, P. P. (2020), How NPM-inspired-change impacted work and HRM in the Irish voluntary sector in an era of austerity. *Employee Relations, 42*(5), 1101–1116. http://doi.org/10.1108/er-01-2020-0003

Orwell, G. (1933). *Down and out in Paris and London.* Harmondsworth: Penguin.

Paine, A., McKay, S., & Moro, D. (2013). Does volunteering improve employability? Insights from the British Household Panel Survey and beyond. *Voluntary Sector Review, 4*(3), 355–376. http://doi.org/10.1332/204080513X13807974909244

Parker, S. (1997). Volunteering: Altruism, markets, careers and leisure. *World Leisure and Recreation, 39*(3), 4–5. https://doi.org/10.1080/10261133.1997.9674070

Pick, D., Holmes, K., & Brueckner, M. (2011). Governmentalities of volunteering: A study of regional Western Australia. *Voluntas, 22*, 390–408. http://doi.org/10.1007/s11266-010-9161-5

Productivity Commission. (2010). *Contribution of the not-for-profit sector.* Canberra: Productivity Commission.

Qi, H. (2020). Conceptualizing volunteering in tourism in China. *Tourism Management Perspectives, 33*, 1–8. http://doi.org/10.1016/j.tmp.2019.100618

Roche, M. (2020). *Are young people replacing older people as the key volunteering group?* London: nfpSynergy.

Rochester, C., Ellis-Paine, A., Howlett S., & Zimmeck M. (2010). *Volunteering in the 21st century.* Basingstoke: Palgrave Macmillan.

Rotatori, D., Lee, E. J., & Sleeva, S. (2021). The evolution of the workforce during the fourth industrial revolution. *Human Resource Development International, 24*(1), 92–103. https://doi.org/10.1080/13678868.2020.1767453

Russell, B. (2016). Measuring the contribution of volunteering to the sustainable development goals: The measurement of volunteering in the Global South. *12th International Conference of the International Society for Third Sector Research* (ISTR) (pp. 1–17). Stockholm.

Shade, L. R., & Jacobson, (2015). Hungry for the job: Gender, unpaid internships, and the creative industries. *The Sociological Review, 63*(S1), 188–205. https://doi.org/10.1111/1467-954X.12249

Shipway, R., & Miles, L. (2020). Bouncing back and jumping forward: Scoping the resilience land-scape of international sports events and implications for events and festivals. *Event Management, 24*(1), 185–196. https://doi.org/10.3727/152599518X15403853721376

Shipway, R., Miles, L., & Gordon, R. (2021). *Crisis and disaster management for sport.* London: Routledge.

Stebbins, R. A. (2000). Obligation as an aspect of leisure experience. *Journal of Leisure Research, 32*(1), 152–155. http://doi.org/10.1080/00222216.2000.11949906

Susskind, D. (2020). *A world without work. Technology, automation and how we should respond.* London: Allen Lane.

Taylor, R. (2004). Extending conceptual boundaries: Work, voluntary work and employment'. *Work, Employment and Society, 18*, 29–49. https://doi.org/10.1177/0950017004040761

Tokyo 2020. (2020). Olympic Games postponed to 2021, accessed at https://tokyo2020.org/en/news/joint-statement-from-international-olympic-committee-and-tokyo2020 on 1st October 2020.

Tuan, Y. (2005). Can volunteerism be promoted through government administration? *Volunteer Service Journal (China)*, Special English edition, 16–23.

UNGA [United Nations General Assembly]. (2014). *The road to dignity by 2030: Ending poverty, trans-forming all lives and protecting the planet. Synthesis report of the Secretary-General on the post-2015 agenda.* New York: United Nations.

UNGA [United Nations General Assembly]. (2015). *Transforming our world: The 2030 agenda for sustain-able development.* New York: United Nations.

UNV [UN Volunteers]. (2018). *2018 state of the world's volunteerism report: The thread that binds.* New York: United Nations.

United Nations. (2020). *The sustainable development goals report 2020.* New York: United Nations.

UNWTO. (2020). Impact of COVID-19 on global tourism made clear as UNWTO counts the cost of standstill, 28th July, accessed at https://www.unwto.org/news/impact-of-covid-19-on-global-tourism-made-clear-as-unwto-counts-the-cost-of-standstill on 1st October 2020.

Warburton, J., & Winterton, R. (2010). The role of volunteering in an era of cultural transition: Can it provide a role identity for older people from Asian cultures? *Diversity, 2*, 1048–1058. https://doi.org/10.3390/d2081048

Winterton, R., Warburton, J., & Oppenheimer, M. (2013). The future of meals on wheels? Reviewing innovative approaches to meal provision for ageing population. *International Journal of Social Welfare, 22*, 141–151. https://doi.org/10.1111/j.1468-2397.2012.00889.x

INDEX

Note: **Bold** page numbers refer to tables and *italic* page numbers refer to figures.

Adams, A. 8
Agrawal, A. 44
Aisbett, L. 322
Alexander, A. 177, 179
Allen, N. J 275, 308
Alonso, A. D. 85
alternative tourism 400, 403
altruism 8; Auckland volunteers 104;
    characteristic of 125–126; and egoism 376,
    382; and instrumentalism 320, 325, 328;
    in New Zealand 107; reciprocal 226–227;
    and self-interest 5, 149, 150–151, 154, 376;
    sentiments of 16
altruistic tourism 122
analytic hierarchy process (AHP) method 274
Andereck, K. 125
Anderson, E. 86
Anderson, H. 300
Andriotis, K. 86
Anheier, H. 203, 204, 205, 206
Appalachian Trail (AT) volunteers: Appalachian
    Trail Conference 114, 115; *Appalachian Trail
    Conservancy Volunteer Leadership Handbook*
    116; corridor monitoring 117–118; guidelines
    116; historical background 114–115; logo
    115; management 115–117; National Park
    Service 114, 115; National Trails System
    Act 115; natural and cultural resources 118;
    organisational plan 116; parks and protected
    area planning and management 113–114;
    recruitment 118; role of volunteers 116–117;
    6,000 volunteers 112–113; task of herding
    volunteers 118; Trail Magic 119; trail work
    117, *117*
Arrow, K. J. 380

Association of Directors of Adult Social
    Services 468
attitudes and behaviour: change in kinds
    of activity, volunteer involvement 467;
    episodic volunteering 466; formal and
    informal volunteering 467–468; growth
    of managerialism 465; new model of
    volunteering 466; volunteering in a digital
    society 466–467; volunteer roles and
    responsibilities 465
Auckland museums: Auckland Art Gallery
    100, **100**; Auckland Council 100; Auckland
    Tourism, Events and Economic Development
    (ATEED) 99; Auckland War Memorial
    Museum 100, **100**; cultural and social
    capital 106–108; government policy 106;
    Maori culture and collections 100–101;
    New Zealand Maritime Museum 100,
    100; nonprofit heritage brands 107; profile
    of volunteers, demographic data 101–103;
    reasons for volunteering 104–105; tourist-
    oriented museums 101–103; visitors 100–101;
    volunteering in bicultural operations in
    multicultural context 99–101; volunteers roles
    and functions 103–104
Auld, C. 61
Australian Football League (AFL): LGBT+
    supporter groups 9; pride groups in sport
    395–397; supporter groups 394–397;
    volunteers doing diversity work 394–397
Australian grassroots associations 136–139; *see
    also* leadership
Australian sport: AFL (*see* Australian Football
    League (AFL)); community sport volunteers
    390–391; demographic variations 390;

511

disability and volunteering 390; diversity and inclusion efforts 389; policy imperative 390; *see also* sport volunteering
Australian Volunteer Program 368
autonomous motivation 60–63, 264–266
Ayer, N. 8
Ayobami, O. K. 379

Baillie Smith, M. 32, 37, 503
Bang, H. 259
Bargeman, B. 362, 366
Bateman, P. 430
Bath-Rosenfeld, R. J. 3
Baudrillard, J. 382
Baum, T. 11, 205, 240
Beck, U. 353
2008 Beijing Olympic Games 224, 419
'being valued' 8, 304, 305, 308, 309, 312
beneficiaries: of charity 338; community as 33; deliver services 202, 203; intended 1, 165; leisure activities 2; project 364; volunteer as 33
benevolent volunteering 394
Benson, A. M. 41, 125, 176, 243, 244, 335
Berkshire Hills Conference 114
Bhati, A. 300, 302
'Big Society,' UK 346
Billis, D. 467
Birchard, W. 113
Black, R. 87
Bladen, C. 205, 206
Boehm, A. 138
Boezeman, E. 273
Bonney, M. S. 353
Bono, B. A. 426
Booth, A. 492
Bosserman, P. 425
Boulding, K. 425
Bowdin, G. 206
Bowles, W. 404
Bradbury, S. 455
Brannick, M. T. 474, 478
Braun, V. 276
Brewis, G. 418
Brian, C. 116
Bridges, D. 404
Bristow, R. S. 5, 118
Brown, P. 304
Brown, S. 124, 125
Brudney, J. L. 134, 249, 250, 254, 273, 278, 477
Bryen, L. 193
Bryon, J. 87
Bulloch S. 461
Burns, D. 503
business events: in China (*see* Chinese business events volunteering); method 225; transitions

in volunteering 230–231; volunteering at 223–224, 230
Business Visits and Events Partnership (BVEP) 208
Bussell, H. 123, 125
Busser, J. A. 263
Butler, B. 430
Bydgoszcz (case study): 2009 Basketball European Championships 73; City Centre for Volunteering 73–74; 2019 European Athletics Championships 73; 2009 European Universities Rowing Championships 73; main tasks of LOC 73; national and international sporting events 72; UEFA U-21 73–75
Byers, T. 355, 356

Caduri, A. 305, 309
CAF World Giving Index 456
Cairncross, G. 86
Caldicott, R. 88, 90, 91, 92
Canadian community sport volunteers 287
Canadian Rockies 50, 51
Carnegie Trust 463
Carnicelli, S. 300, 302, 308
Carron, A. V. 455, 456
Carruthers, C. P. 263
Carvalho, A. 275
Castaneda, Q. 366
casual leisure volunteering 352
Central Product Classification (CPC) Version 2.1 21; classifications for the goods and services, volunteer work 27–28
Chaiechi, T. 300
Chaisinthop, N. 438
Chalip, L. 190, 251
Chambre, S. M. 426
Chanavat, N. 243, 244
Chang, C. 10, 404
charity(ies): in ancient cultures 202; concept of giving 203–204; defined 204; event volunteering (*see* charity event volunteering); factors influencing 206–207; fundraising events 6, 202–205, 208–209, 251; importance of volunteers 202; motivation and trends 206–208; recent development 202–203; rise of episodic volunteering 207–208; time factors 207; volunteering for 205–206
Charity Aid Foundation (CAF) World Giving Index (WGI) survey 475
charity event volunteering **209**; collaborative events 208, 210; organisational events 208, 210; third party events 208, 209; volunteer events 208–209
Chassagne, N. 367
Chen, G. 10

Chen, L. J. 379
Chen, X. 99, 101, 102, 106, 109
Chetkovich, C. A. 137
China Convention/Exhibition/Event
  Society 419
Chinese business events volunteering: auto-
  ethnographic data 419; background of
  419–420; blurred boundaries of volunteering
  229–230; booming of business event industry
  419; collective volunteering phenomenon
  228–229; commercialisation trends 229;
  educational institutions 419–421; event
  organisers 419–421; in-depth interview data
  419; monetary rewards for volunteers 227–
  228; Olympic Games 224–225; reciprocal
  process 421; service learning 418–421;
  2016 Shandong Province Entrepreneurship
  Programs Exhibition 225–226; *Student
  Volunteering at Business Events in China* 418;
  student volunteers 419, 420; volunteer
  motivations 226–227; youths/students
  225–226, 231
Cho, H. 456
Chowdhary, Nimit R. 5
Cigurova, L. 8
Ciucescu, N. 305
civic engagement 430
Clarke, V. 276
Clary, E. G. 99, 104, 258, 262
classic volunteers 58
Clayton, D. 489
Cliffe, R. 304
Clifton, J. 36
Cnaan, R. 150, 151, 332, 333, 334, 336, 341
Cnaan, R. A. 1, 10, 123, 135, 150, 151, 175, 176,
  251, 332, 333, 334, 336, 340
Coghlan, A. 454, 455
Cohen-Callow, A. 308, 310
Cole, D. N. 113
2014 Commonwealth Games 9
community events: ANOVAs testing 198; case
  study 194–196; complexity of goals 190–191;
  definition 190; design and management of
  volunteering 192–194; episodic volunteers
  193; findings **197–198**, 197–199; instrumental
  or celebratory volunteering 191–192;
  National Days of Service 191–192; sample
  195–196, **196**; volunteering as an event 6,
  191–194, 199; volunteering for an event 6,
  191–193, 199
community resilience 506
community sports organisations (CSOs)
  5; analysis of paid work and for-profit
  organisations 145; balance of altruism and
  self-interest 150–151; broader contribution
  to society 148–149; defining 144; in Europe

152–155; formal or informal volunteering
  144; motivations and barriers 149–151;
  numbers of 146; position in leisure market
  152–154; relation to government policy 149;
  role in sports participation and volunteering
  146–148, **147**; social capital and social
  inclusion 146; sociological or political
  approach 145; surveys of 148, 154; theoretical
  conceptualisation 144–145
community sport volunteering 8; Canadian
  287; continuing volunteering, reasons for
  287–289; good role fit 288–289; national
  governing body 144; reaching personal
  goals 289; recognition 290–291; resignation
  291–294; rewards 289–290; rewards and
  recognition 289–291; role of others 287–288;
  study 287
community sustainability 321–324
Compion, S. 253
Connaughton, D. P. 57
Connell, J. 271
conservation volunteer tourism (CVT):
  community 50; discourse 45–46; discursive
  tensions 45–47; growth of 40; interactions
  and flows 41, *42, 43*; knowledge 46–47;
  local involvement and resident perceptions
  47–48; neoliberalism and access to benefits
  48; organisations and projects 50–51;
  political ecology 41–45; political economic
  considerations 47–48; promotional material
  40; sending organisations 40; volunteers
  49–50
continued project-based leisure volunteering
  351–352
continuity theory 59
controlled motivation 60
Cooper, John R. 8
Copeland, J. 99
corporate volunteering: and effects, theoretical
  background 215–216; Enchanted Song
  Festival 215, 218–220; event projects 6;
  GlobeBank Group 218–220; in HeatHouse
  Run 215, 216–218; *2016 Impact Survey*
  215–216; in Poland 214, 216; research method
  216; *2017 Volunteerism Survey* 215
Costa, C. A. 456
Cottrell, S. 124
CouchSurfing.com 474
court-referred volunteering 254
Cousins, J. A. 48
COVID-19 pandemic: to affect local
  communities and nations 295; Auckland
  Museum 100; Australian Volunteer Program
  368; challenges of 11–12, 504; critical societal
  roles 505; international tourism 367, 504–
  505; interviews via Zoom 406; lockdown,

impact of 406, 468; to rebuild tourism 92; spontaneous activity of individuals and groups 468–469; support of health service 468; travel restrictions 10, 412, 437; volunteering in EST 11–12

Cox, T. 418

Coyne, B. S. 456

Coyne, E. J. 456

Crall, A. W. 47

Cramm, J. M. 478

Cricket World Cup 437

Crosbie, R. 162

cultural attractions 97, 99, 108

cultural capital 98, 105, 107

cultural heritage 97–99, **100**, 101, 105, 204, 306

culturally and linguistically diverse (CALD) groups 242–243

Curran, R. 107

2005 Current Population Survey 34

Cushman, F. 382

Cuskelly, G. 7, 58, 59, 61, 241, 429, 447, 449, 454, 496

Darcy, S. 241

Davies, J. 3

Deane, J. 8, 319

Deardorff, D. K. 405

Deci, E. L. 63

dedicated volunteers 58, 112, 302, 389

Deery, M. 85, 101, 486

Democracy in America (Tocqueville) 381

demographics 25, 31, 99, 175, 187, 210, 263, 273, 278, 281, 479; Americans engaged in INV 476; demographic differences 62–63; motivations 263; OF Olympic games 179–180, **180**; profile of volunteers 101–103; role in employment 170–171; variations in sport volunteers in Australia 390; of AT volunteers 118–119

De Nardi, M. 89

Denny-Smith, G. 368

Denscombe, M. 276

Department of Foreign Affairs and Trade (DFAT) 368

destination service volunteering: accommodation facilities 84; arrival points and transport hubs 84; associations 86; campground hosts 88; emergency and rescue settings 84, 88–89; 'Grey Nomad' travellers 88; host volunteers 84; individual perspective 91; meet-and-greet programmes 86–87; model of 89–90; multi-layered perspective 91; multiple stakeholder perspectives 91–92; organisational perspective 91; planning 89; policymaking 92; research agenda 90–92; settings and roles 89, *90*; stakeholders 83, 88;

tour guides 87–88; visitor experience 84, 89; visitor information centres 84, 85–86; *see also* volunteer tourism (VT)

development volunteering 35, 322

Devereux, P. 32

Dickson, A. 425

Dickson, T. J. 176, 177, 179, 335, 336, 348

Digital, Culture, Media and Sport (DCMS) Department 273

'the dimensions of OC' 303

direct volunteers 17, 18, 25

docents 87

Doherty, A. 59, 335, 347

Doherty, A. J. 448, 455, 456

Dolnicar, S. 58

domestic travel volunteering 437–439

Downward, P. 206

Draper, J. 85

Drummond, S. 300

Dubai Expo 504

Dunn, J. 349

Dwiggins-Beeler, R. 304, 309

Eckardt, C. 366

economic value of volunteering: advocacy and recognition purposes 24; calculating 23–25; data uses 23–25; definition of volunteer work (*see* volunteer work); in international statistical system 19–23; measurement at organizational level 25–26; national economic accountants 23; replacement cost approach 24–25; volunteering, definitions of 15–19; volunteer rate 23

Eddins, E. 124

Egerton, M. 477, 480

Egli, B. 292

Einolf, C. 273

elements of volunteer tourism: advantages 125; destination oriented 127; disadvantages 127–128; local community oriented 126; motivations of the volunteers 124–125; tourist oriented 126

Eley, D. 264

Ellemers, N. 273

Elliott-White, M. 485

Ellis Paine, A. 465, 467

emergency volunteers 89

Enchanted Song Festival 215; for talented disabled people 218–220

Engel, S. 322

episodic volunteering 241, 447; genuine episodic volunteers (GEV) 334; habitual episodic volunteers (HEV) 334; long-term committed volunteers (LTVs) 334; volunteer stewardship management models 251

Esping-Andersen, G. 153

ethical dimensions of EST volunteering 9

ethics of volunteering in tourism: as commodity 381–384; as guests 376–377; homo economicus, conceptualisation of 380; international volunteering 376–377; moral reasoning 375; project management 379; proliferation of projects *378*; utilitarianism and egoism 380–381; volunteering and ethical philosophy 380–381; volunteers involvement 376; volunteer tourism or voluntourism (Americanism) 379; volunteer tourists 377, 379
ethnography 492–493
EU Expert Group on the Economic Dimension of Sport (XG ECO) 22
Eurodesk 410
2008 European football championship 259
European Union (EU) Working Group on Sport and Economics, 2006 22
evaluation: of volunteer program 245–246; of volunteers 244–245
Evans, E. 461, 466
Events Management students 10
events, sports and tourism (EST) 1, 56, 64; ethical dimensions 9; organisations 237–239, 243–245; relevant CPC version 2.1 27–28; volunteering in (*see* volunteering in EST)
event volunteering 5–7; business events 6; charity fundraising events 6; community events 6; conscripts 59; corporate volunteering at events 6; enthusiasts 59; instrumentalists 58–59; social legacy (*see* social legacy from event volunteering)
Everingham, P. 9, 363, 367, 368, 369
expectancy-value theory 267
experiential or experimental tourist 125

Facebook 151
Fairley, S. 335, 336, 352
family volunteering 7, 253–254
Farrell, J. M. 176, 450, 455, 457
Fast Israeli Rescue and Search Team (FIRST) 89
fear of volunteerism 127–128
Fedeli, G. 8
Ferrand, A. 243, 244
Ferraro, O. F. 480
festivals: Cherry Blossom Festival, Japan 495; cultural 341; Edinburgh Festivals 504; Enchanted Song Festival 215, 218–220; film 341; in Flanders 194; Hong Kong Arts Festival 495; LolliBop (a children's festival) 341; mega-events 2; multi-day 6; Sundance Film Festival, USA 495; UK music 489
FIBA 70
FIFA 70, 73, 326–327
Filo, K. 335
Finkelstein, M. A. 474, 478
Finn, M. 485

Fire Games 341
first generation of 'latchkey' kids *see* 'Generation X'
Fischer, L. R. 426
Football Association (FA) 146, 152
Forbes, D. 123, 125
formal volunteering (FV) 2, 11, 144, 145, 272, 287, 460–461, 467, 473–474, 479–480
Fort Belknap Indian Community 50
Fredline, L. 58
Freitag, M. 333, 339
Friedman, A. 305
Fukuyama, F. 320
Fukuyasu, M. 87
Fullagar, S. 492
functions, VFI: career and social functions 105, 259; enhancement function 104, 259; protective function 104, 259; understanding function 104, 259; values function 104, 259
future of volunteering and work: COVID-19: seismic change 504–505; and employment in 21st century 500–501; resilience and reinvention for EST volunteering 505–507; as unpaid work 501–503; volunteer tourism 503–504

Gagan, R. 425
Gagne, M. 266
Galley, G. 36
Games Makers (GM) 161
gap year experiences 400
Gardiner, S. 335
Gaskin, K. 465
Gawlowski, R. 4
Gelmez-Burakgazi, S. 417, 418
El Geneidy, S. 365
2008 General Social Survey (GSS) of Canada 475
'Generation X' 464
'Generation Y' 464
genuine episodic volunteers (GEV) 334
Georgeou, N. 322, 405, 503
Getz, D. 190, 199, 206
Giannoulakis, C. 456, 486
'gig' economy, use of 463
Giroux, H. 321, 325
giving, notion of 203–204
global citizenship: action-oriented global citizenship categories 436; critical 439–440; domestic travel volunteering 437–439; environmental 440; future research 439; political citizenship 434; positive and negative polarising conceptions 435; social 439; spiritual 440; through volunteer tourism 436–437; typology of 435, **435**
Global North: changes in population structures 500–501; CVT discourse 45; CVT

organisations 40; demographic change 507; dominance of 3, 46, 49; global perspective 436; international development volunteering 32, 37; political ecology 41; sending and recipient communities 34; in volunteer tourism 438, 503–504

Global South: changes in population structures 500–501; childcare models 505; international development volunteering 32, 49; political ecology 41; sending and recipient communities 34

GlobeBank 216, 218–220

Glyptis, S. 164

goal setting theory 267

Godbey, G. 151

Goldberg-Glen, R. 176

Goldblatt, J. 205

Goss, K. A. 134

Govekar, M. 207

Govekar, P. 207

Grabowski-Faulkner, S. 9

Graeber, D. 501

grassroots associations (GAs) 136–139

Gray, N. J. 46, 51

Gray, P. 430

Griffiths, M. 35, 36, 37, 369

Grimm, K. E. 3, 41, 49

gross domestic product (GDP) 22, 223, 364, 367, 476

guest volunteers 2, 83, 89–90

Gulak-Lipka, P. 4

Gundelach, B. 478

Guntert, S. T. 61, 259, 263

Guo, C. 102

Guttentag, D. 127, 362, 403, 454, 455

Haas, B. 405

habitual episodic volunteers (HEV) 334

Haddock, M. A. 3

Hager, M. A. 273, 278

Hall, C. M. 89, 128, 403, 412, 454, 455

Hallmann, K. 261, 354, 496

Hall, P. D. 153

Hammitt, W. E. 113

Handy, C. 251

Handy, F. 1, 3, 6, 10, 150, 175, 177, 332, 334

Han, H. 454, 455

Hank, K. 477

hard skills 163–164

Harflett, N. 105, 106, 107, 108

Harman, A. 59

Harms, G. 261

Harrington, M. 429

Harvey, J. 455, 456

Haski-Leventhal, D. 254

Haugen, J. 99

Havens, J. J. 475

Hawkins, C. J. 353

Hawksley, C. 503

Hayes, M. 7

HeatHouse 215–219

Heitmann, S. 206

Helms, S. 479

Hemming, H. 135

Henderson, K. A. 126, 425, 426

Henry, J. 41

heritage attractions 97; economic model 302; industrial 298; leisure model 302; motivational dimensions 302; profiling of volunteers 302; railway 300, 302

Heron, B. 34

"hierarchical code of signification" 382

Hill, M. 164

Hirst, A. 164

'holidaymakers' volunteer 124

Holloway, I. 490, 494

Holmes, K. 4, 36, 56, 85, 86, 90, 91, 107, 136, 205, 274, 300, 302, 327, 448

home organisation 191, 200, 250, 253–254

Hoogstad, E. 251

Hook, J. L. 478

Host City Volunteer (HCV) programme 347; balance of contribution 354; casual leisure volunteering 352; Commonwealth Games 350–351; continued project-based leisure volunteering 351–352; development of capacity building 351; event volunteering management 353; Glasgow 2014 352–355; legacy planning 352; serious leisure volunteering 352; social legacies 353–354; social outcomes 351

host organisation 10, 192–195, 198, 250, 253–254, 368

host volunteers 2, 4, 83–84, 88–90, 199, 448, 455

Howard, J. 503

Hoye, R. 241, 322, 485, 496

Huish, R. 505

human resource management (HRM) 145, 192–193, 239–242, 249, 275, 282, 469

human resources (HR) planning 239

Huppert, F. A. 477, 478, 480

Hustinx, L. 6, 175, 332, 334, 338, 340, 466

Hu, W. 96

Huxley, A. 135

Hyde, M. K. 208, 263

'hyphen' approach 254

Ibsen, B. 149

ILO *Manual on the Measurement of Volunteer Work* 24

individual sustainability 321–324

Ineson, E. M. 300

informal volunteering (INV) 10, 11; benefits of 480; defined 144, 473, 474; definition and

measurement 473–475; education 477; factors shaping 476–479; family structure 477–478; and formal volunteering 479–480; future research 480–481; individuals' characteristics 478–479; scope in various countries 475–476; social capital 478; voluntary engagement 478; womens engaged in 477
Innes, P. 89
Instagram 151
institutional sustainability 324–327
insurance and training 7
intercultural competence 404–405
intercultural learning: competencies 400–401; contributions 411–412; empirical research 410; German context 401–402; intercultural competence 404–405, 409–410; intercultural programme design 408–409; limitations and further research 412; methodology 405–406; provider market and characteristics 406; research objectives 405; responses of returned volunteers 411; results 406–409; travel or volunteering 408; voluntourism or volunteering abroad 402–404; *weltwarts* 402
International Association of Athletics Federation 73
International Classification of Non-profit and Third Sector Organizations (ICNP/TSO) 21
international development volunteering: characterisation of place 35–36; evolution of 32–33; international volunteer tourism and place 36–37; scholarship 3; sending and recipient communities, relationships between 34–35; sites for 33
International Labour Organization (ILO) 16, 18–20, 24
International Olympic Committee (IOC) 70, 166, 324, 495
International Paralympic Committee 241
International Recommendations for Tourism Statistics 2008 22
International Red Cross and Red Crescent Societies (IFCRC) 24–25
international service learning 417–418, 422
International Standard Industrial Classification of All Economic Activities Revision 4 (ISIC Rev. 4) 21; section A: culture, communication, and recreation activities 27; section E: environmental protection and animal welfare activities 27; section G: civic, advocacy, political, and international activities 27; section L: other activities 27
international statistical system: connecting volunteer work 20; culture accounts 23; data on consumer products: goods and services – CPC Ver. 2.1 21; data on industries – ISIC-Rev. 4 21; data on occupations – ISCO-08 20; related satellite accounts 21; scale of

volunteering globally 19; sports accounts 22–23; tourism statistics 21–22; volunteer work, definition 16–19; *see also* economic value of volunteering
International Voluntary Services 401
international volunteering 2, 32–37, 364, 369, 376–377, 379, 381–383, 400–402, 406, **407**, 412, 455
International Volunteering Impacts Survey (IVIS) 364
international volunteer tourism 10, 36–37, 434, 436–437, 440, 505
involuntary volunteering 123, 503
Ismail, H. N. B. 379

Jager, U. 274, 282
Jago, L. 85, 101, 486
Jain, P. 163
Jay, E. 203, 204, 207
Jeanes, R. 391, 397
Jepson, A. 495
job characteristics theory 267
Johnson, A. 325
Johnson, G. 303
Johnson, J. E. 259
Jones, E. 34
Jones, I. 493
Jordan, T. A. 304, 305, 308
Journal of Sustainable Tourism 457
Jozefowicz, B. 6
Junek, O. 10

Kainthola, S. 5
Kals, E. 61
Kang, C. 6
Kant, I. 380
Kaplanidou, K. 354, 355
Kaplan, M. 425, 427
Karr, L. B. 252
Kay, P. 58
Kay, T. 455
Keese, J. 36
Kelly, L. 101
Kemp, S. 165
Kennelly, M. 88
Kenyon, J. A. 305
Khasanzyanova, A. 163, 168
Kim, B. J. 262
Kim, D. Y. 177
Kim, E. 58, 354, 447, 449
Kim, M. L. 57, 245, 261
Kim, S. B. 177
Kirk, D. 264
Koo, J. 245
Koutrou, N. 161, 325, 326, 327, 335, 336
Kragt, D. 4
Krasnopolskaya, I. 253

Krause, N. 480
Kreutzer, K. 274, 282
Kunreuther, F. 137

Lammertyn, F. 334
Lamont, M. 88, 90, 91
Laurie, N. 37
Lavery, S. 417
Lawton, L. 96
leadership: barriers 137–139; cause and effect
    relationships 140; "civic torchbearers" 134;
    community organisations 133; focus group
    participants 137–138; *General Social Survey*
    134; good leadership 138; of grassroots
    associations 133–136; literature review
    134–136; methods 136; misuse of power
    139; planning & leadership 308; poor
    behaviour 134–135; results 136–139; skills
    138; 'stalwarts' 135; "village Napoleons"
    135; volunteer leader, defined 134; volunteer
    program 238–239
lean-tos 114
Leask, A. 96, 271
Le Compte, M. D. 491
Lee, S. 62, 126, 437, 477
Lee, Y. 245, 273
legacy(ies): approaches to coding 337; barriers
    336; criterion-based purposive sampling 337;
    enhanced volunteer support 335; and impact
    of volunteering 8–9, 319–320; increased
    levels of volunteering 335; individual
    and community sustainability 321–324;
    organisational and institutional sustainability
    324–327; positive volunteer legacy aspirations
    335; qualitative longitudinal (QL) approach
    336–337
Legget, J. 99
leisure activity, volunteering as 425–427
Leonard, R. 133
Lerdal, K. 102
lesbian, gay, bisexual and trans (LGBT+)
    volunteers 9
Leung, K. K. 365
Leung, Y. F. 113
Leviton, L. C. 273
Levy, S. J. 382
Li, C. 62
Lindsay, P 418
Lindsey, I. 321, 324, 325
Lindsey, R. 144, 461, 467
Lin, Q.-q. 438
Liu C. 99, 109, 365
Liu, T. M. 365
Liu, Y. 85
Li, Y. 480
Local Government Act 2002 106

Local Organising Committees (LOC) 6, 73,
    324, 325
Lockstone-Binney, L. 11, 205, 327, 448, 495
Lockstone, L. 206, 240
locus of causality 63
London 2012 Olympic Games 6, 8, 70, 166,
    175–176, 179, **180**, 325, 495; definitions of
    volunteering prior to 338–339; engagement
    in volunteering 341–342; fleet transport
    167–170; Park Lane Fleet Depot 166–167;
    transport volunteering context 166–170;
    understandings of volunteering after 339–341
London Olympic Games Organising Committee
    (LOCOG) 164–166, 170–171, 325–327
long-term committed volunteers (LTVs) 334
Lorimer, J. 46
Lough, B. J. 32, 33, 34, 35, 400, 404, 411
Luke, S. 489
Lumsden, L. 206
Lupoli, C. A. 50, 364
Lynch, S. 274, 275, 280
Lyons, K. 454, 455

Maas, S. A. 193, 197
Macduff, N. 175, 193
MacKaye, B. 114, 115, 118
Madden, K. 193
Ma, H. C. 417
Mair, J. 101
Manatschal, A. 333, 339
Mangold, K. 37
Marion, J. L. 113
Marx, K. 381, 382
'matching hypothesis' 262
Maull, R. 304, 313
Mawson, H. 390
McAllum, K. 348
McBride, A. M. 34, 35
McCurley, S. 272
McGehee, N. G. 41, 124, 125, 361, 362, 364,
    366, 369, 448, 454, 455, 457
McKenzie, T. 479
Meetings, Incentives, Conventions, and
    Exhibitions (MICE) industry 223
mega events: conceptualising volunteering
    333–335; literature review 333–336; London
    2012 Games 338–342; methodology 336–337;
    previous engagement in volunteering 338;
    volunteer legacy 335–336
mega-sporting events (MSEs) 6, 8; 'active labour
    market' policies 165; Games Makers 161;
    LOCOG 165; London 2012 Olympic Games
    165–166; Manchester Events Volunteers 165;
    in skills-enhancement (*see* skills, MSEs in);
    volunteering at 164–166; volunteer
    manager 238

Meijs, L. C. P. M. 7, 134, 249, 251, 252, 253, 255, 334, 338, 340, 348
Melissen, F. 353
membership management 250, 251–253, 255n1
Meng, B. 454, 455
Miao, Q. 505
Miene, P. 99
'Millennials' *see* 'Generation Y'
model of destination service volunteering 4
Modified Volunteer Functions Inventory for Sports (MVFIS) scale 57
Mohan, J. 461, 467
Monga, M. 57, 456
Montsion, J. M. 35
Morris, P. 435
Morse, W. C. 50
Mostafanezhad, M. 41, 44, 45, 379, 454
motivations 7; at business events 226–227; events, sport, and tourism volunteering 259, **260**, 261; functional approach 258–259; future directions 266–267; practical implications 263–266; reciprocal altruism 226; recruitment 262; retention 262–263; self-determination theory 264–265; utilitarian reasons 226; Volunteer Functions Inventory (VFI) 258–259
motives: affective incentives 58; clusters 58; egoistic 264; financial support 264; fulfilment and matching 261–263; identifying and matching 258–259; normative incentives 58; protective 264; self-development motives 226; socialising/enjoyment 263–264; utilitarian incentives 58; values, social, and enhancement 264
Motta, S. C. 368
Movono, A. 367
Mullan, K. 477, 480
Mullins, L. 274
museums: Auckland (*see* Auckland museums); Metropolitan 98–99; in New Zealand (*see* New Zealand); SLP 102, 107; volunteers 104–105; volunteer tourism 4
'Music for Life' 194

Nagel, S. 292
Nassar, N. 279
National Council for Voluntary Organisations (NVCO) 205
National Days of Service (NDS) 6, 191–194, 198–200, 251, 253
National Environmental Policy Act (NEPA) 117
national governing body (NGB) 144, 146, 152–154
National Health Service 468
National Olympic Committees (NOCs) 166
National Register of Historic Places 118

National Trails System Act (NTSA) 115
Nel, P. 245
neoliberalism 44, 48–50, 320–321, 323–325, 328
Nesbit, R. 134, 135, 139
Netting, F. E. 175
Neulinger, J. 425
New Public Management (NPM) 4, 71, 75, 322, 464, 501
New Zealand: Aotearoa 98–99; Auckland (*see* Auckland museums); little and local 98; Metropolitan museums 98–99; motivational factors 99; museums as cultural heritage visitor attractions in 98–99; policy imperatives 106; and protected natural areas 4; research approach 99; volunteers 104–105
niche tourism 122, 129, 375, 400
niche volunteers 58
Nichols, G. 5, 135, 136, 164, 332, 454
Nicholson, R. 9
Nickels, H. 418
Nieboer, A. P. 478
19th International Conference of Labour Statisticians (ICLS) 16
Ning, R. 383
non-governmental organisations (NGOs) 31, 33–34, 41, 50, 73–74, 118, 139, 215, 366, 367, 400, 504; international voluntary service programmes 10; public management 71
non-profit organisations (NPOs) 22, 145, 194, 228, 402, 456
North-North volunteer tourism programmes 10
not-for-profit sector 2–3, 11, 33–34, 86–87, 114, 145, 299, 502

obligation 10; agreeable 427; ambivalence 430–431; civic engagement 430; culture of 428–429; disagreeable 427; leisure activity 425–427; non-work obligation 428; personal implications 430; *Psychology Today* 432; self-care 428; Serious Leisure Perspective 426–427; service learning 431; sex segregation 426; social interaction 426; study of francophone career volunteers 426; unpaid labor 427; unpleasant tasks 428; volunteering as 427–428
O'Brien, W. 59
O'Connor, M. K. 175
Old Testament 202
Olsson, A. K. 87
Olympic games: ANOVA test (F-test) and post-hoc test 182; 2008 Beijing Olympic Games 224, 419; demographics 179–180; episodic volunteering 177; hosting of 164, 437; implications 186–187; 2004 in Athens, Greece 456; literature review 175–176; London 2012 Olympic Games 6, 70, 166, 175–176, 179, **180**, 325, 495; methods 179, **179**; motivation

174–177, 180–185, **183–184**, 186; motives of olympic volunteers 176–177; Olympic Games Family Assistants 166; 2018 PyeongChang Olympic Games 6, 179, **180**, 495; rankings 180–185, **181–182**; SEVMS scale 177, **185**, 185–186; Sydney 2000 Olympic Games 64, 336, 495; theoretical framework 177–179; transport 166; Vancouver 2010 Winter Olympic Games 6, 175, 179, **180**; volunteers at 164, **178**
'Olympic volunteer,' defined 174
Omoto, A. M. 333, 334, 336
one-day volunteering opportunities 6
one-off and short-term event volunteering 175
Ong, F. 437
online volunteering 63, 241, 430, 502
Onyx, J. 133
Oostlander, J. 63
organisational commitment 7, 61–62, 214–215, 218, 220, 259, 264, 304
organisational culture (OC): 'being valued,' notion of 309; communication 309; dimensions of **303**, 303–304, **311**, 312–313; elements of culture 303–305; engagement of volunteers 305; first glance 306–307; journeying with volunteers 300; literature on 304; methodological approach 306; orientation of volunteers 305; planning & leadership 308; Puffing Billy Railway 298–308; railway heritage attractions 300, 302; relationships and work satisfaction 310–312; time for change 310, 312; value congruence 305; and volunteerism 306–308; and volunteers 302–306
organisational identification 61–62
organisational sustainability 324–327
Organisation for Economic Co-operation and Development (OECD) 19, 501
Organising Committees 343, 350, 352
organization-based volunteers 17, 18
Orwell, G. 501
other-oriented motivations 264, 265
Oxley, L. 435

Page, S. 206
Palacios, C. M. 454, 455
Palmer, D. A. 383
Pappous, A. 161, 325
Paralympic Games 8, 168, 186, 243, 325, 326, 332, 335–337, 342, 489, 494
Paraskevaidis, P. 86
Park, Sang-uk 6
Parker, A. 390
Parker, S. R. 425, 426
Patil, S. 347
Patton, M. 494
Peace Corps and AmeriCorps programs 473

Pearce, P. L. 85
Peluso, N. L. 44
Peng, B.-q. 438
perceived behavioural control (PBC) 62
performance assurance 192, 193
performance evaluations 245
performance management 245, 322
Perpek, E. 479
'personally involved volunteers' 58
Pestoff, V. 464
Petrovic, K. 4, 7
Pettigrew, S. 479
philanthropy 153–154, 203–204, 216, 347, 354
Piatak, J. 272
Plagnol, A. C. 477, 478, 480
Polish Football Association 73, 74
political ecology (PE): conservation and environmental concerns 41; CVT projects 41, *42, 43*; discursive 44; ecotourism 41; political economy 44–45
Posner, B. Z. 134, 140
Preissle, J. 491
Presley, J. 126
Preuss, H. 348
professional volunteering 33
profiling research: author profiling 454; contributors 451–454, **452**; core references 454–456; country profiling 451, 453; elements of 449; episodic volunteering 447–448; host volunteering 448; methods of study 449–450; research institution profiling 453; research productivity *450*, 450–451; source title profiling 453; sport volunteering 448; tourism volunteering 448
programme management 7, 166, 250–253, 255, 255n1
protected natural areas 4
Proudman, R. D. 113
Pryce, J. 300, 304, 305, 307, 313
psychological contract (PC) 59–60; relational 59; transactional 59; volunteer expectations 59–60
psychology of volunteering: becoming a volunteer 57–59; commitment and identification 61–62; demographic differences 62–63; functional approach 57–58; individual differences 63–64; other approaches to volunteer motivation 58–59; personal well-being 56; psychological contract 59–60; remaining a volunteer 59–62; self-determination theory 60–61; social well-being 56; Theory of Planned Behaviour 62
public administration perspective: Bydgoszcz (case study) 72–75; challenges 68; civil engagement 72; disclosure statement and funding 76; international sports events, volunteering in 75, **75**; methodology 69;

social capital 72; and sport, volunteering in 70–71, 75–76; volunteer involvement 71–72
public sector volunteering 68
Puffing Billy Railway (PBR): Australian railway heritage attraction 298–299; Emerald Tourist Railway Board 299–300; journeying with volunteers 300, *301*; into OC 306–308; organisational culture and volunteerism 306–308; Puffing Billy Preservation Society 299; 2016 Volunteer Satisfaction Survey 300, 306, **307**, 307–308
Putnam, R. 72, 106, 134, 139, 148, 323
van Puyvelde, S. 134
PyeongChang 2018 Olympic Games 6, 179, **180**

Qian, X. L. 86
Qi, H. 10, 36
qualitative longitudinal (QL) approach 336–337
qualitative research methods: ethnography in volunteering 492–493; interview *493*, 493–496, *494*; observational guidelines 491, *492*; participant observation 489–492; Virgin Money London Marathon 491, *491*; volunteering experience, feeling and knowledge questions 494, *495*
quantitative research methods: questionnaire administration 487–488; questionnaire design 486–487; sampling 488–489; to support EST volunteering research 485–486
Qur'ãn 202

Ragsdell, G. 495
railway heritage attractions 300, 302
Ralston, R. 164, 206, 300, 314
Rand, A. 381
Randle, M. 58
'ratchet model' 249
Raymond, E. M. 128, 403, 412, 454, 455
reciprocal altruism 227
reciprocity 412
recognition: awards 286; being recognized 290; research on 287; understanding 290–291; volunteer satisfaction 286
recruitment: community events 192–193; 'Community Life' survey 273; cost-effective way 273; difficulties 273–274; digital recruitment strategies 272; expansion of nonprofit sector 272–273; level of formality 280–281; methodology 275–276, *277*; non-coordinated form 273; online questionnaire 278; participation of volunteers in VAs 272; results and discussion 276, 277–278; and selection practices 8; social media 8; tailoring of 8; younger volunteers 273
Reed P. 461
"reflexive volunteering" 376
Rega, I. 379

Reid, F. 9
Reid, S. 492
research: growth phase 10; qualitative approaches 489–496; quantitative approaches 486–489; 'scientificion' 361; shakeout or stabilisation phase 10; start-up phase 10
resignation: dealing with 293; preventing 294; from volunteering 291–292
retention 8, 262–263, 287
'revolving-door,' 'drop-by,' or 'plug-in' volunteering 376
rewards 8, 289–290
Rhoden, S. 300, 302
Ribot, J. C. 44
Richards, J. 417
Richardson, K. M. 87
Ridge, R. D. 99, 258, 262
Ringuet-Riot, C. 61
Roberts, C. 206
Robinson, J. 151
Roche, M. 70
Rochester C. 11, 135, 251, 334, 465, 502, 504
Roesch, S. 304
Rogerson, R. 9
Rotary International 25
Rotolo, T. 426
Rowing World Cup 341
Royal Stakesby Cricket Club (RSCC) 391–393
Roza, L. 253
Ryan, E. M. 63

Sampaio, M. 275
Santos, C. A. 124, 125, 454
Sargeant, A. 203, 204, 207
"satellite accounts" of the non-profit sector 16
Saxton, J. 461, 466
Schaffer, K. B. 426
Schein, E. 303, 305, 312, 313
Scherrer, P. 50
Schervish, P. G. 475
Scheyvens, R. 367
Schlesinger, T. 292
von Schnurbein, G. 193
Schwarz, G. 505
Schwarz, S. 505
secondary management model 250
Seibert, N. 125
Seidel, F. 402
Selby K. 461
selection process: AHP method 274–275; formalised approaches 275; level of formality 280–281; methodology 275–276, *279*; negative outcomes 274; refinement of 280; results and discussion 276, 278–280; standard-conventional practices 274, 278, 281; trustworthy selection methods 274;

unconventional-alternative practices 274, 279; volunteer screening 274
self-determination theory (SDT) 60–61; autonomous motivation 60; autonomy, incentives, and requirements 264–265; autonomy, relatedness, and competence 60; autonomy-supportive leadership 60–61; controlled motivation 60, 61; external and interjected regulation 60; identified and integrated regulation 60; intrinsic and extrinsic motivation 60
self-efficacy theory 267
sending organisations 40, 45, 48, 50, 124, 253, 361, 363–364, 403–404
Senko, J. 47
Serious Leisure Perspective (SLP) 1, 319, 426; activities 431; art lovers 103; as formal and non-occupational 105; museums 102, 107; volunteering 352
service delivery or programme management 250
service learning 254; Chinese business events volunteering 418–421; civic engagement 418; community organisations 417–418; and court-referred volunteering 254; definition 417; educational institutions 417; international 417; non-formal learning 161; numbers of volunteers 418; positive outcomes 417; research on 422; students 417; through volunteering 420; volunteering as type of 420–421
Sharp, B. 347, 354
Sharpe, E. K. 135
Shields, P. O. 273
Shipway, R. 11, 324, 327, 486
Simonson J. 479
Simpson, K 450, 454, 457
single volunteers 253
Sin, H. L. 454, 455
skills, MSEs in: hard skills 163–164; at London 2012 fleet transport 167–169; soft skills 162–163, 170
slow tourism 367
Smit, B. 353
Smith, D. H. 133
Smith, J. A. 305
Smith, K. A. 4, 34, 36, 85, 86, 90, 91, 102, 205, 206, 240, 274, 275, 280, 448, 454, 496
Smith, M. 165
Smith, N. L. 36
Snapchat 151
Snyder, M. 99, 258, 262, 333, 334, 336
Sobocinska, A. 32, 35
social capital 323, **350**, 478–479, 506; bonding 72; bridging dimensions 72, 106, 149; CSO participation 148; development of 57, 69, 75, 162, 164, 171, 347, 354; in local and/or

regional communities 72; resources possessed by volunteers 106–108; women volunteer 63
social global citizenship 439
social legacy from event volunteering: 2014 Commonwealth Games, Glasgow 347; definition 349–350; episodic volunteering 348, 349; Glasgow 2014 352–355; HCV programme (*see* Host City Volunteer (HCV) programme); new models of volunteering 347–348; post-event volunteering 355–356; social indicators of events 350, **350**; volunteering ethos 348–349
social media: community-based volunteers 87; online volunteer 241; recruitment and selection practices 8, 281; rise of 470; surveyed organisations 281; websites and event website 195
soft skills 162–163
Solberg, H. A. 3, 24, 25
South Australian Association of School Parent Clubs 134
Spaaij, R. 243, 390
Sparks, S. 418
Special Events Volunteer Motivation Scale (SEVMS) 175, **177**, **185**, 185–186, 455
"specialist" approach 24
spiritual global citizenship 440
Spitzberg, B. 304
sports clubs: community sports clubs 390–393; community sports organisations 5, 11; German Sports Clubs 244; motivations of volunteers 392–393; in Scotland 144; volunteer experiences 391–393
"sports education" 22
sport volunteering: AFL supporter groups (case study) 394–397; community sports clubs (case study) 391–393; delivering diversity policy and programs 391; diversity amongst community sport volunteers 390–391; diversity and inclusion efforts in Australian Sport 389; pride groups in sport 395–397; public administration perspective 69; role volunteers 389
Spradley, J. P. 490, 491, 494
Springer, S. 324
Stadler, R. 492
'stalwarts' 135
St-Amant, O. 34
Stamer, D. 102
Stammsen, P. 402
Staples, L. 138
Staying Alive surf safety campaign 89
Stebbins, R. A. 10, 105, 107, 351, 352, 426, 430, 503
Steele, J. 50, 246
Storer, C. 205
Storr, R. 389

Strubel, I. T 61
Stuck, S. 477
students' event volunteering 7
Studer, S. 193
Stukas, A. A. 4, 7, 99, 259, 262
Surf Life Saving Queensland (SLSQ)
    88–89
sustainability approach: individual and
    community sustainability 321–324;
    marketisation and individualisation 319;
    organisational and institutional sustainability
    324–327; volunteering impact and legacy
    319–320
Sydney 2000 Olympic Games 64, 336, 495
system of national accounts (SNA) 16

Taheri, B. 123
Talaat, N. 279
Taniguchi, H. 478
Taplin, J. 360, 365
task-specific motivation theory 267
Taylor, M. 72
Taylor, T. 59, 241
'teamers' 401
technology: community-based volunteers 87;
    companies 151; digital 272, 464; information
    technology skills 98, 108, 163, 470;
    interactive training videos 49; internet 272;
    modern banking technology 218; online
    volunteer 501; technology of power 226
Terwiel, F. A. 176
Tesch, R. 491
Theerapappisit, P. 379
Theory of Planned Behaviour (TPB) 267;
    attitudes 62; perceived behavioural control
    (PBC) 62; subjective norms 62
Third Sector 202
Thompson, A. M. 426
Thompson, J. 123
Thomson, A. 355
Tiessen, R. 32, 33, 34
Time Use Survey, Germany 479
Tiraieyari, N. 273
Tiwari, Pinaz 5
de Tocqueville, Alexis: *Democracy in America* 381
Tomazos, K. 9, 489
tourism research: adaptancy phase 361–365;
    advocacy phase 361, 362, 364, 365;
    cautionary phase 361, 362, 365; scientific
    phase 361, 363, 369–370
*Tourism Satellite Account: Recommended
    Methodological Framework* 2008 22
tourism volunteering *see* volunteer tourism (VT)
traditional volunteering 11, 227–229
1840 Treaty of Waitangi – *Te Tiriti o
    Waitangi* 101
Trede, F. 404

trends in volunteering 10, 11; adoption of
    digital media 470; ageing population 463;
    attitudes and behaviour 465–468; changing
    environment for volunteering 461–465;
    changing institutions and weakening of social
    ties 461–462; and COVID-19 468–469;
    dominant paradigm 460; formal and informal
    volunteering 460; growing social isolation
    463–464; growth of consumerism 462;
    impact of marketisation 462; impact of the
    digital revolution 464; inequality and poverty
    462–463; modern managerial methods
    469–470; new public administration regime
    464–465; the non-profit paradigm 460;
    nuclear family 461–462; rise of social media
    470; surveys 461; younger generations 464
20th International Conference of Labour
    Statisticians ((20th ICLS) 18
Twitter 151, 337

UEFA 4, 70, 73–75; 2008 European Football
    Championship 263; UEFA Euro U-21 73, 74;
    Under-21 UEFA Championship or UEFA
    U-21 69, 73
Under-21 UEFA Championship or UEFA U-21
    69, 73
*The 2009 UNESCO Framework for Cultural
    Statistics* 23
UNESCO Institute for Statistics (UIS) 23
United Kingdom Civil Society Almanac 2020 476
United Nations Volunteers (UNV) program 241
UN World Tourism Organization
    (UNWTO) 22
Uriely, N. 89, 123, 129

Vada, S. 125
value congruence 266, 305
value of volunteering 24–25, 56, 150, 323, 505;
    see also economic value of volunteering
Vancouver 2010 Winter Olympic Games 6
Van der Wagen, L. 206
virtual volunteering 241
visitor attractions (VA): in Aotearoa New
    Zealand (*see* New Zealand); categories
    of 96, **96**, 271; cultural and social capital
    resources 106–108; data analysis technique
    276; definition 96; descriptive analysis 276;
    interview respondents' profile 276, **277**;
    mixed-methods approach 275; museum
    volunteers 104–105; policy imperatives 106;
    research approach 99; Scottish VA sector 271–
    272; self-completed questionnaires 275–276;
    semi-structured interview protocol 275–276;
    volunteers' roles and functions 103–104
visitor information centres 85–86
Vogel C. 479
Voluntary Service Overseas (VSO) 35

'volunteerability' 332, 334, 338
volunteer coordinator 238
Volunteer Functions Inventory (VFI) 2, 4, 57, 99, 104, 258–259, 478
Volunteer Graduate Scheme (VGS) 35
volunteering in EST 1–3; contribution of 2; cost of 1–2; COVID-19 pandemic 11–12; critical issues 9–10; definition 1, 10, 15–17, 333, 447; disciplinary approaches 3–4; elements of 1; at events (*see* event volunteering); formal and informal volunteering (*see individual entries*); future of 2–3; global North perspective 3; ICLS definition 26; impacts and legacies 8–9; management process 7–8; outcomes of 6; psychology of 4; public administration 4; pure forms 335; research, new directions in 10–11; research on 2; within tourism (*see* volunteer tourism (VT)); traditional, collective, and dominant forms 334, 340
volunteering organisations 31
volunteer legacy 335–336
volunteer manager 238
volunteer program: defined 237; evaluation of 245–246; evaluation of volunteers 244–245; inducting and training volunteers 240–241; integrating into organisation 239; leadership 238–239; meeting needs of volunteers 241–242; preparing job descriptions 239–240; rationale for volunteer involvement 238; recognising volunteer effort 244; recruiting and retaining volunteers 243–244; reducing barriers to volunteering 242–243; virtual and episodic volunteering 241
2016 Volunteer Satisfaction Survey (VSS) 300
volunteers' future engagement 9
volunteer stewardship management models 7, **250**; episodic volunteers 251; human resource management 249; 'hyphen' approach 254; intermediary management model 250; membership management 250–253, 255n1; programme management 251–253, 255n1; 'ratchet model' 249; secondary management model 250; service delivery or programme management 250; shared management models, intermediary and secondary 253–255; single volunteers or family volunteering 253; smaller events 251; value chain of volunteering 249–250
volunteer support organisation (VSO) 194, 195–196
volunteer tourism (VT) 4–5; autoethnography 368–369; contemporary viewpoint 128; deconstructing 5; defining 83, 123–124, 362, 448; development of Appalachian National Scenic Trail 5; elements of 124–128; ethics of (*see* ethics of volunteering in tourism); evaluation measurements 360; 'Friends of the Park' groups 5; global citizenship through 436–437; guest volunteers 2; 'holidaymakers' volunteer 124; host volunteers 2; impact measurement 360, 363–367; implications 369–370; industry 360; intangible outcomes, importance of 367–369; international 36–37; involuntary volunteering 123; and its impacts 361–363; "methods first approach" 360; micro-social influences 123; museums and protected natural areas 4; research phases (*see* tourism research); and tourist motivations 5
volunteer tourists, defined 361
volunteer work: direct volunteers 18; excluded from volunteer work 18; forms of work and 2008 SNA **17**; internationally accepted economic definition 16–19, 20, 23; in international statistical system (*see* international statistical system); organization-based volunteers 18; persons in 17; *Resolution concerning statistics on work relationships* 18; revised ILO Manual definition 18; revised Labour Force Survey (LFS) survey module 19; Sustainable Development Goals (SDGs) 18–19; working time 18
voluntourism/volunteering abroad 400; commercial and non-commercial providers 403–404, **407–408**; criticisms of commercial voluntourism 403; 'holiday and travel' part 403; intercultural competence 403–404; non-profit organisations and researchers 402–403; tour operators, TUI 403; volunteering organisations 402
Von Hanau, T. 244
Vrasti, W. 35

Wadsworth, M. 1, 10, 150, 332
Wall, G. 96
Wallstam, M. 349, 350
Walton, M. 485
Wang, L. 3, 11, 477, 478, 502
Warburton, J. 273, 274, 278, 279
Warner, S. 261
Wearing, S. 2, 41, 123, 125, 126, 361, 362, 363, 369, 440, 448, 449, 454, 455, 457
Weaver, D. 96
Weerakoon, R. K. 239
Wehner, T. 61
Weiler, B. 87, 88, 90, 91, 92, 454, 455
Weiss-Gal, I. 305, 309
welfare state: Conservative/Corporatist welfare state 153; Liberal (Anglophone) welfare state 153; Universalist welfare state 153
Wen, J. J. 438, 440
western scientific knowledge (WSK) 44
White, L. 206
Wicker, P. 91, 92, 244, 448, 456, 496
Wiehe, E. 3

Wild, C. 215
Wilks, J. 89
Wilks, L. 352, 489
Wilson, J. 426
Wilson, L. M. 99
Wilson, R. 418
2018 Winter Olympic Games 495
Wisner, P. S. 322
Won, H. J. 245
Woodall, J. 324, 326
'workcamps' 401
world cups 237
World Police 341
World Wide Opportunities on Organic Farms
    (WWOOF) 437

Wu, D. C. 259
Wu, Y. 62

Yarnal, C. 86
Yen, C.-L. 437
Yin, R. K. 69
Young-Joo, L. 273
Young, T. 9
YouTube 151

Zahra, A. 366, 369
Zakus, D. H. 61
'zero hours' contracts, use of 463
Zhang, J. J. 57
Zhou, R. 354, 355

Printed in the United States
by Baker & Taylor Publisher Services